THE BOOKS OF THE BIBLE™

NEW TESTAMENT

LECTIO DIVINA FOR THE FAMILY

With my blessing for all families,

Franciscus

Creation, Life and Beauty,

undone by death and wrongdoing,

regained by God's surprising victory,

AS TOLD IN
THE BOOKS OF **THE**

NEW TESTAMENT

CHRISTIAN COMMUNITY BIBLE

LECTIO DIVINA FOR THE FAMILY

Fundación Ramón Pané

With the support of:

PONTIFICIUM CONSILIUM
PRO FAMILIA

The Ramón Pané Foundation takes its name from one of the greatest figures in the evangelization of America. It was founded in 1994 in honor and memory of Ramón Pané, considered the first catechist and evangelizer of America. FRP is an international group of Catholics who want to help all the dioceses, the Episcopal Conferences and Catholic ecclesial movements in their catechetical, missionary and spiritual training. Its main office is in the Archdiocese of Tegucigalpa, Honduras and has an office in the Archdiocese of Miami, USA. Anyone wishing information about our mission and work can write to: emailme@fundacionpane.org.

Pastoral Bible Foundation and Claretian Publications are part of "Claret Publishing Group". CPG is a pastoral endeavor of the Claretian Missionaries. It aims to promote a renewed spirituality rooted in the Word of God and the living tradition of the Church in response to the needs, challenges and pastoral demands of today.

Biblica provides God's Word in multiple languages so people can enter into a relationship with Jesus Christ and grow in him. We work in Africa, East Asia Pacific, Europe, Latin America, Middle East/North Africa, North America, and South Asia. We translate and publish the Bible in the top 100 major spoken languages in the world and are the translation sponsor and worldwide publisher of the New International Version® (NIV®) Bible, the most widely used contemporary English translation in the world.

"**The Word of God is the source of life and spirituality for the family.** All pastoral work on behalf of the family must allow people to be interiorly fashioned and formed as **members of the domestic church through the Church's prayerful reading of Sacred Scripture. The Word of God is not only good news in a person's private life but also a criterion of judgment and a light in discerning** the various challenges that married couples and families encounter." (Relatio Synodi 34)

With deep joy I encourage each family to remember that the Word of God is a source of life, unity and renewal.

This special edition of the New Testament, structured to have an overview of the life of Jesus and the early Christian communities, includes all the books of the New Testament according to the narratives of the four Evangelists. Also there we find helps for the exercise of Lectio Divina in support of the family, designed to strengthen the identity of the nucleus in which values are forged and members educated to virtue.

The Pontifical Council for the Family thanks the Ramón Pané Foundation for this work in several languages, with the blessing of Pope Francis.

For my part I ask God to bless this project and all the members of the families who read and put into practice the teachings of Jesus in the New Testament.

† Vincenzo Paglia

† VINCENZO PAGLIA
President, Pontifical Council for the Family

Fundación Ramón Pané

VALUES FOR MY VIRTUOUS FAMILY

INTRODUCTION

The family is the great institution of humanity. Without the family unit, we would have no one to pass on the culture and values that make a person virtuous. The church, respecting the great challenge set by our Lord Jesus Christ, decided to elevate marriage to the level of a sacrament. God therefore left a tremendous responsibility in the hands of men and women!

If we review the entire history of salvation, we discover the loving plan of God the Father was to form a great family of human beings. Because of the disobedience of our first ancestors, we lost our initial opportunity to be part of God's family. Subsequently our loving Father, through his Son, reworked his plan of love with even stronger bonds. Though we strayed, he did not abandon humanity, promising instead a Messiah and a Savior. In fulfillment of the prophets, God the Father sent his only Son to be born as a human being to a virgin. And God-made-flesh, Jesus Christ the Lord, was born and grew up in a family with a mother and an adoptive father. What could be greater—except for the incarnation—than the fact that God himself chose a family to be a part of where he experienced human life?

God had prepared his people, Israel; and though, as in many families, there were some who were wayward, the faithful still remained. The family of Nazareth, being part of the faithful, taught God's Son, Jesus, the customs and history of God's dealings down through the ages for the benefit of humanity. We could say that human history is the story of how we have learned to listen to the voice of the Creator, to fulfill his will: To build a family! The family itself might be a model of what Christ won for us, when he opened the door to the eternal mansions where we will live forever as the family that God chose.

Jesus himself, when his disciples asked him to teach them to pray, told them that they should address God with a particular word in their language—"Abba," meaning "Daddy"—instead of the more formal "Father" that sounds distinctly authoritarian. Jesus spoke to God in the way that we speak to the person closest to us, someone who has watched us grow and taught us the facts of life. Jesus understood God is so close to us that we have become part of his family. Joseph modeled what it means to be an earthly father. He was the man to whom God entrusted the responsibility of caring for the Son born in the purest womb of Mary. Joseph's example enables us to understand the model for prayer: "Our dearest Father in heaven…"

Those of us who have been fortunate enough to be part of a family, with all the joys and challenges involved, will recognize there is one thing that binds the members of a family together: Love. My parents were married for almost sixty years. I cannot remember a single night when our family went to sleep without saying a prayer; and if there had been an argument or disagreement, at night there would always be a kiss of reconciliation for everyone. So this kind of love is easy for me to talk about, but the fact is not everyone today has had the same experience of family as I had. In my journey through the life of the church, talking to catechists, young people, and faithful believers, I have found many did not have an opportunity like mine. It is hard to imagine what could have happened in their lives, minds, and hearts. Without a loving family to guide them, who taught them about values? Who taught them to align their lives with the truth?

Especially now, when we observe so many acts of aggression between diverse peoples and cultures, the most ferocious attack, which hardly ever appears in the headlines or on the news, is against the family. We all know families who have fallen out over something and have ended up cutting the ties that should endure forever. Families suffer the most because they have the most to lose. Yet this no longer catches our attention; these family breakdowns happening more and more frequently do not appear in the news. In *Evangelii Gaudium* Pope Francis says this:

> The family is experiencing a profound cultural crisis, as are all communities and social bonds. In the case of the family, the weakening of these bonds is particularly serious because the family is the fundamental cell of society, where we learn to live with others despite our differences and to belong to one another; it is also the place where parents pass on the faith to their children. (EG 66)

The family has a basic and fundamental responsibility to love; this is the substance of the sacrament. Love comes to fruition in the family and the children. Here we see something that is key: The family teaches something absolutely essential. Being part of a loving family reveals something intangible: Values for living a virtuous life. And as the family educates its members in this, those values become a reality in their lives.

Following the recent "pre-synod" on the family, our pastors asked us to prepare this program that reflects the findings coming out of the Episcopal Conferences. The synthesis known as *Relatio Synodi* brings together these ideas. We hope to address two issues that have come out of this, with a strong missionary focus.

In paragraph 33 we read:

> **Conversion** also needs to be seen **in the language we use**, so that it might prove to be **effectively meaningful. Proclamation needs to create an experience** where the Gospel of the Family responds to the deepest expectations of the human person: a response to each one's dignity and complete fulfillment in reciprocity, communion and fruitfulness. This does not consist, **not in merely presenting a set of rules, but in espousing values that respond to the needs of those who find themselves today even in the most secularized of countries.**

New language: Nothing could be more appropriate for the needs of today. It is not the content that needs to be adapted, but the "language." Today, the youth of the post-postmodernist generations "X, Y, and Z" must have the same values integrated into their cultural language, the same values expressed in a new way. As St. John Paul II said: "An evangelisation that is new in its passion, new in its methods, new in its expressions." If we do not adopt this new language but continue to express the old values in the old way, they will not be understood, because there is a breakdown in communication between the generations. The older generation is moving toward a new culture. Adults today are often disconected from the new generation. We have no other option but to change our language if we hope to "promote values that respond to today's needs."

This new program offers a response to the findings of the Synodal Fathers for the Family. In their presence, we hope to demonstrate it is possible to pray using the Word of God and *Lectio Divina* as a family. Praying individually and together as a family, the hope is each person will become a light in the darkness—**wisdom and light in discernment**. There could not be a more appropriate time to do this.

This program, known as *The Books of the Bible*, is a different way to read the New Testament. Instead of reading it in the traditional order, it is read in the order it was actually written in. It is the same New Testament but viewed from a different perspective. Over a period of eight weeks, the family members all participate in reading the text. This New Testament does not have chapters and verses—because it is the way it was written and read by the first communities. Reading it in this way offers an opportunity for the whole family to be involved. There are five readings each week. Then the family members talk together at home about what they read. One day of the week is dedicated to praying as a family over transcendental issues connected to values and how these become virtues.

The Christian Community Bible translation we use is backed by the Catholic Bishops' Conference of the Philippines. The English spoken in this translation allows people to meet Jesus through his Word. Our languages and expressions change, so it is important we approach the text through clear and reliable language.

WHAT ARE THE VALUES?

Officially, the church tells us the family is the place where a special effort needs to be made to try out a "new language" in order to "propose values." If we believe there is a need to make an increased investment in values today, then we should provide an initial definition of what we believe values to be:

Values are great ideals that motivate people to maintain appropriate conduct. For example, the patriots of independence forged values (ideals) for their nations. The founders of movements are also motivated by the values they present to their members, who then accept the challenge to use them as points of reference.

Our own families have left us a legacy of values. These values have been put in place for us by our parents, our grandparents, and our ancestors. Think about your grandparents—perhaps they encouraged you to be kind or to work hard. Those families with values pass them on to subsequent generations—their beliefs light the path for us to follow.

There is a "scale of values" with some being more important than others. Everyone has a particular scale of values that motivates them. But how do we form and sustain those values? Today society has made changes to the scale of values. This in turn has placed huge pressure on the family when it comes to maintaining the values that were traditionally so important. Nowadays, there is an emphasis on the outward appearance at the expense of other virtues. Think of the amount of time so many young people spend on their appearance. As they compare themselves to others, this becomes obsessive, going far beyond health and a desire to be well presented.

We must focus on the most important values and make sure these are prioritized on our scale of values. There needs to be a focus on living by values such as respect and care for life from the time of conception until natural death, love, liberty, faithfulness, forgiveness, joy, gratitude, respect for others, and responsibility. Active steps must be taken toward building a life determined by these values. As Pope Francis says:

> The individualism of our postmodern and globalized era favours a lifestyle which weakens the development and stability of personal relationships and distorts family bonds. Pastoral activity needs to bring out more clearly the fact that our relationship with the Father demands and encourages a communion which heals, promotes and reinforces interpersonal bonds. . . . This is a sign of the desire of many people to contribute to social and cultural progress. (*Evangelii Gaudium* 67)

HOW TO PROMOTE VIRTUES

Grand ideals cannot change a society unless they are transformed into virtues. Ideals are simply potential—potential must become reality. Virtue is living according to the values believed in. Therefore, if the value is something "conceptual," virtue is something "dynamic." Values do not exist in and of themselves. No one can purchase three feet of liberty, or two pounds of truth, or two months of love, or three quarts of forgiveness. But real people can be free, truthful, loving, and willing to forgive.

Pope Francis, seeking to clarify the problem of not practicing virtue, tells us:

> The causes of this breakdown include: a lack of opportunity for dialogue in families, the influence of the communications media, a relativistic subjectivism, unbridled consumerism which feeds the market, lack of pastoral care among the poor, the failure of our institutions to be welcoming, and our difficulty in restoring a mystical adherence to the faith in a pluralistic religious landscape. (*Evangelii Gaudium* 70)

The challenge, then, is to move from concept to action. And for that, the church has traditionally used Lectio Divina, the prayerful reading of the Bible, as the most effective way to carry out this transition from values to a virtuous life.

HOW TO USE LECTIO DIVINA IN A FAMILY SETTING

Number 34 in *Relatio Synodi*, a document intended to prepare the Synod on the Family, posed a big challenge. It is this challenge we aim to respond to with this project:

> **The Word of God is the source of life and spirituality for the family.** All pastoral work on behalf of the family must allow people to be interiorly fashioned and formed as members of **the domestic church through the Church's prayerful reading of Sacred Scripture. The Word of God is not only good news in a person's private life but also a criterion of judgment and a light in discerning** the various challenges that married couples and families encounter.

In the past, the Word of God has been used to give pastoral guidance to families, but perhaps without enough understanding of the situations that people find themselves in. The Bible has been understood factually. But this has not always been helpful when offering pastoral direction to a family needing to know how to properly respond to the challenges they face. Therefore, using this program, three important goals will be accomplished:

- A comprehensive appreciation of the New Testament will be acquired

- The practice of Lectio Divina will become a habit of family life

- Wise criteria for specific actions to transform people's lives into virtuous models will be determined.

In this respect Pope Francis reminds us:

> The study of Holy Scripture should be an open door to all believers. It is fundamental that the Word revealed bring to radical fruition the catechism and all other efforts to communicate faith. Evangelization requires familiarity with the Word of God, and this requires that the dioceses, parishes, and all Catholic groups propose a serious and persevering study of the Bible, as well as promote prayerful personal and community reading of Scripture. We are not blindly seeking nor do we need for God to give us a word, for in fact God has spoken; he is no longer the great Unknown, for he has revealed himself. Let us embrace the divine treasure of the revealed Word. (*Evangelii Gaudium* 175)

The habitual practice of Lectio Divina with its five steps, synthesized by Pope Benedict XVI in his Apostolic Exhortation *Verbum Domini* number 87, will help in understanding clearly how to do this. More information about the method can be obtained by reading the additional advice offered about this project online.

"I would like here to review the basic steps of this procedure.

1. It opens with the **reading *(lectio)*** of a text, which leads to a desire to understand its true content: **what does the biblical text say in**

itself? Without this, there is always a risk that the text will become a pretext for never moving beyond our own ideas.

2. Next comes **meditation *(meditatio)***, which asks: **what does the biblical text say to us?** Here, each person, individually but also as a member of the community, must let himself or herself be moved and challenged.

3. Following this comes **prayer *(oratio)***, which asks the question: **what do we say to the Lord in response to his word?** Prayer, as petition, intercession, thanksgiving and praise, is the primary way by which the word transforms us.

4. Finally, lectio divina concludes with **contemplation *(contemplatio)***, during which we take up, as a gift from God, his own way of seeing and judging reality, and ask ourselves **what conversion of mind, heart and life is the Lord asking of us?** In the Letter to the Romans, Saint Paul tells us: "Do not be conformed to this world, but be transformed by the renewal of your mind, that you may prove what is the will of God, what is good and acceptable and perfect" (12:2). Contemplation aims at creating within us a truly wise and discerning vision of reality, as God sees it, and at forming within us "the mind of Christ" (1 Cor 2:16). The word of God appears here as a criterion for discernment: it is "living and active, sharper than any two-edged sword, piercing to the division of soul and spirit, of joints and marrow, and discerning the thoughts and intentions of the heart" (Heb 4:12).

5. We do well also to remember that the process of lectio divina is not concluded until it arrives at **action *(actio)***, which moves the believer to make his or her life a gift for others in charity." (*Verbum Domini* 87)

Take courage! This project is commended to us by God and is intended to transform families. We are open to the working of the Holy Spirit. As Pope Francis said, there is no intention to "domesticate him." Let us remain humble.

> The Church which "goes forth" is a community of missionary disciples who take the first step, who are involved and supportive, who bear fruit and rejoice. An evangelizing community knows that the Lord has taken the initiative, he has loved us first (cf. 1 Jn 4:19), and therefore we can move forward, boldly take the initiative, go out to others, seek those who have fallen away, stand at the crossroads and welcome the outcast. (*Evangelii Gaudium* 24)

We are confident that we have made the right decision. After years of praying for a specific service that focuses on the family, the Ramón Pané Foundation recommends reading the New Testament together with prayer to help in the formation of virtuous families. Our hope is we will evangelize through our example as well as our words.

You will find assistance on our website, *www.fundacionpane.org*, as well as through other materials that complement the program. The challenge has been issued: Let us allow ourselves to be seduced by the Lord; we want to be attentive to his Word. We are going to pray as a family, we will develop and sustain clear values, and with them we will help shape virtuous people. This will be our evangelistic testimony. Long live the Gospel!

May God accompany us on this journey, and may the Sacred Family be a model for us to follow as we meet with Jesus Christ the Lord.

Brother Ricardo Grzona, frp
Executive President
Ramón Pané Foundation

THE DRAMA
OF THE BIBLE
IN SIX ACTS

The Bible is a collection of letters, poems, stories, visions, prophetic oracles, wisdom and other kinds of writing. The first step to good Bible reading and understanding is to engage these collected works as the different kinds of writing that they are, and to read them as whole books. We encourage you to read big, to not merely take in little fragments of the Bible. The introductions at the start of each book will help you to do this.

But it is also important not to view the Bible as a gathering of unrelated writings. Overall, the Bible is a narrative. These books come together to tell God's true story and his plan to set the world right again. This story of the Bible falls naturally into six key major acts, which are briefly summarized below.

> "I had always felt life first as a story:
>
> and if there is a story, there is a story-teller."
>
> G. K. Chesterton

But even more precisely, we can say the story of the Bible is a drama. The key to a drama is that it has to be acted out, performed, lived. It can't remain as only words on a page. A drama is an activated story. The Bible was written so we could enter into its story. It is meant to be lived.

All of us, without exception, live our lives as a drama. We are on stage every single day. What will we say? What will we do? According to which story will we live? If we are not answering these questions with the biblical script, we will follow another. We can't avoid living by someone's stage instructions, even if merely our own.

This is why another key to engaging the Bible well is to recognize that its story has not ended. God's saving action continues. We are all invited to take up our own roles in this ongoing story of redemption and new creation. So, welcome to the drama of the Bible. Welcome to the story of how God intends to renew your life, and the life of the world. God himself is calling you to engage with his word.

Act 1: GOD'S INTENTION

The drama begins (in the first pages of the book of Genesis) with God already on the stage creating a world. He makes a man and a woman, Adam and Eve, and places them in the Garden of Eden to work it and take care of it. The earth is created to be their home. God's intention is for humanity to be in close, trusting relationship with him and in harmony with the rest of creation that surrounds them.

In a startling passage, the Bible tells us that human beings are God's image-bearers, created to share in the task of bringing God's wise and beneficial rule to the rest of the world. Male and female together, we are significant, decision-making, world-shaping beings. This is our vocation, our purpose as defined in the biblical story.

An equally remarkable part of Act 1 is the description of God as coming into the garden to be with the first human beings. Not only is the earth the God-intended place for humanity, God himself comes to make the beautiful new creation his home as well.

God then gives his own assessment of the whole creation: *God saw all that he had made, and it was very good.* Act 1 reveals God's original desire for the world. It shows us that life itself is a gift from the Creator. It tells us what we were made for and provides the setting for all the action that follows.

Act 2: EXILE

Tension and conflict are introduced to the story when Adam and Eve decide to go their own way and seek their own wisdom. They listen to the deceptive voice of God's enemy, Satan, and doubt God's trustworthiness. They decide to live apart from the word that God himself has given them. They decide to be a law to themselves.

The disobedience of Adam and Eve—the introduction of sin into our world—is presented in the Bible as having devastating consequences. Humans were created for healthy, life-giving relationship: with God, with each other, and with the rest of creation. But now humanity must live with the fracturing of all these relations and with the resulting shame, brokenness, pain, loneliness—and death.

Heaven and earth—God's realm and our realm—were intended to be united. God's desire from the beginning was clearly to live with us in the world he made. But now God is hidden. Now it is possible to be in our world and not know him, not experience his presence, not follow his ways, not live in gratitude.

As a result of this rebellion, the first exile in the story takes place. The humans are driven away from God's presence. Their offspring throughout history will seek to find their way back to the source of life. They will devise any number of philosophies and religions, trying to make sense of a fallen, yet haunting world. But death now stalks them, and they will find that they cannot escape it. Having attempted to live apart from God and his good word, humans will find they have neither God nor life.

New questions arise in the drama: Can the curse on creation be overcome and the relationship between God and humanity restored? Can heaven and earth be reunited? Or did God's enemy effectively end the plan and subvert the story?

Act 3: CALLING ISRAEL TO A MISSION

We see the direction of God's redemptive plan when he calls Abraham, promising to make him into a great nation. God narrows his focus and concentrates on one group of people. But the ultimate goal remains the same: to bless all the peoples on earth and remove the curse from creation.

When Abraham's descendants are enslaved in Egypt, a central pattern in the story is set: God hears their cries for help and comes to set them free. God makes a covenant with this new nation of Israel at Mt. Sinai. Israel is called by God to be a light to the nations, showing the world what it means to follow God's ways for living. If they will do this, he will bless them in their new land and will come to live with them.

However, God also warns them that if they are not faithful to the covenant, he will send them away, just as he did with Adam and Eve. In spite of God's repeated warnings through his prophets, Israel seems determined to break the covenant. So God abandons the holy temple—the sign of his presence with his people—and it is smashed by pagan invaders. Israel's capital city Jerusalem is sacked and burned.

Abraham's descendants, chosen to reverse the failure of Adam, have now apparently also failed. The problem this poses in the biblical story is profound. Israel, sent as the divine answer to Adam's fall, cannot escape Adam's sin. God, however, remains committed to his people and his plan, so he sows the seed of a different outcome. He promises to send a new king, a descendant of Israel's great King David, who will lead the nation back to its destiny. The very prophets who warned Israel of the dire consequences of its wrongdoing also pledge that the good news of God's victory will be heard in Israel once again.

Act 3 ends tragically, with God apparently absent and the pagan nations ruling over Israel. But the hope of a promise remains. There is one true God. He has chosen Israel. He will return to his people to live with them again. He will bring justice, peace and healing to Israel, and then to the world. He will do this in a final and climactic way. God will send his anointed one—the Messiah. He has given his word on this.

Act 4: THE SURPRISING VICTORY OF JESUS

"He is the god made manifest . . . the universal savior of human life." These words, referring to Caesar Augustus (found in a Roman inscription from 4 BC in Ephesus), proclaim the gospel of the Roman Empire. This version of the good news announces that Caesar is the lord who brings peace and prosperity to the world.

Into this empire a son of David is born, and he announces the gospel of God's kingdom. Jesus of Nazareth brings the good news of the coming of God's reign. He begins to show what God's new creation looks like. He announces the end of Israel's exile and the forgiveness of sins. He heals the sick and raises the dead. He overcomes the dark spiritual powers. He welcomes sinners and those considered unclean. Jesus renews the nation, rebuilding the twelve tribes of Israel around himself in a symbolic way.

But the established religious leaders are threatened by Jesus and his kingdom, so they have him brought before the Roman governor. During the very week that the Jews were remembering and celebrating Passover—God's ancient rescue of his people from slavery in Egypt—the Romans nail Jesus to a cross and kill him as a false king.

But the Bible claims that this defeat is actually God's greatest victory. How? Jesus willingly gives up his life as a sacrifice on behalf of the nation, on behalf of the world. Jesus takes onto himself the full force of evil and empties it of its power. In this surprising way, Jesus fights and wins Israel's ultimate battle. The real enemy was never Rome, but the spiritual powers that lie behind Rome and every other kingdom whose weapon is death. Through his blood Jesus pays the price and reconciles everything in heaven and on earth to God.

God then publicly declares this victory by reversing Jesus' death sentence and raising him back to life. The resurrection of Israel's king shows that the great enemies of God's creation—sin and death—really have been defeated. The resurrection is the great sign that the new creation has begun.

Jesus is the fulfillment of Israel's story and a new start for the entire human race. Death came through the first man, Adam. The resurrection of the dead comes through the new man, Jesus. God's original intention is being reclaimed.

Act 5: THE RENEWED PEOPLE OF GOD

 If the key victory has already been secured, why is there an Act 5? The answer is that God wants the victory of Jesus to spread to all the nations of the world. The risen Jesus says to his disciples, *"Peace be with you! As the Father has sent me, I am sending you."* So this new act in the drama tells the story of how the earliest followers of Jesus began to spread the good news of God's reign.

According to the New Testament, all those who belong to Israel's Messiah are children of Abraham, heirs of both the ancient promises and the ancient mission. The task of bringing blessing to the peoples of the world has been given again to Abraham's family. Their mission is to live out the liberating message of the good news of God's kingdom.

God is gathering people from all around the world and forming them into assemblies of Jesus-followers—his church. Together they are God's new temple, the place where his Spirit lives. They are the community of those who have pledged their allegiance to Jesus as the true Lord of the world. They have crossed from death into new life, through the power of God's Spirit. They demonstrate God's love across the usual boundaries of race, class, tribe and nation.

Forgiveness of sins and reconciliation with God can now be announced to all. Following in the steps of Jesus, his followers proclaim this gospel in both word and deed. The power of this new, God-given life breaking into the world is meant to be shown by the real-world actions of the Christian community. But the message also has a warning. When the Messiah returns, he will come as the rightful judge of the world.

The Bible is the story of the central struggle weaving its way through the history of the world. And now the story arrives at our own time, enveloping us in its drama.

So the challenge of a decision confronts us. What will we do? How will we fit into this story? What role will we play? God is inviting us to be a part of his mission of re-creation—of bringing restoration, justice and forgiveness. We are to join in the task of making things new, to be a living sign of what is to come when the drama is complete.

Act 6: GOD COMES HOME

 God's future has come into our world through the work of Jesus the Messiah. But for now, the present evil age also continues. Brokenness, wrongdoing, sickness and even death remain. We live in the time of the overlap of the ages, the time of in-between. The final Act is coming, but it has not yet arrived.

We live in the time of invitation, when the call of the gospel goes out to every creature. Of course, many still live as though God doesn't exist. They do not acknowledge the rule of the Messiah. But the day is coming when Jesus will return to earth and the reign of God will become an uncontested reality throughout the world.

God's presence will be fully and openly with us once again, as it was at the beginning of the drama. God's plan of redemption will reach its goal. The creation will experience its own Exodus, finding freedom from its bondage to decay. Pain and tears, regret and shame, suffering and death will be no more.

When the day of resurrection arrives God's people will find that their hope has been realized. The dynamic force of an indestructible life will course through their bodies. Empowered by the Spirit, and unhindered by sin and death, we will pursue our original vocation as a renewed humanity. We will be culture makers, under God but over the world. Having been remade in the image of Christ, we will share in bringing his wise, caring rule to the earth.

At the center of it all will be God himself. He will return and make his home with us, this time in a new heavens and a new earth. We, along with the rest of creation, will worship him perfectly and fulfill our true calling. God will be all in all, and the whole world will be full of his glory.

WHAT NOW?

The preceding overview of the drama of the Bible is meant to give you a framework so you can begin to read the books that make up the story. The summary we've provided is merely an invitation for you to engage the sacred books themselves.

Many people today follow the practice of reading only small, fragmentary snippets of the Bible—verses—and often in isolation from the books of which they are a part. This does not lead to good Bible understanding. We encourage you instead to take in whole books, the way their authors wrote them. This is really the only way to gain deep insight to the Scriptures.

Go deep and read big.

The more you immerse yourself in the script of this drama, the better you will be able to find your own place in the story. The following page, called *Living the Script*, will help you with practical next steps for taking up your role in the Bible's drama of renewal.

LIVING
THE SCRIPT

From the beginning God made it clear that he intends for us to be significant players in his drama. No doubt, it is first and foremost God's story. But we can't passively sit back and just watch what happens. At every stage he invites humans to participate with him.

Here are three key steps to finding your place in the drama:

1. IMMERSE YOURSELF IN THE BIBLE

If we are unfamiliar with the text of the drama itself, there's no chance of living our parts well. Only when we read both deeply and widely in the Bible, marinating in it and letting it soak into our lives, will we be prepared to effectively take up our roles. The more we read the Bible, the better readers we will become. Rather than skimming the surface, we will become skilled at interpreting and practicing what we read.

2. COMMIT TO FOLLOW JESUS

We've all taken part in the brokenness and wrongdoing that came into the story in Act 2. The victory of Jesus in Act 4 now offers us the opportunity to have our lives turned around. Our sins can be forgiven. We can become part of God's story of new creation.

Turn away from your wrongdoing. God has acted through the death and resurrection of the Messiah to deal decisively with evil—in your life and in the life of the world. His death was a sacrifice, and his resurrection a new beginning. Acknowledge that Jesus is the rightful ruler of the world, and commit to follow him and join with God's people.

3. LIVE YOUR PART

Followers of Jesus are gospel players in local communities living out the biblical drama together. But we do not have an exact script for our lines and actions in the drama today. Our history has not yet been written. And we can't just repeat lines from earlier acts in the drama. So what do we do?

We read the Bible to understand what God has already done, especially through Jesus the Messiah, and to know how we carry this story forward. *The Bible helps us answer the key question about everything we say and do: Is this an appropriate and fitting way to live out the story of Jesus today?* This is how we put the Scriptures into action. Life's choices can be messy, but God has given us his word and promised us his Spirit to guide us on the way. You are God's artwork, created to do good works. May your life be a gift of beauty back to him.

THE DRAMA OF THE BIBLE:
A Visual Chronology

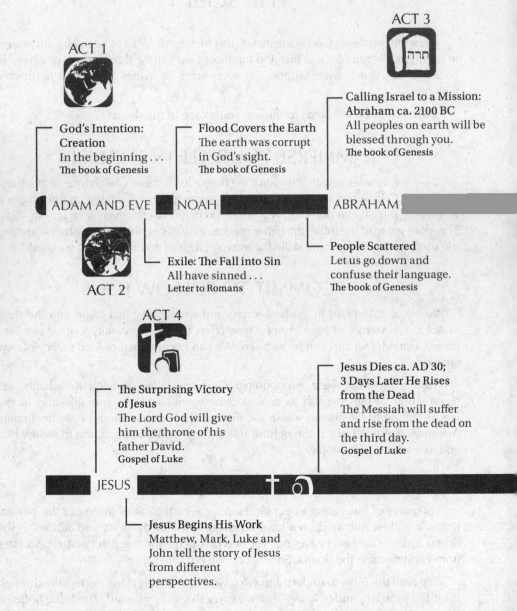

ACT 1

God's Intention: Creation
In the beginning . . .
The book of Genesis

Flood Covers the Earth
The earth was corrupt in God's sight.
The book of Genesis

ACT 3

Calling Israel to a Mission: Abraham ca. 2100 BC
All peoples on earth will be blessed through you.
The book of Genesis

ADAM AND EVE   NOAH   ABRAHAM

ACT 2

Exile: The Fall into Sin
All have sinned . . .
Letter to Romans

People Scattered
Let us go down and confuse their language.
The book of Genesis

ACT 4

The Surprising Victory of Jesus
The Lord God will give him the throne of his father David.
Gospel of Luke

Jesus Dies ca. AD 30; 3 Days Later He Rises from the Dead
The Messiah will suffer and rise from the dead on the third day.
Gospel of Luke

JESUS

Jesus Begins His Work
Matthew, Mark, Luke and John tell the story of Jesus from different perspectives.

Beginning of Kings' Rule
Your house and your kingdom
will endure forever.
The book of Samuel-Kings
Kings begin ruling ca. 1000 BC
Saul
David
Solomon

Kingdoms Exiled
Israel 722 BC
Judah 586 BC

MOSES DAVID

**Moses Leads Israel
out of Slavery**
In your unfailing love
you will lead the people
you have redeemed.
The book of Exodus

Kingdom Divided

Temple Rebuilt
516 BC
In this place I will
grant peace
Prophet Haggai

The Church
Today

ACT 5

God Comes Home
Then I saw "a new
heaven and a new earth."
Revelation

The Renewed People of God
. . . to call all the Gentiles
to the obedience that
comes from faith for
his name's sake.
Letter to Romans

ACT 6

A GUIDE TO
THE BOOKS
OF THE
NEW TESTAMENT

(pause and pray before you read the Scriptures)

The Books of the Bible edition expresses the ancient concept of the fourfold gospel in a fresh way. Here each gospel is placed at the beginning of a group of closely related books. In this way the groups of books can be seen as giving four witnesses to the one gospel of Jesus the Messiah. This cross-shaped presentation of the New Testament highlights the uniqueness of each voice while preserving the unity of the collection.

A WORD ABOUT
THE BOOKS OF THE BIBLE

The Bible isn't a single book. It's a collection of many books that were written, preserved and gathered together so that they could be shared with new generations of readers. Reading, of course, is not an end in itself. Especially in the case of the Bible, reading is a means of entering into the story. Overall, the Bible is an invitation to the reader first to view the world in a new way, and then to become an agent of the world's renewal. Reading is a step in this journey. *The Books of the Bible* is intended to help readers have a more meaningful encounter with the sacred writings and to read with more understanding, so they can take their places more readily within this story of new creation.

Just as the Bible is not a single book, the Bible is more than bare words. Those who wrote its books chose to put them in particular forms, using the literary conventions appropriate to those forms. Many different kinds of writing are found in the Bible: poetry, narrative, wisdom collections, letters, law codes, apocalyptic visions and more. All of these forms must be read as the literature they really are, or else misunderstanding and distortion of meaning are bound to follow. In order to engage the text on its own terms, good readers will honor the agreement between themselves and the biblical writers implied by the choices of particular forms. Good readers will respect the conventions of these forms. In other words, they'll read poetry as poetry, songs as songs, stories as stories, and so forth.

Unfortunately, for some time now the Bible has been printed in a format that hides its literary forms under a mask of numbers. These break the text into bits and sections that the authors never intended. And so *The Books of the Bible* seeks instead to present the books in their distinctive literary forms and structures. It draws on the key insight that visual presentation can be a crucial aid to right reading, good understanding and a better engagement with the Bible.

Specifically, this edition of the Bible differs from the most common current format in several significant ways:

: chapter and verse numbers have been removed from the text;

: the books are presented instead according to the internal divisions that we believe their authors have indicated;

: a single-column setting is used to present the text more clearly and naturally, and to avoid disrupting the intended line breaks in poetry;

: footnotes, section headings and any other additional materials have been removed from the pages of the sacred text;

: individual books that later tradition divided into two or more parts are put back together again; and

: the books have been placed in an order that we hope will help readers understand them better.

Why have we made these changes? First of all, the chapters and verses in the Bible weren't put there by the original authors. The present system of chapter divisions was devised in the thirteenth century, and our present verse divisions weren't added until the sixteenth. Chapters and verses have imposed a foreign structure on the Bible and made it more difficult to read with understanding. Chapter divisions typically don't correspond with the actual divisions of thought. They require readers to make sense of only part of a longer discussion as if it were complete in itself, or else to try to combine two separate discussions into one coherent whole. Moreover, because the Bible's chapters are all roughly the same length, they can at best only indicate sections of a certain size. This hides the existence of both larger and smaller units of thought within biblical books.

When verses are treated as intentional units (as their numbering suggests they should be), they encourage the Bible to be read as a giant reference book, perhaps as a collection of rules or as a series of propositions. Also, when "Bible verses" are treated as independent and free-standing statements, they can be taken selectively out of context and arranged in such a way as to suggest that the Bible supports beliefs and positions that it really doesn't.

It is true that chapter and verse numbers allow ease of reference. But finding passages at this speed may be a dubious benefit since this can encourage ignoring the text *around* the sought out citation. In order to encourage greater understanding and more responsible use of the Bible, we've removed chapter and verse numberings from the text entirely. (A chapter-and-verse range is included at the bottom of each page.)

Because the biblical books were handwritten, read out loud and then hand-copied long before standardized printing, their authors and compilers needed a way to indicate divisions within the text itself. They often did this by repeating a phrase or expression each time they made a transition from one section to another. We can confirm that particular phrases are significant in this way by observing how their placement reinforces a structure that can already be recognized implicitly from other characteristics of a book, such as changes in topic, movement in place or time, or shifts from one kind of writing to another. Through line spacing, we've marked off sections of varying sizes. The smallest are indicated by one blank line, the next largest by two lines, and so on, up to four-line breaks in the largest books. We've also indicated key divisions with a large initial capital letter of new sections. Our goal is to encourage meaningful units to be read in their entirety and so with greater appreciation and understanding.

Footnotes, section headings and other supplemental materials have been removed from the page in order to give readers a more direct and immediate experience of the word of God. At the beginning of each biblical book we've included an invitation to that particular writing with background information on why it was written and how we understand it to be put together. Beyond this, we encourage readers to study the Bible in community. We believe that if they do, they and their teachers, leaders and peers will provide one another with much more information and many more insights than could ever be included in notes added by publishers.

The books of the Bible were written or recorded individually. When they were gathered together, they were placed into a variety of orders. Unfortunately, the order in which today's readers typically encounter these books is yet another factor that hinders their understanding. Paul's letters, for example, have been put in order of length. They are badly out of historical order, and this makes it difficult to read them with an appreciation for where they fit in the course of his life or how they express the development of his thought. The traditional order of the biblical books can also encourage misunderstandings of what kind of writing a particular work is. For example, the book of James has strong affinities with other biblical books in the wisdom tradition. But it's typically placed within a group of letters, suggesting that it, too, should be read as a letter. To help readers overcome such difficulties, we've sought to order the books so that their literary types, their circumstances of composition and the theological traditions they reflect will be evident. Our introductions to each of the different parts of the Bible will explain how we have ordered the books in these sections, and why.

Just as the work of Bible translation is never finished, the work of formatting the Bible on the principles described here will never be completed. Advances in the literary interpretation of the biblical books will undoubtedly enable the work we've begun here to be extended and improved in the years ahead. Yet the need to help readers overcome the many obstacles inherent in the Bible's current format is urgent, so we humbly offer the results of our work to those seeking an improved visual presentation of its sacred books.

We gratefully acknowledge the assistance of many lay people, clergy, scholars and people engaged in active Scripture outreach who've reviewed our work. They've shared their considerable knowledge and expertise with us and continue to provide valuable insights and guidance. However, final responsibility for all of the decisions in this format rests with us. We trust that readers will gain a deeper appreciation for, and a greater understanding of, these sacred texts. Our hope and prayer is that their engagement with *The Books of the Bible* will enable them to take up their own roles in God's great drama of redemption.

The Bible Design Group

Biblica

Colorado Springs, Colorado

March 2011

More information on The Books of the Bible may be found at

Biblica.com/TheBooks

INVITATION TO
THE NEW TESTAMENT

The New Testament is the second of the two major divisions in the Bible, filling the final one-quarter of its pages. It continues the story, begun in the First Testament, of how God is restoring his original purpose in creation by working through the chosen people of Israel. It tells specifically how this story reached its crowning moment in the first century AD as Jesus of Nazareth, Israel's Messiah, answered the question of who God is and what he's like once and for all.

Through his teaching, Jesus revealed the deepest meaning of the laws and institutions God gave to the people of Israel. Through his actions, he demonstrated what human life and community were meant to be, as he brought healing and restoration everywhere he went. And through his death and resurrection, Jesus introduced the forgiveness and life of the age to come into the present age. The New Testament also tells how the followers of Jesus formed a new community and invited people from all over the world to join them. It describes how they worked together to live out the reign of God that Jesus had announced and begun. Finally, the New Testament looks ahead to the day when Jesus will return to renew all of creation and to establish God's justice and peace throughout the earth.

The New Testament tells this story through the words of twenty-six different books that were written for a variety of occasions between the middle and end of the first century. These books vary in length and they represent several different kinds of writing. Most of them are letters, some as short as a single page. On the other hand, a book of history that contains two volumes, Luke-Acts, makes up one quarter of the entire New Testament. There are also books that continue literary traditions developed in the First Testament. James is similar to the wisdom books of Proverbs and Ecclesiastes, and Revelation is an apocalypse like the second half of the book of Daniel.

The New Testament also contains what are traditionally known as the four Gospels: Matthew, Mark, Luke (the first half of Luke-Acts) and John. "Gospel" should not be thought of primarily as a specific kind of writing. The word actually refers to the content of these books: it means good news. In the New Testament, this term refers to the basic content of the message about Jesus that his followers shared far and wide. Thus *The Gospel According to Matthew* (the traditional title of that book) originally meant the good news as told by Matthew. The story of Jesus' life does serve as the framework and foundation for the books of Matthew, Mark, Luke and John, but in important ways these books still differ from one another in their literary character (as the invitations to them will indicate). When we read all of the New Testament's books with an appreciation for when and why they were written, and for the kind of literature they represent, the story of how Jesus brought God's plan to its culmination unfolds before us.

Unfortunately, the order of the books of the New Testament in most printed

Bibles today doesn't help us appreciate these things. For example, since Luke and Acts are two volumes of a single work, they should be read together. The three letters of John are best understood when read with the Gospel of John, since they are all by the same author and reflect the same perspective. But in the traditional order, Luke and Acts are separated by the Gospel of John, and John's letters are separated from his Gospel by most of the New Testament. In addition, the wisdom book of James has been traditionally placed in the middle of a group of letters, suggesting that it should be read as a letter. (It shouldn't.) And in most printed Bibles, the thirteen letters the apostle Paul wrote are presented roughly in order of length. As a result, they're out of historical order. This makes it difficult to read them with an appreciation for where they fit in the context of his life and for how they express the development of his thought.

The order of the New Testament books in this edition seeks to express the ancient concept of the fourfold gospel in a fresh way. The traditional priority of the stories of Jesus is retained, but now each Gospel is placed at the beginning of a group of related books. The presentation of four witnesses to the one gospel of Jesus the Messiah is enhanced by a fuller arrangement that will help readers better appreciate why the books of the New Testament were written and what kind of literature they represent. The four sets of books, each headed by a Gospel, form a cross, as it were, around the central figure of Jesus. Each sheds its light on his story in a unique way.

We have reunited the two volumes of Luke-Acts and placed them first because they provide an overview of the New Testament period. This allows readers to see where most of the other books belong. Next come Paul's letters in the order in which we believe they were most likely written. Luke was one of Paul's co-workers in sharing the good news about Jesus, so it's appropriate to pair Paul's letters with Luke's volumes. The Gospel according to Matthew comes next, together with two books—Hebrews and James—which are also addressed to Jews who believed in Jesus as their Messiah. Then comes the Gospel according to Mark (which many scholars believe was actually the first Gospel to be written), together with the letters of Peter, since Mark seems to tell the story of Jesus' life from Peter's perspective. Also included in this group is the letter of Jude, which is similar to Peter's second letter. Our final group begins with the Gospel according to John, which can suitably come last among the Gospels because it represents a mature reflection, after many years, on the meaning of Jesus' life. The letters of John follow his Gospel. The book of Revelation is appropriately placed last and by itself, since it is unique in literary type and perspective, and since it describes how God's saving plan for all of creation will ultimately be realized.

Israel's continuing story and its climax in
THE LIFE, DEATH
AND RESURRECTION OF
JESUS THE MESSIAH,
the announcement of
GOD'S VICTORY OVER HUMANITY'S
ENEMIES SIN AND DEATH,
and the invitation for
ALL PEOPLES TO BE
RECONCILED TO GOD
and to share in his
RESTORATION OF ALL THINGS,

PRESENTED
IN THE BOOKS OF **THE**
NEW TESTAMENT

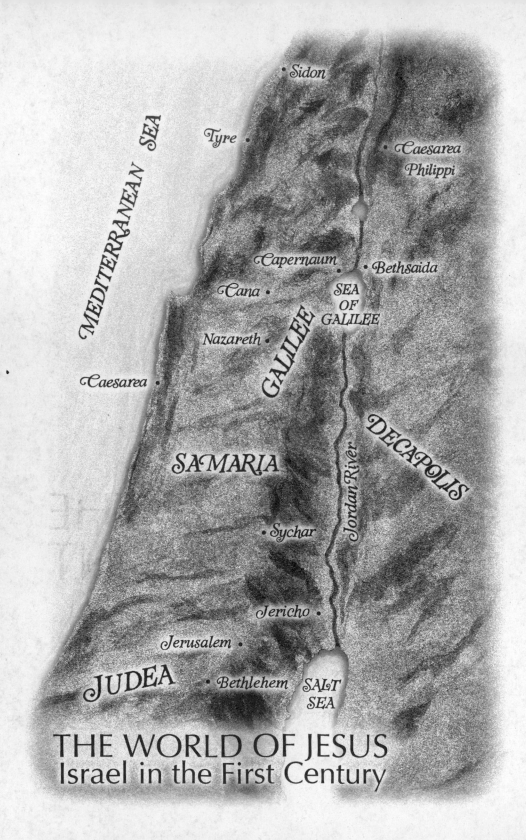

THE WORLD OF JESUS
Israel in the First Century

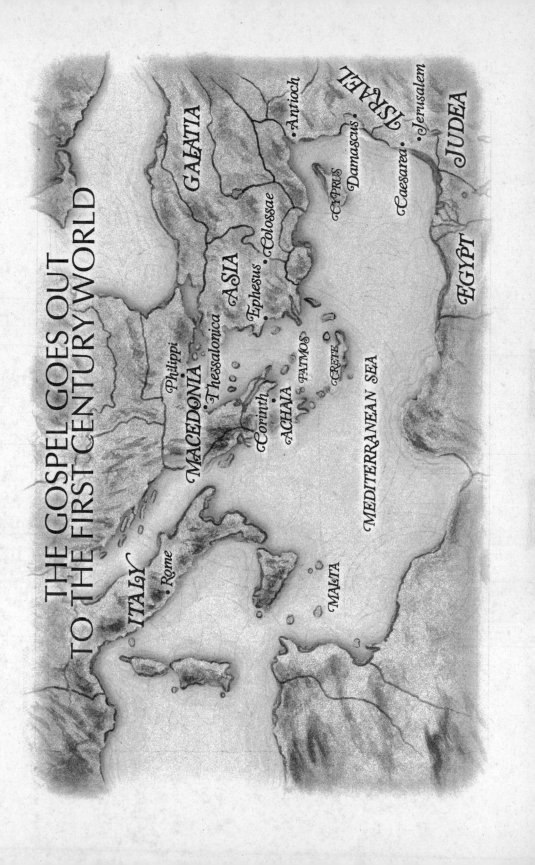

THE GOSPEL GOES OUT
TO THE FIRST CENTURY WORLD

ITALY

Rome

MACEDONIA

Philippi

Thessalonica

ASIA

Ephesus

Colossae

GALATIA

Corinth

ACHAIA

PATMOS

CRETE

MALTA

MEDITERRANEAN SEA

CYPRUS

Antioch

Damascus

ISRAEL

Caesarea

Jerusalem

JUDEA

EGYPT

David Thomason 2010

INVITATION TO
LUKE–ACTS

Luke and Acts are two volumes of a single work. Beginning with the life and ministry of Jesus the Messiah, they trace the history of his followers down to the author's own day, some time after the middle of the first century AD.

Luke wrote this history to serve several important purposes. The first was to assure followers of Jesus that what they'd been taught about him was trustworthy. It's likely that Theophilus, the man who sponsored and helped circulate this work, was a Roman official, since Luke addresses him in his opening dedication as *Theophilus . . . your Excellency*, using the title generally reserved for such officials. Luke speaks of him as someone who's been instructed in the Christian faith and says he wants him to know *the truth of all you have been taught*. Luke no doubt wishes the same for the many people that Theophilus will share the work with.

Luke–Acts also shows that the true God is faithful and can be trusted completely. It does this by documenting how God kept a promise made to the people of Israel by sending them Jesus as their long-awaited Messiah, or King. It then shows how God invited non-Jews (known as Gentiles) to follow Jesus as well. Luke's history thus demonstrates that the extension of God's blessings to people such as Theophilus and his friends represents not a fickle change in plans, but the masterful fulfillment of a plan God has been pursuing over the ages. In the Bible's story, it has been Israel's role all along to bring God's light to the rest of the world. The earliest Jesus-followers take up this calling by announcing Jesus' victory over sin and death to all the nations. This theme runs all the way through both volumes, with Paul and Barnabas telling one Jewish audience:

> For thus we were commanded by the Lord:
>
> > "I have set you as a light to the pagan nations,
> > so that you may bring my salvation to the ends of the earth."

So Luke–Acts tells the story of how God invited first the people of Israel, then the people of all nations, to follow Jesus. The form of Luke's history reflects this message. In the first volume, the movement is towards Jerusalem, the center of Jewish national life. In the second volume, the movement is away from Jerusalem to other nations, closing with Paul proclaiming the kingdom of God in Rome, the capital of the empire.

Compared with other national histories of the time, which often contained twenty or more volumes, Luke's is short. Each of its two volumes covers about 30 years. Like other historians of his day, Luke provides an outline of important events and stocks it with details from the sources available to him: letters, speeches, songs, travel accounts, trial transcripts and biographical anecdotes. (Luke had access to these as a co-worker and traveling companion of the apostle Paul.)

The first volume, the book of Luke, begins with a preliminary section that introduces the main themes of the whole work by telling the story of Jesus' early life. This book then has three main sections:

: The first one describes Jesus' ministry in Galilee, the northern area of the land of Israel (pp. 11–23).
: The second section presents a long journey to Jerusalem, during which Jesus teaches and answers questions about what it means to follow him (pp. 24–41).
: The third describes how Jesus gave his life in Jerusalem and then rose again to be the Ruler and the Savior of the world (pp. 41–52).

The second volume, the book of Acts, has six parts. Each one describes a successive phase in the expansion of the community of Jesus' followers outward from Jerusalem. The divisions between them are marked by variations on the phrase, *the word of God was increasing and spreading.*

: In the first phase, the community is established in Jerusalem and becomes Greek-speaking, enabling it to spread its message throughout the empire (pp. 53–62).
: In the second phase, the community expands into the rest of Palestine (pp. 62–68).
: In the third phase, Gentiles are included in the community along with Jews (pp. 68–73).
: In the fourth part, the community intentionally sends messengers westward into the populous Roman province of Asia (pp. 73–79).
: In the fifth phase, these messengers enter Europe (pp. 79–85).
: In the final phase, the community reaches all the way to the capital of Rome and into the highest levels of society. God's invitation is thus extended to all nations (pp. 85–100).

| LUKE |

S everal people have set themselves to relate the events that have taken place among us, as they were told by the first witnesses, who later became ministers of the word. After I, myself, had carefully gone over the whole story from the beginning, it seemed right for me to give you, Theophilus, an orderly account, so that your Excellency may know the truth of all you have been taught.

I n the days of Herod, king of Judea, there lived a priest named Zechariah, belonging to the priestly clan of Abiah. Elizabeth, Zechariah's wife, also belonged to a priestly family. Both of them were upright in the eyes of God, and lived blamelessly, in accordance with all the laws and commands of the Lord, but they had no child. Elizabeth could not have any and now they were both very old.

Now, while Zechariah and those with him were fulfilling their office, it fell to him by lot, according to the custom of the priests, to enter the Sanctuary of the Lord and burn incense. At the time of offering incense, all the people were praying outside; it was then, that an angel of the Lord appeared to him, standing on the right side of the altar of incense. On seeing the angel, Zechariah was deeply troubled and fear took hold of him.

But the angel said to him, "Don't be afraid, Zechariah, be assured that your prayer has been heard. Your wife Elizabeth will bear you a son and you shall name him John. He will bring joy and gladness to you, and many will rejoice at his birth.

This son of yours will be great in the eyes of the Lord. Listen: he shall never drink wine or strong drink; but he will be filled with the Holy Spirit even from his mother's womb. Through him, many of the people of Israel will turn to the Lord their God. He, himself, will open the way to the Lord, with the spirit and power of the prophet Elijah; he will reconcile fathers and children; and lead the disobedient to wisdom and righteousness, in order to make ready a people prepared for the Lord."

Zechariah said to the angel, "How can I believe this? I am an old man and my wife is elderly, too." The angel replied, "I am Gabriel, who stands before God; and I am the one sent to speak to you, and to bring you this good news! My words will come true in their time. But you would not believe; and now, you will be silent and unable to speak until this has happened."

Meanwhile, the people waited for Zechariah; and they were surprised that he delayed so long in the Sanctuary. When he finally appeared, he could not speak to them; and they realized that he had seen a vision in the Sanctuary. He remained dumb and made signs to them.

When his time of service was completed, Zechariah returned home; and, some time later, Elizabeth became pregnant. For five months she kept to herself, remaining at home, and thinking, "This, for me, is the Lord's doing! This is his time for mercy, and for taking away my public disgrace."

In the sixth month, the angel Gabriel was sent from God, to a town of Galilee called Nazareth. He was sent to a virgin, who was betrothed to a man named Joseph, of the family of David; and the virgin's name was Mary.

The angel came to her and said, "Rejoice, full of grace, the Lord is with you!" Mary was troubled at these words, wondering what this greeting could mean.

But the angel said, "Do not fear, Mary, for God has looked kindly on you. You shall conceive and bear a son; and you shall call him Jesus. He will be great, and shall rightly be called Son of the Most High. The Lord God will give him the kingdom of David, his ancestor; he will rule over the people of Jacob forever; and his reign shall have no end."

Then Mary said to the angel, "How can this be, since I am a virgin?" And the angel said to her, "The Holy Spirit will come upon you and the power of the Most High will overshadow you; therefore, the holy child to be born of you shall be called Son of God. Even your relative, Elizabeth, is expecting a son in her old age, although she was unable to have a child; and she is now in her sixth month. With God nothing is impossible."

Then Mary said, "I am the handmaid of the Lord, let it be done to me as you have said." And the angel left her.

Mary then set out for a town in the hill country of Judah. She entered the house of Zechariah and greeted Elizabeth. When Elizabeth heard Mary's greeting, the baby leapt in her womb. Elizabeth was filled with the Holy Spirit, and, giving a loud cry, said, "You are most blessed among women; and blessed is the fruit of your womb! How is it, that the mother of my Lord comes to me? The moment your greeting sounded in my ears, the baby within me suddenly leapt for joy. Blessed are you, who believed that the Lord's word would come true!"

And Mary said,

> "My soul proclaims the greatness of the Lord,
> my spirit exults in God, my savior!

> He has looked upon his servant, in her lowliness,
> and people, forever, will call me blessed.

> The Mighty One has done great things for me,
> Holy is his Name!

> From age to age, his mercy extends
> to those who live in his presence.

> He has acted with power and done wonders,
> and scattered the proud with their plans.

> He has put down the mighty from their thrones,
> and lifted up those who are downtrodden.

> He has filled the hungry with good things,
> but has sent the rich away empty.

> He held out his hand to Israel, his servant,
> for he remembered his mercy,

> even as he promised to our fathers,
> to Abraham and his descendants forever."

Mary remained with Elizabeth about three months, and then returned home.

When the time came for Elizabeth, she gave birth to a son. Her neighbors and relatives heard that the merciful Lord had done a wonderful thing for her, and they rejoiced with her.

When, on the eighth day, they came to attend the circumcision of the child, they wanted to name him Zechariah after his father. But his mother said, "Not so; he shall be called John." They said to her, "But no one in your family has that name!" and they made signs to his father for the name he wanted to give him. Zechariah asked for a writing tablet, and wrote on it, "His name is John;" and they were very surprised. Immediately, Zechariah could speak again, and his first words were in praise of God.

A holy fear came on all in the neighborhood, and throughout the hill country of Judea the people talked about these events. All who heard of it, pondered in their minds, and wondered, "What will this child be?" For they understood that the hand of the Lord was with him.

Zechariah, filled with the Holy Spirit, sang this canticle:

"Blessed be the Lord God of Israel,
for he has come and redeemed his people.

In the house of David his servant,
he has raised up for us a victorious Savior;

as he promised through his prophets of old,

salvation from our enemies
and from the hand of our foes.

He has shown mercy to our fathers;
and remembered his holy Covenant,

the oath he swore to Abraham, our father,
to deliver us from the enemy,

that we might serve him fearlessly,
as a holy and righteous people,
all the days of our lives.

And you, my child,
shall be called Prophet of the Most High,

for you shall go before the Lord,
to prepare the way for him,

and to enable his people to know of their salvation,
when he comes to forgive their sins.

This is the work of the mercy of our God,
who comes from on high, as a rising sun,

shining on those who live in darkness
and in the shadow of death,

and guiding our feet into the way of peace."

As the child grew up, he was seen to be strong in the Spirit; and he lived in the desert, until the day when he appeared openly in Israel.

At that time, the emperor issued a decree for a census of the whole empire to be taken. This first census was taken when Quirinus was governor of Syria. Everyone had to be registered in his own town. So everyone set out for his own city. Joseph, too, set out from Nazareth of Galilee. As he belonged to the family of David, being a descendant of his, he went to Judea, to David's town of Bethlehem, to be registered with Mary, his wife, who was with child.

They were in Bethlehem when the time came for her to have her child; and she gave birth to a son, her firstborn. She wrapped him in torn rags, and laid him in a feeding trough, because there was no place for them in the inn.

There were shepherds camping in the countryside, taking turns to watch over their flocks by night. Suddenly, an angel of the Lord appeared to them, with the glory of the Lord shining around them.

As they were terrified, the angel said to them, "Don't be afraid; I am here to give you good news, great joy for all the people. Today, a Savior has been born to you in David's town; he is the Messiah and the Lord. Let this be a sign to you: you will find a baby wrapped in torn rags and lying in a feeding trough."

Suddenly, the angel was surrounded by many more heavenly spirits, praising God and saying,

> "Glory to God in the highest,
> and Peace, on earth, to those whom God loves."

When the angels had left them and gone back to heaven, the shepherds said to one another, "Let us go as far as Bethlehem, and see what the Lord has made known to us." So they came hurriedly, and found Mary and Joseph, and the baby lying in the feeding trough. On seeing him, they related what they had been told about the child; and all were astonished on hearing the shepherds.

As for Mary, she treasured all these words, and pondered them in her heart.

The shepherds then returned, giving glory and praise to God for all they had heard and seen, just as the angels had told them.

On the eighth day, the circumcision of the baby had to be performed; he was named Jesus, the name the angel had given him before he was conceived.

When the day came for the purification according to the law of Moses, they brought the baby up to Jerusalem, to present him to the Lord, as it is written in the law of the Lord: Every firstborn male shall be consecrated to God. And they offered a sacrifice, as ordered in the law of the Lord: a pair of turtledoves or two young pigeons.

There lived in Jerusalem, at this time, a very upright and devout man named Simeon; the Holy Spirit was in him. He looked forward to the time when the Lord would comfort Israel; and he had been assured, by the Holy Spirit, that he would not die before seeing the Messiah of the Lord. So, he was led into the temple by the Holy Spirit at the time the parents brought the child Jesus, to do for him according to the custom of the law.

Simeon took the child in his arms, and blessed God, saying,

> "Now, O Lord, you can dismiss your servant in peace,
> for you have fulfilled your word
>
> and my eyes have seen your salvation,
> which you display for all the people to see.
>
> Here is the light you will reveal to the nations,
> and the glory of your people Israel."

His father and mother wondered at what was said about the child. Simeon blessed them, and said to Mary, his mother, "Know this: your son is a sign; a sign established for the falling and rising of many in Israel, a sign of contradiction; and a sword will pierce your own soul, so that, out of many hearts, thoughts may be revealed."

There was also a prophetess named Anna, daughter of Phanuel, of the tribe of Asher. After leaving her father's home, she had been seven years with her husband; and since then, she had been continually about the temple, serving God, as a widow, night and day, in fasting and prayer. She was now eighty-four. Coming up at that time, she gave praise to God, and spoke of the child to all who looked forward to the deliverance of Jerusalem.

When the parents had fulfilled all that was required by the law of the Lord, they returned to their town, Nazareth in Galilee. There, the child grew in stature and strength, and was filled with wisdom: the grace of God was upon him.

Every year, the parents of Jesus went to Jerusalem for the Feast of the Passover, as was customary. And when Jesus was twelve years old, he went up with them, according to the custom of this feast. After the festival was over, they returned, but the boy Jesus remained in Jerusalem; and his parents did not know it.

They assumed that he was in their group of travelers, and, after walking the whole day, they looked for him among their relatives and friends. As they did not find him, they went back to Jerusalem, searching for him; and, on the third day, they found him in the temple, sitting among the teachers, listening to them and asking questions. And all the people were amazed at his understanding and his answers.

His parents were very surprised when they saw him; and his mother said to him, "Son, why have you done this to us? Your father and I were very worried while searching for you." Then he said to them, "Why were you looking for me? Did you not know that I must be in my Father's house?" But they did not understand this answer.

Jesus went down with them, returning to Nazareth, and he continued to be obedient to them. As for his mother, she kept all these things in her heart.

And Jesus increased in wisdom and age, and in divine and human favor.

It was the fifteenth year of the rule of the Emperor Tiberius; Pontius Pilatus was governor of Judea; Herod ruled over Galilee, his brother Philip ruled over the country of Iturea and Trachonitis; and Lysanias ruled over Abilene. Annas and Caiaphas were the High Priests at the time when the word of God came to John, the son of Zechariah, in the desert.

John proclaimed a baptism, for repentant people to obtain forgiveness of sins; and he went through the whole country bordering the Jordan River. It was just as is written in the book of the prophet Isaiah:

> Listen to this voice crying out in the desert,
>
> 'Prepare the way of the Lord,
> make his path straight!
>
> The valleys will be filled
> and the mountains and hills made low.
>
> Everything crooked will be made straight
> and the rough paths smooth;
> and every human being will see the salvation of God!'

John said to the crowds who came out to be baptized by him, "You brood of vipers! How will you escape when divine punishment comes? Produce now, the fruits of a true change of heart; and do not deceive yourselves by saying, 'We have Abraham for our ancestor!' For I tell you, God can make children of Abraham from these stones. The ax is already laid to the root of the tree; and every tree that fails to produce good fruit will be cut down and thrown into the fire."

The people asked him, "What are we to do?" And John answered, "If you have two coats, give one to the person who has none; and if you have food, do the same."

Even tax collectors came to be baptized, and asked him, "Master, what must we do?" John said to them, "Collect no more than your fixed rate." Then some soldiers asked John, "What about us? What are we to do?" And he answered, "Don't take anything by force, or threaten the people by denouncing them falsely. Be content with your pay."

The people were wondering about John's identity, "Could he be the Messiah?" Then John answered them, "I baptize you with water, but the one who is coming will do much more: he will baptize you with the Holy Spirit and fire. As for me, I am not worthy to untie his sandal. He comes with a winnowing fan, to clear his threshing floor, and gather the grain into his barn. But the chaff he will burn, with fire that never goes out."

With these, and many other words, John announced the Good News to the people, until Herod put him in prison. For John had reproached Herod, for living with Herodias, his brother's wife, and for his evil deeds. Then Herod added another crime to all the rest he had committed: he put John in prison.

Now, with all the people who came to be baptized, Jesus, too, was baptized. Then, while he was praying, the heavens opened: the Holy Spirit came down upon him in the bodily form of a dove, and a voice from heaven was heard, "You are my Son, in whom I am well pleased."

When Jesus made his appearance, he had reached the age of thirty years. He was known as the Son of Joseph, whose father and forefathers were:

Heli, Matthat, Levi, Melchi, Jannai, Joseph, Matthathias, Amos, Nahum, Esli, Naggai, Maath, Mattathias, Semein, Josech, Joda, Joanan, Rhesa, Zerubbabel, Shealtiel, Neri, Melchi, Addi, Cosam, Elmadam, Er, Joshua, Eliezer, Jorim, Matthat, Levi, Simeon, Judah, Joseph, Jonam, Eliakim, Melea, Menna, Mattatha, Nathan, David, Jesse, Obed, Boaz, Salmon, Nahson, Amminadab, Adnim, Arni, Hezron, Perez, Judah, Jacob, Isaac, Abraham, Terah, Nahor, Serug, Reu, Peleg, Eber, Shelah, Cainan, Arphaxad, Shem, Noah, Lamech, Methuselah, Enoch, Jared, Malaleel, Cainan, Enos, Seth, and Adam—who was from God.

Jesus was now full of the Holy Spirit. As he returned from the Jordan, the Spirit led him into the desert, where he was tempted by the devil for forty days. He did not eat anything during that time, and at the end he was hungry. The devil then said to him, "If you are the Son of God, tell this stone to turn into bread." But Jesus answered, "Scripture says: People cannot live on bread alone."

Then the devil took him up to a high place, and showed him, in a flash, all the nations of the world. And he said to Jesus, "I can give you power over all the nations; and their wealth will be yours; for power and wealth have been delivered to me; and I give them to whom I wish. All this will be yours, provided you worship me." But Jesus replied, "Scripture says: You shall worship the Lord your God and serve him alone."

Then the devil took him up to Jerusalem, and set him on the highest wall of the temple; and he said, "If you are God's Son, throw yourself down from here; for it is written: God will order his angels to take care of you; and again: They will hold you in their hands, lest you hurt your foot on the stones." But Jesus replied, "It is written: You shall not challenge the Lord your God."

When the devil had exhausted every way of tempting Jesus, he left him, to return another time.

Jesus acted with the power of the Spirit; and on his return to Galilee, the news about him spread throughout all that territory. He began teaching in the synagogues of the Jews and everyone praised him.

When Jesus came to Nazareth, where he had been brought up, he entered the synagogue on the Sabbath, as he usually did. He stood up to read, and they handed him the book of the prophet Isaiah.

Jesus then unrolled the scroll and found the place where it is written:

"The Spirit of the Lord is upon me.
He has anointed me,
to bring good news to the poor;
to proclaim liberty to captives;
and new sight to the blind;
to free the oppressed;
and to announce the Lord's year of mercy."

Jesus then rolled up the scroll, gave it to the attendant and sat down; and the eyes of all in the synagogue were fixed on him. Then he said to them, "Today, these prophetic words come true, even as you listen."

All agreed with him, and were lost in wonder, while he spoke of the grace of God. Nevertheless they asked, "Who is this but Joseph's Son?" So he said, "Doubtless you will quote me the saying: Doctor, heal yourself! Do here, in your town, what they say you did in Capernaum."

Jesus added, "No prophet is honored in his own country. Truly, I say to you, there were many widows in Israel in the days of Elijah, when the heavens withheld rain for three years and six months and a great famine came over the whole land. Yet, Elijah was not sent to any of them, but to a widow of Zarephath, in the country of Sidon. There were also many lepers in Israel in the time of Elisha, the prophet; and no one was healed except Naaman, the Syrian."

On hearing these words, the whole assembly became indignant. They rose up and brought him out of the town, to the edge of the hill on which Nazareth is built, intending to throw him down the cliff. But he passed through their midst and went his way.

Jesus went down to Capernaum, a town of Galilee, and began teaching the people at the Sabbath meetings. They were astonished at the way he taught them, for his word was spoken with authority.

In the synagogue, there was a man possessed by an evil spirit, who shouted in a loud voice, "What do you want with us, Jesus of Nazareth? Have you come to destroy us? I recognize you: you are the Holy One of God." Then Jesus said to him sharply, "Be silent and leave this man!" The evil spirit then threw the man down in front of them, and came out of him without doing him harm.

Amazement seized all these people, and they said to one another, "What does this mean? He commands the evil spirits with authority and power. He orders, and you see how they come out!" And news about Jesus spread throughout the surrounding area.

Leaving the synagogue, Jesus went to the house of Simon. His mother-in-law was suffering from high fever, and they asked him to do something for her. Bending over her, he rebuked the fever, and it left her. Immediately, she got up and waited on them.

At sunset, people suffering from many kinds of sickness were brought to Jesus. Laying his hands on each one, he healed them. Demons were driven out, howling as they departed from their victims, "You are the Son of God!" He rebuked them and would not allow them to speak, for they knew he was the Messiah.

Jesus left at daybreak and looked for a solitary place. People went out in search of him, and finding him, they tried to dissuade him from leaving. But he said, "I have to go to other towns, to announce the good news of the kingdom of God. That is what I was sent to do." And Jesus continued to preach in the synagogues of Galilee.

One day, as Jesus stood by the Lake of Gennesaret, with a crowd gathered around him listening to the word of God, he caught sight of two boats, left at the water's edge by fishermen, now washing their nets. He got into one of the boats, the one belonging to Simon, and asked him to pull out a little from the shore. There he sat, and continued to teach the crowd.

When he had finished speaking, he said to Simon, "Put out into deep water and lower your nets for a catch." Simon replied, "Master, we worked hard all night and caught nothing. But if you say so, I will lower the nets." This they did, and caught such a large number of fish that their nets began to break. They signaled their partners in the other boat to come and help them. They came, and they filled both boats almost to the point of sinking.

Upon seeing this, Simon Peter fell at Jesus' knees, saying, "Leave me, Lord, for I am a sinful man!" For he and his companions were amazed at the catch they had made, and so were Simon's partners, James and John, Zebedee's sons.

Jesus said to Simon, "Do not be afraid. You will catch people from now on." So they brought their boats to land and followed him, leaving everything.

One day, in another town, a man came to Jesus covered with leprosy. On seeing Jesus, the man bowed down to the ground, and said, "Lord, if you want to, you can make me clean."

Stretching out his hand, Jesus touched the man and said, "Yes, I want to. Be clean." In an instant, the leprosy left him. Then Jesus instructed him, "Tell this to no one. But go, and show yourself to the priest. Make an offering for your healing, as Moses prescribed; that will serve as evidence for them."

But the news about Jesus spread all the more; and large crowds came to him, to listen and to be healed of their sickness. As for Jesus, he would often withdraw to solitary places and pray.

One day, Jesus was teaching, and many Pharisees and teachers of the law had come from every part of Galilee and Judea, and even from Jerusalem. They were sitting there, while the power of the Lord was at work to heal the sick. Then some men brought a paralyzed man who lay on his mat. They tried to enter the house to place him before Jesus, but they couldn't find a way through the crowd. So they went up on the roof, and, removing the tiles, they lowered him on his mat into the middle of the crowd, in front of Jesus.

When Jesus saw their faith, he said to the man, "My friend, your sins are forgiven." At once the teachers of the law and the Pharisees began to wonder, "This man insults God! Who can forgive sins, but God alone?"

But Jesus knew their thoughts and asked them, "Why are you reacting like this? Which is easier to say: 'Your sins are forgiven' or 'Get up and walk'? Now you shall know, that the Son of Man has authority on earth to forgive sins." And Jesus said to the paralyzed man, "Get up, take your mat and go home." At once, the man stood before them. He took up the mat he had been lying on, and went home praising God.

Amazement seized the people and they praised God. They were filled with a holy fear, and said, "What wonderful things we have seen today!"

After this, Jesus went out, and noticing a tax collector named Levi, sitting in the tax-office, he said to him, "Follow me!" So Levi, leaving everything, got up and followed Jesus.

Levi gave a great feast for Jesus, and many tax collectors came to his house, and took their places at the table with the other people. Then the Pharisees and their followers complained to Jesus' disciples, "How is it, that you eat and drink with tax collectors and sinners?" But Jesus spoke up, "Healthy people don't need a doctor, but sick people do. I have not come to call the just, but sinners, to a change of heart."

Some people asked him, "The disciples of John fast often and say long prayers, and so do the disciples of the Pharisees. Why is it, that your disciples eat and drink?" Then Jesus said to them, "You can't make wedding guests fast while the bridegroom is with them. But later, the bridegroom will be taken from them; and they will fast in those days."

Jesus also told them this parable: "No one tears a piece from a new coat to put it on an old one; otherwise the new coat will be torn, and the piece taken from the new coat will not match the old coat. No one puts new wine into old wine skins; otherwise the new wine will burst the skins and be spilled, and the skins will be destroyed as well. But new wine must be put into fresh skins. Yet, no one who has tasted old wine is eager to drink new wine, but says, 'The old is good.'"

One Sabbath Jesus was going through a field of grain, and his disciples began to pick heads of grain, crushing them in their hands for food. Some of the Pharisees asked them, "Why do you do what is forbidden on the Sabbath?" Then Jesus spoke up and asked them, "Have you never read what David did when he and his men were hungry? He entered the house of God, took and ate the bread of the offering, and even gave some to his men, though only priests are allowed to eat that bread." And Jesus added, "The Son of Man is Lord and rules over the Sabbath."

On another Sabbath, Jesus entered the synagogue and began teaching. There was a man with a paralyzed right hand, and the teachers of the law and the Pharisees watched him: Would Jesus heal the man on the Sabbath? If he did, they could accuse him.

But Jesus knew their thoughts, and said to the man, "Get up, and stand in the middle." Then he spoke to them, "I want to ask you: what is allowed by the law on the Sabbath? To do good or to do harm, to save life or to destroy it?" And Jesus looked around at them all.

Then he said to the man, "Stretch out your hand." He stretched it out, and his hand was restored, becoming as healthy as the other. But they were furious, and began to discuss with one another how they could deal with Jesus.

At this time, Jesus went out into the hills to pray, spending the whole night in prayer with God. When day came, he called his disciples to him, and chose Twelve of them, whom he called 'apostles': Simon, whom he named Peter, and his brother Andrew; James and John; Philip and Bartholomew; Matthew and Thomas; James son of Alpheus and Simon called the Zealot; Judas son of James, and Judas Iscariot, who would be the traitor.

Coming down the hill with them, Jesus stood in an open plain. Many of his disciples were there, and a large crowd of people, who had come from all parts of Judea and Jerusalem, and from the coastal cities of Tyre and Sidon. They gathered to hear him and to be healed of their diseases. And people troubled by unclean spirits were cured. The entire crowd tried to touch him, because of the power that went out from him and healed them all.

Then, looking at his disciples, Jesus said,

"Fortunate are you who are poor,
for the kingdom of God is yours.

Fortunate are you, who are hungry now,
for you will be filled.

Fortunate are you, who weep now,
for you will laugh.

Fortunate are you, when people hate you,
when they reject you and insult you
and number you among criminals,
because of the Son of Man.

Rejoice in that day, and leap for joy, for a great reward is kept for you in heaven. Remember, that is how the ancestors of the people treated the prophets.

But alas for you, who have wealth,
for you have been comforted now.

Alas for you, who are full,
for you will go hungry.

Alas for you, who laugh now,
for you will mourn and weep.

Alas for you, when people speak well of you,
for that is how the ancestors of the people treated the false prophets.

But I say to you who hear me: Love your enemies, do good to those who hate you. Bless those who curse you, and pray for those who treat you badly. To the one who strikes you on the cheek, turn the other cheek; from the one who takes your coat, do not keep back your shirt. Give to the one who asks, and if anyone has taken something from you, do not demand it back.

Do to others as you would have others do to you. If you love only those who love you, what kind of grace is yours? Even sinners love those who love them. If you do favors to those who are good to you, what kind of grace is yours? Even sinners do the same. If you lend only when you expect to receive, what kind of grace is yours? For sinners also lend to sinners, expecting to receive something in return.

But love your enemies and do good to them, and lend when there is nothing to expect in return. Then will your reward be great, and you will be sons and daughters of the Most High. For he is kind toward the ungrateful and the wicked. Be merciful, just as your Father is merciful.

Don't be a judge of others and you will not be judged; do not condemn and you will not be condemned; forgive and you will be forgiven; give and it will be given to you, and you will receive in your sack good measure, pressed down, full and running over. For the measure you give will be the measure you receive back."

And Jesus offered this example, "Can a blind person lead another blind person? Surely both will fall into a ditch. A disciple is not above the master; but when fully trained, he will be like the master. So why do you pay attention to the speck in your brother's eye, while you have a log in your eye, and are not conscious of it? How can you say to your neighbor, 'Friend, let me take this speck out of your eye,' when you can't remove the log in your own? You hypocrite! First remove the log from your own eye, and then you will see clearly enough to remove the speck from your neighbor's eye.

No healthy tree bears bad fruit, no poor tree bears good fruit. And each tree is known by the fruit it bears: you don't gather figs from thorns, or grapes from brambles. Similarly, the good person draws good things from the good stored in his heart, and an evil person draws evil things from the evil stored in his heart. For the mouth speaks from the fullness of the heart.

Why do you call me, 'Lord! Lord!' and do not do what I say? I will show you what the one is like, who comes to me, and listens to my words, and acts accordingly. That person is like the builder who dug deep, and laid the foundations of his house on rock. The river overflowed, and the stream dashed against the house, but could not carry it off because the house had been well built.

But the one who listens and does not act, is like a man who built his house on the ground without a foundation. The flood burst against it, and the house fell at once: and what a terrible disaster that was!"

When Jesus had finished teaching the people, he went to Capernaum.

A Roman military officer lived there, whose servant was very sick and near to death, a man very dear to him. So when he heard about Jesus, he sent some elders of the Jews to persuade him to come and save his servant's life. The elders came to Jesus and begged him earnestly, saying, "He deserves this of you, for he loves our people and even built a synagogue for us."

Jesus went with them. He was not far from the house, when the Roman officer sent friends to give this message, "Sir, do not trouble yourself, for I am not worthy to welcome you under my roof. You see, I didn't approach you myself. Just give the order, and my servant will be healed. For I myself, a junior officer, give orders to my soldiers, and I say to this one, 'Go!' and he goes; and to the other, 'Come!' and he comes; and to my servant, 'Do this!' and he does it."

On hearing these words, Jesus was filled with admiration. He turned and said to the people with him, "I say to you, not even in Israel have I found such great faith." The people, sent by the captain, went back to his house; there they found that the servant was well.

A little later, Jesus went to a town called Naim. He was accompanied by his disciples and a great number of people. As he reached the gate of the town, a dead man was being carried out. He was the only son of his mother, and she was a widow; there followed a large crowd of townspeople.

On seeing her, the Lord had pity on her and said, "Don't cry." Then he came up and touched the stretcher, and the men who carried it stopped. Jesus then said, "Young man, I say to you, wake up!" And the dead man sat up and began to speak, and Jesus gave him to his mother. A holy fear came over them all, and they praised God saying, "A great prophet has appeared among us. God has visited his people." This news spread throughout Judea and the surrounding places.

John's disciples informed him about all these things. So John called two of his disciples, and sent them to the Lord with this message, "Are you the one we are expecting, or should we wait for another?" These men came to Jesus and said, "John the Baptist sent us to ask you: Are you the one we are to expect, or should we wait for another?"

At that time, Jesus healed many people of their sicknesses and diseases; he freed them from evil spirits and he gave sight to the blind. Then he answered the messengers, "Go back and tell John what you have seen and heard: the blind see again, the lame walk, lepers are made clean, the deaf hear, the dead are raised to life, and the poor are given good news. Now, listen: Fortunate are those who meet me, and are not offended by me."

When John's messengers had gone, Jesus began speaking to the people about John. And he said, "What did you want to see, when you went to the desert? A reed blowing in the wind? What was there to see? A man dressed in fine clothes? But people who wear fine clothes and enjoy delicate food are found in palaces. What did you go out to see? A prophet? Yes, I tell you, and more than a prophet. For John is the one foretold in Scripture in these words:

> I am sending my messenger ahead of you
> to prepare your way.

No one may be found greater than John among those born of women; but, I tell you, the least in the kingdom of God is greater than he.

All the people listening to him, even the tax collectors, had acknowledged the will of God in receiving the baptism of John, whereas the Pharisees and the teachers of the law, in not letting themselves be baptized by him, ignored the will of God.

And Jesus said, "What comparison can I use for the people? What are they like? They are like children sitting in the marketplace, about whom their companions complain,

> 'We piped you a tune
> and you wouldn't dance;
>
> we sang funeral songs
> and you wouldn't cry.'

Remember John: he didn't eat bread or drink wine, and you said, 'He has an evil spirit.' Next, came the Son of Man, eating and drinking; and you say, 'Look, a glutton for food and wine, a friend of tax collectors and sinners.' But the children of Wisdom always recognize her work."

One of the Pharisees asked Jesus to share his meal, so he went to the Pharisee's home, and as usual reclined at the table to eat. And it happened that, a woman of this town, who was known as a sinner, heard that he was in the Pharisee's house. She brought an alabaster jar of perfume, and stood behind him, at his feet, weeping. She wet his feet with tears; she dried them with her hair; she kissed his feet and poured the perfume on them.

The Pharisee who had invited Jesus was watching, and thought, "If this man were a prophet, he would know what sort of person is touching him; isn't this woman a sinner?"

Then Jesus spoke to the Pharisee and said, "Simon, I have something to ask you." He answered, "Speak, master." And Jesus said, "Two people were in debt to the same creditor. One owed him five hundred silver coins, and the other fifty. As they were unable to pay him back, he graciously canceled the debts of both. Now, which of them will love him more?"

Simon answered, "The one, I suppose, who was forgiven more." And Jesus said, "You are right." And turning toward the woman, he said to Simon, "Do you see this woman? You gave me no water for my feet when I entered your house; but she has washed my feet with her tears and dried them with her hair. You didn't welcome me with a kiss; but she has not stopped kissing my feet since she came in. You provided no oil for my head; but she has poured perfume on my feet. This is why, I tell you, her sins, her many sins, are forgiven, because of her great love. But the one who is forgiven little, has little love."

Then Jesus said to the woman, "Your sins are forgiven." The others reclining with him at the table began to wonder, "Now this man claims to forgive sins!" But Jesus again spoke to the woman, "Your faith has saved you; go in peace!"

Jesus walked through towns and countryside, preaching and giving the good news of the kingdom of God. The Twelve followed him, and also some women, who had been healed of evil spirits and diseases: Mary called Magdalene, who had been freed of seven demons; Joanna, wife of Chuza, Herod's steward; Suzanna; and others, who provided for them out of their own funds.

As a great crowd gathered, and people came to him from every town, Jesus began teaching them with a story: "The sower went out to sow the seed. And as he sowed, some of the seed fell along the way, was trodden on, and the birds of the sky ate it up. Some seed fell on rocky ground; and no sooner had it come up than it withered, because it had no water. Some seed fell among thorns; the thorns grew up with the seed and choked it. But some seed fell on good soil and grew, producing fruit, a hundred times as much!" And Jesus cried out, "Listen then, if you have ears to hear!"

The disciples asked him, "What does this story mean?" And Jesus answered, "To you it has been given to know the mystery of the kingdom of God. But to others it is given in the form of stories, or parables, so that,

> seeing, they may not perceive;
> and hearing, they may not understand.

Now, this is the point of the parable:

The seed is the word of God. Those along the wayside are people who hear it; but immediately, the devil comes and takes the word from their minds, for he doesn't want them to believe and be saved. Those on the rocky ground are people who receive the word with joy; but they have no root; they believe for a while, and give way in time of trial. Among the thorns are people who hear the word, but, as they go their way, they are choked by worries, riches, and the pleasures of life; they bring no fruit to maturity. The good soil, instead, are people who receive the word, and keep it, in a gentle and generous mind, and, persevering patiently, they bear fruit.

No one, after lighting a lamp, covers it with a bowl or puts it under the bed; rather, he puts it on a lamp stand, so that people coming in may see the light. In the same way, there is nothing hidden that shall not be uncovered; nothing kept secret, that shall not be known clearly. Now, pay attention and listen well, for whoever produces, will be given more; but from those who do not produce, even what they seem to have will be taken away from them."

Then his mother and his relatives came to him; but they could not get to him because of the crowd. Someone told him, "Your mother and your brothers are standing outside and wish to meet you." Then Jesus answered, "My mother and my brothers are those who hear the word of God and do it."

One day, Jesus got into a boat with his disciples and said to them, "Let us go across to the other side of the lake." So they set out, and as they sailed he fell asleep. Suddenly, a storm came down on the lake, and the boat began to fill with water; and they were in danger. The disciples then went to Jesus to wake him, saying, "Master! Master! We are sinking!" Jesus woke up. He rebuked the wind and the rolling waves; the storm subsided, and all was quiet.

Then Jesus said to them, "Where is your faith?" They had been afraid; now they were astonished and said to one another, "Who can this be? See, he commands even the wind and the sea and they obey him!"

And they sailed to the country of the Gerasenes, which is across the lake from Galilee. As Jesus stepped ashore, a man from the town approached him. This man was possessed by demons, and for a long time he had not worn any clothes. He would not live in a house, but stayed among the tombstones. When he came nearer to Jesus, he screamed and threw himself on the ground before him; and then he shouted, "What do you want with me, Jesus, Son of the Most High God? I beg you, do not torment me," for Jesus had ordered the evil spirit to leave the man.

This spirit had seized him many times, when he had been bound with ropes and chains and kept under control. He would then suddenly break the chains, and be driven by the evil spirit into wild places.

When Jesus asked him, "What is your name?" the man said, "I am Legion," because many demons had entered into him. And they begged Jesus not to command them to go into the bottomless pit. Nearby, on the hillside, a great herd of pigs was feeding; so the demons asked to be allowed to enter the pigs, and Jesus gave them permission. The demons then left the man and entered the pigs, and the herd rushed down the hillside into the lake and was drowned.

When the herdsmen saw what had happened, they fled, and reported it in the town and in the countryside. Then people went out to see what had happened and came to Jesus. There, they saw the man from whom the demons had been driven out. He was clothed and in his right mind, and was sitting at the feet of Jesus. They were afraid. Then people, who had seen it, told them how the man had been healed; and all this crowd from the Gerasene country asked Jesus to depart from them, for a great fear took hold of them. So Jesus got into the boat to return.

It was then, that the man freed of the demons asked Jesus if he could stay with him. But Jesus sent him on his way; "Go back to your family, and tell them how much God has done for you." So the man went away, proclaiming through the whole town how much Jesus had done for him.

When Jesus returned, the people welcomed him, for all had been waiting for him. At that time, a man named Jairus, an official of the synagogue, threw himself at Jesus' feet, and begged him to come to his house because his only daughter, about twelve years old, was dying.

As Jesus was on his way, the crowd pressed from every side. There was a woman who had suffered from a bleeding for twelve years. This woman had spent everything she had on doctors, but none of them had been able to cure her. Now, she came up behind Jesus and touched the fringe of his cloak, and her bleeding stopped at once. Jesus said, "Who touched me?" Everyone denied it; and Peter said, "Master, the crowd is pushing all around you." But Jesus insisted, "Someone touched me, for I felt power go out from me."

The woman knew she had been discovered. She came trembling, and knelt before Jesus. Then she openly confessed why she had touched him, and how she had been instantly cured. And Jesus said to her, "Daughter, your faith has saved you. Go in peace."

While Jesus was still speaking, a messenger arrived from the official's home to tell him, "Your daughter has just died; don't trouble the master any further." But Jesus heard the news, and said to the official, "Do not fear, only believe."

When he entered the house, Jesus allowed no one to follow him, except Peter, James and John, with the father and mother of the child. As all the people were weeping and wailing loudly, Jesus said to them, "Do not weep, she is not dead, but asleep." And they laughed at him, knowing that she was dead. As for Jesus, he took the child by the hand and said to her, "Child, wake up!" And her spirit returned, and she got up at once; then Jesus told them to give her something to eat. The parents were amazed, but Jesus ordered them not to let anyone know what had happened.

Then Jesus called his Twelve disciples and gave them power and authority to drive out all evil spirits and to heal diseases. And he sent them to proclaim the kingdom of God and to heal the sick. He instructed them, "Don't take anything for the journey, neither staff, nor bag, nor bread, nor money; and don't even take a spare tunic. Whatever house you enter, remain there until you leave that place. And wherever they don't welcome you, leave the town and shake the dust from your feet: it will be as a testimony against them."

So they set out, and went through the villages, proclaiming the good news and healing people everywhere.

King Herod heard of all this, and did not know what to think, for people said, "This is John, raised from the dead." Others believed that Elijah, or one of the ancient prophets, had come back to life. As for Herod, he said, "I had John beheaded. Who is this man, about whom I hear such wonders?" And he was anxious to see him.

On their return, the apostles told Jesus everything they had done. Then he took them with him and they withdrew by themselves to a town called Bethsaida. But the crowd heard of this and caught up with him. So he welcomed them, and began speaking about the kingdom of God, curing those who needed healing.

The day was drawing to a close, and the Twelve drew near to tell him, "Send the crowd away, and let them go into the villages and farms around, to find lodging and food, for we are here in a lonely place." But Jesus replied, "You, yourselves, give them something to eat." They answered, "We have only five loaves and two fish. Do you want us to go and buy food for all this crowd?" for there were about five thousand men. Then Jesus said to his disciples, "Make them sit down in groups of fifty."

So they made all of them sit down. Jesus then took the five loaves and two fish, and, raising his eyes to heaven, pronounced a blessing over them; he broke them, and gave them to the disciples to distribute to the crowd. They ate and everyone had enough; and when they gathered up what was left, twelve baskets were filled with broken pieces.

One day, when Jesus was praying alone, not far from his disciples, he asked them, "What do people say about me?" And they answered, "Some say, that you are John the Baptist; others say, that you are Elijah; and still others, that you are one of the prophets of old, risen from the dead." Again Jesus asked them, "But who do you say that I am?" Peter answered, "The Messiah of God." Then Jesus spoke to them, giving them strict orders not to tell this to anyone.

And he added, "The Son of Man must suffer many things. He will be rejected by the elders and chief priests and teachers of the law, and be put to death. Then after three days he will be raised to life."

Jesus also said to all the people, "If you wish to be a follower of mine, deny yourself and take up your cross each day, and follow me! For if you choose to save your life, you will lose it; but if you lose your life for my sake, you will save it. What does it profit you to gain the whole world, if you destroy or damage yourself? If someone feels ashamed of me and of my words, the Son of Man will be ashamed of him, when he comes in his glory, and in the glory of his Father, with his holy angels. Truly, I say to you, there are some here who will not taste death, before they see the kingdom of God."

About eight days after Jesus had said all this, he took Peter, John and James, and went up the mountain to pray. And while he was praying, the aspect of his face was changed, and his clothing became dazzling white. Two men were talking with Jesus: Moses and Elijah. Appearing in the glory of heaven, Moses and Elijah spoke to Jesus about his departure from this life, which was to take place in Jerusalem.

Peter and his companions had fallen asleep; but they awoke suddenly, and they saw his glory and the two men standing with him. As Moses and Elijah were about to leave, Peter—not knowing what to say—said to Jesus, "Master, how good it is for us to be here! Let us make three tents, one for you, one for Moses and one for Elijah." And no sooner had he spoken, than a cloud appeared and covered them; and the disciples were afraid as they entered the cloud. Then these words came from the cloud, "This is my Son, my Beloved, listen to him." And after the voice had spoken, Jesus was there alone.

The disciples kept this to themselves at the time, telling no one of anything they had seen.

The next day, when they came down from the mountain, a large crowd met Jesus. A man among them called out, "Master, I beg you to look at my son, my only child. When the evil spirit seizes him, he suddenly screams. The spirit throws him into a fit, and he foams at the mouth; it scarcely ever leaves him after wearing him out. I begged your disciples to drive it out, but they could not."

Jesus answered, "You faithless people! how disoriented you are! How long must I be with you and put up with you? Bring your son here." And while the boy was being brought, the demon beat him to the ground and threw him into a fit. But Jesus spoke sharply to the evil spirit, healed the boy, and gave him back to his father. And all who saw it were astonished at God's wonderful work.

But while all were amazed at everything Jesus did, he said to his disciples, "Listen, and remember what I tell you now: The Son of Man will be betrayed into the hands of men." But the disciples didn't understand this saying; something prevented them from grasping what he meant, and they were afraid to ask him about it.

One day, the disciples were arguing about which of them was the most important. But Jesus knew their thoughts, so he took a little child and stood him by his side. Then he said to them, "Whoever welcomes this little child in my name, welcomes me; and whoever welcomes me, welcomes the one who sent me. And listen: the one who is found to be the least among you all, is the one who is the greatest."

Then John spoke up, "Master, we saw someone who drives out demons by calling upon your name, and we tried to forbid him, because he doesn't follow you with us." But Jesus said, "Don't forbid him. He who is not against you is for you."

As the time drew near when Jesus would be taken up to heaven, he made up his mind to go to Jerusalem. He sent ahead of him some messengers, who entered a Samaritan village to prepare a lodging for him. But the people would not receive him, because he was on his way to Jerusalem. Seeing this, James and John, his disciples, said, "Lord, do you want us to call down fire from heaven to reduce them to ashes?" Jesus turned and rebuked them, and they went on to another village.

As they went on their way, a man said to him, "I will follow you wherever you go." Jesus said to him, "Foxes have holes and the birds of the air have nests; but the Son of Man has nowhere to lay his head."

To another, Jesus said, "Follow me!" But he answered, "Let me go back now, for, first, I want to bury my father." And Jesus said to him, "Let the dead bury their dead; as for you, leave them, and proclaim the kingdom of God."

Another said to him, "I will follow you, Lord, but first let me say good-bye to my family." And Jesus said to him, "Whoever has put his hand to the plow, and looks back, is not fit for the kingdom of God."

After this, the Lord appointed seventy-two other disciples, and sent them, two by two, ahead of him, to every town and place, where he himself was to go. And he said to them, "The harvest is plentiful, but the workers are few. So you must ask the Lord of the harvest to send workers to his harvest. Courage! I am sending you like lambs among wolves. Set off without purse or bag or sandals; and do not stop at the homes of those you know.

Whatever house you enter, first bless them, saying, 'Peace to this house!' If a friend of peace lives there, the peace shall rest upon that person. But if not, the blessing will return to you. Stay in that house, eating and drinking at their table, for the worker deserves to be paid. Do not move from house to house.

When they welcome you to any town, eat what they offer you. Heal the sick who are there, and say to them: 'The kingdom of God has drawn near to you.'

But in any town where you are not welcome, go to the marketplace and proclaim: 'Even the dust of your town that clings to our feet, we wipe off and leave with you. But know for a certainty that the kingdom of God has drawn near to you.' I tell you, that on the Day of Judgment it will be better for Sodom than for this town.

Alas for you, Chorazin! Alas for you, Bethsaida! So many miracles have been worked in you! If the same miracles had been performed in Tyre and

Sidon, they would already be sitting in ashes and wearing the sackcloth of repentance. Surely for Tyre and Sidon it will be better on the Day of Judgment than for you. And what of you, city of Capernaum? Will you be lifted up to heaven? You will be thrown down to the place of the dead.

Whoever listens to you listens to me, and whoever rejects you rejects me; and he who rejects me, rejects the one who sent me."

The seventy-two disciples returned full of joy. They said, "Lord, even the demons obeyed us when we called on your name." Then Jesus replied, "I saw Satan fall like lightning from heaven. You see, I have given you authority to trample on snakes and scorpions and to overcome all the power of the Enemy, so that nothing will harm you. Nevertheless, don't rejoice because the evil spirits submit to you; rejoice, rather, that your names are written in heaven."

At that time, Jesus was filled with the joy of the Holy Spirit, and said, "I praise you, Father, Lord of heaven and earth, for you have hidden these things from the wise and learned, and made them known to little ones. Yes, Father, such has been your gracious will. I have been given all things by my Father, so that no one knows the Son except the Father, and no one knows the Father except the Son, and he to whom the Son chooses to reveal him."

Then Jesus turned to his disciples and said to them privately, "Fortunate are you to see what you see, for I tell you, that many prophets and kings would have liked to see what you see, but did not see it; and to hear what you hear, but did not hear it."

Then a teacher of the law came and began putting Jesus to the test. And he said, "Master, what shall I do to receive eternal life?" Jesus replied, "What is written in the law? How do you understand it?" The man answered, "It is written: You shall love the Lord your God with all your heart, with all your soul, with all your strength and with all your mind. And you shall love your neighbor as yourself." Jesus replied, "What a good answer! Do this and you shall live." The man wanted to justify his question, so he asked, "Who is my neighbor?"

Jesus then said, "There was a man going down from Jerusalem to Jericho, and he fell into the hands of robbers. They stripped him, beat him and went off, leaving him half-dead.

It happened that a priest was going along that road and saw the man, but passed by on the other side. Likewise a Levite saw the man, and passed by on the other side. But a Samaritan also was going that way; and when he came upon the man, he was moved with compassion. He went over to him, and cleaned his wounds with oil and wine, and wrapped them in bandages. Then he put him on his own mount, and brought him to an inn, where he took care of him.

The next day, he had to set off; but he gave two silver coins to the innkeeper, and said, 'Take care of him, and whatever you spend on him, I will repay when I return.'"

Jesus then asked, "Which of these three, do you think, made himself neighbor to the man who fell into the hands of robbers?" The teacher of the law answered, "The one who had mercy on him." And Jesus said, "Then go and do the same."

As Jesus and his disciples were on their way, he entered a village, and a woman called Martha welcomed him to her house. She had a sister named Mary, who sat down at the Lord's feet to listen to his words. Martha, meanwhile, was busy with all the serving, and finally she said, "Lord, don't you care that my sister has left me to do all the work? Tell her to help me!"

But the Lord answered, "Martha, Martha, you worry and are troubled about many things, whereas only one thing is needed. Mary has chosen the better part, and it will not be taken away from her."

One day, Jesus was praying in a certain place; and when he had finished, one of his disciples said to him, "Lord, teach us to pray, as John also taught his disciples." And Jesus said to them, "When you pray, say this:

> Father,
> may your name be held holy,
> may your kingdom come;
> give us, each day, the kind of bread we need,
> and forgive us our sins;
> for we also forgive all who do us wrong;
> and do not bring us to the test."

Jesus said to them, "Suppose one of you has a friend, and goes to his house in the middle of the night and says, 'Friend, lend me three loaves, for a friend of mine who is traveling has just arrived, and I have nothing to offer him.' Maybe your friend will answer from inside, 'Don't bother me now; the door is locked, and my children and I are in bed, so I can't get up and give you anything.' But I tell you, even though he will not get up and attend to you because you are a friend, yet he will get up because you are a bother to him, and he will give you all you need.

And so I say to you, 'Ask, and it will be given to you; seek, and you will find; knock, and it will be opened to you. For the one who asks receives, and the one who searches finds, and to him who knocks the door will be opened.

If your child asks for a fish, will you give him a snake instead? And if your child asks for an egg, will give him a scorpion? If you sinful people know how to give good gifts to your children, how much more will your heavenly Father give the Holy Spirit to those who ask him."

One day, Jesus was driving out a demon, which was mute. When the demon had been driven out, the mute person could speak, and the people were amazed. Yet some of them said, "He drives out demons by the power of Beelzebul, the chief of the demons." Others wanted to put him to the test, by asking him for a heavenly sign.

But Jesus knew their thoughts, and said to them, "Every nation divided by civil war is on the road to ruin, and will fall. If Satan also is divided, his empire is coming to an end. How can you say that I drive out demons by calling upon Beelzebul? If I drive them out by Beelzebul, by whom do your sons drive out demons? They will be your judges, then.

But if I drive out demons by the finger of God; would not this mean that the kingdom of God has come upon you? As long as a man, strong and well armed, guards his house, his goods are safe. But when a stronger man attacks and overcomes him, the challenger takes away all the weapons he relied on, and disposes of his spoils.

Whoever is not with me is against me, and whoever does not gather with me, scatters.

When the evil spirit goes out of a person, it wanders through dry lands, looking for a resting place; and finding none, it says, 'I will return to my house from which I came.' When it comes, it finds the house swept and everything in order. Then it goes to fetch seven other spirits, even worse than itself. They move in and settle there, so that the last state of that person is worse than the first."

As Jesus was speaking, a woman spoke from the crowd and said to him, "Blessed is the one who gave you birth and nursed you!" Jesus replied, "Truly blessed are those who hear the word of God, and keep it as well."

As the crowd increased, Jesus spoke the following words: "People of the present time are troubled people. They ask for a sign, but no sign will be given to them except the sign of Jonah. As Jonah became a sign for the people of Nineveh, so will the Son of Man be a sign for this generation. The Queen of the South will rise up on Judgment Day with the people of these times and accuse them, for she came from the ends of the earth to hear the wisdom of Solomon; and here, there is greater than Solomon. The people of Nineveh will rise up on Judgment Day with the people of these times and accuse them, for Jonah's preaching made them turn from their sins, and here, there is greater than Jonah.

You do not light a lamp to hide it; rather, you put it on a lamp stand, so that people coming in may see the light.

Your eye is the lamp of your body. If your eye sees clearly, your whole person benefits from the light; but if your eyesight is poor, your whole person is without light. So be careful, lest the light inside you become darkness. If your whole person receives the light, having no part that is dark, you will become light, as when a lamp shines on you."

As Jesus was speaking, a Pharisee asked him to have a meal with him. So he went and sat at table. The Pharisee then wondered why Jesus did not first wash his hands before dinner. But the Lord said to him, "So then, you Pharisees, you clean the outside of the cup and the dish, but inside yourselves you are full of greed and evil. Fools! He who made the outside, also made the inside. But according to you, by the mere giving of alms everything is made clean.

A curse is on you, Pharisees! To the temple you give a tenth of all, including mint and rue and other herbs, but you neglect justice and the love of God. These ought to be practiced, without neglecting the other obligations. A curse is on you, Pharisees, for you love the best seats in the synagogues and to be greeted in the marketplace. A curse is on you, for you are like tombstones of the dead which can hardly be seen; people don't notice them, and make themselves unclean by stepping on them."

Then a teacher of the law spoke up and said, "Master, when you speak like this, you insult us, too." And Jesus answered, "A curse is on you also, teachers of the law. For you prepare unbearable burdens and load them on the people, while you yourselves do not move a finger to help them. A curse is on you, for you build monuments to the prophets your ancestors killed. So you approve and agree with what your ancestors did. Is it not so? They got rid of the prophets, and you build monuments to them!

For that reason the wisdom of God also said: I will send prophets and apostles and these people will kill and persecute some of them. But the present generation will have to answer for the blood of all the prophets that has been shed since the foundation of the world, from the blood of Abel to the blood of Zechariah, who was murdered between the altar and the Sanctuary. Yes, I tell you, the people of this time will have to answer for them all.

A curse is on you, teachers of the law, for you have taken the key of knowledge. You yourselves have not entered, and you prevented others from entering."

As Jesus left that place, the teachers of the law and the Pharisees began to harass him, asking him endless questions, setting traps to catch him in something he might say.

Meanwhile, such a numerous crowd had gathered that they crushed one another. Then Jesus spoke to his disciples in this way,

"Beware of the yeast of the Pharisees, which is hypocrisy. Nothing is covered that will not be uncovered; or hidden, that will not be made known. Whatever you have said in darkness will be heard in daylight, and what you have whispered in hidden places, will be proclaimed from housetops.

I tell you, my friends, do not fear those who put to death the body and, after that, can do no more. But I will tell you whom to fear: Fear the one who, after killing you, is able to throw you into hell. This one you must fear. Don't you buy five sparrows for two pennies? Yet not one of them has been forgotten by God. Even the hairs of your head have been numbered. Don't be afraid! Are you less worthy in the eyes of God than many sparrows?

I tell you, whoever acknowledges me before people, the Son of Man will also acknowledge before the angels of God. But the one who denies me before others will be denied before the angels of God.

There will be pardon for the one who criticizes the Son of Man, but there will be no pardon for the one who slanders the Holy Spirit.

When you are brought before the synagogues, and before governors and rulers, don't worry about how you will defend yourself, or what to say; for the Holy Spirit will teach you at that time what you have to say."

Someone in the crowd spoke to Jesus, "Master, tell my brother to share with me the family inheritance." He replied, "My friend, who has appointed me as your judge or your attorney?" Then Jesus said to the people, "Be on your guard and avoid every kind of greed, for even though you have many possessions, it is not that which gives you life."

And Jesus continued, "There was a rich man, and his land had produced a good harvest. He thought, 'What shall I do, for I am short of room to store my harvest? Alright, I know what I shall do: I will pull down my barns and I will build bigger ones, to store all this grain, which is my wealth. Then I will say to myself: My friend, you have a lot of good things put by for many years. Rest, eat, drink and enjoy yourself.' But God said to him, 'You fool! This very night your life will be taken from you. Tell me, who shall get all you have put aside?' This is the lot of the one who stores up riches for himself and is not wealthy in the eyes of God."

Then Jesus said to his disciples, "I tell you not to worry about your life: What are we to eat? or about your body: What are we to wear? For life is more than food, and the body more than clothing. Look at the crows: they neither sow nor reap; they have no storehouses and no barns; yet God feeds them. In so much, truly, are you different from birds! Which of you, for all your worrying, can add a moment to your span of life? And if you are not able to control such a small thing, why do you worry about the rest?

Look at the wild flowers: they do not spin or weave; but I tell you, even Solomon with all his wealth was not clothed as one of these flowers. If God so clothes the grass in the fields, which is alive today and tomorrow is thrown into the oven, how much more will he clothe you, people of little faith.

Do not set your heart on what you are to eat and drink; stop worrying! Let all the nations of the world run after these things; your Father knows that you need them. Seek, rather, his kingdom, and these things will be given to you as well.

Do not be afraid, little flock, for it has pleased your Father to give you the kingdom. Sell what you have and give alms. Get yourselves purses that do not wear out, and an inexhaustible treasure in the heavens, where no thief comes and no moth destroys. For where your treasure is, there will your heart be also.

Be ready, dressed for service, and keep your lamps lit, like people waiting for their master to return from the wedding. As soon as he comes and knocks, they will open the door to him. Happy are those servants whom the master finds wide-awake when he comes. Truly, I tell you, he will put on an apron, and have them sit at table, and he will wait on them. Happy are those servants, if he finds them awake when he comes at midnight or daybreak!

Pay attention to this: If the master of the house had known at what time the thief would come, he would not have let his house be broken into. You also must be ready, for the Son of Man will come at an hour you do not expect."

Peter said, "Lord, did you tell this parable only for us, or for everyone?" And the Lord replied, "Imagine, then, the wise and faithful steward, whom the master sets over his other servants, to give them wheat at the proper time. Fortunate is this servant if his master, on coming home, finds him doing his work. Truly, I say to you, the master will put him in charge of all his property.

But it may be that the steward thinks, 'My Lord delays in coming,' and he begins to abuse the male servants and the servant girls, eating and drinking and getting drunk. Then the master will come on a day he does not expect, and at an hour he doesn't know. He will cut him off, and send him to the same fate as the unfaithful.

The servant who knew his master's will, but did not prepare and do what his master wanted, will be soundly beaten; but the one who does unconsciously what deserves punishment, shall receive fewer blows. Much will be required of the one who has been given much, and more will be asked of the one who has been entrusted with more.

I have come to bring fire upon the earth, and how I wish it were already kindled! But I have a baptism to undergo, and what anguish I feel until it is finished!

Do you think that I have come to bring peace on earth? No, I tell you, but rather division. From now on, in one house five will be divided: three against two, and two against three. They will be divided, father against son and son against father; mother against daughter and daughter against mother; mother-in-law against her daughter-in-law, and daughter-in-law against her mother-in-law."

12:29–12:53

Jesus said to the crowds, "When you see a cloud rising in the west, you say at once, 'A shower is coming'; and so it happens. And when the wind blows from the south, you say, 'It will be hot'; and so it is. You superficial people! You understand the signs of the earth and the sky, but you don't understand the present times. And why do you not judge for yourselves what is fit? When you go with your accuser before the court, try to settle the case on the way, lest he drag you before the judge, and the judge deliver you to the jailer, and the jailer throw you into prison. I tell you, you will not get out until you have paid the very last penny."

One day, some people told Jesus what had occurred in the temple: Pilate had had Galileans killed, and their blood mingled with the blood of their sacrifices. Jesus asked them, "Do you think that these Galileans were worse sinners than all other Galileans, because they suffered this? No, I tell you. But unless you change your ways, you will all perish, as they did.

And those eighteen persons in Siloah, who were crushed when the tower fell, do you think they were more guilty than all the others in Jerusalem? I tell you: no. But unless you change your ways, you will all perish, as they did."

And Jesus continued, "A man had a fig tree growing in his vineyard, and he came looking for fruit on it, but found none. Then he said to the gardener, 'Look here, for three years now I have been looking for figs on this tree, and I have found none. Cut it down, why should it continue to deplete the soil?' The gardener replied, 'Leave it one more year, so that I may dig around it and add some fertilizer; perhaps it will bear fruit from now on. But if it doesn't, you can cut it down.'"

Jesus was teaching in a synagogue on the Sabbath, and a crippled woman was there. An evil spirit had kept her bent for eighteen years, so that she could not straighten up at all. On seeing her, Jesus called her and said, "Woman, you are freed from your infirmity." Then he laid his hands upon her, and immediately she was made straight and praised God.

But the ruler of the synagogue was indignant, because Jesus had performed this healing on the Sabbath day, and he said to the people, "There are six days in which to work. Come on those days to be healed, and not on the Sabbath!"

But the Lord replied, "You hypocrites! Everyone of you unties his ox or his donkey on the Sabbath, and leads it out of the barn to give it water. And here you have a daughter of Abraham, whom Satan had bound for eighteen years. Should she not be freed from her bonds on the Sabbath?"

When Jesus said this, all his opponents felt ashamed. But the people rejoiced at the many wonderful things that happened because of him.

And Jesus continued, "What is the kingdom of God like? What shall I compare it to? Imagine a person who has taken a mustard seed, and planted it in his garden. The seed has grown, and become like a small tree, so that the birds of the air shelter in its branches."

And Jesus said again, "What is the kingdom of God like? Imagine a woman who has taken yeast, and hidden it in three measures of flour, until it is all leavened."

Jesus went through towns and villages teaching, and making his way to Jerusalem. Someone asked him, "Lord, is it true that few people will be saved?"

And Jesus answered, "Do your best to enter by the narrow door; for many, I tell you, will try to enter and will not be able. When once the master of the house has gone inside and locked the door, you will stand outside. Then you will knock at the door, calling, 'Lord, open to us!' But he will say to you, 'I do not know where you come from.'

Then you will say, 'We ate and drank with you, and you taught in our streets!' But he will reply, 'I don't know where you come from. Away from me, all you workers of evil.'

You will weep and grind your teeth, when you see Abraham, Isaac, and Jacob and all the prophets in the kingdom of God, and you yourselves left outside. Others will sit at table in the kingdom of God, people coming from east and west, from north and south. Some who are among the last, will be first; and some who are among the first, will be last!"

At that time some Pharisees came to Jesus and gave him this warning, "Leave this place and go on your way, for Herod wants to kill you." Jesus said to them, "Go and give that fox my answer: 'I drive out demons, and I heal today and tomorrow, and on the third day I finish my course!' Nevertheless, I must go on my way today, and tomorrow, and for a little longer; for it would not be fitting for a prophet to be killed outside Jerusalem.

O Jerusalem, Jerusalem, you slay the prophets and stone those who are sent to you! How often have I tried to bring together your children, as a bird gathers her young under her wings. But you refused! From now on, you will be left, with your temple. And you will no longer see me until the time when you will say, Blessed is he who comes in the name of the Lord!"

One Sabbath Jesus had gone to eat a meal in the house of a leading Pharisee, and he was carefully watched. In front of him was a man suffering from dropsy; so Jesus asked the teachers of the law and the Pharisees, "Is it lawful to heal on the Sabbath, or not?" But no one answered. Jesus then took the man, healed him, and sent him away. And he said to them, "If your lamb or your ox falls into a well on a Sabbath day, who among you doesn't hurry to pull it out?" And they could not answer.

Jesus then told a parable to the guests, for he had noticed how they tried to take the places of honor. And he said, "When you are invited to a wedding party, do not choose the best seat. It may happen that someone more important than you has been invited; and your host, who invited both of you, will come and say to you, 'Please give this person your place.' What shame is yours when you take the lowest seat!

Whenever you are invited, go rather to the lowest seat, so that your host may come and say to you, 'Friend, you must come up higher.' And this will be a great honor for you in the presence of all the other guests. For whoever makes himself out to be great will be humbled, and whoever humbles himself will be exalted."

Jesus also addressed the man who had invited him, and said, "When you give a lunch or a dinner, don't invite your friends, or your brothers and relatives, or your wealthy neighbors. For surely they will also invite you in return, and you will be repaid. When you give a feast, invite instead the poor, the crippled, the lame and the blind. Fortunate are you then, because they cannot repay you. You will be repaid at the resurrection of the upright."

Upon hearing these words, one of those at the table said to Jesus, "Happy are those who eat at the banquet in the kingdom of God!"

Jesus replied, "A man once gave a feast and invited many guests. When it was time for the feast, he sent his servant to tell those he had invited to come, for everything was ready. But all alike began to make excuses. The first said, 'Please excuse me. I must go and see the piece of land I have just bought.' Another said: 'I am sorry, but I am on my way to try out the five yoke of oxen I have just bought.' Still another said, 'How can I come, when I've just got married?'

The servant returned alone, and reported this to his master. Upon hearing his account, the master of the house flew into a rage, and ordered his servant, 'Go out quickly, into the streets and alleys of the town, and bring in the poor, the crippled, the blind and the lame.'

The servant reported after a while, 'Sir, your orders have been carried out, but there is still room.' The master said, 'Go out to the highways and country lanes, and force people to come in, to ensure that my house is full. I tell you, none of those invited will have a morsel of my feast.'"

One day, when large crowds were walking along with Jesus, he turned and said to them, "If you come to me, unwilling to sacrifice your love for your father and mother, your spouse and children, your brothers and sisters, and indeed yourself, you cannot be my disciple. Whoever does not follow me, carrying his own cross, cannot be my disciple.

Do you build a house without first sitting down to count the cost, to see whether you have enough to complete it? Otherwise, if you, have laid the foundation and are not able to finish it, everyone will make fun of you: 'This fellow began to build and was not able to finish.'

And when a king wages war against another king, does he go to fight without first sitting down to consider whether his ten thousand can stand against the twenty thousand of his opponent? And if not, while the other is still a long way off, he sends messengers for peace talks. In the same way, none of you may become my disciple, if he doesn't give up everything he has.

However good the salt may be, if the salt has lost taste, you cannot make it salty again. It is fit for neither soil nor manure. Let them throw it away. Listen then, if you have ears!"

Meanwhile tax collectors and sinners were seeking the company of Jesus, all of them eager to hear what he had to say. But the Pharisees and the teachers of the law frowned at this, muttering, "This man welcomes sinners and eats with them." So Jesus told them this parable:

"Who among you, having a hundred sheep and losing one of them, will not leave the ninety-nine in the wilderness, and seek the lost one till he finds it? And finding it, will he not joyfully carry it home on his shoulders? Then he will call his friends and neighbors together, and say, 'Celebrate with me, for I have found my lost sheep!' I tell you, in the same way, there will be more rejoicing in heaven over one repentant sinner, than over ninety-nine decent people, who do not need to repent.

What woman, if she has ten silver coins and loses one, will not light a lamp, and sweep the house in a thorough search, till she finds the lost coin? And finding it, she will call her friends and neighbors, and say, 'Celebrate with me, for I have found the silver coin I lost!' I tell you, in the same way, there is rejoicing among the angels of God over one repentant sinner."

Jesus continued, "There was a man with two sons. The younger said to his father, 'Give me my share of the estate.' So the father divided his property between them.

Some days later, the younger son gathered all his belongings and started off for a distant land, where he squandered his wealth in loose living. Having spent everything, he was hard pressed when a severe famine broke out in that land. So he hired himself out to a well-to-do citizen of that place, and was sent to work on a pig farm. So famished was he, that he longed to fill his stomach even with the food given to the pigs, but no one offered him anything.

Finally coming to his senses, he said, 'How many of my father's hired workers have food to spare, and here I am starving to death! I will get up and go back to my father, and say to him, Father, I have sinned against God, and before you. I no longer deserve to be called your son. Treat me then as one of your hired servants.' With that thought in mind, he set off for his father's house.

He was still a long way off, when his father caught sight of him. His father was so deeply moved with compassion that he ran out to meet him, threw his arms around his neck and kissed him. The son said, 'Father, I have sinned against Heaven and before you. I no longer deserve to be called your son.'

But the father turned to his servants: 'Quick!' he said. 'Bring out the finest robe and put it on him! Put a ring on his finger and sandals on his feet! Take the fattened calf and kill it! We shall celebrate and have a feast, for this son of mine was dead, and has come back to life; he was lost, and is found!' And the celebration began.

Meanwhile, the elder son had been working in the fields. As he returned and approached the house, he heard the sound of music and dancing. He called one of the servants and asked what it was all about. The servant answered, 'Your brother has come home safe and sound, and your father is so happy about it that he has ordered this celebration, and killed the fattened calf.'

The elder son became angry, and refused to go in. His father came out and pleaded with him. The son, very indignant, said, 'Look, I have slaved for you all these years. Never have I disobeyed your orders. Yet you have never given me even a young goat to celebrate with my friends. But when this son of yours returns, after squandering your property with loose women, you kill the fattened calf for him!'

The father said, 'My son, you are always with me, and everything I have is yours. But this brother of yours was dead, and has come back to life; he was lost, and is found. And for that we had to rejoice and be glad.'"

At another time Jesus told his disciples, "There was a rich man, whose steward was reported to him because of fraudulent service. He summoned the steward and asked him, 'What is this I hear about you? I want you to render an account of your service, for it is about to be terminated.'

The steward thought to himself, 'What am I to do now? My master will surely dismiss me. I am not strong enough to do hard work, and I am ashamed to beg. I know what I will do: I must make sure that when I am dismissed, there will be people who will welcome me into their homes.'

So he called his master's debtors, one by one. He asked the first debtor, 'How much do you owe my master?' The reply was, 'A hundred jars of oil.' The steward said, 'Here is your bill. Sit down quickly and write fifty.' To the second debtor he put the same question, 'How much do you owe?' The answer was, 'A hundred measures of wheat.' Then the steward said, 'Take your bill and write eighty.'

The master commended the dishonest steward for his astuteness: for the people of this world are more astute, in dealing with their own kind, than are the people of light. And so I tell you: use filthy money to make friends for yourselves, so that, when it fails, these people may welcome you into the eternal homes.

Whoever can be trusted in little things can also be trusted in great ones; whoever is dishonest in slight matters will also be dishonest in greater ones. So if you have been dishonest in handling filthy money, who would entrust you with true wealth? And if you have been dishonest with things that are not really yours, who will give you that wealth which is truly your own?

No servant can serve two masters. Either he does not like the one and is fond of the other, or he regards one highly and the other with contempt. You cannot give yourself both to God and to Money."

The Pharisees, who loved money, heard all this and sneered at Jesus. He said to them, "You do your best to be considered righteous by people. But God knows the heart, and what is highly esteemed by human beings is loathed by God.

The time of the law and the prophets ended with John. Now the kingdom of God is proclaimed, and everyone tries to enter it by force.

It is easier for heaven and earth to pass away than for a single letter of Scripture not to be fulfilled.

Anyone who divorces his wife and marries another commits adultery; and whoever marries a woman divorced by her husband also commits adultery.

Once there was a rich man who dressed in purple and fine linen and feasted every day. At his gate lay Lazarus, a poor man covered with sores, who longed to eat just the scraps falling from the rich man's table. Even dogs used to come and lick his sores. It happened that the poor man died, and angels carried him to take his place with Abraham. The rich man also died, and was buried. From the netherworld where he was in torment, the rich man looked up and saw Abraham afar off, and with him Lazarus at rest.

He called out, 'Father Abraham, have pity on me, and send Lazarus, with the tip of his finger dipped in water, to cool my tongue, for I suffer so much in this fire!'

Abraham replied, 'My son, remember that in your lifetime you were well-off, while the lot of Lazarus was misfortune. Now he is in comfort, and you are in agony. But that is not all. Between your place and ours a great chasm has been fixed, so that no one can cross over from here to you, or from your side to us.'

The rich man implored once more, 'Then I beg you, Father Abraham, send Lazarus to my father's house, where my five brothers live. Let him warn them, so that they may not end up in this place of torment.' Abraham replied, 'They have Moses and the prophets. Let them listen to them.' But the rich man said, 'No, Father Abraham; but if someone from the dead goes to them, they will repent.'

Abraham said, 'If they will not listen to Moses and the prophets, they will not be convinced, even if someone rises from the dead.'"

Jesus said to his disciples, "Scandals will necessarily come and cause people to fall; but woe to the one who brings them about. It would be better for him to be thrown into the sea with a millstone around his neck. Truly, this would be better for that person, than to cause one of these little ones to fall.

Listen carefully: if your brother offends you, tell him, and if he is sorry, forgive him. And if he offends you seven times in one day, but seven times he says to you, 'I'm sorry,' forgive him."

The apostles said to the Lord, "Increase our faith." And the Lord said, "If you have faith, even the size of a mustard seed, you may say to this tree, 'Be uprooted, and plant yourself in the sea!' and it will obey you.

Who among you would say to your servant, coming in from the fields after plowing or tending sheep, 'Go ahead and have your dinner'? No, you tell him, 'Prepare my dinner. Put on your apron, and wait on me while I eat and drink. You can eat and drink afterward.' Do you thank this servant for doing what you told him to do? I don't think so. And therefore, when you have done all that you have been told to do, you should say, 'We are no more than servants; we have only done our duty.'"

On the way to Jerusalem, Jesus passed through Samaria and Galilee, and as he entered a village, ten lepers came to meet him. Keeping their distance, they called to him, "Jesus, Master, have pity on us!" Jesus said to them, "Go, and show yourselves to the priests." Then, as they went on their way, they found they were cured. One of them, as soon as he saw that he was cleansed, turned back, praising God in a loud voice; and throwing himself on his face before Jesus, he gave him thanks. This man was a Samaritan.

Then Jesus asked him, "Were not all ten healed? Where are the other nine? Did none of them decide to return and give praise to God, but this foreigner?" And Jesus said to him, "Stand up and go your way; your faith has saved you."

The Pharisees asked Jesus when the kingdom of God was to come. He answered, "The kingdom of God is not like something you can observe, and say of it, 'Look, here it is!' or 'See, there it is!' for the kingdom of God is within you."

And Jesus said to his disciples, "The time is at hand, when you will long to see one of the glorious days of the Son of Man, but you will not see it. Then people will tell you, 'Look there! Look here!' Do not go with them, do not follow them. As lightning flashes from one end of the sky to the other, so will it be with the Son of Man; but first he must suffer many things, and be rejected by this generation.

As it was in the days of Noah, so will it be on the day the Son of Man comes. In those days people ate and drank and got married; but on the day Noah entered the ark, the flood came and destroyed them all. So it was in the days of Lot: people ate and drank, and bought and sold, and planted and built; but on the day Lot left Sodom, God made fire and sulfur rain down from heaven, which destroyed them all. So will it be on the day the Son of Man is revealed.

On that day, if you are on the rooftop, don't go down into the house to get your belongings; and if you happen to be in the fields, do not turn back. Remember Lot's wife! Whoever tries to save his life will lose it, but whoever gives his life will be born again.

I tell you, though two men are sharing the same bed, it might happen that one will be taken, and the other left; though two women are grinding meal together, one might be taken and the other left."

Then they asked Jesus, "Where will this take place, Lord?" And he answered, "Where the body is, there too will the vultures gather."

Jesus told them a parable, to show them that they should pray continually, and not lose heart. He said, "In a certain town there was a judge, who neither feared God nor people. In the same town there was a widow, who kept coming to him, saying, 'Defend my rights against my adversary!' For a time he refused, but finally he thought, 'Even though I neither fear God nor care about people, this widow bothers me so much, I will see that she gets justice; then she will stop coming and wearing me out."

And Jesus said, "Listen to what the evil judge says. Will God not do justice for his chosen ones, who cry to him day and night, even if he delays in answering them? I tell you, he will speedily do them justice. But, when the Son of Man comes, will he find faith on earth?"

Jesus told another parable to some people, fully convinced of their own righteousness, who looked down on others: "Two men went up to the temple to pray; one was a Pharisee, and the other a tax collector. The Pharisee stood by himself, and said, 'I thank you, God, that I am not like other people, grasping, crooked, adulterous, or even like this tax collector. I fast twice a week, and give a tenth of all my income to the temple.'

In the meantime the tax collector, standing far off, would not even lift his eyes to heaven, but beat his breast, saying, 'O God, be merciful to me, a sinner.' I tell you, when this man went back to his house, he had been reconciled with God, but not the other. For whoever makes himself out to be great will be humbled, and whoever humbles himself will be raised up."

People even brought little children to Jesus to have him touch them; but seeing it, the disciples rebuked these people. So Jesus called the children to him and said, "Let the children come to me and don't stop them, for the kingdom of God belongs to such as these. Truly I tell you, whoever does not receive the kingdom of God like a child will not enter it."

A ruler asked Jesus, "Good master, what shall I do to inherit eternal life?" Jesus said to him, "Why do you call me good? No one is good but God alone. You know the commandments: Do not commit adultery; do not kill; do not steal; do not accuse falsely; honor your father and your mother." And the man said, "I have kept all these commandments from my youth."

Then Jesus answered, "There is still one thing you lack. Sell all you have, and give the money to the poor, and you will have riches in Heaven. And then come, follow me!" When he heard these words, the man became sad, for he was very rich. Jesus noticing this said, "How hard it is for people who have riches to enter the kingdom of God! It is easier for a camel to pass through the eye of a needle, than for a rich person to enter the kingdom of God." The bystanders said, "Who then can be saved?" And Jesus replied, "What is impossible for human beings is possible for God."

Then Peter said, "We left everything we had and followed you." Jesus replied, "Truly, I tell you, whoever has left home or wife, or brothers or parents or children, for the sake of the kingdom of God, will receive much more in this present time, and eternal life in the world to come."

Jesus then took the Twelve aside, and told them, "Now we are going up to Jerusalem, and everything the Prophets have written about the Son of Man will be fulfilled. He will be delivered up to the foreign power. People will mock him, insult him, and spit on him. After they have scourged him, they will kill him, but he will be raised on the third day." The apostles could make nothing of this; the meaning of these words remained a mystery to them, and they did not understand what he said.

When Jesus drew near to Jericho, a blind man was sitting by the road, begging. As he heard the crowd passing by, he inquired what was happening, and they told him that Jesus of Nazareth was going by. Then he cried out, "Jesus, Son of David, have mercy on me!" The people in front of him scolded him. "Be quiet!" they said, but he cried out all the more, "Jesus, Son of David, have mercy on me!"

Jesus stopped, and ordered the blind man to be brought to him; and when he came near, Jesus asked him, "What do you want me to do for you?" And the man said, "Lord, that I may see!" Jesus said, "Receive your sight, your faith has saved you." At once the blind man was able to see, and he followed Jesus, giving praise to God. And all the people who were there also praised God.

Jesus entered Jericho and was passing through it. A man named Zaccheus lived there. He was a tax collector and a wealthy man. He wanted to see what Jesus was like, but he was a short man and could not see him because of the crowd. So he ran ahead and climbed up a sycamore tree. From there he would be able to see Jesus, who was going to pass that way. When Jesus came to the place, he looked up and said to him, "Zaccheus, come down quickly, for I must stay at your house today." So Zaccheus climbed down and received him joyfully.

All the people who saw it began to grumble, and said, "He has gone as a guest to the house of a sinner." But Zaccheus spoke to Jesus, "Half of what I own, Lord, I will give to the poor, and if I have cheated anyone, I will pay him back four times as much." Looking at him Jesus said, "Salvation has come to this house today, for he is also a true son of Abraham. The Son of Man has come to seek and to save the lost."

Jesus was now near Jerusalem, and the people with him thought that God's reign was about to appear. So as they were listening to him, Jesus went on to tell them a parable. He said, "A man of noble birth went to a distant country in order to be crowned king, after which he planned to return home. Before he left, he summoned ten of his servants and gave them ten pounds of silver. He said, 'Put this money to work until I get back.' But his compatriots, who disliked him, sent a delegation after him with this message, 'We do not want this man to be our king.'

He returned, however, appointed as king. At once he sent for the servants, to whom he had given the money, to find out what profit each had made. The first came in, and reported, 'Sir, your pound of silver has earned ten more pounds of silver.'

The master replied, 'Well done, my good servant! Since you have proved yourself faithful in a small matter, I can trust you to take charge of ten cities.' The second reported, 'Sir, your pound of silver earned five more pounds of silver.' The master replied, 'And you, take charge of five cities!'

The third came in, and said, 'Sir, here is your money, which I hid for safekeeping. I was afraid of you, for you are an exacting person: you take up what you did not lay down, and you reap what you did not sow.'

The master replied, 'You worthless servant, I will judge you by your own words! So you knew I was an exacting person, taking up what I did not lay down, and reaping what I did not sow? Why, then, did you not put my money on loan, so that, when I got back, I could have collected it with interest?'

Then the master said to those standing by, 'Take from him that pound, and give it to the one with ten pounds.' But they objected, 'Sir, he already has ten pounds!'

The master replied, 'I tell you, everyone who has will be given more; but from those who have nothing, even what they have will be taken away. As for my enemies who did not want me to be their king, bring them in, and execute them right here in front me!'"

S o Jesus spoke, and then he passed on ahead of them, on his way to Jerusalem. When he drew near to Bethphage and Bethany, close to the Mount of Olives, he sent two of his disciples with these instructions, "Go to the village opposite; and, as you enter it, you will find a colt tied up, that no one has yet ridden. Untie it, and bring it here. And if anyone says to you, 'Why are you untying this colt?' You shall say, 'The Master needs it.'"

So the two disciples went and found things just as Jesus had said. As they were untying the colt, the owner said to them, "Why are you untying the colt?" And they answered, "The Master needs it." So they brought it to Jesus and, throwing their cloaks on the colt, they mounted Jesus on it. And as he went along, people spread their cloaks on the road.

When Jesus came near Jerusalem, to the place where the road slopes down from the Mount of Olives, the whole multitude of his disciples began to rejoice, and to praise God with a loud voice for all the miracles they had seen; and they cried out,

"Blessed is he who comes as king in the name of the Lord.

Peace in heaven, and glory in the highest heavens."

Some Pharisees in the crowd said to him, "Master, rebuke your disciples!" But Jesus answered, "I tell you, if they were to remain silent, the stones would cry out."

When Jesus had come in sight of the city, he wept over it, and said, "If only today you knew the ways of peace! But now they are hidden from your eyes. Yet days will come upon you, when your enemies will surround you with barricades, and shut you in, and press on you from every side. And they will dash you to the ground and your children with you, and not leave stone upon stone within you, for you did not recognize the time and the visitation of your God."

Then Jesus entered the temple area and began to drive out the merchants. And he said to them, "God says in the Scriptures, My house shall be a house of prayer, but you have turned it into a den of robbers!"

Jesus was teaching every day in the temple. The chief priests and teachers of the law wanted to kill him, and the elders of the Jews as well, but they were unable to do anything, for all the people were listening to him and hanging on his words.

One day, when Jesus was teaching the people in the temple and proclaiming the good news, the chief priests and the teachers of the law came with the elders of the Jews, and said to him, "Tell us, what right have you to act like this? Who gives you authority to do all this?"

Jesus said to them, "I also will ask you a question. Tell me: was John's preaching and baptism a work of God, or was it merely something human?" And they argued among themselves, "If we answer that it was a work of God, he will say, 'Why then did you not believe him?' But if we answer that it was merely something human, the people will stone us, for they all regard John as a prophet." So they answered Jesus, "We don't know," and Jesus said to them, "Neither will I tell you what right I have to act like this."

Jesus went on to tell the people this parable, "A man planted a vineyard, and let it out to tenants, before going abroad for a long time.

In due time, he sent a servant to the tenants to get some fruit from the vineyard. But the tenants beat him, and sent him back empty-handed. Again the man sent another servant; they beat him as well, and treated him shamefully, and finally sent him back empty-handed. The owner then sent a third servant, but him they injured and threw out of the vineyard.

The owner then thought, 'What shall I do? I will send my beloved son; surely they will respect him.' However the tenants, as soon as they saw him, said to one another, 'This is the one who will inherit the vineyard. Let us kill him, and the property will be ours!' So they threw him out of the vineyard, and killed him. Now, what will the owner of the vineyard do to them? He will come and destroy those tenants and give the vineyard to others."

On hearing this, some said, "God forbid!" Then Jesus looked directly at them and said, "What does this text of the Scriptures mean:

> The stone which the builders rejected
> has become the keystone?

Everyone who falls on that stone will be broken to pieces, and anyone that stone falls on will be crushed."

The teachers of the law and the chief priests would have liked to arrest him right there, for they realized that Jesus meant this parable for them, but they were afraid of the crowd. So they left, looking for another opportunity.

They sent spies who pretended to be honest men, in order to trap him in his words, and deliver him to the authority and power of the Roman governor. They said to him, "Master, we know that you are true in your words and in your teaching, and your answers do not vary according to who is listening to you; for you truly teach the way of God. Tell us: are we allowed to pay taxes to Caesar or not?"

But Jesus saw through their cunning and said, "Show me a silver coin. Whose image is this, and whose title does it bear?" They answered, "Caesar's." And Jesus said to them, "Return to Caesar the things that are Caesar's, and to God what is God's."

So they were unable to trap him in what he said publicly; they were surprised at his answer, and kept silent.

Then some Sadducees arrived. These people claim that there is no resurrection, and they asked Jesus this question, "Master, in the law Moses told us, 'If anyone dies leaving a wife but no children, his brother must take the wife, and any child born to them will be regarded as the child of the deceased.' Now, there were seven brothers: the first married, but died without children. The second married the woman, but also died childless. And then the third married her, and in this same way all seven died, leaving no children. Last of all the woman died. On the day of the resurrection, to which of them will the woman be a wife? For all seven had her as a wife."

And Jesus replied, "Taking a husband or a wife is proper to people of this world, but for those who are considered worthy of the world to come, and of resurrection from the dead, there is no more marriage. Besides, they cannot die, for they are like the angels. They are sons and daughters of God, because they are born of the resurrection.

Yes, the dead will be raised, as Moses revealed at the burning bush, when he called the Lord the God of Abraham and the God of Isaac and the God of Jacob. For God is God of the living, and not of the dead, for to him everyone is alive."

Some teachers of the law then agreed with Jesus, "Master, you have spoken well." They didn't dare ask him anything else. So Jesus said to them, "How can people say that the Messiah is the Son of David? For David, himself, says in the book of Psalms, The Lord said to my Lord: Sit at my right hand, until I put your enemies under your feet! David, there, calls him Lord; how then can he be his Son?"

Jesus also said to his disciples before all the people, "Beware of those teachers of the law, who like to be seen in long robes, and love to be greeted in the marketplaces, and to take the reserved seats in the synagogues, and the places of honor at feasts. While making a show of long prayers, they devour the property of widows. They will receive a very severe sentence!"

Jesus looked up and saw rich people putting their gifts into the treasury of the temple. He also saw a poor widow, who dropped in two small coins. And he said, "Truly, I tell you, this poor widow put in more than all of them. For all of them gave an offering from their plenty; but she, out of her poverty, gave all she had to live on."

While some people were talking about the temple, remarking that it was adorned with fine stonework and rich gifts, Jesus said to them, "The days will come when there shall not be left one stone upon another of all that you now admire; all will be torn down." And they asked him, "Master, when will this be, and what will be the sign that this is about to take place?"

Jesus said, "Take care not to be deceived, for many will come in my name, saying, 'I am he; the time is near at hand!' Do not follow them. When you hear of wars and troubled times, don't be frightened; for all these things must happen first, even though the end is not so soon."

And Jesus said, "Nations will fight each other and kingdom will oppose kingdom. There will be great earthquakes, famines and plagues; in many places strange and terrifying signs from heaven will be seen. Before all these things happen, people will lay their hands on you and persecute you; you will be delivered to the synagogues and put in prison, and for my sake you will be brought before kings and governors. This will be your opportunity to bear witness.

So keep this in mind: do not worry in advance about what to say, for I will give you words and wisdom that none of your opponents will be able to withstand or contradict.

You will be betrayed even by parents and brothers, by relatives and friends, and some of you will be put to death. But even though, because of my name, you will be hated by everyone, not a hair of your head will perish. By your patient endurance you will save your souls.

When you see Jerusalem surrounded by armies, then know that the time has come when it will be reduced to a wasteland. If you are in Judea, flee to the mountains! If you are in Jerusalem, leave! If you are outside the city, don't enter it!

For these will be the days of its punishment, and all that was announced in the Scriptures will be fulfilled. How hard will it be for pregnant women, and for mothers with babies at the breast! For a great calamity will come upon the land, and wrath upon this people. They will be put to death by the sword, or taken as slaves to other nations; and Jerusalem will be trampled upon by the pagans, until the time of the pagans is fulfilled.

Then there will be signs in sun and moon and stars, and on the earth anguish of nations, perplexed when they hear the roaring of the sea and its waves. People will faint with fear at the mere thought of what is to come upon the world, for the forces of the universe will be shaken. Then, at that time, they will see the Son of Man coming in a cloud with power and great glory.

So, when you see things begin to happen, stand erect and lift up your heads, for your deliverance is drawing near." And Jesus added this comparison, "Look at the fig tree, and all the trees. As soon as their buds sprout, you know that summer is near. In the same way, when you see these things happening, know that the kingdom of God is near. Truly, I tell you, this generation will not pass away, until all this has happened. Heaven and earth will pass away, but my words will not pass away.

Be on your guard: don't immerse yourselves in a life of pleasure, drunkenness and worldly cares, lest that day catch you unaware, like a trap! For, like a snare, will that day come upon all the inhabitants of the earth. But watch at all times and pray, that you may be able to escape all that is going to happen, and to stand before the Son of Man."

In the daytime Jesus used to teach in the temple; then he would leave the city and pass the night on the Mount of Olives. Early in the morning the people would come to the temple to hear him.

The feast of Unleavened Bread, which is called the Passover, was now drawing near, and the chief priests and the teachers of the law wanted to kill Jesus. They were looking for a way to do this, because they were afraid of the people. Then Satan entered into Judas, called Iscariot, one of the Twelve, and he went off to discuss with the chief priests and the officers of the guard how to deliver Jesus to them. They were delighted and agreed to give him money; so he accepted, and from that time he waited for an opportunity to betray him without the people knowing.

Then came the feast of the Unleavened Bread, in which the Passover lamb had to be sacrificed. So Jesus sent Peter and John, saying, "Go and get everything ready for us to eat the Passover meal." They asked him, "Where do you want us to prepare it?" And he said, "When you enter the city, a man will come to you carrying a jar of water. Follow him to the house he enters, and say to the owner, 'The master asks: Where is the room where I may take the Passover meal with my disciples?' He will show you a large, furnished room upstairs, and there you will prepare for us."

Peter and John went off, and having found everything just as Jesus had told them, they prepared the Passover meal.

When the hour came, Jesus took his place at the table and the apostles with him. And he said to them, "I was eager to eat this Passover with you before I suffer; for, I tell you, I shall not eat it again until it is fulfilled in the kingdom of God."

Then they passed him a cup, and when he had given thanks, he said, "Take this, and share it among yourselves; for I tell you that, from now on, I will not drink of the fruit of the vine until the kingdom of God comes." Jesus also took bread, and after giving thanks, he broke it and gave it to them, saying, "This is my body which is given for you. Do this in remembrance of me." And after the supper, he did the same with the cup, saying, "This cup is the new Covenant, sealed in my blood, which is poured out for you.

Yet the hand of the traitor is with me on the table. Know that the Son of Man is going the way marked out for him. But alas for that one who betrays him!" They began to ask one another which of them could do such a thing.

They also began to argue among themselves which of them should be considered the most important. Jesus said, "The kings of the pagan nations rule over them as lords, and the most hard-hearted rulers claim the title, 'Gracious Lord.' But not so with you; let the greatest among you become as the youngest, and the leader as the servant. For who is the greatest, he who sits at the table or he who serves? He who is seated, isn't it? Yet I am among you as one who serves.

You are the ones who have been with me, and stood by me, through my troubles; because of this, just as the kingship has been given to me by my Father, so I give it to you. You will eat and drink at my table in my kingdom, and you will sit on thrones and govern the twelve tribes of Israel.

Simon, Simon, Satan has demanded to sift you like grain, but I have prayed for you that your faith may not fail. And when you have recovered, you shall strengthen your brothers." Then Peter said, "Lord, with you I am ready to go even to prison and death." But Jesus replied, "I tell you, Peter, the cock will not crow this day before you have denied three times that you know me."

Jesus also said to them, "When I sent you without purse or bag or sandals, were you short of anything?" They answered, "No." And Jesus said to them, "But now, the one who has a purse or a bag must take it, or even his coat, and sell it, and but a sword. For Scripture says: He was numbered among criminals. These words have to be fulfilled in me, and everything written about me is now taking place."

Then they said, "See, Lord, here are two swords!" but Jesus answered, "That is enough."

After this, Jesus left to go as usual to the Mount of Olives, and the disciples followed him. When he came to the place, he told them, "Pray that you may not be put to the test."

Then he went a little further, about a stone's throw, and kneeling down he prayed, "Father, if it is your will, remove this cup from me; however, not my will but yours be done." And from heaven there appeared to him an angel, who gave him strength.

As he was in agony, he prayed even more earnestly, and great drops of blood formed like sweat and fell to the ground. When he rose from prayer, he went to his disciples, but found them worn out with grief, and asleep. And he said to them, "Why do you sleep? Get up and pray, so that you may not be put to the test."

Jesus was still speaking when suddenly a crowd appeared, and the man named Judas, one of the Twelve, was leading them. He drew near to Jesus to kiss him, and Jesus said to him, "Judas, with a kiss do you betray the Son of Man?"

Those with Jesus, seeing what would happen, said to him, "Master, shall we use the sword?" And one of them struck the High Priest's servant and cut off his right ear. But Jesus ordered him, "No more of this!" He touched the man's ear and healed him.

Then Jesus spoke to those coming against him, the chief priests, officers of the temple and elders; and he said to them, "Are you looking for a thief, a robber? Do you really need swords and clubs to arrest me? Day after day I was among you, teaching in the temple, and you did not arrest me. But this is the hour of the power of darkness; this is your hour."

Then they seized him and took him away, bringing him to the High Priest's house. Peter followed at a distance.

A fire was kindled in the middle of the courtyard where people were gathered, and Peter sat among them. A maidservant noticed him. Looking at him intently in the light of the fire, she exclaimed, "This man also was with him!" But he denied it, saying, "Woman, I do not know him!"

A little later someone who saw him said, "You are also one of them!" Peter replied, "My friend, I am not!" After about an hour another asserted, "Surely this man was with him, for he is a Galilean."

Again Peter denied it: "My friend, I don't know what you are talking about!" He had not finished saying this, when a cock crowed. The Lord turned around and looked at Peter, and Peter remembered the word which the Lord had spoken: "Before the cock crows, you will deny me three times." Peter went outside, weeping bitterly.

Now the guards, who had arrested Jesus, mocked and beat him. They blindfolded him, struck him, and then asked him, "Who hit you? Tell us, prophet!" And they hurled many other insulting words at him.

At daybreak, the council of the elders of the people, among whom were the chief priests and the teachers of the law, assembled again. Then they had Jesus brought before them, and they began questioning him, "Tell us, are you the Christ?" Jesus replied, "You will not believe, if I tell you, and neither will you answer, if I ask you. But from now on the Son of Man will be seated at the right hand of the power of God."

In chorus they asked, "So you are the Son of God?" And Jesus said to them, "You are right, I am."

Then they said, "What need have we of witnesses? We have heard it from his own lips."

The whole council rose and brought Jesus to Pilate. They gave their accusation: "We found this man subverting our nation, opposing payment of taxes to Caesar, and claiming to be Christ the King."

Pilate asked Jesus, "Are you the King of the Jews?" Jesus replied, "You said so." Turning to the chief priests and the crowd, Pilate said, "I find no basis for a case against this man." But they insisted, "All the country of the Jews is being stirred up by his teaching. He began in Galilee and now he has come all the way here."

When Pilate heard this, he asked if the man was a Galilean. Finding the accused to come under Herod's jurisdiction, Pilate sent Jesus over to Herod who happened to be in Jerusalem at that time.

Herod was delighted to have Jesus before him; for a long time he had wanted to see him because of the reports about him, and he was hoping to see Jesus work some miracle. He piled up question upon question, but got no reply from Jesus.

All the while the chief priests and the scribes remained standing there, vehemently pressing their accusations. Finally, Herod ridiculed him and with his guards mocked him. And when he had put a rich cloak on him, he sent him back to Pilate. Pilate and Herod, who were enemies before, became friends from that day.

Pilate then called together the chief priests and the elders and the people, and said to them, "You have brought this man before me and accused him of subversion. In your presence I have examined him and found no basis for your charges; and neither has Herod, for he sent him back to me. It is quite clear that this man has done nothing that deserves a death sentence. I will therefore have him scourged and then release him." (At Passover, Pilate had to release a prisoner.)

Shouting as one man, the crowd protested, "No! Away with this man! Release Barabbas instead!" This man had been thrown into prison for an uprising in the city and for murder.

Since Pilate wanted to release Jesus, he appealed to the crowd once more, but they shouted back, "Crucify him! Crucify him!" A third time Pilate said to them, "Why, what evil has he done? Since no crime deserving death has been proved, I shall have him scourged and let him go."

But they went on shouting and demanding that Jesus be crucified, and their shouts grew louder. So Pilate decided to pass the sentence they demanded. He released the man they asked for, the one who was in prison for rebellion and murder, and he handed Jesus over in accordance with their wishes.

When they led Jesus away, they seized Simon of Cyrene, arriving from the countryside, and laid the cross on him, to carry it behind Jesus.

A large crowd of people followed him; among them were women, beating their breasts and grieving for him, but Jesus turned to them and said, "Women of Jerusalem, do not weep for me! Weep rather for yourselves and for your children, for the days are coming when people will say, 'Happy are the women without child! Happy are those who have not given birth or nursed a child!'

> And they will say to the mountains, 'Fall on us!'
> and to the hills, 'Cover us!'

For if this is the lot of the green wood, what will happen to the dry?"

Along with Jesus, two criminals also were led out to be executed. There, at the place called the Skull, he was crucified together with two criminals—one on his right and another on his left. (Jesus said, "Father, forgive them, for they do not know what they are doing.") And the guards cast lots to divide his clothes among themselves.

The people stood by, watching. As for the rulers, they jeered at him, saying to one another, "Let the man who saved others now save himself, for he is the Messiah, the chosen one of God!"

The soldiers also mocked him and, when they drew near to offer him bitter wine, they said, "So you are the King of the Jews? Save yourself!" Above Jesus there was an inscription in Greek, Latin and Hebrew, which read, "This is the King of the Jews."

One of the criminals hanging with Jesus insulted him, "So you are the Messiah? Save yourself, and us as well!" But the other rebuked him, saying, "Have you no fear of God, you who received the same sentence as he did? For us it is just: this is payment for what we have done. But this man has done nothing wrong." And he said, "Jesus, remember me, when you come into your kingdom." Jesus replied, "In truth I tell you, today, you will be with me today in paradise."

It was almost midday. The sun was hidden, and darkness came over the whole land until mid-afternoon; and, at that time, the curtain of the Sanctuary was torn in two. Then Jesus gave a loud cry, "Father, into your hands I commend my spirit." And saying that, he gave up his spirit.

The captain, on seeing what had happened, acknowledged the hand of God. "Surely this was an upright man!" he said. And all the people who had gathered to watch the spectacle, as soon as they saw what had happened, went home beating their breasts. But those who knew Jesus, and the women who had followed him from Galilee, remained there at a distance. They witnessed all these things.

Then a member of the Jewish supreme council intervened, a good and righteous man named Joseph, from the Judean town of Arimathea. He had not agreed with the decision and action of his fellow members, and he lived uprightly in the hope of seeing the kingdom of God. Joseph went to Pilate and asked for Jesus' body. He then took it down, wrapped it in a linen cloth, and laid it in a yet unused tomb, cut out of a rock.

It was the day of preparation and the Sabbath was beginning. So the women, who had come with Jesus from Galilee, followed Joseph to see the tomb, and how his body was laid. Returning home, they prepared perfumes and ointments. And on the Sabbath day they rested, as the law required.

On the Sabbath the women rested according to the commandment, but the first day of the week, at dawn, the women went to the tomb with the perfumes and ointments they had prepared. Seeing the stone rolled away from the opening of the tomb, they entered, and were amazed to find that the body of the Lord Jesus was not there.

As they stood there wondering about this, two men in dazzling garments suddenly stood before them. In fright the women bowed to the ground. But the men said, "Why look for the living among the dead? You won't find him here. He is risen. Remember what he told you in Galilee, that the Son of Man had to be given into the hands of sinners, to be crucified, and to rise on the third day." And they remembered Jesus' words.

Returning from the tomb, they told the Eleven and all the others about these things. Among the women, who brought the news, were Mary Magdalene, Joanna, and Mary the mother of James. But however much they insisted, those who heard did not believe the seemingly nonsensical story. Then Peter got up and ran to the tomb. All he saw, when he bent down and looked into the tomb, were the linen cloths, laid by themselves. He went home wondering.

That same day, two followers of Jesus were going to Emmaus, a village seven miles from Jerusalem, and they were talking to each other about all the things that had happened. While they were talking and debating these things, Jesus himself approached and began to accompany them, but their eyes were not able to recognize him.

He asked, "What is it you are talking about?" The two stood still, looking sad. Then the one named Cleophas answered, "Why, it seems you are the only traveler to Jerusalem who doesn't know what has happened there these past few days." And he asked, "What is it?"

They replied, "It is about Jesus of Nazareth. He was a prophet, you know, mighty in word and deed before God and the people. But the chief priests and our rulers sentenced him to death. They handed him over to be crucified. We had hoped that he would redeem Israel.

It is now the third day since all this took place. It is also true that some women of our group have disturbed us. When they went to the tomb at dawn, they did not find his body; and they came and told us that they had had a vision of angels, who said that Jesus was alive. Some of our people went to the tomb and found everything just as the women had said, but they did not find a body in the tomb."

He said to them, "How dull you are, how slow of understanding! Is the message of the prophets too difficult for you to understand? Is it not written that the Christ should suffer all this, and then enter his glory?" Then starting with Moses, and going through the prophets, he explained to them everything in the Scriptures concerning himself.

As they drew near the village they were heading for, Jesus made as if to go farther. But they prevailed upon him, "Stay with us, for night comes quickly. The day is now almost over." So he went in to stay with them. When they were at table, he took the bread, said a blessing, broke it, and gave each a piece.

Then their eyes were opened, and they recognized him; but he vanished out of their sight. And they said to one another, "Were not our hearts burning within us when he was talking to us on the road and explaining the Scriptures?"

They immediately set out and returned to Jerusalem. There, they found the Eleven and their companions gathered together. They were greeted by these words: "Yes, it is true, the Lord is risen! He has appeared to Simon!" Then the two told what had happened on the road to Emmaus, and how Jesus had made himself known, when he broke bread with them.

While they were still talking about this, Jesus himself stood in their midst. (He said to them, "Peace to you.") In their panic and fright they thought they were seeing a ghost, but he said to them, "Why are you upset, and how does such an idea cross your minds? Look at my hands and feet, and see that it is I myself! Touch me, and see for yourselves, for a ghost has no flesh and bones as I have!" (As he said this, he showed his hands and feet.)

Their joy was so great that they still could not believe it, as they were astonished; so he said to them, "Have you anything to eat?" And they gave him a piece of broiled fish. He took it, and ate it before them.

Then Jesus said to them, "Remember the words I spoke to you when I was still with you: Everything written about me in the law of Moses, in the prophets and in the psalms must be fulfilled." Then he opened their minds to understand the Scriptures.

And he said, "So it was written: the Messiah had to suffer, and on the third day rise from the dead. Then repentance and forgiveness in his name would be proclaimed to all nations, beginning from Jerusalem. And you are witnesses of these things. And that is why I will send you what my Father promised. So remain in the city until you are clothed with power from on high."

Jesus led them almost as far as Bethany; then he lifted up his hands and blessed them. And as he blessed them, he withdrew, and was taken to heaven. They worshiped him, and then returned to Jerusalem full of joy; and they were continually in the temple, praising God.

| ACTS |

I n the first part of my work, Theophilus, I wrote of all that Jesus did and taught, from the beginning until the day when he ascended to heaven.

But first he had instructed, through the Holy Spirit, the apostles he had chosen. After his passion, he presented himself to them, giving many signs, that he was alive; over a period of forty days he appeared to them and taught them concerning the kingdom of God. Once, when he had been eating with them, he told them, "Do not leave Jerusalem but wait for the fulfillment of the Father's promise about which I have spoken to you: John baptized with water, but you will be baptized with the Holy Spirit within a few days."

When they had come together, they asked him, "Is it now that you will restore the kingdom of Israel?" And he answered, "It is not for you to know the time and the steps that the Father has fixed by his own authority. But you will receive power when the Holy Spirit comes upon you; and you will be my witnesses in Jerusalem, throughout Judea and Samaria, even to the ends of the earth."

After Jesus said this, he was taken up before their eyes and a cloud hid him from their sight. While they were still looking up to heaven, where he went, suddenly, two men dressed in white stood beside them and said, "Men of Galilee, why do you stand here looking up at the sky? This Jesus, who has been taken from you into heaven, will return in the same way as you have seen him go there."

Then they returned to Jerusalem from the Mount called Olives, which is a fifteen-minute walk away. On entering the city they went to the room upstairs where they were staying. Present there were Peter, John, James and Andrew; Philip and Thomas, Bartholomew and Matthew, James, son of Alpheus; Simon the Zealot and Judas son of James. All of these, together, gave themselves to constant prayer. With them were some women, and also Mary, the mother of Jesus, and his brothers.

It was during this time that Peter stood up in the midst of the community—about one hundred and twenty in all—and he said,

"Brothers, it was necessary that the Scriptures referring to Judas be fulfilled. The Holy Spirit had spoken through David about the one who would lead the crowd coming to arrest Jesus. He was one of our number and had been called to share our common ministry.

(We know that he bought a field with the reward of his sin; yet, he threw himself headlong to his death; his body burst open and all his bowels spilled out. This event became known to all the people living in Jerusalem and they named that field Akeldama in their own language, which means Field of Blood).

In the Book of Psalms it is written:

> Let his house become deserted and
> may no one live in it.

But it is also written:

> May another take his office.

Therefore, we must choose someone from among those who were with us during all the time that the Lord Jesus moved about with us, beginning with John's baptism until the day when Jesus was taken away from us. One of these has to become, with us, a witness to his resurrection."

Then they proposed two: Joseph, called Barsabbas, also known as Justus, and Matthias. They prayed: "You know, Lord, what is in the hearts of all. Show us, therefore, which of the two you have chosen to replace Judas in this apostolic ministry which he deserted to go to the place he deserved."

Then they drew lots between the two and the choice fell on Matthias who was added to the eleven apostles.

When the day of Pentecost came, they were all together in one place. And suddenly, out of the sky, came a sound, like a strong rushing wind; and it filled the whole house where they were sitting. There appeared tongues, as if of fire, which parted and came to rest upon each one of them. All were filled with the Holy Spirit and began to speak other languages, as the Spirit enabled them to speak.

Staying in Jerusalem were religious Jews from every nation under heaven. When they heard this sound, a crowd gathered, all excited, because each heard them speaking in his own language. Full of amazement and wonder, they asked, "Are not all these who are speaking Galileans? How is it, that we hear them in our own native language? Here are Parthians, Medes and Elamites; and residents of Mesopotamia, Judea and Cappadocia; Pontus and Asia; Phrygia, Pamphylia, Egypt; and the parts of Libya belonging to Cyrene; and visitors from Rome; both Jews and foreigners who accept Jewish beliefs, Cretians and Arabians; and all of us hear them proclaiming in our own language what God, the Savior, does."

They were amazed and greatly confused, and they kept asking one another, "What does this mean?" But others laughed and said, "These people are drunk."

Then Peter stood up with the Eleven and, with a loud voice, addressed them, "Fellow Jews and all foreigners now staying in Jerusalem, listen to what I have to say. These people are not drunk as you suppose, for it is only nine o'clock in the morning. Indeed what the prophet Joel spoke about has happened:

> In the last days, God says,
> I will pour out my Spirit on every mortal.

> Your sons and daughters will speak through the Holy Spirit;
> your young men will see visions and
> your old men will have dreams.

> In those days I will pour out my Spirit even on my servants,
> both men and women,
> and they will be prophets.

> I will perform miracles in the sky above
> and wonders on the earth below.
> The sun will be darkened
> and the moon will turn red as blood,
> before the great and glorious Day of the Lord comes.

> And then, whoever calls
> upon the Name of the Lord will be saved.

Fellow Israelites, listen to what I am going to tell you about Jesus of Nazareth. God accredited him and through him did powerful deeds and wonders and signs in your midst, as you well know. You delivered him to sinners to be crucified and killed, and, in this way, the purpose of God, from all times, was fulfilled. But God raised him to life and released him from the pain of death; because it was impossible for him to be held in the power of death. David spoke of him when he said:

> I saw the Lord before me at all times;
> he is by my side,
> that I may not be shaken.

> Therefore, my heart was glad and my tongue rejoiced;
> my body, too, will live in hope.

> Because you will not forsake me in the abode of the dead,
> nor allow your Holy One to experience corruption.

> You have made known to me the paths of life,
> and your presence will fill me with joy.

Friends, I don't need to prove that the patriarch David died and was buried; his tomb is with us to this day. But he knew, that God had sworn to him, that one of his descendants would sit upon his throne and, as he was a prophet, he foresaw and spoke of the resurrection of the Messiah. So he said, that he would not be left in the region of the dead, nor would his body experience corruption.

This Messiah is Jesus; and we are all witnesses that God raised him to life. He has been exalted at God's right side; and the Father has entrusted the Holy Spirit to him; this Spirit, he has just poured upon us, as you now see and hear.

And look: David did not ascend into heaven, but he, himself, said:

> The Lord said to my Lord:
> sit at my right side,
>
> until I make your enemies
> a stool for your feet.

Let Israel, then, know for sure, that God has made Lord and Christ this Jesus, whom you crucified."

When they heard this, they were deeply troubled. And they asked Peter and the other apostles, "What shall we do, brothers?"

Peter answered: "Each of you must repent and be baptized in the name of Jesus Christ, so that your sins may be forgiven. Then, you will receive the gift of the Holy Spirit. For the promise of God was made to you and your children, and to all those from afar, whom our God may call."

With many other words Peter gave the message; and appealed to them, saying, "Save yourselves from this crooked generation." So, those who accepted his word were baptized; some three thousand persons were added to their number that day.

They were faithful to the teaching of the apostles, the common life of sharing, the breaking of bread and the prayers.

A holy fear came upon all the people, for many wonders and miraculous signs were done by the apostles. Now, all the believers lived together, and shared all their belongings. They would sell their property, and all they had, and distribute the proceeds to others, according to their need. Each day, they met together, in the temple area; they broke bread in their homes; they shared their food, with great joy and simplicity of heart; they praised God and won the people's favor. And every day, the Lord added to their number, those who were being saved.

Once when Peter and John were going up to the temple, at three in the afternoon, the hour for prayer, a man, crippled from birth, was being carried in. Every day, they would bring him and put him at the temple gate called "Beautiful;" there, he begged from those who entered the temple.

When he saw Peter and John on their way into the temple, he asked for alms. Then Peter, with John at his side, looked straight at him and said, "Look at us." So he looked at them, expecting to receive something from them. But Peter said, "I have neither silver nor gold, but what I have I give you: In the name of Jesus of Nazareth, the Messiah, walk!"

Then, he took the beggar by his right hand and helped him up. At once, his feet and ankles became firm, and, jumping up, he stood on his feet and began to walk. And he went with them into the temple, walking and leaping and praising God.

All the people saw him walking and praising God; they recognized him as the one who used to sit begging at the Beautiful Gate of the temple, and they were all astonished and amazed at what had happened to him.

While he clung to Peter and John, all the people, struck with astonishment, came running to them in Solomon's Porch, as it was called. When Peter saw the people, he said to them,

"Fellow Israelites, why are you amazed at this? Why do you stare at us, as if it was by some power or holiness of our own, that we made this man walk? The God of Abraham, of Isaac and of Jacob, the God of our ancestors has glorified his servant Jesus, whom you handed over to death and denied before Pilate; when even Pilate had decided to release him. You rejected the Holy and Just One; and you insisted that a murderer be released to you. You killed the Master of life, but God raised him from the dead; and we are witnesses to this. It is his Name, and faith in his Name, that has healed this man, whom you see and recognize. The faith that comes through Jesus has given him wholeness in the presence of all of you.

Yet, I know that you acted out of ignorance, as did your leaders. God has fulfilled, in this way, what he had foretold through all the prophets, that his Messiah would suffer.

Repent, then, and turn to God so that your sins may be wiped out; and the time of refreshment may come by the mercy of God, when he sends the Messiah appointed for you, Jesus. For he must remain in heaven, until the time of the universal restoration, which God spoke of long ago, through his holy prophets.

Moses foretold this, when he said: The Lord God will raise up for you a prophet, like me, from among your own people; you shall listen to him in all that he says to you. Whoever does not listen to that prophet is to be cut off from among his people.

In fact, all the prophets who have spoken, from Samuel onward, have announced the events of these days. You are the children of the prophets, and heirs of the Covenant that God gave to your ancestors, when he said to Abraham: All the families of the earth will be blessed through your descendant. It is to you, first, that God sends his Servant; he raised him to life, to bless you, by turning each of you from your wicked ways."

While Peter and John were still speaking to the people, the priests, the captain of the temple guard and the Sadducees came up to them. They were greatly disturbed, because the apostles were teaching the people, and proclaiming that resurrection from the dead had been proved, in the case of Jesus. Since it was already evening, they arrested them and put them in custody until the following day. But despite this, many of those who heard the Message, believed; and their number increased to about five thousand.

The next day, the Jewish leaders, elders and teachers of the law assembled in Jerusalem. Annas, the High Priest, Caiaphas, John, Alexander, and all who were of the high priestly class were there. They brought Peter and John before them; and began to question them, "How did you do this? Whose name did you use?"

Then Peter, filled with the Holy Spirit, spoke up, "Leaders of the people! Elders! It is a fact, that we are being examined today for a good deed done to a cripple. How was he healed? You, and all the people of Israel, must know, that this man stands before you cured, through the name of Jesus Christ, the Nazorean. You had him crucified. But God raised him from the dead. Jesus is

> the stone rejected by you, the builders,
> which has become the cornerstone.

There is no salvation in anyone else; for there is no other Name given to humankind, all over the world, by which we may be saved."

They were astonished at the boldness of Peter and John, considering that they were uneducated and untrained men. They recognized, also, that they had been with Jesus, but, as the man who had been cured stood beside them, they could make no reply.

So they ordered them to leave the council room while they consulted with one another. They asked, "What shall we do with these men? Everyone who lives in Jerusalem knows, that a remarkable sign has been given through them, and we cannot deny it. But to stop this from spreading any further among the people, let us warn them never again to speak to anyone in the name of Jesus." So they called them back and charged them not to speak, or teach at all, in the name of Jesus.

But Peter and John answered them, "Judge for yourselves, whether it is right in God's eyes, for us to obey you, rather than God. We cannot stop speaking about what we have seen and heard." Then the council threatened them once more and let them go. They could find no way of punishing them because of the people, who glorified God for what had happened; for the man who had been miraculously healed was over forty years old.

As soon as Peter and John were set free, they went to their friends and reported what the chief priests and elders had said to them.

When they heard it, they raised their voices as one, and called upon God, "Sovereign Lord, maker of heaven and earth, of the sea and everything in them, you have put these words in the mouth of David, our father and your servant, through the Holy Spirit:

> Why did the pagan nations rage
> and the people conspire in folly?
>
> The kings of the earth were aligned;
> and the princes gathered together
>
> against the Lord
> and against his Messiah.

For indeed, in this very city, Herod, with Pontius Pilate and the pagans, together, with the people of Israel, conspired against your holy servant, Jesus, whom you anointed. Thus, indeed, they brought about whatever your powerful will had decided, from all time, would happen. But now, Lord, see their threats against us; and enable your servants to speak your word with all boldness. Stretch out your hand, to heal, and to work signs and wonders, through the name of Jesus, your holy servant."

When they had prayed, the place where they were gathered together shook; and they were all filled with the Holy Spirit and began to speak the word of God boldly.

The whole community of believers was one in heart and mind. No one claimed private ownership of any possessions; but rather, they shared all things in common. With great power, the apostles bore witness to the resurrection of the Lord Jesus, for all of them were living in an exceptional time of grace.

There was no needy person among them, for those who owned land or houses, sold them and brought the proceeds of the sale. And they laid it at the feet of the apostles, who distributed it, according to each one's need. This is what a certain Joseph did. He was a Levite from Cyprus, whom the apostles called Barnabas, meaning: "The encouraging one." He sold a field which he owned and handed the money to the apostles.

Another man, named Ananias, in agreement with his wife Sapphira, likewise sold a piece of land; with his wife's knowledge, he put aside some of the proceeds, and the rest he turned over to the apostles.

Then, Peter said to him, "Ananias, how is it, that you let Satan fill your heart; and why do you intend to deceive the Holy Spirit, by keeping some of the proceeds of your land for yourself? Who obliged you to sell it? And, after it was sold, could you not have kept all the money? How could you think of such a thing? You have not deceived us, but God."

Upon hearing these words, Ananias fell down and died. Great fear came upon all who heard of it; the young men stood up, wrapped his body and carried it out for burial.

About three hours later, Ananias's wife came, but she was not aware of what had happened. Peter challenged her, "Tell me, whether you sold that piece of land for this price?" She said, "Yes, that was the price." Peter replied, "How could you, two, agree to put the Holy Spirit to the test? Those who buried your husband are at the door and they will carry you out as well."

With that, she fell dead at his feet. The young men came in, found her dead and carried her out for burial beside her husband. And great fear came upon the whole church; and upon all who heard of it.

Many miraculous signs and wonders were done among the people, through the hands of the apostles. The believers, of one accord, used to meet in Solomon's Porch. None of the others dared to join them, but the people held them in high esteem. So, an ever-increasing number of men and women, believed in the Lord. The people carried the sick into the streets, and laid them on cots and on mats, so, that, when Peter passed by, at least his shadow might fall on some of them. The people gathered from the towns around Jerusalem, bringing their sick and those who were troubled by unclean spirits; and all of them were healed.

The High Priest and all his supporters, that is, the party of the Sadducees, became very jealous of the apostles; so they arrested them and had them thrown into the public jail. But an angel of the Lord opened the door of the prison during the night, brought them out, and said to them, "Go and stand in the temple court and tell the people the whole of this living message." Accordingly, they entered the temple at dawn and resumed their teaching.

When the High Priest and his supporters arrived, they called together the Sanhedrin, that is the full Council of the elders of Israel. They sent word to the jail to have the prisoners brought in. But when the temple guards arrived at the jail, they did not find them inside; so they returned with the news, "We found the prison securely locked, and the prison guards at their post outside the gate; but when we opened the gate, we found no one inside."

Upon hearing these words, the captain of the temple guard and the high priests were baffled, wondering where all of this would end. Just then, someone arrived with the report, "Look, those men whom you put in prison are standing in the temple, teaching the people." Then the captain went off with the guards and brought them back, but without any show of force, for fear of being stoned by the people.

So they brought them in and made them stand before the Council; and the High Priest questioned them, "We gave you strict orders not to preach such a Savior; but you have filled Jerusalem with your teaching; and you intend charging us with the killing of this man." To this, Peter and the apostles replied, "Better for us to obey God, rather than any human authority!

The God of our ancestors raised Jesus, whom you killed by hanging him on a wooden post. God set him at his right hand, as Leader and Savior, to grant repentance and forgiveness of sins to Israel. We are witnesses to all these things, as well as the Holy Spirit, whom God has given to those who obey him."

When the Council heard this, they became very angry and wanted to kill them. But one of them, a Pharisee named Gamaliel, a teacher of the law highly respected by the people, stood up in the Sanhedrin. He ordered the men to be taken outside for a few minutes and then he spoke to the assembly.

"Fellow Israelites, consider, well, what you intend to do to these men. For some time ago, Theudas came forward, claiming to be somebody, and about four hundred men joined him. But he was killed and all his followers were dispersed or disappeared. After him, Judas, the Galilean, appeared, at the time of the census and persuaded many people to follow him. But he, too, perished; and his whole following was scattered. So, in this present case, I advise you to have nothing to do with these men. Leave them alone. If their project or activity is of human origin, it will destroy itself. If, on the other hand, it is from God, you will not be able to destroy it; and you might indeed, find yourselves fighting against God."

The Council let themselves be persuaded. They called in the apostles and had them whipped; and ordered them not to speak again of Jesus, the Savior. Then they set them free.

The apostles went out from the Council, rejoicing that they were considered worthy to suffer disgrace for the sake of the Name. Day after day, both in the temple and in people's homes, they continued to teach, and to proclaim, that Jesus was the Messiah.

In those days, as the number of disciples grew, the so-called Hellenists complained against the so-called Hebrews, because their widows were being neglected in the daily distribution. So the Twelve summoned the whole body of disciples together, and said, "It is not right, that we should neglect the word of God to serve at tables. So, friends, choose from among yourselves seven respected men, full of Spirit and wisdom, that we may appoint them to this task. As for us, we shall give ourselves to prayer, and to the ministry of the word."

5:26–6:4

The whole community agreed; and they chose Stephen, a man full of faith and the Holy Spirit; Philip, Prochorus, Nicanor, Timon, Parmenus and Nicolaus of Antioch, who was a proselyte. They presented these men to the apostles, who, first prayed over them, and then, laid hands upon them.

The word of God continued to spread, and the number of the disciples in Jerusalem increased greatly; and even many priests accepted the faith.

Stephen, full of grace and power, did great wonders and miraculous signs among the people. Some persons then came forward, who belonged to the so-called Synagogue of Freedmen, from Cyrene, Alexandria, Cilicia and Asia. They argued with Stephen. But they could not match the wisdom and the spirit with which he spoke. As they were unable to face the truth, they bribed some men to say, "We heard him speak against Moses and against God."

So they stirred up the people, the elders and the teachers of the law; they took him by surprise, seized him and brought him before the Council. Then they produced false witnesses, who said, "This man never stops speaking against our Holy Place and the law. We even heard him say that Jesus, the Nazorean, will destroy our Holy Place and change the customs which Moses handed down to us." And all who sat in the Council fixed their eyes on him; and his face appeared to them like the face of an angel.

So the High Priest asked him: "Is it true?" He answered, "Brothers and fathers, listen to me.

The God of glory appeared to our father Abraham when he was in Mesopotamia, before he went to live in Haran. And he said to him: 'Leave your land and your relatives and go to the land which I will show you.' So he left the land of the Chaldeans and settled in Haran. After the death of his father, God made him move to this land in which you now dwell. And there, he did not give him anything that was his own, not even the smallest portion of land to put his foot on; but promised to give it to him, in possession, and to his descendants, though he had no child. So God spoke: 'Your descendants shall live in a strange land. They shall be enslaved and maltreated for four hundred years. So, I shall call the nation which they serve as slaves, to render an account for it. They will come out and worship me in this place.'

He made with him, the Covenant of circumcision. And so, at the birth of his son Isaac, Abraham circumcised him on the eighth day. Isaac did the same to Jacob, and Jacob, to the twelve patriarchs.

The patriarchs envied Joseph, so they sold him into Egypt. But God was with him. He rescued him from all his afflictions, granted him wisdom, and made him please Pharaoh, king of Egypt, who appointed him governor of Egypt, and of the whole of his household. Then, there was famine in all the land of Egypt and Canaan; it was a great misery; and our ancestors did not have anything to eat. Upon learning that there was wheat in Egypt, Jacob sent our ancestors there on their first visit. On the second visit, Joseph made himself known to his brothers, and Pharaoh came to know the family of Joseph. Joseph commanded that his father Jacob be brought to him, with the whole of his family of seventy-five persons. Jacob then went down to Egypt, where he and our ancestors died. They were transferred to Shechem, and laid in the tomb that Abraham had bought for a sum of silver, from the sons of Hamor at Shechem.

As the time of promise drew near, which God had made to Abraham, the people increased, and multiplied in Egypt, until came another king, who did not know Joseph. Dealing cunningly with our race, he forced our ancestors to abandon their newborn infants and let them die. At that time, Moses was born, and God looked kindly on him. For three months, he was nursed in the home of his father; and when they abandoned him, Pharaoh's daughter took him and raised him as her own son. So, Moses was educated in all the wisdom of the Egyptians. He was mighty in word and deed. And when he was forty years old, he wanted to visit his own people, the Israelites. When he saw one of them being wronged, he defended the oppressed man and killed the Egyptian. He thought his kinsfolk would understand, that God was sending him to them as a liberator, but they did not understand. On the following day, he came to them as they were fighting and tried to reconcile them, saying: 'You are brothers, why do you hurt each other?' At that moment, the one who was injuring his companion rebuffed him, saying: 'Who appointed you as our leader and judge? Do you want to kill me, as you killed the Egyptian yesterday?' When Moses heard this, he fled, and went to live as a stranger in the land of Midian, where he had two sons.

After forty years, an angel appeared to him in the desert of Mount Sinai in the flame of a burning bush. Moses was astonished at the vision. And as he approached to look at it, he heard the voice of the Lord: 'I am the God of your fathers, the God of Abraham, Isaac and Jacob.' Moses was filled with fear and did not dare look at it. But the Lord said to him: 'Take off your sandals, for the place where you stand is holy ground. I have seen the affliction of my people in Egypt and heard them weeping, and I have come down to free them. And now, get up! I am sending you to Egypt.'

This Moses, whom they rejected, saying: 'Who appointed you leader and judge?' God sent, as leader and liberator, with the assistance of the angel who appeared to him in the bush. He led them out, performing signs and wonders in Egypt, at the Red Sea and in the desert for forty years. This Moses is the one, who said to the Israelites: 'God will give you a prophet, like me, from among your own people.' This is the one, who, in the assembly in the desert, became the mediator between the angel who spoke to him on Mount Sinai and our ancestors; and he received the words of life, that he might communicate them to us.

But him, our ancestors refused to obey, they rejected him, and turned their hearts to Egypt, saying to Aaron: 'Give us gods to lead us, since we do not know what has happened to that Moses, who brought us out of Egypt.' So, in those days, they fashioned a calf, offered sacrifices to their idol, and rejoiced in the work of their hands. So God departed from them, and let them worship the stars of heaven, as it is written in the Book of the Prophets:

'People of Israel,
did you offer me burnt offerings and sacrifices
for forty years in the desert?

No, you carried, instead, the tent of Moloch,
and the star of the god Rehan;

images you made to worship; for this,
I will banish you farther than Babylon.'

Our ancestors had the Tent of Meeting in the desert, for God had directed Moses to build it according to the pattern he had seen. Our ancestors received it, and brought it under the command of Joshua, into the lands of the pagans that they conquered, and whom God expelled before them. They kept it until the days of David, who found favor with God; and asked him to let him build a house for the God of Jacob. However, it was Solomon who built that temple.

In reality, the Most High does not dwell in houses made by human hands, as the Prophet says:

'Heaven is my throne
and earth is my footstool.

What house will you build for me,
says the Lord,

how could you give me a dwelling place?
Was it not I who made all these things?'

But you are a stubborn people. You hardened your hearts and closed your ears. You have always resisted the Holy Spirit, just as your fathers did. Was there a prophet whom your ancestors did not persecute? They killed those who announced the coming of the Just One, whom you have now betrayed and murdered; you, who, received the law through the angels but did not fulfill it."

When they heard this reproach, they were enraged; and they gnashed their teeth against Stephen. But he, full of the Holy Spirit, fixed his eyes on heaven and saw the glory of God, and Jesus at God's right hand; so he declared: "I see the heavens open, and the Son of Man at the right hand of God."

But they shouted and covered their ears with their hands, and rushed together upon him. They brought him out of the city and stoned him; and the witnesses laid down their cloaks at the feet of a young man named Saul. As they were stoning him, Stephen prayed saying: "Lord Jesus, receive my spirit." Then he knelt down and said in a loud voice: "Lord, do not hold this sin against them." And when he had said this, he died.

Saul was there, approving his murder. This was the beginning of a great persecution against the Church in Jerusalem. All, except the apostles, were scattered throughout the region of Judea and Samaria. Devout men buried Stephen and mourned deeply for him. Saul, meanwhile, was trying to destroy the church. He entered house after house and dragged off men and women, and had them put in jail.

At the same time, those who were scattered went about, preaching the word. Philip went down to a town of Samaria and proclaimed the Christ there. All the people paid close attention to what Philip said as they listened to him, and saw the miraculous signs that he did. For, in cases of possession, the unclean spirits came out shrieking loudly. Many people, who were paralyzed or crippled, were healed. So there was great joy in that town.

A certain man named Simon had come to this town, practicing magic. He held the Samaritans spellbound; and passed himself off as a very important person. All the people, from the least to the greatest, put their trust in him, saying, "This is the Power of God, the Great One." And they followed him because he had held them under the spell of his magic for a long time. But when they came to believe Philip, who announced to them the kingdom of God, and Jesus Christ as Savior, both men and women were baptized.

Simon himself, believed, and was baptized, and would not depart from Philip. He was astonished when he saw the miraculous signs and wonders that happened.

Now, when the apostles in Jerusalem heard that the Samaritans had accepted the word of God, they sent Peter and John to them. They went down and prayed for them, that they might receive the Holy Spirit; for he had not as yet come down upon any of them, since they had only been baptized in the name of the Lord Jesus. So Peter and John laid their hands on them and they received the Holy Spirit.

When Simon saw that the Spirit was given through the laying on of the apostles' hands, he offered them money, saying, "Give me, also, this power, so that anyone upon whom I lay my hands may receive the Holy Spirit."

Peter replied, "May you and your money perish, for thinking that the gift of God could be bought with money! You cannot share in this, since you do not understand the things of God. Repent, therefore, of this wickedness of yours and pray to the Lord, that you may be forgiven such a wrong way of thinking; I see you are poisoned with bitterness and in the grip of sin." Simon answered, "Pray to the Lord for me, yourselves, so that none of these things you spoke of will happen to me."

Peter and John gave their testimony and spoke the word of the Lord. And they went back to Jerusalem, bringing the Good News to many Samaritan villages along the way.

An angel of the Lord said to Philip, "Go south, toward the road that goes down from Jerusalem to Gaza, the desert road." So he set out and, it happened that, an Ethiopian was passing along that way. He was an official in charge of the treasury of the queen of the Ethiopians. He had come on pilgrimage to Jerusalem and was on his way home. He was sitting in his carriage and reading the prophet Isaiah.

The Spirit said to Philip, "Go and catch up with that carriage." So Philip ran up and heard the man reading the prophet Isaiah; and he asked, "Do you really understand what you are reading?" The Ethiopian replied, "How can I, unless someone explains it to me?" He then invited Philip to get in and sit beside him. This was the passage of Scripture he was reading:

> He was led like a sheep to be slaughtered;
> like a lamb that is dumb before the shearer,
> he did not open his mouth.

> He was humbled and deprived of his rights.
> Who can speak of his descendants?
> For he was uprooted from the earth.

The official asked Philip, "Tell me, please, does the prophet speak of himself or of someone else?"

Then Philip began to tell him the Good News of Jesus, using this text of Scripture as his starting point. As they traveled down the road, they came to a place where there was some water. Then the Ethiopian official said, "Look, here is water; what is to keep me from being baptized?"

Then he ordered the carriage to stop. Both Philip and the Ethiopian went down into the water and Philip baptized him. When they came out of the water, the Spirit of the Lord took Philip away. The Ethiopian saw him no more, but he continued on his way full of joy.

Philip found himself at Azotus; and he went about, announcing the Good News in all the towns, until he reached Caesarea.

Meanwhile, Saul considered nothing but violence and death for the disciples of the Lord. He went to the High Priest and asked him for letters to the synagogues of Damascus that would authorize him to arrest, and bring to Jerusalem, anyone he might find, man or woman, belonging to the Way.

As he traveled along and was approaching Damascus, a light from the sky suddenly flashed around him. He fell to the ground and heard a voice saying to him, "Saul, Saul! Why do you persecute me?" And he asked, "Who are you, Lord?" The voice replied, "I am Jesus, whom you persecute. Now, get up, and go into the city; there, you will be told what you are to do."

The men who were traveling with him stood there speechless: they had heard the sound, but could see no one. Saul got up from the ground and, opening his eyes, he could not see. They took him by the hand and brought him to Damascus. He was blind; and he did not eat or drink for three days.

There was a disciple in Damascus named Ananias, to whom the Lord called in a vision, "Ananias!" He answered, "Here I am, Lord!" Then the Lord said to him, "Go, at once, to Straight Street and ask, at the house of Judas, for a man of Tarsus named Saul. You will find him praying, for he has just seen in a vision that a man named Ananias has come in and placed his hands upon him, to restore his sight."

Ananias answered, "Lord, I have heard from many sources about this man, and all the harm he has done to your saints in Jerusalem; and now, he is here, with authority from the High Priest, to arrest all who call upon your name." But the Lord said to him, "Go! This man is my chosen instrument, to bring my name to the pagan nations and their kings, and the people of Israel as well. I, myself, will show him how much he will have to suffer for my name."

So Ananias left and went to the house. He laid his hands upon Saul and said, "Saul, my brother, the Lord Jesus, who appeared to you on your way here, has sent me to you, so that you may receive your sight, and be filled with the Holy Spirit." Immediately, something like scales fell from his eyes and he could see; he got up and was baptized. Then he took food and was strengthened.

For several days Saul stayed with the disciples at Damascus, and he soon began to proclaim in the synagogues that Jesus was the Son of God. All who heard were astonished and said, "Is this not the one who cast out, in Jerusalem, all those calling upon this Name? Did he not come here, to bring them bound before the chief priests?"

But Saul grew more and more powerful; and he confounded the Jews living in Damascus when he proved that Jesus was the Messiah.

After a fairly long time, the Jews conspired together to kill him. But Saul became aware of their plan: Day and night they kept watch at the city gate, in order to kill him. So his disciples took him one night and let him down from the top of the wall, lowering him in a basket.

When Saul came to Jerusalem, he tried to join the disciples there, but they were afraid of him, because they could not believe that he was a disciple. But Barnabas took him and brought him to the apostles. He recounted to them, how Saul had seen the Lord on his way, and the words the Lord had spoken to him. He told them, also, how Saul had preached boldly in the name of Jesus.

Then Saul began to live with them. He moved about freely in Jerusalem and preached openly, in the name of the Lord. He also spoke to the Hellenists; and argued with them. But they wanted to kill him. When the believers learned of this, they took him down to Caesarea and sent him off to Tarsus.

Meanwhile, the Church had peace. It was building up throughout all Judea and Galilee and Samaria, with eyes turned to the Lord, and filled with comfort from the Holy Spirit.

A s Peter traveled around, he went to visit the saints who lived in Lydda. There he found a man named Aeneas, who was paralyzed, and had been bedridden for eight years. Peter said to him, "Aeneas, Jesus Christ heals you; get up and make your bed!" And the man got up at once. All the people living in Lydda and Sharon saw him and turned to the Lord.

There was a disciple in Joppa named Tabitha, which means Dorcas, or Gazelle. She was always doing good works and helping the poor. At that time, she fell sick and died. After having washed her body, they laid her in the upstairs room.

As Lydda is near Joppa, the disciples, on hearing that Peter was there, sent two men to him with the request, "Please come to us without delay."

So Peter went with them. On his arrival, they took him upstairs to the room. All the widows crowded around him in tears, showing him the clothes that Dorcas had made while she was with them. Peter made them all leave the room; and then, he knelt down and prayed. Turning to the dead body, he said, "Tabitha, stand up." She opened her eyes, looked at Peter and sat up. Peter gave her his hand and helped her up. Then he called in the saints and widows, and presented her to them alive. This became known throughout all of Joppa; and many people believed in the Lord because of it. As for Peter, he remained for some time in Joppa at the house of Simon, a tanner of leather.

There was, in Caesarea, a man named Cornelius, captain of what was called the Italian Battalion. He was a religious and God-fearing man, together with his whole household. He gave generously to the people and constantly prayed to God.

One afternoon, at about three, he had a vision, in which he clearly saw an angel of God coming toward him, and calling him, "Cornelius!" He stared at the vision with awe and said, "What is it, sir?" And the angel answered, "Your prayers and your alms have just been recalled before God. Now send some men to Joppa and summon a certain Simon, also known as Peter; he is the guest of Simon, a tanner, who lives beside the sea."

As soon as the angel who spoke to him departed, Cornelius called two of his servants, and a devout soldier from among those attached to his service, and, after having explained everything to them, he sent them to Joppa.

The next day, while they were on their journey and approaching the city, Peter went up to the roof, at about noon, to pray. He became hungry and wished to eat, but while they were preparing food, he fell into a trance. The heavens were opened to him and he saw an object that looked like a large sheet coming down, until it rested on the ground by its four corners. In it, were all kinds of four-legged animals of the earth, reptiles and birds.

Then a voice said to him, "Get up, Peter, kill and eat!" But Peter replied, "Certainly not, Lord! I have never eaten any defiled or unclean creature." And again, a second time, the voice spoke, "What God has made clean, you must not call unclean." This happened three times; and then the sheet was taken up again into the sky.

While Peter was still puzzling over the meaning of the vision he had seen, the messengers of Cornelius arrived at the gate, asking for the house of Simon. They called out, to inquire whether Simon, also known as Peter, was staying there. At that moment, as Peter continued pondering on the vision, the Spirit spoke to him, "There are men looking for you; get up and go downstairs and follow them without hesitation, for I have sent them."

So Peter went and said to the men, "I am the one you are looking for. What brings you here?" They answered, "He who sent us is Captain Cornelius. He is an upright and God-fearing man, well respected by all the Jewish people. He has been instructed by a holy angel to summon you to his house, so that he may listen to what you have to say." So Peter invited them in and put them up for the night.

The next day, he went off with them, and some of the believers from Joppa accompanied him. The following day, he arrived in Caesarea, where Cornelius was expecting them; he had called together his relatives and close friends. As Peter was about to enter, Cornelius went to him, fell on his knees and bowed low. But Peter lifted him up saying, "Stand up, for I, too, am a human being."

After talking with him, Peter entered and found many people assembled there. Then he said to them, "You know that it is forbidden for Jews to associate with anyone of another nation, or to enter their houses. But God has made it clear to me that no one should call any person common or unclean; because of this, I came at once when I was sent for. Now, I should like to know why you sent for me."

Cornelius then answered, "Just three days ago at this time, about three in the afternoon, I was praying in my house when a man in shining clothes stood before me and said to me: 'Cornelius, God has heard your prayer, and your alms have been remembered before him. Send someone, therefore, to Joppa and ask for Simon, also known as Peter, who is guest at the house of

Simon the tanner by the sea.' So I sent for you at once and you have been kind enough to come. Now we are all here in God's presence, waiting to hear all that the Lord has commanded you to say."

Peter then spoke to them, "Truly, I realize that God does not show partiality, but in all nations he listens to everyone who fears God and does good. And this is the message he has sent to the children of Israel, the good news of peace he has proclaimed, through Jesus Christ, who is the Lord of all. No doubt you have heard of the event that occurred throughout the whole country of the Jews, beginning from Galilee, after the baptism John preached. You know how God anointed Jesus, the Nazorean with the Holy Spirit, and power. He went about doing good, and healing all who were under the devil's power, because God was with him; we are witnesses of all that he did throughout the country of the Jews, and in Jerusalem itself. Yet, they put him to death, by hanging him on a wooden cross.

But God raised him to life on the third day, and let him manifest himself, not to all the people, but to the witnesses that were chosen beforehand by God—to us, who ate and drank with him after his resurrection from death. And he commanded us to preach to the people, and to bear witness, that he is the one appointed by God, to judge the living and the dead. All the prophets say of him, that everyone who believes in him has forgiveness of sins, through his name."

Peter was still speaking when the Holy Spirit came upon all who listened to the word. And the believers of Jewish origin who had come with Peter were amazed, "Why! God gives and pours the Holy Spirit on foreigners also!" For indeed, this happened: they heard them speaking in tongues and praising God.

Then Peter declared, "Can we refuse to baptize with water these people, who have received the Holy Spirit, just as we have?" So he had them baptized in the name of Jesus Christ. After that, they asked him to remain with them for some days.

News came to the apostles and the brothers and sisters in Judea that even foreigners had received the word of God. So, when Peter went up to Jerusalem, these Jewish believers began to argue with him, "You went to the home of uncircumcised people and ate with them!"

So Peter began to give them the facts as they had happened, "I was at prayer in the city of Joppa when, in a trance, I saw a vision. Something like a large sheet came down from the sky and drew near to me, landing on the ground by its four corners. As I stared at it, I saw four-legged creatures of the earth, wild beasts and reptiles, and birds of the sky. Then I heard a voice saying to me: 'Get up, Peter, kill and eat!' I replied, 'Certainly not, Lord! No common or unclean creature has ever entered my mouth.' A second time the voice from the heavens spoke, 'What God has made clean, you must not call unclean.' This happened three times, and then it was all drawn up into the sky. At that moment, three men, who had been sent to me from Caesarea, arrived at the house where we were staying. The Spirit instructed me to go with them without hesitation; so these six brothers came along with me and we entered into the man's house. He told us how he had seen an angel standing in his house and telling him: 'Send someone to Joppa and fetch Simon, also known as Peter. He will bring you a message by which you and all your household will be saved.'

I had begun to address them when suddenly the Holy Spirit came upon them, just as it had come upon us at the beginning. Then I remembered what the Lord had said: 'John baptized with water, but you shall be baptized with the Holy Spirit.' If, then, God had given them the same gift that he had given us when we believed in the Lord Jesus Christ, who was I to resist God?"

When they heard this they set their minds at rest and praised God saying, "Then God has granted life-giving repentance to the pagan nations as well."

Those who had been scattered, because of the persecution over Stephen, traveled as far as Phoenicia, Cyprus and Antioch, proclaiming the message, but only to the Jews. But there were some natives of Cyprus and Cyrene among them who, on coming into Antioch, spoke also to the Greeks, giving them the good news of the Lord Jesus. The hand of the Lord was with them so that a great number believed and turned to the Lord.

News of this reached the ears of the Church in Jerusalem, so they sent Barnabas to Antioch. When he arrived and saw the manifest signs of God's favor, he rejoiced and urged them all to remain firmly faithful to the Lord; for he, himself, was a good man, filled with the Holy Spirit and faith. Thus large crowds came to know the Lord.

Then Barnabas went off to Tarsus, to look for Saul; and when he found him, he brought him to Antioch. For a whole year, they had meetings with the Church and instructed many people. It was in Antioch that the disciples were first called Christians.

At that time, some prophets went down from Jerusalem to Antioch; and one of them, named Agabus, inspired by the Holy Spirit, foretold that a great famine would spread over the whole world. This actually happened in the days of the Emperor Claudius. So the disciples decided, within their means, to set something aside and to send relief to the brothers and sisters who were living in Judea. They did this and sent their donations to the elders by Barnabas and Saul.

About that time king Herod decided to persecute some members of the Church. He had James, the brother of John, killed with the sword, and when he saw how it pleased the Jews, he proceeded to arrest Peter also.

This happened during the festival of the Unleavened Bread. Herod had him seized and thrown into prison with four squads, each of four soldiers, to guard him. He wanted to bring him to trial before the people after the Passover feast, but while Peter was kept in prison, the whole Church prayed earnestly for him.

On the very night before Herod was to bring him to trial, Peter was sleeping between two soldiers, bound by a double chain, while guards kept watch at the gate of the prison.

Suddenly, an angel of the Lord stood there and a light shone in the prison cell. The angel tapped Peter on the side and woke him saying, "Get up quickly!" At once, the chains fell from Peter's wrists. The angel said, "Put on your belt and your sandals." Peter did so; and the angel added, "Now, put on your cloak and follow me."

Peter followed him out; yet he did not realize that what was happening with the angel was real; he thought he was seeing a vision. They passed the first guard, and then the second, and they came to the iron door leading out to the city, which opened by itself for them. They went out and made their way down a narrow alley, when suddenly the angel left him.

Then Peter recovered his senses and said, "Now I know that the Lord has sent his angel and has rescued me from Herod's clutches and from all that the Jews had in store for me."

Peter then found his bearings and came to the house of Mary, the mother of John also known as Mark, where many were gathered together and were praying. When he knocked at the outside door, a maid named Rhoda came to answer it. On recognizing the voice of Peter she was so overcome with joy that, instead of opening the door, she ran in to announce that Peter was at the door. They said to her, "You are crazy!" And as she insisted, they said, "It must be his angel."

Meanwhile, Peter continued knocking and, when they finally opened the door, they were amazed to see him. He motioned to them with his hand to be quiet and told them how the Lord had brought him out of prison. And he said to them, "Report this to James and to the brothers." Then he left and went to another place.

At daybreak there was a great commotion among the soldiers over what had become of Peter. Herod began a search for him and, not finding him, had the guards questioned and executed. After that, he came down from Judea to Caesarea and stayed there.

At that time, Herod was angry with the people of Tyre and Sidon. By general agreement they appeared before him and, after having won over

Blastus, the king's treasurer, they asked for peace, for their country was supplied with food from the territory of Herod. On the appointed day Herod, clothed in royal robes, sat on his throne and addressed them. So the assembled crowd shouted back, "A god is speaking, not a man!"

The angel of the Lord immediately struck Herod for he did not return the honor to God, and he died eaten by worms.

M eanwhile the word of God was increasing and spreading. Barnabas and Saul carried out their mission and then came back to Jerusalem, taking with them John, also called Mark.

There were at Antioch—in the Church which was there—prophets and teachers: Barnabas, Symeon known as Niger, Lucius of Cyrene, Manaen who had been brought up with Herod, and Saul. On one occasion, while they were celebrating the Lord and fasting, the Holy Spirit said to them, "Set apart for me Barnabas and Saul to do the work for which I have called them." So, after fasting and praying, they laid their hands on them and sent them off.

These then, sent by the Holy Spirit, went down to the port of Seleucia and from there sailed to Cyprus. Upon their arrival in Salamis they proclaimed the word of God in the Jewish synagogue; John was with them as an assistant.

They traveled over the whole island as far as Paphos, where they met a certain magician named Bar-Jesus, a Jewish false prophet, who lived with the governor Sergius Paulus, an intelligent man. He had summoned Barnabas and Saul, and wanted to hear the word of God. But they were opposed by the Elymas (that is, the magician) who tried to turn the governor from the faith.

Then Saul, also known as Paul, full of the Holy Spirit, looked intently at him and said, "You son of the devil, full of all kinds of deceit, and enemy, of all that is right! Will you never stop perverting the straight paths of the Lord? Now, the Lord's hand is upon you; you will become blind and, for a time, you will not see the light of day." At once, a misty darkness came upon him, and he groped about for someone, to lead him by the hand.

The governor saw what had happened; he believed, and was deeply impressed by the teaching about the Lord.

From Paphos, Paul and his companions set sail and came to Perga in Pamphylia. There, John left them and returned to Jerusalem, while they went on from Perga and came to Antioch in Pisidia. On the Sabbath day they entered the synagogue and sat down. After the reading of the law and the prophets, the officials of the synagogue sent this message to them, "Brothers, if you have any word of encouragement for the assembly, please speak up."

So Paul arose, motioned to them for silence and began, "Fellow Isra-elites and, also, all you who fear God, listen. The God of our people Israel chose our ancestors; and after he had made them increase during their stay in Egypt, he led them out by powerful deeds. For forty years he fed them in the desert; and after he had destroyed seven nations in the land of Canaan, he gave them their land as an inheritance. All this took four hundred and fifty years. After that, he gave them Judges, until Samuel the prophet. Then they asked for a king; and God gave them Saul, son of Kish, of the tribe of Benjamin; and he was king for forty years. After that time, God removed him and raised up David as king, to whom he bore witness saying: I have found David, the son of Jesse, a man after my own heart, who will do all I want him to do.

It is from the descendants of David that God has now raised up the promised Savior of Israel, Jesus. Before he appeared, John proclaimed a baptism of repentance for all the people of Israel. As John was ending his life's work, he said: 'I am not what you think I am, for, after me, another one is coming, whose sandal I am not worthy to untie.'

Brothers, children and descendants of Abraham, and you, also, who fear God, it is to you that this message of salvation has been sent. It is a fact, that the inhabitants of Jerusalem, and their leaders, did not recognize Jesus. Yet, in condemning him, they fulfilled the words of the prophets that are read every Sabbath, but not understood. Even though they found no charge against him that deserved death, they asked Pilate to have him executed. And after they had carried out all that had been written concerning him, they took him down from the cross and laid him in a tomb.

But God raised him from the dead, and for many days thereafter, he showed himself, to those who had come up with him from Galilee to Jeru-salem. They have now become his witnesses before the people. We, our-selves, announce to you this Good News: All that God promised our ances-tors, he has fulfilled, for us, their descendants, by raising Jesus, according to what is written in the second psalm:

> You are my Son,
> today I have begotten you.

On raising him from the dead, so that he would never know the decay of death, God fulfilled his promise:

> I will give you the holy blessings,
> the sure ones that I kept for David.

Moreover, in another place it is said:

> You will not allow your holy one to suffer corruption.

Now David was subjected to corruption, for he died, and was laid beside his ancestors, after having served God's purpose in his own time. But the one God raised up—Jesus—did not know corruption. -Through him, fellow Israelites, you have forgiveness of sins, and this is our good news. Whoever believes in him is freed of everything, from which you could not be freed by the law of Moses.

Now, watch out, lest what was said by the prophet happens to you:

> Take care, you cynics;
> be amazed and disappear!
>
> For I am about to do something in your days
> which you would never believe
> even if you had been told."

As Paul and Barnabas withdrew, they were invited to speak again on the same subject the following Sabbath. After that, when the assembly broke up, many Jews and devout God-fearing people followed them; and to these, they spoke, urging them to hold fast to the grace of God.

The following Sabbath almost the entire city gathered to listen to Paul, who spoke a fairly long time about the Lord. But the presence of such a crowd made the Jews jealous. So they began to oppose, with insults, whatever Paul said.

Then Paul and Barnabas spoke out firmly, saying, "It was necessary, that God's word be first proclaimed to you, but since you now reject it, and judge yourselves to be unworthy of eternal life, we turn to non-Jewish people. For thus we were commanded by the Lord:

> I have set you as a light to the pagan nations,
> so that you may bring my salvation to the ends of the earth."

Those who were not Jews rejoiced, when they heard this, and praised the message of the Lord; and all those, destined for everlasting life, believed in it. Thus the word spread, throughout the whole region.

Some of the Jews, however, incited God-fearing women of the upper class, and the leading men of the city, as well, and stirred up an intense persecution against Paul and Barnabas. Finally, they had them expelled from their region. The apostles shook the dust from their feet, in protest against this people, and went to Iconium, leaving; the disciples, filled with joy and the Holy Spirit.

In Iconium Paul and Barnabas likewise went into the Jewish synagogue and preached in such a manner that a great number of Jews and Greeks believed. But the Jews, who would not believe, stirred up the pagan people and poisoned their minds against the brothers. In spite of this, Paul and

Barnabas spent a considerable time there. They spoke fearlessly of the Lord, who confirmed the message of his grace, with the miraculous signs and wonders he gave them power to do.

But the people of the city were divided, some siding with the Jews and some with the apostles. A move was made by pagans and Jews, together with their leaders, to harm the apostles and to stone them. But Paul and Barnabas learned of this and fled to the Lycaonian towns of Lystra and Derbe and to the surrounding countryside, where they continued preaching the Good News.

Paul and Barnabas spent a fairly long time at Lystra. There was a crippled man in Lystra who had never been able to stand or walk. One day, as he was listening to the preaching, Paul looked intently at him and saw that he had the faith to be saved. So he said with a loud voice, "Stand upright on your feet." And the man leaped up and began walking.

When the people saw what Paul had done, they cried out in the language of Lycaonia, "The gods have come to us in human likeness!" They named Barnabas Zeus, and Paul they called Hermes, since he was the chief speaker. Even the priest of the temple of Zeus, which stood outside the town, brought oxen and garlands to the gate; together with the people, he wanted to offer sacrifice to them.

When Barnabas and Paul heard this, they tore their garments, to show their indignation, and rushed into the crowd, shouting, "Friends, why are you doing this? We are human beings, with the same weakness you have, and we are now telling you to turn away from these useless things, to the living God who made the heavens, the earth, the sea and all that is in them. In past generations, he allowed each nation to go its own way, though he never stopped making himself known; for he is continually doing good, giving you rain from heaven and fruitful seasons, providing you with food, and filling your hearts with gladness."

Even these words could hardly keep the crowd from offering sacrifice to them.

Then some Jews arrived from Antioch and Iconium and turned the people against them. They stoned Paul and dragged him out of the town, leaving him for dead. But, when his disciples gathered around him, he stood up and returned to the town. And the next day, he left for Derbe with Barnabas.

After proclaiming the gospel in that town and making many disciples, they returned to Lystra and Iconium, and on to Antioch. They were strengthening the disciples, and encouraging them to remain firm in the faith; for they said, "We must go through many trials to enter the kingdom of God." In each church they appointed elders and, after praying and fast-

14:4–14:23

ing, they commended them to the Lord, in whom they had placed their faith.

Then they traveled through Pisidia, and came to Pamphylia. They preached the word in Perga and went down to Attalia. From there, they sailed back to Antioch, where they had first been commended to God's grace, for the task they had now completed.

On their arrival, they gathered the Church together, and told them all that God had done through them, and how he had opened the door of faith to the non-Jews. They spent a fairly long time there with the disciples.

Some persons, who had come from Judea to Antioch, were teaching the brothers in this way, "Unless you are circumcised, according to the law of Moses, you cannot be saved."

Because of this, there was trouble; and Paul and Barnabas had fierce arguments with them. For Paul told the people to remain as they were, when they became believers. Finally, those who had come from Jerusalem suggested that Paul and Barnabas and some others go up to Jerusalem, to discuss the matter with the apostles and elders.

They were sent on their way by the Church. As they passed through Phoenicia and Samaria they reported how the non-Jews had turned to God; and there was great joy among all the brothers and sisters.

On their arrival in Jerusalem, they were welcomed by the Church, the apostles and the elders, to whom they told all that God had done through them. Some believers, however, who belonged to the party of the Pharisees, stood up and said, that non-Jewish men must be circumcised and instructed to keep the law of Moses. So the apostles and elders met together to consider this matter.

As the discussions became heated, Peter stood up and said to them, "Brothers, you know that from the beginning, God chose me among you, so that non-Jews could hear the Good News from me, and believe. God, who can read hearts, put himself on their side, by giving the Holy Spirit to them, just as he did to us. He made no distinction between us and them, and cleansed their hearts through faith. So, why do you want to put God to the test? Why do you lay on the disciples, a burden that neither our ancestors nor we, ourselves, were able to carry? We believe, indeed, that we are saved through the grace of the Lord Jesus, just as they are."

The whole assembly kept silent as they listened to Paul and Barnabas tell of all the miraculous signs and wonders that God had done, through them, among the non-Jews.

After they had finished, James spoke up, "Listen to me, brothers. Symeon has just explained how God first showed his care, by taking a people for himself from non-Jewish nations. And the words of the prophets agree with this, for Scripture says,

> After this I will return
> and rebuild the booth of David which has fallen;
>
> I will rebuild its ruins
> and set it up again.
>
> Then, the rest of humanity will look for the Lord,
> and all the nations will be consecrated to my Name.
>
> So says the Lord, who does today
> what he decided from the beginning.

Because of this, I think that we should not make difficulties for those non-Jews who are turning to God. Let us just tell them, not to eat food that is unclean from having been offered to idols; to keep themselves from prohibited marriages; and not to eat the flesh of animals that have been strangled; or any blood. For, from the earliest times, Moses has been taught in every place, and every Sabbath his laws are recalled."

Then the apostles and elders, together with the whole Church, decided to choose representatives from among them, to send to Antioch with Paul and Barnabas. These were Judas, known as Barsabbas, and Silas, both leading men among the brothers. They took with them the following letter:

"Greetings from the apostles and elders, your brothers,

to the believers of non-Jewish birth in Antioch, Syria and Cilicia.

We have heard, that some persons from among us have worried you with their discussions, and troubled your peace of mind. They were not appointed by us. But now, it has seemed right to us, in an assembly, to choose representatives, and to send them to you, along with our beloved Barnabas and Paul, who have dedicated their lives to the service of our Lord Jesus Christ. We send you, then, Judas and Silas, who, themselves, will give you these instructions by word of mouth.

We, with the Holy Spirit, have decided not to put any other burden on you except what is necessary: You are to abstain from blood; from the meat of strangled animals; and from prohibited marriages. If you keep yourselves from these, you will do well.

Farewell."

After saying good-bye, the messengers went to Antioch, where they assembled the community and handed them the letter. When they read the news, all were delighted with the encouragement it gave them. Judas and Silas, who were themselves prophets, spoke at length to encourage and strengthen them. After they had spent some time there, the messengers were sent off in peace by the believers; Silas, however, preferred to stay with them and only Judas went off. So Paul and Barnabas continued in Antioch, teaching, and preaching with many others, the word of God.

After some days, Paul said to Barnabas, "Let us return and visit the believers in every town where we proclaimed the word of the Lord, to see how they are getting on." Barnabas wanted to take with them John, also called Mark, but Paul did not think it right to take him, since he had not stayed with them to the end of their mission, but had turned back and left them in Pamphylia. Such a sharp disagreement resulted, that the two finally separated. Barnabas took Mark along with him and sailed for Cyprus. Paul, for his part, chose Silas and left, commended by the brothers and sisters to the grace of the Lord.

He traveled throughout Syria and Cilicia, strengthening the churches there.

Paul traveled on, to Derbe and then to Lystra. A disciple named Timothy lived there, whose mother was a believer of Jewish origin but whose father was a Greek. As the believers at Lystra and Iconium spoke well of him, Paul wanted Timothy to accompany him. So he took him and, because of the Jews of that place, who all knew that his father was a Greek, he circumcised him.

As they traveled from town to town, they delivered the decisions of the apostles and elders in Jerusalem, for the people to obey. Meanwhile, the churches grew stronger in faith, and increased in number, every day.

They traveled through Phrygia and Galatia, because they had been prevented by the Holy Spirit from preaching the message in the province of Asia. When they came to Mysia, they tried to go on to Bithynia, but the Spirit of Jesus did not allow them to do this. So, passing by Mysia, they went down to Troas.

There, one night, Paul had a vision. A Macedonian stood before him and begged him, "Come over to Macedonia and help us!" When he awoke, he told us of this vision; and we understood that the Lord was calling us, to give the Good News to the Macedonian people.

So, we put out to sea from Troas and sailed straight across to Samothrace Island; and the next day, to Neapolis. From there, we went inland to Philippi, the leading city of the district of Macedonia, and a Roman colony. We spent some days in that city.

On the Sabbath, we went outside the city gate, to the bank of the river, where we thought the Jews would gather to pray. We sat down and began speaking to the women who were gathering there. One of them was a God-fearing woman, named Lydia, from the city of Thyatira, a dealer in purple cloth.

As she listened, the Lord opened her heart to respond to what Paul was saying. After she had been baptized, together with her household, she invited us to her house, "If you think I am faithful to the Lord, come and stay at my house." And she persuaded us to accept her invitation.

One day, as we were on our way to the place of prayer, we were met by a slave girl, who had a spirit of divination, and gained much profit for her owners by her fortune-telling.

She followed Paul, and the rest of us, shouting: "These people are servants of the Most High God. They will make known to you a way of salvation." The girl did this for several days, until Paul was annoyed. Then he turned around and said to the spirit, "In the name of Jesus Christ, I command you, come out of her!" The spirit went out of her that very moment.

When her owners realized that all the profits they expected had gone, they seized Paul and Silas and dragged them into the marketplace, before the local authorities. And when they had turned them over to the officials, they said, "These people are Jews and they are disturbing our city. They have come here to introduce customs which are not lawful for us Romans to adopt or practice."

So they set the crowd against them; and the officials tore the clothes off Paul and Silas and ordered them to be flogged. And after inflicting many blows on them, they threw them into prison, charging the jailer to guard them safely. Upon receiving these instructions, he threw them into the inner cell and fastened their feet in the stocks.

About midnight, Paul and Silas were praying and singing hymns to God, and the other prisoners were listening. Suddenly, a severe earthquake shook the place, rocking the prison to its foundations. Immediately, all the doors flew open and the chains of all the prisoners fell off. The jailer woke up to see the prison gates wide open. Thinking that the prisoners had escaped, he drew his sword to kill himself, but Paul shouted to him, "Do not harm yourself! We are all still here."

The jailer asked for a light, then rushed in, and fell at the feet of Paul and Silas. After he had secured the other prisoners, he led them out and asked, "Sirs, what must I do to be saved?" They answered, "Believe in the Lord Jesus Christ and you, and your household, will be saved." Then they spoke the word of God to him and to all his household.

Even at that hour of the night, the jailer took care of them and washed their wounds; and he, and his whole household, were baptized at once. He led them to his house, spread a meal before them and joyfully celebrated with his whole household his new found faith in God.

The next morning, the officials sent police officers with the order, "Let those men go." So the jailer said to Paul and Silas, "The officials have sent an order for you and Silas to be released. You may leave and go in peace."

But Paul said to him, "They flogged us publicly, and jailed us without trial, men who are Roman citizens; and now they want to smuggle us out secretly? Oh no! Let them come themselves and lead us out."

The police officers reported this to the officials, who were afraid when they heard that Paul and Silas were Roman citizens. So they came and apologized to them, took them out and asked them to leave the town.

Once outside the prison, Paul and Silas went to Lydia's house, where they met and encouraged the brothers and sisters, and then departed.

Paul and Silas took the road through Amphipolis and Apollonia, and came to Thessalonica, where there was a Jewish synagogue. As Paul used to do, he went to the synagogue; and on three Sabbaths he held discussions with them about the Scriptures. He explained, and proved to them, that the Messiah had to suffer and rise from the dead, and he said, "Such a Messiah is this Jesus whom I am proclaiming to you."

Some of them were convinced and joined Paul and Silas. So, too, did a great number of Greeks sympathetic to Judaism, and many prominent women.

This only made the Jews jealous; so they gathered some of the good-for-nothing street loafers and formed a mob to start a riot in the town. They came to the house of Jason, in an attempt to bring Paul and Silas before the people's assembly. Not finding them there, they dragged off Jason and some believers to the city authorities shouting, "These people, who have turned the world upside down, have come here also, and Jason has given them hospitality. They all disregard the decrees of the Emperor and claim that there is another King, Jesus."

In this way, they upset the crowd and the city officials who heard them. The officials released Jason and the others on bail.

As soon as night fell, the believers sent Paul and Silas off to Beroea. On their arrival, they went to the Jewish synagogue. Its members were more open-minded than those in Thessalonica and welcomed the message with great enthusiasm. Each day they examined the Scriptures, to see if these things were so. Many of them came to believe, as did numerous influential Greek women, and many men as well.

But when the Jews of Thessalonica came to know, that the word of God had been proclaimed by Paul in Beroea also, they hurried there, to cause a commotion and stir up the crowds. At once, the believers sent Paul away to the coast; but both Silas and Timothy stayed in Beroea. Paul was taken as far as Athens by his escort, who then returned to Beroea with instructions for Silas and Timothy to come to him as soon as possible.

While Paul was waiting for them in Athens, he felt very uneasy at the sight of a city full of idols. He held discussions in the synagogue with the Jews and the God-fearing people, as well as daily debates in the public square with ordinary passersby.

16:38–17:17

Epicureans and Stoic philosophers debated with him, some of them asking, "What is this babbler trying to say?" Others commented, "He sounds like a promoter of foreign gods," because he was heard to speak of Jesus and 'the Resurrection.' So they took Paul and led him off to the Areopagus hall, and said, "We would like to know what this new teaching is that you are talking about. Some of the things we hear you say sound strange to us, and we would like to know what they mean."

Indeed, all Athenian citizens, as well as the foreigners who live there, have as their favorite occupation talking about or listening to the latest news.

Then Paul stood up in the Areopagus hall and said, "Athenian citizens, I note that, in every way, you are very religious. As I walked around, looking at your shrines, I even discovered an altar with this inscription: To an unknown God. Now, what you worship as unknown, I intend to make known to you.

God, who made the world and all that is in it, does not dwell in sanctuaries made by human hands, being as he is Lord of heaven and earth. Nor does his worship depend on anything made by human hands, as if he were in need. Rather, it is he who gives life and breath and everything else, to everyone. From one stock he created the whole human race, to live throughout all the earth, and he fixed the time and the boundaries of each nation. He wanted them to seek him by themselves, even if it was only by groping for him, that they succeed in finding him.

Yet, he is not far from any one of us. For, in him, we live and move, and have our being; as some of your poets have said: for we, too, are his offspring. If we are indeed God's offspring, we ought not to think of divinity as something like a statue of gold or silver or stone, a product of human art and imagination.

But now, God prefers to overlook this time of ignorance; and he calls on all people to change their ways. He has already set a day, on which he will judge the world with justice through a man he has appointed. And, so that all may believe it, he has just given a sign, by raising this man from the dead."

When they heard Paul speak of a resurrection from death, some made fun of him, while others said, "We must hear you on this topic some other time." At that point Paul left. But a few did join him, and believed. Among them were Dionysius, a member of the Areopagus court, a woman named Damaris, and some others.

After this, Paul left Athens and went to Corinth. There, he found a Jew named Aquila, a native of Pontus, who had recently come from Italy with his wife Priscilla, following a decree of the Emperor Claudius, which ordered all Jews to leave Rome. Paul went to visit them, and then stayed and worked with them, because they shared the same trade of tent making. Every Sabbath, he held discussions in the synagogue, trying to convince both Jews and Greeks.

When Silas and Timothy came down from Macedonia, Paul was able to give himself wholly to preaching, and proving to the Jews that Jesus was the Messiah. One day, when they opposed him and insulted him, he shook the dust from his clothes in protest, saying, "Your blood be on your own heads! I am innocent. I am not to blame if, from now on, I go to the non-Jews."

So Paul left there and went to the house of a God-fearing man named Titus Justus, who lived next door to the synagogue. A leading man of the synagogue, Crispus, along with his whole household, believed in the Lord. On hearing Paul, many more Corinthians believed and were baptized.

One night, in a vision, the Lord said to Paul, "Do not be afraid, but continue speaking and do not be silent, for many people in this city are mine. I am with you, so no one will harm you." So Paul stayed a year and a half in that place, teaching the word of God among them.

When Gallio was governor of Achaia, the Jews made a united attack on Paul and brought him before the court. And they accused him, "This man tries to persuade us to worship God in ways that are against the law."

Paul was about to speak in his own defense when Gallio said to the Jews, "If it were a matter of a misdeed or vicious crime, I would have to consider your complaint. But since this is a quarrel about teachings and divine names that are proper to your own law, see to it yourselves: I refuse to judge such matters." And he sent them out of the court.

Then the people seized Sosthenes, a leading man of the synagogue, and beat him in front of the tribunal; but Gallio paid no attention to it.

Paul stayed on with the disciples in Corinth for many days; he then left them and sailed off with Priscilla and Aquila for Syria. And as he was no longer under a vow he had taken, he shaved his head before sailing from Cenchreae.

When they reached Ephesus, he left Priscilla and Aquila behind and entered the synagogue to hold discussions with the Jews. But although they asked him to stay longer, he declined. And he took leave of them saying, "God willing, I will come back to you again." Then he set sail from Ephesus. On landing at Caesarea, he went up to greet the Church, and then went down to Antioch.

After spending some time there, he left and traveled from place to place through Galatia and Phrygia, strengthening the disciples.

A certain Jew named Apollos, a native of Alexandria, arrived at Ephesus. He was an eloquent speaker and an authority on the Scriptures, and he had some knowledge of the way of the Lord. With great enthusiasm he preached, and taught correctly, about Jesus, although he knew only of

John's baptism. As he began to speak boldly in the synagogue, Priscilla and Aquila heard him; so they took him home with them and explained to him the way more accurately. As Apollos wished to go to Achaia, the believers encouraged him and wrote to the disciples there to welcome him. When he arrived, he greatly strengthened those who, by God's grace, had become believers, for he vigorously refuted the Jews, proving from the Scriptures that Jesus is the Messiah.

While Apollos was in Corinth, Paul traveled through the interior of the country and came to Ephesus. There, he found some disciples, whom he asked, "Did you receive the Holy Spirit when you became believers?" They answered, "We have not even heard that anyone may receive the Holy Spirit." Paul then asked, "What kind of baptism have you received?" And they answered, "The baptism of John."

Paul then explained, "John's baptism was for conversion, but he himself said they should believe in the one who was to come, and that one is Jesus." Upon hearing this, they were baptized in the name of the Lord Jesus. Then Paul laid his hands on them and the Holy Spirit came down upon them; and they began to speak in tongues and to prophesy. There were about twelve of them in all.

Paul went into the synagogue; and for three months he preached and discussed there boldly, trying to convince them about the kingdom of God. Some of them, instead of believing, grew obstinate, and criticized the way publicly. So Paul departed from them and took the disciples with him. He taught daily, in the lecture hall of a certain Tyrannus. He did this for two years, so that all those who lived in the province of Asia, both Jews and non-Jews, heard the word of the Lord.

God did extraordinary deeds of power through the hands of Paul. Even handkerchiefs, or cloths that had touched his skin, were laid upon the sick and their illnesses were cured, and evil spirits also departed from them.

Some Jews who traveled around driving out evil spirits, also tried to use the name of the Lord Jesus over those possessed by evil spirits, saying, "I command you, by this Jesus whom Paul preaches." Among them were the seven sons of a Jewish priest, named Sceva. But one day, when they entered a house and dared to do this, the evil spirit said to them, "Jesus, I recognize; and Paul, I know; but who are you?" Then the man with the evil spirit sprang at them and overpowered, first, one and, then, another. And he handled them so violently that they fled from that house naked and mauled. This became known to all the Jews and Greeks living in Ephesus; all of them were very impressed, and the name of the Lord Jesus came to be held in great honor.

Many of those, who had become believers, came forward and openly acknowledged their former practices. Many who had practiced magic arts collected their books and burned them, in front of everyone. When the value of these was assessed, it came to fifty thousand silver coins.

In this way, the word of the Lord spread widely and with power.

When all these events were completed, Paul, led by the Holy Spirit, decided to travel through Macedonia and Achaia, again; and then go on to Jerusalem. And he said, "After I have been there, I must visit Rome also." So he sent two of his assistants, Timothy and Erastus, to Macedonia ahead of him, while he himself stayed on for a time in Asia.

About that time, the city was deeply troubled because of the way. It all began because of a certain silversmith named Demetrius, who made silver models of the temple of the goddess Artemis, and whose business brought a great deal of profit to the workers. He called them together, with others who did similar work, and said, "Friends, you know that our prosperity depends on this work. But, as you can see and hear for yourselves, this Paul has led astray a great number of people, not only here in Ephesus, but also throughout most of the province of Asia. And he has convinced them that gods made by human hands are no gods at all. The danger grows, that not only our trade will be discredited, but even that the temple of the great goddess Artemis will count for nothing. She, whom Asia, and all the world worships, may soon be stripped of her renown."

On hearing this, they became enraged and began shouting, "Great is Artemis of the Ephesians!" The uproar spread throughout the whole city. The mob rushed to the theater, dragging with them Gaius and Aristarchus, two Macedonians, who were Paul's traveling companions. Paul wished to face this crowd, but the disciples would not let him. Some of the officials of the Asian province also, who were friends of Paul, sent him a message, begging him not to show himself in the theater.

Meanwhile, the whole assembly was in an uproar. Some shouted one thing, and some shouted another; and most of them did not know why they were there. Some of the crowd wanted a certain Alexander to speak, whom the Jews put forward. Alexander intended to make a speech of defense before the crowd, but when they recognized that he was a Jew, they chanted all together, for about two hours, "Great is Artemis of the Ephesians!"

Finally, the town clerk was able to calm the mob. He said, "Citizens of Ephesus, who does not know that Ephesus is keeper of the temple of the great Artemis, and of her image which fell from the sky? Since these things are undeniable, you must calm yourselves and do nothing rash. These men, whom you brought here, are not temple-robbers, nor have they spoken ill of our goddess. If Demetrius and his fellow craftsmen want to bring charges against anyone, the courts are open and there are officials. Let them bring charges against each other. If there is anything further that needs to be investigated, let it be done in the lawful assembly. For, as it is today, we are in danger of being charged with rioting, since there is no valid excuse we can give for this wild demonstration." And the town clerk dismissed the assembly.

After the uproar died down, Paul called his disciples together to encourage them. Then he said goodbye and set out on his journey to Macedonia. He traveled throughout those regions and spent himself in speaking and encouraging them. He finally arrived in Greece.

When he had been there for three months, he wanted to set sail for Syria; but as the Jews were plotting against him, he decided to return by way of Macedonia. When he was about to leave for the Asian province, some companions went with him: Sopater, son of Pyrrhus, from Berea, Aristarchus and Secundus from Thessalonica, Gaius from Derbe, Timothy, Tychicus and Trophimus from Asia. So they went ahead, and waited for us in Troas, while we set sail from Philippi, as soon as the festival of Unleavened Bread was over. Five days later, we joined them in Troas, where we spent a week.

On the first day of the week we were together for the breaking of the bread, and Paul, who intended to leave the following day, spoke at length. The discourse went on, until midnight, with many lamps burning in the upstairs room where we were gathered. A young man named Eutychius was sitting on the window ledge, and as Paul kept on talking, Eutychius grew more and more sleepy, until he finally went sound asleep and fell from the third floor to the ground. There, they found him dead.

Paul went down, bent over him and took him in his arms. "Do not be alarmed," he said, "there is life in him." Then he went back upstairs, broke the bread and ate. After that, he kept on talking with them for a long time, until daybreak, and then he left. As for the young man, they lifted him up alive and were greatly comforted.

We went on ahead to the ship and sailed for Assos, where we were to pick up Paul. This was the arrangement, since Paul intended to travel by foot. In fact, we met him at Assos and, taking him aboard, we went on to Mitylene. We sailed from there and arrived off Chios the next day. A day later, we came to Samos; and the following day, we reached Miletus.

Paul had decided to sail past Ephesus, so as not to lose time in Asia, for he was eager to reach Jerusalem by the day of Pentecost, if at all possible.

From Miletus, Paul sent word to Ephesus, summoning the elders of the Church. When they came to him, he addressed them, "You know how I lived among you, from the first day I set foot in the province of Asia; how I served the Lord in humility, through the sorrows and trials that the Jews caused me. You know, that I never held back from doing anything that could be useful for you; I spoke publicly and in your homes; and I urged Jews, and non-Jews, alike, to turn to God and believe in our Lord Jesus.

But now, I am going to Jerusalem, chained by the Spirit, without knowing what will happen to me there. Yet, in every city, the Holy Spirit warns me, that imprisonment and troubles await me. Indeed, I put no value on my life; if only I can finish my race; and complete the service to which I have been assigned by the Lord Jesus, to announce the good news of God's grace.

I now feel sure, that none of you, among whom I have gone about proclaiming the kingdom of God, will ever see me again. Therefore, I declare to you, this day, that my conscience is clear with regard to all of you. For I have spared no effort in fully declaring to you God's will.

Keep watch over yourselves, and over the whole flock the Holy Spirit has placed into your care. Shepherd the Church of the Lord that he has won, at the price of his own blood. I know that, after I leave, ruthless wolves will come among you and not spare the flock. And, from among you, some will arise, corrupting the truth, and inducing the disciples to follow them.

Be on the watch, therefore, remembering that, for three years, night and day, I did not cease to warn everyone, even with tears. Now, I commend you to God, and to his grace-filled word, which is able to make you grow and gain the inheritance that you shall share with all the saints.

I have not looked for anyone's silver, gold or clothing. You, yourselves, know, that these hands of mine have provided for both my needs and the needs of those who were with me. In every way, I have shown you that by working hard one must help the weak, remembering the words that the Lord Jesus himself said, 'Happiness lies more in giving than in receiving.'"

After this discourse, Paul knelt down with them and prayed. Then, they all began to weep and threw their arms around him and kissed him. They were deeply distressed because he had said that they would never see him again. And they went with him even to the ship.

When we had finally taken leave of them, we put out to sea, and sailed straight to Cos, and the next day, to Rhodes; and from there, to Patara. There, we found a ship that made for Phoenicia; we went aboard and set sail. We caught sight of Cyprus but passed it by on our left, as we continued on towards Syria. We landed at Tyre, where the ship had to unload cargo. There, we found the disciples and stayed a week. Warned by the Spirit, they told Paul not to go to Jerusalem.

But when it was time, we departed and continued on our journey. All of them, wives and children included, came out of the city with us, and, on the beach, we knelt down and prayed. After that, we said good-bye to one another; we boarded the ship and they returned home.

We continued our journey, sailing from Tyre to Ptolemais, where we greeted the brothers and sisters and spent a day with them. On the following day, we left; and came to Caesarea. There, we entered the house of Philip, the evangelist; and we stayed with him. He was one of the Seven; and had four unmarried daughters who were gifted with prophecy.

We were there some days, when a prophet named Agabus came down from Judea. Coming to us, he took Paul's belt and bound his own feet and hands with it, saying, Thus speaks the Holy Spirit: "This is how the Jews in Jerusalem will bind the owner of this belt and hand him over to the foreign power."

When we heard this, we, together with these people of Caesarea, begged Paul not to go up to Jerusalem. Then he answered, "Why are you weeping and breaking my heart? For I am ready, not only to be imprisoned, but, also, to die in Jerusalem, for the name of the Lord Jesus." When he would not be persuaded, we gave up and said, "The Lord's will be done."

After this, we got ready; and went up to Jerusalem. With us were some of the disciples of Caesarea, who brought us to the house of a Cypriot, where we were to stay. He was called Mnason and was one of the early disciples.

When we arrived in Jerusalem the brothers welcomed us warmly. The next day, Paul went with us to James' house, where all the elders had gathered. After greeting them, Paul began telling them, in detail, everything God had done among the non-Jews, through his ministry.

After hearing this, they all praised God; but they said, "You see, brother, how many thousands of Jews of Judea have come to believe; and all of them are zealous for the law. Yet, they have heard, that you teach the Jews who live in pagan nations, to depart from Moses, telling them not to have their sons circumcised and to renounce Jewish customs. We shall gather the assembly; for, in any case, they will hear that you have arrived. Then, do as we tell you.

There are four men among us who have made a vow. Take them, and purify yourself, along with them, and pay the sacrifice for them to shave their heads. In that way, everyone will know, that there is nothing true in what they have been told about you; but, that, you go on keeping the law.

As for the non-Jews who have become believers, we sent them a letter to tell them, that they are only obliged not to eat meat offered to idols, or blood, or flesh of strangled animals; and also to avoid prohibited sexual union."

So, the next day, Paul took the men; together with them, he purified himself and entered the temple, to give notice of what day the sacrifice would be offered for each of them, to end his time of purification.

When the seven days were almost over, some Jews from Asia, who saw Paul in the temple, began to stir up the whole crowd. They seized him, shouting, "Fellow Israelites, help! This is the man who is spreading his teaching everywhere against our people, our law and this Sanctuary. And now he has even brought non-Jews into the temple area, defiling this Holy Place." For, they thought they had seen him in the city with Trophimus, a Greek man from Ephesus, and they supposed that Paul had introduced him into the temple.

Then turmoil spread through the whole city. People came running from all sides. They seized Paul and dragged him outside the temple. At once, the gates were shut.

They would have killed him, had not a report reached the commander of the Roman troops, that all of Jerusalem was rioting. At once the commander took some officers and soldiers, and rushed down to the crowd.

When they saw the commander and the soldiers, the crowd stopped beating Paul. The commander went over to Paul, arrested him, and ordered him to be bound with two chains; then he inquired who he was and what he had done. But some in the crowd shouted one thing and others another. As the commander was unable to find out the facts because of the uproar, he ordered Paul to be brought to the fortress. When Paul reached the steps, he actually had to be carried up by the soldiers because of the violence of the mob, for a multitude of people followed shouting, "Kill him!"

Just as he was about to be taken inside, Paul said to the commander, "May I say something to you?" He replied, "So you speak Greek! Are you not the Egyptian, then, who caused a riot some time ago and led a band of four thousand terrorists out into the desert?" Paul answered, "I am a Jew, a citizen of Tarsus, a well-known city in Cilicia. I beg you, let me address these people."

The commander agreed. So Paul, standing on the steps, motioned to the people with his hand and, when they were silent, he began to speak to them in Hebrew.

"Brothers and fathers, listen to what I have to say to you in my defense." When they heard him speaking to them in Hebrew, they became more quiet. So he went on.

"I am a Jew, born in Tarsus in Cilicia, but brought up here, in this city, where I was educated in the school of Gamaliel, according to the strict observance of our law. And I was dedicated to God's service, as are all of you today. As for this way, I persecuted it to the point of death and arrested its followers, both men and women, throwing them into prison.

The High Priest and the whole Council of elders can bear witness to this. From them, I received letters for the Jewish brothers in Damascus; and I set out to arrest those who were there, and bring them back to Jerusalem for punishment. But, as I was traveling along, nearing Damascus, at about noon, a great light from the sky suddenly flashed about me. I fell to the ground and heard a voice saying to me: 'Saul, Saul, why do you persecute me?' I answered: 'Who are you, Lord?' And he said to me: 'I am Jesus, the

Nazorean, whom you persecute.' The men who were with me saw the light, but they did not understand the voice of the one who was speaking to me. I asked: 'What shall I do, Lord?' And the Lord replied: 'Get up and go to Damascus; there, you will be told all that you are destined to do.' Yet, the brightness of that light had blinded me; and, so, I was led by the hand into Damascus by my companions.

There, a certain Ananias came to me. He was a devout observer of the law, and well spoken of by all the Jews who were living there. As he stood by me, he said: 'Brother Saul, recover your sight.' At that moment, I could see; and I looked at him. He, then, said, 'The God of our ancestors has chosen you to know his will, to see the Just One, and to hear the words from his mouth. From now on you shall be his witness before all the pagan people, and tell them all that you have seen and heard. And now, why delay? Get up and be baptized; and have your sins washed away, by calling upon his Name.'

On my return to Jerusalem, I was praying in the temple, when I fell into a trance and saw him. He spoke to me: 'Get ready to leave Jerusalem without delay, because they will not accept your testimony about me.' I answered: 'Lord, they know well, that I imprisoned those who believed in you, and had them beaten in every synagogue; and, while the blood of your witness Stephen was being poured out, I stood by, and approved it, and even guarded the cloaks of his murderers.' Then he said to me: 'Go, for I am sending you far away, to the pagan nations.'"

Up to this point, the crowd listened to Paul, but on hearing the last words, they began to shout, "Kill him! He does not deserve to live!" They were screaming and waving their cloaks and throwing dust into the air. So, the commander ordered Paul to be brought inside the fortress and questioned, after flogging, to find out why they made such an outcry against him.

But when the soldiers had strapped him down, Paul said to the officer standing there, "Is it legal to flog a Roman citizen without a trial?"

On hearing this, the officer went to the commander and said, "What are you doing? That man is a Roman citizen." So the commander came and asked him, "Tell me, are you a Roman citizen?" "Yes," answered Paul. The commander then said, "It cost me a large sum of money to become a Roman citizen." Paul answered, "I am one by birth."

Then those, who were about to question him, backed away; and the commander himself was alarmed, when he realized that he had put a Roman citizen in chains.

The next day, the commander wanted to know for certain, the charges the Jews were making against Paul. So, he released him from prison and called together the High Priest and the whole Council; and they brought Paul down and made him stand before them.

Paul looked directly at the Council and said, "Brothers, to this day, I have lived my life with a clear conscience before God." At that, the High Priest Ananias ordered his attendants to strike him on the mouth. Then Paul said, "God is about to strike you, you whitewashed wall! You sit there, to judge me according to the law, and you break the law, by ordering me to be struck!" At this, the attendants protested, "How dare you insult God's High Priest!" Paul answered, "Brothers, I did not know that he was the High Priest. For Scripture says: You shall not curse the ruler of your people."

Paul knew, that part of the Council were Sadducees and others Pharisees; so he spoke out in the Council, "Brothers, I am a Pharisee, son of a Pharisee. It is for the hope in the resurrection of the dead that I am on trial here."

At these words, an argument broke out between the Pharisees and the Sadducees, and the whole assembly was divided. For the Sadducees claim that, there is neither resurrection, nor angels nor spirits; while the Pharisees acknowledge all these things.

Then, the shouting grew louder; and some teachers of the law of the Pharisee party protested, "We find nothing wrong with this man. Maybe a spirit or an angel has spoken to him."

With this, the argument became so violent that the commander feared that Paul would be torn to pieces by them. He, therefore, ordered the soldiers to go down and rescue him from their midst, and take him back to the fortress.

That night, the Lord stood by Paul and said, "Courage! As you have borne witness to me here, in Jerusalem, so must you do in Rome."

When it was day, certain Jews formed a conspiracy. They bound themselves by an oath, not to eat or drink until they had killed Paul. There were more than forty of them who joined in this conspiracy.

They went to the high priests and the elders, and said, "We have bound ourselves by oath, not to taste food until we have killed Paul. Now then, it is up to you, and the Council, together, to convince the Roman commander to bring him down to you, on the pretext that you want to investigate his case more thoroughly. We, for our part, are prepared to kill him before he gets there."

But the son of Paul's sister heard about the planned ambush. So, he went to the headquarters and informed Paul. Paul sent for one of the officers and said, "Take this young man to the commander, for he has something to report to him." So the officer took him, and brought him to the commander, saying, "The prisoner, Paul, called me, and asked me to bring this boy to you, because he has something to tell you."

The commander took him by the hand and, drawing him aside, asked him privately, "What is it that you have to report to me?" The boy replied, "The Jews have agreed among themselves to ask you tomorrow, to have Paul brought down to the Council, as if to inquire more thoroughly about him. But do not be persuaded by them, for there are more than forty of them ready to ambush him, having bound themselves by an oath not to eat or drink until they have killed him. They are now ready to do it, and are awaiting your decision." The commander let the boy go with this advice, "Do not tell anyone that you gave me this information."

Then the commander summoned two of his officers, and said to them, "Get ready to leave for Caesarea by nine o'clock tonight, with two hundred infantrymen, seventy horsemen and two hundred spearmen. Provide horses, also, for Paul to ride; so that he may be brought safely to Felix, the governor."

He, then, wrote the governor a letter to this effect:

"Claudius Lysias greets

the Most Excellent Governor Felix,

and communicates to him the following:

The Jews had arrested this man, and were about to kill him when I intervened with my troops, and took him out of their hands, since I knew he was a Roman citizen. As I wanted to know what charge they had against him, I presented him before the Sanhedrin; and I discovered, that the accusation related to matters of their law; but there was nothing that deserved death or imprisonment. When I was informed, that the Jews had prepared a plot against this man, I decided to send him to you, and told his accusers to present their complaints before you.

Farewell."

The soldiers acted in accordance with these instructions. They took Paul and brought him to Antipatris by night. On the following day, they returned to the fortress, but the horsemen continued journeying with him. Upon entering Caesarea, they handed the letter to the governor and presented Paul to him. When Felix had read the letter, he asked Paul from which province he was; and when he learned that Paul was from Cilicia, he said to him: "I shall hear your accusers when they come." And he ordered that he be kept in custody, in the palace of Herod.

After five days, Ananias, the High Priest, came down to Caesarea, with some of the elders, and a lawyer named Tertullus. And they presented their case against Paul before the governor. Paul was called in and Tertullus accused him in this way:

"Most Excellent Felix, thanks to you—your labors and your wise reforms—our people now enjoy great peace. We accept all this, in every way, and, in every place, and we are totally grateful to you. So as not to take more of your time, I beg you to listen, briefly, to us, with your usual kindness. We have found, that this man is a pest, he creates division among the Jews throughout the world, and is a leader of the Nazorene sect. He even tried to profane the temple. So we seized him. We would have judged him according to our law, but Lysias, the commandant, intervened in a very violent way, and took him from us. Then he declared that his accusers must present themselves before you. By examining him yourself, you will learn from him, about all that we accuse him of."

The Jews confirmed this, firmly maintaining that all this was so.

Then the governor motioned to Paul, who said:

"As I know, that you have administered this nation for many years, I make my defense with much confidence. You, yourself, can ascertain, that not more than twelve days ago, I went up to Jerusalem to worship; and that, they did not find me disputing with anyone, or inciting the people, either in the temple or in the synagogues, or in the city. So, they cannot prove the things of which they now accuse me.

But this, I admit before you, that I serve the God of our ancestors, according to the Way, that they call a sect. I believe everything written in the law and in the prophets; and I have the same hope in God that they have: that there will be a resurrection of the dead, both the good and the sinners. So, I strive, always, to have a clear conscience, before God and before people.

After many years, I came to bring help to those of my nation, and to offer sacrifices. On that occasion, they found me in the temple; I had been purified, according to the law, and there was no crowd or commotion. Yet, all began, with some Jews from Asia, who ought to be here before you, to accuse me, if they have anything against me. Let these men say what crime they found in me, when I stood before the Sanhedrin; unless, it was for having declared in a loud voice, when I was before them: 'Today, I am being judged, on account of the resurrection of the dead.'"

Felix, who was well-informed about the Way, postponed the case, and said to them, "When the commandant, Lysias, comes down, I will examine the case thoroughly." So he ordered the captain to keep Paul under guard, giving him a certain liberty and without preventing his friends from attending to him.

After some days, Felix came, with his wife Drusilla, who was a Jew. He sent for Paul and let him speak about faith in Christ. But, when Paul spoke about justice, self-control and the future judgment, Felix was frightened, and he said to him: "You may leave now; I shall send for you some other time." Felix was hoping that Paul would give him money, so he sent for him often and conversed with him.

Two years passed, and Felix was succeeded by Porcius Festus; and as Felix wanted to remain on good terms with the Jews, he left Paul in prison.

Three days after Festus arrived in the province, he went up from Caesarea to Jerusalem. There, the chief priests and the elders accused Paul again. In a very hypocritical way, they asked, as a favor from Festus, that Paul be brought to Jerusalem; but they were planning to kill him on the way. Festus answered, that Paul was under custody in Caesarea and, as he, himself, had to go there shortly, he added, "Let those of you, who have the authority, go down with me to Caesarea; and if this man has done anything wrong, let them accuse him."

Festus did not stay in Jerusalem for more than eight or ten days, and then he went to Caesarea. The next day, he took his seat on the tribunal and sent for Paul. When Paul arrived, the Jews, who came from Jerusalem, stood around him, and presented many serious charges that they could not prove. Paul defended himself from all these, saying, "I have not committed any offense against the law of the Jews, or against the temple or against Caesar."

Then Festus, who wanted to please the Jews, asked Paul: "Do you wish to go up to Jerusalem to be tried before me?" Paul answered, "I am on trial before Caesar's tribunal; here, I have to be tried. I have done no wrong to the Jews: you, yourself, know this very well. If I have committed any crime which deserves death, I accept death. But if I have not done anything of which they accuse me, no one can give me up to them. I appeal to Caesar."

So Festus, after conferring with his council, answered, "You have appealed to Caesar. To Caesar, you shall go."

Some days later, king Agrippa, and his sister Bernice, arrived in Caesarea to greet Festus. As they were to stay there several days, Festus told the king about Paul's case, and said to him,

"We have here, a man, whom Felix left as a prisoner. When I was in Jerusalem, the chief priests, and the elders of the Jews, accused him, and asked me to sentence him. I told them, that it is not the custom of the Romans to hand over a man, without giving him an opportunity to defend himself in front of his accusers. So they came, and I took my seat, without delay, on the tribunal, and sent for the man.

When the accusers had the floor, they did not accuse him of any of the crimes that I was led to think he had committed; instead, they quarreled with him, about religion, and about a certain Jesus, who has died, but whom Paul asserted to be alive. I did not know what to do about this case, so I asked Paul if he wanted to go to Jerusalem, to be tried there. But

Paul appealed, to be judged by the emperor. So I ordered, that he be kept in custody until I send him to Caesar." Agrippa said to Festus: "I would like to hear that man." Festus answered him: "Tomorrow, you shall."

On the following day, Agrippa and Bernice arrived, with great ceremony, and entered the audience hall, with the commanders and the elders of the city. Festus ordered that Paul be brought in, and said:

"King Agrippa, and all here present; here, you see this man, about whom the whole community of the Jews came to see me, in Jerusalem, as well as here, protesting loudly, that he must not live. I, for my part, am convinced, that he has not done anything that deserves death. But, after he appealed to be judged by the emperor, I decided to send him on. Well, if I have no definite information, what can I write to Caesar about him? Therefore, I present him before all of you, and especially before you, king Agrippa, that you may examine him, and that I may know what to write. For it seems absurd to me, to send a prisoner, without indicating the charges against him."

Agrippa said to Paul: "You may speak in your own defense." So Paul stretched out his hand and began in this way:

"King Agrippa, you have just heard about the accusations of the Jews. I consider myself fortunate, in having the opportunity, to defend myself against all this, before you, today; for you are an expert in the customs of the Jews and their disputes. Therefore, I beg you to listen to me patiently.

All the Jews know how I have lived, from my youth; how I have lived among my own people, and in Jerusalem. They have always known me; and they can tell you, if they wish, that I have lived as a Pharisee, in the most rigorous sect of our religion. If I am now tried here, it is because of the hope I have, in the promise made by God to our ancestors. The hope of attaining this promise, is behind the fervent worship that our twelve tribes render to God, night and day. Yet, now, O king, the Jews accuse me for this hope! But why refuse to believe, that God raises the dead?

I, myself, in the beginning, thought that I had to use all possible means to counteract the Name of Jesus of Nazareth. This I did, in Jerusalem; and, with the authorization of the chief priests, I put in prison many who believed; and I cast my vote, when they were condemned to death.

I went round the synagogues and multiplied punishments against them, to force them to renounce their faith; such was my rage against them, that I pursued them, even to foreign cities.

With this purpose in mind, I went to Damascus, with full authority, and commissioned by the chief priests. On the way, O king, at midday, I saw a light from heaven, more brilliant than the sun, that dazzled me and those who accompanied me. We, all, fell to the ground; and I heard a voice saying to me, in Hebrew: 'Saul, Saul, why do you persecute me? In vain do you kick against the goad.'

I answered: 'Who are you, Lord?' And the Lord said: 'I am Jesus, whom you persecute. Get up, now, and stand on your feet. I have revealed myself to you, to make you servant and witness to what I have just shown you and to what I will show you later on. I will rescue you from all evil that may come from your own people, or from the pagans, to whom I am sending you. For you shall open their eyes, that they may turn from darkness to light, and from the power of Satan, to God; and, through faith in me, may obtain forgiveness of their sins and a place among those who are sanctified.'

Since that time, king Agrippa, I did not stray from this heavenly vision; on the contrary, I began preaching; first, to those in Damascus, then, to those in Jerusalem and throughout Judea; and, then, to the pagan nations, that they should repent, and turn to God, showing the fruits of true conversion. I was carrying out this mission, when the Jews arrested me in the temple and tried to kill me. But, with the help of God, I still stand here, today, to give my testimony, both to the great and the small.

I do not teach anything, other than what Moses and the prophets announced beforehand: the Messiah had to die; and after being the first to be raised from the dead, he would proclaim the light to his people, as well as to all nations."

As Paul came to this point of his defense, Festus said in a loud voice: "Paul, you are mad; your great learning has deranged your mind!" But Paul answered: "I am not mad, Most Excellent Festus, but everything I have said, is reliable and true. The king is acquainted with all these things, so to him I speak with such confidence. I am convinced, that he knows everything about this case, for these things did not happen in a dark corner. King Agrippa, do you believe the prophets? I know that you do."

Agrippa said to him: "You almost believe that you have already made me a Christian!" Paul answered him: "Whether little or more, I would that, not only you, but all who hear me, this day, may come to be as I am—except for these chains."

Then the king rose and, with him, the governor, Bernice and all the attendants. When they went out, they talked among themselves, and said: "This man has done nothing to deserve death or imprisonment." And Agrippa said to Festus: "Had he not appealed to Caesar, he could have been set free."

When it was decided, that we should sail for Italy, they handed over Paul, and the other prisoners, into the care of an officer of the Augustan battalion, named Julius. We boarded a ship of Adramyttium, bound for the Asian coasts, and we left, accompanied by Aristarchus, a Macedonian from the city of Thessalonica. We arrived at Sidon on the next day. Julius was very kind to Paul, letting him visit his friends and be cared for by them. From there, we sailed along the sheltered coast of Cyprus, because the winds were against us. We sailed across the seas, off Cilicia and Pamphylia, and arrived at Myra, in Lycia. There, the captain found a ship from Alexandria, sailing for Italy, and made us board it.

We sailed slowly for several days, and arrived with great difficulty at Cnidus. As the wind did not allow us to enter that port, we sailed for the shelter of Crete, with the Cape of Salmone within sight. We turned with difficulty and arrived at a place called Good Ports, near the city of Lasea.

Time passed, and the crossing began to be dangerous: we had already celebrated the feast of the Fast. Then Paul said to them: "Friends, I believe that it would not be very wise to proceed with our crossing, for we could lose not only the cargo and the ship, but also our lives." But the Roman officer relied more on the ship's captain, and the owner of the ship, than on the words of Paul. And, as the port was not suitable for wintering, the majority agreed to set out from there, in the hope of reaching the harbor of Crete, called Phoenix, overlooking Africa and Choros, where they could spend the winter.

Then, the south wind began to blow; and they thought that they had gained their purpose; they weighed anchor and sailed along the island of Crete. But a little later, a strong wind called "the northeaster" swept down on them, from across the island. The ship was dragged along and could not face the wind, so that we remained adrift.

As we were crossing under the lee of the small island of Cauda, we managed—but with effort—to secure the lifeboat. After lifting it aboard, they used cables to undergird the hull, and since we feared running aground on the sands of Syrtis, they lowered the sea anchor. So we continued to be dragged along.

The storm lashed at us so strongly that on the next day they began throwing the cargo overboard. On the third day, the sailors, with their own hands, threw out the ship's gear. For several days, neither the sun nor the stars could be seen, and the tempest had not subsided: we lost all hope of saving ourselves.

As we had not eaten for days, Paul stood up among them and said: "Friends, if you had followed my advice when I told you not to set sail from Crete, we would not be in such danger now, and we could have avoided this loss. But now, I invite you to regain courage, for no one among you shall die; only the ship shall be destroyed. Last night, there appeared to me an angel of my God whom I serve, and he said to me: 'Paul, do not be afraid, you must present yourself before Caesar's tribunal; and God has guaranteed you the life of all those who sail with you.'

Have courage, therefore, my friends, for I trust in God, that it will be just as he told me. But we have to run aground on some island."

Near midnight, on the fourteenth night, as we were drifting in the Adriatic Sea, the sailors suspected that land was near. They measured the depth of the water and it was thirty-seven meters. After a while, they measured it again, and it was twenty-seven meters. They feared that we might hit some rocks, so they cast out four anchors from the stern and waited anxiously for morning. Then the sailors tried to escape from the ship, under the pretext of extending the cables of the anchors from the bow; so they lowered the lifeboat into the sea. But Paul said to the captain, and to the soldiers: "If they leave the ship, you cannot be saved." So the soldiers cut the mooring cables of the boat and let it fall.

As they waited for dawn, Paul urged everyone: "For fourteen days you have not eaten anything because of anxious waiting. I ask you to eat, now, if you want to live; be sure, that not even a hair of your head will be lost." Having said this, he took bread, gave thanks to God in everybody's presence, broke it and began to eat. All were encouraged and they, too, ate. They were two hundred and seventy-six persons in all. When they had eaten enough, they threw the wheat into the sea to lighten the boat.

When morning came, they did not recognize the land, but noticed a bay with a beach; so they decided to run the ship aground, if possible. They cast off the anchors and left them in the sea; at the same time, they loosened the ropes of the rudders, hoisted the foresail to the wind and headed for the beach. But they struck a sandbank and the ship ran aground. The bow stuck and was immovable, while the stern was broken up by the violent waves.

The soldiers, then, planned to kill the prisoners, for fear that some of them might escape by swimming. But the captain, who wished to save Paul, did not allow them to do this. He ordered those who knew how to swim, to be the first to jump into the water and head for the shore, and the rest to hold on to planks or pieces of the ship. So all of us reached land safe and sound.

After being saved, we learned that the island was called Malta. The natives were very cordial. They lit a big bonfire and took good care of us all, since it was raining and cold.

Paul gathered a bundle of dried twigs; and as he threw them into the fire, a viper suddenly came out, because of the heat, and entwined itself around his hand. When the natives saw the viper hanging from his hand, they said to one another: "Surely this man is a murderer: he has barely escaped from the raging sea, yet, divine justice will not allow him to live." But Paul shook off the viper into the fire and did not suffer any harm. They waited to see him swell and die; but, after observing him for a while, they saw that nothing happened to him; so they changed their minds and began to say that he was a god.

27:27–28:6

Near this place was an estate owned by the head of the island, named Publius. For three days this man welcomed us hospitably. It so happened, that his father was in bed with fever and dysentery. Paul went to see him; he prayed and laid his hands on him and healed him. Because of this, the rest of the sick people on the island came to see him and were cured. So they showered us with kindness, and, on our departure, they provided us with everything we needed.

After three months, we boarded a ship that had spent the winter at the island. It belonged to an Alexandrian company, and carried the figurehead of Castor and Pollux as insignia. We sailed for Syracuse, staying there for three days; and, after circling the coast, we arrived at Rhegium. On the following day, a south wind began to blow, and, at the end of two days, we arrived at Puteoli, where we found some of our brothers, who invited us to stay with them for a week. And that was how we came to Rome.

There, the brothers and sisters had been informed of our arrival, and came out to meet us as far as the Appian Forum and the Three Taverns. When Paul saw them, he gave thanks to God and took courage. Upon our arrival in Rome, the captain turned the prisoners over to the military governor, but permitted Paul to lodge in a private house, with the soldier who guarded him.

After three days, Paul called together the leaders of the Jews. When they had gathered, he said to them: "Brothers, though I have not done anything against our people, or against the traditions of our fathers, I was arrested in Jerusalem, and handed over to the Romans. They examined me, and wanted to set me free, for they saw nothing in my case that deserved death. But the Jews objected, so I was forced to appeal to Caesar without the least intention of bringing any case against my own people. Therefore, I have asked to see you, and speak with you, since it is because of the hope of Israel, that I bear these chains."

They answered: "We have not received any letter about you from Judea; and none of the brothers who have come from there have brought any message, or said anything against you. But we wish to hear from you, what you think; although we know, already, that everywhere, people speak against this sect that you belong to."

They set a day for him and came in great numbers to his lodging. So Paul explained everything he wanted to tell them regarding the kingdom of God, and tried to convince them concerning Jesus, taking the law of Moses and the prophets as his starting point. This continued from morning till night. Some were convinced by his words, others were not. Finally, the Jews left, still arguing strongly among themselves; and Paul sent them away with this statement: "What the Holy Spirit said has come true, when he spoke to your ancestors, through the prophet Isaiah:

> Go to these people and say to them:
> However much you hear, you will not understand;
> you will see, and see again, but not perceive.
>
> The heart of these people have grown hard;
> they have covered their ears
> and closed their eyes;
>
> lest they should see with their eyes
> and hear with their ears;
> lest their spirit understand,
>
> and I should heal them.

Let it be known to you, that this salvation of God has been sent to the pagans: they will listen."

Paul stayed for two whole years, in a house he, himself, rented, where he received, without any hindrance, all those who came to see him. He proclaimed the kingdom of God, and taught the truth about Jesus Christ, the Lord, quite openly and without any hindrance.

INVITATION TO
1 THESSALONIANS

The book of Acts tells how Paul, Silas, and Timothy brought the good news about Jesus to Europe around AD 51 (see p. 79). They began in northern Greece, which was then known as Macedonia. They went first to the city of Philippi, where many people became followers of Jesus. But a mob attacked Paul and Silas, and local officials beat and imprisoned them and forced them to leave the city. (Timothy was Greek so he was left alone, but Paul and Silas were Jews so they were treated with hostility and suspicion.) The three went to the city of Thessalonica where many more people became Jesus-followers. But another riot broke out. Paul and Silas were accused that they *disregard the decrees of the Emperor and claim that there is another King, Jesus,* and they narrowly escaped with their lives (see p. 81). They went to the nearby city of Berea, where the people listened to them respectfully. But their opponents from Thessalonica came and stirred up the crowds. For his safety, Paul had to be sent away to the city of Athens in Achaia (southern Greece).

Paul was concerned that the believers in Thessalonica might stop following Jesus because of the opposition they were facing. So when Silas and Timothy caught up with him, he sent Timothy (who could make the trip more safely) back to Thessalonica to encourage the believers. When Timothy returned with the welcome news that the Thessalonians had remained faithful, Paul wrote to them to express his joy. He also used the opportunity to provide some teaching and correction the community needed.

Like all of Paul's letters that are preserved in the Bible, this one follows the pattern that was typical for correspondence of the time. There's an opening section that names the sender and the recipients, then offers a good wish. A thanksgiving and prayer often follow. The main body of the letter comes next. Finally, there's a closing section that expresses more good wishes and extends greetings to and from people that the sender and recipients both know.

In the main body of this letter, Paul first talks at length about his relationship with the new believers in Thessalonica. He recalls his time with them and says how grateful he is that they've remained faithful to Jesus. After wishing them a blessing, he makes a transition to provide briefer teaching and instruction on several practical matters. (These are probably things that Timothy told him about after his return visit to Thessalonica.)

: Paul teaches the Thessalonians to avoid sexual immorality, to love one another and to work hard and earn their own livings.

: He explains that believers who die before *the Lord's coming* are not lost. They'll be raised from the dead at this royal, public appearance of the Messiah. But Paul reminds the Thessalonians that Jesus will come back suddenly and unexpectedly.

So they should live in such a way that they won't be ashamed to greet him, whenever he comes.

: Finally, he advises them how to live as a community of Jesus-followers.

In all of his advice and teaching, Paul's basic message is, "Keep up the good work!" Even though he addresses the Thessalonians as his *brothers and sisters*, Paul also says that he, Silas and Timothy treated them the way a mother or father would. This shows the pride and affection they had for these first European followers of Jesus, their dear offspring in the faith.

| 1 THESSALONIANS |

From Paul, Sylvanus and Timothy, to the church of Thessalonica, which is in God, the Father, and in Christ Jesus, the Lord.

May the peace and grace of God be with you.

We give thanks to God, at all times, for you, and remember you in our prayers. We constantly recall, before God, our Father, the work of your faith, the labors of your love, and your endurance, in waiting for Christ Jesus our Lord.

We remember, brothers and sisters, the circumstances of your being called. The gospel we brought you was such, not only in words. Miracles, the Holy Spirit, and plenty of everything, were given to you. You, also, know how we dealt with you, for your sake.

In return, you became followers of us, and of the Lord, when, on receiving the word, you experienced the joy of the Holy Spirit, in the midst of great opposition. And you became a model for the faithful of Macedonia and Achaia, since, from you, the word of the Lord spread to Macedonia and Achaia, and still farther. The faith you have in God has become news in so many places, that we need say no more about it. Others tell, of how you welcomed us, and turned from idols, to the Lord. For you serve the living and true God, and you wait for his Son, from heaven, whom he raised from the dead, Jesus, who frees us from impending trial.

You well know, brothers and sisters, that our visit to you was not in vain. We had been ill-treated and insulted in Philippi but, trusting in our God, we dared announce to you the message of God, and face fresh opposition. Our warnings did not conceal any error or impure motive, nor did we deceive anyone. But, as God had entrusted his gospel to us, as to faithful ministers, we were anxious to please God, who sees the heart, rather than human beings. We never pleased you with flattery, as you know, nor did we try to earn money, as God knows. We did not try to make a name for ourselves among people, either with you, or anybody else, although we were messengers of Christ, and could have made our weight felt.

On the contrary, we were gentle with you, as a nursing mother, who feeds and cuddles her baby. And so great is our concern, that we are ready to give you, as well as the gospel, even our very lives, for you have become very dear to us.

Remember our labor and toil; when we preached the gospel, we worked day and night, so as not to be a burden to you. You are witnesses, with God, that we were holy, just and blameless toward all of you who now believe. We warned each of you, as a father warns his children; we encouraged you, and urged you to adopt a way of life worthy of God, who calls you to share his own glory and kingdom.

This is why we never cease giving thanks to God for, on receiving our message, you accepted it, not as human teaching, but as the word of God. That is what it really is, and, as such, it is at work in you who believe.

Brothers and sisters, you followed the example of the churches of God in Judea, churches of Christ Jesus. For you suffered from your compatriots the same trials they suffered from the Jews, who killed the Lord Jesus and the prophets, and who persecute us. They displease God, and harm all people, when they prevent us from speaking to the pagans, and trying to save them. By doing so, they are heaping up their sins, but, now, judgment is coming upon them.

We are, for a time, deprived of your presence, but not in our heart, and we eagerly long to see you. For we have wanted to visit you, and I, Paul, more than once; but Satan prevented us. In fact, who but you are our hope and our joy? Who but you will be our glorious crown before Jesus, our Lord, when he returns? Yes, indeed, you are our glory and our joy.

As I could no longer bear it, I decided to go alone to Athens, and send you Timothy, our brother and co-worker of God, in the gospel of Christ. I wanted him to encourage you in the faith, and strengthen you, so that none of you might turn back, because of the trials you are now enduring. You know that such is our destiny. I warned you of this, when I was there: "We shall have to face persecution"; and so it was, as you have seen. Therefore, I could not stand it any longer, and sent Timothy to appraise your faith, and see if the Tempter had tempted you, and made our work useless.

But, now, Timothy has just returned with good news of your faith and love. He told us that you remember us kindly, and that you long to see us, as much as we long to see you. What a consolation for us, brothers and sisters, in the midst of our troubles and trials, this faith of yours! It is a breath of life for us, when you stand firm in the Lord. How can we thank God enough, for all the joy that we feel before God, because of you? Day and night, we beg of him, to let us see you again, that we may complete the instruction of the believers.

May God, our Father, and Jesus, our Lord, prepare the way for us to visit you. May the Lord increase, more and more, your love for each other and for all people, as he increases our love for you. May he strengthen you, internally, to be holy and blameless before God, our Father, on the day that Jesus, our Lord, will come with all his saints.

For the rest, brothers, we ask you, in the name of Jesus, the Lord, and we urge you, to live in a way that pleases God, just as you have learned from us. This you do, but try to do still more. You know the instructions we gave you on behalf of the Lord Jesus: the will of God for you is to become holy and not to have unlawful sex.

Let each of you behave toward his wife as a holy and respectful husband, rather than being led by lust, as are pagans, who do not know God. In this matter, let no one offend or wrong a brother. The Lord will do justice in all these things, as we have warned and shown you. God has called us to live, not in impurity but in holiness, and those who do not heed this instruction disobey, not a human, but God, himself, who gives you his Holy Spirit.

Regarding mutual love, you do not need anyone to write to you, because God, himself, taught you how to love one another. You already practice it with all the brothers and sisters of Macedonia, but I invite you to do more. Consider how important it is, to live quietly, without bothering others, to mind your own business, and work with your hands, as we have charged you. In obeying these rules, you will win the respect of outsiders and be dependent on no one.

Brothers and sisters, we want you not to be mistaken about those who are already asleep, lest you grieve as do those who have no hope. We believe that Jesus died and rose; it will be the same for those who have died in Jesus. God will bring them together, with Jesus, and for his sake.

By the same word of the Lord, we assert this: those of us who are to be alive at the Lord's coming, will not go ahead of those who are already asleep. When the command by the archangel's voice is given, the Lord, himself, will come down from heaven, while the divine trumpet call is sounding. Then, those who have died in the Lord, will rise first; as for us who are still alive, we will be brought along with them, in the clouds, to meet the Lord in the celestial world. And we will be with the Lord forever.

So then, comfort one another with these words.

You do not need anyone to write to you about the delay, and the appointed time for these events. You know, that the day of the Lord will come like a thief in the night. When people feel secure, and at peace, the disaster will suddenly come upon them, as the birth pangs of a woman in labor, and they will not escape.

But you, beloved, are not in darkness; so that day will not surprise you like a thief. All of you are citizens of the light and the day; we do not belong to night and darkness. Let us not, therefore, sleep as others do, but remain alert and sober.

Those who sleep, go to sleep at night, and those who drink, get drunk at night. Since we belong to the day, let us be sober, let us put on the breastplate of faith and love, and let the hope of salvation be our helmet. For God has not willed us to be condemned, but to win salvation, through Christ Jesus, our Lord. He died for us, so that, we might enter into life, with him, whether we are still awake or already asleep. Therefore, encourage one another and build up one another, as you are doing now.

Brothers and sisters, I want you to be thankful to those who labor among you, who lead you in the way of the Lord, and also reprimand you. Esteem them highly, and love them for what they are doing. Live at peace among yourselves.

We urge you, to warn the idle, encourage those who feel discouraged, sustain the weak, have patience with everyone. See that no one repays evil for evil, but try to do good, whether among yourselves or toward others.

Rejoice always, pray without ceasing and give thanks to God at every moment. This is the will of God, your vocation as Christians.

Do not quench the Spirit, do not despise the prophets' warnings. Put everything to the test and hold fast to what is good. Avoid evil, wherever it may be.

May the God of peace make you holy and bring you to perfection. May you be completely blameless, in spirit, soul and body, till the coming of Christ Jesus, our Lord; he who called you is faithful and will do it.

B rothers and sisters, pray for us. Greet all the brothers and sisters with a holy kiss. I order you, in the name of the Lord, that this letter be read to all of them.

May the grace of Christ Jesus, our Lord, be with you.

INVITATION TO
2 THESSALONIANS

A short time after he wrote his first letter to the Thessalonians (p. 103), Paul had to write to them again, to correct a false report that he'd said the *day of the Lord* had already come. (He most likely learned about this from whoever carried his first letter to Thessalonica, probably Timothy.) The *day of the Lord* was a phrase the Hebrew prophets used to describe the time when God would win a definitive victory over every opponent and reward *those who believe in him*. The Thessalonians' concern wasn't that this day had come and gone and they'd missed it. Rather, they were concerned that it was now present, meaning that they couldn't expect God to do anything more to deliver them from their enemies. Since they were still enduring *persecution and suffering*, this was very discouraging.

Even before he corrects this false report, Paul reassures the Thessalonians that indeed *God repays, with affliction, those who persecute you, but to you who suffer, he will grant rest*. (He gives this reassurance in his opening thanksgiving and prayer, where he often introduces the main themes of his letters.) Paul then corrects the report by reminding the Thessalonians what he told them when he was with them about how the *day of the Lord* will arrive. It seems he's about to bring his letter to a close, but he then repeats an admonition from his earlier letter (perhaps in response to a further report about their situation). He urges them at greater length not to live in idleness, but to work hard and earn their own livings.

As was common at the time, most of this letter would have been written down by a scribe. But at the end, Paul adds a greeting in his own handwriting, to prove that this letter is genuinely from him. He doesn't want his name attached to any more misrepresentations of his teaching!

| 2 THESSALONIANS |

F rom Paul, Sylvanus and Timothy, to the church of the Thessalonians, which is in God, our Father, and in Christ Jesus, the Lord.

May grace and peace be yours, from God, the Father, and Christ Jesus, the Lord.

B rothers and sisters, we should give thanks to God, at all times, for you. It is fitting to do so, for your faith is growing, and your love for one another, increasing. We take pride in you, among the churches of God, because of your endurance, and your faith in the midst of persecution and sufferings. In this, the just judgment of God may be seen; for you must show yourselves worthy of the kingdom of God, for which you are now suffering.

Indeed, it is just, that God repays, with affliction, those who persecute you, but to you who suffer, he will grant rest, with us, when the Lord Jesus will be shown in his glory, coming from heaven, and surrounded by his court of angels. Then, with flaming fire, will be punished, those who do not recognize God, and do not obey the gospel of Jesus, our Lord.

They will be sent to eternal damnation, far away from the face of the Lord and his mighty glory. On that day, the Lord will be glorified, in the midst of his saints, and reveal his wonders, through those who believe in him, that is, through you, who have received our testimony.

This is why we constantly pray for you; may our God make you worthy of his calling. May he, by his power, fulfill your good purposes, and your work, prompted by faith. In that way, the name of Jesus, our Lord, will be glorified through you, and you, through him, according to the loving plan of God and of Christ Jesus, the Lord.

Brothers and sisters, let us speak about the coming of Christ Jesus, our Lord, and our gathering to meet him. Do not be easily unsettled. Do not be alarmed by what a prophet says, or by any report, or by some letter said to be ours, saying, the day of the Lord is at hand.

Do not let yourselves be deceived, in any way. Apostasy must come first, when the man of sin will appear, that instrument of evil, who opposes and defiles whatever is considered divine and holy, even to the point of sitting in the temple of God and claiming to be God.

Do you not remember, I spoke of it when I was still with you? But you, also, know, what prevents him from appearing, until his due time. The mystery of sin is already at work, but the one who restrains it, at present, has to be taken away. Then, the wicked one will appear, whom the Lord is to sweep away, with the breath of his mouth, and destroy, in the splendor of his coming. This lawless one will appear, with the power of Satan, performing miracles and wonderful signs, at the service of deception. All the deceits of evil will then be used, for the ruin of those who refused to love truth, and be saved. This is why God will send them the power of delusion, that they may believe what is false. So all those who chose wickedness, instead of believing the truth, will be condemned.

But we have to give thanks for you, at all times, dear brothers and sisters in the Lord. For God chose you, from the beginning, to be saved, through true faith, and to be made holy by the Spirit. To this end he called you, through the gospel we preach, for he willed you, to share the glory of Christ Jesus, our Lord.

Because of that, brothers and sisters, stand firm and hold to the traditions that we taught you, by word or by letter. May Christ Jesus, our Lord, who has loved us, may God our Father, who, in his mercy, gives us everlasting comfort and true hope, strengthen you. May he encourage your hearts and make you steadfast in every good work and word.

Finally, brothers and sisters, pray for us that the word of God may spread rapidly and be glorified everywhere, as it was with you. May God guard us from wicked and evil people, since not everyone has faith. The Lord is faithful; he will strengthen you and keep you safe from the evil one. Besides, we have, in the Lord, this confidence, that you are doing, and will continue to do, what we order you. May the Lord direct your hearts to the love of God and to the steadfastness of Christ.

We command you, beloved, to stay away from believers who are living in idleness, contrary to the traditions we passed on to you. You know, how you ought to follow our example: we worked while we were with you. Day and night, we labored and toiled so as not to be a burden to any of you. We had the right to act otherwise, but we wanted to give you an example.

Besides, while we were with you, we said clearly: If anyone is not willing to work, neither should that one eat. However, we heard that some among you live in idleness—busybodies, doing no work. In the name of Christ Jesus, our Lord, we command these people to work and earn their own living. And you, brothers and sisters, do not weary in doing what is right.

If someone does not obey our instruction in this letter, take note and do not have anything to do with him, so that he may be ashamed.

However, do not treat him as an enemy, but warn him as a brother.

M ay the Lord of peace give you his peace at all times and in every way. May the Lord be with you all.

I, Paul, write this greeting with my own hand. This is my signature in all my letters. This is how I write.

May the grace of Christ Jesus our Lord be with you.

INVITATION TO
1 CORINTHIANS

The book of Acts describes how Paul, Silas and Timothy brought the good news about Jesus the Messiah to Macedonia (northern Greece), and then had to flee to Achaia (southern Greece) for their own safety (see p. 81). From Athens Paul sent two letters of encouragement and instruction to the believers he'd left behind in Thessalonica (see pp. 101–111). He then traveled to Corinth, a wealthy and cosmopolitan commercial center. Many people became followers of Jesus there, and he stayed for a year and a half to teach them. But Paul understood that his primary mission was to bring the good news about Jesus to places where it had never been heard before. So he reported back to the Christian leaders in Jerusalem and Antioch, then set out again. Beginning around AD 53 he settled for two years in Ephesus. And since that city was right across the Aegean Sea from Corinth, he was able to continue advising the Corinthian believers through letters and visits.

The Corinthians wrote to Paul, in a letter we no longer have, to ask him some questions and defend some of their practices.

: They'd adopted the common Greek idea that the physical world is bad, so they wanted to free the human spirit from the body. One way they were trying to do this was by denying the body its pleasures. They didn't think that husbands and wives should have sexual relations with each other, and they were encouraging engaged couples not to get married. They asked Paul's advice about this.

: The desire to free the spirit from the body also led some of the Corinthians to deny the resurrection. In their letter they challenged Paul to provide details of the resurrection if he wanted them to believe in it.

: Some of them also wanted to keep attending ceremonial meals held in honor of pagan gods. They argued that their participation in these meals was spiritually harmless because these weren't real gods.

: The Corinthians had also learned that God can give the ability to *speak in tongues,* that is, to speak another language without having to study it first. They were eager to receive this gift and use it in their worship. But they were confused when some of their members began saying things like *a curse on Jesus.*

: Finally, they asked Paul how to take a collection to assist the poor, and how they could be sure this offering would really reach those it was intended to help.

Stephanas, Fortunatus and Achaicus, three members of the community of Jesus-followers in Corinth, carried this letter over to Paul. Around the same time, servants of an Ephesian woman named Chloe returned from doing some business in Corinth and told Paul about additional problems.

: For one thing, the community of Jesus' followers was dividing into factions devoted to one or another of the early Christian leaders. These factions were

modeled after the exclusive schools that gathered around philosophers of the day.
: The Corinthians had apparently misunderstood or misapplied Paul's earlier advice
about how to deal with people in their community who were living immoral lives.
: Chloe's servants also reported that the Corinthians were taking one another to
court in lawsuits;
: that there was a dispute in the church about wearing headcoverings in worship;
: and that when the community gathered for the Lord's Supper, which was
supposed to be a shared meal, the rich were eating by themselves, leaving the
poor to go hungry.

Paul addresses all of these matters in the letter we know as 1 Corinthians. This
letter gives us a glimpse into what life was like in a community of believers twenty
years after Jesus' resurrection. At the same time, it contains practical advice that's still
of great value for communities and believers today. It shows an early Christian leader
teaching, correcting, challenging and even pleading with the friends he's brought
to the faith, trying to help them consistently follow the new way of life that Jesus
introduced.

Paul tells these believers that *for the order of this world is vanishing*, but they
can still give themselves fully to the work of the Lord, knowing that their *labor is
not without fruit*. The coming resurrection of the dead, and the new world it will
introduce, will show the value of all their current efforts. Paul's practical teaching on
how to consistently embody the new life of God's kingdom during a particular scene
in the biblical drama gives us great insight as we seek to take up our own roles today.

| 1 CORINTHIANS |

From Paul, called to be an apostle of Christ Jesus, by the will of God, and from Sosthenes, our brother, to God's Church which is in Corinth; to you, whom God has sanctified in Christ Jesus, and called, to be holy, together, with those, who, everywhere, call upon the name of our Lord Christ Jesus, their Lord and ours.

Receive grace, and peace from God, our Father, and Christ Jesus, our Lord.

I give thanks, constantly, to my God, for you, and for the grace of God given to you, in Christ Jesus. For you have been fully enriched, in him, with words, as well as with knowledge, even as the testimony concerning Christ was confirmed in you. You do not lack any spiritual gift and only await the glorious coming of Christ Jesus, our Lord. He will keep you steadfast to the end, and you will be without reproach, on the day of the coming of our Lord Jesus. The faithful God will not fail you, after calling you to this fellowship with his Son, Christ Jesus, our Lord.

I beg of you, brothers, in the name of Christ Jesus, our Lord, to agree among yourselves, and do away with divisions; please be perfectly united, with one mind and one judgment.

For I heard from people, of Cloe's house, about your rivalries. What I mean is this: some say, "I am for Paul," and others: "I am for Apollos," or "I am for Peter," or "I am for Christ." Is Christ divided, or have I, Paul, been crucified for you? Have you been baptized in the name of Paul?

I thank God that I did not baptize any of you, except Crispus and Gaius, so that no one can say that he was baptized in my name. Well, I have also baptized the Stephanas family. Apart from these, I do not recall having baptized anyone else.

For Christ did not send me to baptize, but to proclaim his gospel. And not with beautiful words! That would be like getting rid of the cross of Christ. The language of the cross remains nonsense for those who are lost. Yet for us who are saved, it is the power of God, as Scripture says:

> I will destroy the wisdom of the wise
> and make fail the foresight of the foresighted.

Masters of human wisdom, educated people, philosophers, you have no reply! And the wisdom of this world? God let it fail.

At first, God spoke the language of wisdom, and the world did not know God through wisdom. Then God thought of saving the believers, through the foolishness that we preach.

The Jews ask for miracles and the Greeks for a higher knowledge, while we proclaim a crucified Messiah. For the Jews, what a great scandal! And for the Greeks, what nonsense! But he is Christ, the power of God, and the wisdom of God, for those called by God among both Jews and Greeks.

In reality, the "foolishness" of God is wiser than humans, and the "weakness" of God is stronger than humans.

Brothers and sisters, look and see whom God has called. Few among you can be said to be cultured or wealthy, and few belong to noble families. Yet God has chosen what the world considers foolish, to shame the wise; he has chosen what the world considers weak, to shame the strong. God has chosen common and unimportant people, making use of what is nothing, to nullify the things that are, so, that, no mortal may boast before God. But, by God's grace, you are in Christ Jesus, who has become our wisdom from God, and who makes us just and holy and free. Scripture says: Let the one who boasts boast of the Lord.

When I came to reveal to you the mystery of God's plan, I did not count on eloquence or on a show of learning. I was determined, not to know anything among you, but Jesus, the Messiah, and a crucified Messiah. I, myself, came; weak, fearful and trembling; my words, and preaching, were not brilliant, or clever to win listeners. It was, rather, a demonstration of spirit and power, so, that, your faith might be a matter, not of human wisdom, but of God's power.

In fact, we do speak of wisdom to the mature in faith, although it is not a wisdom of this world or of its rulers, who are doomed to perish. We teach the mystery, and secret plan, of divine wisdom, which God destined from the beginning, to bring us to glory.

No ruler of this world ever knew this; otherwise, they would not have crucified the Lord of glory. But as Scripture says:

> Eye has not seen,
> ear has not heard,

> nor has it dawned on the mind,
> what God has prepared for those who love him.

God has revealed it to us, through his Spirit, because the Spirit probes everything, even the depth of God.

Who, but his own spirit, knows the secrets of a person? Similarly, no one, but the Spirit of God, knows the secrets of God. We have not received the spirit of the world, but the Spirit who comes from God and, through him, we understand what God, in his goodness, has given us.

So we speak of this, not in terms inspired by human wisdom, but in a language taught by the Spirit, explaining a spiritual wisdom to spiritual persons. The one who remains on the psychological level does not understand the things of the Spirit. They are foolishness for him; and he does not understand, because they require a spiritual experience. On the other hand, the spiritual person judges everything, but no one judges him.

> Who has known the mind of God
> so as to teach him?

But we have the mind of Christ.

I could not, friends, speak to you as spiritual persons but as fleshly people, for you are still infants in Christ. I gave you milk, and not solid food, for you were not ready for it, and, up to now, you cannot receive it, for you are still of the flesh. As long as there is jealousy and strife, what can I say, but that you are at the level of the flesh, and behave like ordinary people.

While one says: "I follow Paul," and the other: "I follow Apollos," what are you, but people still at a human level?

For what is Apollos? What is Paul? They are ministers; and through them, you believed, as it was given by the Lord, to each of them. I planted, Apollos watered the plant, but God made it grow. So neither the one who plants nor the one who waters is anything, but God, who makes the plant grow.

The one who plants and the one who waters work to the same end, and the Lord will pay each, according to their work. We are fellow-workers with God, but you are God's field and building.

I, as a good architect, according to the capacity given to me, I laid the foundation, and another is to build upon it. Each one must be careful how to build upon it. No one can lay a foundation other than the one which is already laid, which is Jesus Christ. Then, if someone builds with gold upon this foundation, another, with silver and precious stones, or with wood, bamboo or straw, the work of each one will be shown for what it is. The day of Judgment will reveal it, because the fire will make everything known. The fire will test the work of everyone. If your work withstands the fire, you will be rewarded; but if your work becomes ashes, you will pay for it. You will be saved, but it will be as if passing through fire.

Do you not know that you are God's temple, and that God's Spirit abides within you? If anyone destroys the temple of God, God will destroy him. God's temple is holy, and you are this temple.

Do not deceive yourselves. If anyone of you considers himself wise in the ways of the world, let him become a fool, so that he may become wise. For the wisdom of this world is foolishness in God's eyes. To this, Scripture says: God catches the wise in their own wisdom. It also says: The Lord knows the reasoning of the wise, that it is useless.

Because of this, let no one boast about human beings, for everything belongs to you; Paul, Apollos, Cephas—life, death, the present and the future. Everything is yours, and you, you belong to Christ, and Christ is of God.

Let everyone, then, see us as the servants of Christ, and stewards of the secret works of God. Being stewards, faithfulness shall be demanded of us; but I do not mind if you, or any human court, judges me. I do not even judge myself; my conscience, indeed, does not accuse me of anything, but that is not enough for me to be set right with God: the Lord is the one who judges me.

Therefore, do not judge before the time, until the coming of the Lord. He will bring to light whatever was hidden in darkness, and will disclose the secret intentions of the hearts. Then, each one will receive praise from God.

Brothers and sisters, you forced me to apply these comparisons to Apollos and to myself. Learn by this example, not to believe yourselves superior by siding with one against the other. How, then, are you more than the others? What have you that you have not received? And if you received it, why are you proud, as if you did not receive it?

So, then, you are already rich and satisfied, and feel like kings, without us! I wish you really were kings, so that we might enjoy the kingship with you!

It seems to me, that God has placed us, the apostles, in the last place, as if condemned to death, and as spectacles for the whole world, for the angels as well as for mortals.

We are fools for Christ, while you show forth the wisdom of Christ. We are weak, you are strong. You are honored, while we are despised. Until now we hunger and thirst, we are poorly clothed and badly treated, while moving from place to place. We labor, working with our hands. People insult us and we bless them, they persecute us and we endure everything; they speak evil against us, and ours are works of peace. We have become like the scum of the earth, like the garbage of humankind until now.

I do not write this to shame you, but to warn you, as very dear children. Because, even though you may have ten thousand guardians in the Christian life, you have only one father; and it was I who gave you life in Christ through the gospel. Therefore, I pray you, to follow my example. With this purpose, I send to you Timothy, my dear and trustworthy son in the service of the Lord. He will remind you, of my way of Christian life, as I teach it in all churches, everywhere.

Some of you thought that I could not visit you and became very arrogant. But I will visit you soon, the Lord willing, and I will see, not what those arrogant people say, but what they can do. Because the kingdom of God is not a matter of words, but of power. What do you prefer, for me to come with a stick, or with love and gentleness?

You have become news, with, a case of immorality, and such a case, that is not even found among pagans. Yes, one of you has taken, as wife, his own stepmother. And you feel proud! Should you not be in mourning, instead, and expel the one who did such a thing? For my part, although I am physically absent, my spirit is with you and, as if present, I have already passed sentence on the man who committed such a sin. Let us meet together, you and my spirit, and in the name of our Lord Jesus, and with his power, you shall deliver him to Satan, for the destruction of the flesh, so that his spirit be saved in the day of Judgment.

This is not the time to praise yourselves. Do you not know that a little yeast makes the whole mass of dough rise? Throw out, then, the old yeast and be new dough. If Christ became our Passover, you should be unleavened bread. Let us celebrate, therefore, the Passover, no longer with old yeast, which is sin and perversity; let us have unleavened bread, that is purity and sincerity.

In my last letter I instructed you not to associate with immoral people. I did not mean, of course, those who do not belong to the church and who are immoral, exploiters, embezzlers or worshipers of idols. Otherwise, you would have to leave this world. What I really meant was, to avoid, and not to mingle with anyone who, bearing the name of brother or sister, becomes immoral, exploiter, slanderer, drunkard, embezzler. In which case, you should not even eat with them.

Why should I judge outsiders? But you, are you not to judge those who are inside? Let God judge those outside, but as for you, drive out the wicked person from among you.

When you have a complaint against a brother, how dare you bring it before pagan judges, instead of bringing it before God's people? Do you not know, that you shall one day judge the world? And if you are to judge the world, are you incapable of judging such simple problems?

Do you not know, that we will even judge the angels? And could you not decide everyday affairs? But when you have ordinary cases to be judged, you bring them before those who are of no account in the Church! Shame on you! Is there not even one among you wise enough to be the arbiter among believers?

But no. One of you brings a suit against another one, and files that suit before unbelievers. It is already a failure that you have suits against each other. Why do you not rather suffer wrong and receive some damage? But no. You wrong and injure others, and those are your brothers and sisters. Do you not know that the wicked will not inherit the kingdom of God?

Make no mistake about it: those who lead sexually immoral lives, or worship idols, or who are adulterers, perverts, sodomites, or thieves, exploiters, drunkards, slanderers or embezzlers will not inherit the kingdom of heaven. Some of you were like that, but you have been cleansed, and consecrated to God and have been set right with God, by the name of the Lord Jesus, and the Spirit of our God.

Everything is lawful for me, but not everything is to my profit. Everything is lawful for me, but I will not become a slave of anything. Food is for the stomach, as the stomach is for food, and God will destroy them both. Yet the body is not for fornication, but for the Lord; and the Lord is for the body. And God, who raised the Lord, will also raise us with his power.

Do you not know that your bodies are members of Christ? And you would make that part of his body become a part of a prostitute? Never! But you well know that when you join yourselves to a prostitute, you become one with her. For Scripture says: The two will become one flesh. On the contrary, anyone united to the Lord becomes one spirit with him.

Avoid unlawful sex entirely. Any other sin a person commits is outside the body; but those who commit sexual immorality sin against their own body.

Do you not know that your body is a temple of the Holy Spirit within you, given by God? You belong no longer to yourselves. Remember at what price you have been bought, and make your body serve the glory of God.

Now I will answer the questions in your letter. It is good for a man not to touch a woman. Yet to avoid immorality, every man should have his own wife and each woman her own husband. Let the husband fulfill his duty of husband and likewise the wife. The wife is not the owner of her own body: the husband is. Similarly, the husband is not the owner of his own body: the wife is.

Do not refuse each other, except by mutual consent, and only for a time, in order to dedicate yourselves to prayer, and then come together again, lest you fall into Satan's trap by lack of self-control. I approve of this abstention, but I do not order it. I would like everyone to be like me, but each has from God a particular gift, some in one way, others differently.

To the unmarried and the widows I say that it would be good for them to remain as I am, but if they cannot control themselves, let them marry, for it is better to marry than to burn with passion.

I command married couples—not I, but the Lord—that the wife should not separate from her husband. If she separates from him, let her not marry again, or let her make peace with her husband. Similarly the husband should not divorce his wife.

To the others I say—from me and not from the Lord—if a brother has a wife who is not a believer but she agrees to live with him, let him not separate from her. In the same manner, if a woman has a husband who is not a believer but he agrees to live with her, let her not separate from her husband. Because the unbelieving husband is sanctified by the wife, and the unbelieving wife is sanctified by the husband who believes. Otherwise, your children also would be apart from God; but as it is, they are consecrated to God.

Now, if the unbelieving husband or wife wants to separate, let them do so. In this case, the Christian partner is not bound, for the Lord has called us to peace. Besides, are you sure, wife, that you could save your husband, and you, husband, that you could save your wife?

Except for this, let each one continue living as he was when God called him, as was his lot set by the Lord. This is what I order in all churches. Let the circumcised Jew not remove the marks of the circumcision when he is called by God, and let the non-Jew not be circumcised when he is called. For the important thing is not, to be circumcised or not, but to keep the commandments of God.

Let each of you, therefore, remain in the state in which you were called by God. If you were a slave when called, do not worry, yet if you can gain your freedom, take the opportunity.

The slave called to believe in the Lord is a freed person belonging to the Lord just as whoever has been called while free, becomes a slave of Christ. You have been bought at a very great price; do not become slaves of a human being.

So then, brothers and sisters, continue living in the state you were before God, at the time of his call.

With regard to those who remain virgins, I have no special commandment from the Lord, but I give some advice, hoping that I am worthy of trust by the mercy of the Lord.

I think this is good in these hard times in which we live. It is good for someone to remain as he is. If you are married, do not try to divorce your wife; if you are not married, do not marry. He who marries does not sin, nor does the young girl sin who marries. Yet they will face disturbing experiences, and I would like to spare you.

I say this, brothers and sisters: time is running out, and those who are married must live as if not married; those who weep as if not weeping; those who are happy as if they were not happy; those buying something as if they had not bought it, and those enjoying the present life as if they were not enjoying it. For the order of this world is vanishing.

I would like you to be free from anxieties. He who is not married is concerned about the things of the Lord and how to please the Lord. While he who is married is taken up with the things of the world and how to please his wife, and he is divided in his interests.

Likewise, the unmarried woman and the virgin are concerned with the service of the Lord, to be holy in body and spirit. The married woman, instead, worries about the things of the world and how to please her husband.

I say this for your own good. I do not wish to lay traps for you, but to lead you to a beautiful life, entirely united with the Lord.

If anyone realizes he will not be behaving correctly with his fiancée because of the ardor of his passion, and that things should take their due course, let him marry; he commits no sin. But if another, of firmer heart, thinks that he can control his passion and decides not to marry so that his fiancée may remain a virgin, he does better. So then, he who marries does well, and he who does not marry does better.

The wife is bound as long as her husband lives. If he dies, she is free to be married to whomsoever she wishes, provided that she does so in the Christian way. However, she will be happier if, following my advice, she remains as she is, and I believe that I also have the Spirit of God.

Regarding meat from the offerings to idols, we know that all of us have knowledge, but knowledge puffs up, while love builds. If anyone thinks that he has knowledge, he does not yet know as he should know, but if someone loves (God), he has been known (by God).

Can we, then, eat meat from offerings to the idols? We know that an idol is without existence and that there is no God but one. People speak indeed of other gods in heaven and on earth and, in this sense, there are many gods and lords. Yet for us, there is but one God, the Father, from whom everything comes, and to whom we go. And there is one Lord, Christ Jesus, through whom everything exists, and through him, we exist.

Not everyone, however, has that knowledge. For some persons, who, until recently, took the idols seriously, that food remains linked to the idol, and eating of it stains their conscience, which is unformed.

It is not food that brings us closer to God. If we eat, we gain nothing, and if we do not eat, we do not lose anything. We are free, of course, but let not your freedom cause others, who are less prepared, to fall. What if others with an unformed conscience see you, a person of knowledge, sitting at the table in the temple of idols? Will not their weak conscience, because of your example, move them to eat also? Then, with your knowledge, you would have caused your weak brother or sister to perish, the one for whom Christ died. When you disturb the weak conscience of your brother or sister, and sin against them, you sin against Christ himself. Therefore, if any food will bring my brother to sin, I shall never eat this food, lest my brother or sister fall.

As for me, am I not free? I am an apostle and I have seen Jesus, the Lord, and you are my work in the Lord. Although I may not be an apostle for others, at least I am one for you. You are, in the Lord, evidence of my apostleship.

Now, this is what I answer to those who criticize me: Have we not the right to be fed? Have we not the right, to bring along with us a sister, as do the other apostles, and the brothers of the Lord, and Cephas? Am I the only one, with Barnabas, bound to work?

What soldier goes to war at his own expense? What farmer does not eat from the vineyard he planted? Who tends a flock, and does not drink from its milk? Are these rights only accepted human practice? No. The law says the same. In the law of Moses it is written: Do not muzzle the ox which threshes grain. Does this mean that God is concerned with oxen, or, rather, with us? Of course, it applies to us. For our sake it was written, that no one plows without expecting a reward for plowing, and no one threshes, without hoping for a share of the crop. Then, if we have sown spiritual riches among you, would it be too much for us to reap some material reward? If others have had a share among you, we could have it all the more.

Yet, we made no use of this right, and we prefer to endure everything, rather than put any obstacle to the gospel of Christ. Do you not know, that those working in the sacred service, eat from what is offered for the temple?

And those serving at the altar, receive their part from the altar. The Lord ordered, likewise, that those announcing the gospel, live from the gospel. Yet, I have not made use of my rights, and, now, I do not write to claim them: I would rather die! No one will deprive me of this glory of mine.

Because I cannot boast of announcing the gospel: I am bound to do it. Woe to me, if I do not preach the gospel! If I preached voluntarily, I could expect my reward, but I have been trusted with this office, against my will. How can I, then, deserve a reward? In announcing the gospel, I will do it freely, without making use of the rights given to me by the gospel.

So, feeling free with everybody, I have become everybody's slave, in order to gain a greater number. To save the Jews, I became a Jew with the Jews, and, because they are under the law, I myself submitted to the law, although I am free from it. With the pagans, not subject to the law, I became one of them, although I am not without a law of God, since Christ is my law. Yet, I wanted to gain those, strangers to the law. To the weak, I made myself weak, to win the weak. So, I made myself all things to all people, in order to save, by all possible means, some of them. This, I do, for the gospel, so that I, too, have a share of it.

Have you not learned anything from the stadium? Many run, but only one gets the prize. Run, therefore, intending to win it, as athletes, who impose upon themselves a rigorous discipline. Yet, for them the wreath is of laurels which wither, while for us, it does not wither.

So, then, I run, knowing where I go. I box, but not aimlessly in the air. I punish my body and control it, lest, after preaching to others, I myself should be rejected.

Let me remind you, brothers and sisters, about our ancestors. All of them were under the cloud and all crossed the sea. All underwent the baptism of the land and of the sea to join Moses; and all of them ate from the same spiritual manna; and all of them drank from the same spiritual drink. For you know, that they drank from a spiritual rock following them, and the rock was Christ. However, most of them did not please God, and the desert was strewn with their bodies.

All of this happened as an example for us, so that we might not become people of evil desires, as they did.

Do not follow idols, as some of them did, and Scripture says: The people sat down to eat and drink and stood up for orgy. Let us not fall into sexual immorality, as some of them did, and in one day, twenty-three thousand of them fell dead. And let us not tempt the Lord, as some of them did, and were killed by serpents; nor grumble, as some of them did, and were cut down by the destroying angel.

These things happened to them, as an example, and they were written as a warning, for us, as the last times come upon us. Therefore, if you think you stand, beware, lest you fall. No trial greater than human endurance has overcome you. God is faithful and will not let you be tempted beyond your strength. He will give you, together with the temptation, the strength to escape and to resist.

Therefore, dear friends, shun the cult of idols.

I address you as intelligent persons; judge what I say. The cup of blessing that we bless, is it not a communion with the blood of Christ? And the bread that we break, is it not a communion with the body of Christ? The bread is one, and so we, though many, form one body, sharing the one bread.

Consider the Israelites. For them, to eat of the victim is to come into communion with its altar.

What does all that mean? That the meat is really consecrated to the idol, or that the idol is a being. However, when the pagans offer a sacrifice, the sacrifice goes to the demons, not to God. I do not want you to come into fellowship with demons. You cannot drink, at the same time, from the cup of the Lord and from the cup of demons. You cannot share in the table of the Lord and in the table of the demons. Do we want, perhaps, to provoke the jealousy of the Lord? Could we be stronger than he?

Everything is lawful for me, but not everything is to my profit. Everything is lawful for me, but not everything builds up: let no one pursue his own interests, but the interests of the other.

Eat, then, whatever is sold at the market, and do not raise questions of conscience about it. Because: the earth and whatever is on it belongs to the Lord. If someone who does not share your faith invites you, go and eat of anything served to you, without problems of conscience. However, if somebody tells you that the meat is from the offerings to idols, then do not eat, out of consideration for those warning you, and for the sake of their conscience.

I say: "In consideration of their conscience," not of yours, for is it convenient, that my rights be misinterpreted by them and their conscience? Is it good that I bring on me criticism, for some good thing I am sharing, and for which I will give thanks?

Then, whether you eat, or drink, or whatever you do, do it for the glory of God. Give no offense to the Jews, or to the Greeks, or to the Church of God, just as I try to please everyone in everything. I do not seek my own interest, but that of many, this is: that they be saved.

Follow my example as I follow the example of Christ. I praise you, because you remember me in everything, and you keep the traditions that I have given you. However, I wish to remind you, that every man has Christ as his head, while the wife has her husband as her head; and God is the head of Christ. If a man prays or prophesies with his head covered, he dishonors his head. On the contrary, the woman who prays or prophesies with her head uncovered, does not respect her head. She might as well cut her hair. If a woman does not use a veil, let her cut her hair; and if it is a shame for a woman to have her hair cut or shaved, then let her use a veil.

Men do not need to cover their heads, for they are the image of God and reflect his glory, while a woman reflects the glory of man. Man was not formed from woman, but woman from man. Nor did God create man for woman, but woman for man. Therefore, a woman must respect the angels, and have on her head the sign of her dependence.

Anyway, the Christian attitude does not separate man from woman, and woman from man, and if God has created woman from man, man is born from woman and both come from God.

Judge for yourselves: is it proper for a woman to pray without a veil? Common sense teaches us that it is shameful for a man to wear long hair, while long hair is the pride of a woman, and it has been given to her precisely as a veil.

If some of you want to argue, let it be known that it is not our custom nor the custom in the churches of God.

To continue with my advice, I cannot praise you, for your gatherings are not for the better but for the worse.

First, as I have heard, when you gather together, there are divisions among you and I partly believe it. There may have to be different groups among you, so that it becomes clear who among you are genuine.

Your gatherings are no longer the Supper of the Lord, for each one eats at once, his own food, and, while one is hungry, the other is getting drunk. Do you not have houses in which to eat and drink? Or perhaps you despise the Church of God and desire to humiliate those who have nothing? What shall I say? Shall I praise you? For this I cannot praise you.

This is the tradition of the Lord that I received, and, that, in my turn, I have handed on to you; the Lord Jesus, on the night that he was delivered up, took bread and, after giving thanks, broke it, saying, "This is my body which is broken for you; do this in memory of me." In the same manner, taking the cup after the supper, he said, "This cup is the new Covenant, in my blood. Whenever you drink it, do it in memory of me." So, then, whenever you eat of this bread and drink from this cup, you are proclaiming the death of the Lord, until he comes.

Therefore, if anyone eats of the bread or drinks from the cup of the Lord unworthily, he sins against the body and blood of the Lord.

Let each one, then, examine himself before eating of the bread and drinking from the cup. Otherwise, he eats and drinks his own condemnation, in not recognizing the Body.

This is the reason why, so many among you are sick and weak, and several have died. But if we examine ourselves, we will not be examined by God, and judged in this way. The Lord's strokes are to correct us, so that we may not be condemned with this world.

So then, brothers, when you gather for a meal, wait for one another and, if someone is hungry, let him eat in his own house. In this way, you will not gather for your common condemnation. The other instructions I shall give, when I go there.

With respect to spiritual gifts, I will remind you of the following: When you were still pagans, you were irresistibly drawn to your dumb idols. I tell you that nobody inspired by the Spirit of God may say, "A curse on Jesus," as no one can say, "Jesus is the Lord," except by the Holy Spirit.

There is diversity of gifts, but the Spirit is the same. There is diversity of ministries, but the Lord is the same. There is diversity of works, but the same God works in all.

The Spirit reveals his presence in each one with a gift that is also a service. One is to speak with wisdom, through the Spirit. Another teaches, according to the same Spirit. To another is given faith, in which the Spirit acts; to another, the gift of healing, and it is the same Spirit. Another works miracles, another is a prophet, another recognizes what comes from the good or evil spirit; another speaks in tongues, and still another interprets what has been said in tongues. And all of this, is the work of the one and only Spirit, who gives to each one, as he so desires.

As the body is one, having many members, and all the members, while being many, form one body, so it is with Christ. All of us, whether Jews or Greeks, slaves or free, have been baptized in one Spirit, to form one body, and all of us have been given, to drink from the one Spirit.

The body has not just one member, but many. If the foot should say, "I do not belong to the body for I am not a hand," it would be wrong: it is part of the body! Even though the ear says, "I do not belong to the body for I am not an eye," it is part of the body. If all the body were eye, how would we hear? And if all the body were ear, how would we smell?

God has arranged all the members, placing each part of the body as he pleased. If all were the same part where would the body be? But there are many members and one body. The eye cannot tell the hand, "I do not need you," nor the head tell the feet, "I do not need you."

Still more, the parts of our body that we most need are those that seem to be the weakest; the parts that we consider lower are treated with much care, and we cover them with more modesty because they are less presentable, whereas the others do not need such attention. God, himself, arranged the body in this way, giving more honor to those parts that need it, so that the body may not be divided, but, rather, each member may care for the others. When one suffers, all of them suffer, and when one receives honor, all rejoice together.

Now, you are the body of Christ, and each of you, individually, is a member of it. So God has appointed us in the Church. First apostles, second prophets, third teachers. Then come miracles, then the gift of healing, material help, administration in the Church and the gift of tongues. Are all apostles? Are all prophets? Are all teachers? Can all perform miracles, or cure the sick, or speak in tongues, or explain what was said in tongues? Be that as it may, set your hearts on the most precious gifts, and I will show you a much better way.

If I could speak all the human and angelic tongues, but had no love, I would only be sounding brass or a clanging cymbal. If I had the gift of prophecy, knowing secret things, with all kinds of knowledge, and had faith great enough to remove mountains, but had no love, I would be nothing. If I gave everything I had to the poor, and even give up my body to be burned, if I am without love, it would be of no value to me.

Love is patient, kind, without envy. It is not boastful or arrogant. It is not ill-mannered, nor does it seek its own interest. Love overcomes anger and forgets offenses. It does not take delight in wrong, but rejoices in truth. Love excuses everything, believes all things, hopes all things, endures all things.

Love will never end. Prophecies may cease, tongues be silent and knowledge disappear. For knowledge grasps something of the truth and prophecy as well. And when what is perfect comes, everything imperfect will pass away. When I was a child, I thought and reasoned like a child, but when I grew up, I gave up childish ways. Likewise, at present, we see dimly, as in a mirror, but, then, it shall be face to face. Now, we know, in part, but then I will know as I am known. Now, we have faith, hope and love, these three, but the greatest of these is love.

Strive, then, for love and set your hearts on spiritual gifts, especially that you may prophesy. The one who speaks in tongues does not speak to people, but to God, for no one understands him; the spirit makes him say things that are not understandable. The prophet, instead, addresses all people, to give them strength, encouragement and consolation. He who speaks in tongues strengthens himself, but the prophet builds the Church.

Would that, all of you spoke in tongues! But, better still, if you were all prophets. The prophet has an advantage over the one speaking in tongues, unless someone explains what was spoken, so that the community may profit. Suppose, brothers and sisters, I go to you and I speak in tongues, of what use will it be to you, if I do not bring you some revelation, knowledge, prophecy or teaching?

When someone plays the flute, or harp, or any musical instrument, if there are no tunes and notes, who will recognize the tune? And if the bugle call is not clear, who will get ready for battle? The same, with you. If your words are not understood, who will know what is said? You will be talking to the moon! There are many languages in the world, and each of them has meaning, but if I cannot find any meaning in what is said, I become a foreigner to the speaker, and the speaker to me.

As you set your heart on spiritual gifts, be eager to build the Church, and you will receive abundantly. Because of this, those who speak in tongues should ask God for the ability to explain what they say.

When I am praying in tongues, my spirit prays, but my mind remains idle. What shall I do, then? I will pray with the spirit and I will pray with my mind. I will sing with the spirit and I will sing with the mind. If you praise God only with your spirit, how will the ordinary person add the "Amen" to your thanksgiving, since the outsider has not understood what you said? Your thanksgiving was indeed beautiful, but it was useless for others.

I give thanks to God because I speak in tongues more than all of you, but when I am in the assembly, I prefer to say five words from my mind, which may teach others, than ten thousand words in tongues.

Brothers and sisters, do not remain as children in your thinking. Be like infants in doing evil, but mature in your thinking. God says in the law:

> I will speak to this people
> through those talking other tongues
> and through lips of foreigners,
> but even so they will not listen to me.

So, speaking in tongues is significant for those who refuse to believe, not for those who believe, while prophecy is a sign for those who believe, not for those who refuse to believe.

Yet, imagine, that the whole Church is gathered together, and all speak in tongues when unbelievers and uninformed people enter. What will they think? That you are crazy. Instead, suppose that each of you speaks as a prophet; as soon as an unbeliever or an uninformed person enters, all of you call him to account and disclose his most secret thinking. Then, falling on his face, he would be urged to worship God and declare that God is truly among you.

What then shall we conclude, brothers? When you gather, each of you can take part with a song, a teaching, or a revelation, by speaking in tongues or interpreting what has been said in tongues. But let all this build up the Church.

Are you going to speak in tongues? Let two or three, at most, speak, each in turn, and let one interpret what has been said. If there is no interpreter, hold your tongue in the assembly and speak to God by yourself.

As for the prophets, let two or three speak, with the others commenting on what has been said. If a revelation comes to one of those sitting by, let the first be silent. Even all of you could prophesy, one by one, for the instruction and encouragement of all. The spirits, speaking through prophets, are submitted to prophets, because God is not a God of confusion, but of peace.

(Let women be silent in the assemblies, as in all the churches of the saints. They are not allowed to speak. Let them be submissive, as the law commands. If there is anything they desire to know, let them consult their husbands at home. For it is shameful for a woman to speak in Church.)

Did the word of God, perhaps, come from you? Or did it come only to you? Anyone among you who claims to be a prophet or a spiritual person, should acknowledge that what I am writing to you is the Lord's command. If he does not recognize that, God will not recognize him.

So, my friends, set your hearts on the gift of prophecy, and do not forbid speaking in tongues. However, everything should be done in a fitting and orderly way.

Let me remind you, brothers and sisters, of the Good News that I preached to you, and which you received, and on which, you stand firm. By that gospel, you are saved, provided that you hold to it, as I preached it. Otherwise, you will have believed in vain.

In the first place, I have passed on to you what I, myself, received: that Christ died for our sins, as Scripture says; that he was buried; that he was raised on the third day, according to the Scriptures; that he appeared to Cephas and then to the Twelve. Afterward, he appeared to more than five hundred brothers and sisters together; most of them are still alive, although some have already gone to rest. Then he appeared to James, and after that, to all the apostles. And last of all, he appeared to the most despicable of them, this is, to me. For I am the last of the apostles, and I do not even deserve to be called an apostle, because I persecuted the Church of God. Nevertheless, by the grace of God, I am what I am, and his grace toward me has not been without fruit. Far from it, I have toiled more than all of them, although, not I, rather the grace of God, in me.

Now, whether it was I or they, this, we preach, and this, you have believed. Well, then, if Christ is preached as risen from the dead, how can some of you say, that there is no resurrection of the dead? If there is no resurrection of the dead, then Christ has not been raised. And if Christ has not been raised, our preaching is empty, and our belief comes to nothing. And we become false witnesses of God, attesting that he raised Christ, whereas he could not raise him, if indeed, the dead are not raised. If the dead are not raised, neither has Christ been raised. And if Christ has not been raised, your faith gives you nothing, and you are still in sin. Also, those who fall asleep, in Christ, are lost. If it is only for this life, that we hope in Christ, we are the most unfortunate of all people.

But no, Christ has been raised from the dead, and he comes before all those who have fallen asleep. A human being brought death; a human being also brings resurrection of the dead. For, as in Adam all die, so, in Christ, all will be made alive. However, each one in his own time: first Christ, then Christ's people, when he comes.

Then, the end will come, when Christ delivers the kingdom to God the Father, after having destroyed every rule, authority and power. For he must reign and put all enemies under his feet. The last enemy to be destroyed will be death. As Scripture says: God has subjected everything under his feet.

When we say that everything is put under his feet, we exclude, of course, the Father, who subjects everything to him. When the Father has subjected everything to him, the Son will place himself under the One who subjected everything to him. From then on, God will be all in all.

Tell me: what are these people doing, who are baptized on behalf of the dead? If the dead cannot be raised, why do they want to be baptized for the dead?

As for us, why do we constantly risk our life? For death is my daily companion. I say that, brothers and sisters, before you, who are my pride in Christ Jesus our Lord. Was it for human interest that I fought in Ephesus like a lion tamer? If the dead are not raised,

> let us eat and drink,
> for tomorrow we shall die!

Do not be deceived; bad theories corrupt good morals. Wake up, and do not sin, because some of you are outstandingly ignorant about God; I say this to your shame.

Some of you will ask: How will the dead be raised? With what kind of body will they come?

You fools! What you sow cannot sprout unless it dies. And what you sow is not the body of the future plant, but a bare grain of wheat or any other seed, and God will give the appropriate body, as he gives to each seed its own body. Now look: not all flesh is the same; one is the flesh of human beings; another the flesh of animals, and, still others, the flesh of birds and of fish. There are, likewise, heavenly bodies and earthly bodies, but the earthly bodies do not shine as do the heavenly ones. The brightness of the sun differs from the brightness of the moon and the stars, and the stars differ from one another in brightness.

It is the same with the resurrection of the dead. The body is sown in decomposition; it will be raised never more to die. It is sown in humiliation, and it will be raised for glory. It is buried in weakness, but the resurrection shall be with power. When buried, it is a natural body, but it will be raised as a spiritual body. For there shall be a spiritual body, as there is, at present, a living body. Scripture says that Adam, the first man, became a living being; but the last Adam has become a life-giving spirit.

The spirit does not appear first, but the natural life, and afterward comes the spirit. The first man comes from the earth and is earthly, while the second one comes from heaven. As it was with the earthly one, so is it with the earthly people. As it is with Christ, so with the heavenly. This is why, after bearing the image of the earthly one, we shall also bear the image of the heavenly one.

This I say, brothers: Flesh and blood cannot share the kingdom of God; nothing of us that is to decay, can reach imperishable life. So, I want to teach you this mystery: although not all of us will die, all of us have to be transformed, in an instant, at the sound of the trumpet. You have heard of the last trumpet; then, in the twinkling of an eye, the dead will be raised, imperishable, while we shall be transformed. For it is necessary that our mortal and perishable being put on the life that knows neither death nor decay.

When our perishable being puts on imperishable life, when our mortal being puts on immortality, the word of Scripture will be fulfilled: Death has been swallowed up by victory.

> Death, where is your victory?
> Death, where is your sting?

Sin is the sting of death, to kill, and the law is what gives force to sin. But give thanks to God, who gives us the victory, through Christ Jesus, our Lord.

So then, my dear brothers and sisters, be steadfast, and do not be moved. Improve constantly, in the work of the Lord, knowing that, with him, your labor is not without fruit.

With regard to the collection in favor of the saints, follow the rules that I gave to the churches of Galatia. On the first day of the week, let each of you put aside what you are able to spare, so that no collection need be made when I come. Then, when I arrive, I will send those whom you approve, with letters of explanation, to carry your gift to Jerusalem. And if it seems better for me to go, they will go with me.

I will visit you after passing through Macedonia, for I want to go only through Macedonia. I would like to stay with you for a while, and perhaps I will spend the winter so that you may help me on my way wherever I go. I do not want to see you now, just in passing, for I really hope to stay with you, if the Lord permits. But I will stay in Ephesus until Pentecost, because I have a door wide open here, even though there are many opponents.

When Timothy comes, make him feel at ease with you. Consider that, like me, he is working for the Lord. Let no one look down on him. Help him continue his journey, so that he may return to me without difficulties. I am expecting him with the brothers.

With respect to our brother Apollos, I have strongly urged him to visit you with the brothers, but he did not want to go at all; he will visit you at his first opportunity.

Be alert, stand firm in the faith, be courageous, be strong. Let love be in all. Now, brothers and sisters, you know that in Achaia, there is none better than Stephanas and his family, and that they have devoted themselves to the service of the holy ones. I urge you to be subject to such persons, and to anyone who works and toils with them.

I am glad about the coming of Stephanas, Fortunatus and Achaicus, who were able to represent you. In fact, they appeased my spirit and yours. Appreciate persons like them.

The churches of Asia greet you. Aquila and Prisca greet you in the Lord, as does the church that gathers in their house. All the brothers and sisters greet you. Greet one another with a holy kiss.

The greeting is from me, Paul, in my own hand. A curse on anyone who does not love the Lord! Maranatha! Come, Lord!

The grace of the Lord Jesus be with you. My love to all, in Christ Jesus.

INVITATION TO
2 CORINTHIANS

In 1 Corinthians, Paul wrote that he was going to stay in Ephesus a little while longer, then visit the churches in Macedonia. He'd pick up the collection they'd taken for the poor, then come to Achaia (see p. 132). So the Corinthians were surprised when he came to their city before going to Macedonia. They were embarrassed, too, because they hadn't been setting aside money and their own collection wasn't ready. They accused Paul of not being true to his word—of saying one thing and then doing another. One man in particular appears to have offered a sharp challenge to his leadership. After this confrontation Paul left abruptly, saying he'd come back to Corinth for their collection and then go on to Macedonia.

Paul returned to Ephesus and sent his co-worker Titus to Corinth with a sharp letter of rebuke. He demanded that the man who'd challenged him be disciplined. Titus was supposed to bring back word of the Corinthians' response. But then Paul had to change his travel plans again. A riot broke out in Ephesus against Jesus' messengers there. Paul had to go into hiding for his own safety (see p. 86). When he was finally able to travel, he went to Troas, where he'd arranged to meet Titus. But when he couldn't find him, he continued on to Macedonia. There he found Titus and learned that the Corinthians had reaffirmed their respect for his authority and disciplined the man who'd challenged him. But Titus also reported a new threat. Some traveling Jewish-Christian teachers had come to Corinth, bearing impressive letters of introduction. They called themselves *super-apostles* and were beginning to win a following. They were demanding that Paul demonstrate his own credentials.

So Paul had several challenges to address before returning to Corinth. He had to assure the Corinthians that all was now forgiven. He had to explain why he'd changed his travel plans yet again. He still needed to help them arrange for the offering. And finally, he had to respond to the self-described *super-apostles*. He did all of these things in the letter we know as 2 Corinthians. It reveals the triumphs and struggles that result when life in the present age meets up with the in-breaking reality of God's kingdom.

The main body of this letter has four parts. Each is introduced by a reference to a place:

: *We want you to know some of the trials we experienced in the province of Asia* (pp. 137–138).

: *So I came to Troas to preach the gospel of Christ, and the Lord opened doors for me. However, I could not be at peace because I did not find my brother Titus there* (pp. 139–142).

: *Know, that, when I came to Macedonia, I had no rest at all, but I was afflicted with all kinds of difficulties: conflict outside and fear within* (pp. 143–145).

: Do not force me to act boldly when I come [to Corinth], as I am determined, and will dare to act against some people, who think that I act from human motives. Human is our condition, but not our fight (pp. 145–148).

In the four parts of this letter, Paul envisions himself in these different locations. Recalling or anticipating the state of his relationship with the Corinthians, he addresses them from four different perspectives. Still, a single theme runs through the whole letter: God will comfort us in all our afflictions, and we can offer this comfort to one another. However, in the final, confrontational section, Paul has to make the Corinthians uncomfortable. This is something he doesn't want to do, but they've left him no choice. But he ends the letter on a hopeful note, calling on them to rejoice in God's *grace*, *love* and *fellowship*.

| 2 CORINTHIANS |

P aul, an apostle of Christ Jesus, by the will of God, and Timothy, our brother, to the church of God in Corinth, and to all the saints in the whole of Achaia.

May you receive grace and peace from God, our Father, and from Christ Jesus, the Lord.

B lessed be God, the Father of Christ Jesus, our Lord, the all-merciful Father, and the God of all comfort! He encourages us in all our trials, so that we may also encourage those in any trial, with the same comfort that we receive from God.

For whenever the sufferings of Christ overflow to us, so, through Christ, a great comfort also overflows. So, if we are afflicted, it is for your comfort and salvation; and if we receive comfort it is also for you. You may experience the same comfort when you come to endure the same sufferings we endure. Our hope for you is most firm; just as you share in our sufferings, so shall you also share in our consolation.

Brothers and sisters, we want you to know some of the trials we experienced in the province of Asia. We were crushed; it was too much; it was more than we could bear and we had already lost all hope of coming through alive. We felt branded for death, but this happened that we might no longer rely on ourselves but on God, who raises the dead. He freed us from such a deadly peril and will continue to do so. We trust he will continue protecting us, but you must help us with your prayers. When such a favor is obtained by the intercession of many, so will there be many to give thanks to God on our behalf.

There is something we are proud of: our conscience tells us that we have lived in this world with the openness and sincerity that comes from God. We have been guided, not by human motives, but by the grace of God, especially in relation to you. There were no hidden intentions in my letter, but only what you can read and understand. I trust that what you now only partly realize, you will come to understand fully, and so be proud of us, as we shall also be proud of you on the Day of the Lord Jesus.

With this assurance, I wanted to go and visit you first and this would have been a double blessing for you, for I would have left you to go through Macedonia, and I would have come back to you on my way back from Macedonia, and you would have sent me on my way to Judea. Have I planned this without thinking at all? Or do I change my decisions on the spur of the moment, so that I am between No and Yes?

God knows that our dealing with you is not Yes and No, just as the Son of God, Christ Jesus, whom we—Silvanus, Timothy and I—preach to you, was not Yes and No; with him it was simply Yes. In him all the promises of God have come to be a Yes, and we also say in his name: Amen! giving thanks to God. God, himself, has anointed us and strengthens us, with you, to serve Christ; he has marked us with his own seal, in a first outpouring of the Spirit, in our hearts.

God knows, and I swear to you by my own life, that if I did not return to Corinth, it was because I wanted to spare you. I do not wish to lord it over your faith, but to contribute to your happiness; for regarding faith, you already stand firm.

So I gave up a visit that would, again, be a distressing one. If I make you sad, who will make me happy, if not you, whom I have grieved? Remember what I wrote you, "May it be that when I come, I do not feel sad because of you, who should, rather, make me happy." I trust in everyone and I am sure that my joy will be the joy of you all.

So afflicted and worried was I, when I wrote to you, that I even shed tears. I did not intend to cause you pain, but, rather, to let you know of the immense love that I have for you.

If anyone has caused me pain, he has hurt not me but in some measure, (I do not wish to exaggerate) all of you. The punishment that he received from the majority is enough for him. Now you should, rather, forgive and comfort him, lest excessive sorrow discourage him. So I beg you to treat him with love.

This is why I wrote to you, to test you and to know if you would obey in everything. The one you forgive, I also forgive. And what I forgave, if, indeed, I had anything to forgive, I forgave, for your sake, in the presence of Christ, lest Satan take advantage of us; for we know his designs.

So I came to Troas to preach the gospel of Christ, and the Lord opened doors for me. However, I could not be at peace because I did not find my brother Titus there. So I took leave of them and went to Macedonia.

Thanks be to God, who always leads us in the triumphant following of Christ and, through us, spreads the knowledge of him everywhere, like an aroma. We are Christ's fragrance, rising up to God, and perceived by those who are saved, as well as by those who are lost. To the latter, it smells of death and leads them to death. To others, it is the fragrance of life and leads to life.

But who is worthy of such a mission? Unlike so many, who make money out of the word of God, we speak with sincerity: everything comes from God, and is said in his presence, in Christ.

Am I, again, commending myself? Or do I need to present to you letters of recommendation, as some do; or should I ask you for those letters? You are the letter. This letter is written in your inner self, yet all can read and understand it. Yes, who could deny that you are Christ's letter, written by us—a letter written, not with ink, but with the Spirit of the living God, carved not in slabs of stone, but in hearts of flesh.

This is how we are sure of God, through Christ. As for us, we would not dare consider that something comes from us: our ability comes from God. He has even enabled us to be ministers of a new covenant, no longer depending on a written text, but on the Spirit. The written text kills, but the Spirit gives life.

The ministry of the law carved on stones brought death; it was, nevertheless, surrounded by glory, and, we know, that the Israelites could not fix their eyes on the face of Moses, such was his radiance, though fleeting. How much more glorious will the ministry of the Spirit be! If there is greatness in a ministry which used to condemn, how much more will there be, in the ministry that brings holiness? This is such a glorious thing that, in comparison, the former's glory is like nothing. That ministry was provisory and had only moments of glory; but ours endures, with a lasting glory.

Since we have such a great ambition, we are quite confident—unlike Moses, who covered his face with a veil. Otherwise, the Israelites would have seen his passing radiance fade.

They became blind, however; until this day, the same veil prevents them from understanding the Old Covenant, and they do not realize that, in Christ, it is nullified. Up to this very day, whenever they read Moses, the veil remains over their understanding but, for whoever turns to the Lord, the veil shall be removed. The Lord is Spirit, and where the Spirit of the Lord is, there is freedom.

So, with unveiled faces, we all reflect the glory of the Lord, while we are transformed into his likeness, and experience his glory, more and more by the action of the Lord, who is Spirit.

Since this is our ministry, mercifully given to us, we do not weaken. We refuse to stay with half-truths through fear; we do not behave with cunning, or falsify the message of God, but, manifesting the truth, we commend ourselves to the conscience of everyone, in the sight of God.

In fact, if the gospel we proclaim remains obscure, it is obscure only for those who go to their own destruction. The god of this world has blinded the minds of these unbelievers, lest they see the radiance of the glorious gospel of Christ, who is God's image. It is not ourselves we preach, but Christ Jesus, as Lord; and, for Jesus' sake, we are your servants. God, who said, Let the light shine out of darkness, has also made the light shine in our hearts, to radiate, and to make known the glory of God, as it shines in the face of Christ.

However, we carry this treasure in vessels of clay, so that this all-surpassing power may not be seen as ours, but as God's. Trials of every sort come to us, but we are not discouraged. We are left without answer, but do not despair; persecuted but not abandoned, knocked down but not crushed. At any moment, we carry, in our person, the death of Jesus, so, that, the life of Jesus may also be manifested in us. For we, the living, are given up continually to death, for the sake of Jesus, so, that, the life of Jesus may appear in our mortal existence. And as death is at work in us, life comes to you.

We have received the same spirit of faith referred to in Scripture, that says: I believed and so I spoke. We also believe, and so we speak. We know that he, who raised the Lord Jesus, will also raise us, with Jesus, and bring us, with you, into his presence. Finally, everything is for your good, so that grace will come more abundantly upon you, and great will be the thanksgiving for the glory of God.

Therefore, we are not discouraged. On the contrary, while our outer being wastes away, the inner self is renewed, from day to day. The slight affliction, that quickly passes away, prepares us for an eternal wealth of glory, so great, and beyond all comparison. So, we no longer pay attention to the things that are seen, but to those that are unseen, for the things that we see last for a moment, but that which cannot be seen is eternal.

We know that, when our earthly dwelling, or, rather, our tent, is destroyed, we may count on a building from God, a heavenly dwelling, not built by human hands, that lasts forever. Therefore, we long and groan: Why may we not put on this heavenly dwelling over that which we have? (Indeed, are we sure, that, we shall still be wearing our earthly dwelling and not be unclothed?)

As long as we are in the field-tent, we, indeed, bemoan our unbearable fate, for we do not want this clothing to be removed from us; we would, rather, put the other, over it, that the mortal body may be absorbed by true life. This is God's purpose for us, and he has given us the Spirit, as a pledge of what we are to receive.

So we feel confident always. We know, that, while living in the body, we are exiled from the Lord, living by faith, without seeing; but we dare to think, that we would rather be away from the body, to go and live with the Lord. So, whether we have to keep this house or lose it, we only wish to please the Lord. Anyway, we all have to appear before the tribunal of Christ, for each one to receive what he deserves, for his good or evil deeds in the present life.

So, we know the fear of the Lord, and we try to convince people, while we live openly before God. And I trust, that, you know, in your conscience what we truly are. Once more, we do not try to win your esteem; we want to give you a reason to feel proud of us, that you may respond to those who heed appearances and not the reality. Now, if I have spoken foolishly, let God alone hear; if what I have said makes sense, take it for yourselves.

Indeed, the love of Christ holds us, and we realize, that, if he died for all, all have died. He died for all, so, that, those who live, may live no longer for themselves, but for him, who died, and rose again for them. And so, from now on, we do not regard anyone from a human point of view; and even if we once knew Christ personally, we should now regard him in another way.

For that same reason, the one who is in Christ is a new creature. For him, the old things have passed away; a new world has come. All this is the work of God, who, in Christ, reconciled us to himself, and who entrusted to us the ministry of reconciliation. Because, in Christ, God reconciled the world with himself, no longer taking into account their trespasses, and entrusting to us the message of reconciliation.

So we present ourselves as ambassadors, in the name of Christ, as if God, himself, makes an appeal to you, through us. Let God reconcile you; this, we ask you, in the name of Christ. He had no sin, but God made him bear our sin, so, that, in him, we might share the holiness of God.

Being God's helpers, we beg you: let it not be in vain, that you received this grace of God. Scripture says:

> At the favorable time I listened to you,
> on the day of salvation I helped you.

This is the favorable time, this is the day of salvation.

We are concerned, not to give anyone an occasion to stumble or criticize our mission. Instead, we prove, we are true ministers of God, in every way, by our endurance in so many trials, in hardships, afflictions, floggings, imprisonment, riots, fatigue, sleepless nights and days of hunger.

People can notice, in our upright life, knowledge, patience and kindness, action of the Holy Spirit, sincere love, words of truth, and power of God. So we fight with the weapons of justice, to attack, as well as to defend.

Sometimes, we are honored, at other times, insulted; we receive criticism as well as praise. We are regarded as liars, although we speak the truth; as unknown, though we are well known; as dead, and yet we live. Punishments come upon us, but we have not, as yet, been put to death. We appear to be afflicted, yet always joyful; we seem to be poor, but we enrich many; we have nothing, but we possess everything!

Corinthians! I have spoken to you frankly and I have uncovered my inner thought. My heart is wide open to you, but you feel uneasy, because of your closed heart: repay us with the same measure—I speak to you as to my children—open wide your hearts also.

Do not make unsuitable covenants with those who do not believe: can justice walk with wickedness? Or can light coexist with darkness, and can there be harmony between Christ and Satan? What union can there be between one who believes and one who does not believe? God's temple must have no room for idols, and we are the temple of the living God. As Scripture says;

> I will dwell and live in their midst,
> I will be their God and they shall be my people.

Therefore:

> Come out from their midst
> and separate from them,
>
> says the Lord.

> Do not touch anything unclean
> and I will be gracious to you.

> I will be a father to you,
> that you may become my sons and daughters,
>
> says the all-powerful God.

Since we have such promises, dear friends, let us purify ourselves from all defilement of body and spirit, and complete the work of sanctification, in the fear of God.

Welcome us in your hearts! We have injured no one. We have harmed no one, we have cheated no one. I do not say this to condemn you: I have just said, that you are in our heart, so, that, together, we live, together, we die. I have great confidence in you and I am indeed proud of you. I feel very much encouraged and my joy overflows, in spite of all this bitterness.

Know, that, when I came to Macedonia, I had no rest at all, but I was afflicted with all kinds of difficulties: conflict outside and fear within. But God, who encourages the humble, gave me comfort with the arrival of Titus, not only because of his arrival, but, also, because you had received him very well. He told me about your deep affection for me; you were affected by what happened. You worried about me, and this made me rejoice all the more.

If my letter caused you pain, I do not regret it. Perhaps I did regret it, for I saw that the letter caused you sadness, for a moment, but, now, I rejoice, not because of your sadness, but because this sadness brought you to repentance. This was a sadness from God, so, that, no evil came to you, because of me. Sadness from God brings firm repentance, that leads to salvation, and brings no regret, but worldly grief produces death. See what this sadness from God has produced in you: What concern for me! What apologies! What indignation and fear! What a longing to see me, to make amends and do me justice!

You have fully proved that you were innocent in this matter. In reality, I wrote to you, not on account of the offender or of the offended, but, that you may be conscious of the concern you have for me before God. I was encouraged by this.

In addition to this consolation of mine, I rejoice, especially, to see Titus very pleased with the way you all reassured him. I had no cause to regret my praise of you to him. You know that I am always sincere with you; likewise my praise of you to Titus has been justified. He now feels much more affection for you, as he remembers the obedience of all, and the respect and humility with which you received him. Really, I rejoice, for I can be truly proud of you.

Now, I want you to know about a gift of divine grace among the Churches of Macedonia. While they were so afflicted and persecuted, their joy overflowed, and their extreme poverty turned into a wealth of generosity. According to their means—even beyond their means—they wanted to share, in helping the saints.

They asked us for this favor, spontaneously, and with much insistence, and, far beyond anything we expected, they put themselves at the disposal of the Lord, and of us by the will of God. Accordingly, I urged Titus to complete, among you, this work of grace, since he began it with you. You excel in everything: in the gifts of faith, speech and knowledge; you feel concern for every cause and, besides, you are first in my heart. Excel, also, in this generous service.

This is not a command; I make known to you the determination of others, to check the sincerity of your fraternal concern. You know well, the generosity of Christ Jesus, our Lord. Although he was rich, he made himself poor, to make you rich, through his poverty.

I only make a suggestion, because you were the first, not only in cooperating, but in beginning this project a year ago. So complete this work and, according to your means, carry out what you decided, with much enthusiasm. When there is a good disposition, everything you give is welcomed, and no one longs for what you do not have. I do not mean that others should be at ease and you burdened. Strive for equality; at present, give from your abundance what they are short of, and, in some way, they, also, will give from their abundance, what you lack. Then, you will be equal and what Scripture says shall come true: To the one who had much, nothing was in excess; to the one who had little, nothing was lacking.

Blessed be God, who inspires Titus with such care for you! He not only listened to my appeal but he wanted to go and see you on his own initiative. I am sending with him the brother who has gained the esteem of the churches in the work of the gospel; moreover, they appointed him to travel with us in this blessed work we are carrying on, for the glory of the Lord, but, also, because of our personal enthusiasm.

We decided on this, so that, no one could suspect us, with regard to this generous fund that we are administering. Let us see to it, that all may appear clean, not only before God but also before people. We also send with them, another brother, who, on several occasions, has shown us his zeal and, now, is more enthusiastic, because of his confidence in you.

You, then, have Titus, our companion and minister, to serve you, and, with him, you have our brothers, representatives of the churches, and a glory to Christ. Show them how you love, and prove, before the churches, all the good things I said to them about you.

It is not necessary for me to write to you about assistance to the saints. I know your readiness and I praised you before the Macedonians. I said, "In Achaia they have been ready for the collection since last year." And your enthusiasm carried most of them along. So I send you these brothers of ours. May all my praise of you not fall flat in this case! May you be ready, as I said. If some Macedonians come with me, let them not find you unprepared. What a shame for me—and perhaps for you—after so much confidence!

So I thought it necessary to ask our brothers to go ahead of us and see you, to organize this blessed work you have promised. It shall come from your generosity and not be an imposed task.

Remember: the one who sows meagerly will reap meagerly, and there shall be generous harvests for the one who sows generously. Each of you should give as you decided personally, and not reluctantly, as if obliged. God loves a cheerful giver. And God is able to fill you with every good thing, so that you have enough of everything, at all times, and may give abundantly for any good work.

Scripture says:

> He distributed, he gave to the poor,
> his good works last forever.

God, who provides the sower with seed, will also provide him with the bread he eats. He will multiply the seed for you and also increase the interest on your good works. Become rich in every way, and give abundantly. What you give will become, through us, a thanksgiving to God.

For this sacred relief, after providing the saints with what they need, will result in much thanksgiving to God. This will be a test for them; they will give thanks, because you obey the requirements of Christ's gospel and share generously with them, and with all. They shall pray to God for you, and feel affection for you, because the grace of God overflows in you.

Yes, thanks be to God, for his indescribable gift!

It is I, Paul, who, by the humility and kindness of Christ, appeal to you; the Paul "who is timid among you and bold when far away from you!"

Do not force me to act boldly when I come, as I am determined, and will dare to act against some people, who think that I act from human motives. Human is our condition, but not our fight.

Our weapons for this fight are not human, but they have divine power, to destroy strongholds—those arguments and haughty thoughts that oppose the knowledge of God. We compel all understanding, that they obey Christ. So, I am prepared to punish any disobedience, when you should show perfect obedience.

See things as they really are. If someone is convinced that he belongs to Christ, let him consider, that, just as he is Christ's, so am I. Although, I may seem too confident in the authority that the Lord gave me for building you up and not for pulling you down, I will not be put to shame for saying this. Do not think that I can only frighten you with letters. "His letters are severe and strong," some say, "but as he is, he has no presence and he is a poor speaker." To such people I say, "Be careful: what my letters say from afar, is what I will do when I come."

How could I venture to equate or compare myself with some people, who proclaim their own merits? Fools! They measure themselves with their own measure, and compare themselves with themselves. As for me, I will not boast beyond measure, for I will not go past the limits that the God of true measure has set for me: He gave the measuring stick when he made me set foot in your place.

It is not the same when someone goes beyond his field, to where he has not been able to set foot. But I am he who first reached you with the gospel of Christ. I am not making myself important where others have worked. On the contrary, we hope that, as your faith increases, so too, our area of ministry among you will be enlarged, without going beyond our limit. So, we shall bring the gospel to places beyond yours, without entering into the field of others, or boasting, and making ourselves important, where the work is already done. Let the one who boasts, boast in the Lord. It is not the one who commends himself who is approved, but the one whom the Lord commends.

May you bear with me in some little foolishness! But surely you will. I confess that I share the jealousy of God for you, for I have promised you, in marriage, to Christ, the only spouse; to present you to him, as a pure virgin. And this is my fear: the serpent that seduced Eve, with cunning, could also corrupt your minds, and divert you from Christian sincerity. Someone, now, comes, and preaches another Jesus, different from the one we preach, or you are offered a different spirit from the one you have received, with a different gospel from the one you have accepted—and you agree!

I do not see how I am inferior to those super-apostles. Does my speaking leave much to be desired? Perhaps, but not my knowledge, as I have abundantly shown to you in every way.

Perhaps my fault was, that I humbled myself, in order to uplift you, or that, I gave you the gospel free of charge. I called upon the services of other churches, and served you with the support I received from them. When I was with you, although I was in need, I did not become a burden to anyone. The friends from Macedonia gave me what I needed. I have taken care, not to be a burden to you in anything, and I will continue to do so. By the truth of Christ within me, I will let no one in the land of Achaia stop this boasting of mine.

Why? Because I do not love you? God knows that I do! Yet, I do, and I will continue to do so, to silence any people anxious to appear as equal to me: this is my glory. In reality, they are false apostles, deceivers, disguised as apostles of Christ. It is not surprising: if Satan disguises himself as an angel of light, his servants can easily disguise themselves as ministers of salvation, until they receive what their deeds deserve.

I say again: Do not take me for a fool, but if you do take me as such, bear with me, that I may sing my own praises a little. I will not speak with the Lord's authority, but as a fool, bringing my own merits to prominence. As some people boast of human advantages, I will do the same. Fortunately, you bear rather well with fools, you, who are so wise! You tolerate being enslaved, and exploited, robbed, treated with contempt and slapped in the face. What a shame, that I acted so weakly with you!

But if others are so bold, I shall also dare, although I may speak like a fool. Are they Hebrews? So am I. Are they Israelites? So am I. Are they descendants of Abraham? So am I. Are they ministers of Christ? (I begin to talk like a madman) I am better than they.

Better than they, with my numerous labors. Better than they, with the time spent in prison. The beatings I received are beyond comparison. How many times have I found myself in danger of death! Five times, the Jews sentenced me to thirty-nine lashes. Three times, I was beaten with a rod. Once I was stoned. Three times, I was shipwrecked; and once, I spent a night and a day, adrift on the high seas.

I have been continually in hazards of traveling; because of rivers, because of bandits, because of my fellow Jews, or because of the pagans; in danger, in the city, in the open country, at sea; in danger from false brothers. I have worked, and often labored without sleep, I have been hungry and thirsty and starving, cold, and without shelter.

Besides these, and other things, there was my daily concern for all the churches. Who is weak, that I do not feel weak as well? Whoever stumbles, am I not on hot bricks?

If it is necessary to boast, let me proclaim the occasions on which I was found weak. The God and Father of Jesus the Lord—may he be blessed for ever!—knows that I speak the truth. At Damascus, the governor under king Aretas placed the city under guard in order to arrest me, and I had to be let down in a basket, through a window in the wall. In that way, I slipped through his hands.

It is useless to boast; but if I have to, I will go on, to some visions and revelations of the Lord.

I know a certain Christian: fourteen years ago he was taken up to the third heaven. Whether in the body or out of the body, I do not know, God knows. But I know that this man, whether in the body or out of the body—I do not know, God knows—was taken up to Paradise, where he heard words that cannot be told: things which humans cannot express.

Of that man I can indeed boast, but of myself I will not boast except of my weaknesses. If I wanted to boast, it would not be foolish of me, for I would speak the truth. However, I better give up, lest somebody think more of me than what is seen in me, or heard from me. Lest I become proud, after so many and extraordinary revelations; I was given a thorn in my flesh, a true messenger of Satan, to slap me in the face. Three times, I prayed to the Lord, that it leave me, but he answered, "My grace is enough for you; my great strength is revealed in weakness."

Gladly, then, will I boast of my weakness, that the strength of Christ may be mine. So I rejoice, when I suffer infirmities, humiliations, want, persecutions: all for Christ! For when I am weak, then I am strong.

I have acted as a fool but you forced me. You should have been the ones commending me. Yet I do not feel outdone by those super-apostles, even though

I am nothing. All the signs of a true apostle are found in me: patience in all trials, signs, miracles and wonders.

Now, in what way were you not treated like the rest of the churches? Only in this: I was not a burden to you—forgive me for this offense!

For the third time, I plan to visit you, and I will not be a burden to you, for I am not interested in what you have, but only in you. Children should not have to collect money for their parents, but the parents, for their children. As for me, I am ready to spend whatever I have, and even my whole self, for all of you. If I love you so much, am I to be loved less?

Well, I was not a burden to you, but was it not a trick to deceive you? Tell me: Did I take money from you through any of my messengers? I asked Titus to go to you and I sent another brother with him. But did Titus take money from you? Have we not both acted in the same spirit?

Perhaps you think that we are again apologizing; but no: we speak in Christ and before God, and I do this for you, dear friends, to build you up. I fear that, if I go and see you, I might not find you as I would wish, and you, in turn, might not find me to your liking. I might see rivalries, envy, grudges, disputes, slanders, gossip, conceit, disorder. Let it not be, that, in coming again to you, God humbles me because of you, and I have to grieve over so many of you, who live in sin, on seeing that, they have not yet given up an impure way of living, their wicked conduct, and the vices they formerly practiced.

This will be my third visit to you. Any charge must be decided upon by the declaration of two or three witnesses. I have said and I say again, being still far away, just as I did on my second visit, I say, to you who lived in sin, as well as to the rest: when I return to you, I will not have pity. You want to know if Christ is speaking through me? So you will. He is not used to dealing weakly with you, but rather he acts with power. If he was crucified in his weakness, now he lives by the strength of God; and so we are weak with him, but we will be well alive with him, because God acts powerfully with you.

Examine yourselves: are you acting according to faith? Test yourselves. Can you assert that Christ Jesus is in you? If not, you have failed the test. I hope you recognize that we ourselves have not failed it.

We pray God, that you may do no wrong, not that we wish to be acknowledged, but we want you to do right, even if, in this, we appear to have failed. For we do not have power against the truth, but only for the truth. We rejoice, if we are weak, while you are strong, for all we hope, is that you become perfect. This is why I am writing now, so that when I come, I may not have to act strictly, and make use of the authority the Lord has given me for building up, and not for destroying.

Finally, brothers and sisters, be happy, strive to be perfect, have courage, be of one mind and live in peace. And the God of love and peace will be with you. Greet one another with a holy kiss. All the saints greet you.

The grace of Christ Jesus the Lord, the love of God and the fellowship of the Holy Spirit be with you all.

INVITATION TO
GALATIANS

It's difficult to know exactly when and where Paul wrote his letter to *the churches in Galatia*. He doesn't say where he's writing from, as he does in his letters to Thessalonica and Corinth. And while he says he's writing on behalf of *all the brothers and sisters who are with me*, he doesn't say who these brothers and sisters are. Many interpreters believe that Galatians may actually be the earliest of Paul's letters. However, its themes and language are so close to the letter he sent to the church in Rome that it's quite probable Galatians was written about the same time as Romans. This would mean he wrote it from Corinth around AD 56 or 57, while arranging for the collection to be sent to the poor in Judea. When Paul tells the Galatians he's been eager to remember the poor, and that they should do good to all people, especially to those who belong to the family of believers, he may be referring to this collection.

Galatia was a Roman province in central Asia Minor. The book of Acts reports that Paul traveled through this province on each of the three journeys he made to spread the good news about Jesus. On one of these occasions he needed to stop and recuperate from an illness and he met the people he later sent this letter to. (As he reminds them, *it was an illness that first gave me the opportunity to announce the gospel to you*.) The Galatians received Paul warmly and cared for him, and through his message they came to believe in Jesus.

But some people Paul calls *agitators* later came to Galatia and made some unsettling claims. Paul consistently taught that Gentiles (non-Jews) didn't have to keep the Jewish law in order to be Jesus-followers. But these agitators insisted that the apostles in Jerusalem taught just the opposite, that Gentiles who believed in Jesus had to be circumcised, keep kosher, and observe the Sabbath and annual Jewish festivals. The agitators also claimed that Paul insisted on these things elsewhere, and that he'd only relaxed these requirements for the Galatians to get on their good side. In response to these claims, the Galatians had already begun *to observe this and that day, and the new moon, and this period and that year*, and they were considering being circumcised, too.

So in his letter Paul first has to answer these charges against himself. He then has to correct the idea that certain Jewish practices have to be added to what they already have. He reaffirms the core message that faith in the Messiah is the basis of membership in God's new community.

Paul could defend himself by appealing to the apostles in Jerusalem, since their message is actually the same as his. But he doesn't. Instead, he insists that *the gospel we preached* was received directly *as a revelation from Jesus Christ*. Paul explains that he really had very little contact with the apostles for the first part of his ministry. But when he finally did visit them to make sure his message wouldn't be contested everywhere he went, they affirmed his teaching and welcomed him as their partner. But even after that, Paul wasn't dependent on their endorsement. Once he publicly rebuked Cephas (Peter), one of the leading apostles, for backing away from their shared message.

After addressing the charges against himself, Paul proceeds to his main argument, which is that Gentiles who become followers of Jesus don't need to be circumcised or keep other key provisions of the law. He begins by asking the Galatians about their own experience. He points out that God sent them the Holy Spirit before they were even considering Jewish religious observances.

Paul then makes two different appeals to the story of Abraham in the Scriptures. First he notes that Abraham, the source of spiritual blessings for both Jews and Gentiles, *believed God, and, because of this, was held to be a just man*. This was 430 years before the law was given to Moses. God promised Abraham that *all the nations*, meaning Gentiles like the Galatians, would be blessed through him. The implications are that *those who take the way of faith receive the same blessing as Abraham*. The new worldwide family which had been promised to Abraham is created by faith in Messiah Jesus, not by keeping the law. The biblical drama had been pointing to this all along.

Paul explains that he's making his second appeal *as an allegory*, using characters and events in Abraham's story to represent spiritual realities. He observes that Abraham had two sons, but only one was to share in the inheritance. This was Isaac, the son born in freedom, who symbolizes being justified by faith. Ishmael, the other son, was born into slavery and represents *pretending to become righteous through the observance of the law*. If you really want to be included in the blessings that God promised to Abraham and his descendants, Paul tells the Galatians, stand firm in faith and *do not submit, again, to the yoke of slavery*, the law.

In the midst of these arguments, Paul breaks off twice to appeal directly to the Galatians on the basis of his relationship with them (*You had begun your race well, who, then, hindered you on the way?*). He's writing to people who once took care of him when he was ill. He cares about them deeply, and it grieves him to send them such a strongly-worded letter of correction.

Once he's established that Gentile believers don't need to be circumcised or follow the Jewish law, Paul has to address one more concern. If people don't have the law to restrain them, what's to keep them from running wild? He explains that the Holy Spirit lives inside the believers, giving them the power and the desire to live as God wishes. Instead of external restraint, there will be inner transformation. Paul concludes his main argument by describing what this transformation should look like. He describes the character qualities that make up the *fruit of the Spirit* and how these qualities should be lived out in the community of Jesus-followers.

Paul ends this letter, like some of his others, with a greeting in his own handwriting. This gives him the opportunity to repeat his main theme: *Let us no longer speak of the circumcised and of non-Jews, but of a new creation*.

| GALATIANS |

From Paul, an apostle sent, not by humans nor by human mediation, but by Christ Jesus, and by God the Father, who raised him from the dead;

I, and all the brothers and sisters who are with me, greet the churches in Galatia: may you receive grace and peace from God, our Father, and from Christ Jesus, our Lord.

He gave himself for our sins, to rescue us from this evil world, in fulfillment of the will of God the Father:

Glory to him for ever and ever. Amen.

I am surprised at how quickly you have abandoned God, who called you, according to the grace of Christ, and have gone to another gospel. Indeed, there is no other gospel, but some people, who are sowing confusion among you, want to turn the gospel of Christ upside down.

But even if we, ourselves, were giving you another gospel, different from the one we preached to you, or if it were an angel from heaven, I would say: let God's curse be on him! As I have said, I now say again: if anyone preaches the gospel in a way other than you received it, fire that one! Are we to please humans or obey God? Do you think that I try to please people? If I were still trying to please people, I would not be a servant of Christ.

Let me remind you, brothers and sisters, that the gospel we preached to you is not a human message, nor did I receive it from anyone, I was not taught of it; but it came to me, as a revelation from Christ Jesus. You have heard of my previous activity in the Jewish community; I furiously persecuted the Church of God and tried to destroy it. For I was more devoted to the Jewish religion than many fellow Jews of my age, and I defended the traditions of my ancestors more fanatically.

But one day, God called me, out of his great love, he, who had chosen me from my mother's womb; and he was pleased to reveal, in me, his Son, that I might make him known among the pagan nations. Then, I did not seek human advice nor did I go up to Jerusalem, to those who were apostles before me. I immediately went to Arabia, and from there, I returned, again, to Damascus. Later, after three years, I went up to Jerusalem to meet Cephas, and I stayed with him for fifteen days. But I did not see any other apostle except James, the Lord's brother. On writing this to you, I affirm before God that I am not lying.

After that, I went to Syria and Cilicia. The churches of Christ in Judea did not know me personally; they had only heard of me: "He, who once persecuted us, is now preaching the faith he tried to uproot." And they praised God because of me.

After fourteen years, I, again, went up to Jerusalem with Barnabas, and Titus came with us. Following a revelation, I went, to lay before them the gospel that I am preaching to the pagans. I had a private meeting with the leaders—lest I should be working, or have worked, in a wrong way. But they did not impose circumcision, not even on Titus who is Greek, and who was with me. But there were some intruders, and false brothers, who had gained access to watch over the way we live the freedom Christ, has given us. They would have us enslaved by the law, but we refused to yield, even for a moment; so that the truth of the gospel remain intact, for you.

The others, the more respectable leaders—it does not matter what they were before: God pays no attention to the status of a person—gave me no new instructions. They recognized that I have been entrusted to give the Good News to the pagan nations, just as Peter has been entrusted to give it to the Jews. In the same way that God made Peter the apostle of the Jews, he made me the apostle of the pagans.

James, Cephas and John acknowledged the graces God gave me. Those men, who were regarded as the pillars of the Church, stretched out their hand to me and Barnabas, as a sign of fellowship; we would go to the pagans, and they, to the Jews. We should only keep in mind, the poor among them. I have taken care to do this.

When, later, Cephas came to Antioch, I confronted him, since he deserved to be blamed. Before some of James' people arrived, he used to eat with non-Jewish people. But when they arrived, he withdrew, and did not mingle anymore with them, for fear of the Jewish group. The rest of the Jews followed him in this pretense, and even Barnabas was part of this insincerity. When I saw that they were not acting in line with the truth of the gospel, I said to Cephas publicly: If you, who are Jewish, agreed to live like the non-Jews, setting aside the Jewish customs, why do you, now, compel the non-Jews to live like Jews?

We are Jews by birth; we are not pagan sinners. Yet, we know that a person is justified, not by practicing the law, but by faith in Christ Jesus. So, we have believed in Christ Jesus, that we may receive true righteousness, from faith in Christ Jesus, and not from the practices of the law, because no one will be justified by the works of the law.

Now, if in our own effort to be justified in Christ, we, ourselves, have been found to be sinners, then Christ would be at the service of sin. Not so! But look: if we do away with something and then restore it, we admit we did wrong.

As for me, the very law brought me, to die to the law, that I may live for God. I am crucified with Christ. Do I live? It is no longer me; Christ lives in me. My life, in this body, is life through faith in the Son of God, who loved me and gave himself for me. In this way, I don't ignore the gift of God, for, if justification comes through the practice of the law, Christ would have died for nothing.

How foolish you are, Galatians! How could they bewitch you after Jesus Christ has been presented to you as crucified? I shall ask you only this: Did you receive the Spirit by the practice of the law, or by believing the message? How can you be such fools: you begin with the Spirit and end up with the flesh!

So, you have experienced all this in vain! Would that, it were not so! Did God give you the Spirit, and work miracles among you because of your observance of the law, or because you believed in his message? Remember Abraham: he believed God, and, because of this, was held to be a just man. Understand, then, that those who follow the way of faith are sons and daughters of Abraham.

The Scriptures foresaw that, by the way of faith, God would give true righteousness to the non-Jewish nations. For God's promise to Abraham was this: In you shall all the nations be blessed. So, now, those who take the way of faith receive the same blessing as Abraham, who believed; but those who rely on the practice of the law are under a curse, for it is written: Cursed is everyone who does not always fulfill everything written in the law.

It is plainly written that no one becomes righteous in God's way, by the law: by faith the righteous shall live. Yet the law gives no place to faith, for according to it: the one who fulfills the commandments shall have life through them.

Now Christ rescued us from the curse of the law, by becoming cursed himself, for our sake, as it is written: there is a curse on everyone who is hanged on a tree. So the blessing granted to Abraham, reached the pagan nations in, and, with Christ, and we received the promised Spirit, through faith.

Brothers, listen to this comparison. When anyone has made his will in the prescribed form, no one can annul it or add anything to it. Well now, what God promised Abraham was for his descendant. Scripture does not say: for the descendants, as if they were many. It means only one: this will be for your descendant, and this is Christ. Now I say this: if God has made a testament in due form, it cannot be annulled by the law, which came four hundred and thirty years later; God's promise cannot be canceled. But if we now inherit for keeping the law, it is not because of the promise. Yet, that promise was God's gift to Abraham.

Why then, the law? It was added because of transgressions; but was only valid until the descendant would come, to whom the promise had been made; and it was ordained through angels by a mediator. A mediator means that there are parties, and God is one.

Does the law, then, compete with the promises of God? Not at all! Only if we had been given a law capable of raising life, could righteousness be the fruit of the law. But the Scriptures have declared, that we are all prisoners of sin. So, the only way to receive God's promise is to believe in Jesus Christ.

Before the time of faith had come, the law confined us, and kept us in custody, until the time in which faith would show up. The law, then, was serving as a slave, to look after us until Christ came, so that we might be justified by faith. With the coming of faith, we are no longer submitted to this guidance.

Now, in Christ Jesus, all of you are sons and daughters of God, through faith. All of you, who were given to Christ through Baptism, have put on Christ. Here, there is no longer any difference between Jew or Greek, or between slave or freed, or between man and woman: but all of you are one, in Christ Jesus. And because you belong to Christ, you are of Abraham's race and you are to in

But listen, as long as the heir is a child, he does not differ at all from a slave, although he is owner of everything. He is subject to those who care for him, and who are entrusted with his affairs, until the time set by his father comes. In the same way, we, as children, were first subjected to the created forces that govern the world. But when the fullness of time came, God sent his Son. He came, born of woman, and subject to the law, in order to redeem the subjects of the law, that we might receive adoption, as children of God. And because you are children, God has sent into your hearts, the spirit of his Son, who cries out: Abba! that is, Father!

You, yourself, are no longer a slave, but a son or daughter, and yours is the inheritance, by God's grace.

When you did not know God, you served those who are not gods. But now that you have known God—or, rather, he has known you—how can you turn back to weak and impoverished created things? Do you want to be enslaved again? Will you again observe this and that day, and the new moon, and this period and that year...? I fear I may have wasted my time with you.

I implore you, dearly beloved, do as I do, just as I became like you. You have not offended me in anything. Remember, that it was an illness that first gave me the opportunity to announce the gospel to you. Although my illness was a trial to you, you did not despise or reject me, but received me, as an angel of God, as Christ Jesus.

Where is this bliss? For I can testify, that you would have even plucked out your eyes to give them to me. But now, have I become your enemy for telling you the truth?

Those who show consideration to you are not sincere; they want to separate you from me, so that you may show interest in them. Would, that you were surrounded with sincere care at all times, and not only from me when I am with you!

My children! I still suffer the pains of childbirth, until Christ is formed in you. How I wish I could be there with you, at this moment, and find the right way of talking to you.

Tell me, you who desire to submit yourselves to the law, did you listen to it? It says, that Abraham had two sons, one by a slave woman, the other by the free woman, his wife. The son of the slave woman was born in the ordinary way; but the son of the free woman was born in fulfillment of God's promise.

Here we have an allegory and the figures of two Covenants. The first is the one from Mount Sinai, represented through Hagar: her children have slavery for their lot. We know that Hagar was from Mount Sinai in Arabia: she stands for the present city of Jerusalem, which is in slavery with her children.

But the Jerusalem above, who is our mother, is free. And Scripture says of her:

> Rejoice, barren woman
> without children,
>
> break forth in shouts of joy,
> you who do not know the pains of childbirth,
>
> for many shall be the children of the forsaken mother,
> more than of the married woman.

You, dearly beloved, are children of the promise, like Isaac. But, as at that time, the child born according to the flesh persecuted Isaac, who was born according to the spirit, so is it now. And what does Scripture say? Cast out the slave woman and her son, for the son of the slave cannot share the inheritance with the son of the free woman.

Brethren, we are not children of the slave woman, but of the free woman.

Christ freed us, to make us really free. So remain firm, and do not submit, again, to the yoke of slavery. I, Paul, say this to you: if you receive circumcision, Christ can no longer help you. Once more, I say, to whoever receives circumcision: you are now bound to keep the whole law. All you, who pretend to become righteous through the observance of the law, have separated yourselves from Christ, and have fallen away from grace.

As for us, through the Spirit and faith, we eagerly wait for the hope of righteousness. In Christ Jesus, it is irrelevant, whether we be circumcised or not; what matters is, faith, working through love.

You had begun your race well, who, then, hindered you on the way? Why did you stop obeying the truth? This was not in obedience to God, who calls you: in fact, a little leaven is affecting the whole of you. I am personally convinced, that you will not go astray, but the one who confuses you, whoever he may be, shall receive punishment.

I, myself, brothers, could I not preach circumcision? Then, I would no longer be persecuted. But where would be the scandal of the cross? Would, that those who confuse would castrate themselves!

You, brothers and sisters, were called to enjoy freedom; I am not speaking of that freedom which gives free rein to the desires of the flesh, but of that which makes you slaves of one another through love. For the whole law is summed up in this sentence: You shall love your neighbor as yourself. But if you bite and tear each other to pieces, be careful lest you all perish.

Therefore, I say to you: walk according to the Spirit and do not give way to the desires of the flesh! For the desires of the flesh war against the Spirit, and the desires of the Spirit are opposed to the flesh. Both are in conflict with each other, so that you cannot do everything you would like. But when you are led by the Spirit you are not under the law.

You know what comes from the flesh: fornication, impurity and shamelessness, idol worship and sorcery, hatred, jealousy and violence, anger, ambition, division, factions, and envy, drunkenness, orgies and the like. I again say to you what I have already said: those who do these things shall not inherit the kingdom of God.

But the fruit of the Spirit is charity, joy and peace, patience, understanding of others, kindness and fidelity, gentleness and self-control. For such things there is no law or punishment. Those who belong to Christ have crucified the flesh with its vices and desires.

If we live by the Spirit, let us live in a spiritual way. Let us not be conceited; let there be no rivalry or envy of one another.

Brethren, in the event of someone falling into a sin, you, who are spiritual, shall set him aright with the spirit of kindness. Take care; for you, too, may be tempted. Carry each other's burdens and so fulfill the law of Christ. If anyone thinks he is something, when in fact he is nothing, he deceives himself. Let each one examine his own conduct and boast for himself, if he wants to do so, but not before others. In this, let each one carry his own things.

He who receives the teaching of the word ought to share the good things he has with the one who instructs him. Do not be fooled. God cannot be deceived. You reap what you sow. The person who sows for the benefit of his own flesh shall reap corruption and death from the flesh. He who sows in the spirit shall reap eternal life from the Spirit. Let us do good without being discouraged; in due time, we shall reap the reward of our constancy. So, while there is time, let us do good to all, and especially to our family in the faith.

See these large letters I use when I write to you in my own hand! Those who are most anxious to put on a good show in life, are trying to persuade you to be circumcised. The only reason they do this, is to avoid being persecuted for the cross of Christ. Not for being circumcised do they observe the law: what interests them is the external rite. What a boast for them, if they had you circumcised!

For me, I do not wish to take pride in anything, except in the cross of Christ Jesus, our Lord. Through him, the world has been crucified to me, and I to the world.

Let us no longer speak of the circumcised and of non-Jews, but of a new creation. Let those who live according to this rule receive peace and mercy: they are the Israel of God! Let no one trouble me any longer: for my part, I bear in my body the marks of Jesus.

May the grace of Christ Jesus our Lord be with your spirit, brothers and sisters. Amen.

INVITATION TO
ROMANS

The book of Acts reports how all the Jews and Greeks who lived in the province of Asia heard the word of the Lord during the two years Paul spent in Ephesus, the capital and most influential city in that province (see p. 84). Since Paul and others had previously preached in the surrounding regions, the good news about Jesus had now been proclaimed throughout the entire eastern part of the Roman Empire. Paul understood that his primary mission was to bring the message about Jesus to places where it had never been heard before. So he began to make plans to travel to the western part of the empire.

Paul knew there was already a strong community of Jesus-followers in Rome that could provide a base of operations for his western trip. While he was in Corinth arranging for the delivery of the collection (around AD 57 or 58), he wrote to them, explaining:

> I have been very careful, however, and I am proud of this, not to preach in places where Christ is already known, and not to build upon foundations laid by others ... But, now, there is no more place for me in these regions, and, as I have wanted for so long, to go and see you, I hope to visit you, when I go to Spain. Then, you could help me go to that nation, once I have fully enjoyed your company.

But Paul had to do more than just ask for assistance, because the Roman church wasn't necessarily willing to help him. Even though it was made up of both Jews and Gentiles, its particular focus was on bringing the good news about Jesus to Jews. But Paul was well known as an apostle to the Gentiles. And so he had to make the case for why this church should support him. A woman named Phoebe, a leader in the church of Cenchreae (a small city near Corinth), was planning to travel to Rome, and this gave Paul the opportunity to send a letter with her asking the Romans to support his western journey.

Romans is the longest and most complex of Paul's letters, but it follows the same general pattern as the others. It has an *opening section* where Paul introduces himself and his key message, and a *closing section* where he explains his travel plans and sends greetings. In between, the *main body* of the letter has two basic parts. Like many of Paul's other letters, it begins with a *teaching section*. It then ends with a *practical section* that describes how this teaching should be followed in everyday life. A short song of praise to God comes in between these two parts and marks the division between them.

Opening Section: Introduction of Paul and His Message (p. 163)
Main Body: (pp. 163–181)
   Teaching Section (pp. 163–177)
    (Song of Praise) (p. 177–178)
   Practical Section (pp. 178–181)
Closing Section: Travel Plans and Greetings (pp. 181–183)

Paul uses his opening self-introduction and thanksgiving to stress his main theme, namely, that *this Good News; it is God's power, saving those who believe, first, the Jews, and then, the Greeks*. Paul proclaims boldly that he is an apostle, set apart to make the royal announcement about the Lordship of Jesus to the world, even to those in the capital city of the Roman Empire. Paul is calling the Gentiles to faith and obedience to the one true God. God's plan for the world has been revealed in the life, death and resurrection of a descendant of the renowned Jewish king David: Jesus the Messiah.

The teaching section itself is divided into three parts by the way Paul alternates between two approaches. He develops his argument for a time, and then he takes a step back to address anticipated questions and objections. This pattern is repeated three times. Paul always answers objections emphatically: "Of course not!" "By no means!" "Certainly not!" But he isn't just looking back on the argument he's developed and defending it. He's actually using his responses to keep advancing the argument itself.

The flow of this part of the letter echoes the themes of the ancient Jewish story of slavery and rescue. When Israel (Abraham's descendants) fell into captivity in Egypt, God came to save them. He gave them his law and brought them through the wilderness and into their own promised land as an inheritance. Now Paul explains that humanity is in slavery due to the entrance of sin and death to the world. But God has come to rescue both Jews and Gentiles through the death and resurrection of Jesus. A new worldwide family is being created. Baptism into Jesus breaks the power of evil and brings freedom. The Holy Spirit leads the way into this new life that will be complete in a new inheritance—a redeemed creation.

Next Paul faces the difficult question of why many within Israel itself fail to believe in Jesus as the Messiah. Within the larger purposes of God, it turns out that Israel's rejection of Jesus has actually brought life to the rest of the world. But even now the offer of this life through the Messiah is held out to the Jews.

Having explained and defended his teaching and mission, Paul concludes the main body of the letter with a practical section. He challenges the Romans to live the kind of new life, both individually and in community, that shows they've been restored to fellowship with God through Jesus Christ. *The night is almost over; and day is at hand*—so it is time to *discard, therefore, everything that belongs to darkness*.

Paul ends this long letter by showing that the Jewish sacred writings always looked ahead to the inclusion of the Gentiles. He then shares his travel plans, formally asks for the church's support, and passes along greetings to and from mutual friends. He closes with a final wish that all the Gentiles might come to *the faith proclaimed to them*, exactly the phrase he uses at the start of this letter to the assembly of Jesus-followers living directly under the shadow of Caesar.

| ROMANS |

From Paul, a servant of Jesus Christ, an apostle, called and set apart for God's Good News, the very promises he foretold through his prophets in the sacred Scriptures, regarding his Son, who was born in the flesh a descendant of David, and has been recognized as the Son of God, endowed with Power, upon rising from the dead, through the Holy Spirit.

Through him, Jesus Christ, our Lord, and for the sake of his name, we received grace, and mission in all the nations, for them to accept the faith.

All of you, the elected of Christ, are part of them, you, the beloved of God in Rome, called to be holy:

May God our Father, and the Lord Jesus Christ, give you grace and peace.

First of all, I give thanks to my God, through Jesus Christ, for all of you, because your faith is spoken of all over the world. And God, whom I serve in spirit, by announcing the Good News of his Son, is my witness, that I remember you in my prayers at all times. I pray constantly that, if it is his will, he make it possible for me to visit you. I long to see you, and share some spiritual blessings with you, to strengthen you. In that way, we will encourage each other, by sharing our common faith.

You must know, brothers and sisters, that, many times, I have made plans to go to you, but, till now, I have been prevented. I would like to harvest some fruits among you, as I have done among other nations. Whether Greeks or foreigners, cultured or ignorant, I feel under obligation to all. Hence, my eagerness to proclaim the gospel also to you, who are in Rome.

For I am not ashamed at all, of this Good News; it is God's power, saving those who believe, first, the Jews, and then, the Greeks. This Good News shows us the saving justice of God; a justice that saves, exclusively by faith, as the Scripture says: The upright one shall live by faith.

For the wrath of God is being revealed from heaven, against all ungodliness, and injustice, of those who have silenced the truth by their wicked ways. For everything that could have been known about God, was clear to them: God himself made it plain. Because his invisible attributes—his everlasting power and divinity—are made visible to reason, by means of his works, since the creation of the world.

So they have no excuse, for they knew God, and did not glorify him, as was fitting; nor did they give thanks to him. On the contrary, they lost themselves in their reasoning, and darkness filled their minds.

Believing themselves wise, they became foolish: they exchanged the glory of the immortal God, for the likes of mortal human beings, birds, animals and reptiles. Because of this, God gave them up to their inner cravings; they did shameful things and dishonored their bodies.

They exchanged God's truth for a lie; they honored and worshiped created things, instead of the Creator, to whom be praise for ever, Amen! Because of that, God gave them up to shameful passions: their women exchanged natural sexual relations for unnatural ones. Similarly, the men, giving up natural sexual relations with women, were lustful of each other: they did, men with men, shameful things, bringing upon themselves the punishment they deserve for their wickedness. And since they did not think that God was worth knowing, he gave them up to their senseless minds, so that they committed all kinds of obscenities.

And so, they are full of injustice, perversity, greed, evil; they are full of jealousy, murder, strife, deceit, bad will and gossip. They commit calumny, offend God, are haughty; they are proud, liars, clever in doing evil. They are rebellious toward their parents, senseless, disloyal, cold-hearted and merciless. They know of God's judgment, which, declares worthy of death, anyone living in this way; yet, not only do they do all these things, they even applaud anyone who does the same.

Therefore, you have no excuse, whoever you are, if you are able to judge others. For, in judging your neighbor, you condemn yourself, for you practice what you are judging. We know, that the condemnation of God will justly reach those who commit these things, and do you think that by condemning others, you will escape from the judgment of God, you, who are doing the same?

This would be taking advantage of God, and his infinite goodness, patience and understanding; and not to realize that, his goodness is in order to lead you to conversion. If your heart becomes hard and you refuse to change, then you are storing for yourself a great punishment on the day of judgment, when God will appear as just judge.

He will give each one his due, according to his actions. He will give everlasting life to those who seek glory, honor and immortality, and persevere in doing good. But anger and vengeance will be the lot of those who do not serve truth, but injustice. There will be suffering and anguish, for everyone committing evil, first the Jew, then the Greek. But God will give glory, honor and peace to whoever does good, first, the Jew, then, the Greek, because one is not different from the other before God.

Those, who, without knowing the law, committed sin, will perish without the law; and whoever committed sin knowing the law, will be judged by that law. What makes us righteous before God is not hearing the law, but obeying it. When the non-Jews, who do not have the law, practice naturally, what the law commands, they are giving themselves a law, showing that the commandments of the law are engraved in their minds. Their conscience, speaking within them also shows it, when they condemn or approve their actions. The same is to happen on the day when God, according to my gospel, will judge people's secret actions, in the person of Jesus Christ.

But, suppose you call yourself a Jew: you have the law as foundation, and feel proud of your God. You know the will of God, and the law teaches you to distinguish what is better, and, so, you believe you are the guide for the blind, light in darkness, a corrector of the foolish, and instructor of the ignorant, because you possess, in the law, the formulation of true knowledge. Well, then, you who teach others, why don't you teach yourself? If you say that one must not steal, why do you steal? You say, one must not commit adultery, yet you commit it! You say, you hate idols, but you steal into their temples! You feel proud of the law, yet, you do not obey it, and you dishonor your God. In fact, as the Scripture says, the other nations despise the name of God because of you.

Circumcision is of value to you, if you obey the law; but if you do not obey, it is as if you were not circumcised. On the contrary, if those who are uncircumcised, obey the commandments of the law, do you not think that, in spite of them being pagans, they make themselves like the circumcised? The one who obeys the law, without being marked in his body with circumcision, will judge you, who have been marked with circumcision, and who have the law, which you do not obey. For external things do not make a true Jew, nor is real circumcision that which is marked on the body. A Jew must be so interiorly; the heart's circumcision belongs to spirit, and not to a written law; he who lives in this way will be praised, not by people, but by God.

Then, what is the advantage of being a Jew? And what is the use of circumcision? It is important from any point of view. In the first place, it was to the Jews that God entrusted his word.

Well now, if some of them were not faithful, will their unfaithfulness do away with the faithfulness of God? Of course not! Rather, it will be proved, that God is truthful, every human a liar, as the Scripture says:

> it will be proved,
> that your words are true and you will be the winner,
> if they want to judge you.

If our wickedness shows God to be just, would it be right to say that God is unjust when he gets angry and punishes us? (I speak in a human way.)

– Not at all because, otherwise, how could God judge the world?

– But if my lie makes the truth of God more evident, thus increasing his glory, is it correct to call me a sinner?

– Then, your only choice would be to sin, so that good may come of it. Some slanderers say that this is my teaching, but they will have to answer for those words.

Do we have, then, any advantage? Not really. For we have just demonstrated that all, Jews and non-Jews, are under the power of sin, as the Scripture says:

> Nobody is good, not even one,
> no one understands,
> no one looks for God.
>
> All have gone astray
> and have become base.
>
> There is no one doing what is good,
> not even one.
>
> Their throats are open tombs,
> their words deceit.
>
> Their lips hide the poison of vipers,
> from their mouths come bitter curses.
>
> They run to where they can shed blood,
> leaving behind ruin and misery.
>
> They do not know the way of peace.
> There is no fear of God before their eyes.

Now, we know, that whatever the Scripture says, it is said for the people of the law, that is for the Jews. Let all be silent, then, and recognize, that the whole world is guilty before God. Still more: no mortal will be worthy, before God, by performing the demands of the law. What comes from the law is the consciousness of sin.

But, now it has been revealed, altogether apart from the law, as it was already foretold in the law and the prophets: God makes us righteous by means of faith in Jesus Christ, and this is applied to all who believe, without distinction of persons. Because all have sinned and all fall short of the glory of God; and all are graciously forgiven and made righteous, through the redemption effected in Christ Jesus. For God has given him to be the victim, whose blood obtains us forgiveness, through faith.

So God shows us, how he makes us righteous. Past sins are forgiven, which God overlooked till now. For, now, he wants to reveal his way of righteousness: how he is just, and how he makes us righteous, through faith in Jesus.

Then, what becomes of our pride? It is excluded. How? Not through the law and its observances, but through another law, which is faith. For we hold, that people are in God's grace, by faith, and not because of all the things ordered by the law. Otherwise, God would be the God of the Jews; but is he not God of pagan nations as well? Of course he is, for there is only one God, and he will save, by faith, the circumcised Jews, as well as the uncircumcised nations. Do we, then, deny the value of the law, because of what we say of faith? Of course not; rather, we place the Law in its proper place.

Let us consider Abraham, our father in the flesh. What has he found? If Abraham attained righteousness because of his deeds, he could be proud. But he cannot be this before God; because Scripture says: Abraham believed God, who took it into account, and held him to be a just man.

Now, when someone does a work, salary is not given as a favor, but as a debt that is paid. Here, on the contrary, someone who has no deeds to show, but believes in him, who makes sinners righteous before him: such faith is taken into account, and that person is held as righteous. David congratulates, in this way, those who become righteous, by the favor of God, and not by their actions:

> Blessed are those
> whose sins are forgiven
> and whose offenses are forgotten;
>
> blessed the one,
> whose sin God does not take into account!

Is this blessing only for the circumcised, or is it also for the uncircumcised? We have just said, that, because of his faith, Abraham was made a just man, but when did this happen? After Abraham was circumcised, or before? Not after, but before. He received the rite of circumcision, as a sign of the righteousness given him, through faith, when he was still uncircumcised, that he might be the father of all those uncircumcised who come to faith and are made just. And, he was to be the father of the Jews, provided that, besides being circumcised, they also imitate the faith Abraham showed before being circumcised.

If God promised Abraham, or rather his descendants, that the world would belong to him, this was not because of his obeying the law, but because he was just, and a friend of God, through faith. If, now, the promise is kept for those who rely on the law, then faith has no power, and nothing is left of the promise. For it is proper of the law, to bring punishment, and it is only when there is no law, that it is possible to live without breaking the law.

For that reason, faith is the way, and all is given, by grace; and the promises of Abraham are fulfilled for all his descendants, not only for his children according to the law, but, also, for all the others, who have believed.

Abraham is the father of all of us, as it is written: I will make you the father of many nations. He is our father, in the eyes of Him, who gives life to the dead, and calls into existence, what does not yet exist, for this is the God in whom he believed.

Abraham believed, and hoped against all expectation, thus, becoming the father of many nations, as he had been told: See how many will be your descendants. He did not doubt, although his body could no longer give life—he was about a hundred years old—and, in spite of his wife, Sarah, being unable to have children. He did not doubt, nor did he distrust the promise of God, and, by being strong in faith, he gave glory to God: he was convinced, that, He who had given the promise, had power to fulfill it.

This was taken into account, for him to attain righteousness. This was taken into account: these words of Scripture are not only for him, but for us, too, because we believe in him, who raised Jesus, our Lord, from among the dead, he, who was delivered for our sins, and raised to life, for us to receive true righteousness.

By faith, we have received true righteousness, and we are at peace with God, through Jesus Christ, our Lord. Through him, we obtain this favor, in which we remain, and we even boast to expect the glory of God.

Not only that, we also boast even in trials, knowing that trials produce patience, from patience comes merit; merit is the source of hope, and hope does not disappoint us, because the Holy Spirit has been given to us, pouring into our hearts the love of God.

Consider, moreover, the time that Christ died for us: when we were still helpless and unable to do anything. Few would accept to die for an upright person; although, for a very good person, perhaps someone would dare to die. But see how God manifested his love for us: while we were still sinners, Christ died for us; and we have become just, through his blood. With much more reason now he will save us from any condemnation. Once enemies, we have been reconciled with God through the death of his Son; with much more reason, now we may be saved, through his life. Not only that, but we even boast in God because of Christ Jesus, our Lord, through whom we have been reconciled.

Therefore, sin entered the world through one man; and through sin, death; and later on, death spread to all humankind, because all sinned. As long as there was no law, they could not speak of disobedience, but sin was already in the world. This is why, from Adam to Moses, death reigned among them, although their sin was not disobedience, as in Adam's case—this was not the true Adam, but foretold the other, who was to come.

Such has been the fall, but God's gift goes far beyond. All died, because of the fault of one man, but how much more does the grace of God spread, when the gift he granted, reaches all, from this unique man, Jesus Christ. Again, there is no comparison between the gift, and the offense of one man. The disobedience that brought condemnation was of one sinner, whereas the grace of God brings forgiveness to a world of sinners. If death reigned through the disobedience of one and only one person, how much more, will there be a reign of life, for those who receive the grace, and the gift of true righteousness, through the one person, Jesus Christ.

Just as one transgression brought sentence of death to all, so, too, one man's good act has brought justification and light to all; and, as the disobedience of only one, made all sinners, so the obedience of one person, allowed all to be made just and holy.

The law itself, introduced later on, caused sin to increase; but where sin increased, grace abounded all the more, and, as sin caused death to reign, so grace will reign, in its own time, and, after making us just, and friends of God, will bring us to eternal life, through Jesus Christ, our Lord.

Then, what shall we say? Shall we keep on sinning, so that grace may come more abundantly? Can we live, again, in sin? Of course not: we are now dead regarding sin.

Don't you know, that in baptism, which unites us to Christ, we are all baptized and plunged into his death? By this baptism in his death, we were buried with Christ and, as Christ was raised from among the dead by the glory of the Father, we begin walking in a new life. If we have been joined to him by dying a death like his, so shall we be, by a resurrection like his.

We know, that our old self was crucified with Christ, so as to destroy what of us was sin, so that, we may no longer serve sin—if we are dead, we are no longer in debt to sin. But, if we have died with Christ, we believe we will also live with him. We know, that Christ, once risen from the dead, will not die again, and death has no more dominion over him. For, by dying, he is dead to sin, once and for all, and, now, the life that he lives, is life with God.

So you, too, must consider yourselves dead to sin, and alive to God, in Christ Jesus. Do not allow sin any control over your mortal bodies; do not submit yourselves to its evil inclinations, and do not give your members over to sin, as instruments to do evil. On the contrary, offer yourselves, as persons returned from death to life, and let the members of your body be as holy instruments, at the service of God. Sin will not lord it over you again, for you are not under the law, but under grace.

I ask again: are we to sin because we are not under the law, but under grace? Certainly not. If you have given yourselves up to someone as his slave, you are to obey the one who commands you, aren't you? Now, with sin, you go to death, and by accepting faith, you go the right way. Let us give thanks to God, for, after having sin as your master, you have been given to another, that is, to the doctrine of faith, to which you listen willingly. And being free from sin, you began to serve true righteousness—you see, that I speak in a very human way, taking into account that you are not fully mature.

There was a time, when you let your members be slaves of impurity and disorder, walking in the way of sin; convert them, now, into servants of righteousness, to the point of becoming holy.

When you were slaves of sin, you did not feel under obligation to righteousness, but what were the fruits of those actions, of which you are now ashamed? Such things bring death. Now, however, you have been freed from sin and serve God. You are bearing fruit, and growing in holiness, and the result will be life everlasting. So, on one side is sin: its reward, death; on the other side, is God: He gives us, by grace, life everlasting, in Christ Jesus, our Lord.

You, my friends, understand law. The law has power only while a person is alive. The married woman, for example, is bound, by law, to her husband while he is alive; but if he dies, she is free from her obligations as a wife. If she gives herself to another, while her husband is alive, she will be an adulteress; but once the husband dies, she is free, and if she gives herself to another man, she is not an adulteress.

It was the same with you, brothers and sisters: you have died to the law with the person of Christ, and you belong to another, who has risen from among the dead, so that we may produce fruit for God. When we lived as humans used to do, the law stirred up the desires for all that is sin, and they worked in our bodies with fruits of death. But we have died to what was holding us; we are freed from the law, and no longer serve a written law—which was the old; with the spirit, we are in the new.

Then, shall we say that the law is part of sin? Of course not! However, I would not have known sin, had it not been for the law. I would not be aware of greed, if the law did not tell me: Do not covet. Sin took advantage of the commandment, to stir in me all kinds of greed; whereas, without a law, sin lies dead.

First, there was no law and I lived. Then the commandment came, and gave life to sin, and I died. It happened, that the law of life had brought me death. Sin took advantage of the commandment. It lured me, and killed me, through the commandment.

But the law itself is holy, just and good. Is it possible, that something good, brings death to me? Of course not. This comes from sin, that may be seen as sin, when it takes advantage of something good, to kill: the commandment let sin appear fully sinful.

We know, that the law is spiritual; as for me, I am flesh, and have been sold to sin. I cannot explain what is happening to me, because I do not do what I want, but, on the contrary, the very things I hate. Well then, if I do the evil I do not want to do, I agree, that the law is good; but, in this case, I am not the one striving toward evil, but it is sin, living in me. I know, that what is right, does not abide in me, I mean, in my flesh. I can want to do what is right, but I am unable to do it. In fact, I do not do the good I want, but the evil I hate. Therefore, if I do what I do not want to do, I am not the one striving toward evil, but sin, which is in me.

I discover, then, this reality: though I wish to do what is right, the evil within me asserts itself first. My inmost self, agrees and rejoices with the law of God, but I notice in my body, another law, challenging the law of the spirit, and delivering me, as a slave to the law of sin, written in my members. Alas, for me! Who will free me from this being, which is only death? Let us give thanks to God, through Jesus Christ, our Lord!

So, with my conscience, I am a servant of the law of God, and with my mortal body, I serve the law of sin.

This contradiction no longer exists for those who are in Jesus Christ. For, in Jesus Christ, the law of the spirit of life has set me free from the law of sin and death. The law was without effect, because flesh was not responding. Then God, planning to destroy sin, sent his own Son, in the likeness of those subject to the sinful human condition; by doing this, he condemned the sin, in this human condition. Since then, the perfection intended by the law would be fulfilled, in those not walking in the way of the flesh, but in the way of the spirit.

Those walking according to the flesh tend toward what is flesh; those led by the spirit, to what is spirit. Flesh tends toward death, while spirit aims at life and peace. What the flesh seeks is against God: it does not agree, it cannot even submit to the law of God. So, those walking according to the flesh cannot please God.

Yet, your existence is not in the flesh, but in the spirit, because the

Spirit of God is within you. If you did not have the Spirit of Christ, you would not belong to him. But Christ is within you; though the body is branded by death, as a consequence of sin, the spirit is life and holiness. And, if the Spirit of him, who raised Jesus from the dead, is within you, he, who raised Jesus Christ from among the dead, will also give life to your mortal bodies. Yes, he will do it, through his Spirit, who dwells within you.

Then, brothers, let us leave the flesh and no longer live according to it. If not, we will die. Rather, walking in the spirit, let us put to death the body's deeds, so that we may live.

All those who walk in the Spirit of God are sons and daughters of God. Then, no more fear: you did not receive a spirit of slavery, but the spirit that makes you sons and daughters, and every time, we cry, "Abba! (this is Dad!) Father!" the Spirit assures our spirit, that we are sons and daughters of God. If we are children, we are heirs, too. Ours will be the inheritance of God, and we will share it with Christ; for, if we now suffer with him, we will also share glory with him.

I consider, that the suffering of our present life cannot be compared with the glory that will be revealed, and given to us. All creation is eagerly expecting the birth, in glory, of the children of God. For, if now, the created world was unable to attain its purpose, this did not come from itself, but from the one who subjected it. But it is not without hope; for even the created world, will be freed from this fate of death, and share the freedom and glory of the children of God.

We know, that the whole creation groans and suffers the pangs of birth. Not creation alone, but even ourselves; although the Spirit was given to us, as a foretaste of what we are to receive, we groan in our innermost being, eagerly awaiting the day, when God will give us full rights, and rescue our bodies as well.

In hope, we already have salvation. But, if we saw what we hoped for, there would no longer be hope: how can you hope for what is already seen? So, we hope for what we do not see, and we will receive it, through patient hope.

Likewise, the Spirit helps us in our weakness; for we do not know how to pray as we ought, but that very Spirit intercedes for us, without words, as if with groans. And he, who sees inner secrets, knows the desires of the Spirit, for he asks for the holy ones, what is pleasing to God.

We know that in everything, God works for the good of those who love him, whom he has called, according to his plan. Those whom he knew beforehand, he has also predestined, to be like his Son, similar to him, so, that, he may be the Firstborn among many brothers and sisters. And so, those whom God predestined, he called; and those whom he called, he makes righteous; and to those whom he makes righteous, he will give his glory.

What shall we say after this? If God is with us, who shall be against us? If he did not spare his own Son, but gave him up for us all, how will he not give us all things with him? Who shall accuse those chosen by God: He takes away their guilt. Who will dare to condemn them? Christ, who died, and better still, rose, and is seated at the right hand of God, interceding for us?

Who shall separate us from the love of Christ? Will it be trials, or anguish, persecution or hunger, lack of clothing, or dangers or sword? As the Scripture says:

> For your sake, we are being killed all day long;
> they treat us like sheep to be slaughtered.

No, in all of this, we are more than conquerors, thanks to him, who has loved us. I am certain, that neither death nor life, neither angels nor spiritual powers, neither the present nor the future, nor cosmic powers, were they from heaven, or from the deep world below, nor any creature whatsoever, will separate us from the love of God, which we have, in Jesus Christ, our Lord.

I tell you, sincerely, in Christ, and my conscience assures me in the Holy Spirit, that I am not lying: I have great sadness and constant anguish for the Jews. I would even desire, that, I myself, suffer the curse of being cut off from Christ, instead of my brethren: I mean, my own people, my kin. They are Israelites, whom God adopted, and on them, rests his glory. Theirs, are the Covenants, the law, the worship and the promises of God. They are descendants of the patriarchs, and from their race, Christ was born, he, who, as God, is above all distinctions. Blessed be He forever and ever: Amen!

We cannot say that the promise of God has failed. For not all Israelites belong to Israel. And not because they are of the race of Abraham, are they all his children, for it was said to him: The children of Isaac will be called your descendants. This means, that the children of God are not identified with the race of Abraham, but only with the children born to him, because of the promise of God. To such a promise, this text refers: I shall return about this time, and Sarah will have a son. And, listen: Rebecca, the wife of our father Isaac, became pregnant, and, before the twins were born, or had done anything, right or wrong, in order that God's purpose of election might continue, not on the merits, but of who is called, she was told: The elder will serve the younger, as the Scripture says: I chose Jacob and rejected Esau.

Shall we say, that God is unjust? Of course not. However, God said to Moses:

> I shall forgive whom I forgive,
> and have pity on whom I have pity.

So, what is important is, not that we worry or hurry, but that God has compassion.

And he says in Scripture, to Pharaoh: I made you, Pharaoh, to show my power in you, and for the whole world to know my name. And so, God takes pity on whom he wishes, and hardens the heart of whomsoever he wishes.

Maybe you say: "Why, then, does God complain, if it is impossible to evade his decision?" But you, my friend, who are you, to call God to account? Should the clay pot say to its maker: Why did you make me like this? Is it not up to the potter, to make from the same clay, a vessel for beauty, and a vessel for menial use?

Thus, God endures, very patiently, vessels that deserve his wrath, fit to be broken, and through them, he wants to show his wrath, and the extent of his power. But, he also wants to show the riches of his glory in others, in vessels of mercy, prepared for glory. And he called us, not only from among the Jews, but from among the pagans, too, as he said, through the prophet Hosea:

> I will call "my people," those that were not my people,
> and "my beloved," the one who was not beloved.

> And in the same place, where they were told,
> "You are not my people,"
> they will be called children of the living God.

With regard to Israel, Isaiah proclaims:

> Even if the Israelites are as numerous as the sand of the sea,
> only a few will be saved.
> This is a matter that the Lord will settle in Israel,
> without fail or delay.

Isaiah also announced:

> If the Almighty Lord had not left us some descendants,
> we would have become like Sodom and similar to Gomorrah.

What are we saying, then? That the pagans, who were not aiming at true righteousness, found it (I speak of righteousness through faith); while Israel, striving to observe a law of righteousness, lost the purpose of the law.

Why? Because they relied on the observance of the law, not on faith. And they stumbled over the stumbling stone (Christ), as it was said:

> Look, I am laying in Zion a stone, that will make people stumble,
> a rock, that will make them fall;
> but whoever relies on him will not be deceived.

My brothers and sisters, I wish, with all my heart, that the Jews be saved, and I pray to God for them. I can testify, that they are zealous for God, but this is not the way. They don't know God's way of righteousness, and they try to achieve their own righteousness: this is why they did not enter God's way of righteousness. For Christ is the aim of the law, and it is, then, that the believer reaches this righteousness.

Moses, indeed, speaks of becoming just through the law; he writes: The one who obeys the law will find life through it. But the righteousness coming from the faith says, instead: Do not say in your heart: Who will go up to heaven? (because, in fact, Christ came down from there) or who will go down to the world below? (because, in fact, Christ came up, from among the dead). True righteousness, coming from faith, also says: The word of God is near you, on your lips and in your hearts. This is the message that we preach, and this is faith.

You are saved, if you confess with your lips that Jesus is Lord, and, in your heart, you believe that God raised him from the dead. By believing from the heart, you obtain true righteousness; by confessing the faith with your lips, you are saved. For Scripture says: No one who believes in him will be ashamed. Here, there is no distinction between Jew and Greek; all have the same Lord, who is very generous with whoever calls on him. Truly, all who call upon the name of the Lord will be saved.

But how can they call upon the name of the Lord without having believed in him? And how can they believe in him, without having first heard about him? And how will they hear about him, if no one preaches about him? And how will they preach about him, if no one sends them? As Scripture says: How beautiful are the feet of the messenger of good news. Although, not everyone obeyed the good news, as Isaiah said: Lord, who has believed in our preaching? So, faith comes from preaching, and preaching is rooted in the word of Christ.

I ask: Have the Jews not heard? But, of course, they have. Because the voice of those preaching

> resounded all over the earth,
> and their voice was heard,
> to the ends of the world.

Then, I must ask: Did Israel not understand? Moses was the first to say:

> I will make you jealous of a nation that is not a nation,
> I will excite your anger against a senseless nation.

Isaiah dares to add more:

> I was found by those not looking for me;
> I have shown myself to those not asking for me.

While referring to Israel, the same Isaiah says:

> I hold out my hands the whole day long
> to a disobedient and rebellious people.

And so I ask: Has God rejected his people? Of course not! I, myself, am an Israelite, a descendant of Abraham, from the tribe of Benjamin. No, God has not rejected the people he knew beforehand. Don't you know what the Scripture says of Elijah, when he was accusing Israel before God? He said: "Lord, they have killed your prophets, destroyed your altars, and I alone remain; and now they want to kill me." What was God's answer? "I kept for myself seven thousand who did not worship Baal." In the same way, now, there is a remnant in Israel, those who were chosen, by grace. It is said: by grace, not because of what they did. Otherwise, grace would not be grace.

What then? What Israel was looking for, it did not find, but those whom God elected found it. The others hardened their hearts, as Scripture says:

> God made them dull of heart and mind;
> to this day, their eyes cannot see nor their ears hear.

David says:

> May they be caught and trapped at their banquets;
> may they fall, may they be punished.

> May their eyes be closed so that they cannot see
> and their backs be bent forever.

Again, I ask: Did they stumble so as to fall? Of course not. Their stumbling allowed salvation to come to the pagan nations, and, this, in turn, will stir up the jealousy of Israel. If Israel's shortcoming made the world rich, if the pagan nations grew rich with what they lost, what will happen when Israel is restored?

Listen to me, you who are not Jews: I am spending myself, as an apostle to the pagan nations, but I hope my ministry will be successful enough to awaken the jealousy of those of my race, and, finally, to save some of them. If the world made peace with God, when they remained apart, what will it be, when they are welcomed? Nothing less than, a passing from death to life.

When the first fruits are consecrated to God, the whole is consecrated. If the roots are holy, so will be the branches. Some branches have been cut from the olive tree, while you, as a wild olive tree, have been grafted in their stead, and you are benefiting from their roots and sap. Now, therefore, do not be proud, and despise the branches, because you do not support the roots, the roots support you. You may say, "They cut off the branches to graft me." Well and good! But they were cut off because they did not believe, while you stand, by faith. Then, do not pride yourself on this too much, rather, beware: if God did not spare the natural branches, even less will he spare you.

Admire, at the same time, both the goodness and severity of God: he was severe with the fallen, and he is generous with you, as long as you remain faithful. Otherwise, you will be cut off. If they do not keep on rejecting the faith they will be grafted in, for God is able to graft them back again. If you were taken from the wild olive tree, to which you belonged, and, in spite of being a different species, you were grafted into the good olive tree, it will be much easier, and natural, for them to be grafted into their own tree.

I want you to understand the mysterious decree of God, lest you be too confident: a part of Israel will remain hardened, until the majority of pagans have entered. Then, the whole of Israel will be saved, as Scripture says:

> From Zion will come the Liberator,
> who will purify the descendants of Jacob from all sin.

> And this is the Covenant I will make with them:
> I will take away from them their sins.

Regarding the gospel, the Jews are opponents, but it is for your benefit. Regarding election, they are beloved, because of their ancestors; because the call of God, and his gifts, cannot be nullified.

Through the disobedience of the Jews, the mercy of God came to you who did not obey God. They, in turn, will receive mercy, in due time, after this disobedience, that brought God's mercy to you. So, God has submitted all to disobedience, in order to show his mercy to all.

> How deep are the riches, the wisdom and knowledge of God!
> His decisions cannot be explained,
> nor his ways understood!

> Who has ever known God's thoughts?
> Who has ever been his adviser?

> Who has given him something first,
> so that God had to repay him?

> For everything comes from him,
> has been made by him
> and has to return to him.

> To him be the glory for ever! Amen.

I beg you, dearly beloved, by the mercy of God, to give yourselves, as a living and holy sacrifice, pleasing to God; that is the kind of worship for you, as sensible people. Don't let yourselves be shaped by the world where you live, but, rather, be transformed, through the renewal of your mind. You must discern the will of God: what is good, what pleases, what is perfect.

The grace that God has given me, allows me to tell each of you: don't pretend too much, but think with sober judgment, each, according to the measure of faith that God has assigned.

See, the body is one, even if formed by many members, but not all of them with the same function. The same with us; being many, we are one body in Christ, depending on one another. Let each one of us, therefore, serve, according to our different gifts. Are you a prophet? Then give the insights of faith. Let the minister fulfill his office; let the teacher teach, the one who encourages, convince.

You must, likewise, give, with an open hand, preside with dedication, and be cheerful in your works of charity.

Let love be sincere. Hate what is evil and hold to whatever is good. Love one another and be considerate. Out do one another, in mutual respect. Be zealous in fulfilling your duties. Be fervent in the spirit, and serve God.

Have hope and be cheerful. Be patient in trials and pray constantly. Share with other Christians in need. With those passing by, be ready to receive them.

Bless those who persecute you; bless, and do not wish evil on anyone. Rejoice with those who are joyful, and weep with those who weep. Live in peace with one another. Do not dream of extraordinary things; be humble and do not hold yourselves as wise.

Do not return evil for evil, but let everyone see your good will. Do your best to live in peace with everybody. Beloved, do not avenge yourselves, but let God be the one who punishes, as Scripture says: Vengeance is mine, I will repay, says the Lord. And it adds:

> If your enemy is hungry, feed him;
> if he is thirsty, give him to drink;

> by doing this you will heap burning coals upon his head.

Do not let evil defeat you, but conquer evil with goodness.

Let everyone be subject to the authorities. For there is no authority that does not come from God, and the offices have been established by God. Whoever, therefore, resists authority, goes against a decree of God, and those who resist deserve to be condemned.

In fact, who fears authority? Not those who do good, but those who do evil. Do you want to be without fear of a person in authority? Do good and you will receive praise. They are the stewards of God, for your good. But if you do not behave, fear them, for they do not carry arms in vain; they are at the service of God when they judge and punish wrongdoers.

It is necessary to obey, not through fear, but as a matter of conscience. In the same way, you must pay taxes, and the collectors are God's officials. Pay to all what is due them; to whomsoever you owe contributions, make a contribution; to whom taxes are due, pay taxes; to whom respect is due, give respect; to whom honor is due, give honor.

Do not be in debt to anyone. Let this be the only debt of one to another: Love. The one who loves his or her neighbor fulfills the law. For the commandments: Do not commit adultery, do not kill, do not covet, and whatever else, are summarized in this one: You will love your neighbor as yourself. Love cannot do the neighbor any harm; so love fulfills the whole law.

You know what hour it is. This is the time to awake, for our salvation is, now, nearer than when we first believed; the night is almost over, and day is at hand. Let us discard, therefore, everything that belongs to darkness, and let us put on the armor of light. As we live in the full light of day, let us behave with decency; no banquets with drunkenness, no promiscuity or licentiousness, no fighting or jealousy. Put on, rather, the Lord Jesus Christ, and do not be led by the will of the flesh nor follow its desires.

Welcome those weak in faith and do not criticize their scruples. Some think they can eat any food, while others, less liberated, eat only vegetables. If you eat, do not despise those who abstain; if you abstain, do not criticize those who eat, for God has welcomed them. Who are you to pass judgment on the servant of another? Whether he stands or falls, the one concerned is his master. But he will not fall, for his master is able to keep him standing.

Some judge one day to be better than the other; let us act according to our own opinion. The one who distinguishes among days, does that for the Lord; and the one who eats, eats for the Lord and in eating, gives thanks to the Lord. And the one who does not eat, does it for the Lord, and gives him thanks as well.

In fact, none of us lives for himself, nor dies for himself. If we live, we live for the Lord, and if we die, we die for the Lord. Either in life or in death, we belong to the Lord; It was for this purpose that Christ both died and came to life again, to be Lord, both of the living and of the dead.

Then you, why do you criticize your brother or sister? And you, why do you despise them? For we will all appear at the tribunal of God. It is written:

> I swear by myself—word of the Lord—
> every knee will bend before me, a
> nd every tongue shall give glory to God.

So each of us will account for himself before God.

Therefore, let us not continue criticizing one another; let us try, rather, never to put in the way of our brother anything that would make him stumble or fall. I know, I am sure of this in the Lord Jesus, that nothing is unclean in itself, it is only unclean for those who consider it unclean. But if you hurt your brother or sister because of a certain food, you are no longer walking according to love. Let not your eating cause the loss of one for whom Christ died.

Don't put yourself in the wrong with something good. The kingdom of God is not a matter of food or drink; it is justice, peace, and joy in the Holy Spirit, and if you serve Christ in this way, you will please God and be praised by people. Let us look, then, for what strengthens peace and makes us better.

Do not destroy the work of God because of food. All food is clean, but it is wrong for you to make others fall by what you eat. And it may be better not to eat meat, or drink wine, or anything else that causes your brother or sister to stumble.

Keep your own belief before God, and happy are you, if you never act against your own belief. Instead, whoever eats something, in spite of his doubt, is condemned by his conscience, because whatever we do against our conscience is sinful.

We, the strong and liberated, should bear the weakness of those who are not strong, instead of pleasing ourselves. Let each of us bring joy to our neighbors, helping them for the good purpose, for building up. Christ, himself, did not look for his own contentment, as Scripture says: The insults of those insulting you fell upon me. And we know, that whatever was written in the past, was written for our instruction, for both perseverance and comfort, given us by the Scripture, sustain our hope. May God, the source of all perseverance and comfort, give to all of you, to live in peace in Christ Jesus, that you may be able to praise, in one voice God, Father of Christ Jesus, our Lord.

Welcome, then, one another, as Christ welcomed you for the glory of God. Look: Christ put himself at the service of the Jewish world, to fulfill the promises made by God to their ancestors; here, you see God's faithfulness. The pagans, instead, give thanks to God for his mercy, as Scripture says:

> Because of that, I will sing
> and praise your name among the pagans.

And, in another place:

> Rejoice, pagan nations, with God's people.

And, again:

> Praise the Lord, all people,
> and let all nations speak of his magnificence.

Isaiah says:

> A descendant of Jesse will come
> who will rule the pagan nations
> and they will hope in him.

May God, the source of hope, fill you with joy and peace, in the faith, so, that, your hope may increase, by the power of the Holy Spirit.

As for me, brothers and sisters, I am convinced, that you have goodwill, knowledge, and the capacity to advise each other; nevertheless, I have written boldly in some parts of this letter, to remind you of what you already know. I do this, according to the grace God has given to me, when I was sent to the pagan nations. I dedicated myself to the service of the Good News of God, as a minister of Christ Jesus, in order to present the non-Jews to God, as an agreeable offering, consecrated by the Holy Spirit. This service of God is, for me, a cause of pride, in Christ Jesus.

Of course, I would not dare to speak of other things, but what Christ, himself, has done, through me, my words and my works, with miracles and signs, by the power of the Holy Spirit—so, that, non-Jews may obey the faith. In this way, I have extended the Good News to all parts, from Jerusalem to Illyricum.

I have been very careful, however, and I am proud of this, not to preach in places where Christ is already known, and not to build upon foundations laid by others. Let it be as Scripture says:

> Those not told about him will see,
> and those who have not heard will understand.

This work has prevented me from going to you. But, now, there is no more place for me in these regions, and, as I have wanted for so long, to go and see you, I hope to visit you, when I go to Spain. Then, you could help me go to that nation, once I have fully enjoyed your company.

Right now, I am going to Jerusalem, to help that community. Know, that the churches of Macedonia and Achaia have decided to make a contribution, for the poor among the believers of Jerusalem. They have decided to do that, and, in fact, they were indebted to them. For the non-Jews have shared the spiritual goods of the Jews, and, now, they must help them materially. So, I am to complete this task, and give over the amount that has been collected. Then, I will go to you, and from there, to Spain. And I am sure, that when I go to you, I will go with all the blessings of God.

I beg of you, brothers and sisters, by Christ Jesus our Lord, and by the love of the Spirit, to join me in the fight, praying to God, for me; pray, that I may avoid the snares of the enemies of faith in Judea, and, that, the community of Jerusalem may welcome the help I bring. And so, I will go to you with joy, and, God willing, be refreshed in your company. The God of peace be with you. Amen.

I recommend to you, our sister, Phoebe, deaconess of the church of Cenchreae. Please receive her, in the name of the Lord, as it should be among brothers and sisters in the faith, and help her in whatever is necessary, because she helped many; among them, myself.

Greetings to Prisca and Aquilas, my helpers in Christ Jesus. To save my life, they risked theirs; I am very grateful to them, as are all the churches of the pagan nations.

Greetings also to the church that meets in their house. Greetings to my dear Epaenetus, the first in the province of Asia to believe in Christ.

Greet Mary, who worked so much for you.

Greetings to Andronicus and Junias, my relatives and companions in prison; they are well known apostles and served Christ before I did.

Give greetings to Ampliatus, whom I love so much in the Lord.

Greetings to Urbanus, our fellow worker, and to my dear Stachys.

Greetings to Apelles, who suffered for Christ, and the family of Aristobulus.

Greetings to my relative Herodion and those in the household of Narcissus, who work in the Lord's service.

Greetings to Tryphaena and Tryphosa, who toil for the Lord's sake.

Greetings to Rufus, elected of the Lord, and his mother who was a second mother to me.

Greetings to Asyncritus, Phlegon, Hermes, Patrobas, Hermas and the brothers and sisters staying with them.

Greetings to Philologus and Julia, Nereus and his sister, Olympas and all the holy ones in Christ Jesus with them.

Greet one another with a holy kiss.

All the churches of Christ send their greetings.

Brothers and sisters, I beg of you, to be careful of those who are causing divisions and troubles, in teaching you a different teaching, from the one you were taught. Keep away from them, because those persons do not serve Christ our Lord, but their own interests, deceiving, with their soft and entertaining language, those who are simple of heart. Everybody knows, that you are very obedient, and because of that, I am happy, but I want you to be sensible in doing good, and firm against evil. The God of peace will soon crush Satan, and place him under your feet.

May Christ Jesus, our Lord, bless you. Timothy, who is with me, sends you greetings, and so do Lucius, Jason and Sosipatros, my relatives.

I, Tertius, the writer of this letter, send you greetings in the Lord.

Greetings from Gaius, who has given me lodging and in whose house the church meets. Greetings from Erastus, treasurer of the city, and from our brother Quartus.

Glory be to God!

He is able to give you strength, according to the Good News I proclaim, announcing Christ Jesus.

Now is revealed the mysterious plan, kept hidden for long ages in the past.

By the will of the eternal God it is brought to light, through the prophetic books, and all nations shall believe the faith proclaimed to them.

Glory to God, who alone is wise, through Christ Jesus, for ever! Amen.

INVITATION TO
COLOSSIANS

Around AD 58 the apostle Paul left his base in Ephesus and traveled to Jerusalem. He went there to deliver the collection for the poor that the followers of Jesus in Macedonia and Achaia had taken. Afterward he planned to bring the good news about Jesus into the western part of the Roman Empire. But his presence in Jerusalem sparked a city-wide riot by those who misunderstood and opposed his work. He was taken into custody by Roman officials, who held him for interrogation (see pp. 88–90). Paul had several hearings and trials, but his case was repeatedly delayed. After two years, he invoked his rights as a Roman citizen and asked to have Caesar hear his case in person. So he was taken to Rome, where he spent at least two more years awaiting trial. But while he was a prisoner he was able to continue his work of guiding the young communities of Jesus-followers throughout the empire by instructing and encouraging them through letters and messengers.

Paul had worked with a man named Epaphras when he was in Ephesus. Epaphras was originally from the city of Colossae, about a hundred miles to the east. Paul sent him to bring the good news about Jesus to his city and two nearby cities, Laodicea and Hierapolis. Epaphras was later arrested and brought to Rome as a prisoner himself. He told Paul what was happening in these cities. Even though Paul hadn't ever met the followers of Jesus there, they knew who he was and respected his leadership. So Paul wrote two letters, which we know as Colossians and Ephesians, to teach and encourage them.

Epaphras told Paul that the community of believers in Colossae was strong and growing, but that it was also threatened by some of the same influences Paul had needed to correct elsewhere. The Colossians were mostly Gentiles, but like the Galatians they were being pressured to be circumcised, keep kosher and observe the Sabbath and other Jewish holy days. Some of them, like the Corinthians, were priding themselves on having visions and getting secret spiritual knowledge. Many apparently also thought that harsh treatment of the body would somehow liberate their spirits. Paul recognized that in all these ways they were trying to add something to the complete salvation they'd already received when they believed in Jesus. So he wrote them a letter whose basic message is, "When you've got Messiah Jesus, you've got it all!"

Paul begins this letter by laying the foundation he needs to make this point. Since the Colossians don't know him personally, Paul introduces himself as a co-worker of their friend Epaphras. He explains that they're always in his prayers and says how grateful he is for their faith. He then reminds them of the message they've believed, particularly stressing that the Son of God has made everything, that he rules over everything and that he's reconciling everything to God. From a Roman prison cell Paul writes that the Son is the firstborn over all creation, and all things, including thrones or powers or rulers or authorities, were created through him and for him. The true power in the world is not on Caesar's throne, but is found in the Messiah's cross.

Paul explains that his own struggles and exertions are for their sake and for the sake of others like them, to bring them to spiritual maturity. He then challenges the Colossians to live their faith to the fullest. This means not trying to add anything to what Jesus has already done for them, but rather recognizing that they already have everything they need in Jesus himself. Paul encourages them to see themselves as people who've entered into a new kind of life, in which their personal character and community relationships will be transformed. He also stresses the watchful, prayerful attitude the community should have as it seeks to bring the message about Jesus to others.

In closing, Paul introduces Tychicus, who's carrying this letter to the believers in Colossae. He also describes his other messenger, the former runaway slave Onesimus (see p. 203), as a *faithful and dear brother*, hoping the community will welcome him back as a fellow believer. He sends greetings from their friend Epaphras, and alerts the church that another of his co-workers, Mark, may be coming to them soon. He exhorts their leader, Archippus, to persevere in his duties. In this way Paul, even in his imprisonment, continues to direct the work of bringing the good news about Jesus to the Gentiles. He proclaims the empowering and liberating truth for the nations that *There is no room for distinction between Greek or Jew, circumcised or uncircumcised, barbarian, foreigner, slave or free, but Christ is all, and in all.*

| COLOSSIANS |

Paul, apostle of Christ Jesus, by the will of God, and Timothy, our brother, to the saints in Colossae, our faithful brothers and sisters in Christ:

Receive grace and peace from God, our Father, and Christ Jesus, our Lord.

Thanks be to God, the Father of Christ Jesus, our Lord! We constantly pray for you, for we have known of your faith in Christ Jesus, and of your love for all the saints. Indeed, you await in hope the inheritance reserved for you in heaven, of which, you have heard through the word of truth. This gospel, already present among you, is bearing fruit, and growing throughout the world, as it did among you, from the day you accepted it, and understood the gift of God, in all its truth.

He who taught you, Epaphras, our dear companion in the service of Christ, faithful minister of Christ on our behalf, has reminded me of the love you have for me, in the Spirit. Because of this, from the day we received news of you, we have not ceased praying to God for you, that you may attain the full knowledge of his will, through all the gifts of wisdom and spiritual understanding.

May your lifestyle be worthy of the Lord and completely pleasing to him. May you bear fruit in every good work and grow in the knowledge of God.

May you become strong, in everything, by a sharing of the glory of God, so that you may have great endurance and persevere in joy.

Constantly give thanks to the Father, who has empowered us to receive our share in the inheritance of the saints, in his kingdom of light. He rescued us from the power of darkness and transferred us to the kingdom of his beloved Son. In him, we are redeemed and forgiven.

He is the image of the unseen God,
and for all creation, he is the firstborn,
for, in him, all things were created,
in heaven and on earth,
visible and invisible:
thrones, rulers, authorities, powers...

All was made through him and for him.

He is before all
and all things hold together, in him.

And he is the head of the body, that is the Church,
for he is the first, the first raised from the dead,
that he may be the first in everything,
for God was pleased to let fullness dwell in him.

Through him, God willed to reconcile all things to himself,
and through him, through his blood shed on the cross,
God establishes peace,
on earth as in heaven.

You, yourselves, were once estranged, and opposed to God, because of your evil deeds, but now, God has reconciled you, in the human body of his Son, through his death, so that you may be without fault, holy and blameless before him. Only stand firm upon the foundation of your faith, and be steadfast in hope. Keep in mind the gospel you have heard, which has been preached to every creature under heaven, and of which I, Paul, became a minister.

At present, I rejoice when I suffer for you; I complete, in my own flesh, what is lacking in the sufferings of Christ, for the sake of his body, which is the church. For I am serving the church since God entrusted to me the ministry to make the word of God fully known. I mean that mysterious plan that, for centuries and generations, remained secret, and which God has now revealed to his holy ones.

God willed to make known to them the riches, and even the glory, that his mysterious plan reserved for the pagan nations: Christ is in you, the hope for glory.

This Christ, we preach. We warn, and teach everyone true wisdom, aiming to make everyone perfect, in Christ. For this cause I labor and struggle, with the energy of Christ working powerfully in me.

I want you to know how I strive for you, for those of Laodicea, and for so many who have not met me personally. I pray, that all may be encouraged. May you be established in love, that you may obtain all the riches of a full understanding, and know the mystery of God, Christ himself. For, in him, are hidden all the treasures of wisdom and knowledge.

So, let no one deceive you with persuasive arguments. Although I am far from you, my spirit is with you, and I rejoice in recalling how well-disciplined you are, and how firm in the faith of Christ.

If you have accepted Christ Jesus as Lord, let him be your doctrine. Be rooted and built up in him; let faith be your principle, as you were taught, and your thanksgiving, overflowing.

See that no one deceives you with philosophy or any hollow discourse; these are merely human doctrines, not inspired by Christ, but by the wisdom of this world. For in him, dwells the fullness of God, in bodily form. He is the head of all cosmic power and authority, and, in him, you have everything.

In Christ Jesus, you were given a circumcision, but not by human hands, which removed completely from you the carnal body: I refer to baptism. On receiving it, you were buried with Christ; and you also rose with him, for having believed in the power of God, who raised him from the dead.

You were dead. You were in sin and uncircumcised at the same time. But God gave you life with Christ. He forgave all our sins. He canceled the record of our debts, those regulations which accused us. He did away with all that, and nailed it to the cross. Victorious through the cross, he stripped the rulers and authorities of their power, humbled them before the eyes of the whole world, and dragged them behind him, as prisoners.

So, then, let no one criticize you in matters of food or drink, or about observance of animal festivals, new moons or the Sabbath. These things were only shadows of what was to come, whereas the reality is the person of Christ. Do not let anyone disqualify you, insisting on humbling practices and worship of angels. In fact, they are only good to satisfy self-indulgence, instead of holding firmly to the head, Christ. It is he who nourishes and gives unity to the whole body by a complex system of nerves and ligaments, making it grow according to the plan of God.

If you have really died with Christ, and are rid of the principles of the world, why do you now let yourselves be taught as if you belonged to the world? "Do not eat this, do not taste that, do not touch that..." These are human rules and teachings, referring to things that are perishable, that wear out and disappear. These doctrines may seem to be profound because they speak of religious observance and humility and of disregarding the body. In fact, they are useless as soon as the flesh rebels.

So then, if you are risen with Christ, seek the things that are above, where Christ is seated at the right hand of God. Set your mind on the things that are above, not on earthly things. For you have died and your life is now hidden with Christ in God. When Christ, who is your life, reveals himself, you also will be revealed with him in glory.

Therefore, put to death what is earthly in your life, that is immorality, impurity, inordinate passions, wicked desires and greed, which is a way of worshiping idols. These are the things that arouse the wrath of God.

For a time, you followed this way and lived in such disorders. Well then, reject all that: anger, evil intentions, malice; and let no abusive words be heard from your lips.

Do not lie to one another. You have been stripped of the old self and its way of thinking; to put on the new, which is being renewed, and is to reach perfect knowledge, and the likeness of its creator. There is no room for distinction between Greek or Jew, circumcised or uncircumcised, barbarian, foreigner, slave or free, but Christ is all, and in all.

Clothe yourselves, then, as is fitting for God's chosen people, holy and beloved of him. Put on compassion, kindness, humility, meekness, and patience to bear with one another, and forgive, whenever there is any occasion to do so. As the Lord has forgiven you, forgive one another. Above all, clothe yourselves with love, which binds everything together in perfect harmony. May the peace of Christ overflow in your hearts; for this end you were called, to be one body. And be thankful.

Let the word of God dwell in you, in all its richness. Teach and admonish one another with words of wisdom. With thankful hearts, sing to God psalms, hymns and spontaneous praise. And whatever you do or say, do it in the Name of Jesus, the Lord, giving thanks to God, the Father, through him.

Wives, submit yourselves to your husbands, as you should do in the Lord. Husbands, love your wives and do not get angry with them. Children, obey your parents in everything, because that pleases the Lord. Parents, do not be too demanding of your children, lest they become discouraged.

Servants, obey your masters in everything; not only while they are present, to gain favor with them, but sincerely, because you fear the Lord. Whatever you do, do it wholeheartedly, working for the Lord, and not for humans. You well know, that the Lord will reward you with the inheritance. You are servants, but your Lord is Christ. Every evildoer will be paid back for whatever wrong has been done, for God does not make exceptions in favor of anyone.

As for you, masters, give your servants what is fair and reasonable, knowing that you yourselves have a Master in heaven.

Be steadfast in prayer, and even spend the night praying and giving thanks. Pray, especially, for us and our preaching: may the Lord open a door for us, that we may announce the mystery of Christ. Because of this, I am in chains; pray, then, that I may be able to reveal this mystery as I should.

Deal wisely with those who do not belong to the Church; take advantage of every opportunity. Let your conversation be pleasing, with a touch of wit. Know how to speak to everyone in the best way.

Tychicus will give news of me. He is our dear brother and, for me, a faithful assistant and fellow worker for the Lord. I am purposely sending him, to give you news of me, and to encourage you. With him, I am sending Onesimus, our faithful and dear brother, who is one of yours. They will tell you about everything that is happening here.

My companion in prison, Aristarchus, greets you, as does Mark, the cousin of Barnabas, about whom you have already received instructions. If he calls on you, receive him warmly. Jesus, called Justus, also greets you. They are the only Jewish people working with me for the kingdom of God, and because of that, they have been a comfort to me.

Greetings from your countryman Epaphras, a good servant of Christ Jesus. He constantly battles for you, through his prayer that you be perfect, and firm in whatever God asks of you. I assure you, that he has worked hard for you, as well as for those at Laodicea and Hierapolis.

Greetings from Luke, our dear doctor and from Demas. Greet the brothers and sisters of Laodicea, and don't forget Nympha and the church that gathers in her house.

After reading this letter, see that it is read in the Church of the Laodiceans, and have the letter they received, read in yours. And say to Archipus, "Do not forget the ministry given to you in the Lord."

Greetings in my own hand, Paul. Remember, that I am in chains. Grace be with you.

INVITATION TO
EPHESIANS

Besides Colossians, Paul sent at least two more letters with Tychicus and Onesimus from Rome (see p. 186). One of them has traditionally been known as Ephesians, but it may not actually have been written to believers in the city of Ephesus. The original letter hasn't survived, but there are many early copies, and some of the most accurate are addressed simply *to the saints*, not *to the saints in Ephesus*. If this letter had been written to the Ephesians, Paul would have included lengthy personal greetings at the end, since he spent two years in Ephesus and got to know many people there. Instead, he tells his readers that he's heard about their faith, and says they've no doubt heard about him as well. So, like Colossians, this is a letter from Paul to a group of believers he's never met personally.

One possibility is that this is actually the letter to Laodicea mentioned at the end of Colossians (see p. 191). The followers of Jesus in Laodicea fit the profile for the recipients of this letter very well. They had the same kind of relationship with Paul that the Colossians did: they knew he was in prison, and that his sufferings were for their benefit. On the other hand, if Paul were writing to the Laodiceans, we would expect him to introduce himself as a co-worker of their friend Epaphras. But Epaphras isn't mentioned here. So another possibility is that this is a general letter intended to circulate among the churches of western Asia Minor, to address problems they all had in common.

Even though we don't know exactly who the intended recipients were, we can at least tell from the letter that they were Gentiles who'd come to believe in Jesus. Paul addresses them as *you, the non-Jews*. He draws a contrast between *we who were the first to put our hope in Christ*, meaning himself and his fellow Jews, and *you who were included in Christ when you heard the message of truth*. They seem to have lived in a place where there was little direct Jewish influence. They weren't being encouraged to follow certain aspects of the law as if this were needed to support their faith and help restrain their desires. Indeed, they don't seem to have been concerned enough about controlling their actions, and had to be exhorted to live better lives.

As he often does in his letters, Paul uses the opening thanksgiving and prayer (which are quite lengthy in this case) to introduce his main theme. He writes that *He revealed his almighty power in Christ when he raised him from the dead, and had him sit at his right hand in heaven, far above all rule, power, authority, dominion, or any other supernatural force that could be named*. In this way, God brought everything together under the rule of Jesus the Messiah. Paul echoes a phrase from Psalm 8—*God put all things under the feet of Christ*—to show that Jesus is the truly human one. Jesus fulfills the original human calling to rule over the creation properly. Paul immediately draws the implication from this, in the first part of the main body of his letter, that Jews and Gentiles have been brought together into one body, with Jesus at the head. This means that Gentiles who believe in Jesus are no longer foreigners and strangers, but fellow citizens with God's people and also members of his household. As Paul puts it, God is creating *one New Man* through the reconciling work of Jesus.

Paul tells his readers he's praying they'll understand the implications of their new identity. In the rest of the letter's main body, he explains those implications. These believers are part of a body that God has given the resources to ensure that each of its members becomes godly and mature. So they must give up their former way of life and practice purity in daily living and integrity in their relationships. As in the case of Colossians, the responsibilities of those in and under authority—husbands and wives, parents and children, servants and masters—are used as an important example of the new kind of relationships God is expecting. Paul also cautions his readers that by seeking to live a new kind of life in this world, they're entering a spiritual battle. God's people must be on their guard and arm themselves with all the resources that God has provided—*the whole armor of God*.

Paul's closing greetings are understandably brief, because this is a letter to people he's never met and doesn't know well. While we can't determine exactly who they were, all who seek to take up their roles in God's drama will gain from this big-picture overview of salvation in Christ. It documents God's dramatic transformation of human communities when the message of truth about the exalted Jesus is heard and believed, looking ahead to the day God will *unite, when the fullness of time had come, everything in heaven and on earth.*

| EPHESIANS |

Paul, an apostle of Christ Jesus, by the will of God, to the saints in
Ephesus, to you, who share Christian faith:

receive grace and peace from God, our Father, and from Jesus, the Lord.

Blessed be God, the Father of Christ Jesus our Lord, who, in Christ, has
blessed us from heaven, with every spiritual blessing.

> God chose us, in Christ, before the creation of the world,
> to be holy, and without sin in his presence.

> From eternity he destined us, in love,
> to be his adopted sons and daughters, through Christ Jesus,
> thus fulfilling his free and generous will.

> This goal suited him:
> that his loving-kindness, which he granted us in his beloved
> might finally receive all glory and praise.

> For, in Christ, we obtain freedom, sealed by his blood,
> and have the forgiveness of sins.

> In this, appears the greatness of his grace,
> which he lavished on us.

> In all wisdom and understanding,
> God has made known to us his mysterious design,
> in accordance with his loving-kindness, in Christ.

> In him, and under him, God wanted to unite,
> when the fullness of time had come,
> everything in heaven and on earth.

> By a decree of him, who disposes all things,
> according to his own plan and decision,

> we, the Jews, have been chosen and called,
> and we were awaiting the Messiah,
> for the praise of his glory.

> You, on hearing the word of truth,
> the gospel that saves you,
> have believed in him.

> And, as promised, you were sealed with the Holy Spirit,
> the first pledge of what we shall receive,
> on the way to our deliverance, as a people of God,
> for the praise of his glory.

I have been told of your faith and your affection toward all the believers, so I always give thanks to God, remembering you in my prayers.

May the God of Christ Jesus our Lord, the Father of glory, reveal himself to you, and give you a spirit of wisdom and revelation, that you may know him.

May he enlighten your inner vision, that you may appreciate the things we hope for, since we were called by God.

May you know how great is the inheritance, the glory, God sets apart for his saints;

may you understand, with what extraordinary power, he acts in favor of us who believe.

He revealed his almighty power in Christ when he raised him from the dead, and had him sit at his right hand in heaven, far above all rule, power, authority, dominion, or any other supernatural force that could be named, not only in this world, but in the world to come as well.

Thus has God put all things under the feet of Christ and set him above all things, as head of the church, which is his body, the fullness of him, who fills all in all.

You were dead, through the faults and sins. Once, you lived through them, according to this world, and followed the Sovereign Ruler who reigns between heaven and earth, and who goes on working, in those who resist the faith. All of us belonged to them, at one time, and we followed human greed; we obeyed the urges of our human nature and consented to its desires. By ourselves, we went straight to the judgment, like the rest of humankind.

But God, who is rich in mercy, revealed his immense love. As we were dead through our sins, he gave us life, with Christ. By grace, you have been saved! And he raised us to life, with Christ, giving us a place with him in heaven.

In showing us such kindness, in Christ Jesus, God willed to reveal, and unfold in the coming ages, the extraordinary riches of his grace. By the grace of God, you have been saved, through faith. This has not come from you: it is God's gift. This was not the result of your works, so you are not to feel proud. What we are, is God's work. He has created us, in Christ Jesus, for the good works he has prepared, that we should devote ourselves to them.

Remember, that you were pagans, even in your flesh; and the Jews, who call themselves Circumcised (because of a surgical circumcision), called you Uncircumcised. At that time, you were without Christ, you did not belong to the community of Israel; the Covenants of God, and his promises, were not for you; you had no hope, and were without God in this world. But now, in Christ Jesus, and by his blood, you, who were once far off, have come near.

For Christ is our peace; he, who has made the two people, one; destroying, in his own flesh, the wall—the hatred—which separated us. He abolished the law, with its commands and precepts. He made peace, in uniting the two people, in him; creating, out of the two, one New Man. He destroyed hatred and reconciled us both to God, through the cross, making the two, one body.

He came to proclaim peace; peace to you who were far off, peace to the Jews who were near. Through him, we—the two people—approach the Father, in one Spirit.

Now, you are no longer strangers or guests, but fellow citizens of the holy people: you are of the household of God. You are the house, whose foundations are the apostles and prophets, and whose cornerstone is Christ Jesus. In him, the whole structure is joined together, and rises, to be a holy temple, in the Lord. In him, you, too, are being built, to become the spiritual Sanctuary of God.

For this reason, I, Paul, came to be the prisoner of Christ, for you, the non-Jews. You may have heard of the graces God bestowed on me, for your sake. By a revelation, he gave me the knowledge of his mysterious design, as I have explained in a few words. On reading them, you will have some idea of how I understand the mystery of Christ.

This mystery was not made known to past generations, but only now, through revelations, given to holy apostles and prophets, by the Spirit. Now, the non-Jews share the inheritance; in Christ Jesus, the non-Jews are incorporated, and are to enjoy the Promise.

This is the Good News, of which I have become minister, by a gift of God; a grace he gave me, when his power worked in me.

This grace, was given to me, the least, among all the holy ones: to announce to the pagan nations, the immeasurable riches of Christ, and to make clear to all, how the mystery, hidden from the beginning, in God, the Creator of all things, is to be fulfilled.

Even the heavenly forces and powers will now discover, through the church, the wisdom of God in its manifold expression, as the plan is being fulfilled, which God designed from the beginning, in Christ Jesus, our Lord. In him, we receive boldness and confidence to approach God.

So I ask you, not to be discouraged at seeing the trials I endure for you, but, rather, to feel proud because of them.

And, now, I kneel in the presence of the Father, from whom, every family in heaven and on earth has received its name.

May he strengthen in you, the inner self, through his Spirit, according to the riches of his glory;

may Christ dwell in your hearts, through faith;

may you be rooted and founded in love.

All of this, so that you may understand, with all the holy ones, the width, the length, the height and the depth—in a word, that you may know the love of Christ, that surpasses all knowledge, that you may be filled, and reach the fullness of God.

Glory to God, who shows his power in us, and can do much more than we could ask or imagine; glory to him, in the Church, and in Christ Jesus, through all generations, for ever and ever. Amen.

Therefore, I, the prisoner of Christ, invite you, to live the vocation you have received. Be humble, kind, patient, and bear with one another in love.

Make every effort to keep, among you, the unity of spirit, through bonds of peace. Let there be one body, and one Spirit, just as one hope is the goal of your calling by God. One Lord, one faith, one baptism; one God, the Father of all, who is above all, and works through all, and is in all.

But to each of us, divine grace is given, according to the measure of Christ's gift. Therefore, it is said:

> When he ascended to the heights,
> he brought captives
> and gave his gifts to people.

He ascended, what does it mean, but, that he had also descended to the lower parts of the world? He, himself, who went down, then ascended far above all the heavens, to fill all things. As for his gifts, to some, he gave to be apostles; to others, prophets, or even evangelists; or pastors and teachers. So, he prepared those who belong to him, for the ministry, in order to build up the Body of Christ, until we are all united, in the same faith and knowledge of the Son of God. Thus, we shall become the perfect Man, upon reaching maturity, and sharing the fullness of Christ.

Then, no longer shall we be like children, tossed about by any wave, or wind of doctrine; and deceived by the cunning of people, who drag them along into error. Rather, speaking the truth, in love, we shall grow in every way, toward him, who is the head, Christ. From him, comes the growth of the whole body, to which a network of joints gives order and cohesion, taking into account, and making use of, the function of each one. So, the body builds itself, in love.

I say to you, then, and with insistence I advise you, in the Lord: do not imitate the pagans, who live an aimless kind of life. Their understanding is in darkness, and they remain in ignorance, because of their blind conscience, very far from the life of God. As a result of their corruption, they have abandoned themselves to sensuality, and have eagerly given themselves to every kind of immorality.

But it is not for this, that you have followed Christ. For, I suppose, that you heard of him, and received his teaching, which is seen in Jesus himself. You must give up your former way of living, the old self, whose deceitful desires bring self-destruction. Renew yourselves, spiritually, from inside, and put on the new self, or self, according to God, that is created in true righteousness and holiness.

Therefore, give up lying; let all of us speak the truth to our neighbors, for we are members of one another. Be angry, but do not sin: do not let your anger last until the end of the day, lest you give the devil a foothold.

Let the one who used to steal, steal no more, but busy himself, working usefully with his hands, so that he may have something to share with the needy. Do not let even one bad word come from your mouth, but only good words, that will encourage when necessary, and be helpful to those who hear.

Do not sadden the Holy Spirit of God, who you were marked with. He will be your distinctive mark on the day of salvation. Do away with all quarreling, rage, anger, insults and every kind of malice: be good and understanding, forgiving one another, as God forgave you, in Christ.

As most beloved children of God, strive to imitate him. Follow the way of love, the example of Christ, who loved you. He gave himself up for us, and became the offering and sacrificial victim, whose fragrance rises to God. And, since you are holy, there must not be among you, even a hint of sexual immorality, or greed, or any kind of impurity: these should not be named among you. So, too, for scandalous words, nonsense and foolishness, which are not fitting; instead, offer thanksgiving to God.

Know this: no depraved, impure, or covetous person, who serves the god 'Money,' shall have part in the kingdom of Christ and of God. Let no one deceive you with empty arguments, for these are the sins which God is about to condemn in people, who do not obey. Do not associate with such people. You were once darkness, but, now, you are light, in the Lord. Behave as children of light; the fruits of light are kindness, justice and truth, in every form.

You, yourselves, search out what pleases the Lord, and take no part in works of darkness, that are of no benefit; expose them instead. Indeed, it is a shame even to speak of what those people do in secret, but as soon as it is exposed to the light, everything becomes clear; and what is unmasked, becomes clear through light. Therefore it is said:

> "Awake, you who sleep,
> arise from the dead,
> that the light of Christ may shine on you."

Pay attention to how you behave. Do not live as the unwise do, but as responsible persons. Try to make good use of the present time, because these days are evil. So do not be foolish, but understand what the will of the Lord is.

Do not get drunk: wine leads to levity; but be filled with the Holy Spirit. Gather together to pray, with psalms, hymns and spiritual songs. Sing, and celebrate the Lord in your heart, giving thanks to God, the Father, in the name of Christ Jesus, our Lord, always, and for everything.

Let all kinds of submission to one another, become obedience to Christ. So wives, to their husbands, as to the Lord.

The husband is the head of his wife, as Christ is the head of the church, his body, of whom he is also the Savior. And as the church submits to Christ, so let a wife submit in everything to her husband.

As for you, husbands, love your wives, as Christ loved the church, and gave himself up for her. He washed her, and made her holy, by baptism in the word. As he wanted a radiant church, without stain or wrinkle or any blemish, but holy and blameless, he, himself, had to prepare, and present her to himself.

In the same way, husbands should love their wives, as they love their own bodies. He, who loves his wife, loves himself. And no one has ever hated his body; he feeds and takes care of it. That is just what Christ does for the Church, because we are members of his body.

Scripture says: Because of this, a man shall leave his father and mother, to be united with his wife, and the two shall become one flesh. This is a very great mystery, and I refer to Christ and the Church. As for you, let each one love his wife as himself, and let the wife respect her husband.

Children, obey your parents, for, this is right: Honor your father and your mother. And this is the first commandment that has a promise: that you may be happy and enjoy long life in the land. And you, fathers, do not make rebels of your children, but educate them, by correction and instruction, which the Lord may inspire.

Servants, obey your masters of this world with fear and respect, with simplicity of heart, as if obeying Christ. Do not serve, only when you are watched, or in order to please others, but become servants of Christ, who do God's will, with all your heart. Work willingly, for the Lord, and not for humans, mindful that the good each one has done, whether servant or free, will be rewarded by the Lord.

And you, masters, deal with your servants in the same way, and do not threaten them, since you know that they, and you, have the same Lord, who is in heaven, and he treats all fairly.

Finally, be strong in the Lord, with his energy and strength. Put on the whole armor of God, to be able to resist the cunning of the devil. Our battle is not against human forces, but against the rulers and authorities and their dark powers, that govern this world. We are struggling against the spirits and supernatural forces of evil.

Therefore, put on the whole armor of God, that, in the evil day, you may resist, and stand your ground, making use of all your weapons. Take truth as your belt, justice as your breastplate, and zeal as your shoes, to propagate the gospel of peace. Always hold in your hand, the shield of faith, to repel the flaming arrows of the devil. Finally, use the helmet of salvation, and the sword of the Spirit, that is, the word of God.

Pray, at all times, as the Spirit inspires you. Keep watch, together with sustained prayer and supplication for all the holy ones. Pray, also, for me, so that when I speak, I may be given words, to proclaim bravely, the mystery of the gospel. Even when in chains, I am an ambassador of God; may he give me the strength to speak as I should.

I also want you to know how I am and what I am doing.

Tychicus, our beloved brother and faithful minister in the Lord, will tell you everything. I am sending him precisely to give you news of us and comfort you all.

May peace and love, with faith from God, the Father, and from Christ Jesus, the Lord, be with the brothers and sisters. And may his blessing be with all who love Christ Jesus, our Lord, with undying love.

INVITATION TO
PHILEMON

From prison in Rome, Paul sent his friends Tychicus and Onesimus to Asia Minor to deliver the letters we know as Colossians and Ephesians. Tychicus hadn't ever met the people Paul was writing to, so Paul had to introduce him in these letters. Onesimus was originally from Colossae and the people there would have known him. Even so, Paul also had to write on his behalf; in fact, he had to write a separate letter for him. This was because Onesimus had been the slave of a wealthy Colossian named Philemon, who hosted the community of Jesus-followers in his own home. Onesimus had run away, probably robbing Philemon in the process, and had ended up in Rome. There he became a follower of Jesus. He'd been helping Paul in prison, but now Paul needed him to return to Colossae. Paul hoped that Philemon would not only forgive Onesimus, but welcome him *no longer as a slave, but better than a slave. For he is a very dear brother to me.*

Paul's brief letter to Philemon stresses the change in Onesimus' life. His name means *useful* in Greek, and Paul tells Philemon that while Onesimus had formerly been *useless* (a servant he couldn't count on), he could now be useful to both of them. The letter reminds Philemon how much he owes Paul, since it was Paul's own co-workers who brought the good news of Jesus to his city. Paul addresses his letter not just to Philemon but also to Archippus, another leader of the church, and to Apphia (probably Philemon's wife), likely hoping that they would help persuade Philemon to do as he was asking. Even so, he doesn't put Philemon under any obligation. He ultimately appeals to him on the basis of love, but also promises to honor the demands of justice by making whatever restitution Philemon required.

It's most likely that Paul's appeal was successful. This letter, and the other two that Onesimus and Tychicus were carrying, would probably not have been preserved otherwise. One tradition says that Onesimus was not only freed to work with the churches, but eventually became the leader of the large and influential community of believers in Ephesus. In his life, therefore, we have a specific example of the kind of transformation that occurred in thousands of lives as the good news about Jesus spread throughout the Roman Empire.

| PHILEMON |

From Paul, a prisoner of Christ Jesus, and from our brother Timothy, to Philemon, our friend and fellow worker, to our dear sister Apphia, to Archippus, faithful companion in our soldiering, and to all the Church gathered in your house.

Grace and peace be with you from God, the Father, and Jesus Christ, the Lord.

I never cease to give thanks to my God when I remember you in my prayers, for I hear of your love and faith toward the Lord and all the holy ones. And I pray, that the sharing of your faith may make known all the good that is ours in Christ. I had great satisfaction and comfort on hearing of your charity, because the hearts of the saints have been cheered by you, brother.

Because of this, although in Christ I have the freedom to command what you should do, yet I prefer to request you, in love. The one talking is Paul, the old man, now prisoner for Christ. And my request is on behalf of Onesimus, whose father I have become while I was in prison.

This Onesimus has not been helpful to you, but now he will be helpful, both to you and to me. In returning him to you, I am sending you my own heart. I would have liked to keep him at my side, to serve me, on your behalf, while I am in prison for the gospel, but I did not want to do anything without your agreement, nor impose a good deed upon you without your free consent.

Perhaps Onesimus has been parted from you for a while so that you may have him back forever, no longer as a slave, but better than a slave. For he is a very dear brother to me, and he will be even dearer to you. And so, because of our friendship, receive him, as if he were I myself. And if he has caused any harm, or owes you anything, charge it to me. I, Paul, write this and sign it with my own hand: I will pay it... without further mention of your debt to me, which is you yourself. So, my brother, please do me this favor, for the Lord's sake. Give me this comfort in Christ.

Confident of your obedience, I write to you, knowing you will do even more than I ask. And one more thing, get a lodging ready for me because, thanks to all your prayers, I hope to return to you.

Epaphras, my fellow prisoner in Christ Jesus, sends greetings. So do Mark, Aristarchus, Demas and Luke, my assistants.

May the grace of the Lord Christ be with you. Amen!

INVITATION TO
PHILIPPIANS

On his second journey to bring the good news about Jesus to the people of the Roman empire, the apostle Paul helped establish a community of Jesus-followers in the city of Philippi (see pp. 79–81). The people of that community became his friends and supporters for the rest of his life. When they heard he'd been taken to Rome as a prisoner, they collected money to assist him and sent it with one of their members, a man named Epaphroditus, who stayed in Rome to help take care of Paul.

Unfortunately, Epaphroditus became very sick and nearly died. When he recovered, Paul decided to send him back to Philippi because he knew how concerned his friends were for him. Paul sent a letter with Epaphroditus to thank the Philippians for the friendship and support they'd always shown him, and particularly on this occasion.

In his letter, Paul also offers some challenges and encouragement. He knows that the Philippians are experiencing a lot of opposition, just as he is, so he appeals to his own life as an example of how they should respond. He reports that throughout the whole palace guard—that is, right in the center of Caesar's realm—he's been able to make the royal announcement boldly that Jesus is Lord. Paul's desire is that the Philippians will be encouraged, like most of the brothers and sisters around him, to become confident in the Lord and dare all the more to proclaim the gospel without fear.

Paul also knows that some people in the community at Philippi are having trouble getting along, so he urges them to stand firm in the one Spirit, striving together as one for the faith of the gospel without being frightened in any way by those who oppose you. Composing or quoting an amazing song of praise right in the middle of his letter, Paul urges the Philippians to have the same servant attitude that Jesus had. Jesus didn't use his high position for his own advantage, but humbled himself even to the point of death—all for the sake of others. This is the new way of life in God's kingdom.

Paul reminds the Philippians that they don't need to be circumcised, as some people were apparently teaching they did, and he warns them that they shouldn't live like those who are controlled by their desires. All of these themes are interwoven throughout the letter, which doesn't develop systematically the way some of Paul's other letters do, but flows freely, as one friend writes to another.

The dominant note in this letter is joy. Even though Paul is a prisoner, and even though he and his friends are experiencing strong opposition, he's rejoicing. So he urges the Philippians to rejoice, too, in the partnership they have in helping others meet Jesus and in the reward they can anticipate when their work is finished. Our citizenship is in God's realm, Paul says, and so we eagerly await the Savior's return to us. Then he will transform our lowly bodies to become like his glorious resurrected body.

| PHILIPPIANS |

F rom Paul and Timothy, servants of Christ Jesus, to the saints in Philippi, with their bishops and deacons; to you all in Christ Jesus:

May grace and peace be yours from God, our Father, and Christ Jesus the Lord.

I give thanks to my God, each time I remember you, and when I pray for you, I pray with joy. I cannot forget all you shared with me in the service of the gospel, from the first day, until now. Since God began such a good work, in you, I am certain, that he will complete it in the day of Christ Jesus.

This is my hope for you, for I carry you all, in my heart: whether I am in prison, or defending and confirming the gospel, you are with me and share the same grace.

God knows, that I love you dearly, with the love of Christ Jesus, and in my prayers, I ask that your love may lead you, each day, to a deeper knowledge and clearer discernment, that you may have good criteria for everything. So you may be pure of heart, and come, blameless, to the day of Christ, filled with the fruit of holiness, that comes through Christ Jesus, for the glory and praise of God.

I want you to know, brothers and sisters, that what has happened to me has served to advance the gospel. Actually the whole praetorian guard, and even those outside the palace, know that I am in chains for Christ. And what is more, my condition, as prisoner, has encouraged most of our brothers, who are now emboldened, to proclaim the word of God more openly and without fear.

Some, it is true, are moved by envy and rivalry, but others preach Christ with a good intention. These latter are moved by love and realize that I am here to defend the gospel. The others announce Christ to challenge me. They do not act with a pure intention but think they are making my prison more unbearable. But, in any case, whether they are sincere or showing off, Christ is proclaimed and, because of this, I rejoice and have no regrets.

I know that all this will be a grace for me, because of your prayers, and the help given by the Spirit of Christ. I am hopeful, even certain, that I shall not be ashamed. I feel as assured now, as before, that Christ will be exalted through my person, whether I live or die.

For to me, living is for Christ, and dying is even better. But if I am to go on living, I shall be able to enjoy fruitful labor. Which shall I choose? So I feel torn between the two. I desire greatly to leave this life and to be with Christ, which will be better by far, but it is necessary for you that I remain in this life. And because I am convinced of this, I know that I will stay, and remain with you, for your progress and happiness in the faith. I will surely come to you again, and give you more reason for being proud of belonging to Christ Jesus.

Try, then, to adjust your lives according to the gospel of Christ. May I see it when I come to you, and if I cannot come, may I at least hear that you stand firm in the same spirit, striving to uphold the faith of the gospel with one heart. Do not be afraid of your opponents. This will be a sign, that they are defeated and you are saved, that is, saved by God. For, through Christ, you have been granted, not only to believe in Christ, but also to suffer for him. And you now share the same struggle that you saw I had, and that I continue to have, as you know.

If I may advise you, in the name of Christ, and if you can hear it, as the voice of love; if we share the same Spirit, and are capable of mercy and compassion, then I beg of you, make me very happy: have one love, one spirit, one feeling, do nothing through rivalry or vain conceit. On the contrary, let each of you gently consider the others, as more important than yourselves. Do not seek your own interest, but, rather, that of others. Your attitude should be the same as Jesus Christ had:

> Though he was in the form of God,
> he did not regard equality with God as something to be grasped,
>
> but emptied himself,
> taking on the nature of a servant, made in human likeness,
> and, in his appearance, found, as a man,
>
> He humbled himself by being obedient, to death,
> death on the cross.

> That is why God exalted him
> and gave him the name which outshines all names,
>
> so, that, at the name of Jesus all knees should bend
> in heaven, on earth and among the dead,
>
> and all tongues proclaim, that Christ Jesus is the Lord,
> to the glory of God the Father.

Therefore, my dearest friends, as you always obeyed me while I was with you, even more, now, that I am far from you, continue working out your salvation "with fear and trembling." It is God who makes you, not only wish but also, carry out what pleases him. Do everything without grumbling, so, that, without fault or blame, you will be children of God, without reproach, among a crooked and perverse generation. You are a light among them, like stars in the universe, holding to the word of life. I shall feel proud of you, on the day of Christ, on seeing that my effort and labor have not been in vain. And if I am being poured out, as a libation over the sacrifice, and the offering of your faith, I rejoice and continue to share your joy; and, you, likewise should rejoice and share my joy.

The Lord Jesus lets me hope that I may soon send you Timothy, and have news of you. With this, I will feel encouraged. For I have no one so concerned for you as he is. Most follow their own interest, not those of Christ Jesus. But Timothy has proved himself, as you know. Like a son at the side of his father, he has been with me at the service of the gospel. Because of that, I hope to send him to you as soon as I see how things work out for me. Nevertheless, the Lord lets me think that I, myself, shall be coming soon.

I judged it necessary to send back to you Epaphroditus, who worked and fought at my side, and whom you sent, to help me in my great need. In fact, he missed you very much and was still more worried, because you had heard of his sickness. He was, indeed, sick, and almost died, but God took pity on him, and on me, sparing me greater sorrow. And so, I am eager to send him to you, so that, on seeing him, you will be glad and I will be at peace. Receive him, then, with joy, as is fitting in the Lord. Consider highly persons like him, who almost died for the work of Christ; he risked his life to serve me, on your behalf, when you could not help me.

Finally, my brothers and sisters, rejoice in the Lord.

It is not a burden for me to write, again, the same things, and for you, it is safer. Beware of the dogs, beware of the bad workers; beware of the circumcised. We are the true circumcised people, since we serve according to the Spirit of God, and our confidence is in Christ Jesus, rather than in our merits.

I, myself, do not lack those human qualities in which people have confidence. If some of them seem to be accredited with such qualities, how much more am I! I was circumcised when eight days old. I was born of the race of Israel, of the tribe of Benjamin; I am a Hebrew, born of Hebrews. With regard to the law, I am a Pharisee, and such was my zeal for the law that I persecuted the Church. As for being righteous according to the law, I was blameless.

But once I found Christ, all those things that I might have considered as profit, I reckoned as loss. Still more, everything seems to me, as nothing, compared with the knowledge of Christ Jesus, my Lord. For his sake, I have let everything fall away, and I now consider all as garbage, if, instead, I may gain Christ. May I be found in him, not having a righteousness of my own, that comes from the law, but with the righteousness that God gives, to those who believe.

May I know him, and experience the power of his resurrection, and share in his sufferings, and become like him, in his death, and attain, through this, God willing, the resurrection from the dead!

I do not believe I have already reached the goal, nor do I consider myself perfect, but I press on till I conquer Christ Jesus, as I have already been conquered by him. No, brothers and sisters, I do not claim to have claimed the prize yet. I say only this: forgetting what is behind me, I race forward, and run toward the goal, my eyes on the prize, to which God has called us from above, in Christ Jesus. Let all of us who claim to be perfect, have the same way of thinking, but if there is something on which you differ, God will make it clear to you. Meanwhile, let us go forward, from the point we have each attained.

Unite in imitating me, brothers and sisters, and look at those who walk in our way of life. For many live as enemies of the cross of Christ. I have said it to you many times, and now I repeat it with tears: they are heading for ruin; their belly is their god, and they feel proud of what should be their shame. They only think of earthly things.

For us, our citizenship is in heaven, from where we await the coming of our Savior, Jesus Christ, the Lord. He will transfigure our lowly body, making it like his own body, radiant in glory, through the power which is his, to submit everything to himself.

Therefore, my brothers and sisters, whom I love and long for, you, my glory and crown, be steadfast in the Lord. I beg Evodia and Syntyche to agree with each other, in the Lord. And you, Sycygus, my true companion, I beg you to help them. Do not forget that they have labored with me in the service of the gospel, together with Clement, and my other fellow-workers, whose names are written in the Book of Life.

Rejoice in the Lord, always! I say it again: rejoice, and may everyone experience your gentle and understanding heart. The Lord is near: do not be anxious about anything. In everything, resort to prayer and supplication, together, with thanksgiving, and bring your requests before God. Then, the peace of God, which surpasses all understanding, will keep your hearts and minds in Christ Jesus.

Finally, brothers and sisters, fill your minds with whatever is truthful, holy, just, pure, lovely and noble. Be mindful of whatever deserves praise and admiration. Put into practice what you have learned from me, what I passed on to you, what you heard from me or saw me doing, and the God of peace will be with you.

I rejoice in the Lord because of your concern for me. You were indeed concerned for me before, but you had no opportunity to show it. I do not say this because of being in want; I have learned to manage with what I have. I know what it is to be in want and what it is to have plenty. I am trained for both: to be hungry or satisfied, to have much or little. I can do all things in him who strengthens me.

However, you did right in sharing my trials. You Philippians, remember that, in the beginning, when we first preached the gospel, after I left Macedonia, you, alone, opened for me a debit and credit account, and when I was in Thessalonica, twice you sent me what I needed.

It is not your gift that I value, but rather, the interest increasing in your own account. Now, I have enough, and more than enough, with everything Epaphroditus brought me, on your behalf, and which I received as "fragrant offerings pleasing to God." God, himself, will provide you with everything you need, according to his riches, and show you his generosity in Christ Jesus. Glory to God, our Father, for ever and ever: Amen.

G reet all who believe in Christ Jesus. The brothers and sisters with me greet you. All the believers here greet you, especially those from Caesar's household. The grace of Christ Jesus, the Lord, be with your spirit.

INVITATION TO
1 TIMOTHY

After being held prisoner in Rome for at least two years, the apostle Paul was released. He continued his work of bringing the good news about Jesus to new places and guiding and strengthening the communities he'd founded.

A particular challenge awaited him in the city of Ephesus, where he'd lived for two years and helped start a strong community of Jesus-followers. Just before his arrest and imprisonment, while he was on his way to Jerusalem with the offering for the poor, Paul had a sense that some of the leaders in Ephesus would distort the genuine message they'd heard, to try to get rich and win personal followings. So he arranged a special meeting to warn them about this (see pp. 86–87). After he was released from prison, Paul discovered that some of these leaders had done just what he'd anticipated. They'd misapplied some Jewish practices and borrowed others from the philosophies of the day to create a regimen they expected believers to follow to supplement their faith in Jesus. Like those who opposed Paul in other places, they didn't allow certain foods, forbade marriage and stressed controversial speculations as the means to spiritual progress. At the same time, they were tolerant of immoral behavior. It appears their teaching was being spread particularly by younger widows, who had lots of energy and free time because they were being supported by the church.

Paul was apparently only able to make a brief visit to Ephesus after his release before traveling to Macedonia on other business. He couldn't address the problems he'd discovered by writing directly to the leaders in Ephesus, since many of them were now unsympathetic to his message and questioning his authority. So Paul left his co-worker Timothy in Ephesus and wrote him a letter that he hoped would give him the power and influence to begin setting things in order until he could get back to Ephesus in person. While the letter is addressed to Timothy, it's clear that Paul expected him to share much of it with the community.

Paul begins by restating why he's left Timothy in Ephesus. He defends his own apostleship in the process. He states that he's deposed two of the community's leaders, Hymenaeus and Alexander, because they've departed from the genuine teaching about Jesus. He urges the community to respect those in authority and strive for a *quiet and peaceful life, in godliness and respect*—the opposite of the moral and social chaos the upstart leaders have created.

Paul explains what kind of people the community should have as its leaders, so it can reject those who aren't qualified and replace them with those who are. He also shows how to avoid the problem of younger widows going about from house to house spreading bad influences: only godly older widows should be supported; younger ones should remarry and devote themselves to family life. Paul includes a special warning toward the end of the letter about the dangers of greed, which seems to be behind much of the trouble in Ephesus.

His letter alternates between instruction that's directed primarily at the community and some very personal words to Timothy (for example, *Let no one reproach you on account of your youth*). It's likely that Timothy read much of the letter out loud to the others in the community. In fact, as Paul offers a final encouragement to Timothy, he also includes a greeting to them. He hopes they'll recognize the qualities of genuine leadership he's modeled over the years as he's invested so much in them.

Throughout the letter Paul uses the phrase *Christ Jesus*—that is, Messiah Jesus—which emphasizes the kingly rule of Jesus. This helped remind the church that Jesus is their real leader and is the clearest model of authentic leadership.

| 1 TIMOTHY |

From Paul, apostle of Christ Jesus, by a command of God, our Savior, and of Christ Jesus, our hope, to Timothy, my true son in the faith.

May God the Father, and Christ Jesus, our Lord, give you grace, mercy and peace.

When I left for Macedonia, I urged you to remain in Ephesus, to warn certain persons not to teach false doctrine, or to concern themselves with fables and endless genealogies. These give rise to discussions, rather than promoting a better service of God, through faith. The aim of our warning is love, which comes from a pure mind, a good conscience and sincere faith.

Some have turned away from such motivation and have strayed into useless discussions. They claim to be teachers of the law when, in fact, they understand neither what they say nor the things they speak about.

We know that the law is good, as long as it serves its purpose. The law is not for the righteous, but for the lawless, and for the wicked and sinful, for those who do not respect God, and religion, for those who kill their parents, for murderers, for those who indulge in unlawful sex and homosexuality, for kidnappers and exploiters, for liars and perjurers, and for all that is contrary to sound doctrine, to the gospel of the God of glory and happiness, which was entrusted to me.

I give thanks to Christ Jesus, our Lord, who is my strength, who has considered me trustworthy, and appointed me to his service, although I had been a blasphemer, a persecutor and a fanatical enemy. However, he took mercy on me, because I did not know what I was doing when I opposed the faith; and the grace of our Lord was more than abundant, together with faith and love that are in Christ Jesus.

This saying is true and worthy of belief: Christ Jesus came into the world to save sinners, of whom I am the first. Because of that, I was forgiven; Christ Jesus wanted to display his utmost patience, so that I might be an example for all who are to believe, and obtain eternal life. To the King of ages, the only God, who lives beyond every perishable and visible creation—to him, be honor and glory forever. Amen!

Timothy, my son, I command you to fight the good fight, fulfilling the prophetic words pronounced over you. Hold onto faith and a good conscience, unlike those who, ignoring conscience, have finally wrecked their faith. Among them are Hymeneus and Alexander, whom I have delivered to Satan, to be taught not to blaspheme.

First of all, I urge that petitions, prayers, intercessions and thanksgiving be made for everyone, for rulers of states, and all in authority, that we may enjoy a quiet and peaceful life, in godliness and respect. This is good and pleases God. For he wants all to be saved, and come to the knowledge of truth. As there is one God, there is one mediator between God and humankind, Christ Jesus, himself human, who gave his life for the redemption of all. This is the testimony, given in its proper time, and of this, God has made me apostle and herald. I am not lying, I am telling the truth: He made me teacher of the nations regarding faith and truth.

I want the men, in every place, to lift pure hands, in prayer, to heaven, without anger and dissension.

Let women dress with simplicity and modesty, not adorned with fancy hairstyles, gold, jewels and expensive clothes, but with good works, as is fitting for women serving God. Let a woman quietly receive instruction and be submissive. I allow no woman to teach, or to have authority over men. Let them be quiet. For Adam was created first and then Eve. Adam was not deceived; it was the woman who was deceived and fell into sin. But she will be saved through motherhood, provided that her life be orderly and holy, in faith and love.

If someone aspires to the overseer's ministry, he is, without a doubt, looking for a noble task. It is necessary, that the overseer (or bishop) be beyond reproach, the husband of one wife, responsible, judicious, of good manners, hospitable and skillful in teaching. He must not be addicted to wine, or quarrelsome, but gentle and peaceful, and not a lover of money, but a man whose household is well-managed, with obedient and well-mannered children. If he cannot govern his own house, how can he lead the assembly of God?

He must not be a recent convert, lest he become conceited, and fall into the same condemnation as the devil. Moreover, he must enjoy a good reputation among the outsiders, lest people speak evil about him, and he fall into the snare of the devil.

Deacons, likewise, must be serious and sincere, and moderate in drinking wine, not greedy for money; they must keep the mystery of faith with a clear conscience. Let them be first tried and, if found blameless, be accepted as deacons. In the same way, the women must be conscientious, not given to gossip, but reserved and trustworthy.

A deacon must be husband of one wife, and must know how to guide his children and manage his household. Those who serve well as deacons will win honorable rank, with authority to speak of Christian faith.

I give you these instructions, although I hope I will see you soon. If I delay, you will know how you ought to conduct yourself in the household of God, that is, the Church of the living God, which is the pillar and foundation of the truth. How great, indeed, is the mystery of divine blessing!

> He was shown in the flesh
> and sanctified by the spirit;
>
> presented to the angels
> and proclaimed to all nations.
>
> The world believed in him:
> He was taken up in glory!

The Spirit tells us, clearly, that in the last days, some will defect from the faith, and follow deceitful spirits and devilish doctrines, led by lying hypocrites, whose consciences have been branded with the stamp of infamy.

These persons forbid marriage, and condemn the use of certain foods, which God created for those who know the truth, and which the believers receive with thanksgiving. Everything created by God is good, and all food is lawful; nothing is to be rejected, if we receive it with thanksgiving, for it is blessed with the word of God, and prayer, and made holy.

If you explain these things to the brothers and sisters, you will prove to be a good servant of Christ Jesus, nourished by the teachings of faith, and the sound doctrine that you have followed. Reject irreligious fables and old wives' tales. Train yourself in godliness. Physical training is of limited value; godliness, instead, is useful in every way, holding promise for the present life and for the life to come. Here, you have a sure doctrine you can trust. We toil and endure, because we trust in the living God, the Savior of all, especially of those who believe.

Command and teach these things. Let no one reproach you on account of your youth. Be a model to the believers, in the way you speak and act, in your love, your faith and purity of life. Devote yourself to reading, preaching and teaching, until I come.

Do not neglect the spiritual gift conferred on you with prophetic words, when the elders laid their hands upon you. Think about it, and practice it, so that your progress may be seen by all. Take heed of yourself, and attend to your teaching. Be steadfast in doing this, and you will save both yourself and your hearers.

Do not rebuke an older man; on the contrary, advise him, as if he were your father. Treat the young as your brothers, the elder women, as mothers and the young girls, as your sisters, with great purity.

Take care of widows who are really widows. If a widow has children or grandchildren, they should, first, learn their family duties, and give their parents financial help. This is correct and pleases God.

A true widow is one who, on being left alone, has set her hope on God, praying day and night to God, and asking him for help. On the contrary, a widow who lives for pleasure is dead even while she lives. Warn them about this, that they may be blameless. Those who do not take care of their own, especially those of their household, have denied the faith, and are worse than unbelievers.

Let no one be put on the list of widows unless she is sixty years old and has been married only once. She must be commended for her good works and the education of her children. Has she offered hospitality, washed the feet of the saints, helped the suffering and practiced other good deeds?

Do not accept younger widows; they may have other desires than for Christ and want to marry; then they deserve condemnation, for breaking their first commitment. Besides, they form the habit of being idle, going from house to house. And it is not just idleness! They become gossips and busybodies, saying what they should not.

So I want young widows to marry and have children, to rule their household and give adversaries no grounds for criticism. Some have already strayed, to follow Satan. If any Christian woman has widows in her family, let her assist them; in this way, the church will not be burdened, and may assist those who are truly widows.

Let the elders, who preside well, receive double compensation, especially those who labor in preaching and teaching. Scripture says: Do not muzzle the ox while it threshes grain, and: The worker deserves his wages.

Do not accept accusations against an elder except on the evidence of two or three witnesses. If he continues to sin, rebuke him in the presence of the community, as a warning to the rest.

I urge you, in the presence of God and Christ Jesus, and of the holy angels, to obey these rules with impartiality, without making distinctions.

Do not be hasty in the laying on of hands, thus becoming an accomplice in the sins of others. Keep yourself free from blame.

The sins of some people are plain to see, even before they are examined; the sins of others are known only later on.

Likewise, good deeds are conspicuous; even when they are not, they cannot remain hidden.

(Do not drink only water but take a little wine to help your digestion, because of your frequent illness.)

Let those who are slaves always show respect to their masters, so that no one may speak ill of God and his teaching. Those, whose masters are Christians, should not show less respect, under the pretext that, they are members of the church. On the contrary, they must give a better service, since they are doing good works, on behalf of believers, and dear friends.

Teach and stress these things. Whoever teaches in some other way, not following the sound teaching of our Lord Christ Jesus, and true religious instruction, is conceited, and understands nothing. This one is crazy about controversies and discussions, that result in envy, insults, blows and constant arguments between people of depraved minds, and far from the truth. For them, religion is merely for financial gain.

In reality, religion is a treasure, if we are content with what we have. We brought nothing into the world and we will leave it with nothing. Let us, then, be content with having food and clothing. Those who strive to be rich fall into temptations and traps. A lot of foolish and harmful ambitions plunge them into ruin and destruction. Indeed, the love of money is the root of every evil. Because of this greed, some have wandered away from the faith, bringing on themselves afflictions of every kind.

But you, man of God, shun all this. Strive to be holy and godly. Live in faith and love, with endurance and gentleness. Fight the good fight of faith and win everlasting life, to which you were called, when you made the good profession of faith, in the presence of so many witnesses.

Now, in the presence of God, who gives life to all things, and of Jesus Christ, who expressed before Pontius Pilate the authentic profession of faith: preserve the revealed message to all. Keep yourself pure and blameless, until the glorious coming of Christ Jesus, our Lord, who God will bring about at the proper time; he, the magnificent sovereign, King of kings and

Lord of lords. To him, alone, immortal, who lives in unapproachable light, and whom no one has ever seen or can see, to him, be honor and power, for ever and ever. Amen!

Command the rich of this world not to be arrogant, or to put their trust in the uncertainty of wealth. Let them, rather, trust in God, who generously gives us all we need for our happiness. Let them do good, be rich in good deeds, and be generous; let them share with others. In this way, they shall heap up a sound capital for the future, and gain true life.

Timothy, guard what has been entrusted to you; avoid useless and profane words, as well as discussions arising from false knowledge. Some have lost the faith in accepting such knowledge.

The grace of God be with you all.

INVITATION TO
TITUS

After the apostle Paul was released from prison in Rome, he discovered that renegade leaders were preying on the community of Jesus-followers that he'd helped establish in Ephesus. He left his longtime co-worker Timothy in that city with a letter authorizing him to replace those leaders and restore order. A similar situation on the island of Crete required Paul to commission another long-time collaborator, Titus, to act as his representative there.

Like his first letter to Timothy, Paul's letter to Titus is addressed to his co-worker but meant for the people of the community to hear as well. Paul confers his own authority on Titus and instructs him to appoint godly leaders and oppose predatory teachings. After describing the proper qualifications for community leadership, Paul identifies the teaching that must be opposed. From what he says, it's similar to the one in Ephesus: a combination of selective Jewish observances (such as being circumcised and abstaining from certain foods) and the pursuit of controversial speculations. Like the teaching in Ephesus, it wasn't helping people live purer lives. Instead, it was making them unfit for doing anything good. Therefore, in the instructions Paul gives to the members of the community about how to live out their varying stations in life, he stresses how they can and should do what is good. *For the grace of God has appeared, bringing salvation to all*, he says, so that God's people can live a new kind of life.

Paul ends his letter with some personal instructions to Titus. He reveals that he's planning to fulfill his longtime dream of bringing the good news about Jesus to the western part of the empire. He's expecting to spend the winter in Nicopolis, a city on the west coast of Macedonia that will provide an excellent jumping-off point for this trip. He trusts that his co-workers will help restore order to the communities in the eastern part of the empire in time to accompany him on this new venture.

| TITUS |

$\mathbf{F}$rom Paul, servant of God, apostle of Christ Jesus, at the service of God's chosen people, so that they may believe, and reach the knowledge of truth and godliness.

The eternal life we are waiting for was promised from the very beginning, by God, who never lies, and as the appointed time had come, he made it known, through the message entrusted to me by a command of God, our Savior.

Greetings to you, Titus, my true son in the faith we share.

May grace and peace be with you from God the Father and Christ Jesus our Lord.

$\mathbf{I}$ left you in Crete because I wanted you to put right, what was defective, and appoint elders in every town, following my instructions. They must be blameless, married only once, whose children are believers, and not open to the charge of being immoral and rebellious. Since the overseer (or bishop) is the steward of God's House, he must be beyond reproach: not proud, hot-headed, over-fond of wine, quarrelsome, or greedy for gain.

On the contrary, he must be hospitable, a lover of what is good, wise, upright, devout and self-controlled. He must hold to the message of faith, just as it was taught, so that, in his turn, he may teach sound doctrine, and refute those who oppose it.

You know, that there are many rebellious minds, talkers of nonsense, deceivers, especially the party of the circumcised. They have to be silenced when they go around disturbing whole families, teaching, for low gain, what should not be taught. A Cretan, one of their own prophets, has said, "Cretans: always liars, wicked beasts and lazy gluttons." This is true. For this reason, rebuke them sharply, if you want them to have a sound faith, instead of heeding Jewish fables, and practices of people who reject the truth.

To the pure everything is pure; to the corrupt and unbelieving, nothing is pure: their minds and consciences have been defiled. They pretend to know God, but deny him with their deeds. They are detestable, disobedient, and unfit for doing anything good.

Let your words strengthen sound doctrine. Tell the older men to be sober, serious, wise, sound in faith, love and perseverance.

The older women, in like manner, must behave as befits holy women, not given to gossiping or drinking wine, but as good counselors, able to teach younger women to love their husbands and children, to be judicious and chaste, to take care of their households, to be kind, and submissive to their husbands, lest our faith be attacked.

Encourage the young men, to be self-controlled. Set them an example by your own way of doing. Let your teaching be earnest and sincere, and your preaching, beyond reproach. Then, your opponents will feel ashamed and will have nothing to criticize.

Teach slaves to be subject to their masters, and to give satisfaction in every respect, instead of arguing. They must not steal from them, but be trustworthy. In this way, they will draw everyone to admire the doctrine of God our Savior.

For the grace of God has appeared, bringing salvation to all, teaching us to reject an irreligious way of life, and worldly greed, and to live in this world, as responsible persons, upright and serving God, while we await our blessed hope—the glorious manifestation of our great God and Savior Christ Jesus. He gave himself for us, to redeem us from every evil, and to purify a people he wanted to be his own, and dedicated to what is good.

Teach these things, encourage, and reprove with all authority. Let no one despise you.

Remind the believers, to be submissive to rulers and authorities, to be obedient, and to be ready for every good work. Tell them to insult no one; they must not be quarrelsome, but gentle and understanding with everyone.

We ourselves were once foolish, disobedient and misled. We were slaves of our desires, seeking pleasures of every kind. We lived in malice and envy, hateful, and hating each other. But God, our Savior, revealed his eminent goodness and love for humankind, and saved us, not because of good deeds we may have done, but for the sake of his own mercy, to the water of rebirth and renewal, by the Holy Spirit poured over us through Christ Jesus our Savior, so that, having been justified by his grace, we should become heirs, in hope of eternal life.

This is the truth. I want you to insist on these things, for those who believe in God must excel in good deeds; that is what matters, and is profitable to us. Avoid stupid arguments, discussions about genealogies, and quarrels about the law, for they are useless and unimportant.

If anyone promotes sects in the church, warn him once, and then, a second time. If he still continues, break with him, knowing that such a person is misled, and sinful, and stands self-condemned.

When I send Artemas or Tychicus to you, try to come to me at Nicopolis, as soon as possible, for I have decided to spend the winter there. Do your best to send Zenas, the lawyer, and Apollos, on their way soon, and see to it that they have everything they need. Our people must learn, to be outstanding in good works, and to face urgent needs, instead of remaining idle and useless.

All who are with me send greetings. Greet those who love us in the faith.

Grace be with you all.

INVITATION TO
2 TIMOTHY

Paul left his co-worker Timothy in the city of Ephesus to deal with some renegade leaders in the community of Jesus-followers. Timothy was unable to do this, and Paul needed to go back to Ephesus himself. There he suffered a great deal of harm from Alexander, one of these leaders, and he was once again imprisoned and taken to Rome. He expected that this time he wouldn't be released, but would be tried and executed. Since most of his other co-workers were either on different assignments or had deserted him, Paul wrote to Timothy and asked him to come to Rome quickly. He was concerned that winter might prevent travel, or his trial might reach its conclusion, before he could see one of his most dependable co-workers again. Paul wanted both to enjoy his company and assistance and to challenge and encourage him about the uncertain future.

Things in Ephesus had not gone as Paul or Timothy expected. Paul had ordered both Alexander and another renegade leader, Hymenaeus, to step down. But both men were continuing to oppose Paul. Others had joined their ranks, including Phygelus, Hermogenes and Philetus. They were still misdirecting people into a corrupted version of the faith that stressed debate and dissension rather than purity and obedience. Paul believed Timothy was feeling discouraged and intimidated. So his letter includes challenges to stay faithful to the true message—even if this meant suffering or death—and warnings against the dangers of the false teaching. Paul reminds Timothy that *in the last days*, that is, before the open appearance of Jesus as king, *there will be difficult times*. False teachers, treacherous and insincere people, persecutions and more will all challenge the faithfulness of Jesus-followers.

Paul urges Timothy to remember the gospel message: *Christ Jesus, risen from the dead, Jesus, son of David*. He points out that the sacred writings Timothy has known since he was a child are *inspired by God* and will make him thoroughly equipped for every good work. Knowing of Timothy's sincere faith, we can be confident that Paul's letter helped his longtime protégé to be able to say at the end of his own life, as Paul himself did, *I have fought the good fight, I have finished the race, I have kept the faith*.

| 2 TIMOTHY |

From Paul, apostle of Christ Jesus, by the will of God, for the sake of his promise of eternal life, in Christ Jesus, to my dear son Timothy.

May grace, mercy and peace be with you, from God, the Father, and Christ Jesus our Lord.

I give thanks to God, whom I serve with a clear conscience, the way my ancestors did, as I remember you constantly, day and night, in my prayers. I recall your tears, and I long to see you, that I may be filled with joy. I am reminded of your sincere faith, so like the faith of your grandmother Lois and of your mother Eunice, which I am sure you have inherited.

For this reason, I invite you to fan into a flame, the gift of God you received, through the laying on of my hands. For God did not confer on us a spirit of fearfulness, but of strength, love and good judgment. Do not be ashamed of testifying to our Lord, nor of seeing me in chains. On the contrary, do your share in laboring for the gospel, with the strength of God. He saved us and called us—a calling which proceeds from his holiness. This did not depend on our merits, but on his generosity and his own initiative. This calling, given to us from all time, in Christ Jesus has just been manifested with the glorious appearance of Christ Jesus, our Lord, who destroyed death, and brought life and immortality to light, in his gospel. Of this message, I was made herald, apostle and teacher.

For its sake, I now suffer this trial, but I am not ashamed, for I know in whom I have believed, and I am convinced, that he is capable of taking care of all I have entrusted to him, until that day.

Follow the pattern of the sound doctrine which you have heard from me, concerning faith, and love in Christ Jesus. Keep this precious deposit, with the help of the Holy Spirit, who lives within us.

You must know, that those from Asia have turned away from me, including Phygelus and Hermogenes. May the Lord show his mercy to the household of Onesiphorus, because he often comforted me, and was not ashamed when he found out that I was in prison. On the contrary, he showed courage, searched for me and found me. May the Lord grant, that he find mercy on that day. You know better than I, all the services he rendered in Ephesus.

You, my son, be strong with the grace you have in Christ Jesus. Entrust to reliable people everything you have learned from me in the presence of many witnesses, that they may instruct others.

Labor like a good soldier of Christ Jesus. No soldier gets involved in civilian trade; the soldier's aim is to please his commanding officer. No athlete is crowned, unless he competes according to the rules. And again, the farmer who tills the land is the first to enjoy the fruits of the harvest. Think over what I am telling you; the Lord will give you understanding in everything.

Remember Christ Jesus, risen from the dead, Jesus, son of David, as preached in my gospel. For this gospel I labor, and even wear chains like an evildoer, but the word of God is not chained. And, so, I bear everything, for the sake of the chosen people, that they, too, may obtain the salvation given to us, in Christ Jesus, and share eternal glory. This statement is true:

> If we have died with him,
> we shall also live with him;
>
> If we endure with him,
> we shall also reign with him;
>
> If we deny him,
> he will also deny us;
>
> If we are unfaithful,
> he remains faithful for he cannot deny himself.

Remind your people of these things, and urge them, in the presence of God, not to fight over words, which does no good, but only ruins those who listen. Be for God, an active and proven minister, a blameless worker, correctly handling the word of truth. Do not take part in useless conversations, alien to the faith. This leads to a greater impiety. Such teaching spreads like gangrene: I am thinking of Hymeneus and Philetus. They strayed from the truth, holding that the resurrection has already taken place; and with this, they upset the faith of some. But the solid foundations laid by God are not shaken; on them, it is written: The Lord knows those who are his, and: Let him who confesses the name of the Lord turn away from evil.

In a large house, we find, not only vessels of gold and silver, but also of wood and clay. Some are reserved for special uses, others, for ordinary ones. All who clean themselves of what I speak of, will become a noble vessel, useful to the Lord, prepared for any holy purpose.

So shun the passions of youth and seek righteousness, faith, love and peace, together with those who call upon the Lord with a pure heart. Avoid stupid and senseless discussions, since such are the cause of misunderstanding. God's servant must not be quarrelsome, but kind to all, always teaching, and patient with those who do not understand, and gently correcting opponents; perhaps God may grant them to repent and discover the truth, withdrawing them from the snare of the devil, who held them captive to his own will.

Be quite sure, that there will be difficult times in the last days. People will become selfish, lovers of money, boastful, conceited, gossips, disobedient to their parents, ungrateful, unholy. They will be unable to love and to forgive; they will be slanderers, without self-control, cruel, enemies of good, traitors, shameless, full of pride, more in love with pleasure than with God. They will keep the appearance of piety, while rejecting its demands. Keep away from such people.

Of the same kind, are those who enter houses and captivate weak women, full of sins, swayed by all kinds of passion, who are always learning, but never grasping knowledge of the truth. These people of corrupt mind and false faith, oppose the truth, just as Jannes and Jambres opposed Moses. Yet, they may not go very far, for their folly will be clear to all, as in the case of those two.

You, instead, have closely followed my teaching, my way of life, my projects, faith, patience, love, endurance, persecutions and sufferings. You know what happened to me at Antioch, Iconium and Lystra. How many trials I had to bear! Yet, the Lord rescued me from them all. All who want to serve God, in Christ Jesus, will be persecuted; while evil persons and impostors will go from bad to worse, deceiving and being deceived.

As for you, continue with what you have learned, and what has been entrusted to you, knowing from whom you received it. Besides, you have known the Scriptures from childhood; they will give you the wisdom that leads to salvation, through faith in Christ Jesus. All Scripture is inspired by God, and is useful for teaching, refuting error, for correcting and training in Christian life. Through Scripture, the man of God is made expert and thoroughly equipped for every good work.

In the presence of God and Christ Jesus, who is to judge the living and the dead, and by the hope I have of his coming, and his kingdom, I urge you to preach the word, in season and out of season, reproving, rebuking, or advising, always with patience, and providing instruction. For the time is coming, when people will no longer endure sound doctrine, but, following their passions, they will surround themselves with teachers to please their itching ears. And they will abandon the truth to hear fables. So be prudent, do not mind your labor, give yourself to your work as an evangelist, fulfill your ministry.

As for me, I am already poured out as a libation, and the moment of my departure has come. I have fought the good fight, I have finished the race, I have kept the faith. Now, there is laid up for me the crown of righteousness, with which the Lord, the just judge, will reward me, on that day, and not only me, but all those who have longed for his glorious coming.

D o your best to come to me quickly. You must know, that Demas has deserted me, for the love of this world: he returned to Thessalonica. Crescens has gone to Galatia and Titus to Dalmatia. Only Luke remains with me. Get Mark and bring him with you, for he is a useful helper in my work. I sent Tychicus to Ephesus.

Bring with you the cloak I left at Troas, in Carpos' house, and also the scrolls, especially the parchments. Alexander, the metalworker, has caused me great harm. The Lord will repay him for what he has done. Distrust him, for he has been very much opposed to our preaching.

At my first hearing in court, no one supported me; all deserted me. May the Lord not hold it against them. But the Lord was at my side, giving me strength, to proclaim the word fully, and let all the pagans hear it. So I was rescued from the lion's mouth. The Lord will save me from all evil, bringing me to his heavenly kingdom. Glory to him for ever and ever. Amen!

Greetings to Prisca and Aquila, and to the family of Onesiphorus. Erastus remained in Corinth. I left Trophimus sick in Miletus.

Try to come here before the winter. Eubulus, Pudens, Linus, Claudia and all the brothers and sisters send you greetings. The Lord be with your spirit.

May grace be with you all.

INVITATION TO
MATTHEW

The book known as Matthew is an account of the life and teaching of Jesus. While tradition says the disciple Matthew wrote it, the author never identifies himself. But he may be giving us a clue to his identity when he includes, at a strategic place in the book, a saying of Jesus that isn't recorded anywhere else: *every teacher of the law, who becomes a disciple of the kingdom of heaven, is like a householder, who can produce from his store things both new and old*. This clue, and the character of the book itself, suggest that the author was actually someone highly trained in the Hebrew Scriptures, rather than a tax collector like Matthew.

It's hard to tell exactly where and when this book was written. But much of what it says can be best understood by those who are familiar with Israel's Scriptures, so we can be reasonably sure it was written within a community of Jews who believed in Jesus as their Messiah. Its author was most likely, in other words, a teacher of the law who had been instructed about the kingdom of heaven that Jesus was now establishing on earth. He wrote to tell his fellow Jews how Jesus, the promised king, was creating a new community by bringing the ancient Jewish story to its climax. This book uses a combination of literary forms (an ancestor list; action sequences; collected teachings) to show that God is fulfilling his ancient promises to Israel through the life and ministry of Jesus of Nazareth.

To portray Jesus as the culmination of the work God began through Israel, the author starts the book with a list of Jesus' ancestors. The list highlights how Jesus was the son (descendant) of David, Israel's most famous king, and the son of Abraham, Israel's founding patriarch. In other words, Jesus is the true Israelite and the long-awaited Messiah. The list is arranged to show Jesus coming at the beginning of the seventh group of seven generations since Abraham. The seventh seven was, for the Jews, a time of special celebration, so the message is that Jesus came to bring a special time of God's blessing to the world.

After this opening ancestor list, the author tells the story of Jesus' life. He draws several parallels at the beginning of the story between Jesus and Moses. For example, like Moses, Jesus narrowly escapes death when a ruler attempts to kill all Hebrew baby boys. Just as Moses spent forty years in the desert, Jesus spends forty days in the desert before beginning his ministry. As these parallels develop, they show that just as Moses was the founder of the original nation of Israel, Jesus came as the founder of a renewed Israel.

Jesus also embodies this renewed Israel himself. His experience echoes the themes of Israel's experience under Moses. But where Israel failed to follow God, Jesus obeys. Soon after God rescued Israel from slavery in Egypt and formed them into a nation, two key events happened. Right after a covenant-making ceremony in the desert, the people fell to the temptation of worshipping other gods. Later, Israel crossed the Jordan River and followed their leader Joshua into the land God had promised them. The book of Matthew shows how two corresponding events took place at the beginning of Jesus' own ministry. Jesus goes down to the Jordan River and is baptized, in a ceremony that demonstrates his loyalty to God's covenant with Israel. Then Jesus goes into the desert and is also tempted. But he resists the enticement to evil and triumphs over God's adversary. In all of this Matthew reveals Jesus as starting a movement to renew Israel, inviting the people to a new beginning with their God.

But the author draws the most important parallel between Jesus and Moses by the way he organizes his work as a whole. Moses gave the people of Israel the Torah (or law) and it was traditionally divided into five books. In Matthew the teachings of Jesus are organized into five long speeches, which are inserted into the story at intervals. Just as Moses went up Mount Sinai to receive the law, Jesus goes up on a mountain to give his first speech. In these ways Jesus is revealed as the new Moses, and his teaching becomes the foundation of the multinational community that now constitutes the people of God.

To show us how important these five speeches are, the author marks them all in the same way. Each one begins with the disciples coming to Jesus for teaching. Each one ends with a variation of the phrase, *When Jesus had finished these sayings . . .* These five speeches express five different themes, and these themes run through the episodes in the story that lead up to them. And so the core of the book is divided into five thematic sections consisting of story plus teaching. These sections address five key aspects of the kingdom of heaven:

: The first section reveals that this kingdom is based on a way of *righteous* living in which outward action expresses inward character (pp. 238–246).

: The second section demonstrates how Jesus chose twelve disciples as a symbol of the renewed Israel and sent them out on a *mission* to announce the coming of the kingdom of heaven (pp. 247–251).

: The third section explores the *mystery* of the kingdom: it's hard to recognize and easy to misunderstand, but it's nevertheless actively growing throughout the world (pp. 252–258).

: The fourth section shows how the kingdom of heaven creates a new *family*, the community of Jesus' followers (pp. 258–265).

: The fifth section shows that the *destiny* of this kingdom is for its citizens to be scattered throughout the world by their enemies, giving them the opportunity to tell people everywhere about Jesus (pp. 265–278).

After this new Torah has been given, the book concludes with the story of how Jesus performed a great new act of redemption for his people. In the ancient story of Israel's exodus, a Passover meal was celebrated and then the deliverance came. In this story, Jesus celebrates the Passover with his disciples and then gives his life for the sake of the world. He is then raised from the dead, the dawn of a day of new creation. Jesus announces that he has been enthroned as king: *All authority has been given to me in heaven and on earth*. At the beginning of Matthew, Jesus' birth was announced with the name *Emmanuel*, which means "God with us." At the end of the book, Jesus sends his closest followers to *go, therefore, and make disciples of all nations*, promising them, *I am with you always*.

| MATTHEW |

This is the account of the genealogy of Jesus Christ, son of David, son of Abraham.

Abraham was the father of Isaac, Isaac the father of Jacob, Jacob the father of Judah and his brothers.

Judah was the father of Perez and Zerah (their mother was Tamar), Perez was the father of Hezron, and Hezron of Aram. Aram was the father of Aminadab, Aminadab of Nahshon, Nahshon of Salmon.

Salmon was the father of Boaz. His mother was Rahab. Boaz was the father of Obed. His mother was Ruth. Obed was the father of Jesse.

Jesse was the father of David, the king. David was the father of Solomon. His mother had been Uriah's wife.

Solomon was the father of Rehoboam. Then came the kings: Abijah, Asaph, Jehoshaphat, Joram, Uzziah, Jotham, Ahaz, Hezekiah, Manasseh, Amon, Josiah.

Josiah was the father of Jechoniah and his brothers at the time of the deportation to Babylon.

After the deportation to Babylon, Jechoniah was the father of Salathiel and Salathiel of Zerubbabel.

Zerubbabel was the father of Abiud, Abiud of Eliakim, and Eliakim of Azor. Azor was the father of Zadok, Zadok the father of Akim, and Akim the father of Eliud. Eliud was the father of Eleazar, Eleazar of Matthan, and Matthan of Jacob.

Jacob was the father of Joseph, the husband of Mary, and from her came Jesus who is called the Christ—the Messiah.

There were then fourteen generations from Abraham to David, and fourteen generations from David to the deportation to Babylon, and fourteen generations from the deportation to Babylon to the birth of Christ.

This is how Jesus Christ was born: Mary his mother had been given to Joseph in marriage, but before they lived together, she was found to be pregnant through the Holy Spirit.

Then Joseph, her husband, made plans to divorce her in all secrecy. He was an upright man, and in no way did he want to disgrace her.

While he was pondering over this, an angel of the Lord appeared to him in a dream and said, "Joseph, descendant of David, do not be afraid to take Mary as your wife. She has conceived by the Holy Spirit, and now she will bear a son. You shall call him 'Jesus' for he will save his people from their sins."

All this happened in order to fulfill what the Lord had said through the prophet: The virgin will conceive and bear a son, and he will be called Emmanuel, which means: God-with-us. When Joseph awoke, he did what the angel of the Lord had told him to do, and he took his wife to his home. He did not have any marital relations with her. When she gave birth to a son, Joseph gave him the name Jesus.

When Jesus was born in Bethlehem, in Judea, during the days of king Herod, wise men from the East arrived in Jerusalem. They asked, "Where is the newborn king of the Jews? We saw the rising of his star in the East and have come to honor him."

When Herod heard this he was greatly disturbed, and with him all Jerusalem. He immediately called a meeting of all high-ranking priests and teachers of the law, and asked them where the Messiah was to be born.

"In the town of Bethlehem in Judea," they told him, "for this is what the prophet wrote:

> And you, Bethlehem, in the land of Judah,
> you are by no means the least among the clans of Judah,
>
> for from you will come a leader,
> one who is to shepherd my people Israel."

Then Herod secretly called the wise men and asked them the precise time the star appeared. He sent them to Bethlehem with these instructions, "Go and get accurate information about the child. As soon as you have found him, report to me, so that I, too, may go and honor him."

After the meeting with the king, they set out. The star that they had seen in the East went ahead of them and stopped over the place where the child was. The wise men were overjoyed on seeing the star again. They went into the house, and when they saw the child with Mary his mother, they knelt and worshiped him. They opened their bags and offered him their gifts of gold, incense and myrrh.

In a dream they were warned not to go back to Herod, so they returned to their home country by another way.

After the wise men had left, an angel of the Lord appeared in a dream to Joseph and said, "Get up, take the child and his mother and flee to Egypt, and stay there until I tell you, for Herod will soon be looking for the child in order to kill him."

Joseph got up, took the child and his mother, and left that night for Egypt, where he stayed until the death of Herod. In this way, what the Lord had said through the prophet was fulfilled: I called my son out of Egypt.

When Herod found out that he had been tricked by the wise men, he was furious. He gave orders to kill all the boys in Bethlehem and its neighborhood who were two years old or under. This was done, according to what he had learned from the wise men about the time when the star appeared.

In this way, what the prophet Jeremiah had said was fulfilled:

> A cry is heard in Ramah,
> wailing and loud lamentation:
>
> Rachel weeps for her children. S
> he refuses to be comforted,
> for they are no more.

After Herod's death, an angel of the Lord appeared in a dream to Joseph and said, "Get up, take the child and his mother, and go back to the land of Israel, because those who tried to kill the child are dead." So Joseph got up, took the child and his mother, and went to the land of Israel.

But when Joseph heard that Archilaus had succeeded his father Herod as king of Judea, he was afraid to go there. Joseph was given further instructions in a dream, and went to the region of Galilee.

There he settled, in a town called Nazareth. In this way, what was said by the prophets was fulfilled: He shall be called a Nazarene.

In the course of time, John the Baptist appeared in the desert of Judea and began to proclaim his message: "Change your ways; the kingdom of heaven is at hand!" It was about him that the prophet Isaiah had spoken when he said:

> A voice is shouting in the desert,
> 'Prepare a way for the Lord;
> make his paths straight!'

John had a leather garment around his waist and wore a cloak of camel's hair; his food was locusts and wild honey. People came to him from Jerusalem, from all Judea and from the whole Jordan valley, and they were baptized by him in the Jordan, as they confessed their sins.

When he saw several Pharisees and Sadducees coming to where he baptized, he said to them, "Brood of vipers! Who told you that you could escape the punishment that is to come? Let it be seen that you are serious in your conversion; and do not think: We have Abraham for our father. I tell you, that God can raise children for Abraham from these stones! The ax is already laid to the roots of the trees; any tree that does not produce good fruit will be cut down and thrown in the fire.

I baptize you in water for a change of heart, but the one who is coming after me is more powerful than I am; indeed, I am not worthy to carry his sandals. He will baptize you with the Holy Spirit and fire. He has the winnowing fan in his hand; and he will clear out his threshing floor. He will gather his wheat into the barn; but the chaff, he will burn in inextinguishable fire."

At that time, Jesus arrived from Galilee and came to John at the Jordan, to be baptized by him. But John tried to prevent him, and said, "How is it, you come to me? I should be baptized by you!"

But Jesus answered him, "Let it be like that for now; so that we may fulfill the right order." John agreed.

As soon as he was baptized, Jesus came up out of the water. All at once, the heavens opened and he saw the Spirit of God come down, like a dove, and rest upon him. At the same time, a voice from heaven was heard, "This is my Son, the Beloved; he is my Chosen One."

Then the Spirit led Jesus into the desert, that he might be put to the test by the devil. After Jesus fasted forty days and nights he was famished.

Then the tempter came to him and said, "If you are the Son of God, order these stones to turn into bread." But Jesus answered, "Scripture says: One does not live on bread alone, but on every word that comes from the mouth of God."

Then the devil took Jesus to the Holy City, set him on the highest wall of the temple, and said to him, "If you are the Son of God, throw yourself down, for scripture says:

> God has given orders to his angels concerning you.
> Their hands will hold you up,
> lest you hurt your foot against a stone."

Jesus answered, "But scripture also says: You shall not put the Lord your God to the test."

Then the devil took Jesus to a very high mountain, and showed him all the nations of the world in all their greatness and splendor. And he said, "All this I will give you, if you kneel down and worship me." Then Jesus answered, "Be off, Satan! Scripture says: Worship the Lord your God and serve him alone!"

Then the devil left him; and angels came to serve him.

When Jesus heard that John had been arrested, he withdrew into Galilee. He left Nazareth and went to live in Capernaum, a town by the lake of Galilee, at the border of Zebulun and Naphtali.

In this way, the word of the prophet Isaiah was fulfilled:

> Land of Zebulun and land of Naphtali,
> crossed by the Road of the Sea;
> and you, who live beyond the Jordan, Galilee,
> land of pagans:
>
> The people who lived in darkness
> have seen a great light;
>
> on those who live in the land of the shadow of death,
> a light has shone.

From that time on, Jesus began to proclaim his message, "Change your ways: the kingdom of heaven is near."

As Jesus walked by the lake of Galilee, he saw two brothers, Simon called Peter, and Andrew his brother, casting a net into the lake, for they were fishermen. He said to them, "Come, follow me; and I will make you fish for people."

At once they left their nets and followed him.

He went on from there and saw two other brothers, James, the son of Zebedee, and his brother John, in a boat with their father Zebedee, mending their nets. Jesus called them.

At once, they left the boat, and their father, and followed him.

Jesus went around all Galilee, teaching in their synagogues, proclaiming the good news of the kingdom, and curing all kinds of sickness and disease among the people.

The news about him spread through the whole of Syria; and the people brought all their sick to him, and all those who suffered: the possessed, the deranged, the paralyzed; and he healed them all. Large crowds followed him from Galilee and the Ten Cities, from Jerusalem, Judea, and from across the Jordan.

When Jesus saw the crowds, he went up the mountain. He sat down and his disciples gathered around him. Then he spoke and began to teach them:

> Fortunate are those who are poor in spirit,
> for theirs is the kingdom of heaven.
>
> Fortunate are those who mourn;
> they shall be comforted.
>
> Fortunate are the gentle;
> they shall possess the land.
>
> Fortunate are those who hunger and thirst for justice,
> for they shall be satisfied.
>
> Fortunate are the merciful,
> for they shall find mercy.
>
> Fortunate are those with pure hearts,
> for they shall see God.
>
> Fortunate are those who work for peace;
> they shall be called children of God.
>
> Fortunate are those who are persecuted for the cause of
>   righteousness,
> for theirs is the kingdom of heaven.

Fortunate are you, when people insult you and persecute you and speak all kinds of evil against you because you are my followers. Be glad and joyful, for a great reward is kept for you in God. For that is how this people persecuted the prophets who lived before you.

You are the salt of the earth. But if salt has lost its saltiness, how can it be made salty again? It has become useless. It can only be thrown away and people will trample on it.

You are the light of the world. A city built on a mountain cannot be hidden. No one lights a lamp and covers it; instead, it is put on a lamp stand, where it gives light to everyone in the house. In the same way, your light must shine before others, so that they may see the good you do, and praise your Father in heaven.

Do not think that I have come to annul the law and the prophets. I have not come to annul them, but to fulfill them. I tell you this: as long as heaven and earth last, not the smallest letter or dot in the law will change, until all is fulfilled.

So then, whoever breaks the least important of these commandments, and teaches others to do the same, will be the least in the kingdom of heaven. On the other hand, whoever obeys them, and teaches others to do the same, will be great in the kingdom of heaven.

I tell you, if your sense of right and wrong is not keener than that of the Lawyers and the Pharisees, you will not enter the kingdom of heaven.

You have heard, that it was said to our people in the past: Do not commit murder; anyone who murders will have to face trial. But now, I tell you: whoever gets angry with a brother or sister will have to face trial. Whoever insults a brother or sister is liable, to be brought before the council. Whoever calls a brother or sister "Fool!" is liable, of being thrown into the fire of hell. So, if you are about to offer your gift at the altar, and you remember that your brother has something against you, leave your gift there, in front of the altar; go at once, and make peace with your brother, and then come back and offer your gift to God.

Don't forget this: be reconciled with your opponent quickly when you are together on the way to court. Otherwise he will turn you over to the judge, who will hand you over to the police, who will put you in jail. There, you will stay, until you have paid the last penny.

You have heard that it was said: Do not commit adultery. But I tell you this: anyone who looks at a woman with lustful intent, has already committed adultery with her in his heart.

So, if your right eye causes you to sin, pluck it out and throw it away! It is much better for you to lose a part of your body, than to have your whole body thrown into hell. If your right hand causes you to sin, cut it off and throw it away! It is better for you to lose a part of your body, than to have your whole body thrown into hell.

It was also said: Anyone who divorces his wife, must give her a written notice of divorce. But what I tell you is this: if a man divorces his wife, except in the case of unlawful union, he causes her to commit adultery. And the man who marries a divorced woman commits adultery.

You have also heard that people were told in the past: Do not break your oath; an oath sworn to the Lord must be kept. But I tell you this: do not take oaths. Do not swear by the heavens, for they are God's throne; nor by the earth, because it is his footstool; nor by Jerusalem, because it is the city of the great king. Do not even swear by your head, because you cannot make a single hair white or black. Let your 'Yes' mean 'Yes' and your 'No' mean 'No.' Anything else you say comes from the evil one.

You have heard, that it was said: An eye for an eye and a tooth for a tooth. But I tell you this: do not oppose evil with evil; if someone slaps you on your right cheek, turn and offer the other. If someone sues you in court for your shirt, give him your coat as well. If someone forces you to go one mile, go two miles with him. Give when asked, and do not turn your back on anyone who wants to borrow from you.

You have heard, that it was said: Love your neighbor and do not do good to your enemy. But this I tell you: love your enemies; and pray for those who persecute you, so that you may be children of your Father in Heaven. For he makes his sun rise on both the wicked and the good; and he gives rain to both the just and the unjust.

If you love those who love you, what is special about that? Do not even tax collectors do as much? And if you are friendly only to your friends, what is so exceptional about that? Do not even the pagans do as much? As for you, be perfect, as your heavenly Father is perfect.

Be careful not to make a show of your good deeds before people. If you do so, you do not gain anything from your Father in heaven. When you give something to the poor, do not have it trumpeted before you, as do those who want to be noticed in the synagogues and in the streets, in order to be praised by people. I assure you, they have their reward.

If you give something to the poor, do not let your left hand know what your right hand is doing, so that your gift remains really secret. Your Father, who sees what is kept secret, will reward you.

When you pray, do not be like those who want to be noticed. They love to stand and pray in the synagogues or on street corners, in order to be seen by everyone. I assure you, they have their reward. When you pray, go into your room, close the door, and pray to your Father who is with you in secret; and your Father who sees what is kept secret will reward you.

When you pray, do not use a lot of words, as the pagans do; for they believe that, the more they say, the more chance they have of being heard. Do not be like them. Your Father knows what you need, even before you ask him.

This, then, is how you should pray:

> Our Father in heaven,
> holy be your name,
> your kingdom, come,
> your will, be done
> on earth, as in heaven.
> Give us today, our daily bread.
> Forgive us our debts,
> as we forgive those who are in debt to us.
> Do not bring us to the test,
> but deliver us from the evil one.

If you forgive others their wrongdoings, your Father in heaven will also forgive yours. If you do not forgive others, then your Father will not forgive you.

When you fast, do not put on a miserable face, as do the hypocrites. They put on a gloomy face, so that people can see they are fasting. I tell you this: they have been paid in full already. When you fast, wash your face and make yourself look cheerful, because you are not fasting for appearances or for people, but for your Father, who sees beyond appearances. And your Father, who sees what is kept secret, will reward you.

Do not store up treasures for yourself here, on earth, where moth and rust destroy it; and where thieves can steal it. Store up treasures for yourself with God, where no moth or rust can destroy it, nor thief come and steal it.

For where your treasures is, there, also, will your heart be.

The lamp of the body is the eye; if your eyes are sound, your whole body will be full of light. If your eyes are diseased, your whole body will be full of darkness. If, then, the light in you is darkness, how great is that darkness!

No one can serve two masters; for he will either hate one and love the other; or he will be loyal to the first and look down on the second. You cannot, at the same time, serve God and money.

Therefore, I tell you, not to be worried about food and drink for yourself, or about clothes for your body. Is not life more important than food; and is not the body more important than clothes? Look at the birds of the air; they do not sow, they do not harvest, and do not store food in barns; and yet, your heavenly Father feeds them. Are you not more worthy than they are?

Can any of you add a day to your life by worrying about it? Why are you so worried about your clothes? Look at how the flowers in the fields grow. They do not toil or spin. But I tell you, that not even Solomon, in all his glory, was clothed like one of these. If God so clothes the grass in the field, which blooms today and is to be burned in an oven tomorrow, how much more will he clothe you? What little faith you have!

Do not worry, and say: What are we going to eat? What are we going to drink? or: What shall we wear? The pagans busy themselves with such things; but your heavenly Father knows that you need them all. Set your heart, first, on the kingdom and righteousness of God; and all these things will also be given to you. Do not worry about tomorrow, for tomorrow will worry about itself. Each day has enough trouble of its own.

Do not judge; and you will not be judged. In the same way you judge others, you will be judged; and the measure you use for others will be used for you. Why do you look at the speck in your brother's eye, and not see the plank in your own eye? How can you say to your brother, 'Come, let me take the speck from your eye,' as long as that plank is in your own? Hypocrite, remove the plank out of your own eye; then, you will see clearly, to remove the speck out of your brother's eye.

Do not give what is holy to the dogs, or throw your pearls before pigs. They might trample on them, and then turn on you and tear you to pieces.

Ask, and you will receive; seek, and you will find; knock, and the door will be opened. For everyone who asks, receives; whoever seeks, finds; and to him who knocks, the door will be opened. Would any of you give a stone to your son, when he asks for bread? Or give him a snake, when he asks for a fish? However bad you may be, you know how to give good things to your children. How much more, then, will your Father in heaven give good things to those who ask him!

So, do to others whatever you would that others do to you: there, you have the law and the prophets.

Enter through the narrow gate: for wide is the gate, and broad is the road, that leads to destruction, and many go that way. How narrow is the gate that leads to life; and how rough, the road; few there are, who find it.

Beware of false prophets: they come to you in sheep's clothing; but inside, they are voracious wolves. You will recognize them by their fruits. Do you ever pick grapes from thorn bushes; or figs, from thistles?

A good tree always produces good fruit. A rotten tree produces bad fruit. A good tree cannot produce bad fruit; and a rotten tree cannot bear good fruit. Any tree that does not bear good fruit is cut down and thrown into the fire. So then, you will know them by their fruit.

Not everyone who says to me, 'Lord! Lord!' will enter the kingdom of heaven, but the one who does the will of my heavenly Father. Many will say to me on that day, 'Lord, Lord, did we not speak in your name? Did we not cast out devils and perform many miracles in your name?' Then I will tell them openly, 'I have never known you; away from me, you evil people!'

"Therefore, anyone who hears these words of mine, and acts according to them, is like a wise man, who built his house on rock. The rain poured down, the rivers flooded, and the wind blew and struck that house. But it did not collapse, because it was built on rock. But anyone who hears these words of mine, and does not act accordingly, is like a fool who built his house on sand. The rain poured, the rivers flooded, and the wind blew and struck that house; it collapsed, and what a terrible collapse that was!"

When Jesus had finished this discourse, the crowds were struck by the way he taught, because he taught with authority, unlike their teachers of the law.

W hen Jesus came down from the mountain, large crowds followed him.

Then a leper came forward. He knelt before him and said, "Sir, if you want to, you can make me clean." Jesus stretched out his hand, touched him, and said, "I want to, be clean again." At that very moment, the man was cleansed from his leprosy. Then Jesus said to him, "See that you do not tell anyone; but go to the priest, have yourself declared clean, and offer the gift that Moses commanded as evidence for them."

When Jesus entered Capernaum, an army captain approached him, to ask his help, "Sir, my servant lies sick at home. He is paralyzed and suffers terribly." Jesus said to him, "I will come and heal him."

The captain answered, "I am not worthy to have you under my roof. Just give an order and my boy will be healed. For I myself, a junior officer, give orders to my soldiers. And if I say to one, 'Go!' he goes; and if I say to another, 'Come!' he comes; and if I say to my servant, 'Do this!' he does it."

When Jesus heard this, he was astonished; and said to those who were following him, "I tell you, I have not found such faith in Israel. I say to you, many will come from east and west and sit down with Abraham, Isaac and Jacob at the feast in the kingdom of heaven; but the heirs of the kingdom will be thrown out into extreme darkness; there, they will wail and grind their teeth."

Then Jesus said to the captain, "Go home now. As you believed, so let it be." And at that moment, his servant was healed.

Jesus went to Peter's house and found Peter's mother-in-law in bed with fever. He took her by the hand and the fever left her; she got up and began to wait on him.

Toward evening, they brought to Jesus many people possessed by evil spirits; and with a word, he drove out the spirits. He also healed all who were sick. In this way, what was said by the prophet Isaiah was fulfilled:

> He bore our infirmities
> and took on himself our diseases.

When Jesus saw the crowd pressing around him, he gave orders to cross to the other side of the lake. A teacher of the law approached him; and said, "Master, I will follow you wherever you go." Jesus said to him, "Foxes have holes and birds have nests, but the Son of Man has nowhere to lay his head."

Another disciple said to him, "Lord, let me go and bury my father first." But Jesus said to him, "Follow me, and let the dead bury their dead."

Jesus got into the boat and his disciples followed him. Without warning, a fierce storm burst upon the lake, with waves sweeping the boat. But Jesus was asleep.

The disciples woke him up and cried, "Lord save us! We are lost!" But Jesus answered, "Why are you so afraid, you of little faith?" Then he stood up and rebuked the wind and sea; and it became completely calm.

The disciples were astonished. They said, "What kind of man is he? Even the winds and the sea obey him."

When Jesus reached Gadara, on the other side, he was met by two men, possessed by devils, who came out from the tombs. They were so fierce that no one dared to pass that way. They cried out, "Son of God, leave us alone! Have you come here to torment us before the time?"

Some distance away there was a large herd of pigs feeding. So the demons begged him, "If you drive us out, send us into that herd of pigs." Jesus ordered them, "Go!" So the demons left the men and went into the pigs. The whole herd rushed down the cliff into the lake and was drowned.

The men in charge of the pigs ran off to the town, where they told the whole story; and also what had happened to the men possessed with the demons. The whole town went out to meet Jesus; and when they saw him, they begged him to leave their region.

Jesus got back into the boat, crossed the lake again, and came to his hometown. Here, they brought to him a paralyzed man, lying on a bed. Jesus saw their faith and said to the paralytic, "Courage, my son! Your sins are forgiven."

Some teachers of the law said within themselves, "This man insults God." Jesus was aware of what they were thinking; and said, "Why have you such evil thoughts? Which is easier to say: 'Your sins are forgiven' or 'Stand up and walk'? But that you may know, that the Son of Man has power on earth to forgive sins," he said to the paralyzed man, "Stand up! Take your stretcher and go home!" The man got up, and went home.

When the crowds saw this, they were filled with awe, and praised God for giving such power to human beings.

As Jesus moved on from there, he saw a man named Matthew, at his seat in the custom-house; and he said to him, "Follow me!" And Matthew got up and followed him. Now it happened, while Jesus was at table in Matthew's house, many tax collectors and sinners joined Jesus and his disciples. When the Pharisees saw this, they said to his disciples, "Why is it, that your master eats with sinners and tax collectors?"

When Jesus heard this, he said, "Healthy people do not need a doctor, but sick people do. Go, and find out what this means: What I want is mercy, not sacrifice. I did not come to call the righteous, but sinners."

Then the disciples of John came to him with the question, "How is it, that we and the Pharisees fast on many occasions, but not your disciples?"

Jesus answered them, "How can you expect wedding guests to mourn as long as the bridegroom is with them? The time will come, when the bridegroom will be taken away from them, and then, they will fast.

No one patches an old coat with a piece of unshrunken cloth, for the patch will shrink and tear an even bigger hole in the coat. In the same way, you don't put new wine into old wine skins. If you do, the wine skins will burst and the wine will be spilt. No, you put new wine into fresh skins; then both are preserved."

While Jesus was speaking to them, an official of the synagogue came up to him, bowed before him and said, "My daughter has just died, but come and place your hands on her, and she will live." Jesus stood up and followed him with his disciples.

Then a woman, who had suffered from a severe bleeding for twelve years, came up from behind and touched the edge of his cloak; for she thought, "If I only touch his cloak, I will be healed." Jesus turned, saw her and said, "Courage, my daughter, your faith has saved you." And from that moment, the woman was cured.

When Jesus arrived at the official's house and saw the flute players and the excited crowd, he said, "Get out of here! The girl is not dead. She is only sleeping!" And they laughed at him. But once the crowd had been turned out, Jesus went in and took the girl by the hand, and she stood up. The news of this spread through the whole area.

As Jesus moved on from there, two blind men followed him, shouting, "Son of David, help us!" When he was about to enter the house, the blind men caught up with him; and Jesus said to them, "Do you believe that I am able to do what you want?" They answered, "Yes, sir!"

Then Jesus touched their eyes and said, "As you have believed, so let it be." And their eyes were opened. Then Jesus gave them a stern warning, "Be careful that no one knows about this." But as soon as they went away, they spread the news about him through the whole area.

As they were going away, some people brought to Jesus a man who was dumb, because he was possessed by a demon. When the demon was driven out, the dumb man began to speak. The crowds were astonished and said, "Nothing like this has ever been seen in Israel." But the Pharisees said, "He drives away demons with the help of the prince of demons."

Jesus went around all the towns and villages, teaching in their synagogues and proclaiming the good news of the kingdom; and he cured every sickness and disease. When he saw the crowds, he was moved with pity; for they were harassed and helpless, like sheep without a shepherd. Then he said to his disciples, "The harvest is abundant, but the workers are only few. Ask the master of the harvest to send workers to gather his harvest."

Jesus called his Twelve disciples to him, and gave them authority over unclean spirits, to drive them out, and to heal every disease and sickness.

These are the names of the Twelve apostles: first Simon, called Peter, and his brother Andrew; James, the son of Zebedee, and his brother John; Philip and Bartholomew; Thomas and Matthew, the tax collector; James, the son of Alphaeus, and Thaddaeus; Simon, the Canaanite, and Judas Iscariot, the man who would betray him.

Jesus sent these Twelve on mission, with the instructions: "Do not visit pagan territory and do not enter a Samaritan town. Go, instead, to the lost sheep of the people of Israel.

Go, and proclaim this message: The kingdom of heaven is near. Heal the sick, bring the dead back to life, cleanse the lepers, and drive out demons. Freely have you received, freely give. Do not carry any gold or silver or money in your purses. Do not take a traveling bag, or an extra shirt, or sandals, or a walking stick: workers deserve to be compensated.

When you come to a town or a village, look for a worthy person, and stay there until you leave.

When you enter the house, wish it peace. If the people are worthy people, your peace will rest on them; if they are not worthy people, your blessing will come back to you.

And if you are not welcomed, and your words are not listened to, leave that house or that town, and shake the dust off your feet. I assure you, it will go easier for the people of Sodom and Gomorrah on the day of judgment, than it will for the people of that town.

Look, I send you out like sheep among wolves. You must be as clever as snakes and as innocent as doves. Be on your guard with people, for they will hand you over to their courts, and they will flog you in their synagogues. You will be brought to trial before rulers and kings because of me, so that you may witness to them and the pagans.

But when you are arrested, do not worry about what you are to say, or how you are to say it; when the hour comes, you will be given what you are to say. For it will not be you who speak, but the Spirit of your Father, speaking through you.

Brother will hand over his brother to death, and a father his child;

children will turn against their parents and have them put to death. Everyone will hate you because of me, but whoever stands firm to the end will be saved.

When they persecute you in one town, flee to the next. I tell you the truth, you will not have passed through all the towns of Israel before the Son of Man comes.

A student is not above his teacher, nor a slave above his master. A student should be content to become like his teacher, and the slave like his master. If the head of the household has been called Beelzebul, how much more, those of his household! So, do not be afraid of them!

There is nothing covered that will not be uncovered. There is nothing hidden that will not be made known. What I am telling you in the dark, you must speak in the light. What you hear in private, proclaim from the housetops.

Do not be afraid of those who kill the body, but have no power to kill the soul. Rather, be afraid of him who can destroy both body and soul in hell. For a few cents you can buy two sparrows. Yet not one sparrow falls to the ground without your Father knowing. As for you, every hair of your head has been counted. Do not be afraid: you are worth more than many sparrows!

Whoever acknowledges me before others, I will acknowledge before my Father in heaven. Whoever rejects me before others, I will reject before my Father in heaven.

Do not think that I have come to establish peace on earth. I have not come to bring peace, but a sword. For I have come to set

> a man against his father,
> and a daughter against her mother,
> a daughter-in-law against her mother-in-law.
> Each one will have as enemies, those of one's own family.

Whoever loves father or mother more than me, is not worthy of me. And whoever loves son or daughter more than me, is not worthy of me. And whoever does not take up his cross and follow me, is not worthy of me. Whoever finds his life will lose it; but whoever loses his life, for my sake, will find it.

Whoever welcomes you, welcomes me; and whoever welcomes me, welcomes him who sent me. The one who welcomes a prophet, as a prophet, will receive the reward of a prophet; the one who welcomes a just man, because he is a just man, will receive the reward of a just man. And if anyone gives even a cup of cold water to one of these little ones, because he is my disciple, I assure you, he will not go unrewarded."

When Jesus had finished giving his twelve disciples these instructions, he went on from there, to teach and to proclaim his message in their towns. When John the Baptist heard in prison about the deeds of Christ, he sent a message by his disciples, asking him, "Are you the one who is to come, or should we expect someone else?"

Jesus answered them, "Go back and report to John what you hear and see: the blind see, the lame walk, the lepers are made clean, the deaf hear, the dead are brought back to life, and the poor hear the good news; and how fortunate is the one who does not take offense at me!"

As the messengers left, Jesus began to speak to the crowds about John: "When you went out to the desert, what did you expect to see? A reed swept by the wind? What did you go out to see? A man dressed in fine clothes? People who wear fine clothes live in palaces. What did you really go out to see? A prophet? Yes, indeed, and even more than a prophet. He is the man of whom Scripture says:

> I send my messenger ahead of you,
> to prepare the way before you.

I tell you this: no one greater than John the Baptist has arisen from among the sons of women; and yet, the least in the kingdom of heaven is greater than he. From the days of John the Baptist until now, the kingdom of heaven is something to be conquered; and violent men seize it.

Up to the time of John, there was only prophesy: all the prophets and the law. And if you believe me, John is indeed that Elijah, whose coming was predicted. Let anyone with ears listen!

Now, to what can I compare the people of this day? They are like children sitting in the marketplace, about whom their companions complain: 'We played the flute for you, but you would not dance. We sang a funeral song, but you would not cry!'

For John came fasting, and people said, 'He is possessed by a demon!' Then, the Son of Man came. He ate and drank; and people said, 'Look at this man: a glutton and drunkard, a friend of tax collectors and sinners!' Yet, wisdom is vindicated by her works."

Then Jesus began to denounce the cities in which he had performed most of his miracles, because the people there did not change their ways. "Alas for you Chorazin and Bethsaida! If the miracles worked in you had taken place in Tyre and Sidon, the people there would have repented long ago in sackcloth and ashes. But I assure you, for Tyre and Sidon; it will be more bearable for Tyre and Sidon on the day of judgment than for you. And you,

Capernaum, will you be lifted up to heaven? You will be thrown down to the place of the dead! For if the miracles which were performed in you had been performed in Sodom, it would still be there today! But I tell you, it will be more bearable for Sodom on the day of judgment than for you."

On that occasion, Jesus said, "Father, Lord of heaven and earth, I praise you; because you have hidden these things from the wise and learned, and revealed them to simple people. Yes, Father, this was your gracious will.

Everything has been entrusted to me by my Father. No one knows the Son except the Father; and no one knows the Father except the Son, and those to whom the Son chooses to reveal him.

Come to me, all you who are weary and burdened, and I will give you rest. Take my yoke upon you and learn from me, for I am gentle and humble of heart; and you will find rest. For my yoke is easy; and my burden is light."

It happened that, Jesus was walking through the wheat fields on a Sabbath. His disciples were hungry; and they began to pick some heads of wheat, to crush and to eat the grain. When the Pharisees noticed this, they said to Jesus, "Look at your disciples! They are doing what is prohibited on the Sabbath!"

Jesus answered, "Have you not read what David did, when he and his men were hungry? He went into the House of God, and they ate the bread offered to God, though neither he nor his men had the right to eat it, but only the priests. And have you not read in the law, how, on the Sabbath, the priests in the temple desecrate the Sabbath, yet they are not guilty?

I tell you, there is greater than the temple here. If you really knew the meaning of the words: It is mercy I want, not sacrifice, you would not have condemned the innocent.

Besides, the Son of Man is Lord of the Sabbath."

Jesus then left that place and went into one of their synagogues. A man was there with a paralyzed hand, and the people who wanted to bring a charge against Jesus asked him, "Is it permitted to heal on the Sabbath?"

But he said to them, "What if one of you has a sheep and it falls into a pit on the Sabbath? Will you not take hold of your sheep and lift it out? Is a human being less worthy of help than a sheep? Therefore, it is permitted to do good on the Sabbath." Then Jesus said to the man, "Stretch out your arm." He stretched it out and it was completely restored, as sound as the other one.

Then the Pharisees went out, and made plans to get rid of Jesus. As Jesus was aware of their plans, he left that place. Many people followed him, and he cured all who were sick. But he gave them strict orders not to make him known.

In this way, Isaiah's prophecy was fulfilled:

> Here is my servant, whom I have chosen;
> the one I love, and with whom I am pleased.
>
> I will put my spirit upon him;
> and he will announce my judgment to the nations.
>
> He will not argue or shout,
> nor will his voice be heard in the streets.
>
> The bruised reed he will not crush,
> nor snuff out the smoldering wick
>
> until he brings justice to victory,
> and in him, all the nations will put their hope.

Then some people brought to him a possessed man, who was blind and mute. Jesus healed the man; who was then able to speak and see. All in the crowd were amazed and said, "Could he be the Son of David?" When the Pharisees heard this, they said, "It is by Beelzebul, prince of the devils, that this man drives out devils."

Jesus, knowing their thoughts, said to them, "Every kingdom that is divided against itself is destroyed; and every city, or family, that is divided against itself will not last long. So, if Satan drives out Satan, he is divided: how then can his reign endure? And, if it is by Beelzebul that I drive out devils, by whom do your own people drive them out? For this reason, they will be your judges.

But, if it is by the Spirit of God that I drive out devils, then the kingdom of God has already come upon you. How can anyone break into the strong man's house and make off with his belongings, unless he first ties him up? Only then can he plunder his house.

The one who is not with me, is against me; and the one who does not gather with me, scatters.

And so, I tell you this: people can be forgiven any sin and any evil thing they say against God, but blasphemy against the Spirit will not be forgiven. The one who speaks against the Son of Man, will be forgiven; but the one who speaks against the Holy Spirit will not be forgiven, neither in this age nor in the age to come.

If you have a healthy tree, its fruit will be healthy; if you have a rotten tree, its fruit will be rotten. You can know a tree by its fruit. You brood of vipers, how can you say anything good, when you are so evil? For the mouth speaks what fills the heart. A good person produces good things from his good store, and an evil person produces evil things from his evil store.

I tell you this: on the day of judgment, people will have to give an account of any careless word they have spoken. Your own words will declare you either innocent or guilty."

Then, some teachers of the law and some Pharisees spoke up, "Teacher, we want to see a sign from you." Jesus answered them, "An evil and unfaithful people want a sign; but no sign will be given, them except the sign of the prophet Jonah. In the same way, as Jonah spent three days and three nights in the belly of the whale, so will the Son of Man spend three days and three nights in the heart of the earth.

At the judgment, the people of Nineveh will rise with this generation, and condemn it; because they reformed their lives at the preaching of Jonah, and here, there is greater than Jonah. At the judgment, the Queen of the South will stand up and condemn you. She came from the ends of the earth to hear the wisdom of Solomon; and here, there is greater than Solomon.

When an evil spirit goes out of a person, it wanders over arid wastelands, looking for a place to rest, but it cannot find any. Then it says: 'I will go back to my house which I had to leave.' So it goes back, and finds the house empty, clean, and in order. Off it goes again, to bring back with itself, this time, seven spirits, more evil than itself. They move in, and settle there; so that this person is, finally, in a worse state at the end, than he was at the beginning. This is what will happen to this evil generation."

While Jesus was talking to the people, his mother and his brothers wanted to speak to him, and they waited outside. So someone said to him, "Your mother and your brothers are standing outside; they want to speak with you."

Jesus answered, "Who is my mother? Who are my brothers?" Then he pointed to his disciples and said, "Look! Here are my mother and my brothers. Whoever does the will of my Father in heaven is my brother and sister and mother."

That same day, Jesus left the house and sat down by the lakeside. Many people gathered around him. So he got into a boat, and sat down, while the crowds stood on the shore; and he spoke to them in parables about many things.

Jesus said, "The sower went out to sow; and, as he sowed, some seeds fell along the path; and the birds came and ate them up. Other seeds fell on rocky ground, where there was little soil, and the seeds sprouted quickly, because the soil was not deep. But as soon as the sun rose, the plants were scorched; and they withered, because they had no roots. Again, other seeds fell among thistles; and the thistles grew and choked the plants. Still, other seeds fell on good soil and produced a crop: some a hundredfold, others sixty, and others thirty. If you have ears, then hear!"

Then his disciples came to him and said, "Why do you speak to them in parables?"

Jesus answered, "To you it has been given to know the secrets of the kingdom of heaven, but not to these people. For the one who has will be given more; and he will have in abundance. But the one who does not have will be deprived of even what he has. That is why I speak to them in parables;

> because they look and do not see;
> they hear; but they do not listen or understand.

In them, the words of the prophet Isaiah are fulfilled:

> However much you hear, you do not understand;
> however much you see, you do not perceive.

> For the heart of this people has grown dull.
> Their ears hardly hear and their eyes dare not see.

> If they were to see with their eyes,
> hear with their ears
> and understand with their heart,

> they would turn back, and I would heal them.

But blessed are your eyes, because they see; and your ears, because they hear.

For I tell you, many prophets and righteous people have longed to see the things you see, but they did not see them; and to hear the things you hear, but they did not hear them.

Now listen to the parable of the sower.

When a person hears the message of the kingdom, but does not take it seriously, the devil comes and snatches away what was sown in his heart. This is the seed that fell along the footpath.

The seed that fell on rocky ground stands for the one who hears the word, and accepts it at once with joy. But such a person has no roots, and endures only for a while. No sooner is he harassed or persecuted because of the word, than he gives up.

The seed that fell among the thistles is the one who hears the word; but then, the worries of this life and the love of money choke the word; and it does not bear fruit.

As for the seed that fell on good soil, it is the one who hears the word and understands it; this seed bears fruit and produces a hundred, or sixty, or thirty times more."

Jesus told the people another parable, "The kingdom of heaven can be compared to a man, who sowed good seed in his field. While everyone was asleep, his enemy came, and sowed weeds among the wheat, and went away.

When the plants sprouted and produced grain, the weeds also appeared. Then, the servants of the owner came, and said to him, 'Sir, was it not good seed that you sowed in your field? Where did the weeds come from?'

He answered them, 'This is the work of an enemy.' They asked him, 'Do you want us to go and pull up the weeds?' He told them, 'No, when you pull up the weeds, you might uproot the wheat with them. Let them grow together, until harvest; and, at harvest time, I will say to the workers: Pull up the weeds first, tie them in bundles and burn them; then gather the wheat into my barn.'"

Jesus offered them another parable: "The kingdom of heaven is like a mustard seed that a man took and sowed in his field.

It is smaller than all other seeds, but once it is fully grown, it is bigger than any garden plant; like a tree, the birds come and rest in its branches."

He told them another parable, "The kingdom of heaven is like the yeast that a woman took, and hid in three measures of flour, until the whole mass of dough began to rise."

Jesus taught all these things to the crowds by means of parables; he did not say anything to them without using a parable. This fulfilled what was spoken by the Prophet:

I will speak in parables.
I will proclaim things kept secret since the beginning of the
world.

Then he sent the crowds away and went into the house. And his disciples came to him, saying, "Explain to us the parable of the weeds in the field." Jesus answered them, "The one who sows the good seed is the Son of Man. The field is the world; the good seed are the people of the kingdom; the weeds are those who follow the evil one. The enemy who sows the weeds is the devil; the harvest is the end of time, and the workers are the angels.

Just as the weeds are pulled up and burned in the fire, so will it be at the end of time. The Son of Man will send his angels, and they will weed out of his kingdom all that is scandalous and all who do evil. And these will be thrown into the blazing furnace, where there will be weeping and gnashing of teeth. Then the just will shine, like the sun, in the kingdom of their Father. If you have ears, then hear.

The kingdom of heaven is like a treasure, hidden in a field. The one who finds it, buries it again; and so happy is he, that he goes and sells everything he has, in order to buy that field.

Again, the kingdom of heaven is like a trader, who is looking for fine pearls. Once he has found a pearl of exceptional quality, he goes away, sells everything he has and buys it.

Again, the kingdom of heaven is like a big fishing net, let down into the sea, in which every kind of fish has been caught. When the net is full, it is dragged ashore. Then they sit down and gather the good fish into buckets, but throw the bad away. That is how it will be at the end of time; the angels will go out to separate the wicked from the just, and to throw the wicked into the blazing furnace, where they will weep and gnash their teeth."

Jesus asked, "Have you understood all these things?" "Yes," they answered. So he said to them, "Therefore, every teacher of the law, who becomes a disciple of the kingdom of heaven, is like a householder, who can produce from his store things both new and old."

When Jesus had finished these parables, he left that place. He went to his hometown and taught the people in their synagogue. They were amazed and said, "Where did he get this wisdom and these special powers? Isn't he the carpenter's son? Isn't Mary his mother and aren't James, Joseph, Simon and Judas his brothers? Aren't all his sisters living here? Where did he get all these things?" And so they took offense at him.

Jesus said to them, "The only place where prophets are not welcome is his hometown and in his own family." And he did not perform many miracles there because of their lack of faith.

At that time, the reports about Jesus reached king Herod. And he said to his servants, "This man is John the Baptist. John has risen from the dead, and that is why miraculous powers are at work in John."

Herod had, in fact, ordered that John be arrested, bound in chains and put in prison, because of Herodias, the wife of his brother Philip. For John had said to Herod, "It is not right for you to have her as your wife." Herod wanted to kill him but he did not dare, because he feared the people, who regarded John as a prophet.

On Herod's birthday the daughter of Herodias danced among the guests; she so delighted Herod that he promised under oath to give her anything she asked for. The girl, following the advice of her mother, said, "Give me the head of John the Baptist, here, on a dish."

The king was very displeased, but because he had made his promise under oath, in the presence of his guests, he ordered it to be given to her. So he had John beheaded in prison, and his head brought on a dish and given to the girl. The girl then took it to her mother.

Then John's disciples came, took his body and buried it. Then they went and told Jesus.

When Jesus heard of it, he set out by boat for a secluded place, to be alone. But the people heard of it, and they followed him on foot from their towns. When Jesus went ashore, he saw the crowd gathered there, and he had compassion on them. And he healed their sick.

Late in the afternoon, his disciples came to him and said, "We are in a lonely place and it is now late. You should send these people away, so that they can go to the villages and buy something for themselves to eat."

But Jesus replied, "They do not need to go away; you give them something to eat." They answered, "We have nothing here but five loaves and two fishes." Jesus said to them, "Bring them here to me."

Then he made everyone sit down on the grass. He took the five loaves and the two fishes, raised his eyes to heaven, pronounced the blessing, broke the loaves, and handed them to the disciples to distribute to the people. And they all ate, and everyone had enough; then the disciples gathered up the leftovers, filling twelve baskets. About five thousand men had eaten there, besides women and children.

Immediately, Jesus obliged his disciples to get into the boat and go ahead of him to the other side, while he sent the crowd away.

And having sent the people away, he went up the mountain by himself, to pray. At nightfall, he was there alone. Meanwhile, the boat was very far from land, dangerously rocked by the waves, for the wind was against it.

At daybreak, Jesus came to them, walking on the sea. When they saw him walking on the sea, they were terrified, thinking that it was a ghost. And they cried out in fear. But at once, Jesus said to them, "Courage! Don't be afraid. It's me!" Peter answered, "Lord, if it is you, command me to come to you on the water."

Jesus said to him, "Come!" And Peter got out of the boat, and walked on the water to go to Jesus. But seeing the strong wind, he was afraid, and began to sink; and he cried out, "Lord, save me!" Jesus immediately stretched out his hand and took hold of him, saying, "Man of little faith, why did you doubt?"

As they got into the boat, the wind dropped. Then those in the boat bowed down before Jesus, saying, "Truly, you are the Son of God!"

They came ashore at Gennesaret. The local people recognized Jesus and spread the news throughout the region. So they brought to him all the sick people, begging him to let them touch just the hem of his cloak. All who touched it became perfectly well.

Then, some Pharisees, and teachers of the law, who had come from Jerusalem, gathered around Jesus. And they said to him, "Why don't your disciples follow the tradition of the elders? For they, they don't wash their hands before eating."

Jesus answered, "And you, why do you break God's command for the sake of your traditions? For God commanded: Do your duty to your father and your mother, and: Whoever curses his father or his mother is to be put to death. But you say, that anyone may say to his father or mother, 'What you could have expected from me, is given to God.' In this case, according to you, a person is freed from his duty to his father and mother. And so, you have nullified the command of God for the sake of your traditions.

Hypocrites! Isaiah rightly prophesied of you when he said:

> This people honors me with their lips,
> but their heart is far from me.
> The worship they offer me is worthless,
> for they only teach human rules."

Jesus then called the people to him, and said to them, "Listen and understand: What enters into the mouth does not make a person unclean. What defiles a person is what comes out of his mouth."

After a while the disciples gathered around Jesus and said, "Do you know that the Pharisees were offended by what you said?" Jesus answered, "Every plant which my heavenly Father has not planted shall be uprooted. Pay no attention to them! They are blind, leading the blind. When a blind person leads another, the two will fall into a pit."

Peter said to him, "Explain this parable to us." Jesus replied, "So even you, too, are dull? Do you not see, that whatever enters the mouth goes into the stomach, and then out of the body? But what comes out of the mouth comes from the heart, and that is what makes a person unclean.

Indeed, it is from the heart that evil desires come: murder, adultery, immorality, theft, lies, slander. These are the things that make a person unclean; but eating without washing the hands does not make a person unclean."

Leaving that place, Jesus withdrew to the region of Tyre and Sidon. A Canaanite woman from the area, came and cried out, "Lord, Son of David, have pity on me! My daughter is tormented by a demon." But Jesus did not answer her, not even a word. So his disciples approached him and said, "Send her away! See how she is shouting after us."

Then Jesus said to her, "I was sent only to the lost sheep of the nation of Israel."

But the woman was already kneeling before Jesus, and said, "Sir, help me!" Jesus answered, "It is not right to take the bread from the children and throw it to puppies." The woman replied, "That is true, sir, but even puppies eat the crumbs which fall from their master's table." Then Jesus said, "Woman, how great is your faith! Let it be as you wish." And her daughter was healed at that moment.

From there, Jesus went to the shore of Lake Galilee, and then went up into the hills, where he sat down. Great crowds came to him, bringing the dumb, the blind, the lame, the crippled, and many with other infirmities. People carried them to the feet of Jesus, and he healed them. All were astonished when they saw the dumb speaking, the lame walking, the crippled healed, and the blind able to see; and they glorified the God of Israel.

Jesus called his disciples and said to them, "I am filled with compassion for these people; they have already followed me for three days and now have nothing to eat. I do not want to send them away fasting, or they may faint on the way." His disciples said to him, "And where shall we find enough bread in this wilderness to feed such a crowd?" Jesus said to them, "How many loaves do you have?" They answered, "Seven, and a few small fish."

Jesus ordered the people to sit on the ground. Then, he took the seven loaves and the small fish, and gave thanks to God. He broke them and gave them to his disciples, who distributed them to the people.

They all ate and were satisfied, and the leftover pieces filled seven wicker baskets. Four thousand men had eaten, besides women and children. Then Jesus sent the crowd away, got into the boat and went to Magdala.

The Pharisees and Sadducees appeared. They wanted to put Jesus to the test and asked him for some heavenly sign.

Jesus answered, "(When evening comes, you say, 'It will be a good day, for the sky is red.' And in the morning you say, 'Stormy weather today, for the sky in the east is red.' If you know how to interpret the appearance of the sky, why can't you interpret the signs of the times?) An evil and unbelieving people want a sign, but no sign will be given them, except the sign of Jonah."

And Jesus left them and went away.

When the disciples went to the other side, they forgot to take bread. Jesus said to them, "Pay attention, and beware of the yeast of the Pharisees and Sadducees." But the disciples said to one another, "He means, the bread we did not bring."

Aware of this, Jesus said to them, so he said to them, "You of little faith! Why are you arguing among yourselves about having no bread? Do you still not understand? Do you not remember the five loaves, for the five thousand; and how many baskets you took up? Or the seven loaves for the four thousand, and how many wicker baskets you took up?

How can you not understand, that I was not talking about bread, when I said to you: Beware of the yeast of the Pharisees and Sadducees?" Then they understood, that he was not talking about yeast for bread, but about the teaching of the Pharisees and Sadducees.

After that, Jesus came to Caesarea Philippi. He asked his disciples, "Who do people say the Son of Man is?" They said, "For some of them, you are John the Baptist; for others Elijah, or Jeremiah, or one of the prophets."

Jesus asked them, "But you, who do you say I am?" Peter answered, "You are the Messiah, the Son of the living God." Jesus replied, "It is well for you, Simon Barjona, for it is not flesh or blood that has revealed this to you, but my Father in heaven.

And now I say to you: You are Peter; and on this Rock I will build my Church; and never will the powers of death overcome it.

I will give you the keys of the kingdom of heaven: whatever you bind on earth shall be bound in heaven; and whatever you unbind on earth shall be unbound in heaven."

Then he ordered his disciples not to tell anyone that he was the Christ.

From that day, Jesus began to make it clear to his disciples that he must go to Jerusalem; that he would suffer many things from the Jewish authorities, the chief priests and the teachers of the law; and that he would be killed and be raised on the third day.

Then Peter took him aside and began to reproach him, "Never, Lord! No, this must never happen to you!" But he turned and said to Peter, "Get behind me, Satan! You are an obstacle in my path. You are thinking not as God does, but as people do."

Then Jesus said to his disciples, "If you want to follow me, deny yourself. Take up your cross and follow me. For whoever chooses to save his life will lose it, but the one who loses his life, for my sake, will find it. What will one gain by winning the whole world, if he destroys his soul? Or what can a person give, in exchange for his life?

Know, that the Son of Man will come, in the glory of his Father with the holy angels, and he will reward each one according to his deeds. Truly, I tell you, there are some standing here who will not taste death, before they see the Son of Man coming in his kingdom."

Six days later, Jesus took with him Peter and James, and his brother John, and led them up a high mountain, where they were alone. Jesus' appearance was changed before them: his face shone like the sun, and his clothes became white as snow. Then suddenly, Moses and Elijah appeared to them, talking with Jesus.

Peter spoke up and said to Jesus, "Master, it is good for us to be here. If you wish, I will make three tents: one for you, one for Moses, and one for Elijah."

Peter was still speaking, when a bright cloud covered them with its shadow; and a voice from the cloud said, "This is my Son, the Beloved, my Chosen One. Listen to him."

On hearing the voice, the disciples fell to the ground, full of fear. But Jesus came, touched them, and said, "Stand up, do not be afraid!" When they raised their eyes, they no longer saw anyone except Jesus. And as they came down the mountain, Jesus commanded them not to tell anyone what they had seen, until the Son of Man be raised from the dead.

The disciples asked him, "Why do the teachers of the law say that Elijah must come first?" Jesus answered, "So it is: first comes Elijah; and he will restore all things. But I tell you, Elijah has already come; and they did not recognize him; and they treated him as they pleased. And they will also make the Son of Man suffer."

Then the disciples understood that Jesus was referring to John the Baptist.

When they came to the crowd, a man approached Jesus, knelt before him and said, "Sir, have pity on my son, who is an epileptic and suffers terribly. He has often fallen into the fire, and at other times into the water. I brought him to your disciples but they could not heal him."

Jesus replied, "O you people, faithless and misled! How long must I be with you? How long must I put up with you? Bring him here to me." And Jesus commanded the evil spirit to leave the boy, and the boy was immediately healed.

Later, the disciples approached Jesus and asked him privately, "Why couldn't we drive out the spirit?" Jesus said to them, "Because you have little faith. I say to you: if only you had faith the size of a mustard seed, you could tell that mountain to move from here to there, and the mountain would obey. Nothing would be impossible for you. (Only prayer and fasting can drive out this kind of spirit.")

While Jesus was in Galilee with the Twelve, he said to them, "The Son of Man will be delivered into the hands of men, and they will kill him. But he will rise on the third day." The Twelve were deeply grieved.

When they returned to Capernaum, the temple tax collectors came to Peter and asked him, "Does your master pay the temple tax?" He answered, "Yes."

Peter then entered the house; and immediately, Jesus asked him, "What do you think, Simon? Who pay taxes or tribute to the kings of the earth: their sons or strangers and aliens?" Peter replied, "Strangers and aliens." And Jesus told him, "The sons, then, are tax-free. But, so as not to offend these people, go to the sea, throw in a hook, and open the mouth of the first fish you catch. You will find a coin in it. Take the coin and give it to them for you and for me."

At that time, the disciples came to Jesus and asked him, "Who is the greatest in the kingdom of heaven?"

Then Jesus called a little child, set the child in the midst of the disciples, and said, "I assure you, that, unless you change, and become like little children, you cannot enter the kingdom of heaven. Whoever becomes humble, like this child, is the greatest in the kingdom of heaven, and whoever receives such a child, in my name, receives me.

If any of you should cause one of these little ones, who believe in me, to stumble and fall, it would be better for him to be thrown into the depths of the sea with a great millstone around his neck.

Woe to the world, because of so many scandals! Scandals necessarily come, but woe to the one who causes a scandal.

If your hand or foot causes you to sin, cut it off and throw it away. It is better for you to enter life without a hand or a foot, than to be thrown into the eternal fire with two hands and two feet. And if your eye causes you to sin, tear it out and throw it away. It is better for you to enter life with one eye, than to be thrown into the fire of hell with two eyes.

See that you do not despise any of these little ones; for I tell you, their angels in heaven continually see the face of my heavenly Father.

(The Son of Man has come to save the lost).

What do you think of this? If someone has a hundred sheep and one of them strays, won't he leave the ninety-nine on the hillside, and go to look for the stray one? And I tell you, when he finally finds it, he is more pleased about it, than about the ninety-nine that did not go astray. It is the same with your Father in heaven. Your Father in heaven doesn't want even one of these little ones to perish.

If your brother has sinned against you, go and point out the fault to him, when the two of you are alone; and if he listens to you, you have won back your brother. If he doesn't listen to you, take with you one or two others, so that the case may be decided by the evidence of two or three witnesses. And if he refuses to listen to them, tell it to the assembled Church. But if he does not listen to the Church, then regard him as a pagan, or a tax collector.

I say to you: whatever you bind on earth, heaven will keep bound; and whatever you unbind on earth, heaven will keep unbound.

In like manner, I say to you, if, on earth, two of you agree in asking for anything, it will be granted to you by my heavenly Father; for where two or three are gathered in my name, I am there, among them."

Then Peter asked him, "Lord, how many times must I forgive the offenses of my brother or sister? Seven times?" Jesus answered, "No, not seven times, but seventy-seven times.

This story throws light on the kingdom of Heaven: A king decided to settle accounts with his servants. Among the first of them was one who owed him ten thousand pieces of gold. As the man could not repay the debt, the king commanded that he be sold as a slave with his wife, his children and all his goods, as repayment.

The servant threw himself at the feet of the king and said, 'Give me time, and I will pay you back everything.' The king took pity on him, and not only set him free, but even canceled his debt.

When this servant left the king's presence, he met one of his fellow servants, who owed him a hundred pieces of silver. He grabbed him by the throat and almost choked him, shouting, 'Pay me what you owe!' His fellow servant threw himself at his feet and begged him, 'Give me time, and I will pay everything.' But the other did not agree, and sent him to prison until he had paid all his debt.

Now the servants of the king saw what had happened. They were extremely upset, and so they went and reported everything to their lord. Then the lord summoned his servant and said, 'Wicked servant, I forgave you all that you owed me when you begged me to do so. Weren't you bound to have pity on your fellow servant, as I had pity on you?' The lord was now angry. He handed the wicked servant over to be punished, until he had paid the whole debt."

Jesus added, "So will my heavenly Father do with you, unless you sincerely forgive your brothers and sisters."

When Jesus had finished these sayings, he left Galilee and arrived at the border of Judea, on the other side of the Jordan River. Large crowds followed him; and there, too, he healed their sick.

Some Pharisees approached him. They wanted to test him and asked, "Is a man allowed to divorce his wife for any reason he wants?"

Jesus replied, "Have you not read, that, in the beginning, the Creator made them male and female? And the Creator said: Therefore, a man shall leave father and mother, and be joined to his wife, and the two shall become one body. So, they are no longer two, but one body. Let no one separate what God has joined."

They asked him, "Then why did Moses command us to write a bill of dismissal in order to divorce?" Jesus replied, "Moses knew the hardness of your hearts, so he allowed you to divorce your wives; but it was not so in the beginning. Therefore, I say to you: whoever divorces his wife, unless it be for immorality, and marries another, commits adultery."

The disciples said, "If that is the condition of a married man, it is better not to marry." Jesus said to them, "Not everybody can accept what you have just said, but only those who have received this gift. There are eunuchs born so, from their mother's womb. Some have been made that way by others. But there are some who have given up the possibility of marriage, for the sake of the kingdom of heaven. Let the one who can accept it, accept it."

Then little children were brought to Jesus, that he might lay his hands on them and pray for them. But the disciples scolded those who brought them. Jesus then said, "Let the children be! Don't hinder them from coming to me; for the kingdom of heaven belongs to those who are humble, like these children." Jesus laid his hands on them and went away.

It was then, that a young man approached him and asked, "Master, what good work must I do to receive eternal life?" Jesus answered, "Why do you ask me about what is good? One, only, is good. If you want to enter eternal life, keep the commandments." The young man said, "Which commandments?" Jesus replied, "Do not kill; do not commit adultery; do not steal; do not bear false witness; honor your father and mother. And love your neighbor as yourself."

The young man said to him, "I have kept all these commandments. What do I still lack?" Jesus answered, "If you wish to be perfect, go, sell all that you possess, and give the money to the poor; and you will have treasure in heaven. Then come back and follow me."

On hearing this, the young man went away sad, for he was a man of great wealth.

Jesus said to his disciples, "Truly I say to you: it will be hard for one who is rich to enter the kingdom of heaven. Yes, believe me: it is easier for a camel to go through the eye of the needle than for the one who is rich to enter the kingdom of heaven."

On hearing this, the disciples were astonished and said, "Who, then, can be saved?" Jesus looked at them and answered, "For human beings it is impossible, but for God all things are possible."

Then Peter spoke up and said, "You see, we have given up everything to follow you. What, then, will there be for us?"

Jesus answered, "You, who have followed me, listen to my words: on the

Day of Renewal, when the Son of Man sits on his throne in glory, you, also, will sit, on twelve thrones, to judge the twelve tribes of Israel. As for those who have left houses, brothers, sisters, father, mother, children or property for my Name's sake, they will receive a hundredfold, and be given eternal life. Many who are now first, will be last, and many who are now last, will be first.

This story throws light on the kingdom of heaven: A landowner went out early in the morning, to hire workers for his vineyard. He agreed to pay each worker the usual daily wage, and sent them to his vineyard.

He went out again, at about nine in the morning, and, seeing others idle in the town square, he said to them, 'You also, go to my vineyard, and I will pay you what is just.' So they went.

The owner went out at midday, and, again, at three in the afternoon, and he made the same offer. Again he went out, at the last working hour—the eleventh—and he saw others standing around. So he said to them, 'Why do you stand idle the whole day?' They answered, 'Because no one has hired us.' The master said, 'Go, and work in my vineyard.'

When evening came, the owner of the vineyard said to his manager, 'Call the workers and pay them their wage, beginning with the last and ending with the first.' Those who had gone to work at the eleventh hour came up, and were each given a silver coin. When it was the turn of the first, they thought they would receive more. But they, too, received one silver coin. On receiving it, they began to grumble against the landowner.

They said, 'These last, hardly worked an hour; yet, you have treated them the same as us, who have endured the heavy work of the day and the heat.' The owner said to one of them, 'Friend, I have not been unjust to you. Did we not agree on one silver coin per day? So, take what is yours and go. I want to give to the last the same as I give to you. Don't I have the right to do as I please with what is mine? Why are you envious when I am kind?'

So will it be: the last will be first, the first will be last."

When Jesus was going to Jerusalem, he took the twelve disciples aside and said to them, "See, we are going to Jerusalem. There, the Son of Man will be betrayed to the chief priests and the teachers of the law; and they will condemn him to death. They will hand him over to the foreigners, who will mock him, scourge him and crucify him. But he will be raised to life on the third day."

Then the mother of James and John came to Jesus with her sons, and she knelt down, to ask a favor. Jesus said to her, "What do you want?" And she answered, "Here, you have my two sons. Grant, that they may sit, one at your right hand and one at your left, in your kingdom."

Jesus said to the brothers, "You do not know what you are asking. Can you drink the cup that I am about to drink?" They answered, "We can."

Jesus replied, "You will indeed drink my cup; but to sit at my right or at my left is not for me to grant. That will be for those, for whom my Father has prepared it."

The other ten heard all this, and were angry with the two brothers. Then Jesus called them to him and said, "You know, that the rulers of nations behave like tyrants, and the powerful oppress them. It shall not be so among you: whoever wants to be great in your community, let him minister to the community. And if you want to be the first of all, make yourself the servant of all. Be like the Son of Man, who came not to be served, but to serve, and to give his life to redeem many."

As they left Jericho, a great crowd followed them on the way. Two blind men were sitting by the roadside; and when they heard that Jesus was passing by, they began to call out, "Son of David, have mercy on us!" The people told them to keep quiet. But they shouted even louder, "Lord, Son of David, have mercy on us!" Jesus stopped, called out to them and asked, "What do you want me to do for you?" They said, "Lord, open our eyes."

Jesus was moved with compassion and touched their eyes. Immediately, they recovered their sight, and they began to follow Jesus.

When they drew near Jerusalem and arrived at Bethphage, on the Mount of Olives, Jesus sent two of his disciples, saying, "Go to the village ahead, and there, you will find a donkey tied up, with its colt by her. Untie them and bring them to me. If anyone says something to you, say that the Lord needs them, and that he will send them back immediately."

This happened in fulfillment of what the prophet said:

> Say to the daughter of Zion:
> See, your king comes to you in all simplicity,
>
> riding on a donkey,
> a beast of burden, with its colt.

The disciples went, as Jesus had instructed them, and they brought the donkey with its colt. Then they threw their cloaks on its back, and Jesus sat on them.

Many people also spread their cloaks on the road, while others cut leafy branches from the trees and spread them on the road. The people who walked ahead of Jesus, and those who followed him, began to shout,

> "Hosanna to the Son of David!
>
> Blessed is he who comes in the name of the Lord!
>
> Hosanna in the highest!"

When Jesus entered Jerusalem, the whole city was disturbed. The people asked, "Who is this man?" And the crowd answered, "This is the Prophet Jesus from Nazareth of Galilee."

Jesus went into the temple, and drove out all who were buying and selling in the temple area. He overturned the tables of the money changers, and the stools of those who sold pigeons. And he said to them, "It is written: My house shall be called a house of prayer. But you have turned it into a den of thieves."

The blind and the lame came to him in the temple, and Jesus healed them.

The chief priests and the teachers of the law saw the wonderful things that Jesus did, and the children shouting in the temple area, "Hosanna to the Son of David!" They became angry and said to Jesus, "Do you hear what they say?" Jesus answered them, "Yes. But have you never read this text:

> From the mouths of children and infants
> you have perfect praise?"

So leaving them, he went out of the city and came to Bethany, where he spent the night.

While returning to the city early in the morning, Jesus felt hungry. He noticed a fig tree by the road, went up to it and found nothing on it but leaves. So he said to the tree, "Never again bear fruit!" And immediately, the fig tree withered.

When the disciples saw this, they were astonished and said, "How did the fig tree suddenly dry up?" Jesus said, "Truly, I say to you: if you had faith and did not doubt, not only could you do what I did to the fig tree, but you could even say to that mountain, 'Go, and throw yourself into the sea!' and it would be done. Whatever you ask for in prayer, full of faith, you will receive."

Jesus had entered the temple and was teaching, when the chief priests, the teachers of the law and the Jewish authorities came to him, and asked, "What authority have you to act like this? Who gave you authority to do all this?"

Jesus answered them, "I will also ask you one question. If you answer me, then I will also tell you by what authority I do these things." Where did John's baptism come from? From heaven or from people?"

They discussed this among themselves, saying, "If we say, 'From heaven,' he will say, 'Then why did you not believe him?' And if we say, 'The baptism of John was merely something human', we've got to beware of the people, for all consider John to be a prophet." So they answered Jesus, "We do not know."

And Jesus said to them, "Neither will I tell you by what authority I do these things."

Jesus went on to say, "What do you think of this? A man had two sons. He went to the first and said to him, 'Son, go and work today in my vineyard.' And the son answered, 'I don't want to.' But later he thought better of it and went. Then the father went to his other son and said the same thing to him. This son replied, 'I will go, sir,' but he did not go.

Which of the two did what the father wanted?" They answered, "The first." And Jesus said to them, "Truly, I say to you: the publicans and the prostitutes are ahead of you on the way to the kingdom of heaven. For John came, to show you the way of goodness, and you did not believe him; but the publicans and the prostitutes did. You were witnesses of this, but you neither repented nor believed him.

Listen to another example: There was a landowner who planted a vineyard. He put a fence around it, dug a hole for the wine press, built a watchtower, leased the vineyard to tenants, and then, went to a distant country. When harvest time came, the landowner sent his servants to the tenants to collect his share of the harvest. But the tenants seized his servants, beat one, killed another, and stoned a third.

Again, the owner sent more servants; but they were treated in the same way.

Finally, he sent his son, thinking, 'They will respect my son.' But when the tenants saw the son, they thought, 'This is the one who is to inherit the vineyard. Let us kill him, and his inheritance will be ours.' So they seized him, threw him out of the vineyard and killed him.

Now, what will the owner of the vineyard do with the tenants when he comes?" They said to him, "He will bring those evil men to an evil end, and lease the vineyard to others, who will pay him in due time."

And Jesus replied, "Have you never read what the Scriptures say?

> The stone which the builders rejected
> has become the cornerstone.
> This was the Lord's doing,
> and we marvel at it.

Therefore I say to you: the kingdom of heaven will be taken from you, and given to a people who will produce its fruit.

(Whoever falls on this stone, he will be broken to pieces; on whomsoever this stone falls, he will be ground to dust.)"

When the chief priests and the Pharisees heard these parables, they realized that Jesus was referring to them. They would have arrested him, but they were afraid of the crowd, who regarded him as a prophet.

Jesus continued speaking to them in parables:
"This story throws light on the kingdom of heaven: A king gave a wedding banquet for his son. He sent his servants to call the invited guests to the banquet, but the guests refused to come.

Again, he sent other servants, instructing them to say to the invited guests, 'I have prepared a banquet, slaughtered my fattened calves and other animals, and now, everything is ready. Come to the wedding!' But they paid no attention and went away, some to their farms, and some to their work. Others seized the servants of the king, insulted them and killed them.

The king was furious. He sent his troops to destroy those murderers and burn their city. Then he said to his servants, 'The wedding banquet is prepared, but the invited guests were not worthy. Go instead to the main streets, and invite everyone you find to the wedding feast.'

The servants went out into the streets and gathered all they found, good and bad alike, so that the hall was filled with guests.

The king came in to see the wedding guests, and he noticed a man not wearing a wedding garment. So he said to him, 'Friend, how did you get in without the wedding clothes?' But the man remained silent. So the king said to his servants, 'Bind his hands and feet and throw him into the outer darkness, where there is weeping and gnashing of teeth.'

For many are called, but few are chosen."

The Pharisees went away, considering how they could trap Jesus by his own words. They sent to him their disciples, along with members of Herod's party, saying, "Master, we know that you are an honest man, and truly teach God's way. You are not influenced by others, nor are you afraid of anyone. So tell us what you think: is it against the law to pay taxes to Caesar or not?"

But Jesus understood their evil intentions, and said to them, "Hypocrites, why are you trying to trap me? Show me the coin with which you pay taxes."

They showed him a silver coin, and Jesus said to them, "Whose head is this, and whose name?" They answered, "Caesar's." Then Jesus replied, "So give to Caesar what is Caesar's, and give to God what is God's."

Astonished by his answer, they left him and went away.

That same day, some of the Sadducees came to Jesus. Since they claim that there is no resurrection, they questioned him in this way: "Master, Moses said, that if a man dies without any children, his brother must take the wife and have a child, who will be considered the child of the deceased man. Now, there were seven brothers. The first married a woman, but he died; since he had no children, he left his wife to his brother. The same thing happened to the second brother, and to the third, until the seventh. Then, last of all, the woman died. Now, in the resurrection of the dead, to which of the seven will she be wife, for they all had her as wife?"

Jesus answered, "You are totally wrong, because you understand neither the Scriptures nor the power of God. First of all, in the resurrection of the dead, neither men nor women will marry, but they will be like the angels in heaven. As for the resurrection of the dead, have you never reflected on what God said to you: I am the God of Abraham, the God of Isaac, and the God of Jacob? He is God, not of the dead but of the living."

The people who heard him were astonished at his teaching.

When the Pharisees heard how Jesus had silenced the Sadducees, they assembled together. One of them, a lawyer, questioned him to test him, "Teacher, which commandment of the law is the greatest?"

Jesus answered, "You shall love the Lord your God with all your heart, with all your soul, and with all your mind. This is the first and the most important of the commandments. The second is like it: You shall love your neighbor as yourself. The whole law and the prophets are founded on these two commandments."

While the Pharisees were assembled, Jesus asked them, "What do you think of the Messiah? Whose son is he?" They answered, "David's."

Jesus then asked them, "Why did David, inspired by God, call the Messiah Lord? For David says in a psalm:

> The Lord said to my Lord:
> Sit at my right hand
>
> until I put your enemies
> under your feet.

If David calls him Lord, how can he be his son?"

No one could answer him, not even a word. From that day on, no one dared question him anymore.

Then Jesus said to the crowds and to his disciples,

"The teachers of the law and the Pharisees have sat down on the chair of Moses. So you shall do and observe all they say; but do not do as they do, for they do not do what they say. They tie up heavy burdens and load them on the shoulders of the people, but they do not even lift a finger to move them. They do everything in order to be seen by people: they wear very wide bands of the law around their foreheads, and robes with large tassels. They enjoy the first places at feasts and the best seats in the synagogues, and they like being greeted in the marketplace, and being called 'Master' by the people.

But you, do not let yourselves be called Master, because you have only one Master, and all of you are brothers and sisters. Neither should you call anyone on earth Father, because you have only one Father, he who is in heaven. Nor should you be called Leader, because Christ is the only Leader for you. Let the greatest among you be the servant of all. For whoever makes himself great shall be humbled, and whoever humbles himself shall be made great.

But woe to you, teachers of the law and Pharisees, you hypocrites! You shut the door to the kingdom of heaven in people's faces. You, yourselves, do not enter it, nor do you allow others to do so.

Woe to you, scribes and Pharisees, you hypocrites! You devour widows' property; and as a show, you pray long prayers! Therefore, you shall receive greater condemnation. Woe to you, teachers of the law and Pharisees, you hypocrites! You travel by sea and land to make a single convert; yet, once he is converted, you make him twice as fit for hell as yourselves!

Woe to you, blind guides! You say: To swear by the temple is not binding; but, to swear by the gold of the temple is binding. Foolish men! Blind men! Which is of more worth: the gold in the temple, or the temple which makes the gold a sacred treasure? You say: To swear by the altar is not binding, but to swear by the offering on the altar is binding. How blind you are! Which is of more value: the offering on the altar, or the altar which makes the offering sacred? Whoever swears by the altar, is swearing by the altar and by everything on it. Whoever swears by the temple, is swearing by the temple, and by God, who dwells in the temple. Whoever swears by heaven, is swearing by the throne of God, and by him, who is seated on it.

Woe to you, teachers of the law and Pharisees, you hypocrites! You do not forget the mint, anise and cumin seeds when you demand the tenth of everything; but then, you forget what is most fundamental in the law: justice, mercy and faith! You should have done these things without neglecting the others. Blind guides! You strain out a mosquito, but swallow a camel.

Woe to you, teachers of the law and Pharisees, you hypocrites! You fill the plate and the cup, with theft and violence, and then pronounce a blessing over them. Blind Pharisee! Purify the inside first, then the outside, too, will be purified.

Woe to you, teachers of the law and Pharisees, you hypocrites! You are like whitewashed tombs, beautiful in appearance; but, inside, there are only dead bones and uncleanness. In the same way, you appear religious to others, but you are full of hypocrisy and wickedness within.

Woe to you, teachers of the law and Pharisees, you hypocrites! You build tombs for the prophets, and decorate the monuments of the righteous. You say: Had we lived in the time of our ancestors, we would not have joined them in shedding the blood of the prophets. So, you, yourselves, confess to be the descendants of those who murdered the prophets. And now, finish off what your ancestors began!

Serpents, race of vipers! How can you escape condemnation to hell? Therefore, indeed, I send prophets, wise men and teachers to you; but some you will murder and crucify; some, you will flog in your synagogues; some, you will drive from one city to the next.

Because of this, you will be accountable for all the innocent blood that has been shed on the earth, from the blood of upright Abel to the blood of Zechariah, son of Barachiah, whom you murdered between the altar and the Sanctuary. Truly I say to you: the present generation will pay for all this.

Jerusalem, Jerusalem! You murder the prophets and stone those sent to you by God. How often would I have gathered your children together, just as a hen gathers her chicks under her wings; but you refused! Look! Your house shall be left to you, deserted! I tell you, that you will no longer see me, until you say: Blessed is he who comes in the name of the Lord!

Jesus left the temple, and as he was walking away, his disciples came to him and pointed out to him the imposing temple buildings. But he said, "You see all this? Truly I say to you: not one stone will be left upon another here. All will be torn down."

Later when Jesus was sitting on the Mount of Olives, the disciples approached him privately and asked, "Tell us, when this will take place. What sign will be given us of your coming, and the end of the world?"

Jesus answered, "Be on your guard; and let no one mislead you. Many will come in my name, saying: 'I am the Messiah,' and they will mislead many people. You will hear about wars, and rumors of wars; but do not be troubled, for these things must happen; but the end is still to come. Nations will fight one another, and kingdoms oppose one another. There will be famine, and earthquakes in different places; but all this is only the beginning, the first pains of childbirth.

Then, they will arrest you; they will torture and kill you. All nations will hate you, for you bear my name. In those days, many will be led into sin; they will betray and hate one another. False prophets will appear and mislead many; and because of such great wickedness, love in many people will grow cold. But the one who holds out to the end will be saved. The Good News of the kingdom will be proclaimed throughout the world, to all the nations, a Testament to all peoples. Then will the end come.

When you see what the prophet Daniel spoke about, the idol of the invader, set up in the temple (let the reader understand!), then, let those in Judea flee to the mountains.

If you are on the housetop, do not come down to take anything with you. If you are in the field, do not turn back to fetch your coat. How hard it will be for pregnant women, and for mothers with babies at the breast! Pray, that you don't have to flee in winter, or on a Sabbath; for there will be great tribulation, such as was never known, from the beginning of the world until now, and is never to be known again. And if that time were not to be shortened, no one would survive. But God will shorten those days, for the sake of his chosen ones. Then, if anyone says to you, 'Look! The Messiah is here! He is there!', do not believe it. For false Messiahs and false prophets will appear, and perform signs and wonders so great, that they would deceive even God's chosen people, if that were possible. See, I have told you everything ahead of time.

So, if anyone tells you, 'He is in the desert,' do not go. If they say, 'He is in the inner rooms,' do not believe it. For the coming of the Son of Man will be like lightning, which flashes from the east even to the west. Wherever the body is, the vultures will gather.

And later, after that distress,

> the sun will grow dark,
> the moon will not give its light,
>
> the stars will fall from the skies,
> and the whole universe will be shaken.

Then the sign of the Son of Man will appear in heaven. As all the nations of the earth beat their breasts, they will see the Son of Man coming, in the clouds of heaven, with divine power and great glory. He will send his angels to sound the trumpet; and they will gather his chosen ones from the four winds, from one end of the earth to the other.

Learn a lesson from the fig tree: when its branches grow tender and its leaves begin to sprout, you know that summer is near. In the same way, when you see all these things, know that the time is near, even at the door. Truly I say to you, this generation will not pass away until all these things have happened. Heaven and earth will pass away, but my words will not pass away.

But, as for that Day and that Hour, no one knows when it will come, not even the angels of God, nor the Son, but only the Father.

At the coming of the Son of Man, it will be just as it was in the time of Noah. In those days before the Flood, people were eating and drinking, and marrying, until that day when Noah went into the ark. Yet, they did not know what would happen, until the flood came and swept them away. So will it be, at the coming of the Son of Man: of two men in the field, one will be taken and the other left; of two women grinding wheat together at the mill, one will be taken and the other left.

Stay awake then, for you do not know on what day your Lord will come. Obviously, if the owner of the house knew at what time the thief was coming, he would certainly stay up and not allow his house to be broken into. So be alert, for the Son of Man will come at the hour you least expect.

Imagine a faithful and prudent servant, whom his master has put in charge of his household, to give them food at the proper time. Fortunate, indeed, is that servant, whom his master will find at work when he comes. Truly I say to you, his lord will entrust him with everything he has.

Not so with the bad servant, who thinks, 'My master is delayed.' And he begins to ill-treat his fellow servants, while eating and drinking with drunkards. But his master will come on the day he does not know, and at the hour he least expects. He will punish that servant severely; and place with him with the hypocrites. There will be weeping and gnashing of teeth.

This story throws light on what will happen in the kingdom of heaven: Ten bridesmaids went out with their lamps to meet the bridegroom. Five of them were foolish, and five were sensible.

The careless bridesmaids took their lamps as they were, and did not take extra oil. But those who were sensible, took flasks of oil with their lamps. As the bridegroom delayed, they all grew drowsy and fell asleep.

But at midnight, a cry rang out, 'The bridegroom is here, come out and meet him!' All the maidens woke up at once, and trimmed their lamps. Then the foolish ones said to the sensible ones, 'Give us some oil, for our lamps are going out.' The sensible ones answered, 'There may not be enough for us and for you. You had better go to those who sell, and buy some for yourselves.'

When the bridegroom came, the foolish maidens were out buying oil, but those who were ready went with him into the wedding feast, and the doors were shut.

Later the other bridesmaids arrived and called out, 'Lord, Lord, open to us!' But he answered, 'Truly I do not know you.'

So stay awake, for you do not know the day nor the hour.

Imagine someone who, before going abroad, summoned his servants to entrust his property to them. He gave five talents of silver to one servant, two talents to another servant, and one talent to a third, to each, according to his ability; and he went away. He who received five talents went at once to do business with the talents, and gained another five. The one who received two talents did the same, and gained another two. But the one who received one talent dug a hole in the ground, and hid his master's money.

After a long time, the master of those servants returned and asked for a reckoning. The one who had received five talents came with another five talents, saying, 'Lord, you entrusted me with five talents, but see, I have gained five more.' The master answered, 'Well done, good and faithful servant, since you have been faithful in a few things, I will entrust you in charge of many things. Come and share the joy of your master.'

Then the one who had received two talents came and said, 'Lord, you entrusted me with two talents; with them I have gained two more.' The master said, 'Well done, good and faithful servant, since you have been faithful in little things, I will entrust you in charge of many things. Come and share the joy of your master.'

Finally, the one who had received one talent came and said, 'Master, I know that you are a hard man. You reap what you have not sown, and gather what you have not scattered. I was afraid, so I hid your money in the ground. Here, take what is yours!' But his master replied, 'Wicked and worthless servant, you know that I reap where I have not sown, and gather where I have not scattered. You should have deposited my money in the bank, and given it back to me with interest on my return.

Therefore, take the talent from him, and give it to the one who has ten. For to all those who have, more will be given, and they will have an abundance; but from those who are unproductive, even what they have will be taken from them. As for that useless servant, throw him out into outer darkness, where there will be weeping and gnashing of teeth.'

When the Son of Man comes in his glory with all his angels, he will sit on the throne of his glory. All the nations will be brought before him; and, as a shepherd separates the sheep from the goats, so will he do with them, placing the sheep on his right hand and the goats on his left.

The king will say to those on his right, 'Come, blessed of my Father! Take possession of the kingdom prepared for you from the beginning of the world. For I was hungry, and you fed me. I was thirsty, and you gave me something to drink. I was a stranger, and you welcomed me into your home. I was naked, and you clothed me. I was sick, and you visited me. I was in prison, and you came to see me.'

Then the righteous will ask him, 'Lord, when did we see you hungry, and give you food; thirsty, and give you something to drink; or a stranger, and welcome you; or naked, and clothe you? When did we see you sick, or in prison, and go to see you?' The king will answer, 'Truly I say to you: just as you did it for one of the least of these brothers or sisters of mine, you did it to me.'

Then he will say to those on his left, 'Go, cursed people, out of my sight, into the eternal fire, which has been prepared for the devil and his angels! For I was hungry, and you did not give me anything to eat; I was thirsty, and you gave me nothing to drink; I was a stranger, and you did not welcome me into your house; I was naked, and you did not clothe me; I was sick, and in prison, and you did not visit me.'

They, too, will ask, 'Lord, when did we see you hungry, thirsty, naked or a stranger, sick or in prison, and did not help you?' The king will answer them, 'Truly I say to you: just as you did not do it for one of the least of these, you did not do it for me.'

And these will go into eternal punishment; but the just, to eternal life."

When Jesus had finished all he wanted to say, he told his disciples, "You know that in two days' time it will be the Passover, and the Son of Man will be handed over to be crucified."

Then the chief priests and the elders of the people gathered together, at the palace of the High Priest, whose name was Caiaphas, and they agreed to arrest Jesus and to kill him. But they said, "Not during the feast, lest there be an uprising among the people."

While Jesus was in Bethany, in the house of Simon the leper, a woman came up to him, carrying an alabaster jar of expensive perfume. She poured it on Jesus' head as he was at table. Seeing this, the disciples became indignant and said, "What a useless waste! The perfume could have been sold for a large sum, and the money given to the poor."

Jesus was aware of this, and said to them, "Why are you troubling this woman? What she has done for me is indeed a good work. You have the poor with you always; but me, you will not have always. When she anointed my body with perfume, she was preparing me for my burial. Truly I say to you: wherever the gospel is proclaimed, all over the world, what she has done will be told in memory of her."

Then one of the Twelve, who was called Judas Iscariot, went to the chief priests and said, "How much will you give me if I hand him over to you?" They promised to give him thirty pieces of silver; and from then on, he kept looking for the best way to hand Jesus over to them.

On the first day of the Festival of Unleavened Bread, the disciples came to Jesus and said to him, "Where do you want us to prepare the Passover meal for you?" Jesus answered, "Go into the city, to the house of a certain man, and tell him, 'The Master says: My hour is near, and I will celebrate the Passover with my disciples in your house.'"

The disciples did as Jesus had ordered, and prepared the Passover meal.

When it was evening, Jesus sat at table with the Twelve. While they were eating, Jesus said, "Truly I say to you: one of you will betray me." They were deeply distressed, and they asked him, one after the other, "You do not mean me, do you, Lord?"

He answered, "The one who dips his bread with me will betray me. The Son of Man is going as the Scriptures say he will. But alas for that one who betrays the Son of Man: better for him not to have been born." Judas, the one who would betray him, also asked, "You do not mean me, Master, do you?" Jesus replied, "You have said it."

While they were eating, Jesus took bread, said a blessing and broke it, and gave it to his disciples saying, "Take and eat: this is my body." Then he took a cup, and gave thanks, and passed it to them, saying, "Drink this, all of you, for this is my blood, the blood of the Covenant, which is poured out for many for the forgiveness of sins. Yes, I say to you: From now on I will not taste the fruit of the vine, until that day when I drink new wine with you in my Father's kingdom."

After singing psalms of praise, they went out to the Mount of Olives. Then Jesus said to them, "You will falter tonight because of me, and all of you will fall. For Scripture says:

> I will strike the shepherd
> and the sheep will be scattered.

But after my resurrection, I will go before you to Galilee."

Peter responded, "Even though all stumble and fall, I will never fall away!" Jesus replied, "Truly I say to you: this very night, before the cock crows, you will deny me three times." Peter said, "Even if I must die with you, I will never deny you!" And all the disciples said the same thing.

Jesus came with them to a place called Gethsemane, and he said to his disciples, "Sit here while I go over there to pray."

He took Peter and the two sons of Zebedee with him, and he began to be overwhelmed by anguish and distress. And he said to them, "My soul is full of sorrow, even to death. Remain here and stay awake with me."

He went a little farther and fell to the ground, with his face touching the earth, and prayed, "Father, if it is possible, take this cup away from me. Yet, not what I will, but what you will." He went back to his disciples and found them asleep; and he said to Peter, "Could you not stay awake with me for one hour? Stay awake and pray, so that you may not fall into temptation. The spirit indeed is willing, but the flesh is weak."

He went away again, and prayed, "Father, if this cup cannot be taken away from me without my drinking it, your will must be done." When he came back to his disciples, he, again, found them asleep, for they could not keep their eyes open. So leaving them again, Jesus went to pray for the third time, saying the same words.

Then he came back to his disciples and said to them, "You can sleep on now and take your rest! The hour has come, and the Son of Man will be handed over to sinners. Get up, let us go! See, the betrayer is here!"

Jesus was still speaking when Judas, one of the Twelve, arrived. With him was a crowd armed with swords and clubs, who had been sent by the chief priests and the elders of the people. The traitor had given them a sign: "The one I kiss, he is the man; arrest him!" Judas went directly to Jesus and said, "Greetings, Rabbi!" and he kissed him. Jesus said to him, "Friend, do what you came to do." Then they laid hands on Jesus, and arrested him.

One of those who were with Jesus drew his sword, and struck at the servant of the High Priest, cutting off his ear. Then Jesus said to him, "Put your sword back in its place! For all who take hold of the sword will die by the sword. Do you not know that I could call on my Father, and he would at once send me more than twelve legions of angels? If Scripture says that these things must be, should Scripture not be fulfilled?"

At that hour, Jesus said to the crowd, "Why do you come to arrest me with swords and clubs, as if I were a robber? Day after day, I sat among you, teaching in the temple, yet, you did not arrest me. But all this has happened in fulfillment of what the Prophets said." Then all his disciples deserted Jesus and fled.

Those who had arrested Jesus took him to the house of the High Priest Caiaphas, where the teachers of the law and the elders were assembled.

Peter followed Jesus at a distance, as far as the courtyard of the High Priest; he entered and sat with the guards, waiting to see the end.

The chief priests and the whole Supreme Council needed some false evidence against Jesus, so that they might put him to death. But they were unable to find any, even though false witnesses came forward. At last, two men came forward and declared, "This man said, 'I am able to destroy the Temple of God and rebuild it in three days.'"

The High Priest stood up and asked Jesus, "What is the evidence against you? Have you no answer to the things they testify against you?" But Jesus remained silent.

So the High Priest said to him, "In the name of the living God, I command you to tell us: Are you the Messiah, the Son of God?" Jesus answered, "You have said it yourself. But I tell you: from now on, you will see the Son of Man, seated at the right hand of God most powerful, and coming on the clouds of heaven."

Then the High Priest tore his clothes, saying, "He has blasphemed. What more evidence do we need? You have heard the blasphemy! What is your decision?" They answered, "He must die!" Then they spat in his face and slapped him, while others hit him with their fists, saying, "Messiah, prophesy! Who hit you?"

Meanwhile, as Peter sat outside in the courtyard, a young servant-girl said to him, "You also were with Jesus of Galilee." But he denied it before everyone, saying, "I do not know what you are talking about."

Later, as Peter was going out through the gateway, another servant-girl saw him and said to the bystanders, "This man was with Jesus of Nazareth."

Peter again denied it with an oath, saying, "I do not know the man."

After a little while, those who were standing there approached Peter and said to him, "Surely you are one of the Galileans: your accent gives you away." Peter began to justify himself with curses and oaths, protesting that he did not know Jesus. Just then, a cock crowed.

And Peter remembered the words of Jesus, "Before the cock crows, you will deny me three times." And going out, he wept bitterly.

Early in the morning, all the chief priests and the elders of the people met together, to look for ways of putting Jesus to death. They had him bound, and delivered him to Pilate, the governor.

When Judas, the traitor, realized that Jesus had been condemned, he was filled with remorse, and returned the thirty pieces of silver to the chief priests and the elders, saying, "I have sinned by betraying an innocent man to death." They answered, "What does it matter to us? That is your concern." So, throwing down the money in the temple, he went away and hanged himself.

The chief priests picked up the money and said, "This money cannot be put into the temple treasury, for it is the price of blood." So they conferred together, and decided to buy the potter's field with the money, and to make it a cemetery for foreigners. That is why, to this day, that place has been called Field of Blood.

What the prophet Jeremiah said was fulfilled: They took the thirty pieces of silver, the price which the Sons of Israel estimated as his value, and they gave them for the potter's field, as the Lord commanded me.

Jesus stood before the governor. Pilate asked him, "Are you the king of the Jews?" Jesus answered, "You say so."

The chief priests and the elders of the people accused him, but he made no answer. Pilate said to him, "Do you hear all the charges they bring against you?" But he did not answer even one question, so that the governor wondered greatly.

At Passover, it was customary for the governor to release any prisoner the people asked for. Now, there was a well-known prisoner called Barabbas. When the people had gathered, Pilate asked them, "Whom do you want me to set free: Barabbas, or Jesus called the Messiah?" for he knew that Jesus had been handed over to him out of envy.

While Pilate was sitting in court, his wife sent him this message, "Have nothing to do with that holy man. Because of him, I had a dream last night that disturbed me greatly."

But the chief priests and the elders of the people stirred up the crowds, to ask for the release of Barabbas and the death of Jesus. When the governor asked them again, "Which of the two do you want me to set free?" they answered, "Barabbas!" Pilate said to them, "And what shall I do with Jesus called the Messiah?" All answered, "Crucify him!" Pilate asked, "Why? What evil has he done?" But they shouted louder, "Crucify him!"

Pilate saw that he was getting nowhere, and that there could be a riot. He asked for water, washed his hands before the people, and said, "I am innocent of this man's blood. Do what you want!" And all the people answered, "His blood be on us and on our children!"

Then Pilate set Barabbas free, but had Jesus scourged, and handed over to be crucified.

The Roman soldiers took Jesus into the palace of the governor and the whole troop gathered around him. They stripped him and dressed him in a purple cloak. Then, weaving a crown of thorns, they forced it onto his head, and placed a reed in his right hand. They knelt before Jesus and mocked him, saying, "Hail, king of the Jews!" They spat on him, took the reed from his hand and struck him on the head with it.

When they had finished mocking him, they pulled off the purple cloak and dressed him in his own clothes, and led him out to be crucified.

On the way they met a man from Cyrene called Simon, and forced him to carry the cross of Jesus. When they reached the place called Golgotha, which means the Skull, they offered him wine mixed with gall. He tasted it but would not drink it.

There they crucified him, and divided his clothes among themselves, casting lots to decide what each one should take. Then they sat down to guard him. The statement of his offense was displayed above his head, and it read, "This is Jesus, the King of the Jews." They also crucified two thieves with him, one on his right hand and one on his left.

The people passing by shook their heads and insulted him, saying, "Aha! You, who destroy the temple and in three days rebuild it, save yourself—if you are God's Son—and come down from the cross!"

In the same way the chief priests, the elders and the teachers of the law mocked him. They said, "The man who saved others cannot save himself. Let the king of Israel come down from his cross and we will believe in him.

He trusted in God; let God rescue him if God wants to, for he himself said, 'I am the Son of God.'"

Even the thieves who were crucified with him insulted him.

From midday, darkness fell over all the land until mid-afternoon. At about three o'clock, Jesus cried out in a loud voice, "Eloi, Eloi, lamma sabbacthani?" which means: My God, my God, why have you forsaken me? As soon as they heard this, some of the bystanders said, "He is calling for Elijah." And one of them ran, took a sponge and soaked it in vinegar and, putting it on a reed, gave it to him to drink. Others said, "Leave him alone, let us see whether Elijah will come to save him."

Then Jesus cried out again in a loud voice and gave up his spirit.

At that very moment, the curtain of the temple Sanctuary was torn in two from top to bottom, the earth quaked, rocks were split, tombs were opened, and many holy people who had died were raised to life. They came out of the tombs after the Resurrection of Jesus, entered the Holy City, and appeared to many.

The captain and the soldiers who were guarding Jesus, having seen the earthquake and everything else that had happened, were terribly afraid, and said, "Truly, this was God's Son."

There were also many women there, who watched from a distance; they had followed Jesus from Galilee and had seen to his needs. Among them were Mary Magdalene, Mary the mother of James and Joseph, and the mother of Zebedee's sons.

When it was evening, there came a wealthy man from Arimathea, named Joseph, who was also a disciple of Jesus. He went to Pilate and asked for the body of Jesus, and the governor ordered that the body be given to him. So Joseph took the body of Jesus, wrapped it in a clean linen sheet, and laid it in his own new tomb, that he had cut in the rock. Then he rolled a huge stone across the entrance to the tomb and left. Mary Magdalene and the other Mary remained, sitting there in front of the tomb.

On the following day, which is after the day of preparation, the chief priests and the Pharisees went to Pilate and said to him, "Sir, we remember that when that impostor was still alive, he said, 'After three days I will rise again.' Therefore, have his tomb secured until the third day, lest his disciples come and steal the body, and say to the people: He is risen from the dead. That would be a deception worse than the first." Pilate answered them, "You have soldiers, go and take all the necessary precautions." So they went to the tomb and secured it, sealing the stone, placing the tomb under guard.

After the Sabbath, at dawn on the first day of the week, Mary Magdalene and the other Mary went to visit the tomb. Suddenly there was a violent earthquake: an angel of the Lord descending from heaven, came to the stone, rolled it from the entrance of the tomb, and sat on it. His appearance was like lightning and his garment white as snow. When they saw the angel, the guards were struck with terror.

The angel said to the women, "Do not be afraid, for I know that you are looking for Jesus, who was crucified. He is not here, for he is risen as he said. Come, see the place where they laid him; then go at once and tell his disciples that he is risen from the dead, and is going before you to Galilee. You will see him there. This is my message for you."

In fear, yet with great joy, the women left the tomb and ran to tell the news to his disciples.

Suddenly, Jesus met them on the way and said, "Rejoice!" The women approached him, embraced his feet and worshiped him. But Jesus said to them, "Do not be afraid! Go and tell my brothers to set out for Galilee; there, they will see me."

As the women proceeded on their way, some of the guards went into the city, and reported to the chief priests all that had happened. The chief priests met with the elders, and decided to give the soldiers a large sum of money, with this order, "Say that his disciples came by night while you were asleep, and stole the body of Jesus. If Pilate comes to know of this, we will explain the situation and keep you out of trouble." The soldiers accepted the money and did as they were told. This story has circulated among the Jews until this day.

As for the eleven disciples, they went to Galilee, to the mountain where Jesus had told them to go. When they saw Jesus, they bowed before him, although some doubted.

"All authority has been given to me in heaven and on earth. Go, there-fore, and make disciples of all nations. Baptize them in the Name of the Father and of the Son and of the Holy Spirit, and teach them to observe all that I have commanded you. I am with you always, even to the end of the world."

INVITATION TO
HEBREWS

The author of the book of Hebrews doesn't give his name and doesn't say who he's writing to. But the book itself reveals much about who wrote it, and why, and who it's written to.

The recipients are clearly Jews who've come to believe in Jesus as their Messiah. They are facing persecution and are in danger of falling away from the faith. The author expects them to be familiar with specific details of Israel's history and customs, and he also addresses them as followers of Jesus. They seem to have lived in Italy, since the author sends them greetings from those from Italy—that is, their friends from back home who are now traveling elsewhere in the Roman Empire.

The book seems to have been written before AD 70, when Jewish sacrifices ended with the destruction of the temple in Jerusalem, since it asks, if sacrifices could make us right with God, would they not have stopped being offered? Whatever the specifics of their situation, the recipients seem to have the option of escaping persecution by identifying themselves as Jews rather than as followers of Jesus. The author warns them not to do this. He explains that through Jesus, God has established a *new Covenant* that reveals the meaning and fulfills the purposes of the covenant God previously established through Moses. God now wants people to belong to him through this new covenant.

To convince his readers of this, the author of Hebrews alternates between teachings—such as reviews of Israel's history and the temple worship arrangements—and challenges based on the truths these teachings disclose. The book is essentially made up of four teaching-exhortation pairs (although it concludes with a further section that describes the practical implications of its truths for the community's life together). They develop these four topics:

: Jesus is much greater than the angels, so the salvation he announced is much greater than the message spoken through angels, that is, in the law of Moses (pp. 287–289).

: Jesus is our *apostle* (meaning someone sent by God on a specific mission). The apostles Moses and Joshua brought the people of Israel into a promised land and into God's rest, but the promised land and rest Jesus brings us into is a much greater one (pp. 289–291).

: Jesus is our *high priest*, and his advocacy for us in that position is much more effective than that of the priests appointed by the law of Moses (pp. 291–298).

: We must respond to all that God has done through Jesus by stepping out in *faith*, that is, by living in light of unseen heavenly realities. This is what faithful people have done throughout the ages, as they have waited for God to bring his heavenly realm back together with the earth once again (pp. 298–301).

The first section is really a prelude, and the fourth section is an application of the earlier ones. The core of the book is therefore found in the second and third sections. These sections are introduced intentionally by the statement, *Therefore, holy brothers, partners in a heavenly calling, consider Jesus, the **apostle**, and **high priest** of our faith*.

The goal of the whole book is to demonstrate that the final realities God has revealed in the new covenant are vastly superior to the temporary ones of the old covenant. Readers are encouraged to respond to every situation, including the threat of persecution, in light of the new reality revealed by Jesus the Messiah. This means not seeking refuge in a previous identity, but rather being willing to suffer if necessary to remain faithful to Jesus. The author encourages his readers to stay faithful by reminding them that they're receiving a kingdom that cannot be shaken.

| HEBREWS |

God has spoken, in the past, to our ancestors, through the prophets in many different ways, although never completely; but, in our times, he has spoken definitively to us, through his Son.

He is the one God appointed heir of all things, since, through him, he unfolded the stages of the world.

He is the radiance of God's glory, and bears the stamp of God's hidden being, so that, his powerful word upholds the universe. And after taking away sin, he took his place, at the right hand of the divine Majesty, in heaven.

So he is now far superior to angels, just as the name he received sets him apart from them. To what angel did God say:

> You are my son,
> I have begotten you today?

And to what angel did he promise:

> I shall be a father to him
> and he will be a son to me?

On sending his Firstborn to the world, God says:

> Let all the angels adore him.

Whereas, about angels, we find words like these:

> God sends the angels like wind,
> makes his servants flames of fire.

But of the Son, we read this:

> Your throne, O God, will last forever and ever;
> a rule of justice is your rule.
> You loved righteousness and hated wickedness;
> therefore God, your God, has anointed you with the oil of gladness,
> above your fellow kings.

And also, these words:

> Lord, in the beginning you placed the earth on its foundation
> and the heavens are the work of your hands.
>
> They will disappear, but you remain.
> They, all, wear out, like a garment;
> you will fold them like a cloak,
> and, change them.
>
> You, on the contrary, are always the same
> and your years will never end.

God never said to any of his angels:

> Sit here at my right side
> until I put your enemies
> as a footstool under your feet.

For all these spirits are only servants, and God sends them to help those who shall be saved.

So, we must pay the closest attention to the preaching we heard, lest we drift away. If words, spoken through angels, became law, and all disobedience or neglect received its due reward, how could we, now, escape, if we neglect such powerful salvation? For the Lord, himself, announced it first, and it was later confirmed by those who heard it. God confirmed their testimony by signs, wonders, and miracles of every kind—especially by the gifts of the Holy Spirit, that he distributed, according to his will.

The angels were not given dominion over the new world of which we are speaking. Instead, someone declared in Scripture:

> What is man, that you should be mindful of him,
> what is the son of man that you should care for him?
>
> For a while you placed him a little lower than the angels,
> but you crowned him with glory and honor.
> You have given him dominion over all things.

When it is said, that God gave him dominion over all things, nothing is excluded. As it is, we do not yet see his dominion over all things. But Jesus, who suffered death, and for a little while, was placed lower than the angels, has been crowned with honor and glory. For the merciful plan of God demanded that he experience death, on behalf of everyone.

God, from whom all come, and by whom all things exist, wanted to bring many children to glory, and he thought it fitting to make perfect, through suffering, the initiator of their salvation. So, he who gives, and those who receive holiness, are one. He, himself, is not ashamed of calling us brothers and sisters, as we read:

> Lord, I will proclaim your name to my brothers;
> I will praise you in the congregation.

He also says: I will trust in God; here I am, and the children God has given me. And because all those children share one same nature of flesh and blood, Jesus, likewise, had to share this nature. This is why his death destroyed the one holding the power of death, that is the devil, and freed those who remained in bondage all their lifetime, because of the fear of death.

Jesus came, to take by the hand, not the angels but the human race. So, he had to be like his brothers and sisters, in every respect, in order to be the high priest, faithful to God and merciful to them, a priest, able to ask pardon, and atone for their sins. Having been tested through suffering, he is able to help those who are tested.

Therefore, holy brothers, partners in a heavenly calling, consider Jesus, the apostle, and high priest of our faith.

He is faithful to God, who appointed him, just as Moses was a faithful steward over God's household; but Jesus deserves much greater honor than Moses, since he who builds the house is greater than the house. As every house has a builder, God is the builder of all. It is said, that Moses was found faithful, as a servant of God over all his household, and as witness of a former revelation from God. Christ came as the Son, to whom the house belongs; and we are his household, provided that, we stand firm in hope and courage.

Listen to what the Holy Spirit says:

> If only you would hear God's voice today!
> Do not be stubborn,
>
> as they were in the place called Rebellion,
> when your ancestors challenged me in the desert,
> although they had seen my deeds for forty years.
>
> That is why I was angry with those people and said:
> Their hearts are always going astray
> and they do not understand my ways.

> I was angry and made a solemn vow:
> They will never enter my rest.

So, brothers, be careful, lest some of you come to have an evil and unbelieving heart, that falls away from the living God. Encourage one another, day by day, as long as it is called today. Let no one become hardened in the deceitful way of sin. We are associated with Christ, provided we hold steadfastly to our initial hope, until the end.

Scripture says:

> If you hear God's voice,
> do not be stubborn a
> s they were in the place called Rebellion.

Who are those who, having heard, still rebelled? They were all those who came out of Egypt with Moses. With whom was God angry for forty years? With those who sinned and whose bodies fell in the desert. To whom did God swear, that they would not enter into his rest? To those who had disobeyed. We see, then, that unbelief prevented them from reaching their rest.

Therefore, let us fear while we are invited to enter the rest of God, lest any of you be left behind. We received the gospel, exactly as they did, but hearing the message did them no good, because they did not share the faith of those who did listen. We are now to enter this rest, because we believed, as it was said:

> I was angry and made a solemn vow:
> they will never enter my rest

—that is, the rest of God after he created the world. In another part, it was said about the seventh day: And God rested on the seventh day from all his works. But, now, it is said: They will not enter my rest. We must conclude, that some will enter the rest of God, and that those who first received the good , did not, because of their disobedience. Yet God, again, assigns a day when he says: today, and declares, through David, many years later:

> If you hear God's voice today,
> do not be stubborn.

So, it was not Joshua who let them enter the land of rest; otherwise, God would not have assigned another day, later on. Then, some other rest, or Sabbath, is reserved for the people of God. For those who enter this rest of God, rest from all their works, as God rests from his work.

Let us strive, then, to enter the rest, and not to share the misfortune of those who disobeyed. For the word of God is living and effective, sharper than any two-edged sword. It pierces, to the division of soul and spirit, of joints and marrow, and judges the intentions and thoughts of the heart. All creation is transparent to him; everything is uncovered and laid bare, to the eyes of him, to whom we render account.

We have a great high priest, Jesus, the Son of God, who has entered heaven. Let us, then, hold fast to the faith we profess. Our high priest is not indifferent to our weaknesses, for he was tempted, in every way, just as we are, yet, without sinning. Let us, then, with confidence, approach the throne of grace. We will obtain mercy and, through his favor, help in due time.

Every high priest is taken from among mortals, and appointed, to be their representative before God, to offer gifts, and sacrifices for sin. He is able to understand the ignorant and erring, for he, himself, is subject to weakness. This is why he is bound to offer sacrifices, for his sins, as well as, for the sins of the people. Besides, one does not presume to take this dignity, but takes it only when called by God, as Aaron was.

Nor did Christ become high priest in taking upon himself this dignity, but it was given to him, by the one who says:

> You are my son,
> I have begotten you today.

And in another place:

> You are a priest forever,
> in the priestly order of Melchizedek.

Christ, in the days of his mortal life, offered his sacrifice with tears and cries. He prayed to him, who could save him from death, and he was heard, because of his humble submission. Although he was Son, he learned, through suffering, what obedience was, and, once made perfect, he became the source of eternal salvation, for those who obey him. This is how God proclaimed him Priest in the order of Melchizedek.

About this, we have much to say, but it is difficult to explain, for you have become dull in understanding. You should be teachers by this time, but, in fact, you need to be taught, again, the basic elements of God's teaching. You need milk, not solid food. Those fed with milk are still infants: this refers to those who have not been tested in the way of righteousness. Solid food is for adults, who have trained themselves to distinguish good from evil.

Therefore, let us leave the elementary teaching about Christ, and move forward, to a more advanced knowledge, without laying, again, the foundation, that is: turning away from dead works, faith in God, the teaching about baptisms and laying on of hands, the resurrection of the dead and the final judgment. This is what we shall do, God permitting.

In any case, it would be impossible to renew, again, through penance, those who have once been enlightened, and have tasted the heavenly gift, and received the Holy Spirit, tasted the beauty of the word of God, and the wonders of the supernatural world. If, in spite of this, they have ceased to believe, and have fallen away, it is impossible to move them a second time to repentance, when they are crucifying, on their own account, the Son of God, and spurning him publicly. Soil that drinks the rain falling continually on it and produces profitable grass for those who till it, receives the blessings of God, but the soil that produces thorns and bushes is poor soil, and in danger of being cursed. In the end, it will be burned.

Yet, even though we speak like this, we are more optimistic, dear friends, regarding you and your salvation. God is not unjust, and will not forget everything you have done for love of his name; you have helped, and still help, the believers. We desire each of you to have, until the end, the same zeal for reaching what you have hoped for. Do not grow careless, but imitate those, who, by their faith and determination, inherit the promise.

Remember God's promise to Abraham. God wanted to confirm it with an oath, and, as no one is higher than God, he swore by himself: I shall bless you and give you many descendants. By just patiently waiting, Abraham obtained the promise.

People are used to swearing by someone higher than themselves, and their oath affirms everything that could be denied. So God committed himself, with an oath, in order to convince those who were to wait for his promise, that he would never change his mind. Thus, we have two certainties, in which it is impossible that God be proved false: promise and oath. That is enough to encourage us strongly, when we leave everything, to hold to the hope set before us. This hope is like a steadfast anchor of the soul, secure and firm, thrust beyond the curtain of the temple, into the Sanctuary itself, where Jesus has entered ahead of us—Jesus, high priest for ever, in the order of Melchizedek.

Scripture says that Melchizedek, king of Salem, priest of the Most High God, came out to meet Abraham, who returned from defeating the kings. He blessed Abraham, and Abraham gave him a tenth of everything.

Let us note, that the name Melchizedek means king of Justice, and that king of Salem means king of Peace. There is no mention of father, mother or genealogy; nothing is said about the beginning or the end of his life. In this, he is the figure of the Son of God, the priest who remains forever.

See, then, how great Melchizedek was. Even Abraham gave him a tenth of the spoils! When the descendants of Levi are consecrated priests, they are commanded to collect tithes from their people, that is, from their kindred, though these also are descended from Abraham. Here, however, Melchizedek, who does not belong to the family of the Levites, is given tithes from Abraham. Still more, he blesses him, the man of God's promise. There is no doubt, that he who blesses is higher than the one who is blessed. In the first case, we see that, tithes are received by those who are mortals; here, instead, Melchizedek is mentioned, as one who lives on.

When Abraham pays the tenth, it is, so to speak, the Levites, receivers of the tithes, who pay the tithe, because, in a way, Levi was still in the body of Abraham, his ancestor, when Melchizedek met him.

The institutions of the chosen people are founded upon the Levitical priesthood, but with it, they could not attain what is perfect and permanent. If that were possible, why would there be need of another priest, after the order of Melchizedek, instead of Aaron's? If there is a change in the priesthood, the law also has to be changed. Jesus, to whom all this has reference, was from a tribe that never served at the altar. All know, that he belonged to the tribe of Judah, that is not mentioned by Moses, when he speaks of the priesthood.

All this, however, becomes clear, if this priest, after the likeness of Melchizedek, has, in fact, received his mission, not on the basis of any human law, but by the power of an immortal life. Because Scripture says:

> You are a priest, forever,
> in the priestly order of Melchizedek.

With this, the former disposition is removed as insufficient and useless (for the law did not bring anything to perfection). At the same time, a better hope is given to us: that of drawing near to God.

This change is confirmed by God's oath. When the others became priests, God did not compromise himself with an oath, but Jesus is confirmed with an oath, as it is said:

> The Lord has sworn
> and will not change his mind:
> you are a priest forever.

Therefore, Jesus is our assurance of a better Covenant.

The former priests were many, since, as mortal men, they could not remain in office. But Jesus remains forever, and the priesthood shall not be taken from him. Consequently, he is able to save, for all time, those who approach God, through him. He always lives, to intercede on their behalf.

It was fitting, that our high priest be holy, undefiled, set apart from sinners, and exalted above the heavens; a priest, who does not, first, need to offer sacrifice for himself, before offering for the sins of the people, as high priests do. He offered himself in sacrifice, once, and for all. And, whereas, the law elected weak men as high priests, now, after the law, the word of God, with an oath, appointed the Son, made perfect forever.

The main point of what we are saying is that we have a high priest. He is seated at the right hand of the divine majesty, in heaven, where he serves as minister of the true temple and Sanctuary, set up not by any mortal, but by the Lord.

A high priest is appointed to offer to God gifts and sacrifices, and Jesus, also, has to offer some sacrifice. Had he remained on earth, he would not be a priest, since others offer the gifts, according to the law. In fact, the ritual celebrated by those priests is only an imitation, and shadow of the heavenly Sanctuary. We know the word of God to Moses, with regard to the construction of the holy tent. He said: You are to make everything according to the pattern shown to you on the mountain.

Now, however, Jesus enjoys a much higher ministry, in being the mediator of a better Covenant, founded on better promises. If all had been perfect in the first Covenant, there would have been no need for another one. Yet God sees defects when he says:

> The days are coming—it is the word of the Lord—
> when I will draw up a new Covenant
>
> with the people of Israel
> and with the people of Judah.
>
> It will not be like the Covenant
> that I made with their ancestors
>
> on the day I took them by the hand
> and led them out of Egypt.
>
> They did not keep my Covenant,
> and so I myself have forsaken them,
>
> says the Lord.
>
> But this is the Covenant
> that I will make with the people of Israel
> in the days to come:
> I will put my laws into their minds
> and write them on their hearts.

> I will be their God
> and they will be my people.

> None of them will have to teach one another
> or say to each other: Know the Lord,

> for they will know me
> from the least to the greatest.

> I will forgive their sins
> and no longer remember their wrongs.

Here, we are being told of a new Covenant; which means, that the first one had become obsolete, and what is obsolete, and aging, is soon to disappear.

The first Covenant had rites and regulations. There was also a Sanctuary—an earthly one. A first tent was prepared, with the lamp stand, the table and the bread of the presence; this is called the Holy Place. Behind the second curtain, there is a second Sanctuary, called the Most Holy Place, with the gold altar for the burning of incense, and the Ark of the Covenant, fully covered with gold. The ark contained a golden jar holding the manna, Aaron's rod that had sprouted leaves and the two slabs of the Covenant. Above the ark, the two cherubim of glory overshadowed the Seat of Mercy. But we cannot, here, describe it in detail.

With everything arranged as described, the priests continually enter the first room, to fulfill their ministry; but the high priest enters, only once a year, the second one, and not without bringing the blood, which he will offer for himself and for the sins of the people. By this, the Holy Spirit teaches us that the way into the inner Sanctuary is not open, as long as the first tent still stands. Here is a teaching, by means of figures, for the present age: the gifts and sacrifices presented to God cannot bring the people offering them to interior perfection. These are no more than food, drink, and different kinds of cleansing by water; all these are human regulations, awaiting a reformation.

But, now, Christ has appeared, as the high priest, with regard to the good things of these new times. He passed through a Sanctuary more noble and perfect, not made by hands, that is, not created. He did not take with himself the blood of goats and bulls, but his own blood, when he entered, once, and for all, into this Sanctuary, after obtaining definitive redemption. If the sprinkling of people, defiled by sin, with the blood of goats and bulls, or with the ashes of a heifer, provides them with exterior cleanness and holiness, how much more will it be, with the blood of Christ? He, moved by the eternal spirit, offered himself, as an unblemished victim, to God, and his blood cleanses us from dead works, so that we may serve the living God.

So, Christ is the mediator of a new Covenant, or testament. His death made atonement for the sins committed under the old testament, and the promise is handed over, to all who are called to the everlasting inheritance. With every testament, it is necessary to wait until its author has died. For a testament infers death, and has no value while the maker of it is still alive.

That is why the first Covenant was not ratified without blood. Moses proclaimed to the assembled people, all the commandments of the law; then, he took the blood of bulls and goats, and mixed it with water, and with these, he sprinkled the book, itself, and all the people, using scarlet, wool and hyssop, saying: This is the blood of the Covenant that God commanded you. In the same way, he sprinkled with blood, the Sanctuary, and all the objects of the ritual. According to the law, almost all cleansings have to be performed with blood; there is no forgiveness without the shedding of blood.

It was necessary, that mere copies of supernatural realities be purified, but, now, these realities need better sacrifices. Christ did not enter some sanctuary made by hands, a copy of the true one, but heaven itself. He is now in the presence of God, on our behalf. He had not to offer himself many times, as the high priest does: he, who, may return every year, because the blood is not his own. Otherwise, he would have suffered many times, from the creation of the world. But no; he manifested himself only now, at the end of the ages, to take away sin by sacrifice, and, as humans die only once, and afterward are judged, in the same way, Christ sacrificed himself, once to take away the sins of the multitude. There will be no further question of sin, when he comes again, to save those waiting for him.

The religion of the law is only a shadow of the good things to come; it has the patterns but not the realities. So, year after year, the same sacrifices are offered, without bringing the worshipers to what is the end. If they had been cleansed once and for all, they would no longer have felt guilt, and would have stopped offering the same sacrifices. But no, year after year their sacrifices witness to their sins, and never, will the blood of bulls and goats take away these sins.

This is why, on entering the world, Christ says:

> You did not desire sacrifice and offering;
> you were not pleased with burnt offerings and sin offerings.

Then I said:

> "Here I am. It was written of me in the scroll.
> I will do your will, O God."

First he says:

> Sacrifice, offerings, burnt offerings and sin offerings
> you did not desire nor were you pleased with them
> —although they were required by the law.

Then he says:

> Here I am to do your will.

This is enough to nullify the first will and establish the new. Now, by this will of God, we are sanctified, once, and for all, by the sacrifice of the body of Christ Jesus. So, whereas every priest stands, daily, by the altar, offering, repeatedly, the same sacrifices, that can never take away sins, Christ has offered, for all times, a single sacrifice for sins, and has taken his seat at the right hand of God, waiting, until God puts his enemies as a footstool under his feet. By a single sacrifice he has brought those who are sanctified to what is perfect forever.

This also was testified by the Holy Spirit. For after having declared:

> This is the Covenant that I will make with them
> in the days to come—says the Lord—
>
> I will put my laws in their hearts
> and write them on their minds.

He says:

> Their sins and evil deeds
> I will remember no more.

So, if sins are forgiven, there is no longer need of any sacrifice for sin.

So, my friends, we are assured of entering the Sanctuary, by the blood of Jesus who opened, for us, this new and living way, passing through the curtain, that is, his body. Because we have a high priest in charge of the house of God, let us approach, with a sincere heart, with full faith, interiorly cleansed from a bad conscience, and our bodies washed, with pure water.

Let us hold fast to our hope, without wavering, because he, who promised, is faithful. Let us consider, how we may spur one another to love and good works. Do not abandon the assemblies, as some of you do, but encourage one another, and all the more, since the Day is drawing near.

If we sin, willfully, after receiving knowledge of the truth, there is no longer sacrifice for sin, but only the fearful prospect of judgment and of fire which devours the rebellious. Anyone who disregards the law of Moses is put to death, without mercy, on the testimony of two or three witnesses. What, then, do you think it will be, for those who have despised the Son of

God? How severely shall he be punished, for having defiled the blood of the covenant, by which they were sanctified, and for having insulted the spirit given to them? For we know the one, who says: Revenge is mine, I will repay. And also: The Lord will judge his people. What a dreadful thing, to fall into the hands of the living God.

Remember the first days, when you were enlightened. You had to undergo a hard struggle in the face of suffering. Publicly, you were exposed to humiliations and trials, and had to share the sufferings of others who were similarly treated. You showed solidarity with those in prison; you were dispossessed of your goods, and accepted it gladly, for you knew, you were acquiring a much better and more durable possession. Do not now throw away your confidence, that will be handsomely rewarded. Be patient in doing the will of God, and the promise will be yours:

> A little, a little longer—says Scripture—
> and he who is coming will come;
> he will not delay.
>
> My righteous one will live if he believes;
> but if he distrusts,
> I will no longer look kindly on him.

We are not among those who withdraw and perish, but among those who believe, and win personal salvation.

F aith is the assurance of what we hope for, being certain of what we cannot see. Because of their faith, our ancestors were approved.

By faith, we understand that the stages of creation were disposed by God's word, and what is visible came from what cannot be seen.

Because of Abel's faith his offering was more acceptable than that of his brother Cain, which meant he was upright, and God, himself, approved his offering. Because of this faith he cried to God, as said in Scripture, even after he died.

By faith, Enoch was taken to heaven, instead of experiencing death: he could not be found, because God had taken him. In fact, it is said, that before being taken up, he had pleased God. Yet, without faith, it is impossible to please him: no one draws near to God, without first believing, that he exists, and that he rewards those who seek him earnestly.

By faith, Noah was instructed of events which could not yet be seen and, heeding what he heard, he built a boat, in which to save his family. The faith of Noah condemned the world, and he reached holiness, born of faith.

It was by faith, that Abraham, called by God, set out for a country that would be given to him as an inheritance; for he parted without knowing where he was going. By faith, he lived as a stranger in that promised land. There, he lived in tents, as did Isaac and Jacob, beneficiaries of the same promise. Indeed, he looked forward to that city of solid foundation, of which God is the architect and builder.

By faith, Sarah, herself, received power to become a mother, in spite of her advanced age; since she believed that, he, who had made the promise, would be faithful. Therefore, from an almost impotent man, were born descendants, as numerous as the stars of heaven, as many as the grains of sand on the seashore.

Death found all these people strong in their faith. They had not received what was promised, but they had looked ahead, and had rejoiced in it, from afar, saying that they were foreigners and travelers on earth. Those who speak in this way prove, that they are looking for their own country. For, if they had longed for the land they had left, it would have been easy for them to return, but no, they aspired to a better city, that is, a supernatural one; so God, who prepared the city for them, is not ashamed of being called their God.

By faith, Abraham went to offer Isaac, when God tested him. And so, he, who had received the promise of God, offered his only son, although God had told him: Isaac's descendants will bear your name. Abraham reasoned, that God is capable even of raising the dead, and he received back his son, which has a figurative meaning.

By faith, also, Isaac blessed the future of Jacob and Esau. By faith, Jacob, before he died, blessed both children of Joseph, and worshiped, as he leaned on his staff. By faith, Joseph, when about to die, warned the children of Israel of their exodus and gave orders about his remains.

By faith, the parents of the newly-born Moses hid him for three months, for they saw, the baby was very beautiful, and they did not fear the order of Pharaoh. By faith, Moses, already an adult, refused to be called son of Pharaoh's daughter. He preferred to share ill treatment with the people of God, rather than enjoy the passing pleasures of sin. He considered the humiliation of Christ a greater treasure than the wealth of Egypt, and he looked ahead to his reward. By faith, he left Egypt, without fearing the king's anger, and he persevered, as someone who could see the Invisible.

By faith, Moses had the Passover celebrated, sprinkling the doors with blood, so that the Destroyer would not kill their first-born sons. By faith they crossed the Red Sea, as if on dry land, while the Egyptians, who tried to cross it, were swallowed by the waters and drowned.

By faith, the walls of Jericho crumbled and fell, after Israel had marched round them for seven days; by faith, also, the prostitute Rahab escaped death, which befell the unbelievers, for having welcomed the spies.

Do I need to say more? There is not enough time to speak of Gideon,

Barak, Samson, Jephthah, David, as well as Samuel and the prophets. Through faith, they fought and conquered nations, established justice, saw the fulfillment of God's promises, shut the mouths of lions, quenched raging fire, escaped the sword, were healed of their sicknesses; they were weak people, who were given strength, to be brave in battle and repulse foreign invaders.

Some women recovered their dead by resurrection, but there were others—persecuted and tortured believers—who, for the sake of a better resurrection, refused to do what would have saved them. Others suffered chains and prison. They were stoned, sawn in two, killed by the sword. They fled, from place to place, with no other clothing than the skins of sheep and goats, lacking everything, afflicted, ill-treated. These people, of whom the world was not worthy, had to wander through wastelands and mountains, and take refuge in the dens of the land.

However, although all of them were praised because of their faith, they did not enjoy the promise, because God had us in mind, and saw beyond. And he did not want them to reach perfection, except with us.

What a cloud of innumerable witnesses surround us! So, let us be rid of every encumbrance, and especially of sin, to persevere in running the race marked out before us.

Let us look to Jesus, the founder of our faith, who will bring it to completion. For the sake of the joy reserved for him, he endured the cross, scorning its shame, and then, sat at the right of the throne of God. Think of Jesus, who suffered so many contradictions from evil people, and you will not be discouraged or grow weary. Have you already shed your blood in the struggle against sin?

Do not forget the comforting words that Wisdom addresses to you as children:

> My son, pay attention when the Lord corrects you
> and do not be discouraged when he punishes you.
>
> For the Lord corrects those he loves
> and chastises everyone he accepts as a son.

What you endure, is in order to correct you. God treats you like sons, and what son is not corrected by his father? If you were without correction, which has been received by all, (as is fitting for sons), you would not be sons, but bastards. Besides, when our parents, according to the flesh, corrected us, we respected them. How much more should we be subject to the Father of spirits, to have life? Our parents corrected us as they saw fit, with a view to this very short life; but God corrects us, for our own good, that we may share his holiness.

All correction is painful at the moment, rather than pleasant; later, it brings the fruit of peace, that is, holiness, to those who have been trained by it.

Lift up, then, your drooping hands, and strengthen your trembling knees; make level the ways for your feet, so that the lame may not be disabled, but healed.

Strive for peace with all, and strive to be holy, for without holiness, no one will see the Lord.

See that no one falls from the grace of God, lest a bitter plant spring up and its poison corrupt many among you. Let no one be immoral or irreligious, like Esau, who sold his birthright for a single meal. You know, that later, when he wished to get the blessing, he was rejected, although he pleaded with tears.

What you have come to, is nothing known to the senses: nor heat of a blazing fire, darkness and gloom and storms, blasts of trumpets or such a voice that the people pleaded, that no further word be spoken. For they could not endure the order that was given: Every man or beast reaching the mountain shall be stoned. The sight was so terrifying, that Moses said: I tremble with fear.

But you came near to Mount Zion, to the City of the living God, to the heavenly Jerusalem, with its innumerable angels. You have come to the solemn feast, the assembly of the firstborn of God, whose names are written in heaven. There is God, Judge of all, with the spirits of the upright, brought to perfection. There is Jesus, the mediator of the new Covenant, with the sprinkled blood that cries out more effectively than Abel's.

Be careful not to reject God when he speaks. If those who did not heed the prophet's warnings were not spared on earth, how much more shall we be punished, if we do not heed the One warning us from heaven? His voice, then, shook the earth, but, now, he says: Once more, I will shake not only the earth but also the heavens.

The words once more indicate the removal of everything that can be shaken, that is, created things, and only those that cannot be shaken will remain. Such is the kingdom that we receive. Let us, then, be grateful, and offer to God a worship pleasing to him, with reverence and awe. Our God is indeed a consuming fire.

L et mutual love continue. Do not neglect to offer hospitality; you know, that some people have entertained angels without knowing it. Remember prisoners, as if you were with them in chains, and the same for those who are suffering. Remember, that you also have a body.

Marriage must be respected by all, and husband and wife, faithful to each other. God will punish the immoral and the adulterous.

Do not depend on money. Be content with having enough for today, for God has said:

I will never forsake you or abandon you,

and we shall confidently answer:

The Lord is my helper, I will not fear;
what can man do to me?

Remember your leaders, who taught you the word of God. Consider their end, and imitate their faith. Christ Jesus is the same today, as yesterday, and forever.

Do not be led astray by all kinds of strange teachings. Your heart will be strengthened by the grace of God rather than by foods of no use to anyone. We have an altar, from which those still serving in the temple cannot eat.

After the high priest has offered the blood in the Sanctuary for the sins of the people, the carcasses of the animals are burnt outside the camp. For this same reason, Jesus, to purify the people with his own blood, suffered his Passion outside the Holy City. Let us, therefore, go to him, outside the sacred area, sharing his shame. For we have, here, no lasting city, and we are looking for the one to come.

Let us, then, continually offer, through Jesus, a sacrifice, of praise to God, that is the fruit of lips, celebrating his name. Do not neglect good works and common life, for these are sacrifices pleasing to God. Obey your leaders and submit to them, for they are concerned for your souls, and are accountable for them. Let this be a joy for them, rather than a burden, which would be of no advantage for you.

Pray for us, for we believe our intentions are pure, and that we only want to act honorably in all things. Now, I urge you, all the more, to pray for me, that I may be given back to you the sooner.

May God give you peace, he, who brought back, from among the dead, Jesus our Lord, the Great Shepherd of the sheep, whose blood seals the eternal Covenant.

He will train you in every good work, that you may do his will, for it is he who works in us what pleases him, through Jesus Christ, to whom all glory be for ever and ever. Amen!

B rothers, I beg you, to take these words of encouragement. For my part, I will add few words. Know, that our brother Timothy has been released. If he comes soon, I will visit you with him. Greetings to all your leaders and to the saints. Greetings from those in Italy.

Grace be with you all.

INVITATION TO
JAMES

Jesus had several brothers, and one of them was named James. After Jesus' death and resurrection, James became one of the most important leaders of the community of his followers in Jerusalem. James was respected for the advice he gave and for the wise decisions he helped the community make (see, for example, pp. 77–79). Later in his life he decided to write down some of his best teachings and advice and send them to other Jewish believers in Jesus who were scattered throughout the Roman Empire. What he wrote to them has become known as the book of James.

This book begins like a letter because it's being sent to people at a distance. But it's actually not very much like other letters of the time. Instead, it's a collection of short sayings, perhaps ones that James repeated often as he advised people. It also includes slightly longer discussions of practical topics. These discussions could have been taken from sermons that James gave, since they use the same techniques employed by speakers of the day. For example, sometimes James anticipates and answers a question someone might ask. Or, he may pose a question to his audience himself and then respond based on how he thinks they would have answered. Also, unlike most letters, this book doesn't treat its topics in logical or sequential order. Instead, it interweaves various themes as James raises subjects, leaves them, and then comes back to them again. The conversational style, the short, pithy sayings and the interweaving of themes all make this book similar to the wisdom writing found in the books of Proverbs and Ecclesiastes.

Like those wisdom books, the book of James concentrates primarily on questions of daily living in God's good creation. When James discusses directly what it means to be wise, he explains that wisdom is demonstrated in practical conduct: *the wisdom that comes from above is pure and peace-loving. Persons with this wisdom show understanding, and listen to advice; they are full of compassion and good works; they are impartial and sincere.* The practical issues he considers include concern for the poor, the responsible use of wealth, control of the tongue, purity of life, unity within the community of Jesus-followers, and above all patience and endurance during times of trial. We can see that the people James wrote to faced many challenges as they sought to practice *in the sight of God, our Father, pure and blameless religion.* As we face similar challenges today, his godly wisdom remains as valuable a guide to living fully human lives as it was when he first shared it centuries ago.

| JAMES |

J ames, a servant of God, and of the Lord Jesus Christ,

sends greetings to the twelve tribes scattered among the nations.

C onsider yourselves fortunate, my brothers and sisters, when you meet with every kind of trial, for you know, that the testing of your faith makes you steadfast. Let your steadfastness become perfect, with deeds, that you, yourselves, may be perfect and blameless, without any defect.

If any of you is lacking in wisdom, ask God, who gives to all easily and unconditionally. But ask with faith, not doubting, for the one who doubts is like a wave driven and tossed on the sea by the wind. Such a person should not expect anything from the Lord, since the doubter has two minds and his conduct will always be insecure.

Let the believer who is poor, boast, in being uplifted, and let the rich one boast, in being humbled, because he will pass away like the flower of the field. The sun rises and its heat dries the grass; the flower withers and its beauty vanishes. So, too, will the rich person fade away, even in the midst of his pursuits.

Happy are those who patiently endure trials, because, afterward, they will receive the crown of life, which the Lord promised to those who love him. No one, when tempted, should say, "This temptation comes from God." God is never tempted, and he can never tempt anyone. Instead, each of us is lured, and enticed, by our own evil desire. Once this desire has conceived, it gives birth to sin, and sin, when fully grown, gives birth to death.

Do not be deceived, my beloved. Every good and perfect gift comes from above, from the Father of Light, in whom there is no change, or shadow of a change. By his own will, he gave us life, through the word of truth, that we might be a kind of offering to him, among his creatures.

My beloved, be quick to hear but slow to speak, and slow to anger, for human anger does not fulfill the justice of God. So get rid of any filth, and reject the prevailing evil, and welcome the word that has been planted in you, and has the power to save you.

Be doers of the word, and not just hearers, lest you deceive yourselves. The hearer, who does not become a doer, is like that one, who looked at himself in the mirror; he looked, and then promptly forgot what he was like. But those who fix their gaze on the perfect law of freedom, and hold onto it, not listening and then forgetting, but acting on it, will find blessing on their deeds.

Those who think they are religious, but do not restrain their tongue, deceive themselves, and their religion is in vain. In the sight of God, our Father, pure and blameless religion lies in helping the orphans, and widows in their need, and keeping oneself from the world's corruption.

My brothers and sisters, if you truly believe in our glorified Lord, Jesus Christ, you will not discriminate between persons. Suppose a person enters the synagogue where you are assembled, dressed magnificently and wearing a gold ring; at the same time, a poor person enters dressed in rags. If you focus your attention on the well-dressed and say, "Come and sit in the best seat," while, to the poor one you say, "Stay standing, or else sit down at my feet," have you not, in fact, made a distinction between the two? Have you not judged, using a double standard?

Listen, my beloved brothers and sisters, did God not choose the poor of this world to receive the riches of faith, and to inherit the kingdom, which he has promised to those who love him? Yet, you despise them! Is it not the rich who are against you, and drag you to court? Do they not insult the holy name of Christ by which you are called?

If you keep the law of the kingdom, according to Scripture: Love your neighbor as yourself, you do well; but if you make distinctions between persons, you break the law, and are condemned by the same law. For whoever keeps the whole law, but fails, in one aspect, is guilty of breaking it all. For he who said, Do not commit adultery, also said, Do not kill. If, then, you do not commit adultery but you do commit murder, you have broken the law. Therefore, speak and behave like people who are going to be judged by the law of freedom. There will be justice, without mercy, for those who have not shown mercy, whereas, mercy has nothing to fear of judgment.

What good is it, my brothers and sisters, to profess faith, without showing works? Such faith has no power to save you. If a brother or sister is in need of clothes or food, and one of you says, "May things go well for you; be warm and satisfied," without attending to their material needs, what good is that? So, it is, for faith without deeds: it is totally dead.

Say to whoever challenges you, "You have faith and I have good deeds; show me your faith apart from actions and I, for my part, will show you my faith in the way I act." Do you believe there is one God? Well enough, but do not forget, that the demons, also, believe, and tremble with fear!

You foolish one, do you have to be convinced, that faith without deeds is useless? Think of our father Abraham. Was he not justified by the act of offering his son Isaac on the altar? So you see, his faith was active, along with his deeds, and became perfect by what he did. The word of Scripture was thus fulfilled, Abraham believed in God so he was considered a righteous person and he was called the friend of God.

So you see, a person is justified by works, and not by faith alone. Likewise, we read of Rahab, the prostitute, that she was acknowledged and saved, because she welcomed the spies, and showed them another way to leave.

So, just as the body is dead without its spirit, so faith, without deeds is also dead.

My brothers and sisters, don't all be teachers! You know that, as teachers, we will be judged most strictly; in fact, we make mistakes, like everybody else. A person who commits no offense in speech is perfect, and capable of ruling the whole self. We put a bit into the horse's mouth to master it and, with this, we control its whole body. The same is true of ships: however big they are, driven by strong winds, they are guided by a tiny rudder. In the same way, the tongue is a tiny part of the body, but it is capable of great things.

A small flame is enough to set a huge forest on fire. The tongue is a similar flame; it is, in itself, a whole world of evil. It infects the whole being, and sets fire to our world, with the very fire of hell. Wild animals, birds, reptiles and sea creatures of every kind are, and have been ruled, by the human species. Nobody, however, can control the tongue; it is an untiring whip, full of deadly poison. We use it to bless God, our Father, and also, to curse those made in God's likeness. From the same mouth come both blessing and curse.

Brothers and sisters, this should not be the case. Can both fresh and salt water gush from the same source? Can a fig tree produce olives or a grapevine give figs? Neither is the sea able to give fresh water.

If you consider yourself wise and learned, show it by your good life, and let your actions, in all humility, be an example for others. But if your heart is full of bitter jealousy, and ambition, do not try to show off; that would be covering up the truth; this kind of wisdom does not come from above, but from the world, and it is earthly and devilish. Wherever there is jealousy and ambition, you will also find discord, and all that is evil. Instead, the wisdom that comes from above is pure and peace-loving. Persons with this wisdom show understanding, and listen to advice; they are full of compassion and good works; they are impartial and sincere. Peacemakers, who sow peace, reap a harvest of justice.

What causes these fights and quarrels among you? Is it not your cravings, that make war within your own selves? When you long for something you cannot have, you kill for it, and when you do not get what you desire, you squabble and fight. The fact is, you do not have what you want, because you do not pray for it. You pray for something, and you do not get it, because you pray with the wrong motive, of indulging your pleasures. You adulterers! Don't you know, that making friends with the world makes you enemies of God? Therefore, whoever chooses to be the world's friend becomes God's enemy.

Can you not see the point of the saying in Scripture: "The longing of the spirit, he sent to dwell in us, is a jealous longing?" But God has something better to give, and Scripture also says,

> God opposes the proud
> but he gives his favor to the humble.

Give in, then, to God; resist the devil, and he will flee from you. Draw close to God and he will come close to you. Clean your hands, you sinners, and purify your hearts, you doubters. Recognize your distress, be miserable and weep. Turn your laughter into tears and your joy into sadness. Humble yourselves before the Lord and he will raise you up.

Brothers and sisters, do not criticize one another. Anyone who speaks against, or condemns another, speaks against the law, and condemns the law. If, however, you condemn the law, you are no longer an observer of the law, but a judge of it. There is only one lawgiver and one judge: he who has the power to save or condemn. So you, who are you, to judge your neighbor?

Listen now, you who speak like this, "Today or tomorrow we will go off to this city and spend a year there; we will do business and make money." You have no idea what tomorrow will bring. What is your life? No more than a mist, which appears for a moment and then disappears. Instead of this, you should say, "God willing, we will live and do this or that." But no! You boast of your plans: this brazen pride is wicked. Anyone who knows what is good, and does not do it, sins.

So, now, for what concerns the rich, cry and weep, for the misfortunes that are coming upon you. Your riches are rotting, and your clothes, eaten up by the moths. Your silver and gold have rusted, and their rust grows into a witness against you. It will consume your flesh, like fire, for having piled up riches, in these, the last days.

You deceived the workers who harvested your fields, but, now, their wages cry out to the heavens. The reapers' complaints have reached the ears of the Lord of hosts. You lived in luxury and pleasure in this world, thus, fattening yourselves for the day of slaughter. You have easily condemned, and killed the innocent since they offered no resistance.

Be patient then, beloved, until the coming of the Lord. See how the sower waits for the precious fruits of the earth, looking forward, patiently, to the autumn and spring rains. You, also, be patient, and do not lose heart, because the Lord's coming is near.

Beloved, do not fight among yourselves and you will not be judged. See, the judge is already at the door. Take for yourselves, as an example of patience, the suffering of the prophets, who spoke in the Lord's name. See how those who were patient are called blessed. You have heard of the patience of Job and know how the Lord dealt with him in the end. For the Lord is merciful and shows compassion.

Above all, my beloved, do not swear, either by heaven or by earth, or make a habit of swearing. Let your yes be yes and your no be no, lest you become liable for judgment.

Are any among you, discouraged? They should pray. Are any of you happy? They should sing songs to God. If anyone is sick, let him call on the elders of the Church. They shall pray for him, anointing him with oil in the name of the Lord. The prayer said in faith will save the sick person; the Lord will raise him up and if he has committed any sins, he will be forgiven.

There will be healing, if you confess your sins to one another, and pray for each other. The prayer of the upright man has great power, provided he perseveres. Elijah was a human being, like ourselves, and when he prayed, earnestly, for it not to rain, no rain fell for three and a half years. Then he prayed again: the sky yielded rain and the earth produced its fruit.

Brothers, if any one of you strays far away from the truth, and another person brings him back to it, be sure of this: he who brings back a sinner from the wrong way, will save his soul from death and win forgiveness for many sins.

INVITATION TO
MARK

The book of Mark is one of four accounts of the life and teachings of Jesus in the New Testament. Its author doesn't identify himself by name, and he doesn't say who he's writing to. But we can determine a lot about these things from the book itself.

First, it's clear that this book is written for a Roman audience—that is, for people whose first language was Latin, who lived at a distance from the land of Israel, and who were not familiar with Jewish customs. The book is written in Greek, the common language of the time, but it uses many Latin terms. The author explains Jewish customs, and he translates quotations from Jesus that are in Aramaic. He also notes that Simon of Cyrene, who carried Jesus' cross, was the *father of Alexander and Rufus*, expecting that his audience will know who these men are. A man named Rufus was a leader in the church at Rome.

Another thing we can tell from the book is that its author either witnessed Jesus' ministry personally or heard about Jesus from an eyewitness. The book includes many details which an eyewitness would recall. At one point we're told that Peter *remembered* that Jesus had cursed the fig tree. Such a detail could only have been provided originally by Peter himself. The book therefore may well be the "memoirs" of Peter as Jesus' disciple.

But why was it written? As we read through its pages, we're struck by the recurring emphasis on the need to be willing to suffer and even give one's life in order to remain faithful to Jesus. One clue we have to this purpose comes in the way that Peter's brash boasting of loyalty to Jesus and his subsequent denial are related unflinchingly, with only a hint of his later restoration. The portrayal seems intended to challenge believers not to deny Jesus in the same way Peter had. But it must have been offered at a time when Peter's standing in the Roman church was so high that not even this portrayal would have diminished it. This time would have been right after Peter's death at the hands of the emperor Nero around AD 65. (In that case, Peter's memoirs would have been written down, as tradition suggests, by his younger friend and co-worker John Mark, who was with him in Rome at the end of his life—see p. 352.)

The kind of witness to Jesus by Roman believers that the hour called for is modeled by the Roman centurion at Jesus' death: *Truly, this man was the Son of God*. The book appears to be written, therefore, to challenge and encourage believers in Rome to remain faithful to Jesus in the face of Nero's persecution.

While it accomplishes this goal by telling the story of Jesus' life, it has a much faster-moving plot than other biographies of the day. It's much more like the dramas that were presented on the stage for Greek and Roman audiences. In these dramas, the tension would build until reaching a point of crisis and climax. After this the tension would be steadily defused as conflicting parties put a plan into action to secure their threatened interests. The ultimate clash of these plans produced an "overturning" of the situation that had formerly prevailed, in favor of a new one.

In Mark the tension centers around the identity of Jesus. If we think of the book as a drama, we may say that in its opening half, the tension is over the question: Who is this man? This tension builds over the course of three acts:

: In the first act, Jesus teaches and heals the crowds that swarm to him (pp. 315–318).
: In the second act, Jesus encounters more conflict and opposition (pp. 319–323).
: In the third act, the disciples struggle more to understand who Jesus is (pp. 323–328).

Each act begins with a reference to Jesus calling or commissioning his disciples, and each one ends with an episode that calls attention to the question of his identity. The episode at the end of the third act shows Jesus healing a blind man in two stages, so that he slowly comes to see. This reflects the experience of the disciples, who have only gradually come to recognize who Jesus is. Then in the central episode of the whole story—between its two halves—Peter confesses that Jesus is the Messiah (p. 328), the one bringing God's reign to earth.

Now the overt conflict begins. As the Messiah, Jesus has come to introduce a radical new way of life that will undercut existing power relationships. (*If someone wants to be first, let him be last of all and servant of all.*) This is threatening to those who are currently in power. As he and his disciples travel to Jerusalem for the Passover Festival, Jesus warns them three times that he will be betrayed and executed, but adds that in the ultimate triumph of God's plan, he will then rise from the dead. The second half of the drama depicts this outcome, and it too does so in three acts:

: In the first act (which, significantly, also ends with the healing of a blind man), Jesus and his disciples travel to Jerusalem (pp. 328–333).
: In the second act, Jesus teaches in the temple and clashes with the established leadership (pp. 333–338).
: In the final act, this leadership executes its plan and has Jesus arrested and crucified, seemingly "overturning" all he has done. But then God "overturns" their deed and raises Jesus to life (pp. 338–344).

Readers of the story are thus called to be faithful to Jesus, even if this means suffering the same fate he did. This is how God will continue to overturn the existing order and establish the way of life that Jesus taught. Implicit in this is the promise that God will "overturn" the death of believers just as he did that of Jesus. They too will be vindicated and raised to new life.

| MARK |

This is the beginning of the Good News of Jesus Christ, the Son of God. It is written in the book of Isaiah, the prophet,

> "I am sending my messenger ahead of you,
> to prepare your way.

> Let the people hear the voice calling in the desert:

> Prepare the way of the Lord,
> level his paths."

So John began to baptize in the desert; he preached a baptism of repentance, for the forgiveness of sins. All Judea and all the people from the city of Jerusalem went out to John to confess their sins, and to be baptized by him in the river Jordan.

John was clothed in camel's hair and wore a leather belt around his waist. His food was locusts and honey. He preached to the people, saying, "After me comes one who is more powerful than I am; I have baptized you with water, but he will baptize you in the Holy Spirit."

At that time, Jesus came from Nazareth, a town of Galilee, and was baptized by John in the Jordan. And the moment he came up out of the water, heaven opened before him, and he saw the Spirit coming down on him like a dove. And these words were heard from heaven, "You are my Son, the Beloved, the One I have chosen."

Then the Spirit drove him into the desert. Jesus stayed in the desert forty days and was tempted by Satan. He was with the wild animals, but angels ministered to him.

After John was arrested, Jesus went into Galilee and began preaching the Good News of God. He said, "The time has come; the kingdom of God is at hand. Change your ways and believe the Good News."

As Jesus was walking along the shore of Lake Galilee, he saw Simon and his brother Andrew casting a net into the lake, for they were fishermen. And Jesus said to them, "Follow me, and I will make you fish for people." At once, they abandoned their nets and followed him. Jesus went a little farther on, and saw James and John, the sons of Zebedee; they were in their boat mending their nets. Immediately, Jesus called them and they followed him, leaving their father Zebedee in the boat with the hired men.

They went into the town of Capernaum and Jesus taught in the synagogue on the Sabbath day. The people were astonished at the way he taught, for he spoke as one having authority, and not like the teachers of the law.

It happened that, a man with an evil spirit was in their synagogue, and he shouted, "What do you want with us, Jesus of Nazareth? Have you come to destroy us? I know who you are: you are the Holy One of God." Then Jesus faced him and said with authority, "Be silent, and come out of this man!" The evil spirit shook the man violently and, with a loud shriek, came out of him.

All the people were astonished, and they wondered, "What is this? With what authority he preaches! He even gives orders to evil spirits and they obey him!" And Jesus' fame spread throughout all the country of Galilee.

On leaving the synagogue, Jesus went to the home of Simon and Andrew, with James and John. As Simon's mother-in-law was sick in bed with fever, they immediately told him about her. Jesus went to her and, taking her by the hand, raised her up. The fever left her and she began to wait on them. That evening, at sundown, people brought to Jesus all the sick and those who had evil spirits: the whole town was pressing around the door. Jesus healed many who had various diseases, and drove out many demons; but he did not let them speak, for they knew who he was.

Very early in the morning, before daylight, Jesus went off to a lonely place where he prayed. Simon and the others went out also, searching for him; and when they found him, they said, "Everyone is looking for you." Then Jesus answered, "Let us go to the nearby villages so that I may preach there too; for that is why I came."

So Jesus set out to preach in all the synagogues throughout Galilee; he also cast out demons.

A leper came to Jesus and begged him, "If you want to, you can make me clean." Moved with pity, Jesus stretched out his hand and touched him, saying, "I do want to; be clean." The leprosy left the man at once and he was made clean. As Jesus sent the man away, he sternly warned him, "Don't tell anyone about this, but go and show yourself to the priest; and for the cleansing, bring the offering ordered by Moses; in this way, you will give to them your testimony."

However, as soon as the man went out, he began spreading the news everywhere, so that Jesus could no longer openly enter any town. But even though he stayed in the rural areas, people came to him from everywhere.

After some days, Jesus returned to Capernaum. As the news spread that he was in the house, so many people gathered, that there was no longer room even outside the door. While Jesus was preaching the word to them, some people brought to him a paralyzed man.

The four men who carried him couldn't get near Jesus because of the crowd, so they opened the roof above the room where Jesus was and, through the hole, lowered the man on his mat. When Jesus saw the faith of these people, he said to the paralytic, "My son, your sins are forgiven."

Now, some teachers of the law, who were sitting there, wondered within themselves, "How can he speak like this, insulting God? Who can forgive sins except God?"

At once, Jesus knew in his spirit what they were thinking, and asked, "Why do you wonder? Is it easier to say to this paralyzed man, 'Your sins are forgiven,' or to say, 'Rise, take up your mat and walk?' But now you shall know, that the Son of Man has authority on earth to forgive sins."

And he said to the paralytic, "Stand up, take up your mat and go home." The man rose and, in the sight of all those people, he took up his mat and went out. All of them were astonished and praised God, saying, "Never have we seen anything like this!"

When Jesus went out again, beside the lake, a crowd came to him, and he taught them. As he walked along, he saw a tax collector sitting in his office. This was Levi, the son of Alpheus. Jesus said to him, "Follow me!" And Levi got up and followed him.

And it so happened that, when Jesus was eating in Levi's house, tax collectors and sinners sat with him and his disciples; there were a lot of them, and they used to follow Jesus.

But Pharisees, men educated in the law, when they saw Jesus eating with sinners and tax collectors, said to his disciples, "Why does your master eat and drink with tax collectors and sinners?"

Jesus heard them, and answered, "Healthy people don't need a doctor, but sick people do. I did not come to call the righteous, but sinners."

One day, when the Pharisees and the disciples of John the Baptist were fasting, some people asked Jesus, "Why is it, that both the Pharisees and the disciples of John fast, but yours do not?" Jesus answered, "How can the wedding guests fast while the bridegroom is with them? As long as they have the bridegroom with them, they cannot fast. But the day will come, when the bridegroom will be taken from them, and on that day they will fast.

No one sews a piece of new cloth on an old coat, because the new patch will shrink and tear away from the old cloth, making a worse tear. And no one puts new wine into old wine skins, for the wine would burst the skins, and then both the wine and the skins would be lost. But new wine, new skins!"

One Sabbath he was walking through grain fields. As his disciples walked along with him, they began to pick the heads of grain and crush them in their hands. Then the Pharisees said to Jesus, "Look! They are doing what is forbidden on the Sabbath!"

And he said to them, "Have you never read what David did in his time of need; when he and his men were very hungry? He went into the House of God, when Abiathar was High Priest, and ate; the bread of offering, which only the priests are allowed to eat, and he also gave some to the men who were with him." Then Jesus said to them, "The Sabbath was made for man, not man for the Sabbath. So the Son of Man is master even of the Sabbath."

Again, Jesus entered the synagogue. A man, who had a paralyzed hand, was there; and some people watched Jesus: would he heal the man on the Sabbath? If he did, they could accuse him.

Jesus said to the man with the paralyzed hand, "Stand here, in the center." Then he asked them, "What does the law allow us to do on the Sabbath? To do good or to do harm? To save life or to kill?" But they were silent.

Then Jesus looked around at them with anger and deep sadness at their hardness of heart. And he said to the man, "Stretch out your hand." He stretched it out, and his hand was healed. As soon as the Pharisees left, they met with Herod's supporters, looking for a way to destroy Jesus.

Jesus and his disciples withdrew to the lakeside, and a large crowd from Galilee followed him. A great number of people also came from Judea, Jerusalem, Idumea, Transjordan, and from the region of Tyre and Sidon, for they had heard of all that he was doing.

Because of the crowd, Jesus told his disciples to have a boat ready for him, to prevent the people from crushing him. He healed so many, that all who had diseases kept pressing toward him to touch him. Even the people who had evil spirits, whenever they saw him, they would fall down before him and cry out, "You are the Son of God." But he warned them sternly not to tell anyone who he was.

Then Jesus went up into the hill country, and called those he wanted, and they came to him. He appointed Twelve to be with him, and he called them 'apostles.' He wanted to send them out to preach; and he gave them authority to drive out demons.

These are the Twelve: Simon, to whom he gave the name Peter; James, son of Zebedee, and John his brother, to whom he gave the name Boanerges, which means 'men of thunder'; Andrew, Philip, Bartholomew, Matthew, Thomas, James son of Alpheus, Thaddeus, Simon the Cananean, and Judas Iscariot, the one who betrayed him.

They went home. The crowd began to gather again and they couldn't even have a meal. Knowing what was happening, his relatives came to take charge of him. "He is out of his mind," they said. Meanwhile, the teachers of the law, who had come from Jerusalem, said, "He is in the power of Beelzebul: the chief of the demons helps him to drive out demons."

Jesus called them to him, and began teaching them by means of stories, or parables. "How can Satan drive out Satan? If a nation is divided by civil war, that nation cannot stand. If a family divides itself into groups, that family will not survive. In the same way, if Satan has risen against himself and is divided, he will not stand; he is finished. No one can break into the house of a strong man in order to plunder his goods, unless he first ties up the strong man. Then indeed, he can plunder his house.

Truly, I say to you, every sin will be forgiven humankind, even insults to God, however numerous. But whoever slanders the Holy Spirit will never be forgiven. He carries the guilt of his sin forever."

This was their sin when they said, "He has an unclean spirit in him."

Then his mother and his brothers came. As they stood outside, they sent someone to call him. The crowd sitting around Jesus told him, "Your mother and your brothers are outside asking for you." He replied, "Who are my mother and my brothers?"

And looking around at those who sat there, he said, "Here are my mother and my brothers. Whoever does the will of God is brother and sister and mother to me."

Again, Jesus began to teach by the lake; but such a large crowd gathered about him, that he got into a boat and sat in it on the lake, while the crowd stood on the shore. He taught them many things through parables. In his teaching he said,

"Listen! The sower went out to sow. As he sowed, some of the seed fell along a path; and the birds came and ate it up. Some of the seed fell on rocky ground, where it had little soil; it sprang up immediately, because it had no depth; but when the sun rose and burned it, it withered, because it had no roots. Other seed fell among thorn bushes; and the thorns grew and choked it; so it didn't produce any grain. But some seed fell on good soil, grew and increased and yielded grain; some seed produced thirty times as much, some sixty, and some one hundred times as much." And Jesus added, "Listen then, if you have ears."

When the crowd went away, some who were around him with the Twelve asked about the parables.

He answered them, "The mystery of the kingdom of God has been given to you. But for those outside, everything comes in parables, so, that,

> the more they see, they don't perceive;
> the more they hear, they don't understand;
>
> otherwise they would be converted and pardoned."

Jesus said to them, "Don't you understand this parable? How, then, will you understand any of the parables?

What the sower is sowing is the word. Those along the path, where the seed fell, are people who hear the word, but as soon as they hear it, Satan comes and takes away the word that was sown in them.

Other people receive the word like rocky ground. As soon as they hear the word, they accept it with joy. But they have no roots, so it lasts only a little while. No sooner does trouble or persecution come because of the word, than they fall.

Others receive the seed, as seed among thorns. After they hear the word, they are caught up in the worries of this life, false hopes of riches and other desires. All these come in and choke the word, so that finally it produces nothing.

And there are others who receive the word as good soil. They hear the word, take it to heart and produce: some thirty, some sixty, and some one hundred times as much."

Jesus also said to them, "When the light comes, is it put under a basket or a bed? Surely it is put on a lamp stand. Whatever is hidden will be disclosed, and whatever is kept secret will be brought to light. Listen then, if you have ears!"

And he also said to them, "Pay attention to what you hear. In the measure you give, so shall you receive, and still more will be given to you. For to the one who produces something, more will be given; and from him who does not produce anything, even what he has will be taken away from him."

Jesus also said, "In the kingdom of God it is like this: a man scatters seed upon the soil. Whether he is asleep or awake, be it day or night, the seed sprouts and grows; he knows not how. The soil produces of itself; first, the blade; then, the ear; then the full grain in the ear. And when it is ripe for harvesting, they take the sickle for the cutting: the time for the harvest has come."

Jesus also said, "What is the kingdom of God like? To what shall we compare it? It is like a mustard seed which, when sown, is the smallest of all the seeds scattered upon the soil. But once sown, it grows up and becomes the largest of the plants in the garden; and even grows branches so big, that the birds of the air can take shelter in its shade."

Jesus used many such stories, in order to proclaim the word to them in a way that they would be able to understand. He would not teach them without parables; but privately, to his disciples, he explained everything.

On that same day, when evening had come, Jesus said to them, "Let's go across to the other side of the lake." So they left the crowd, and took him along in the boat he had been sitting in, and other boats set out with him. Then a storm gathered and it began to blow a gale. The waves spilled over into the boat, so that it was soon filled with water. Jesus was in the stern, sleeping on a cushion.

They woke him up, and said, "Master, don't you care if we drown?" And rising up, Jesus rebuked the wind, and ordered the sea, "Quiet now! Be still!" The wind dropped, and there was a great calm. Then Jesus said to them, "Why are you so frightened? Do you still have no faith?"

But they were terrified, and they said to one another, "Who can this be? Even the wind and the sea obey him!"

They arrived at the other side of the lake, in the region of the Gerasenes. No sooner did Jesus leave the boat than he was met by a man with evil spirits, who had come from the tombs. The man lived among the tombs, and no one could restrain him, even with a chain. He had often been bound with fetters and chains; but he would pull the chains apart and smash the fetters; and no one had the strength to control him. Night and day he stayed among the tombs on the hillsides, and was continually screaming, and beating himself with stones.

When he saw Jesus from afar, he ran and fell at his feet, and cried with a loud voice, "What do you want with me, Jesus, Son of the Most High God? For God's sake, I beg you, do not torment me!" He said this, because Jesus had commanded, "Evil spirit, come out of the man!" When Jesus asked the evil spirit, "What is your name?" it replied, "Legion is my name, for we are many." And it kept begging Jesus, not to send them out of that region.

Now a great herd of pigs was feeding on the hillside, and the evil spirits begged him, "Send us to the pigs, and let us go into them." So Jesus let them

go. The evil spirits came out of the man and went into the pigs; and imme-
diately, the herd rushed down the cliff; and all were drowned in the lake.
The herdsmen fled, and reported this in the town and in the countryside.
So all the people came to see what had happened.

They came to Jesus, and saw the man freed of the evil spirits, sitting
there, clothed and in his right mind; the same man who had been possessed by the legion. They were afraid. And when those who had seen it,
told what had happened to the man and to the pigs, the people begged Jesus
to leave their neighborhood.

When Jesus was getting into the boat, the man, who had been possessed, begged to stay with him. Jesus would not let him, and said, "Go
home to your people, and tell them how much the Lord has done for you,
and how he has had mercy on you." So he went throughout the country of
Decapolis, telling everyone how much Jesus had done for him; and all the
people were astonished.

Jesus then crossed to the other side of the lake; and while he was still on the
shore, a large crowd gathered around him. Jairus, an official of the synagogue, came up and, seeing Jesus, threw himself at his feet; and begged
him earnestly, "My little daughter is at the point of death. Come and lay
your hands on her, so that she may get well and live."

Jesus went with him, and many people followed, pressing around him.
Among the crowd was a woman who had suffered from bleeding for twelve
years. She had suffered a lot at the hands of many doctors and had spent
everything she had, but instead of getting better, she was worse. Because
she had heard about Jesus, this woman came up behind him and touched
his cloak, thinking, "If I just touch his clothing, I shall get well." Her flow of
blood dried up at once, and she felt in her body that she was healed of her
complaint.

But Jesus was conscious that healing power had gone out from him,
so he turned around in the crowd, and asked, "Who touched my clothes?"
His disciples answered, "You see how the people are crowding around you.
Why do you ask who touched you?" But he kept looking around to see who
had done it. Then the woman, aware of what had happened, came forward,
trembling and afraid. She knelt before him, and told him the whole truth.

Then Jesus said to her, "Daughter, your faith has saved you. Go in peace
and be free of this illness."

While Jesus was still speaking, some people arrived from the official's
house to inform him, "Your daughter is dead. Why trouble the Master any
further?" But Jesus ignored what they said, and told the official, "Do not
fear, just believe." And he allowed no one to follow him except Peter, James,
and John, the brother of James.

When they arrived at the house, Jesus saw a great commotion, with people weeping and wailing loudly. Jesus entered, and said to them, "Why all this commotion and weeping? The child is not dead, but asleep."

They laughed at him. So Jesus sent them outside, and went with the child's father and mother and his companions into the room, where the child lay. Taking her by the hand, he said to her, "Talitha kumi!" which means, "Little girl, get up!"

The girl got up at once and began to walk around. (She was twelve years old.) The parents were amazed, greatly amazed. Jesus strictly ordered them not to let anyone know about it; and he told them to give her something to eat.

Leaving that place, Jesus returned to his own country, and his disciples followed him. When the Sabbath came, he began to teach in the synagogue, and most of those who heard him were astonished. But they said, "How did this come to him? What kind of wisdom has been given to him, that he also performs such miracles? Who is he but the carpenter, the Son of Mary, and the brother of James and Joses and Judas and Simon? His sisters, too, are they not here among us?" So they took offense at him.

And Jesus said to them, "Prophets are despised only in their own country, among their relatives, and in their own family." And he could work no miracles there, but only healed a few sick people, by laying his hands on them. Jesus himself was astounded at their unbelief.

Jesus then went around the villages, teaching. He called the Twelve to him, and began to send them out two by two, giving them authority over evil spirits. And he ordered them to take nothing for the journey, except a staff: no food, no bag, no money in their belts. They were to wear sandals and were not to take an extra tunic.

And he added, "In whatever house you are welcomed, stay there until you leave the place. If any place doesn't receive you, and the people refuse to listen to you, leave after shaking the dust off your feet. It will be a testimony against them."

So they set out to proclaim that this was the time to repent. They drove out many demons and healed many sick people by anointing them.

King Herod also heard about Jesus, because his name had become well-known. Some people said, "John the Baptist has been raised from the dead, and that is why miraculous powers are at work in him." Others thought, "He is Elijah," and others, "He is a prophet like the prophets of times past." When Herod was told of this, he thought, "I had John beheaded; yet, he has risen from the dead!"

For this is what had happened: Herod had ordered John to be arrested;

and had had him bound and put in prison because of Herodias, the wife of his brother Philip. Herod had married her; and John had told him, "It is not right for you to live with your brother's wife." So Herodias held a grudge against John and wanted to kill him; but she could not, because Herod respected John. He knew John to be an upright and holy man, and kept him safe. And he liked listening to him; although he became very disturbed whenever he heard him.

Herodias had her chance on Herod's birthday, when he gave a dinner for all the senior government officials, military chiefs, and the leaders of Galilee. On that occasion, the daughter of Herodias came in and danced; and she delighted Herod and his guests. The king said to the girl, "Ask me for anything you want and I will give it to you." And he went so far as to say with many oaths, "I will give you anything you ask, even half my kingdom." She went out and said to her mother, "What shall I ask for?" The mother replied, "The head of John the Baptist." The girl hurried to the king and made her request, "I want you to give me the head of John the Baptist, here and now, on a dish."

The king was very displeased, but he would not refuse in front of his guests because of his oaths. So he sent one of the bodyguards, with orders to bring John's head. He went and beheaded John in prison; then he brought the head on a dish and gave it to the girl. And the girl gave it to her mother. When John's disciples heard of this, they came and took his body and buried it.

The apostles returned and reported to Jesus all they had done and taught. Then he said to them, "Let us go off by ourselves into a remote place and have some rest." For there were so many people coming and going that the apostles had no time even to eat. And they went away in the boat to a secluded area by themselves.

But people saw them leaving, and many could guess where they were going. So, from all the towns, they hurried there on foot, arriving ahead of them.

As Jesus went ashore, he saw a large crowd, and he had compassion on them, for they were like sheep without a shepherd. And he began to teach them many things.

It was now getting late, so his disciples came to him and said, "This is a lonely place and it is now late. You should send the people away, and let them go to the farms and villages around here, to buy themselves something to eat."

Jesus replied, "You, yourselves, give them something to eat." They answered, "If we are to feed them, we need two hundred silver coins to go and buy enough bread." But Jesus said, "You have some loaves; how many?

Go and see." The disciples found out and said, "There are five loaves and two fish."

Then he told them to have the people sit down, together in groups, on the green grass. This they did, in groups of hundreds and fifties. And Jesus took the five loaves and the two fish and, raising his eyes to heaven, he pronounced a blessing, broke the loaves, and handed them to his disciples to distribute to the people. He also divided the two fish among them.

They all ate and everyone had enough. The disciples gathered up what was left, and filled twelve baskets with broken pieces of bread and fish. Five thousand men had eaten there.

Immediately, Jesus obliged his disciples to get into the boat and go ahead of him to the other side, toward Bethsaida, while he himself sent the crowd away. And having sent the people off, he went by himself to the hillside to pray.

When evening came, the boat was far out on the lake, while he was alone on the land. Jesus saw his disciples straining at the oars, for the wind was against them; and before daybreak he came to them, walking on the lake, and he was going to pass them by.

When they saw him walking on the lake, they thought it was a ghost and cried out; for they all saw him and were terrified. But, at once, he called to them, "Courage! It is I; don't be afraid!" Then Jesus got into the boat with them, and the wind died down. They were completely astonished, for they had not really grasped the fact of the loaves; their minds were dull.

Having crossed the lake, they came ashore at Gennesaret, where they tied up the boat. As soon as they landed, people recognized Jesus, and ran to spread the news throughout the countryside. Wherever he was, they brought to him the sick lying on their mats; and wherever he went, to villages, towns or farms, they laid the sick in the marketplace, and begged him to let them touch just the fringe of his cloak. And all who touched him were cured.

One day, the Pharisees gathered around Jesus, and with them were some teachers of the law who had just come from Jerusalem.

They noticed that some of his disciples were eating their meal with unclean hands, that is, without washing them. Now the Pharisees, and in fact all the Jews, never eat without washing their hands, for they follow the tradition received from their ancestors. Nor do they eat anything, when they come from the market, without first washing themselves. And there are many other traditions they observe; for example, the ritual washing of cups, pots and plates.

So the Pharisees and the teachers of the law asked him, "Why do your disciples not follow the tradition of the elders, but eat with unclean hands?"

Jesus answered, "You shallow people! How well Isaiah prophesied of you when he wrote:

> This people honors me with their lips,
> but their heart is far from me.
>
> The worship they offer me is worthless,
> for what they teach are only human rules.

You even put aside the commandment of God to hold fast to human tradition."

And Jesus commented, "You have a fine way of disregarding the commandments of God in order to enforce your own traditions! For example, Moses said: Do your duty to your father and your mother, and: Whoever curses his father or his mother is to be put to death. But according to you, someone could say to his father or mother, 'I already declared Corban (which means "offered to God") what you could have expected from me.' In this case, you no longer require him to do anything for his father or mother; and so you nullify the word of God through the tradition you have handed on. And you do many other things like that."

Jesus then called the people to him again and said to them, "Listen to me, all of you, and try to understand. Nothing that enters a person from the outside can make that person unclean. It is what comes from within that makes a person unclean. Let everyone who has ears listen."

When Jesus got home and was away from the crowd, his disciples asked him about this saying, and he replied, "So even you are dull? Do you not see that whatever comes from outside cannot make a person unclean, since it enters not the heart but the stomach, and is finally passed out?"

Thus Jesus declared that all foods are clean.

And he went on, "What comes out of a person is what defiles him, for evil designs come out of the heart: theft, murder, adultery, jealousy, greed, maliciousness, deceit, indecency, slander, pride and folly. All these evil things come from within and make a person unclean."

When Jesus left that place, he went to the border of the Tyrian country. There, he entered a house, and did not want anyone to know he was there; but he could not remain hidden. A woman, whose small daughter had an evil spirit, heard of him, and came and fell at his feet. Now this woman was a pagan, a Syrophoenician by birth, and she begged him to drive the demon out of her daughter.

Jesus told her, "Let the children be fed first, for it is not right to take the children's bread and throw it to the puppies." But she replied, "Sir, even the puppies under the table eat the crumbs from the children's bread." Then Jesus said to her, "You may go your way; because of such a response, the demon has gone out of your daughter." And when the woman went home, she found her child lying in bed, and the demon gone.

Again, Jesus set out: from the country of Tyre he passed through Sidon and, skirting the sea of Galilee, he came to the territory of Decapolis. There, a deaf man, who also had difficulty in speaking, was brought to him. They asked Jesus to lay his hand upon him.

Jesus took him apart from the crowd, put his fingers into the man's ears, and touched his tongue with spittle. Then, looking up to heaven, he said with a deep sigh, "Ephphata!" that is, "Be opened!"

And immediately, his ears were opened, his tongue was loosened, and he began to speak clearly. Jesus ordered them not to tell anyone about it; but the more he insisted, the more they proclaimed it. The people were completely astonished and said, "He has done all things well; he makes the deaf hear and the dumb speak."

Soon afterward, Jesus was in the midst of another large crowd, that obviously had nothing to eat. So he called his disciples and said to them, "I feel sorry for these people, because they have been with me for three days and now have nothing to eat. If I send them to their homes hungry, they will faint on the way; some of them have come a long way."

His disciples replied, "Where, in a deserted place like this, could we get enough bread to feed these people?" He asked them, "How many loaves have you?" And they answered, "Seven."

Then he ordered the crowd to sit down on the ground. Taking the seven loaves and giving thanks, he broke them, and handed them to his disciples to distribute. And they distributed them among the people. They also had some small fish. So Jesus said a blessing, and asked that these be shared as well.

The people ate and were satisfied, and they picked up the broken pieces left over, seven baskets full. Now those who had eaten were about four thousand in number. Jesus sent them away, and immediately got into the boat with his disciples, and went to the region of Dalmanutha.

The Pharisees came and started to argue with Jesus. Hoping to embarrass him, they asked for some heavenly sign. Then his spirit was moved. He gave a deep sigh and said, "Why do the people of this present time ask for a sign? Truly, I say to you, no sign shall be given to this people." Then he left them, got into the boat again, and went to the other side of the lake.

The disciples had forgotten to bring more bread, and had only one loaf with them in the boat. Then Jesus warned them, "Keep your eyes open, and beware of the yeast of the Pharisees and the yeast of Herod." And they said to one another, "He saw that we have no bread."

Aware of this, Jesus asked them, "Why are you talking about the loaves you are short of? Do you not see or understand? Are your minds closed? Have you eyes that don't see and ears that don't hear? And do you not remember when I broke the five loaves among five thousand? How many baskets full of leftovers did you collect?" They answered, "Twelve." "And having distributed seven loaves to the four thousand, how many wicker baskets of leftovers did you collect?" They answered, "Seven." Then Jesus said to them, "Do you still not understand?"

When they came to Bethsaida, Jesus was asked to touch a blind man who was brought to him. He took the blind man by the hand and led him outside the village. When he had put spittle on his eyes and laid his hands upon him, he asked, "Can you see anything?" The man, who was beginning to see, replied, "I see people! They look like trees, but they move around." Then Jesus laid his hands on his eyes again and the man could see perfectly. His sight was restored and he could see everything clearly.

Then Jesus sent him home, saying, "Do not return to the village."

Jesus set out with his disciples for the villages around Caesarea Philippi; and on the way he asked them, "Who do people say I am?" And they told him, "Some say, you are John the Baptist; others say, you are Elijah or one of the prophets."

Then Jesus asked them, "But you, who do you say I am?" Peter answered, "You are the Messiah." And he ordered them not to tell anyone about him.

Jesus then began to teach them that the Son of Man had to suffer many things and be rejected by the elders, the chief priests and the teachers of the law. He would be killed, and after three days rise again. Jesus said all this quite openly, so that Peter took him aside and began to protest strongly. But Jesus, turning around, and looking at his disciples, rebuked Peter, saying, "Get behind me, Satan! You are thinking not as God does, but as people do."

Then Jesus called the people and his disciples, and said, "If you want to follow me, deny yourself; take up your cross and follow me. For if you choose to save your life, you will lose it; and if you lose your life for my sake, and for the sake of the gospel, you will save it.

What good is it, to gain the whole world, while destroying your soul? There is nothing more precious than your soul. I tell you, if anyone is ashamed of me and of my words, among this adulterous and sinful people, the Son of Man will also be ashamed of him, when he comes in the glory of his Father with the holy angels."

And he went on to say, "Truly I tell you, there are some here who will not die before they see the kingdom of God coming with power."

Six days later, Jesus took with him Peter and James and John, and led them up a high mountain. There, his appearance was changed before their eyes. Even his clothes shone, becoming as white as no bleach of this world could make them. Elijah and Moses appeared to them; the two were talking with Jesus.

Then Peter spoke and said to Jesus, "Master, it is good that we are here; let us make three tents, one for you, one for Moses, and one for Elijah." For he did not know what to say: they were overcome with awe. But a cloud formed, covering them in a shadow, and from the cloud came a voice, "This is my Son, the Beloved: listen to him!" And suddenly, as they looked around, they no longer saw anyone except Jesus with them.

As they came down the mountain, he ordered them to tell no one what they had seen, until the Son of Man had risen from the dead. So they kept this to themselves, although they discussed with one another what 'to rise from the dead' could mean.

Finally they asked him, "Why, then, do the teachers of the law say that Elijah must come first?" Jesus answered them, "Of course Elijah will come first, so that everything may be as it should be. But why do the Scriptures say that the Son of Man must suffer many things and be despised? I tell you that Elijah has already come; and they have treated him as they pleased, as the Scriptures say of him."

When they came to the place where they had left the disciples, they saw many people around them and some teachers of the law arguing with them. When the people saw Jesus, they were astonished and ran to greet him.

He asked, "What are you arguing about with them?" A man answered him from the crowd, "Master, I brought my son to you, for he has a spirit, deaf and mute. Whenever the spirit seizes him, it throws him down and he foams at the mouth, grinds his teeth and becomes stiff all over. I asked your disciples to drive the spirit out, but they could not."

Jesus replied, "You faithless people! How long must I be with you? How long must I put up with you? Bring him to me." And they brought the boy to him.

As soon as the spirit saw Jesus, it shook and convulsed the boy, who fell on the ground and began rolling about, foaming at the mouth. Then Jesus asked the father, "How long has this been happening to him?" He replied, "From childhood. And it has often thrown him into the fire and into the water to destroy him. If you can do anything, have pity on us and help us."

Jesus said to him, "Why do you say, 'If you can?' All things are possible for one who believes." Immediately, the father of the boy cried out, "I do believe, but help the little faith I have."

Jesus saw that the crowd was increasing rapidly, so he ordered the evil spirit, "Dumb and deaf spirit, I command you: Leave the boy and never enter him again." The evil spirit shook and convulsed the boy and with a terrible shriek came out. The boy lay like a corpse and people said, "He is dead." But Jesus took him by the hand and raised him; and the boy stood up.

After Jesus had gone indoors, his disciples asked him privately, "Why couldn't we drive out the spirit?" And he answered, "Only prayer can drive out this kind, nothing else."

After leaving that place, they made their way through Galilee; but Jesus did not want people to know where he was because he was teaching his disciples. And he told them, "The Son of Man will be delivered into the hands of men. They will kill him, but three days after he has been killed, he will rise." The disciples, however, did not understand these words and they were afraid to ask him what he meant.

They came to Capernaum and, once inside the house, Jesus asked them, "What were you discussing on the way?" But they did not answer, because they had been arguing about who was the greatest.

Then he sat down, called the Twelve and said to them, "If someone wants to be first, let him be last of all and servant of all." Then he took a little child, placed him in their midst, and putting his arms around him he said to them, "Whoever welcomes a child such as this in my name, welcomes me; and whoever welcomes me, welcomes not me, but the One who sent me."

John said to him, "Master, we saw someone who drove out demons by calling upon your name, and we tried to forbid him, because he does not belong to our group." Jesus answered, "Do not forbid him, for no one who works a miracle in my name can soon after speak evil of me. For whoever is not against us is for us.

If anyone gives you a drink of water because you belong to Christ and bear his name, truly, I say to you, he will not go without reward.

If anyone should cause one of these little ones who believe in me to stumble and sin, it would be better for him to be thrown into the sea with a great millstone around his neck.

If your hand makes you fall into sin, cut it off! It is better for you to enter life without a hand, than with two hands to go to hell, to the fire that never goes out. And if your foot makes you fall into sin, cut it off! It is better for you to enter life without a foot, than with both feet to be thrown into hell. And if your eye makes you fall into sin, tear it out! It is better for you to enter the kingdom of God with one eye, than, keeping both eyes, to be thrown into hell, where

> the worms that eat them never die,
> and the fire never goes out.

The fire itself will preserve them.

Salt is a good thing; but if it loses its saltiness, how can you make it salty again? Have salt in yourselves and be at peace with one another."

Jesus then left that place and went to the province of Judea, beyond the Jordan River. Once more, crowds gathered around him and, once more, he taught them, as he always did. Some (Pharisees came and) put him to the test with this question: "Is it right for a husband to divorce his wife?" He replied, "What law did Moses give you?" They answered, "Moses allowed us to write a certificate of dismissal in order to divorce."

Then Jesus said to them, "Moses wrote this law for you, because you have hearts of stone. But in the beginning of creation God made them male and female; and because of this, man has to leave father and mother and be joined to his wife; and the two shall become one body. So, they are no longer two, but one body. Therefore, let no one separate what God has joined."

When they were indoors at home, the disciples again asked him about this, and he told them, "Whoever divorces his wife and marries another, commits adultery against his wife; and the woman who divorces her husband and marries another, also commits adultery."

People were bringing their little children to him to have him touch them; and the disciples rebuked them for this.

When Jesus noticed it, he was very angry and said, "Let the children come to me and don't stop them, for the kingdom of God belongs to such as these. Truly, I say to you, whoever does not receive the kingdom of God like a child will not enter it." Then he took the children in his arms and, laying his hands on them, blessed them.

Just as Jesus was setting out on his journey again, a man ran up, knelt before him and asked, "Good Master, what must I do to have eternal life?"

Jesus answered, "Why do you call me good? No one is good but God alone. You know the commandments: Do not kill; do not commit adultery; do not steal; do not bear false witness; do not cheat; honor your father and mother." The man replied, "I have obeyed all these commandments since my childhood."

Then Jesus looked steadily at him and loved him; and he said, "For you one thing is lacking. Go, sell what you have, and give the money to the po and you will have riches in heaven. Then, come, and follow me." On he these words, his face fell and he went away sorrowful, for he was a man of great wealth.

Jesus looked around and said to his disciples, "How hard it is for those who have riches to enter the kingdom of God!" The disciples were shocked at these words, but Jesus insisted, "Children, how hard it is to enter the kingdom of God! It is easier for a camel to go through the eye of the needle than for one who is rich to enter the kingdom of God."

They were more astonished than ever and wondered, "Who, then, can be saved?" Jesus looked steadily at them and said, "For human beings it is impossible, but not for God; all things are possible with God."

Peter spoke up and said, "We have given up everything to follow you." Jesus answered, "Truly, there is no one who has left house, or brothers or sisters, or father or mother, or children, or lands, for my sake, and for the gospel, who will not receive his reward. I say to you: even in the midst of persecution, he will receive a hundred times as many houses, brothers, sisters, mothers, children, and lands in the present time; and, in the world to come, eternal life. Do pay attention: many who now are the first will be last, and the last, first."

They were on the road going up to Jerusalem, and Jesus was walking ahead. The Twelve were anxious, and those who followed were afraid. Once more Jesus took the Twelve aside to tell them what was to happen to him. "You see we are going up to Jerusalem, and the Son of Man will be given over to the chief priests and the teachers of the law. They will condemn him to death, and hand him over to the foreigners, who will make fun of him, spit on him, scourge him, and kill him; but three days later he will rise."

James and John, the sons of Zebedee, came to Jesus and said to him, "Master, we want you to grant us what we are going to ask of you." And he said, "What do you want me to do for you?" They answered, "Grant us to sit, one at your right hand and one at your left, when you come in your glory."

But Jesus said to them, "You don't know what you are asking. Can you drink the cup that I drink, or be baptized in the way I am baptized?" They answered, "We can." And Jesus told them, "The cup that I drink, you will drink; and you will be baptized in the way that I am baptized; but to sit at my right hand or at my left is not mine to grant. It has been prepared for others."

On hearing this, the other ten were angry with James and John. Jesus then called them to him and said, "As you know, the so-called rulers of the nations behave like tyrants, and those in authority oppress the people. But it shall not be so among you; whoever would be great among you must be your servant, and whoever would be first among you shall make himself slave of all. Think of the Son of Man, who has not come to be served but to serve, and to give his life to redeem many."

They came to Jericho. As Jesus was leaving Jericho with his disciples and a large crowd, a blind beggar, Bartimaeus, the son of Timaeus, was sitting by the roadside. On hearing that it was Jesus of Nazareth passing by, he began to call out, "Son of David, Jesus, have mercy on me!" Many people scolded him and told him to keep quiet, but he shouted all the louder, "Son of David, have mercy on me!"

Jesus stopped and said, "Call him." So they called the blind man, saying, "Take heart! Get up, he is calling you!" He immediately threw aside his cloak, jumped up and went to Jesus.

Then Jesus asked him, "What do you want me to do for you?" The blind man said, "Master, let me see again!" And Jesus said to him, "Go your way, your faith has made you well." And, immediately, he could see, and he followed Jesus along the road.

When they drew near to Jerusalem and arrived at Bethphage and Bethany, at the Mount of Olives, Jesus sent two of his disciples with these instructions, "Go to the village ahead of you and, as you enter it, you will find there a colt tied up that no one has ridden. Untie it and bring it here. If anyone says to you, 'What are you doing?' give this answer, 'The Lord needs it, but he will send it back immediately.'"

They went off and found the colt, out in the street, tied at the door. As they were untying it, some of the bystanders asked, "Why are you untying that colt?" They answered as Jesus had told them, and the people allowed them to continue.

They brought the colt to Jesus, threw their cloaks on its back, and Jesus sat upon it. Many people also spread their cloaks on the road, while others spread leafy branches from the fields. Then the people who walked ahead, and those who followed behind Jesus, began to shout,

"Hosannah!

Blessed is he who comes in the name of the Lord!

Blessed is the kingdom of our father David, which comes!

Hosannah in the highest!"

So Jesus entered Jerusalem and went into the temple. And after he had looked all around, as it was already late, he went out to Bethany with the Twelve.

The next day, when they were leaving Bethany, he felt hungry. In the distance, he noticed a fig tree covered with leaves; so he went to see if he could find anything on it. When he reached it, he found nothing but leaves, for it was not the season for figs. Then Jesus said to the fig tree, "May no one ever eat your fruit!" And his disciples heard these words.

When they reached Jerusalem, Jesus went to the temple, and began to drive away all the people he saw buying and selling there. He overturned the tables of the money changers and the stools of those who sold pigeons. And he would not let anyone carry anything through the temple area.

Jesus then taught the people, "Does not God say in the Scriptures: My house will be called a House of Prayer for all the nations? But you have turned it into a den of thieves."

The chief priests and the teachers of the law heard of this; and they tried to find a way to destroy him. They were afraid of him, because all the people were astonished by his teaching.

When evening came, Jesus left the city.

Early next morning, as they walked along the road, the disciples saw the fig tree withered to its roots. Peter then said to him, "Master, look! The fig tree you cursed has withered."

And Jesus replied, "Have faith in God. Truly, I say to you, if you say to this mountain, 'Be taken up and cast into the sea,' and have no doubt in your heart, but believe that what you say will happen, it will be done for you. Therefore, I tell you, whatever you ask in prayer, believe that you have received it, and it shall be done for you. And when you stand to pray, if you have anything against anyone, forgive, so that your heavenly Father may also forgive your sins."

They were once again in Jerusalem. As Jesus was walking in the temple, the chief priests, the teachers of the law and the elders came to him and asked, "What authority do you have to act like this? Who gave you authority to do the things you do?"

Jesus said to them, "I will ask you a question, only one, and if you give me an answer, then I will tell you what authority I have to act like this. Was John's preaching and baptism a work of God, or was it merely something human? Answer me."

And they kept arguing among themselves, "If we answer that it was a work of God, he will say, 'Why then did you not believe him?'" But neither could they answer before the people that the baptism of John was merely something human, for everyone regarded John as a prophet. So they answered Jesus, "We don't know," and Jesus said to them, "Neither will I tell you what authority I have to act as I do."

Using parables, Jesus went on to say, "A man planted a vineyard, put a fence around it, dug a hole for the wine press and built a watch tower. Then he leased the vineyard to tenants and went abroad.

In due time, he sent a servant to receive from the tenants the fruit of the vineyard. But they seized the servant, struck him and sent him back empty-handed. Again, the man sent another servant. They also struck him on the head and treated him shamefully. He sent another, and they killed him. In the same way they treated many others: some they beat up and others they killed. One was still left, his beloved son. And so, last of all, he sent him to the tenants, for he said, 'They will respect my son.'

But those tenants said to one another, 'This is the one who is to inherit the vineyard. Let's kill him and the property will be ours.' So they seized him and killed him, and threw him out of the vineyard. Now, what will the owner of the vineyard do? He will come and destroy those tenants and give the vineyard to others."

And Jesus added, "Have you not read this text of the Scriptures:

> The stone which the builders rejected
> has become the keystone;
>
> this is the Lord's doing,
> and we marvel at it?"

They wanted to arrest him, for they realized that Jesus meant this parable for them, but they were afraid of the crowd; so they left him and went away.

They sent to Jesus some Pharisees with members of Herod's party, with the purpose of trapping him by his own words. They came and said to Jesus, "Master, we know that you are truthful; you are not influenced by anyone, and your answers do not vary according to who is listening to you, but you truly teach God's way. Tell us, is it against the law to pay taxes to Caesar? Should we pay them or not?"

But Jesus saw through their trick and answered, "Why are you testing me? Bring me a silver coin and let me see it." They brought him one and Jesus asked, "Whose image is this, and whose name?" They answered, "Caesar's." Then Jesus said, "Give back to Caesar what is Caesar's, and to God, what is God's."

And they were greatly astonished.

The Sadducees also came to Jesus. Since they claim that there is no resurrection, they questioned him in this way, "Master, in the Scriptures Moses gave us this law: If anyone dies and leaves a wife but no children, his brother must take the woman, and, with her, have a baby, who will be considered the child of his deceased brother. Now, there were seven brothers. The first married a wife, but he died without leaving any children. The second took the wife, and he also died, leaving no children. The same thing happened to the third. In fact, all seven brothers died, leaving no children. Last of all, the woman died. Now, in the resurrection, to which of them will she be wife? For all seven brothers had her as wife."

Jesus replied, "Is this not the reason you are mistaken, that you do not understand the Scriptures or the power of God? When they rise from the dead, men and women do not marry, but are like the angels in heaven.

Now, about the resurrection of the dead, have you never had thoughts about the burning bush in the book of Moses? God said to Moses: I am the God of Abraham, the God of Isaac and the God of Jacob. He is the God, not of the dead, but of the living. You are totally wrong."

A teacher of the law had been listening to this discussion and admired how Jesus answered them. So he came up and asked him, "Which commandment is the first of all?"

Jesus answered, "The first is: Hear, Israel! The Lord, our God, is One Lord; and you shall love the Lord, your God, with all your heart, with all your soul, with all your mind and with all your strength. And after this comes a second commandment: You shall love your neighbor as yourself. There is no commandment greater than these two."

The teacher of the law said to him, "Well spoken, Master; you are right when you say that he is one, and there is no other besides him. To love him with all our heart, with all our understanding and with all our strength, and to love our neighbor as ourselves is more important than any burnt offering or sacrifice."

Jesus approved this answer and said, "You are not far from the kingdom of God." And after that, no one dared to ask him any more questions.

As Jesus was teaching in the temple, he said, "The teachers of the law say that the Messiah is the Son of David. How can that be? For David, himself, inspired by the Holy Spirit, declared:

> The Lord said to my Lord,
> 'Sit at my right hand,
>
> until I put your enemies
> under your feet!'

If David, himself, calls him Lord, in what way can he be his Son?"

Many people came to Jesus, and listened to him gladly.

As he was teaching, he also said to them, "Beware of those teachers of the law, who enjoy walking around in long robes and being greeted in the marketplace; and who like to occupy reserved seats in the synagogues; and the first places at feasts. They even devour the widow's and the orphan's goods, while making a show of long prayers. How severe a sentence they will receive!"

Jesus sat down opposite the temple treasury, and watched the people dropping money into the treasury box; and many rich people put in large offerings. But a poor widow also came and dropped in two small coins.

Then, Jesus called his disciples and said to them, "Truly I say to you, this poor widow put in more than all those who gave offerings. For all of them gave from their plenty; but she gave from her poverty, and put in everything she had, her very living."

As Jesus left the temple, one of his disciples said, "Look, Master, at the enormous stones and wonderful buildings here!" And Jesus answered, "You see these great buildings? Not one stone will be left upon another, but all will be torn down."

After a while, when Jesus was sitting on the Mount of Olives, facing the temple, Peter, James, John and Andrew approached him privately and asked, "Tell us when this will be. What sign will be given us before all this happens?"

Then Jesus began to tell them, "Don't let anyone mislead you. Many will come in my name, saying, 'I am he,' and they will deceive many people.

When you hear of wars and threats of war, don't be troubled; this must occur, but the end is not yet. Nation will fight nation and kingdom will oppose kingdom. There will be earthquakes everywhere and famines, too. And these will be like the first pains of childbirth. Be on your guard, for you will be arrested and taken to court. You will be beaten in synagogues; and you will stand before governors and kings for my sake, to bear witness before them. For the preaching of the gospel to all nations has to come first.

So, when you are arrested and brought to trial, don't worry about what you are to say; for you shall say what will be given to you in that hour. It is not you who speak, but the Holy Spirit.

Brother will betray brother, even to death, and the father his child. Children will turn against their parents and have them put to death. You will be hated by all for my name's sake, but whoever holds out to the end will be saved.

So, when you see the desolating abomination set in the place where it should not be (may the reader understand!), then let those in Judea flee to the mountains. If you are on the housetop, don't come down to take anything with you. If you are in the field, don't turn back to fetch your cloak. How hard it will be then for pregnant women and mothers with babies at the breast! Pray, that it may not happen in winter. For this will be a time of distress, such as was never known, from the beginning, when God created the world, until now; and is never to be known again. So, that, if the

Lord had not shortened that time, no one would survive; but he decided to shorten it, for the sake of those whom he has chosen.

And if anyone says to you at that time, 'Look, here is the Messiah! Look, he is there!'—do not believe it. For false messiahs and false prophets will arise and perform signs and wonders in order to deceive even God's chosen people, if that were possible. Be on your guard then; I have told you everything ahead of time.

> Later on in those days, after that disastrous time,
> the sun will grow dark, the moon will not give its light,
>
> the stars will fall out of the sky,
> and the whole universe will be shaken.

Then people will see the Son of Man coming in the clouds with great power and glory. And he will send the angels to gather his chosen people from the four winds, from the ends of the earth to the ends of the sky.

Learn a lesson from the fig tree: as soon as its branches become tender and it begins to sprout leaves, you know that summer is near. In the same way, when you see these things happening, know that the time is near, even at the door. Truly, I say to you, this generation will not pass away until all this has happened. Heaven and earth will pass away, but my words will not pass away.

But, regarding that day and that hour, no one knows when it will come, not even the angels, not even the Son, but only the Father.

Be alert and watch, for you don't know when the time will come. When a man goes abroad and leaves his home, he puts his servants in charge, giving to each one some responsibility; and he orders the doorkeeper to stay awake. So stay awake, for you don't know when the Lord of the house will come, in the evening or at midnight, when the cock crows or before dawn. If he comes suddenly, do not let him catch you asleep.

And what I say to you, I say to all: Stay awake!"

It was now two days before the feast of the Passover and Unleavened Bread. The chief priests and the teachers of the law were looking for a way to arrest Jesus on a false charge, and put him to death; but they said, "Not during the Festival, for there might be trouble among the people."

Jesus was in Bethany in the house of Simon the leper. As he was reclining at dinner, a woman entered carrying an alabaster jar of expensive perfume, made of pure nard. She broke the jar and poured the perfumed oil on Jesus' head. Then some of them became angry and said, "What a useless waste of perfume. It could have been sold for more than three hundred silver coins and the money given to the poor." And they criticized her.

But Jesus said, "Let her alone; why are you troubling her? What she has just done for me is a very charitable work. At any time you can help the poor, for you always have them with you; but you will not have me forever. This woman did what she had to do: she anointed my body for burial, before I die. Truly, I say to you, wherever the Good News is proclaimed, and this will be throughout the world, what she has done will be told in praise of her."

Then Judas Iscariot, one of the Twelve, went off to the chief priests, in order to betray Jesus to them. On hearing him, they were excited and promised to give him money. So Judas started planning the best way to hand Jesus over to them.

On the first day of the Festival of Unleavened Bread, the day when the Passover Lamb was killed, the disciples asked him, "Where would you have us go to prepare the Passover meal for you?"

So Jesus sent two of his disciples with these instructions, "Go into the city, and there, a man will come to you carrying a jar of water. Follow him to the house he enters and say to the owner, 'The Master says, Where is the room where I may eat the Passover meal with my disciples?' Then he will show you a large room upstairs, already arranged and furnished. There, you will prepare for us." The disciples went off. When they reached the city, they found everything just as Jesus had told them; and they prepared the Passover meal.

When it was evening, Jesus arrived with the Twelve. While they were at table eating, Jesus said, "Truly, I tell you, one of you will betray me, one who shares my meal." They were deeply distressed at hearing this and asked him, one after the other, "You don't mean me, do you?" And Jesus answered, "It is one of you Twelve, one who dips his bread in the dish with me. The Son of Man is going as the Scriptures say he will. But alas for that man by whom the Son of Man is betrayed; better for him if he had never been born."

While they were eating, Jesus took bread, blessed it and broke it, and gave it to them. And he said, "Take this. It is my body." Then he took a cup; and after he had given thanks, he passed it to them and they all drank from it. And he said, "This is my blood, the blood of the Covenant, poured out for many. Truly, I say to you, I will not taste the fruit of the vine again, until that day when I drink the new wine in the kingdom of God."

After singing psalms of praise, they went out to the Mount of Olives.

And Jesus said to them, "All of you will be dismayed and fall away; for the Scripture says:

> I will strike the shepherd
> and the sheep will be scattered.

But after I am raised, I will go to Galilee ahead of you."

Then Peter said to him, "Even though all the others fall away, I will not." And Jesus replied, "Truly I say to you, today, this very night, before the cock crows twice, you will deny me three times." But Peter insisted, "Though I have to die with you, I will never deny you." And all of them said the same.

They came to a place which is called Gethsemane; and Jesus said to his disciples, "Sit here while I pray."

But he took Peter, James and John along with him, and, becoming filled with fear and distress, he said to them, "My soul is full of sorrow, even to death. Remain here and stay awake."

Then he went a little further on and fell to the ground, praying that, if possible, this hour might pass him by. Jesus said, "Abba, Father, all things are possible for you. Take this cup away from me. Yet, not what I want, but what you want."

Then he came and found them asleep; and he said to Peter, "Simon, are you sleeping? Couldn't you stay awake for one hour? Stay awake and pray, all of you, so that you may not slip into temptation. The spirit indeed is willing, but the body is weak. And, going away, he prayed, saying the same words. When he came back to the disciples, he found them asleep again. They could not keep their eyes open; and they did not know what to say to him.

When he came back the third time, he said to them, "Are you still sleeping and resting? It is all over, the time has come: the Son of Man is now given into the hands of sinners. Get up, let us go! Look: the one who betrays me is approaching."

While Jesus was still speaking, Judas, one of the Twelve, came up. With him was a crowd armed with swords and clubs, who had been sent by the chief priests, the teachers of the law and the elders. The traitor had arranged a signal for them, "The one I kiss, he is the man. Arrest him, and take him away under guard."

So, when he came, he went directly to Jesus, and said, "Master! Master!" and kissed him. Then they seized Jesus and arrested him. One of the bystanders drew his sword and struck out at the High Priest's servant, cutting off his ear.

Jesus turned to them and said, "So, you have set out against a robber! Did you need swords and clubs to arrest me? Day after day, I was among you, teaching in the temple, and you did not arrest me. But let the Scriptures be fulfilled." Then they all deserted him and fled.

A young man, covered by nothing but a linen cloth, followed Jesus. When they took hold of him, he left the cloth in their hands and fled away naked.

They led Jesus to the High Priest; and all the chief priests assembled, with the elders and the teachers of the law. Peter had followed him at a distance; and went right into the courtyard of the High Priest, where he sat with the guards, warming himself at the fire.

Now the chief priests and the whole Council tried to find some evidence against Jesus so that they might put him to death; but they were unable to find anything. Even though many came up to speak falsely against him, their evidence did not agree. At last, some stood up and gave this false witness: "We heard him say, 'I will destroy this temple made by human hands, and, in three days, I will build another, not made by human hands." But even so, their evidence did not agree.

The High Priest then stood up in the midst of them and asked Jesus, "Have you no answer at all? What about this evidence against you?" But Jesus was silent and made no reply.

The High Priest put a second question to him, "Are you the Christ, the Son of the Blessed One?" Then Jesus answered, "I am, and you will see the Son of Man seated at the right hand of the Most Powerful, and coming with the clouds of heaven around him." Then the High Priest, tearing his garments to show his horror, said, "What more evidence do we need? You have just heard his blasphemous words. What is your decision?" They all condemned Jesus, saying, "He must die."

Some of them began to spit on Jesus; and, blindfolding him, they struck him and said, "Play the prophet!" And the guards set upon him with blows.

While Peter was below, in the courtyard, a servant-girl of the High Priest came by. Noticing Peter beside the fire, she looked straight at him and said, "You also were with Jesus, the Nazarene." But he denied it, "I don't know or understand what you are talking about." And he went out through the gateway, and a cock crowed.

The servant-girl saw him there and told the bystanders, "This man is one of them." But Peter denied it again. After a little while, those standing nearby said to Peter, "Of course you are one of them; you are a Galilean, aren't you?" And Peter began to justify himself with curses and oaths, "I don't know the man you are talking about."

Just then a cock crowed a second time, and Peter remembered what Jesus had said to him, "Before the cock crows twice, you will deny me three times." And he broke down and wept.

Early in the morning, the chief priests, the elders and the teachers of the law (that is, the whole Council or Sanhedrin) had their plan ready. They put Jesus in chains, led him away and handed him over to Pilate.

Pilate asked him, "Are you the King of the Jews?" Jesus answered, "You say so." As the chief priests accused Jesus of many things, Pilate asked him again, "Have you no answer at all? See how many charges they bring against you." But Jesus gave no further answers, much to Pilate's surprise.

At every Passover festival, Pilate used to free any prisoner the people asked for. Now there was a man called Barabbas, jailed with the rioters who had committed murder in the uprising. When the crowd went up to ask Pilate the usual favor, he said to them, "Do you want me to set free the King of the Jews?" for he realized that the chief priests had handed Jesus over to him out of envy. But the chief priests stirred up the crowd to ask, instead, for the release of Barabbas. Pilate replied, "And what shall I do with the man you call King of the Jews?" The crowd shouted back, "Crucify him!" Pilate asked, "What evil has he done?" But they shouted the louder, "Crucify him!"

As Pilate wanted to please the people, he freed Barabbas; and, having had Jesus flogged, Pilate handed him over to be crucified.

The soldiers took him inside the courtyard, known as the praetorium, and called the rest of their companions. They clothed him in a purple cloak, and twisting a crown of thorns, they forced it onto his head. Then they began saluting him, "Long life to the King of the Jews!" With a stick they gave him blows on the head and spat on him; then they knelt down, pretending to worship him.

When they had finished mocking him, they pulled off the purple cloak and put his own clothes on him.

The soldiers led him out of the city to crucify him. On the way, they met Simon of Cyrene, father of Alexander and Rufus, who was coming in from the country; and forced him to carry the cross of Jesus.

When they had led him to the place called Golgotha, which means the Skull, they offered him wine mixed with myrrh, but he would not take it. Then they nailed him to the cross, and divided his clothes among themselves, casting lots to decide what every man should take.

It was about nine o'clock in the morning when they crucified him. The statement of his offense was displayed above his head, and it read, "The King of the Jews." They also crucified two robbers with him, one on his right and one on his left. And the Scripture was fulfilled which says: And with lawless ones he was numbered.

People passing by laughed at him, shook their heads and jeered, "Aha! So, you are able to tear down the temple and build it up in three days? Save yourself now, and come down from the cross!"

In the same way the chief priests and the teachers of the law mocked him, saying to one another, "The man who saved others cannot save himself. Let's see the Messiah, the King of Israel, come down from his cross, and then we will believe in him." Even the men who were crucified with Jesus insulted him.

When noon came, darkness fell over the whole land and lasted until three o'clock; and at three o'clock Jesus cried out in a loud voice, "Eloi, Eloi, lamma sabachthani?" which means, "My God, my God, why have you deserted me?" As soon as they heard these words, some of the bystanders said, "Listen! He is calling for Elijah." And one of them went quickly to fill a sponge with bitter wine, and putting it on a reed, gave it to him to drink, saying, "Now let's see whether Elijah comes to take him down."

But Jesus uttered a loud cry and gave up his spirit. And immediately, the curtain that enclosed the temple Sanctuary was torn in two, from top to bottom.

The captain, who was standing in front of him, saw how Jesus died and heard the cry he gave; and he said, "Truly, this man was the Son of God."

There were also some women watching from a distance; among them were Mary Magdalene, Mary the mother of James the younger and of Joses, and Salome, who had followed Jesus when he was in Galilee and saw to his needs. There were also others who had come up with him to Jerusalem.

It was now evening, and, as it was Preparation Day, that is the day before the Sabbath, Joseph of Arimathea boldly went to Pilate and asked for the body of Jesus. Joseph was a respected member of the Council, who was, himself, waiting for the kingdom of God.

Pilate was surprised that Jesus should have died so soon; so he summoned the captain and inquired if Jesus was already dead. After hearing the captain, he let Joseph have the body.

Joseph took it down and wrapped it in the linen sheet he had bought. He laid the body in a tomb that had been cut out of the rock, and rolled a stone across the entrance to the tomb. Now Mary of Magdala and Mary the mother of Joses took note of where the body had been laid.

When the Sabbath was over, Mary of Magdala, Mary the mother of James, and Salome bought spices so that they might go and anoint the body. And very early in the morning, on the first day of the week, just after sunrise, they came to the tomb.

They were saying to one another, "Who will roll back the stone for us from the entrance to the tomb?" But, as they looked up, they noticed that the stone had already been rolled away. It was a very big stone.

As they entered the tomb, they saw a young man in a white robe seated on the right, and they were amazed. But he said to them, "Don't be alarmed; you are looking for Jesus of Nazareth who was crucified; he has been raised and is not here. This is, however, the place where they laid him. Now go, and tell his disciples and Peter: Jesus is going ahead of you to Galilee; you will see him there, just as he told you." The women went out and fled from the tomb, for terror and amazement had seized them. And they were so afraid that they said nothing to anyone.

After Jesus rose early on the first day of the week, he appeared first to Mary of Magdala, from whom he had driven out seven demons. She went and reported the news to his followers, who were now mourning and weeping. But when they heard that he lived, and had been seen by her, they would not believe it.

After this he showed himself in another form to two of them, as they were walking into the country. These men also went back and told the others, but they did not believe them.

Later Jesus showed himself to the Eleven while they were at table. He reproached them for their unbelief, and hardness of heart, in refusing to believe those who had seen him after he had risen.

Then he told them, "Go out to the whole world and proclaim the Good News to all creation. The one who believes and is baptized will be saved; the one who refuses to believe will be condemned. Signs like these will accompany those who have believed: in my name they will cast out demons and speak new languages; they will pick up snakes, and if they drink anything poisonous, they will be unharmed; they will lay their hands on the sick, and they will be healed."

So then, after speaking to them, the Lord Jesus was taken up into heaven and took his place at the right hand of God. The Eleven went forth and preached everywhere, while the Lord worked with them and confirmed the message by the signs that accompanied it.

16:8–16:20

INVITATION TO
1 PETER

In the final years of his life and ministry, in the early AD 60's, the apostle Peter was a leader of the church in Rome. From there he continued to encourage and challenge believers in other parts of the empire. Peter learned that the communities of Jesus-followers in the Roman provinces of Pontus, Galatia, Cappadocia, Asia and Bithynia (all located in what is now Turkey) were experiencing persecution. He wrote to urge them to remain faithful to Jesus and to live godly lives, to show their opponents that they were really blameless.

Peter shares introductory greetings and then he writes an extended blessing to God. Jesus' resurrection has brought the believers into an inheritance *reserved . . . in heaven* for them. Peter tells them this is *the grace you will receive, when Jesus Christ appears*, when God will reunite heaven and earth. Following this profound statement of Christian hope, Peter's letter has three main sections:

: He first tells his readers to *be holy, in all your conduct.* He reminds them that as Gentiles, they once lived in ignorance (they didn't know the ways of God). But they're now a *holy community*, part of God's own people, called to a new way of life. Peter here uses language and images drawn from the description of God's people in the First Testament. This new life, Peter insists, is to be lived out specifically in their community—in their relationships with one another.

: Peter then describes one effect of this way of life: it will impress those who would accuse and persecute them without just cause. *Live a blameless life, among the pagans; so, when they accuse you falsely of any wrong, they may see your good works and give glory to God, on the day he comes to them.* Once again Peter teaches that this must be achieved practically, in the world of human relationships.

: Finally, Peter comes directly to his purpose for writing. He acknowledges that his readers are suffering for their faith, but he explains that this is only to be expected: *do not be surprised at the testing, by fire, which is taking place among you, as though something strange were happening to you.* The Messiah himself suffered, and their fellow believers throughout the world are undergoing the same kind of sufferings, so they should bear up patiently and faithfully. Peter can even tell them to rejoice *to share in the sufferings of Christ, because, on the day his glory is revealed, you will also fully rejoice.*

Peter's letter was delivered by Silas, a man who also worked with the apostle Paul (see pp. 78–81). Peter introduces Silas in the letter and explains that he helped write it. As Silas visited each of the communities this letter was addressed to, he brought the message that he and Peter recognized was needed: followers of Jesus are waiting for the day God will visit them, and even in the face of suffering they can live in a way that shows that they belong to God.

| 1 PETER |

F rom Peter, apostle of Jesus Christ, to all those living as aliens in the Dispersion, in Pontus, Galatia, Cappadocia, Asia and Bithynia, to those whom God, the Father, has called, according to his plan, and made holy, by the Spirit, to obey Jesus Christ, and be purified by his blood: may grace and peace increase among you.

L et us praise God, the Father of our Lord Jesus Christ, for his great mercy. In raising Jesus Christ from the dead, he has given us new life, and a living hope. The inheritance that does not corrupt, nor goes bad, nor passes away, was reserved for you, in heaven, since God's power shall keep you faithful, until salvation is revealed, in the last days.

There is cause for joy, then, even though you may, for a time, have to suffer many trials. Thus will your faith be tested, like gold in a furnace. Gold, however, passes away, but faith, worth so much more, will bring you, in the end, praise, glory and honor, when Jesus Christ appears.

You have not, yet, seen him, and, yet, you love him; even without seeing him, you believe in him, and experience a heavenly joy beyond all words, for you are reaching the goal of your faith: the salvation of your souls.

This was the salvation for which the prophets so eagerly looked when, in days past, they foretold the favor of God, with regard to you. But they could only investigate when the Spirit of Christ present within them, pointed out the time and the circumstances, of this—the sufferings of Christ, and the glories which would follow.

It was revealed to them, that they were working, not for themselves, but for you. Thus, in these days, after the Holy Spirit has been sent from heaven, the gospel's preachers have taught you these mysteries, which even the angels long to see.

So, then, let your spirit be ready. Be alert, with confident trust, in the grace you will receive, when Jesus Christ appears. Like obedient children, do not return to your former life, given over to ignorance and passions. Imitate the one who called you. As he is holy, so you, too, be holy, in all your conduct, since Scripture says: Be holy for I am holy.

You call upon a Father who makes no distinction between persons, but judges, according to each one's deeds; take seriously, then, these years which you spend in a strange land. Remember, that you were freed from the useless way of life of your ancestors, not with gold and silver, but with the precious blood of the Lamb without spot or blemish. God, who has known Christ before the world began, revealed him to you in the last days. Through him, you have faith in God, who raised him from the dead, and glorified him, in order that you might put all your faith and hope in God.

In obeying the truth, you have gained interior purification, from which comes sincere mutual love. Love one another, then, with all your heart, since you are born again, not from mortal beings, but with enduring life, through the word of God, who lives and remains forever. It is written:

> All flesh is grass
> and its glory like the flowers of the field.
>
> The grass withers and the flower falls,
> but the word of the Lord endures forever.

This word, is the gospel, which has been brought to you.

So, give up all evil and deceit, hypocrisy, envy, and every kind of gossip. Like newborn children, seek, eagerly, for the pure milk of the word, that will help you grow and reach salvation. Did you not taste the goodness of the Lord? He is the living stone, rejected by people, but chosen by God, and precious to him; set yourselves close to him, so that, you, too, become living stones, built into a spiritual temple, a holy community of priests, offering spiritual sacrifices that please God, through Jesus Christ. Scripture says:

> See, I lay in Zion
> a chosen and precious cornerstone;
>
> whoever believes in him
> will not be disappointed.

This means honor, for you who believed, but for unbelievers, also

> the stone which the builders rejected
> has become the cornerstone

and

> it is a stone to stumble over,
> a rock which lays people low.

They stumble over it, in rejecting the word, but the plan of God is fulfilled in this.

You are a chosen race, a community of priest-kings, a consecrated nation, a people God has made his own, to proclaim his wonders. For he called you, from your darkness, to his own wonderful light. At one stage, you were no people, but, now, you are God's people, you had not received his mercy, but, now, you have been given mercy.

Beloved, while you are strangers and exiles, I urge you, not to indulge in selfish passions, that wage war on the soul. Live a blameless life, among the pagans; so, when they accuse you falsely of any wrong, they may see your good works and give glory to God, on the day he comes to them.

For the Lord's sake, respect all human authority: the king as chief authority, the governors, as sent by him, to punish evildoers, and to encourage those who do good. And God wants you to do good, so that you may silence those fools who ignorantly criticize you. Behave as free people, but do not speak of freedom as a license for vice; you are free men, and God's servants. Reverence each person, love your brothers and sisters, fear God and show respect to the emperor.

Servants must respect their masters, not only those who are good and understanding, but those who are difficult. For there is merit in putting up with unprovoked suffering, for the sake of God. What merit would there be in taking a beating, when you have done wrong? But if you endure punishment when you have done well, that is a grace before God.

This is your calling: remember Christ, who suffered for you, leaving you an example, so that you may follow in his way.

> He did no wrong
> and there was no deceit in his mouth.

He did not return insult, for insult, and, when suffering, he did not curse, but put himself in the hands of God, who judges justly. He went to the cross, bearing our sins on his own body, on the cross, so that we might die to sin, and live an upright life. For, by his wounds, you have been healed. You were like stray sheep, but you have come back to the Shepherd and Guardian of your souls.

In the same way, wives must be submissive to their husbands. If any of them resists the word, they will be won over, without words, by the conduct of their wives. It will be enough for them, to see your responsible and blameless conduct.

Do not be taken up with outward appearances: hairstyles, gold necklaces and clothes. There is something more permanent, that shines from within a person: a gentle and peaceful disposition. This is really precious in God's eyes. This was the way the holy women of the past dressed. They put their trust in God, and were obedient to their husbands, namely, Sarah, who had such respect for Abraham, that she called him her lord. You are her children, if you do what is right, and are not afraid.

Husbands, in your turn, be sensible in your life together. Be considerate, realizing that the woman is of a more frail disposition, and that you both share in the gift of life. This will prevent anything from coming in the way of your prayer.

Finally, you should all be of one mind: share each other's troubles with mutual affection, be compassionate and humble. Do not repay evil for evil, or answer one insult with another. Give a blessing, instead, since this is what you have been called to do, and so you will receive the blessing. For

> if you seek life
> and want to see happiness,
>
> keep your tongue from evil
> and your mouth from speaking deceit.
>
> Turn away from evil and do good;
> seek peace and pursue it.
>
> Because the Lord's eyes are turned to the just
> and his ears listen to their appeal.
>
> But the Lord frowns on evildoers.

Who can harm you if you devote yourselves to doing good? If you suffer for the sake of righteousness, happy are you. Do not fear what they fear or be disturbed as they are, but bless the Lord Christ in your hearts. Always have an answer ready, when you are called upon, to account for your hope, but give it simply and with respect. Keep your conscience clear, so that those who slander you may be put to shame by your upright, Christian living. Better to suffer for doing good, if it is God's will, than for doing wrong.

Remember how Christ died, once, and for all, for our sins. He, the just one, died for the unjust, in order to lead us to God. In the body, he was put to death, in the spirit, he was raised to life, and it was then, that he went to preach to the imprisoned spirits. They were the generation who did not believe, when God, in his great patience, delayed punishing the world, while Noah was building the ark, in which a small group of eight persons escaped, through water. That was a type of the baptism that now saves you; this baptism is not a matter of physical cleansing, but of asking God to reconcile us, through the resurrection of Christ Jesus. He has ascended to heaven, and is at the right hand of God, having subjected the angels, Dominions and Powers.

Given that Christ suffered in his human life, arm yourselves with this certainty: the one who suffers in his body has broken with sin, so as to spend the rest of his life following the will of God, and not human passions.

You have given enough time, in the past, to living as the pagans do: a life of excess, evil passions, drunkenness, orgies and worship of idols. They now find it strange, that you are no longer swept along with them in this ruinous flood, and then abuse you for it. But they will be accountable to the one who is ready to judge the living and the dead. The gospel has been preached to many who are now dead. As humans, they received a deadly sentence, but through the spirit, they shall live for God.

The end of all things is near; keep your minds calm and sober, for prayer. Above all, let your love for one another be sincere, for love covers a multitude of sins. Welcome one another into your houses without complaining. Serve one another with the gifts each of you received, thus becoming good managers of the varied graces of God. If you speak, deliver the word of God; if you have a special ministry, let it be seen as God's power, so that, in everything, God may be glorified, in Jesus Christ. To him, belong glory and power forever and ever. Amen.

My dear people, do not be surprised at the testing, by fire, which is taking place among you, as though something strange were happening to you. Instead, you should be glad to share in the sufferings of Christ, because, on the day his glory is revealed, you will also fully rejoice. You are fortunate, if you are insulted because of the name of Christ, for the Spirit of glory rests on you. I suppose that none of you should suffer for being a murderer, a thief, a criminal or an informer; but if anyone suffers on account of being a Christian, do not consider it a disgrace; rather, let this name bring glory to God.

The time of judgment has come, and it begins with God's household. If its beginning so affects us, what will be the end of those, who refuse to believe in the gospel?

> If the just one is barely saved,
> what will happen to the sinner and unbeliever?

So, then, if you suffer, according to God's will, entrust yourself to the faithful creator, and continue to do good.

I now address myself to those elders among you; I, too, am an elder, and a witness to the sufferings of Christ, hoping to share the glory that is to be revealed. Shepherd the flock which God has entrusted to you, guarding it, not out of obligation, but, willingly, for God's sake; not as one looking for a reward, but with a generous heart; do not lord it over, those in your care, rather be an example to your flock. Then, when the Chief Shepherd appears, you will be given a crown of unfading glory.

In the same way, let the younger ones among you respect the authority of the elders. All of you must clothe yourselves with humility, in your dealings with one another, because

> God opposes the proud
> but gives his grace to the humble.

Bow down, then, before the power of God, so that he will raise you up at the appointed time. Place all your worries on him, since he takes care of you.

Be sober and alert, because, your enemy, the devil prowls about, like a roaring lion, seeking someone to devour. Stand your ground, firm in your faith, knowing, that our brothers and sisters, scattered throughout the world, are confronting similar sufferings. God, the giver of all grace, has called you, to share in Christ's eternal glory, and after you have suffered a little, he will bring you to perfection: he will confirm, strengthen and establish you forever. Glory be to him forever and ever. Amen.

I have had these few lines of encouragement, written to you by Silvanus, our brother, whom I know to be trustworthy. For I wanted to remind you of the kindness of God, really present in all this. Hold on to it.

Greetings from the community in Babylon, gathered by God, and from my son, Mark.

Greet one another with a friendly embrace. Peace to you all who are in Christ.

INVITATION TO
2 PETER

Around AD 65 the apostle Peter was imprisoned by the emperor Nero in Rome. He realized that he would soon be executed. Since he was an eyewitness of the ministry of Jesus, he decided to write another letter to the believers he'd written to before, assuring them that what they'd been taught about Jesus was true and accurate. *It seems fitting, that as long as I live in the tent of this body*, he wrote, *knowing that my tent may soon be folded up, as our Lord Jesus Christ has shown me. I will, nonetheless, endeavor to see, that, after my departure, you will be constantly reminded of all this.*

It was particularly important for Peter to write to these believers again because some people had been telling them that since Jesus hadn't returned already, his return couldn't be expected at all. (*What has become of his promised coming?*) Because they didn't expect any future judgment, these false teachers lived immoral lives. Their teaching was undermining the faith and confidence of many believers. Their conduct was giving the assembly of Jesus-followers a bad reputation and encouraging others to excuse immorality themselves. (Peter likely learned about the threat of these teachers from a letter sent by Jude, another of Jesus' brothers, to warn believers against them. Peter's letter echoes Jude's in many places. See pp. 361–362.)

In his letter, Peter first challenges his readers to godly living, and then answers the false teachers' skepticism by stressing that he, along with James and John, personally saw the glory and majesty of Jesus *when we were with him on the holy mountain* (see p. 329). All will see this same glory when Jesus returns. Peter reminds his readers that the prophetic message in the Scriptures testifies to Jesus' return as well. (For the early Christian communities "the Scriptures" would refer to the First Testament.)

Peter then observes that false teachers have slipped in among the people of God throughout their history, so his readers shouldn't be surprised that this is also happening in their own day. In powerful imagery, he describes the false teachers' destructive effect on the community and the judgment that awaits them.

In the final section of his letter, Peter addresses the false teachers' denial of Jesus' return head-on. He explains that the Messiah is indeed coming back, but his return has been delayed, because God *gives you time, because he does not want anyone to perish, but that all may come to conversion*. The proper response to this delay is to live holy and godly lives so as to be in a position to welcome the Lord gladly when he does return. *We wait for a new heaven and a new earth, in which justice reigns, according to God's promise*. Since this is our hope, Peter concludes, we should make every effort to be found spotless and to remain at peace with God.

| 2 PETER |

Symeon Peter, a servant and apostle of Jesus Christ, to those who have been sanctified by our God and Savior Jesus Christ, and have received a faith as precious as ours: may grace and peace abound in you, through the knowledge of God and of Jesus, our Lord.

His divine power has given us everything we need for life and piety. First, the knowledge of the One who called us through his own glory and Might, by which we were given the most extraordinary and precious promises. Through them, you share in the divine nature, after repelling the corruption and evil desires of this world.

So, strive with the greatest determination, and increase your faith, with goodness, goodness with knowledge, knowledge with moderation, moderation with constancy, constancy with piety, piety with mutual affection, mutual affection with charity. If all these riches are in you, so as to abound in you, you will not be idle and useless; you will, rather, be rooted in the knowledge of Jesus Christ, our Lord. Whoever is not aware of this, is blind and shortsighted, and is forgetful of the cleansing of former sins.

Therefore, brothers and sisters, strive, more and more, to respond to the call of God, who chose you. If you do so, you will never stumble. Moreover, you will be generously granted entry to the eternal kingdom of our Lord and Savior Jesus Christ.

So, I shall always remind you of these things, though you know them, and remain firm in the truth that you have. It seems fitting, that as long as I live in the tent of this body, I refresh your memory of them, knowing that my tent may soon be folded up, as our Lord Jesus Christ has shown me. I will, nonetheless, endeavor to see, that, after my departure, you will be constantly reminded of all this.

Indeed, what we taught you about the power, and the return of Christ Jesus our Lord, was not drawn from myths or formulated theories. We, ourselves, were eyewitnesses of his majesty, when he received glory and honor from God, the Father, when, from the magnificent glory, this most extraordinary word came upon him: "This is my beloved Son, this is my Chosen One." We, ourselves, heard this voice from heaven, when we were with him on the holy mountain.

Therefore, we believe most firmly in the message of the prophets, which you should consider rightly, as a lamp shining in a dark place, until the break of day, when the Morning Star shines in your hearts.

Know this well: no prophecy of Scripture can be handed over to private interpretation, since no prophecy comes from human decision, for it was men of God, moved by the Holy Spirit, who spoke.

Just as there have been false prophets in the midst of the people of Israel, so will there be false teachers among you. They will introduce harmful sects and, by denying the Master who saved them, they will bring upon themselves sudden perdition. Many, nonetheless, will imitate their vices, and, because of them, the way of truth will be discredited. They will take advantage of you, with deceitful words, for the sake of money. But the judgment made upon them, long ago, is not idle, and the destruction awaiting them is not asleep.

In fact, God did not pardon the angels who sinned, but cast them into hell, confining them in the dark pits, keeping them there, until the day of judgment. Neither did he pardon the ancient world, when he unleashed the waters of the flood upon the world of wicked people, but protected only Noah, the preacher of righteousness, along with seven others. God also condemned the cities of Sodom and Gomorrah, reducing them to ashes, to serve as a warning to the wicked in the future. But he saved Lot, a good man, deeply afflicted by the unbridled conduct of those vicious people. For Lot, a righteous man, who lived in their midst, suffered, day after day, in the goodness of his heart, as he saw and heard of their crimes.

So, then, the Lord knows how to free from trial, those who serve him, and keep the wicked for punishment, on the day of judgment.

He will do this, especially, for certain people who follow the baser desires of their nature, and despise the Lord's majesty. Proud and daring they are, not afraid of insulting fallen spirits while the angels, who are superior to them in strength and power, do not permit themselves any injurious accusation in the presence of the Lord.

Those people are like irrational animals, born to be caught and killed; after they have slandered what they cannot understand, they will end, like animals and they will suffer the repayment of their wickedness.

They delight in giving themselves to depravity, even in the daytime;

they are deceiving you, even when they are sharing your table. With their eyes always looking for adultery, they do not tire of sinning, and seducing weak souls. They are full of greed—an accursed people.

They abandoned the right way and followed Balaam, son of Beor, who was attached to what he gained from his wrongdoing. But he was rebuked for his sin: his she-ass began to speak with a human voice, stopping the prophet in his madness. These people are like waterless springs, clouds driven by a storm which move swiftly, into the blackest darkness.

With their boastful and empty discourses, they encourage the lust and impure desire of those, who have just freed themselves from the common errors.

They promise freedom, when, they, themselves, are slaves of corruption: for people are slaves to whatever dominates them. Indeed, after being freed from worldly vices through the knowledge of the Lord and Savior Jesus Christ, they returned to those vices, and surrendered to them; and their present state has become worse than the first. It would have been better, for them, not to know the way of holiness, than, knowing it, to turn away from the sacred doctrine that they had been taught. In their case, these proverbs are relevant: "The dog turns back to its own vomit," and: "Hardly has the pig been washed, than it again wallows in the mud."

Dearly beloved, this is the second letter I write to you. In both of them, I have intended to remind you of sound doctrine. Do not forget the words of the holy prophets, and the teaching of our Lord and Savior, as you heard it, through his apostles.

Remember, first of all, that, in the last days, scoffers will appear, their mockery serving their evil desires. And they will say, "What has become of his promised coming? Since our fathers in faith died, everything still goes on, as it was from the beginning of the world." Indeed, they deliberately ignore, that, in the beginning, the heavens existed first, and earth appeared from the water, taking its form by the word of God. By the same word of God, this world perished in the Flood. Likewise, the word of God maintains the present heavens and earth, until their destruction, by fire; they are kept for the day of judgment, when the godless will be destroyed. Do not forget, beloved, that with the Lord, one day is like a thousand years, and a thousand years is like one day. The Lord does not delay in fulfilling his promise, though some speak of delay; rather, he gives you time, because he does not want anyone to perish, but that all may come to conversion. The Day of the Lord is to come like a thief. Then, the heavens will dissolve with a great noise; the elements will melt away by fire, and the earth, with all that is on it, will be burned up.

Since all things are to vanish, how holy and religious your way of life must be, as you wait for the day of God, and long for its coming, when the heavens will dissolve in fire, and the elements melt away in the heat. We wait for a new heaven and a new earth, in which justice reigns, according to God's promise.

Therefore, beloved, as you wait in expectation of this, strive, that God may find you rooted in peace, without blemish or fault.

And consider, that God's patience is for our salvation, as our beloved brother, Paul, wrote to you, with the wisdom given him. He speaks of these things in all his letters. There are, however, some points in them that are difficult to understand, which people, who are ignorant, and immature in their faith, twist, as they do with the rest of the Scriptures, to their own destruction.

So then, dearly beloved, as you have been warned, be careful, lest those people who have gone astray, deceive you, in turn, and drag you along, making you stumble, and finally fall away. Grow in the grace and knowledge of our Lord and Savior Jesus Christ: to him be glory, now, and to the day of eternity. Amen.

INVITATION TO
JUDE

Jesus had several brothers, including James and Jude. James is better known, since he was a prominent leader in the church at Jerusalem (see p. 305). Much less is known about Jude, but he too was clearly a church leader, since he wrote to believers with authority in this letter that bears his name. It's not clear exactly who was meant to receive this letter, although the references to angels, to the history of Israel and to specific writings suggest that it was addressed to Jews who believed in Jesus as their Messiah.

But the problem that occasioned the letter is quite clear. Jude warns his readers about certain individuals who have secretly slipped in among them, whose teaching and example are threatening *the faith God has given, once, for all, to the saints*. These false teachers, on the basis of supposedly inspired dreams, reject authority and pollute their own bodies, engage in immorality and refuse discipline. Even though they claim to bring God's message, they really *are worldly people, and do not have the Holy Spirit*.

The believers' response to them must be active resistance. They must contend for the faith by rejecting both the teaching and the example of these men and cleansing their community. *Try to convince those who doubt*, Jude instructs them, *others you will save, snatching them from condemnation. Treat the others with compassion, but also with prudence*. He assures them that as they do these things, they can entrust themselves to God their Savior.

It appears that the apostle Peter received a copy of Jude's letter and wrote a similar one of his own to show that Jude was faithfully presenting the teaching of the apostles of the Lord Jesus Christ (see p. 353).

| JUDE |

J ude, servant of Jesus Christ, and brother of James, to those called to the
faith, beloved by God, the Father, and kept in Christ Jesus.

May mercy, peace and love abound in you.

M ost beloved, I had wanted to write to you about the salvation we all
share, but, now, I feel I must urge you to fight for the faith God has
given, once, for all, to the saints.

Some individuals have slipped into your midst, godless people, who
were, long ago, marked down for condemnation. They make use of the
grace of our God as a license for immorality, and deny our only Master and
Lord Jesus Christ.

Although you may be aware of it, I wish to remind you, that the Lord
saved his people from the land of Egypt, but later delivered to death, those
who did not believe. He did the same with the angels, who did not keep their
rank, but abandoned their dwelling places. God enclosed them in eternal
prisons, in the pit of darkness, until the great day of judgment. Sodom and
Gomorrah, and the surrounding cities that prostituted themselves, and
were lured into unnatural unions, are also a warning of the punishment of
eternal fire. In spite of all this, these people, now, do the same: in their rav-
ings, they debase their bodies, scorn the celestial authorities, blaspheme
against the angels.

When the archangel Michael fought against the devil, and disputed
about the body of Moses, he did not dare insult him, but simply said, "May
the Lord rebuke you!" Not so, these people, they insult and scorn what they
cannot understand; what they know by instinct, like animals, they use
for their corruption. Woe to them! They follow the footsteps of Cain, and
like Balaam, go astray, because of money: they will, finally, perish, like the
rebellious Korah. When you celebrate your love-meals, they spoil everything, coming only for the food, and shamelessly seeing to their own needs.

They are like clouds, carried along by the wind, which never bring rain, like trees, without fruit at the end of autumn, twice dead when uprooted. The scum of their vices is splashed, like foam on the rough waves of the sea, they are like shooting stars, which the thick darkness engulfs for ever. The patriarch Enoch, the seventh after Adam, said these words about them: The Lord comes with thousands of angels, to judge everyone, and call the wicked to account, for all the evil deeds they committed; he will punish all the injurious words, the impious sinners uttered against him. All these are discontented, who curse their lot and follow their passions. Their mouth is full of arrogant words, and they flatter people for their own interest.

But, most beloved, remember what the apostles of Christ Jesus, our Lord, announced to you. They said to you, "At the end of time, there will be scoffers, led by their desires, which are those of godless people." Actually, these people are those who cause divisions, they are worldly people, and do not have the Holy Spirit.

But, dearly beloved, build your life on the foundation of your most holy faith, praying in the Holy Spirit. Remain firm, in the love of God, welcoming the mercy of Jesus Christ, our Lord, which leads to eternal life.

Try to convince those who doubt; others you will save, snatching them from condemnation. Treat the others with compassion, but also with prudence, shunning even the clothes that touched their body.

T o the one God, who is able to keep you from all sin, and bring you, happy and without blemish before his own glory, to the one God, who saves us, through Jesus Christ, our Lord, to him be glory, honor, might and power, from past ages, now and forever. Amen.

INVITATION TO
JOHN

These are recorded, so that you may believe that Jesus is the Christ, the Son of God. Believe, and you will have life through his name! This is how the author of the book of John explains his purpose in telling Jesus' story, making the issue of belief central.

The author doesn't identify himself by name; he simply describes himself as *the disciple Jesus loved*. But we can still recognize who wrote this book, since the different occurrences of this phrase show that this disciple was one of those closest to Jesus. We know the phrase doesn't refer to Peter, since he's named separately. From the stories of Jesus that others have recorded, we can see that this disciple could only have been John. So the book's traditional title correctly identifies its author. John may have described himself anonymously out of humility, to show that he had come to understand everything about himself in light of his relationship with Jesus.

In the beginning . . . John opens his book with a poetic prologue that mirrors the first words of the Bible. This shows his readers that he's going to tell the story of Jesus as a story of new creation. His intention is confirmed by many other features of the book. John's prologue describes a light shining in the darkness, as at the first creation. The book of Genesis reveals that the first creation was completed in six days, followed by a seventh day of rest. For the Jews the number seven came to represent completeness and wholeness, a finished work of God revealing his purpose for the world. John uses the number seven in multiple ways to structure his book, showing that the finished work of Jesus reveals God's plan to renew his creation and bring us the gift of life.

After his prologue, John tells the story of Jesus in two main parts:

: The first part (pp. 366–388) describes his public ministry.

: The second part (pp. 388–400) narrates the end of Jesus' life, recording the private instructions he gave to those who believed in him, and then depicts his death and resurrection.

The book ends with an epilogue that was likely added to correct the misunderstanding that John wouldn't die until Jesus returned.

The action in the first part takes place in seven sections. Most of these sections describe trips that Jesus made to Judea and back, usually to attend one of the religious festivals that were celebrated in Jerusalem.

The first section places Jesus in Judea and provides a model of the structure of the rest of the book. It relates how John the Baptist testified on three successive days that Jesus was the Messiah, and then how, on the fourth day, Jesus called some of his first followers. Three days later, on the seventh day, Jesus did his first miraculous sign, and his disciples believed in him. In the next section Jesus goes to Jerusalem for the Passover Festival. This pattern of "seven, then the Passover" can be seen in the book as a whole. There are seven sections in the first part, then the entire second part is devoted to the Passover weekend on which Jesus gave his life for the world. Each of these seven sections closes with a report on how different groups of people responded to Jesus—either in faith or in unbelief.

In the first part of the book, a total of seven powerful signs are also related. These signs point to Jesus' identity as the one whom God has sent. (They don't correspond exactly with the section divisions, but they help mark them off.) At the end of this part of the book, John marvels, *Even though Jesus had done so many miraculous signs among them, they didn't believe in him*. Near the conclusion of the whole book, John invites the reader to respond differently: *There were many other signs that Jesus gave in the presence of his disciples, but they are not recorded in this book. These are recorded, so that you may believe* . . .

John also records seven instances when Jesus reveals his identity through the phrase *I am*. Earlier in the Bible's drama God had revealed himself by this name to the people of Israel. God had chosen Israel to bring blessing and life to the rest of the world. These seven phrases run throughout the book, tying its parts together and connecting Jesus closely to Israel's history. Jesus explains that he is the bread of life; the light of the world; the gate for the sheep; the good shepherd; the resurrection and the life; the way, the truth and the life; and the true vine. These show us that Jesus embodies the deepest meaning and truest fulfillment of Israel's story.

As Jesus does miraculous signs and participates in religious festivals, his identity is disclosed symbolically. It's then interpreted as he teaches and answers questions. He feeds five thousand people by multiplying several loaves of bread, for example, and he then explains to the crowd that he's the *true bread from heaven*. The Festival of Tabernacles recalled how, when the Jews were living in the desert, God provided water for them and went ahead of them as a pillar of fire to light the way. Jesus calls out at this feast, *Let anyone who is thirsty come to me; and let the one who believes in me drink*, and he declares, *I am the Light of the world*.

The way John closes his book confirms that the power of a new creation has broken into this world. On the sixth day of the first creation God made the first man, Adam. On the sixth day of Jesus' last week, the Roman governor Pilate announces Jesus with the words, *Behold the man!* The book of Genesis records that after creating the heavens and the earth, God rested on the seventh day. John records that Jesus is dead and resting in the grave on the Sabbath, the seventh day. Then in the story of how Jesus was powerfully raised from the dead, John notes twice that this took place *on the first day after the Sabbath*. So John has taken us from *in the beginning* to a new beginning. Jesus the Messiah has defeated sin and death, the great enemies of God's good creation. Jesus has been raised to a new life. John invites his readers to find this new resurrection life themselves by believing in Jesus.

| JOHN |

In the beginning was the Word.
And the Word was with God
and the Word was God;
he was in the beginning with God.

All things were made through him,
and without him nothing came to be.

Whatever has come to be, found life in him;
life, which for human beings, was also light,
light that shines in darkness,
light that darkness could not overcome.

A man came, sent by God;
his name was John.

He came to bear witness,
as a witness to introduce the Light,
so that all might believe through him.

He was not the Light,
but a witness to introduce the Light;
for the Light was coming into the world,
the true Light that enlightens everyone.

He was in the world,
and through him the world was made,
the very world that did not know him.

He came to his own,
yet his own people did not receive him;
but to all who received him,
he empowers to become children of God,
for they believe in his name.

These are born, but not by seed,
or carnal desire, nor by the will of man:
they are born of God.

And the Word was made flesh and dwelt among us;
and we have seen his glory, the glory of the only Son of the Father:
fullness of truth and loving-kindness.

John bore witness to him openly, saying,
"This is the one who comes after me,
but he is already ahead of me,
for he was before me."

From his fullness we have all received,
favor upon favor.

For God had given us the law through Moses,
but Truth and Loving-kindness
came through Jesus Christ.

No one has ever seen God,
but God-the-only-Son made him known:
the one, who is in and with the Father.

This was the testimony of John, when the Jews sent priests and Levites to ask him, "Who are you?" John recognized the truth, and did not deny it. He said, "I am not the Messiah."

And they asked him, "Then who are you? Elijah?" He answered, "I am not." They said, "Are you the Prophet?" And he answered, "No." Then they said to him, "Tell us who you are, so that we can give some answer to those who sent us. How do you see yourself?" And John said, quoting the prophet Isaiah, "I am the voice of one crying out in the wilderness: Make straight the way of the Lord!"

Those who had been sent were Pharisees; and they put a further question to John, "Then why are you baptizing, if you are not the Messiah, or Elijah, or the Prophet?" John answered, "I baptize you with water, but among you stands one whom you do not know; although he comes after me, I am not worthy to untie the strap of his sandal."

This happened in Bethabara beyond the Jordan, where John was baptizing.

The next day, John saw Jesus coming toward him, and said, "There is the Lamb of God, who takes away the sin of the world! It is he of whom I said: A man comes after me, who is already ahead of me, for he was before me. I myself did not know him, but I came baptizing to prepare for him, so that he might be revealed in Israel."

And John also gave this testimony, "I saw the Spirit coming down on him, like a dove from heaven, and resting on him. I myself did not know him, but God, who sent me to baptize, told me, 'You will see the Spirit coming down, and resting on the one who baptizes with the Holy Spirit.' Yes, I have seen! And I declare that this is the Chosen One of God!"

On the following day, John was standing there again, with two of his disciples. As Jesus walked by, John looked at him and said, "There is the Lamb of God." On hearing this, the two disciples followed Jesus. He turned and saw them following, and he said to them, "What are you looking for?" They answered, "Rabbi (which means Master), where are you staying?" Jesus said, "Come and see." So they went and saw where he stayed, and spent the rest of that day with him. It was about four o'clock in the afternoon.

Andrew, the brother of Simon Peter, was one of the two who heard what John had said, and followed Jesus. Early the next morning, he found his brother Simon and said to him, "We have found the Messiah" (which means the Christ), and he brought Simon to Jesus. Jesus looked at him and said, "You are Simon, son of John, but you shall be called Cephas" (which means Rock).

The next day, Jesus decided to set off for Galilee. He found Philip and said to him, "Follow me." Philip was from Bethsaida, the town of Andrew and Peter. Philip found Nathanael and said to him, "We have found the one Moses wrote about in the law, and the prophets: he is Jesus, son of Joseph, from Nazareth."

Nathanael replied, "Can anything good come from Nazareth?" Philip said to him, "Come and see." When Jesus saw Nathanael coming, he said of him, "Here comes an Israelite, a true one; there is nothing false in him." Nathanael asked him, "How do you know me?" And Jesus said to him, "Before Philip called you, you were under the fig tree, and I saw you."

Nathanael answered, "Master, you are the Son of God! You are the king of Israel!" But Jesus replied, "You believe because I said, 'I saw you under the fig tree.' But you will see greater things than that.

Truly, I say to you, you will see the heavens opened, and the angels of God ascending and descending upon the Son of Man."

Three days later there was a wedding at Cana in Galilee, and the mother of Jesus was there. Jesus was also invited to the wedding with his disciples. When all the wine provided for the celebration had been served, and they had run out of wine, the mother of Jesus said to him, "They have no wine." Jesus replied, "Woman, what concern is that to you and me? My hour has not yet come."

However his mother said to the servants, "Do whatever he tells you."

Nearby were six stone water jars, set there for ritual washing as practiced by the Jews; each jar could hold twenty or thirty gallons. Jesus said to the servants, "Fill the jars with water." And they filled them to the brim. Then Jesus said, "Now draw some out and take it to the steward." So they did.

The steward tasted the water that had become wine, without knowing from where it had come; for only the servants who had drawn the water knew. Immediately he called the bridegroom, and said, "Everyone serves the best wine first, and when people have drunk enough, he serves that which is ordinary. But you have kept the best wine until the end."

This miraculous sign was the first, and Jesus performed it at Cana in Galilee. In this way he showed his glory, and his disciples believed in him.

After this, Jesus went down to Capernaum with his mother, his brothers and his disciples; and they stayed there for a few days.

As the Passover of the Jews was at hand, Jesus went up to Jerusalem. In the temple court he found merchants selling oxen, sheep and doves, and money-changers seated at their tables. Making a whip of cords, he drove them all out of the temple court, together with the oxen and sheep. He knocked over the tables of the money-changers, scattering the coins, and ordered the people selling doves, "Take all this away, and stop making a marketplace of my Father's house!"

His disciples recalled the words of Scripture: Zeal for your house devours me like fire.

The Jews then questioned Jesus, "Where are the miraculous signs which give you the right to do this?" And Jesus said, "Destroy this temple and in three days I will raise it up." The Jews then replied, "The building of this temple has already taken forty-six years, and will you raise it up in three days?"

Actually, Jesus was referring to the temple of his body. Only when he had risen from the dead did his disciples remember these words; then they believed both the Scripture and the words Jesus had spoken.

Jesus stayed in Jerusalem during the Passover Festival, and many believed in his name, when they saw the miraculous signs he performed. But Jesus did not trust himself to them, because he knew all of them. He had no need of evidence about anyone, for he himself knew what there was in each one.

Among the Pharisees there was a ruler of the Jews named Nicodemus. He came to Jesus by night and said, "Rabbi, we know that you have come from God to teach us, for no one can perform miraculous signs like yours unless God is with him."

Jesus replied, "Truly, I say to you, no one can see the kingdom of God unless he is born again from above."

Nicodemus said, "How can there be rebirth for a grown man? Who could go back to his mother's womb and be born again?" Jesus replied, "Truly, I say to you: No one can enter the kingdom of God without being born of water and Spirit. What is born of the flesh is flesh, and what is born of the Spirit is spirit. Because of this, don't be surprised when I say, 'You must be born again from above.'

The wind blows where it pleases and you hear its sound, but you don't know where it comes from or where it is going. It is like that with everyone who is born of the Spirit."

Nicodemus asked again, "How can this be?" And Jesus answered, "You are a teacher in Israel, and you don't know these things!

Truly, I say to you, we speak of what we know and we witness to the things we have seen, but you don't accept our testimony. If you don't believe when I speak of earthly things, what then, when I speak to you of heavenly things? No one has ever gone up to heaven except the one who came from heaven, the Son of Man.

As Moses lifted up the serpent in the desert, so must the Son of Man be lifted up, so that whoever believes in him may have eternal life.

Yes, God so loved the world that he gave his only Son that whoever believes in him may not be lost, but may have eternal life. God did not send the Son into the world to condemn the world; instead, through him the world is to be saved. Whoever believes in him will not be condemned. He who does not believe is already condemned, because he has not believed in the name of the only Son of God.

This is how Judgment is made: Light has come into the world, and people loved darkness rather than light, because their deeds were evil. For whoever does wrong hates the light, and doesn't come to the light, for fear that his deeds will be seen as evil. But whoever lives according to the truth comes into the light, so that it can be clearly seen that his works have been done in God."

After this, Jesus went into the territory of Judea with his disciples. He stayed there with them and baptized. John was also baptizing in Aenon, near Salim, where water was plentiful; people came to him and were baptized. This happened before John was put in prison.

Now John's disciples had been questioned by a Jew about spiritual cleansing, so they came to John and said, "Rabbi, the one who was with you across the Jordan, and about whom you spoke favorably, is now baptizing, and all are going to him."

John answered, "No one can receive anything, except what has been given to him from heaven. You yourselves are my witnesses that I said, 'I am not the Christ, but I have been sent before him.' Only the bridegroom has the bride; but the friend of the bridegroom stands by and listens, and rejoices to hear the bridegroom's voice. My joy is now full. It is necessary that he increase, but that I decrease.

He who comes from above is above all; he who comes from the earth belongs to the earth, and his words belong to the earth. He who comes from heaven speaks of the things he has seen and heard; he bears witness to these things, but no one accepts his testimony. Whoever does receive his testimony acknowledges the truthfulness of God.

The one sent by God speaks God's words, and gives the Spirit unstintingly. The Father loves the Son and has entrusted everything into his hands. Whoever believes in the Son lives with eternal life; but he who will not believe in the Son will never know life, and always faces the justice of God."

The Lord knew that the Pharisees were informed about him; people said that Jesus was attracting and baptizing more disciples than John; but in fact it was not Jesus himself who was baptizing, but his disciples. So Jesus left Judea and returned to Galilee. He had to cross Samaria.

He came to a Samaritan town called Sychar, near the land that Jacob had given to his son Joseph. Jacob's well is there. Tired from his journey, Jesus sat down by the well; it was about noon. Now a Samaritan woman came to draw water, and Jesus said to her, "Give me a drink." His disciples had just gone into town to buy some food.

The Samaritan woman said to him, "How is it that you, a Jew, ask me, a Samaritan and a woman, for a drink?" (For Jews, in fact, have no dealings with Samaritans.) Jesus replied, "If you only knew the gift of God! If you knew who it is, who is asking you for a drink, you yourself would have asked me, and I would have given you living water."

The woman answered, "Sir, you have no bucket, and this well is deep; where is your living water? Are you greater than our ancestor Jacob, who gave us this well; he drank from it himself, together with his sons and his cattle?"

Jesus said to her, "Those who drink of this water will be thirsty again; but those, who drink of the water that I shall give, will never be thirsty; for the water, that I shall give, will become in them a spring of water, welling up to eternal life."

The woman said to him, "Give me this water, that I may never be thirsty, and never have to come here to draw water." Jesus said, "Go, call your husband, and come back here." The woman answered, "I have no husband." And Jesus replied, "You are right to say, 'I have no husband'; for you have had five husbands, and the one you have now is not your husband. What you said is true."

The woman then said to him, "I see you are a prophet; tell me this: Our ancestors came to this mountain to worship God; but you Jews, do you not claim that Jerusalem is the only place to worship God?"

Jesus said to her, "Believe me, woman, the hour is coming when you shall worship the Father, but that will not be on this mountain nor in Jerusalem. You worship what you do not know; we worship what we know, because salvation is from the Jews. But the hour is coming, and is even now here, when the true worshipers will worship the Father in Spirit and truth; for that is the kind of worshippers the Father wants. God is Spirit, and those who worship him must worship in Spirit, and truth."

The woman said to him, "I know that the Messiah (that is the Christ) is coming. When he comes, he will tell us everything." And Jesus said, "I who am talking to you, I am he."

At this point the disciples returned, and were surprised that Jesus was speaking with a woman; however, no one said, "What do you want?" or, "Why are you talking with her?" So the woman left her water jar and ran to the town. There she said to the people, "Come and see a man who told me everything I did! Could he not be the Christ?" So they left the town and went to meet him.

In the meantime, the disciples urged Jesus, "Master, eat." But he said to them, "I have food to eat that you don't know about." And the disciples wondered, "Has anyone brought him food?" Jesus said to them, "My food is to do the will of the one who sent me, and to carry out his work.

You say that in four months there will be the harvest; now, I say to you, look up and see the fields white and ready for harvesting. People who reap the harvest are paid for their work, and the fruit is gathered for eternal life, so that sower and reaper may rejoice together.

Indeed the saying holds true: One sows and another reaps. I sent you to reap where you didn't work or suffer; others have worked, and you are now sharing in their labors."

In that town many Samaritans believed in him when they heard the woman who declared, "He told me everything I did." So, when they came to him, they asked him to stay with them, and Jesus stayed there two days. After that, many more believed because of his own words, and they said to the woman, "We no longer believe because of what you told us; we have heard for ourselves, and we know that this is the Savior of the world."

When the two days were over, Jesus left for Galilee. Jesus himself said that no prophet is recognized in his own country. Yet the Galileans welcomed him when he arrived, because of all the things which he had done in Jerusalem during the Festival, and which they had seen. For they, too, had gone to the feast.

Jesus went back to Cana of Galilee, where he had changed the water into wine. At Capernaum there was an official, whose son was ill, and when he heard that Jesus had come from Judea to Galilee, he went and asked him to come and heal his son, for he was at the point of death.

Jesus said, "Unless you see signs and wonders, you will not believe!" The official said, "Sir, come down before my child dies." And Jesus replied, "Go, your son lives!"

The man had faith in the word that Jesus spoke to him, and went his way. As he was approaching his house, his servants met him, and gave him the good news, "Your son has recovered!" So he asked them at what hour the child began to recover, and they said to him, "The fever left him yesterday, at about one o'clock in the afternoon." And the father realized that that was the time when Jesus had told him, "Your son lives!" And he became a believer, he and all his family.

Jesus performed this second miraculous sign when he returned from Judea to Galilee.

After this, there was a feast of the Jews, and Jesus went up to Jerusalem. Now, by the Sheep Gate in Jerusalem, there is a pool (called Bethzatha in Hebrew) surrounded by five galleries. In these galleries lay a multitude of sick people: blind, lame and paralyzed.

(All were waiting for the water to move, for at times an angel of the Lord would descend into the pool and stir up the water; and the first person to enter the pool, after this movement of the water, would be healed of whatever disease that he had.)

There was a man who had been sick for thirty-eight years. Jesus saw him, and because he knew how long this man had been lying there, he said to him, "Do you want to be healed?" And the sick man answered, "Sir, I have no one to put me into the pool when the water is disturbed; so while I am still on my way, another steps down before me."

Jesus then said to him, "Stand up, take your mat and walk!" And at once the man was healed, and he took up his mat and walked.

Now that day happened to be the Sabbath. So the Jews said to the man who had just been healed, "It is the Sabbath, and the law doesn't allow you to carry your mat." He answered them, "The one who healed me said to me, 'Take up your mat and walk!'" They asked him, "Who is the one who said to you: Take up your mat and walk?" But the sick man had no idea who it was who had cured him, for Jesus had slipped away among the crowd that filled the place.

Afterward Jesus met him in the temple court and told him, "Now you are well; don't sin again, lest something worse happen to you." And the man went back and told the Jews that it was Jesus who had healed him. So the Jews persecuted Jesus because he performed healings like that on the Sabbath.

Jesus replied, "My Father goes on working and so do I." And the Jews tried all the harder to kill him, for Jesus not only broke the Sabbath observance, but also made himself equal with God, calling God his own Father.

Jesus said to them, "Truly, I assure you, the Son cannot do anything by himself, but only what he sees the Father do. And whatever he does, the Son also does. The Father loves the Son and shows him everything he does; and he will show him even greater things than these, so that you will be amazed.

As the Father raises the dead and gives them life, so the Son gives life to whom he wills. In the same way, the Father judges no one, for he has entrusted all judgment to the Son, and he wants all to honor the Son, as they honor the Father. Whoever ignores the Son, ignores as well the Father who sent him.

Truly, I say to you, anyone who hears my word and believes him who sent me, has eternal life; and there is no judgment for him, because he has passed from death to life.

Truly, the hour is coming and has indeed come, when the dead will hear the voice of the Son of God and, on hearing it, will live. For the Father has life in himself, and he has given to the Son also to have life in himself. And he has empowered him as well to carry out Judgment, for he is Son of Man.

Do not be surprised at this: the hour is coming when all those lying in tombs will hear my voice and come out; those who have done good shall rise to live, and those who have done evil will rise to be condemned.

I can do nothing of myself. As I hear, so I judge, and my judgment is just, because I seek not my own will, but the will of him who sent me.

If I bore witness to myself, my testimony would be worthless. But Another One is bearing witness to me, and I know that his testimony is true when he bears witness to me. John also bore witness to the truth when you sent messengers to him, but I do not seek such human testimony; I recall this for you, so that you may be saved.

John was a burning and shining lamp, and for a while you were willing to enjoy his light. But I have greater evidence than that of John—the works which the Father entrusted to me to carry out. The very works I do bear witness: the Father has sent me. Thus he who bears witness to me is the Father who sent me. You have never heard his voice and have never seen his likeness; therefore, as long as you do not believe his messenger, his word is not in you.

You search in the Scriptures, thinking that in them you will find life; yet Scripture bears witness to me. But you refuse to come to me, that you may live. I am not seeking human praise; but I know that the love of God is not within you, for I have come in my Father's name and you do not accept me. If another comes in his own name, you will accept him. As long as you seek praise from one another, instead of seeking the glory which comes from the only God, how can you believe?

Do not think that I shall accuse you to the Father. Moses himself, in whom you placed your hope, accuses you. If you believed Moses, you would believe me, for he wrote of me. But if you do not believe what he wrote, how will you believe what I say?

Moses gave you the law, didn't he? But none of you keep the law. Why, then, do you want to kill me?"

The people replied, "You have a demon; who wants to kill you?" Jesus said to them, "I performed just one deed, and you are all astounded by it. But remember the circumcision ordered by Moses—actually it was not Moses but the ancestors who began this practice. You circumcise a man even on the Sabbath, and you would break the law if you refused to do so because of the Sabbath. How is it, then, that you are indignant with me because I healed the whole person on the Sabbath? Do not judge by appearances, but according to what is right."

After this, Jesus went to the other side of the Sea of Galilee, near Tiberias, and large crowds followed him, because of the miraculous signs they saw, when he healed the sick. So he went up into the hills and sat down there with his disciples. Now the Passover, the feast of the Jews, was at hand.

Then lifting up his eyes, Jesus saw the crowds that were coming to him, and said to Philip, "Where shall we buy bread so that these people may eat?" He said this to test Philip, for he himself knew what he was going to do. Philip answered him, "Two hundred silver coins would not buy enough bread for each of them to have a piece."

Then one of Jesus' disciples, Andrew, Simon Peter's brother, said, "There is a boy here who has five barley loaves and two fish; but what good are these for so many?"

Jesus said, "Make the people sit down." There was plenty of grass there, so the people, about five thousand men, sat down. Jesus then took the loaves, gave thanks, and distributed them to those who were seated. He did the same with the fish, and gave them as much as they wanted. And when they had eaten enough, he told his disciples, "Gather up the pieces left over, that nothing may be lost."

So they gathered them up and filled twelve baskets with bread, that is, with pieces of the five barley loaves left over by those who had eaten.

When the people saw the miracle which Jesus had performed, they said, "This is really the Prophet, the one who is to come into the world." Jesus realized that they would come and take him by force to make him king; so he fled to the hills by himself.

When evening came, the disciples went down to the shore. After a while, they got into a boat to make for Capernaum on the other side of the sea, for it was now dark and Jesus had not yet come to them. But the sea was getting rough because a strong wind was blowing.

They had rowed about three or four miles, when they saw Jesus walking on the sea, and he was drawing near to the boat. They were frightened, but he said to them, "It is I! Don't be afraid!"

They wanted to take him into the boat, but immediately, the boat was at the shore to which they were going.

Next day, the people, who had stayed on the other side, realized that only one boat had been there, and that Jesus had not entered it with his disciples; but rather, the disciples had gone away alone. Other boats from Tiberias landed near the place where all these people had eaten the bread. When they saw that neither Jesus nor his disciples were there, they got into the boats and went to Capernaum looking for Jesus.

When they found him on the other side of the lake, they asked him, "Master, when did you come here?"

Jesus answered, "Truly, I say to you, you look for me, not because of the signs which you have seen, but because you ate bread and were satisfied. Work then, not for perishable food, but for the lasting food which gives eternal life. The Son of Man will give it to you, for he is the one on whom the Father has put his mark."

Then the Jews asked him, "What shall we do? What are the works that God wants us to do?" And Jesus answered them, "The work God wants is this: that you believe in the One whom God has sent."

They then said, "Show us miraculous signs, that we may see and believe you. What sign do you perform? Our ancestors ate manna in the desert; as Scripture says: They were given bread from heaven to eat."

Jesus then said to them, "Truly, I say to you, it was not Moses who gave you the bread from heaven. My Father gives you the true bread from heaven. The bread God gives is the One who comes from heaven and gives life to the world." And they said to him, "Give us this bread always."

Jesus said to them, "I am the bread of life; whoever comes to me shall never be hungry, and whoever believes in me shall never be thirsty. Nevertheless, as I said, you refuse to believe, even when you have seen. Yet all those whom the Father gives me will come to me, and whoever comes to me, I shall not turn away. For I have come from heaven, not to do my own will, but the will of the One who sent me.

And the will of him who sent me is that I lose nothing of what he has given me, but instead that I raise it up on the last day. This is the will of the

Father, that whoever sees the Son and believes in him shall live eternal life; and I will raise him up on the last day."

The Jews murmured because Jesus had said, "I am the bread which comes from heaven." And they said, "This man is the son of Joseph, isn't he? We know his father and mother. How can he say that he has come from heaven?"

Jesus answered them, "Do not murmur among yourselves. No one can come to me unless he is drawn by the Father who sent me; and I will raise him up on the last day. It has been written in the Prophets: They shall all be taught by God. So whoever listens and learns from the Father comes to me.

For no one has seen the Father except the One who comes from God; he has seen the Father. Truly, I say to you, whoever believes has eternal life.

I am the bread of life. Though your ancestors ate the manna in the desert, they died. But here you have the bread from heaven, so that you may eat of it, and not die.

I am the living bread from heaven; whoever eats of this bread will live forever. The bread I shall give is my flesh, and I will give it for the life of the world."

The Jews were arguing among themselves, "How can this man give us his flesh to eat?" So Jesus replied, "Truly, I say to you, if you do not eat the flesh of the Son of Man and drink his blood, you have no life in you. The one who eats my flesh and drinks my blood lives eternal life, and I will raise him up on the last day.

My flesh is really food, and my blood is truly drink. Those who eat my flesh and drink my blood, live in me, and I in them. Just as the Father, who is life, sent me, and I have life from the Father, so whoever eats me will have life from me. This is the bread from heaven; not like that of your ancestors, who ate and later died. Those who eat this bread will live forever."

Jesus spoke in this way in Capernaum when he taught them in the synagogue.

After hearing this, many of Jesus' followers said, "This language is very hard! Who can accept it?"

Jesus was aware that his disciples were murmuring about this, and so he said to them, "Does this offend you? Then how will you react when you see the Son of Man ascending to where he was before? It is the spirit that gives life, not the flesh. The words that I have spoken to you are spirit and they are life. But among you there are some who do not believe."

From the beginning, Jesus knew who would betray him. So he added, "As I have told you, no one can come to me unless it is granted by the Father."

After this many disciples withdrew and no longer followed him. Jesus asked the Twelve, "Will you also go away?" Peter answered him, "Lord, to whom shall we go? You have the words of eternal life. We now believe and know that you are the Holy One of God."

Jesus said to them, "I chose you, the Twelve, did I not? Yet one of you is a devil." Jesus spoke of Judas Iscariot, the son of Simon. He, one of the Twelve, was to betray him.

After this, Jesus went around Galilee; he would not go about in Judea, because the Jews wanted to kill him. Now the Jewish feast of the Tents was at hand. So the brothers of Jesus said to him, "Don't stay here; go instead to Judea and let your disciples see the works you are doing. Anyone who wants to be known doesn't work secretly. Since you are able to do these things, show yourself to the world."

His brothers spoke like this because they didn't believe in him. Jesus said to them, "My time has not yet come, but your time is always here.

The world cannot hate you; but it hates me because I bear witness and I show that its deeds are evil. Go up to the feast! I am not going to this feast, because my time has not yet come."

Jesus said these things, and remained in Galilee. But after his brothers had gone to the festival, he also went up, not publicly but in secret. The Jews were looking for him at the festival and asked, "Where is he?" There was a lot of talk about him among the people. Some said, "He is a good man," but others replied, "No, he is misleading the people." For fear of the Jews no one spoke openly about him.

When the festival was half over, Jesus went to the temple and began to teach. The Jews marveled and said, "How is it, that he knows Scriptures when he has had no teacher?"

And Jesus answered them, "My teaching is not mine, but it comes from the One who sent me. Anyone who does the will of God shall know whether my teaching is from God, or whether I speak on my own authority.

Those who speak on their own authority wish to gain honor for themselves. But the one who seeks the glory of him who sent him is truthful, and there is no reason to doubt him."

Some of the people of Jerusalem said, "Is this not the man they want to kill? And here he is speaking freely, and they don't say a word to him? Can it be, that the rulers know that this is really the Christ? Yet we know where this man comes from; but when the Christ appears, no one will know where he comes from."

So Jesus announced in a loud voice in the temple court where he was teaching, "You say that you know me and know where I come from! I have not come of myself; I was sent by the One who is true, and you don't know him. I know him, for I come from him, and he sent me."

They would have arrested him, but no one laid hands on him because his time had not yet come. Many people in the crowd, however, believed in him and said, "When the Christ comes, will he give more signs than this man?"

The Pharisees heard all these rumors among the people; they and the chief priests sent officers of the temple to arrest him. Jesus then said, "I shall be with you a little longer; after that, I shall go to him who sent me. You will look for me and you will not find me. Where I am you cannot come."

The Jews said to one another, "Where does this man intend to go, where we shall not find him? Will he go abroad to the Jews dispersed among the Greek nations, and teach the Greeks also? What does he mean when he says, 'You will look for me and not find me,' and, 'Where I am going you cannot come'?"

On the last and greatest day of the festival, Jesus stood up and proclaimed, "Let anyone who is thirsty come to me; and let the one who believes in me drink, for the Scripture says: Out of the believer's heart shall flow rivers of living water."

Jesus was referring to the Spirit, which those who believe in him were to receive; the Spirit had not yet been given, because Jesus had not yet entered into his glory.

Many who had been listening to these words began to say, "This is the Prophet." Others said, "This is the Christ." But some wondered, "Would the Christ come from Galilee? Doesn't Scripture say that the Christ is a descendant of David and from Bethlehem, the city of David?" The crowd was divided over him. Some wanted to arrest him, but no one laid hands on him.

The officers of the temple went back to the chief priests, who asked them, "Why didn't you bring him?" The officers answered, "No one ever spoke like this man." The Pharisees then said, "So you, too, have been led astray! Have any of the rulers or any of the Pharisees believed in him? Only these cursed people, who have no knowledge of the law!"

Yet one of them, Nicodemus, who had gone to Jesus earlier, spoke out, "Does our law condemn people without first hearing them and knowing the facts?" They replied, "Do you, too, come from Galilee? Look it up and see for yourself that no prophet is to come from Galilee."

And they all went home.

As for Jesus, he went to the Mount of Olives.

At daybreak Jesus appeared in the temple again. All the people came to him, and he sat down and began to teach them.

Then the teachers of the law and the Pharisees brought in a woman who had been caught in the act of adultery. They made her stand in front of everyone. "Master," they said, "this woman has been caught in the act of adultery. Now the law of Moses orders that such women be stoned to death;

but you, what do you say?" They said this to test Jesus, in order to have some charge against him.

Jesus bent down and started writing on the ground with his finger. And as they continued to ask him, he straightened up and said to them, "Let anyone among you who has no sin be the first to throw a stone at her." And he bent down, again, writing on the ground.

As a result of these words, they went away, one by one, starting with the elders, and Jesus was left alone, with the woman standing before him. Then Jesus stood up and said to her, "Woman, where are they? Has no one condemned you?" She replied, "No one." And Jesus said, "Neither do I condemn you; go away and don't sin again."

Jesus spoke to them again, "I am the Light of the world; the one who follows me will not walk in darkness, but will have light and life." The Pharisees replied, "Now you are speaking on your own behalf, your testimony is worthless."

Then Jesus said, "Even though I bear witness to myself, my testimony is true, for I know where I have come from and where I am going. But you do not know where I came from or where I am going.

You judge by human standards; as for me, I don't judge anyone. But if I had to judge, my judgment would be valid for I am not alone: the Father who sent me is with me. In your law it is written that the testimony of two witnesses is valid; so I am bearing witness to myself, and the Father who sent me bears witness to me."

They asked him, "Where is your Father?" Jesus answered, "You don't know me or my Father; if you knew me, you would know my Father as well."

Jesus said these things when he was teaching in the temple area, in the place where they received the offerings. No one arrested him, because his hour had not yet come.

Again, Jesus said to them, "I am going away, and though you look for me, you will die in your sin. Where I am going you cannot come." The Jews wondered, "Why does he say that we can't come where he is going? Will he kill himself?"

But Jesus said, "You are from below and I am from above; you are of this world and I am not of this world. That is why I told you that you will die in your sins. And you shall die in your sins, unless you believe that I am He."

They asked him, "Who are you?"; and Jesus said, "Just what I have told you from the beginning. I have much to say about you and much to condemn; but the One who sent me is truthful and everything I learned from him, I proclaim to the world."

They didn't understand that Jesus was speaking to them about the Father. So Jesus said, "When you have lifted up the Son of Man, then you will know that I am He and that I do nothing of myself, but I say just what the Father taught me. He who sent me is with me and has not left me alone; because I always do what pleases him."

As Jesus spoke like this, many believed in him. Jesus went on to say to the Jews who believed in him, "You will be my true disciples, if you keep my word. Then you will know the truth, and the truth will set you free." They answered him, "We are the descendants of Abraham and have never been slaves of anyone. What do you mean by saying: You will be free?"

Jesus answered them, "Truly, I say to you, whoever commits sin is a slave. But the slave doesn't stay in the house forever; the son stays forever. So, if the Son makes you free, you will be really free.

I know that you are the descendants of Abraham; yet you want to kill me because my word finds no place in you. For my part, I speak of what I have seen in my Father's presence, but you do what you have learned from your father."

They answered him, "Our father is Abraham." Then Jesus said, "If you were Abraham's children, you would do as Abraham did. But now you want to kill me, the one who tells you the truth—the truth that I have learned from God. That is not what Abraham did; what you are doing are the works of your father."

The Jews said to him, "We are not illegitimate children; we have one Father, God." Jesus replied, "If God were your Father you would love me, for I came forth from God, and I am here. And I didn't come by my own decision, but it was he himself who sent me. Why do you not understand my teaching? It is because you cannot bear my message.

The father you spring from is the devil, and you will carry out the evil wishes of your father, who has been a murderer from the beginning. He didn't uphold the truth for, in him, there is no truth; and now, when he speaks for himself, he lies. He is a liar and the father of lies.

Now I speak the truth and you don't believe me. Who among you can find anything false in me? Then, if I speak the truth, why do you not believe me? He who is of God hears the words of God; you don't hear because you are not of God."

The Jews retorted, "So we are right in saying that you are a Samaritan and are possessed by a demon." Jesus said, "I am not possessed, and you try to shame me when I give honor to my Father. I don't care about my own glory; there is One who cares for me and he will be the judge.

Truly, I say to you, if anyone keeps my word, he will never experience death." The Jews replied, "Now we know that you have a demon. Abraham died and the prophets as well, but you say, 'Whoever keeps my word will never experience death.' Who do you claim to be? Do you claim to be greater than our father Abraham, who died? And the prophets who also died?"

Then Jesus said, "If I were to praise myself, it would count for nothing.

But he who gives glory to me is the Father, the very one you claim as your God, although you don't know him. I know him, and if I were to say that I don't know him, I would be a liar like you. But I know him and I keep his word.

As for Abraham, your ancestor, he looked forward to the day when I would come; and he rejoiced when he saw it."

The Jews then said to him, "You are not yet fifty years old and you have seen Abraham?" And Jesus said, "Truly, I say to you, before Abraham was, I am." They then picked up stones to throw at him, but Jesus hid himself and left the temple.

As Jesus walked along, he saw a man who had been blind from birth. His disciples asked him, "Master, was he born blind because of a sin of his, or of his parents?"

Jesus answered, "Neither was it for his own sin nor for his parents' sin. He was born blind so that God's power might be shown in him. While it is day we must do the work of the One who sent me; for the night will come when no one can work. As long as I am in the world, I am the light of the world."

As Jesus said this, he made paste with spittle and clay, and rubbed it on the eyes of the blind man. Then he said, "Go and wash in the Pool of Siloam." (This word means sent.) So the blind man went and washed and came back able to see.

His neighbors, and all the people who used to see him begging, wondered. They said, "Isn't this the beggar who used to sit here?" Some said, "He's the one." Others said, "No, but he looks like him." But the man himself said, "I am he." Then they asked him, "How is it, that your eyes were opened?" And he answered, "The man called Jesus made a mud paste, put it on my eyes and said to me, 'Go to Siloam and wash.' So I went, and washed, and I could see." They asked, "Where is he?" and the man answered, "I don't know."

The people brought the man who had been blind to the Pharisees. Now it was a Sabbath day when Jesus made mud paste and opened his eyes. The Pharisees asked him again, "How did you recover your sight?" And he said, "He put paste on my eyes, and I washed, and now I see." Some of the Pharisees said, "That man is not from God, for he works on the Sabbath"; but others wondered, "How can a sinner perform such miraculous signs?" They were divided, and they questioned the blind man again, "What do you think of this man who opened your eyes?" And he answered, "He is a prophet!"

After all this, the Jews refused to believe that the man had been blind and had recovered his sight; so they called his parents and asked them, "Is this your son? You say that he was born blind, how is it, that he now sees?" The parents answered, "He really is our son and he was born blind; but how it is that he now sees, we don't know, neither do we know who opened his eyes. Ask him, he is old enough. Let him speak for himself."

The parents said this because they feared the Jews, who had already agreed that whoever confessed Jesus to be the Christ was to be expelled from the synagogue. Because of that his parents said, "He is old enough, ask him."

So, a second time, the Pharisees called the man who had been blind, and they said to him, "Tell us the truth; we know that this man is a sinner." He replied, "I don't know whether he is a sinner or not; I only know that I was blind and now I see." They said to him, "What did he do to you? How did he open your eyes?" He replied, "I have told you already and you would not listen. Why do you want to hear it again? Do you also want to become his disciples?"

Then they started to insult him. "Become his disciple yourself! We are disciples of Moses. We know that God spoke to Moses; but as for this man, we don't know where he comes from."

The man replied, "It is amazing that you don't know where the man comes from, and yet he opened my eyes! We know that God doesn't listen to sinners, but if anyone honors God and does his will, God listens to him. Never, since the world began, has it been heard that anyone opened the eyes of a person who was born blind. If this man were not from God, he could do nothing."

They answered him, "You were born a sinner and now you teach us!" And they expelled him.

Jesus heard that they had expelled him. He found him and said, "Do you believe in the Son of Man?" He answered, "Who is he, that I may believe in him?" Jesus said, "You have seen him and he is speaking to you." He said, "Lord, I believe"; and he worshiped him.

Jesus said, "I came into this world to carry out a judgment: Those who do not see shall see, and those who see shall become blind." Some Pharisees stood by and asked him, "So we are blind?" And Jesus answered, "If you were blind, you would not be guilty. But you say, 'We see'; this is the proof of your sin."

Truly, I say to you, anyone who does not enter the sheepfold by the gate, but climbs in some other way, is a thief and a robber. But the shepherd of the sheep enters by the gate. The keeper opens the gate to him and the sheep hear his voice; he calls each of his sheep by name and leads them out. When he has brought out all his own, he goes before them, and the sheep follow him for they know his voice. A stranger they will not follow, but rather they will run away from him, because they don't recognize a stranger's voice."

Jesus used this comparison, but they did not understand what he was saying to them.

So Jesus said, "Truly, I say to you, I am the gate of the sheep. All who came were thieves and robbers, and the sheep did not hear them. I am the gate. Whoever enters through me will be saved; he will go in and out freely and find food.

The thief comes to steal and kill and destroy, but I have come that they may have life, life in all its fullness.

I am the good shepherd. The good shepherd gives his life for the sheep. Not so the hired hand, or any other person who is not the shepherd, and to whom the sheep do not belong. They abandon the sheep as soon as they see the wolf coming; then the wolf snatches and scatters the sheep. This is because the hired hand works for pay and cares nothing for the sheep.

I am the good shepherd. I know my own and my own know me, as the Father knows me and I know the Father. Because of this, I give my life for my sheep.

I have other sheep which are not of this fold. These I have to lead as well, and they shall listen to my voice. Then there will be one flock, since there is one shepherd.

The Father loves me, because I lay down my life in order to take it up again. No one takes it from me, but I lay it down freely. It is mine to lay down and to take up again: this mission I received from my Father."

Because of these words, the Jews were again divided. Many of them said, "He has a demon and is out of his mind. Why listen to him?" But others said, "A man possessed doesn't speak in this way. Can a demon open the eyes of the blind?"

The time came for the feast of the Dedication. It was winter, and Jesus walked back and forth in the portico of Solomon. The Jews then gathered around him and said to him, "How long will you keep us in doubt? If you are the Messiah, tell us plainly." Jesus answered, "I have already told you, but you do not believe. The works I do in my Father's name proclaim who I am, but you don't believe because, as I said, you are not my sheep.

My sheep hear my voice and I know them; they follow me and I give them eternal life. They shall never perish, and no one will ever steal them from me. What my Father has given me, is greater than all things else. To snatch it out of the Father's hand, no one is able! I and the Father are One."

The Jews then picked up stones to throw at him; so Jesus said, "I have openly done many good works among you, which the Father gave me to do. For which of these do you stone me?"

The Jews answered, "We are not stoning you for doing a good work, but for insulting God; you are only a man, and you make yourself God."

Then Jesus replied, "Is this not written in your law: I said, you are gods? So those who received this word of God were called gods, and the Scripture is always true. What then should be said of the one anointed, and sent into the world, by the Father? Am I insulting God when I say, 'I am the Son of God'?

If I am not doing the works of my Father, do not believe me. But if I do them, even if you have no faith in me, believe because of the works I do; and know that the Father is in me, and I in the Father."

Again they tried to arrest him, but Jesus escaped from their hands. He went away again to the other side of the Jordan, to the place where John had baptized, and there he stayed.

Many people came to Jesus, and said, "John worked no miracles, but he spoke about you, and everything he said was true." And many in that place became believers.

There was a sick man named Lazarus who was from Bethany, the village of Mary and her sister Martha. This is the same Mary, who anointed the Lord with perfume and wiped his feet with her hair. Her brother Lazarus was sick.

So the sisters sent this message to Jesus, "Lord, the one you love is sick." On hearing this, Jesus said, "This illness will not end in death; rather it is for God's glory, and the Son of God will be glorified through it."

It is a fact that Jesus loved Martha and her sister and Lazarus; yet, after he heard of the illness of Lazarus, he stayed two days longer in the place where he was. Only then did he say to his disciples, "Let us go into Judea again." They replied, "Master, recently the Jews wanted to stone you. Are you going there again?"

Jesus said to them, "Are not twelve working hours needed to complete a day? Those who walk in the daytime shall not stumble, for they see the light of this world. But those who walk at night stumble, for there is no light in them."

After that, Jesus said to them, "Our friend Lazarus has fallen asleep, but I am going to wake him up." The disciples replied, "Lord, a sick person who sleeps will recover." But Jesus had referred to Lazarus' death, while they thought that he had meant the repose of sleep. So Jesus said plainly, "Lazarus is dead; and for your sake I am glad I was not there, so that you may believe. But let us go to him." Then Thomas, called the Twin, said to his fellow disciples, "Let us also go, that we may die with him."

When Jesus came, he found that Lazarus had been in the tomb for four days. As Bethany is near Jerusalem, about two miles away, many Jews had come to Martha and Mary, after the death of their brother, to comfort them.

When Martha heard that Jesus was coming, she went to meet him, while Mary remained sitting in the house. Martha said to Jesus, "If you had been here, my brother would not have died. But I know that whatever you ask from God, God will give you." Jesus said, "Your brother will rise again."

Martha replied, "I know that he will rise in the resurrection, at the last day." But Jesus said to her, "I am the resurrection. Whoever believes in me, though he die, shall live. Whoever lives and believes in me will never die. Do you believe this?"

Martha then answered, "Yes, Lord, I have come to believe that you are the Christ, the Son of God, he who is coming into the world."

After that, Martha went and called her sister Mary secretly, saying, "The Master is here and is calling for you." As soon as Mary heard this, she rose and went to him. Jesus had not yet come into the village, but was still in the place where Martha had met him.

The Jews, who were with Mary in the house consoling her, also came. When they saw her get up and go out, they followed her, thinking that she was going to the tomb to weep.

When Mary came to the place where Jesus was and saw him, she fell at his feet and said, "Lord, if you had been here, my brother would not have died." When Jesus saw her weeping, and the Jews also weeping, who had come with her, he was moved to the depths of his spirit and troubled. Then he asked, "Where have you laid him?" They answered, "Lord, come and see." Jesus wept.

The Jews said, "See how he loved him!" But some of them said, "If he could open the eyes of the blind man, could he not have kept this man from dying?"

Jesus, again deeply moved, drew near to the tomb. It was a cave with a stone laid across the entrance. Jesus said, "Take the stone away." Martha said to him, "Lord, by now he will smell, for this is the fourth day." Jesus replied, "Have I not told you that, if you believe, you will see the glory of God?" So they removed the stone.

Jesus raised his eyes and said, "Father, I thank you, for you have heard me. I knew that you hear me always; but my prayer was for the sake of these people, that they may believe that you sent me." When Jesus had said this, he cried out in a loud voice, "Lazarus, come out!"

The dead man came out, his hands and feet bound with linen strips, and his face wrapped in a cloth. Jesus said to them, "Untie him, and let him go."

Many of the Jews who had come with Mary believed in Jesus when they saw what he did; but some went to the Pharisees and told them what Jesus had done. So the chief priests and the Pharisees called together the Council.

They said, "What are we to do? For this man keeps on performing many miraculous signs. If we let him go on like this, all the people will believe in him and, as a result of this, the Romans will come and destroy our Holy Place and our nation."

Then one of them, Caiaphas, who was High Priest that year, spoke up, "You know nothing at all! It is better to have one man die for the people than to let the whole nation be destroyed."

In saying this Caiaphas did not speak for himself, but being High Priest that year, he foretold like a prophet that Jesus would die for the nation, and not for the nation only, but also would die in order to gather into one the scattered children of God. So, from that day on, they were determined to kill him.

Because of this, Jesus no longer moved about freely among the Jews. He withdrew instead to the country near the wilderness, and stayed with his disciples in a town called Ephraim.

The Passover of the Jews was at hand, and people from everywhere were coming to Jerusalem to purify themselves before the Passover. They looked for Jesus and, as they stood in the temple, they talked with one another, "What do you think? Will he come to the festival?" Meanwhile the chief priests and the elders had given orders that anyone who knew where he was should let them know, so that they could arrest him.

Six days before the Passover, Jesus came to Bethany, where he had raised Lazarus, the dead man, to life. Now they gave a dinner for him, and while Martha waited on them, Lazarus sat at the table with Jesus.

Then Mary took a pound of costly perfume, made from genuine spike-nard, and anointed the feet of Jesus, wiping them with her hair. And the whole house was filled with the fragrance of the perfume.

Judas Iscariot—the disciple who was to betray Jesus—remarked, "This perfume could have been sold for three hundred silver coins, and the money given to the poor." Judas, indeed, had no concern for the poor; he was a thief, and as he held the common purse, he used to help himself to the funds.

But Jesus spoke up, "Leave her alone. Was she not keeping it for the day of my burial? (The poor you always have with you, but you will not always have me.)"

Many Jews heard that Jesus was there and they came, not only because of Jesus, but also to see Lazarus whom he had raised from the dead. So the chief priests thought about killing Lazarus as well, for many of the Jews were drifting away because of him, and believing in Jesus.

The next day, many people who had come for the festival heard that Jesus was to enter Jerusalem. So they took branches of palm trees and went out to meet him. And they cried out,

"Hosanna!

Blessed is he who comes in the name of the Lord!

Blessed is the king of Israel!"

Jesus found a donkey and sat upon it, as Scripture says:

> Do not fear, city of Zion!
> See, your king is coming,
> sitting on the colt of a donkey!

The disciples were not aware of this at first, but after Jesus was glorified, they realized that this had been written about him, and that this was what had happened to him.

The people who came with him bore witness, and told how he had called Lazarus out of the tomb and raised him from the dead. It was because of this miraculous sign, which Jesus had given, that so many people welcomed him. In the meantime the Pharisees said to one another, "We are getting nowhere; the whole world has gone after him."

There were some Greeks who had come up to Jerusalem to worship during the feast. They approached Philip, who was from Bethsaida in Galilee, and asked him, "Sir, we wish to see Jesus." Philip went to Andrew, and the two of them told Jesus.

Then Jesus said, "The hour has come for the Son of Man to be glorified. Truly, I say to you, unless the grain of wheat falls to the earth and dies, it remains alone; but if it dies, it produces much fruit.

Those who love their life destroy it, and those who despise their life in this world save it even to everlasting life.

Whoever wants to serve me, let him follow me; and wherever I am, there shall my servant be also. If anyone serves me, the Father will honor him.

Now my soul is in distress. Shall I say, 'Father, save me from this hour'? But, to face all this, I have come to this hour. Father, glorify your name!" Then a voice came from heaven, "I have glorified it, and I will glorify it again."

People standing there heard something and said it was thunder; but others said, "An angel was speaking to him." Then Jesus declared, "This voice did not come for my sake but for yours. Now sentence is being passed on this world; now the prince of this world is to be cast down. And when I am lifted up from the earth, I shall draw all people to myself." With these words Jesus referred to the kind of death he was to die.

The crowd answered him, "We have been told in the law that the Messiah stands forever. How can you say that the Son of Man shall be lifted up? What kind of Son of Man is that?"

Jesus said to them, "The light will be with you a little longer. Walk while you have the light, lest the darkness overtake you. If you walk in the darkness, you do not know where you are going. While you have the light, believe in the light and become children of light."

After Jesus had said this, he withdrew, and kept himself hidden.

Even though Jesus had done so many miraculous signs among them, they didn't believe in him. Indeed the words spoken by the prophet Isaiah had to be fulfilled:

> Lord, who has believed what we proclaimed?
> To whom have the ways of God the Savior been made known?

They could not believe. Isaiah had said elsewhere:

> He let their eyes become blind
> and their hearts hard,
>
> so that they could neither see
> nor understand, nor be converted—otherwise,
> I would have healed them.

Isaiah said this when he saw the his glory, and his words refer to him.

Many of them, however, believed in Jesus, even among the rulers, but they did not acknowledge him because of the Pharisees, lest they be put out of the Jewish community. They preferred the favorable opinion of people, rather than God's approval.

Yet Jesus had said, and even cried out, "Whoever believes in me, believes not in me, but in him who sent me. And whoever sees me, sees him who sent me. I have come into the world as light, so that whoever believes in me may not remain in darkness.

If anyone hears my words and does not keep them, I am not the one to condemn him; for I have come, not to condemn the world, but to save the world. The one who rejects me, and does not receive my words, already has a judge: the very words I have spoken will condemn him on the last day.

For I have not spoken on my own authority; the Father, who sent me, has instructed me what to say and how to speak. I know that his commandment is eternal life, and that is why the message I give, I give as the Father instructed me."

I t was before the feast of the Passover. Jesus realized that his hour had come to pass from this world to the Father; and as he had loved those who were his own in the world, he would love them with perfect love.

They were at supper, and the devil had already put into the mind of Judas, son of Simon Iscariot, to betray him. Jesus knew that the Father had entrusted all things to him, and as he had come from God, he was going to God. So he got up from the table, removed his garment, and taking a towel, wrapped it around his waist. Then he poured water into a basin, and began to wash the disciples' feet, and to wipe them with the towel he was wearing.

When he came to Simon Peter, Simon asked him, "Why, Lord, do you want to wash my feet?" Jesus said, "What I am doing you cannot understand now, but afterward you will understand it." Peter replied, "You shall never wash my feet!"

Jesus answered him, "If I do not wash you, you can have no part with me." Then Simon Peter said, "Lord, wash not only my feet, but also my hands and my head!"

Jesus replied, "Whoever has taken a bath does not need to wash (except the feet), for he is clean all over. You are clean, though not all of you." Jesus knew who was to betray him; because of this he said, "Not all of you are clean."

When Jesus had finished washing their feet, he put on his garment again, went back to the table, and said to them, "Do you understand what I have done to you? You call me Master and Lord, and you are right, for so I am. If I, then, your Lord and Master, have washed your feet, you also must wash one another's feet. I have given you an example, that as I have done, you also may do.

Truly, I say to you, the servant is not greater than his master, nor is the messenger greater than he who sent him. Understand this, and blessed are you, if you put it into practice.

I am not speaking of you all, because I know the ones I have chosen, and the Scripture has to be fulfilled which says: The one who shares my table will rise up against me. I tell you this now before it happens, so that when it does happen, you may know that I am He.

Truly, I say to you, whoever welcomes the one I send, welcomes me; and whoever welcomes me, welcomes the One who sent me."

After saying this, Jesus was distressed in spirit, and said plainly, "Truly, one of you will betray me." The disciples then looked at one another, wondering whom he meant. One of the disciples, the one Jesus loved, was reclining near Jesus; so Simon Peter signaled him to ask Jesus whom he meant.

And the disciple, who was reclining near Jesus, asked him, "Lord, who is it?" Jesus answered, "I shall dip a piece of bread in the dish, and he to whom I give it, is the one."

So Jesus dipped the bread in the dish and gave it to Judas Iscariot, the son of Simon. As Judas took the piece of bread, Satan entered into him. Jesus then said to him, "What you are going to do, do quickly."

None of the others, reclining at the table, understood why Jesus had said this to Judas. As Judas had the common purse, they may have thought that Jesus was telling him, "Buy what we need for the feast," or, "Give something to the poor." Judas left as soon as he had eaten the bread. It was night.

When Judas had gone out, Jesus said, "Now is the Son of Man glorified, and God is glorified in him. God will glorify him, and he will glorify him very soon.

My children, I am with you for only a little while; you will look for me, but as I already told the Jews, now I tell you: where I am going you cannot come. I give you a new commandment: Love one another! Just as I have loved you, you also must love one another. By this everyone will know that you are my disciples, if you have love for one another."

Simon Peter said to him, "Lord, where are you going?" Jesus answered, "Where I am going you cannot follow me now, but afterward you will." Peter said, "Lord, why can't I follow you now? I am ready to give my life for you." "To give your life for me?" Jesus asked Peter. "Truly I tell you, the cock will not crow, before you have denied me three times."

"Do not be troubled! Trust in God and trust in me! In my Father's house there are many rooms; otherwise, I would not have told you that I go to prepare a place for you. After I have gone and prepared a place for you, I shall come again and take you to me, so that where I am, you also may be. Yet you know the way where I am going."

Thomas said to him, "Lord, we don't know where you are going; how can we know the way?" Jesus said, "I am the way, the truth and the life; no one comes to the Father but through me. If you know me, you will know the Father also; indeed you know him, and you have seen him."

Philip asked him, "Lord, show us the Father, and that is enough." Jesus said to him, "What! I have been with you so long and you still do not know me, Philip? Whoever sees me sees the Father; how can you say, 'Show us the Father'? Do you not believe that I am in the Father and the Father is in me?

All that I say to you, I do not say of myself. The Father who dwells in me is doing his own work. Believe me when I say that I am in the Father and the Father is in me; at least believe it on the evidence of these works that I do.

Truly, I say to you, the one who believes in me will do the same works that I do; and he will even do greater than these, for I am going to the Father. Everything you ask in my name, I will do, so that the Father may be glorified in the Son. Indeed, anything you ask, calling upon my name, I will do it.

If you love me, you will keep my commandments; and I will ask the Father, and he will give you another Helper to be with you forever, the Spirit of truth whom the world cannot receive, because it neither sees him nor knows him. But you know him, for he is with you, and will be in you.

I will not leave you orphans, I am coming to you. A little while and the world will see me no more, but you will see me, because I live and you will also live. On that day you will know that I am in my Father, and you in me, and I in you.

Whoever keeps my commandments is the one who loves me. If he loves me, he will also be loved by my Father; I too shall love him and show myself clearly to him."

Judas—not Judas Iscariot—asked Jesus, "Lord, how can it be that you will show yourself clearly to us and not to the world?" Jesus answered him, "If anyone loves me, he will keep my word and my Father will love him; and we will come to him and live with him. But if anyone does not love me, he will not keep my words; and these words that you hear are not mine, but the Father's who sent me.

I told you all this while I am still with you. From now on the Helper, the Holy Spirit whom the Father will send in my name, will teach you all things, and remind you of all that I have told you.

Peace be with you! My peace I give to you; not as the world gives peace do I give it to you. Do not be troubled! Do not be afraid! You heard me say, 'I am going away, but I am coming to you.' If you loved me, you would be glad that I go to the Father, for the Father is greater than I.

I have told you this now before it takes place, so that when it does happen you may believe. There is very little left for me to tell you, for the prince of this world is at hand, although there is nothing in me that he can claim. But see, the world must know that I love the Father, and that I do what the Father has taught me to do. Come now, let us go.

I am the true vine and my Father is the vine grower. If any of my branches doesn't bear fruit, he breaks it off; and he prunes every branch that does bear fruit, that it may bear even more fruit.

You are already made clean by the word I have spoken to you. Live in me as I live in you. The branch cannot bear fruit by itself, but has to remain part of the vine; so neither can you, if you don't remain in me.

I am the vine and you are the branches. As long as you remain in me and I in you, you bear much fruit; but apart from me you can do nothing. Whoever does not remain in me is thrown away, as they do with branches, and they wither. Then they are gathered and thrown into the fire and burned.

If you remain in me and my words remain in you, you may ask whatever you want, and it will be given to you. My Father is glorified when you bear much fruit: it is then that you become my disciples.

As the Father has loved me, so I have loved you. Remain in my love! You will remain in my love if you keep my commandments, just as I have kept my Father's commandments and remain in his love.

I have told you all this, that my own joy may be in you, and your joy may be complete. This is my commandment: Love one another as I have loved you! There is no greater love than this, to give one's life for one's friends; and you are my friends, if you do what I command you.

I shall not call you servants any more, because servants do not know what their master is about. Instead, I have called you friends, since I have made known to you everything I learned from my Father.

You did not choose me; it was I who chose you and sent you to go and bear fruit, fruit that will last. And everything you ask the Father in my name, he will give you.

This is my command, that you love one another.

If the world hates you, remember that the world hated me before you. This would not be so if you belonged to the world, because the world loves its own. But you are not of the world, since I have chosen you from the world; because of this the world hates you.

Remember what I told you: the servant is not greater than his master; if they persecuted me, they will also persecute you. If they kept my word, they will keep yours as well. All this they will do to you on account of my name, because they do not know the One who sent me.

If I had not come and spoken to them, they would have no sin, but now they have no excuse for their sin. Those who hate me hate my Father.

If I had not done among them what no one else has ever done, they would have no sin. But after they have seen all this, they hate me and my Father, and the words written in their law become true: They hated me for no reason.

From the Father, I will send you the Spirit of truth. When this Helper has come from the Father, he will be my witness, and you, too, will be my witnesses, for you have been with me from the beginning.

I tell you all this to keep you from stumbling and falling away. They will put you out of the synagogue. Still more, the hour is coming, when anyone who kills you will claim to be serving God; they will do this, because they have not known the Father or me. I tell you all these things now so that, when the time comes, you may remember that I told you about them.

I did not tell you about this in the beginning, because I was with you. But now I am going to the One who sent me, and none of you asks me where I am going; instead you are overcome with grief, because of what I have said.

Believe me, it is better for you that I go away, because as long as I do not go away, the Helper will not come to you. But if I go away, I will send him to you, and when he comes, he will vindicate the truth before a sinful world; and he will vindicate the paths of righteousness and justice.

What is the world's sin, in regard to me? Disbelief. What is the path of righteousness? It is the path I walk, by which I go to the Father; and you shall see me no more. What is the path of justice? It is the path on which the prince of this world will always stand condemned.

I still have many things to tell you, but you cannot bear them now. When he, the Spirit of truth comes, he will guide you into the whole truth.

For he will not speak of his own authority, but will speak what he hears, and he will tell you about the things which are to come. He will take what is mine and make it known to you; in doing this, he will glorify me. All that the Father has is mine; for this reason, I told you that the Spirit will take what is mine, and make it known to you.

A little while, and you will see me no more; and then a little while, and you will see me."

Some of the disciples wondered, "What does he mean by, 'A little while, and you will not see me; and then a little while, and you will see me'? And why did he say, 'I go to the Father'?" And they said to one another, "What does he mean by 'a little while'? We don't understand."

Jesus knew that they wanted to question him; so he said to them, "You are puzzled because I told you that in a little while you will see me no more, and then a little while later you will see me.

Truly, I say to you, you will weep and mourn while the world rejoices. You will be sorrowful, but your sorrow will turn to joy. A woman in childbirth is in distress because her time is at hand. But after the child is born, she no longer remembers her suffering because of her great joy: a human being is born into the world.

You feel sorrowful now, but I will see you again, and your hearts will rejoice; and no one will take your joy from you. When that day comes you will not ask me anything. Truly, I say to you, whatever you ask the Father in my name, he will give you. So far you have not asked for anything in my name; ask, and receive, that your joy may be full.

I have taught you all these things in veiled language, but the time is coming when I shall no longer speak in veiled language, but will speak to you plainly about the Father.

When that day comes, you will ask in my name; and it will not be necessary for me to ask the Father for you, for the Father himself loves you, because you have loved me, and you believed that I came from the Father. As I came from the Father, and have come into the world, so I am leaving the world, and going to the Father."

The disciples said to him, "Now you are speaking plainly and not in veiled language! Now we see that you know all things, even before we question you. Because of this we believe that you came from God."

Jesus answered them, "You say that you believe? The hour is coming, indeed it has come, when you will be scattered, each one to his home, and you will leave me alone. Yet I am not alone, for the Father is with me.

I have told you all this, so that in me you may have peace. You will have trouble in the world; but, courage! I have overcome the world."

After saying this, Jesus lifted up his eyes to heaven and said, "Father, the hour has come! Give glory to your Son, that the Son may give glory to you. You have given him power over all humanity, so that he may give eternal life to all those you entrusted to him. For this is eternal life: to know you, the only true God, and the One you sent, Jesus Christ.

I have glorified you on earth and finished the work that you gave me to do. Now, Father, give me, in your presence, the same glory I had with you before the world began.

I have made your name known to those you gave me from the world. They were yours, and you gave them to me, and they kept your word. And now they know that whatever you entrusted to me, is indeed from you. I have given them the teaching I received from you, and they accepted it, and know in truth that I came from you; and they believe that you sent me.

I pray for them. I do not pray for the world, but for those who belong to you, and whom you have given to me. Indeed all I have is yours, and all you have is mine; and now they are my glory. I am no longer in the world, but they are in the world, and I come to you. Holy Father, keep those you have given me in your name, so that they may be one, as we also are.

When I was with them, I kept them safe in your name; and not one was lost, except the one who was already lost, and in this, the Scripture was fulfilled. And now I come to you; in the world I speak these things, so that those whom you gave me, might have joy—all my joy within themselves.

I have given them your word; and the world has hated them, because they are not of the world, just as I am not of the world, I do not ask you to remove them from the world, but to keep them from the evil one. They are not of the world, just as I am not of the world. Consecrate them in the truth. Your word is truth.

I have sent them into the world as you sent me into the world; and for their sake, I go to the sacrifice by which I am consecrated, so that they too may be consecrated in truth.

I pray not only for these. but also for those who through their word will believe in me. May they all be one, as you Father are in me and I am in you. May they be one in us, so that the world may believe that you have sent me.

I have given them the glory you have given me, that they may be one as we are one: I in them and you in me. Thus they shall reach perfection in unity; and the world shall know that you have sent me, and that I have loved them, just as you loved me.

Father, since you have given them to me, I want them to be with me where I am, and see the glory you gave me, for you loved me before the foundation of the world.

Righteous Father, the world has not known you, but I have known you, and these have known that you have sent me. As I revealed your name to them, so will I continue to reveal it, so that the love with which you loved me may be in them, and I also may be in them."

When Jesus had finished speaking, he went with his disciples to the other side of the Kidron Valley. There was a garden there which Jesus entered with his disciples.

Now Judas, who betrayed him, knew the place, since Jesus had often met there with his disciples. So Judas took soldiers and some servants from the chief priests and Pharisees, and they went to the garden with lanterns, torches and weapons.

Jesus knew all that was going to happen to him; he stepped forward and asked, "Who are you looking for?" They answered, "Jesus the Nazarene." Jesus said, "I am he." Judas, who betrayed him, stood there with them.

When Jesus said, "I am he," they moved backwards and fell to the ground. He then asked a second time, "Who are you looking for?" and they answered, "Jesus the Nazarene." Jesus replied, "I told you that I am he. If you are looking for me, let these others go." So what Jesus had said came true: "I have not lost one of those you gave me."

Simon Peter had a sword; he drew it and struck Malchus, the High Priest's servant, cutting off his right ear. But Jesus said to Peter, "Put your sword into its sheath! Shall I not drink the cup which the Father has given me?"

The guards and the soldiers, with their commander, seized Jesus and bound him; and they took him first to Annas. Annas was the father-in-law of Caiaphas, who was the High Priest that year; and it was Caiaphas who had told the Jews, "It is better that one man should die for the people."

Simon Peter and another disciple followed Jesus. Because this disciple was known to the High Priest, they let him enter the courtyard of the High Priest along with Jesus, but Peter had to stay outside at the door. The other disciple, who was known to the High Priest, went out and spoke to the maidservant at the gate and brought Peter in. Then this maidservant on duty at the door said to Peter, "So you also are one of his disciples?" But he answered, "I am not."

Now the servants and the guards had made a charcoal fire and were standing and warming themselves, because it was cold. Peter was also with them warming himself.

The High Priest questioned Jesus about his disciples and his teaching. Jesus answered him, "I have spoken openly to the world; I have always taught in places where the Jews meet together, either at the assemblies in synagogues or in the temple. I did not teach secretly. Why then do you question me? Ask those who heard me, they know what I said."

At this reply one of the guards standing there gave Jesus a blow on the face, saying, "Is that the way to answer the High Priest?" Jesus said to him, "If I have said something wrong, point it out. But if I spoke correctly, why strike me?"

Then Annas sent him, bound, to Caiaphas, the High Priest.

Now Simon Peter stood there warming himself. They said to him, "Surely you also are one of his disciples." He denied it, and answered, "I am not!" One of the High Priest's servants, a kinsman of the one whose ear Peter had cut off, asked, "Did I not see you with him in the garden?" Again Peter denied it, and at once the cock crowed.

Then they led Jesus from the house of Caiaphas to the headquarters of the Roman governor. It was now morning. The Jews didn't go inside, lest they be made unclean by entering the house of a pagan, and therefore not allowed to eat the Passover meal. So Pilate came outside and asked, "What charge do you bring against this man?"

They answered, "If he were not a criminal, we would not be handing him over to you." Pilate said, "Take him yourselves and judge him according to your own law." But they replied, "We ourselves are not allowed to put anyone to death."

According to what Jesus himself had foretold, it was clear what kind of death he would die.

Pilate then entered the court again, summoned Jesus and asked him, "Are you the King of the Jews?" Jesus replied, "Are you saying this on your own initiative; or have others told you about me?"

Pilate answered, "Am I a Jew? Your own nation and the chief priests have handed you over to me. What have you done?" Jesus answered, "My kingship does not come from this world. If I were a king, like those of this world, my servants would have fought to save me from being handed over to the Jews. But my kingship is not of this world."

Pilate asked him, "So you are a king?" And Jesus answered, "Just as you say, I am a king. For this I was born and for this I have come into the world, to bear witness to the truth. Everyone who is on the side of truth hears my voice." Pilate said, "What is truth?"

Pilate then went out to the Jews again and said, "I find no crime in this man. Now, according to custom, I must release a prisoner to you at the Passover. With your agreement I will release to you the King of the Jews." But they insisted and cried out, "Not this man, but Barabbas!" Now Barabbas was a robber.

Then Pilate had Jesus taken away and scourged. The soldiers twisted thorns into a crown and put it on his head. They threw a cloak of royal purple around his shoulders; and they began coming up to him and saluting him, "Hail, King of the Jews!" and they struck him on the face.

Pilate went outside yet another time and said to the Jews, "Look, I am bringing him out, and I want you to know that I find no crime in him." Jesus then came out wearing the crown of thorns and the purple cloak, and Pilate pointed at him, saying, "Behold the man!"

On seeing him the chief priests and the guards cried out, "Crucify him! Crucify him!" Pilate said, "Take him yourselves and have him crucified, for I find no case against him." The Jews then said, "We have a law, and according to the law this man must die because he made himself Son of God."

When Pilate heard this he was more afraid. And coming back into the court he asked Jesus, "Where are you from?" But Jesus gave him no answer. Then Pilate said to him, "You will not speak to me? Do you not know that I have power to release you, just as I have power to crucify you?" Jesus replied, "You would have no power over me unless it had been given to you from above; therefore the one who handed me over to you is more guilty."

From that moment Pilate tried to release him, but the Jews cried out, "If you release this man, you are no friend of Caesar. Anyone who makes himself a king is defying Caesar."

When Pilate heard this, he had Jesus brought outside to the place called the Stone Floor—in Hebrew Gabbatha—and sat down in the judgment seat. It was the day of preparation for the Passover, about noon. Pilate said to the Jews, "Behold your king!" But they cried out, "Away! Take him away! Crucify him!" Pilate replied, "Shall I crucify your king?" And the chief priests answered, "We have no king but Caesar!"

Then Pilate handed Jesus over to them to be crucified.

They took Jesus, and led him away. Bearing his cross, Jesus went out of the city to what is called the Place of the Skull, in Hebrew Golgotha. There he was crucified, and with him two others, one on either side, and Jesus in the middle.

Pilate had a notice written and fastened to the cross, which read: JESUS THE NAZARENE, THE KING OF THE JEWS. Many Jewish people saw this title, because the place where Jesus was crucified was very close to the city; and the title was written in Hebrew, Latin and Greek. The chief priests said to Pilate, "Do not write 'The King of the Jews'; but, 'This man claimed to be King of the Jews.'" Pilate answered them, "What I have written, I have written."

When the soldiers crucified Jesus, they took his clothes and divided them into four parts, one part for each of them. But as the tunic was woven in one piece from top to bottom, they said, "Let us not tear it, but cast lots to decide who will get it." This fulfilled the words of Scripture:

> They divided my clothing among them;
> they cast lots for my garment.

This was what the soldiers did.

Near the cross of Jesus stood his mother, his mother's sister Mary, who was the wife of Cleophas, and Mary of Magdala. When Jesus saw the mother, and the disciple whom he loved, he said to the mother, "Woman, this is your son." Then he said to the disciple, "This is your mother." And from that moment the disciple took her to his own home.

Jesus knew all was now finished and, in order to fulfill what was written in Scripture, he said, I am thirsty. A jar full of bitter wine stood there; so, putting a sponge soaked in the wine on a twig of hyssop, they raised it to his lips. Jesus took the wine and said, "It is accomplished." Then he bowed his head and gave up the spirit.

As it was Preparation Day, the Jews did not want the bodies to remain on the cross during the Sabbath, for this Sabbath was a very solemn day. They asked Pilate to have the legs of the condemned men broken, so that the bodies might be taken away.

The soldiers came and broke the legs of the first man and of the other man, who had been crucified with Jesus. When they came to Jesus, they saw that he was already dead, so they did not break his legs. One of the soldiers, however, pierced his side with a lance, and immediately there came out blood and water.

The one who saw that, has testified to it, and his testimony is true; he knows he speaks the truth, so that you also might believe. All this happened to fulfill the words of Scripture: Not one of his bones shall be broken. Another text says: They shall look on him whom they have pierced.

After this, Joseph of Arimathea approached Pilate, for he was a disciple of Jesus, though secretly, for fear of the Jews. And he asked Pilate to let him remove the body of Jesus. Pilate agreed; so he came and took away the body.

Nicodemus, the man who first visited Jesus by night, also came and brought a jar of myrrh mixed with aloes, about seventy-five pounds. They took the body of Jesus and wrapped it in linen cloths with the spices, following the burial customs of the Jews.

There was a garden in the place where Jesus had been crucified, and, in the garden, a new tomb in which no one had ever been laid. And therefore, because the sepulcher was nearby, and the Jewish day of preparation was coming to a close, they placed the body of Jesus there.

Now, on the first day after the Sabbath, Mary of Magdala came to the tomb early in the morning while it was still dark, and she saw that the stone blocking the tomb had been moved away. She ran to Peter, and the other disciple whom Jesus loved, and she said to them, "They have taken the Lord out of the tomb and we don't know where they have laid him."

Peter then set out with the other disciple to go to the tomb. They ran together, but the other disciple outran Peter and reached the tomb first. He bent down and saw the linen cloths lying flat, but he did not enter.

Then Simon Peter came, following him, and entered the tomb; he, too, saw the linen cloths lying flat. The napkin, which had been around his head, was not lying flat like the other linen cloths, but lay rolled up in its place. Then the other disciple, who had reached the tomb first, also went in; he saw and believed. Scripture clearly said that Jesus must rise from the dead, but they had not yet understood that.

The disciples went back to their homes.

Mary stood weeping outside the tomb; and as she wept, she bent down to look inside. She saw two angels in white, sitting where the body of Jesus had been, one at the head, and the other at the feet. They said, "Woman, why are you weeping?" She answered, "Because they have taken my Lord and I don't know where they have put him."

As she said this, she turned around and saw Jesus standing there, but she did not recognize him. Jesus said to her, "Woman, why are you weeping? Who are you looking for?" She thought it was the gardener and answered him, "Sir, if you have taken him away, tell me where you have put him, and I will go and take him away."

Jesus said to her, "Mary!" She turned, and said to him, "Rabboni!"— which means Master. Jesus said to her, "Do not touch me, because I have not yet ascended to the Father. But go to my brothers and say to them: I am ascending to my Father, who is your Father, to my God, who is your God."

So Mary of Magdala went and announced to the disciples, "I have seen the Lord, and this is what he said to me."

On the evening of that day, the first day after the Sabbath, the doors were locked where the disciples were, because of their fear of the Jews. But Jesus came, and stood among them, and said to them, "Peace be with you!" Then he showed them his hands and his side. The disciples, seeing the Lord, were full of joy.

Again Jesus said to them, "Peace be with you! As the Father has sent me, so I send you." After saying this, he breathed on them, and said to them, "Receive the Holy Spirit! Those whose sins you forgive, they are forgiven; those whose sins you retain, they are retained."

Thomas, the Twin, one of the Twelve, was not with them when Jesus came. The other disciples told him, "We have seen the Lord." But he replied, "Until I have seen in his hands the print of the nails, and put my finger in the mark of the nails and my hand in his side, I will not believe."

Eight days later, the disciples were again inside the house and Thomas was with them. Although the doors were locked, Jesus came and stood in their midst and said, "Peace be with you!" Then he said to Thomas, "Put your finger here, and see my hands; stretch out your hand, and put it into my side. Do not continue in your unbelief, but believe!"

Thomas said, "You are my Lord and my God." Jesus replied, "You believe because you see me, don't you? Happy are those who have not seen and yet have come to believe."

There were many other signs that Jesus gave in the presence of his disciples, but they are not recorded in this book. These are recorded, so that you may believe that Jesus is the Christ, the Son of God. Believe, and you will have life through his name!

After this, Jesus revealed himself to the disciples by the Lake of Tiberias. He appeared to them in this way: Simon Peter, Thomas who was called the Twin, Nathanael of Cana in Galilee, the sons of Zebedee and two other disciples were together; and Simon Peter said to them, "I'm going fishing." They replied, "We will come with you." And they went out and got into the boat, but that night they caught nothing.

When the sun came up, Jesus was standing on the shore, but the disciples did not know that it was Jesus. Jesus called out, "Friends, have you anything to eat?" They answered, "Nothing." Then he said to them, "Throw the net on the right side of the boat and you will find something." When they had lowered the net, they were not able to pull it in because of the great number of fish.

Then the disciple Jesus loved said to Peter, "It's the Lord!" At these words, "It's the Lord!" Simon Peter put on his clothes, for he was stripped for work, and jumped into the water. The other disciples came in the boat, dragging the net full of fish; they were not far from land, about a hundred meters.

When they landed, they saw a charcoal fire with fish on it, and some bread. Jesus said to them, "Bring some of the fish you've just caught." So Simon Peter climbed into the boat and pulled the net to shore. It was full of big fish—one hundred and fifty-three—but, in spite of this, the net was not torn.

Jesus said to them, "Come and have breakfast." And not one of the disciples dared to ask him, "Who are you?" for they knew it was the Lord. Jesus came and took the bread and gave it to them, and he did the same with the fish.

This was the third time that Jesus revealed himself to his disciples after rising from the dead.

After they had finished breakfast, Jesus said to Simon Peter, "Simon, son of John, do you love me more than these do?" He answered, "Yes, Lord, you know that I love you." And Jesus said, "Feed my lambs."

A second time Jesus said to him, "Simon, son of John, do you love me?" And Peter answered, "Yes, Lord, you know that I love you." Jesus said to him, "Look after my sheep." And a third time he said to him, "Simon, son of John, do you love me?"

Peter was saddened because Jesus asked him a third time, "Do you love me?" and he said, "Lord, you know everything; you know that I love you."

Jesus then said, "Feed my sheep! Truly, I say to you, when you were young, you put on your belt and walked where you liked. But when you grow old, you will stretch out your hands, and another will put a belt around you, and lead you where you do not wish to go."

Jesus said this to make known the kind of death by which Peter was to glorify God. And he added, "Follow me!"

Peter looked back and saw that the disciple Jesus loved was following as well, the one who had reclined close to Jesus at the supper, and had asked him, "Lord, who is to betray you?" On seeing him, Peter asked Jesus, "Lord, what about him?" Jesus answered, "If I want him to remain until I come, is that any concern of yours? Follow me!"

Because of this, the rumor spread in the community that this disciple would not die. Yet Jesus did not say to Peter, "He will not die," but, "Suppose I want him to remain until I come back, what concern is that of yours?"

It is this disciple who testifies about the things and has written these things down, and we know that his testimony is true. But Jesus did many other things; if all were written down, I think the world itself could not contain the books that should be written.

INVITATION TO
1 JOHN

The letter known as 1 John was sent to a group of believers who were in a deeply troubled situation. Many within their community had abandoned the original faith in Jesus as the Messiah. This was because they couldn't reconcile the teaching that God had come to earth in a human body with the prevailing Greek idea that physical matter is evil and only spirit is good. This prevailing idea also led them to conclude that anything they did in their bodies had no spiritual consequences, so they indulged in activities they'd been taught were sinful. They also showed little concern for the needs of others. Despite their denial that Jesus had come in the flesh, their immoral lives and their lack of practical love, they still claimed that they belonged to God. They asserted they had a special source of spiritual insight, and that the rest of the group didn't know the truth as they did. They made their rejection of the original teaching about Jesus emphatic by leaving the community of those who still held to it. Those left behind were deeply shaken, uncertain about everything they'd been taught.

Someone close to this group of believers, who was an eyewitness of the life and ministry of Jesus, sent them a letter to reassure them that the real truth was what they'd *heard, from the beginning*. This writer doesn't identify himself by name, but it's very likely that he was the apostle John. Some phrases in this letter show close similarities to the book of John, for example, *How did the love of God appear among us? God sent his only Son into this world, that we might have life, through him*.

The letter doesn't develop systematically and logically; rather, it weaves together several main themes:

: it testifies to the reality of the Son of God's coming in the flesh;
: it warns believers not to let anyone deceive them;
: it refutes the claims of those who've left the group;
: it reassures believers that they have full access to the truth;
: and it emphasizes godly living and practical caring as the signs of those who genuinely know God.

| 1 JOHN |

This is what has been, from the beginning, and what we have heard, and have seen with our own eyes, what we have looked at, and touched with our hands, I mean the Word who is Life...

The Life made itself known. We have seen Eternal Life and we bear witness; and we are telling you of it. It was with the Father and made himself known to us.

So, we tell you, what we have seen and heard, that you may be in fellowship with us, and us, with the Father, and with his Son, Jesus Christ.

And we write this, that our joy may be complete.

We heard his message, from him, and announce it to you: God is light and there is no darkness in him.

If we say we are in fellowship with him, while we walk in darkness, we lie, instead of being in truth. But if we walk in the light, as he is in the light, we are in fellowship with one another; and the blood of Jesus, the Son of God, purifies us from all sin.

If we say, "We have no sin," we deceive ourselves, and the truth is not in us. If we confess our sins, he, who is faithful and just, will forgive us our sins, and cleanse us from all wickedness.

If we say that we do not sin, we make God a liar, his word is not in us.

My little children, I write to you, that you may not sin. But if anyone sins, we have an intercessor with the Father, Jesus Christ, the Just One. He is the sacrificial victim, for our sins, and the sins of the whole world.

How can we know that we know him? If we fulfill his commands.

If you say, "I know him," but do not fulfill his commands, you are a liar and the truth is not in you. But if you keep his word, God's love is made complete in you. This is how we know that we are in him:

he who claims to live in him, must live as he lived.

My dear friends, I am not writing you a new commandment, but reminding you of an old one, one you had from the beginning. This old commandment is the word you have heard.

But, in a way, I give it as a new commandment, that is true in him, and in you, because the darkness is passing away, and the true light already shines.

If you claim to be in the light, but hate your brother, you are still in darkness.

If you love your brothers and sisters, you remain in the light, and nothing in you will make you fall. But if you hate your brother, you are in the dark, and walk in darkness, without knowing where you go, for the darkness has blinded you.

> My dear children, I write this to you:
> you have already received the forgiveness of your sins,
> through the name of Jesus.
> Fathers, I write this to you:
> you know him, who is from the beginning.
> Young men, I write this to you:
> you have overcome the evil one.
> My dear children, I write to you,
> because you already know the Father.
> Fathers, I write to you,
> because you know him,
> who is from the beginning.
> Young men, I write to you,
> because you are strong,
> and the word of God lives in you,
> who have, indeed, overcome the evil one.

Do not love the world, or what is in it. If anyone loves the world, the love of the Father is not in him.

> For everything in the world—
> the craving of the flesh,
> the greed of eyes
> and people boasting of their superiority—
> all this, belongs to the world, not to the Father.

The world passes away, with all its craving, but those who do the will of God remain for ever.

My dear children, it is the last hour. You were told, that an antichrist would come; but several antichrists have already come, by which, we know, that it is, now, the last hour.

They went out, from us, though they did not really belong to us. Had they belonged to us, they would have remained with us. So, it became clear, that, not all of us were really ours.

But you have the anointing from the Holy One, so that all of you have true wisdom.

I write to you, not because you lack knowledge of the truth, but because you already know it, and lies have nothing in common with the truth. Who is the liar?

The one who denies that Jesus is the Christ.

This is an antichrist, who denies both the Father and the Son. The one who denies the Son is without the Father, and those who acknowledge the Son also have the Father.

Let what you heard, from the beginning, remain in you. If what you heard from the beginning, remains in you, you too, will remain in the Son and in the Father. And this is the promise he, himself, gave us: eternal life.

I write this to you, thinking of those who try to lead you astray.

You received from him, an anointing, and it remains in you, so you do not need someone to teach you. His anointing teaches you all things. It speaks the truth and does not lie to you; so remain in him, and keep what he has taught you.

And now, my children, live, in him, so that when he appears in his glory, we may be confident, and not ashamed, before him when he comes.

You know, that he is the Just One: know, then, that anyone living justly is born of God.

See what singular love the Father has for us: we are called children of God, and we really are. This is why the world does not know us, because it did not know him.

Beloved, we are God's children, and what we shall be has not, yet, been shown. Yet, when he appears in his glory, we know, that we shall be like him, for, then, we shall see him as he is. All who have such a hope, try to be pure, as he is pure.

Anyone who commits a sin, acts as an enemy of the law of God; any sin acts wickedly, because all sin is wickedness. You know, that he came to take away our sins, and that there is no sin in him. Whoever remains in him, has no sin, whoever sins, has not seen, or known him.

My little children, do not be led astray; those who do what is right are upright, just as Jesus Christ is upright. But those who sin belong to the devil, for the devil sins from the beginning.

This is why the Son of God was shown to us, he was to undo the works of the devil.

Those born of God do not sin, for the seed of God remains in them; they cannot sin, because they are born of God.

What is the way to recognize the children of God, and those of the devil? The one, who does not do what is right, is not of God; so, too, the one who does not love his brother or sister.

For this is the message taught to you, from the beginning: we must love one another. Do not imitate Cain, who killed his brother, for he belonged to the Evil One. Why did he kill him? Because he, himself, did evil, and his brother did good.

So, be not surprised, brothers, if the world hates us; we love our brothers and sisters, and with this, we know, that we have passed from death to life. The one who does not love, remains in death.

The one who hates his brother is a murderer, and, as you know, eternal life does not remain in the murderer.

This is how we have known what love is: he gave his life for us. We, too, ought to give our life for our brothers and sisters.

If anyone enjoys the riches of this world, but closes his heart when he sees his brother or sister in need, how will the love of God remain in him? My dear children, let us love, not only with words and with our lips, but in truth and in deed.

Then, we shall know that we are of the truth, and we may calm our conscience in his presence. Every time it reproaches us, let us say: God is greater than our conscience, and he knows everything.

When our conscience does not condemn us, dear friends, we may have complete confidence in God. Then, whatever we ask, we shall receive, since we keep his commands and do what pleases him.

His command is, that we believe in the name of his Son Jesus Christ, and that, we love one another, as he has commanded us.

Whoever keeps his commands remains in God and God in him. It is by the Spirit God has given us, that we know he lives in us.

My beloved, do not trust every inspiration. Test the spirits, to see, whether they come from God, because many false prophets are now in the world.

How will you recognize the Spirit of God? Any spirit recognizing Jesus as the Christ, who has taken our flesh, is of God. But any spirit that does not recognize Jesus, is not from God, it is the spirit of the antichrist. You have heard of his coming, and even, now, he is in the world.

You, my dear children, are of God, and you have already overcome these people, because the one who is in you, is more powerful than he who is in the world.

They are of the world and the world inspires them, and those of the world listen to them.

We are of God, and those who know God, listen to us, but those who are not of God, ignore us. This is how we know the spirit of truth, and the spirit of falsehood as well.

My dear friends, let us love one another, for love comes from God. Everyone who loves, is born of God and knows God.

Those who do not love have not known God, for God is love.

How did the love of God appear among us? God sent his only Son into this world, that we might have life, through him.

This is love: not that we loved God, but that, he first loved us and sent his Son, as an atoning sacrifice for our sins.

Dear friends, if such has been the love of God, we, too, must love one another.

No one has ever seen God, but if we love one another, God lives in us, and his love comes to its perfection in us.

How may we know that we live in God and he in us? Because God has given us his Spirit.

We ourselves have seen, and declare, that the Father sent his Son to save the world. Those who confess that Jesus is the Son of God, God remains in them, and they in God.

We have known the love of God and have believed in it. God is love. The one who lives in love, lives in God, and God in him.

When do we know, that we have reached a perfect love? When, in this world, we are like him, in everything, and expect, with confidence, the Day of Judgment.

There is no fear in love. Perfect love drives away fear, for fear has to do with punishment; those who fear do not know perfect love.

So, let us love one another, since he loved us first.

If you say, "I love God," while you hate your brother or sister, you are a liar. How can you love God, whom you do not see, if you do not love your brother, whom you see? We received from him, this commandment: let those who love God also love their brothers.

All those, who believe that Jesus is the Anointed, are born of God; whoever loves the Father, loves the Son. How may we know, that we love the children of God? If we love God and fulfill his commands,

for God's love requires us to keep his commands. In fact, his commandments are not a burden

because all those born of God overcome the world. And the victory, which overcomes the world, is our faith. Who has overcome the world? The one who believes that Jesus is the Son of God.

Jesus Christ was acknowledged through water, but also through blood. Not only water, but water and blood.

And the Spirit, too, witnesses to him, for the Spirit is truth.

There are, then, three testimonies; the Spirit, the water and the blood, and these three witnesses agree.

If we accept human testimony, with greater reason must we accept that of God, given in favor of his Son. If you believe in the Son of God, you have God's testimony in you.

But those who do not believe, make God a liar, since they do not believe his words when he witnesses to his Son.

What has God said? That he has granted us eternal life, and this life is in his Son. The one who has the Son has life, those who do not have the Son of God do not have life.

I write you, then, all these things, that you may know, that you have eternal life, all you, who believe in the name of the Son of God.

Through him we are fully confident that whatever we ask, according to his will, he will grant us. If we know that he hears us whenever we ask, we know that we already have what we asked of him.

If you see your brother committing sin, a sin which does not lead to death, pray for him, and God will give life to your brother. I speak, of course, of the sin which does not lead to death. There is also a sin that leads to death; I do not speak of praying about this. Every kind of wrongdoing is sin, but not all sin leads to death.

We know, that those born of God do not sin, but the one who was born of God, protects them, and the evil one does not touch them.

We know, that we belong to God, while the whole world lies in evil.

We know, that the Son of God has come and has given us power to know the truth. We are in him who is true, his Son Jesus Christ. He is the true God, and eternal life.

My dear children, keep yourselves from idols.

INVITATION TO
2 JOHN

The same person who wrote 1 John also had to write to other communities where the false teachers he opposed might go to spread their ideas and practices. A letter he wrote to another community has been preserved for us as 2 John. Its author addresses the community he's writing to as a *Lady* and calls its members her *children*. He describes the members of his own community as the *children of your chosen sister*. (This was apparently typical of early followers of Jesus. There's a similar greeting at the end of 1 Peter.) The writer identifies himself as a leader by using the title *elder*.

Apparently some people from this community had just come to visit him and he was pleased to learn they were walking in the truth—that is, they were maintaining the teaching they had heard from the beginning. But he had to warn the community (probably sending this letter with those returning home) not to support the false teachers in any way: *Even in greeting him, you would become an accomplice in his wicked deeds.* Despite its brevity, this letter expresses all of the themes that receive a more extensive development in 1 John.

| 2 JOHN |

I, the elder,

to the chosen Lady and her children, whom I love sincerely—and with me, all who know the truth—because of this same truth, which is, and will be, in us forever.

Grace, mercy and peace be with you, in the name of God, the Father, and of his Son, Christ Jesus, in truth and love.

I rejoiced greatly on meeting some of your children, who live in accordance with the truth, according to the command we have received from the Father. And now, I ask you, Lady—I write to you, not a new commandment, but that which we had, from the beginning—I ask you: let us love one another.

This is love: to walk according to his commandments. And this is the commandment: that you walk in love, as you have learned from the beginning.

Many deceivers have gone out into the world, people who do not acknowledge that Jesus is the Christ, who came in the flesh. They are impostors and antichrists. Take care of yourselves, that you do not lose the fruit of your labors, but receive a perfect reward. Everyone who goes beyond, and does not remain within the teaching of Christ, does not have God. The one who remains in the teaching, has both the Father and the Son. If anyone comes to you, and does not bring this teaching, do not receive him into your houses, or even greet him. Even in greeting him, you would become an accomplice in his wicked deeds.

I have many things to write to you, but I prefer not to use paper and ink. I hope to meet you and speak to you personally, that our joy may be full.

The children of your chosen sister greet you.

INVITATION TO
3 JOHN

While 2 John was written to warn a community of Jesus-followers against providing material assistance to false teachers, 3 John was written to address the opposite situation: to insist that a community provide a base of operations for traveling preachers who were walking in the truth. John had sent a letter to this community introducing and commending certain individuals, but Diotrephes, a leader in the community, refused to accommodate them. He opposed John's authority to the point of actually expelling anyone who supported the people he'd sent. A man named Gaius, however, put these preachers up in his own home, enabling them to carry out their mission. Word got back to John both of Diotrephes' resistance and of Gaius' loyalty. In this letter John sends Gaius a message of thanks and encouragement by the hand of Demetrius, another man he hopes will receive support. He also promises to come soon and set matters right.

| 3 JOHN |

I, the elder,

to my dear friend Gaius, whom I love sincerely.

Dear friend, may everything go well with you and may you enjoy health of body and soul. I greatly rejoiced with the friends who arrived, and testified to your faithfulness to the truth, namely, how you walk in the truth. Nothing gives me greater joy, than to know, that my children live in the truth.

Beloved, you do well to care for the brothers and sisters as you do. I mean, those coming from other places. They spoke of your charity before the assembled Church. It will be well, to provide them with what they need, to continue their journey, as if you did it for God. In reality, they have set out on the road, for his name without accepting anything from the pagans. We should receive such persons, making ourselves their cooperators in the work of the truth.

I have written these words to the Church. But Diotrephes, who is anxious to preside over it, does not acknowledge our authority. So, when I come, I will not cease reproaching his manner of acting, since he discredited us with words of evil intent. And not content with that, he does not receive the friends, and even restrains those who want to receive them, and expels them from the Church.

Dear friend, do not imitate evil, but only the good. Whoever does good is of God. Whoever does evil does not know God. Now, about Demetrius: everyone praises him, even the truth itself. We, too, praise him, and you know that our testimony is true.

I have many things to tell you, but I do not want to do it in writing. I hope to see you soon, and we will talk face to face.

Peace be with you. Your friends greet you. Greet the friends for me, each one by name.

INVITATION TO
REVELATION

The Roman Empire, like most kingdoms in the ancient world, portrayed itself as the divinely intended ruler over the earth. It justified its economic and political control on spiritual grounds. The religion of the empire included the worship of the traditional Roman gods and the veneration of the Caesars as divine beings. This tendency toward emperor worship began in earnest with Caesar Augustus, the one who oversaw the transition of Rome from a republic to an empire. The following inscription, from Asia Minor in 9 BC, shows how Caesar's rule was proclaimed in both political and religious terms:

> The providence which has ordered the whole of our life, showing concern and zeal, has ordained the most perfect consummation for human life by giving to it Augustus, by filling him with virtue for doing the work of a benefactor among men, and by sending in him, as it were, a savior for us and those who come after us, to make war to cease, to create order everywhere; the birthday of the god Augustus was the beginning for the world of the gospel that has come to men through him.

By the time of the emperor Domitian (AD 81–96), this gospel of the *pax Romana*, or Roman Peace, was well established. The wealthy cities of western Asia Minor were competing with one another for the emperor's favor and patronage, proclaiming his divinity and promoting a cult of emperor worship. Any resistance to this cult would put a city's hopes of imperial favor in jeopardy. But believers in Jesus who lived in these cities acknowledged a different Savior, and they worshiped only the true God.

God sent a message to these believers through a Jewish Christian prophet named John. He circulated among seven cities in the Roman province of Asia Minor, challenging and encouraging Jesus' followers in each place. On the island of Patmos, John received a vision in which he saw that the cult of emperor worship would soon become deadly to followers of Jesus. Believers needed to be warned to be on their guard against any compromise, and to be *faithful, even to death* in order to receive life as their *crown of life*.

John wrote down his vision and sent it as a circular letter to be read aloud in the churches under his care. He wanted it to be understood as a word directly from God, so he described it as a *prophecy*. John communicated the vision he received through a particular literary form, called *apocalypse*, which was well known in his day, even though it's unfamiliar to us now. This form was perfectly suited to his task. In an apocalypse, a visitor from heaven uses vivid symbols to disclose the secrets of the unseen world and the future. This visitor typically takes the recipient of the vision on a journey through heaven and offers a review of history leading up to a present crisis between good and evil. The vision enables the recipients to understand the spiritual dimensions of their situation and to respond to the crisis by remaining loyal to God. (The book itself is named Revelation, or Apocalypse, meaning *unveiling*.)

The vision report that John sent to the churches of Asia has four main parts. Each one is marked by a version of the phrase *in the Spirit*.

: In the first part, John is in the Spirit on Patmos and receives a vision on the Lord's Day. In this vision, Jesus speaks words of warning and encouragement to each of the seven churches (pp. 422–425).

: In the second part, John relates how he was taken in the Spirit into heaven and saw Jesus being exalted because he had redeemed humanity through his sacrifice. John also saw Jesus begin to execute God's judgment against his enemies, while protecting those who belonged to him. Next, the first coming of the Messiah and the threat against the early Christian community are depicted symbolically. John sees that Jesus will be victorious in the end, but in the meantime there is a call for endurance (pp. 425–438).

: This extended vision is interrupted by the third part of the book. John is taken in the Spirit to a wilderness, where he is shown the true spiritual state of the Roman Empire. Despite Rome's pretensions to glory, it is really drunken, greedy, blasphemous and immoral—and doomed to destruction (pp. 438–442).

: The long vision that begins in the second part of the book then continues to its conclusion. It depicts the triumph of the Messiah over all his enemies (pp. 442–444).

: Afterwards John is taken in the Spirit onto a mountain, where, in the fourth part of the book, he sees the new Jerusalem coming down out of heaven. The city is portrayed as the home of the true ruler over all things; it's the reality of which Rome is the parody. The vision closes with the promise that God's faithful servants will reign over the new creation (pp. 444–445).

While the symbols in the book may appear strange at first, the meaning of many of them becomes clear when viewed in light of John's circumstances and of the imagery found in other parts of the Bible. The number twelve, for example, which occurs repeatedly in the description of the new Jerusalem, describes the people of God, since there were twelve tribes of Israel and twelve apostles of Jesus. When John writes that the woman in the third part of the book is seated on seven mountains, he's identifying this character with Rome, the city of seven hills. With some care and reflection on the book's first-century setting, modern readers can interpret many of its symbols.

Revelation was written to warn followers of Jesus living in a specific place how they needed to respond to the challenge of a particular time. But the book also functions as the appropriate conclusion to the entire drama of the Bible. John's closing vision incorporates images from the Garden of Eden, the first story in the Bible. The world will experience a fresh beginning: *The One seated on the throne said, "See, I make all things new."* But until then, all who would reign with Jesus need to know that they can triumph only by following the path of Jesus. *This is, for the holy ones, the time of endurance and faith.*

| REVELATION |

The Revelation of Jesus Christ. God gave it to him, to let his servants know what is soon to take place.
He sent his angel to make it known to his servant, John,
who reports everything he saw, for this is the word of God, and the declaration of Jesus Christ.
Happy is the one who reads aloud these prophetic words,
and happy those who hear them, and treasure everything written here,
for the time is near.

From John,

to the seven churches of Asia:
receive grace and peace from him who is, who was, and who is to come,
and from the seven spirits of God, which are before his throne,
and from Jesus Christ, the faithful witness, the firstborn of the dead, the ruler of the kings of the earth.
To him who loves us, and has washed away our sins with his own blood,
making us a kingdom, and priests for God, his Father,
to him, be the glory and power, for ever and ever. Amen.

> See, he comes with the clouds,
> and everyone will see him,
>
> even those who pierced him;
> on his account, all the nations of the earth will beat their breast.
> Yes. It will be so.

"I am the Alpha and the Omega," says the Lord God, "the one who is, and who was, and who is to come: the Master of the universe."

I, John, your brother, who shares with you, in Jesus, the sufferings, the kingdom and the patient endurance, was on the island of Patmos, because of the word of God and witnessing to Jesus. On the Lord's day, the spirit took possession of me and I heard a voice behind me, which sounded like a trumpet, "Write down all that you see, in a book, and send it to the seven churches; of Ephesus, Smyrna, Pergamum, Thyatira, Sardis, Philadelphia and Laodicea."

I turned to see who was speaking to me; behind me were seven golden lamp stands and, in the middle of these, I saw someone, like a son of man, dressed in a long robe, tied with a golden girdle.

His head and his hair are white, as wool, or as snow, and his eyes are like flames of fire. His feet are like burnished bronze when it has been refined in a furnace. His voice is like the roaring of the waves.

I saw seven stars in his right hand, and a sharp, double-edged sword coming out of his mouth; his face shone, like the sun in all its brilliance.

Seeing him, I fell at his feet, like one dead; but he touched me with his right hand and said, "Do not be afraid. It is I, the First and the Last. I am the living one; I was dead; and now I am alive, for ever and ever; and mine are the keys of death and the netherworld. Now write what you have seen, both what is and what is yet to come. Know the secret of the seven stars you saw in my right hand, and the seven golden lamp stands: the seven stars are the angels of the seven churches, and the seven lamp stands are the seven churches.

Write this, to the angel of the church in Ephesus,

"Thus says the one who holds the seven stars in his right hand, and who walks among the seven golden lamp stands:

I know your works, your difficulties and your patient suffering. I know, you cannot tolerate evildoers, but have tested those who call themselves apostles, and have proved them to be liars. You have persevered, and have suffered for my name without losing heart.

Nevertheless, I have this complaint against you: you have lost your first love. Remember from where you have fallen, and repent, and do what you used to do before. If not, I will come to you, and remove your lamp stand from its place; this, I will do, unless you repent. Yet, it is in your favor, that you hate the doings of the Nicolaitans, which I also hate.

Let anyone who has ears, listen to what the Spirit says to the churches: To the victor I will give to eat of the tree of life, which is in God's paradise."

Write this to the angel of the church in Smyrna,

"Thus says the first and the last, he who was dead, and returned to life:
I know your trials and your poverty: you are rich, indeed. I know, how you are slandered, by those who pretend to be Jews, but are not, for they are, in fact, the synagogue of Satan. Do not be afraid of what will happen to you. The devil will throw some of you into prison, to test you, and there will be ten days of trials. Remain faithful, even to death, and I will give you the crown of life.

Let anyone who has ears, listen to what the Spirit says to the churches: The victor has nothing to fear, from the second death."

Write this, to the angel of the church in Pergamum,

"Thus says the one who has the sharp, double-edged sword:
I know where you live, where Satan's throne is, but you cling, firmly, to my name; you have not renounced me, not even in the days when Antipas, my faithful witness, was killed; in your place, where Satan lives.

Nevertheless, I have a few complaints against you: Some, among you, hold the teaching of Balaam, who taught Balak how to make the Israelites stumble, by eating food sacrificed to idols, and committing adultery. Also, among you, some follow the teaching of the Nicolaitans. Therefore, repent; if not, I will come to you, soon, to attack these people, with the sword of my mouth.

Let anyone who has ears, listen to what the Spirit says to the churches: To the victor, I will give the hidden manna. And I will also give a white stone, with a new name written on it, which no one knows, except the one who receives it."

Write this, to the angel of the church in Thyatira,

"Thus says the Son of God, whose eyes are like flames of fire, and whose feet are like burnished bronze. I know your works: your love, faith, service, patient endurance; and your later works, greater than the first.

Nevertheless, I have a complaint against you: you tolerate your Jezebel, this woman, who calls herself a prophetess; and is deceiving my servants; she teaches them prostitution, and the eating of food sacrificed to idols. I have given her time to repent, but she is unwilling to leave her prostitution. So, I am going to throw her onto a bed, and inflict severe trials on her partners in adultery, unless they repent of their evil. I will strike her children dead, and all the churches will know, that I am he, who probes the heart and mind; I will give each of you what your conduct deserves.

Listen to me, now, the rest of you in Thyatira. You do not hold with this teaching, and have not learned 'the secrets,' as they are called, which are, in fact, those of Satan. So I have no cause to reproach you, only, hold on to what you have, until I come. To the victor, who keeps to my ways to the end, I will give power over the nations, to rule them with an iron rod, and shatter them like earthen pots; he will be like me, who received this power from my Father. Moreover, I will give him the Morning Star.

Let anyone who has ears, listen to what the Spirit says to the churches."

Write this, to the angel of the church in Sardis,

"Thus says he, who holds the seven spirits of God and the seven stars:

I know your worth: you think you live, but you are dead. Wake up, and strengthen that which is not already dead. For I have found your works to be imperfect in the sight of my God. Remember what you were taught; keep it, and change your ways. If you do not repent, I will come upon you, like a thief, at an hour you least expect.

Yet, there are some left in Sardis who have not soiled their robes; these will come with me, dressed in white, since they deserve it. The victor will be dressed in white, and I will never erase his name from the book of life; instead, I will acknowledge it before my Father and his angels.

Let anyone who has ears, listen to what the Spirit says to the churches."

Write this, to the angel of the church in Philadelphia,

"Thus says he who is holy and true, who holds the key of David; if he opens, nobody shuts, and if he shuts, nobody opens.

I know your worth; I have opened a door before you, which nobody can close, because you have kept my word, and not renounced me, in spite of your lack of power. I am giving you some of the synagogue of Satan, who call themselves Jews, but they are only liars. I will make them fall at your feet, and recognize that I have loved you.

Because you have kept my words with patient endurance, I, for my part, will keep you safe in the hour of trial, that is coming upon the whole world, to test the people of the earth. I am coming soon; hold fast to what you have, lest anyone take your crown.

I will make the victor into a column, in the Sanctuary of my God, where he will stay, forever. I will write on him the name of my God, and the name of the city of my God, the new Jerusalem, which comes down, from my God in heaven, and my own new name. Let anyone who has ears, listen to what the Spirit says to the churches."

Write this, to the angel of the church in Laodicea,

"Thus says the Amen, the faithful and true witness, the beginning of God's creation:

I know your works: you are neither cold nor hot. Would, that, you were cold or hot! You are lukewarm, neither hot nor cold; so I will spit you out of my mouth. You think you are rich, and have piled up so much, that you need nothing, but you do not realize, that you are wretched, and to be pitied; poor, blind and naked.

I advise you, to buy from me gold, that has been tested by fire, so that you may be rich, and white clothes to wear, so that your nakedness may not shame you; and ointment for your eyes, that you may see. I reprimand and correct all those I love. Be earnest, and change your ways.

Look, I stand at the door and knock. If you hear my call, and open the door, I will come in to you, and have supper with you, and you, with me. I will let the victor sit with me, on my throne, just as I was victorious, and took my place with my Father, on his throne. Let anyone who has ears, listen to what the Spirit says to the churches."

After this, I looked up, to the wall of the sky, and saw an open door. The voice which I had first heard speaking to me, like a trumpet, said, "Come up here and I will show you what will come in the future."

Immediately, I was seized by the spirit. There, in heaven, was a throne, and one sitting on it. He who sat there, looked like jasper and carnelian, and round the throne, was a rainbow, resembling an emerald.

In a circle, around the throne, are twenty-four thrones, and seated on these, are twenty-four elders, dressed in white clothes, with golden crowns on their heads. Flashes of lightning come forth from the throne, with voices and thunderclaps. Seven flaming torches burn before the throne; these are the seven spirits of God.

Before the throne, there is a platform, transparent, like crystal. Around and beside the throne, stand four living creatures, full of eyes, both in front and behind. The first living creature is like a lion, the second, like a bull; the third has the face of a man, and the fourth looks like a flying eagle. Each of the four living creatures has six wings, full of eyes, all around as well as within; day and night, they sing without ceasing,

> Holy, holy, holy is the Lord God,
> master of the universe,
> who was, and is, and is to come.

Whenever the living creatures give glory, honor and thanks to the one on the throne, he who lives for ever and ever, the twenty-four elders fall down before him, and worship the one who lives for ever and ever. They lay their crowns in front of the throne and say,

> Our Lord and God, worthy are you
> to receive glory, honor and power!

> For you have created all things;
> by your will they came to be and were made.

Then, I saw in the right hand of him who was seated on the throne, a scroll, written on both sides, sealed with seven seals. A mighty angel exclaimed, in a loud voice, "Who is worthy to open this and break the seals?"

But no one in heaven or on earth, or in the netherworld, was found able to open the book and read it. I wept much, when I saw that no one was found worthy to open the book and read it. Then, one of the elders said to me, "Do not weep. Look, the lion of the tribe of Judah, the shoot of David, has conquered; he will open the book of the seven seals."

And I saw next to the throne, with its four living creatures, and the twenty-four elders, a Lamb, standing, although it had been slain. I saw him with seven horns and seven eyes, which are the seven spirits of God, sent out to all the earth.

The Lamb moved forward, and took the book from the right hand of him who was seated on the throne. When he took it, the four living creatures and the twenty-four elders bowed before the Lamb. They all held in their hands, harps, and golden cups full of incense, which are the prayers of the holy ones.

This is the new song they sang:

> You are worthy to take the book
> and open its seals,
>
> for you were slain,
> and by your blood, you purchased, for God,
> people, of every race, language and nation;
>
> and you made them a kingdom, and priests for our God,
> and they shall reign over the land.

I went on looking; I heard the noise of a multitude of angels, gathered around the throne, the living creatures and the elders, numbering millions of millions, crying out with a loud voice:

> Worthy is the Lamb, who was slain, to receive
> power and riches, wisdom and strength,
> honor, glory and praise.

Then, I heard the voice of the whole universe, heaven, earth, sea, and the place of the dead; every creature cried out:

> To him who sits upon the throne, and to the Lamb,
> be praise, honor, glory and power, for ever and ever.

And the four living creatures said, Amen, while the elders bowed down and worshiped.

I saw the Lamb opening the first of the seven seals, and I heard one of the four living creatures cry out, with a voice like thunder, "Come and see!"

A white horse appeared, and its rider had a bow. He was crowned, and he went out as a conqueror, and he will conquer.

When he opened the second seal, I heard the second living creature cry out, "Come!" Then, another horse, the color of fire, came out. Its rider was ordered to take peace away from the earth, that people might kill one another; so he was given a great sword.

When he opened the third seal, I heard the third creature cry out, "Come!" This time, it was a black horse, and its rider held a balance in his hand. Then, from the midst of the four living creatures, a voice was heard: "A measure of wheat for a piece of silver, and three measures of barley for a piece, as well! Do not spoil the oil or the wine."

When he opened the fourth seal, I heard a cry from the fourth living creature, "Come!" A greenish horse appeared, its rider was called Death, and the Netherworld rode behind him. He was allowed to utterly destroy, by sword, famine, pestilence and wild beasts, a fourth of the inhabitants of the earth.

When he opened the fifth seal, I saw, under the altar, the spirits of those who proclaimed the word of God, and were slain, for its sake. They began to cry aloud, "Holy and righteous Lord, how long will it be, before you render justice, and avenge our blood on the inhabitants of the earth?" Then, each one of them was given a white garment, and they were told to wait a little while, until the number of their brothers and sisters, and fellow servants, who would be killed, as they had been, would be completed.

And my vision continued. When the Lamb opened the sixth seal, there was a violent earthquake. The sun became black, as a mourning dress, and the whole moon turned blood-red, and the stars in the sky fell to the earth, like dry figs falling from a fig tree shaken by a hurricane. The sky was folded up like rolled parchment; there was no mountain or continent that was not removed from its place. The kings of the earth and their ministers, the generals, the rich and the powerful, and all the people, slaves, as well as free persons, hid, in caves, or among rocks, on the mountains, saying, "Fall on us, mountains and rocks, and hide us, for we are afraid of him who sits on the throne, and of the wrath of the Lamb. The great day of his wrath has come, and who can endure it?"

After this, there were four angels standing at the four corners of the earth, holding back the four winds, to prevent their blowing against the earth, the sea, and the trees. I saw another angel, ascending from the sunrise, carrying the seal of the living God, and he cried out with a loud voice, to the four angels empowered to harm the earth and the sea, "Do not harm the earth or the sea or the trees, until we have sealed the servants of our God upon their foreheads."

Then, I heard the number of those marked with the seal: a hundred and forty-four thousand, from all the tribes of the people of Israel:

from the tribe of Judah, twelve thousand were sealed;
from the tribe of Reuben, twelve thousand;
from the tribe of Gad, twelve thousand;
from the tribe of Asher, twelve thousand;
from the tribe of Naphtali, twelve thousand;
from the tribe of Manasseh, twelve thousand;
from the tribe of Simeon, twelve thousand;
from the tribe of Levi, twelve thousand;
from the tribe of Issachar, twelve thousand;
from the tribe of Zebulun, twelve thousand;
from the tribe of Joseph, twelve thousand;
from the tribe of Benjamin, twelve thousand.

After this, I saw a great crowd, impossible to count, from every nation, race, people and tongue, standing before the throne, and the Lamb, clothed in white, with palm branches in their hands, and they cried out with a loud voice,

"Who saves, but our God,
who sits on the throne,
and the Lamb?"

All the angels were around the throne, the elders and the four living creatures; they, then, bowed before the throne, with their faces to the ground, to worship God. They said,

Amen.
Praise, glory,
wisdom, thanks, honor,
power and strength
to our God forever and ever.
Amen!

At that moment, one of the elders spoke up, and said to me, "Who are these people clothed in white, and where did they come from?" I answered, "Sir, it is you who know this."

The elder replied, "They, are those who have come out of the great persecution; they have washed, and made their clothes white, in the blood of the Lamb.

> This is why they stand before the throne of God,
> and serve him, day and night, in his Sanctuary.

> He, who sits on the throne,
> will spread his tent over them.

> Never again, will they suffer hunger or thirst,
> or be burned by the sun, or any scorching wind.

> For the Lamb, near the throne,
> will be their Shepherd,
> and he will bring them to springs of life-giving water,
> and God will wipe away their tears."

When the Lamb opened the seventh seal, there was silence in heaven, for about half an hour.

Then, I looked at the seven angels standing before God, who were given seven trumpets.

Another angel came, and stood before the altar of incense, with a golden censer. He was given much incense to be offered, with the prayers of all the holy ones, on the golden altar before the throne; and the cloud of incense rose, with the prayers of the holy ones, from the hands of the angel, to the presence of God. Then, the angel took the censer, and filled it with burning coals from the altar, and threw them on the earth: and there came thunder, lightning and earthquakes.

The seven angels with the seven trumpets prepared to sound them. When the first angel blew his trumpet, there came hail and fire, mixed with blood, which fell on the earth. And a third of the earth was burned up with a third of the trees and the green grass.

When the second angel blew his trumpet, something, like a great mountain, was thrown into the sea, and a third of the sea was turned into blood. At once, a third of the living creatures in the sea died, and a third of the ships perished.

When the third angel sounded his trumpet, a great star fell from heaven, like a ball of fire, on a third of the rivers and springs. The star is called Wormwood, and a third of the waters was turned into wormwood, and many people died because of the water, which had turned bitter.

The fourth angel blew his trumpet, and a third of the sun, the moon, and the stars was affected. Daylight decreased one third, and the light at night as well.

And my vision continued: I noticed an eagle flying through the highest heaven, and crying with a loud voice, "Woe, woe, woe to the inhabitants of the land, when the last three angels sound their trumpets."

And the fifth angel blew his trumpet. I, then, saw a star fall from heaven to earth. The star was given the key to the depths of the abyss. He opened the abyss, and a cloud of smoke rose, as if from a great furnace, which darkened the sun and the air.

Locusts came from this smoke and spread throughout the earth. They were given the same harmful power as the scorpions of the earth. Then, they were told not to harm the meadows, the green grass or the trees, but only the people who do not bear the seal of God upon their foreheads. They were not to kill them, but only torture them for five months. This pain is like the sting of scorpions. In those days, people will look for death, but will not find it; they will long to die, but death will elude them. These locusts look like horses equipped for battle; they wear golden crowns on their heads, and their faces are like those of human beings. Their hair is like women's hair, and their teeth, like lion's teeth; their chests are like iron breastplates; and the noise of their wings, like the roar of an army of chariots and horses, rushing for battle.

Their tails are like those of scorpions and have stings; the power they have to torture people for five months is in their tails. These locusts have a king, who is the angel of the abyss, whose name in Hebrew is Abaddon, or Apollyon in Greek (Destruction).

The first woe has passed. Two others are to come.

The sixth angel blew his trumpet. Then, I heard a voice calling from the corners of the golden altar before God. It said to the sixth angel, who had just sounded the trumpet, "Release the four angels chained at the banks of the great river Euphrates."

And the four angels were released, who had been waiting for this year, this month, this day and this hour, ready to utterly destroy a third of humankind. The number of the soldiers on horses was two hundred million; this is the number I heard.

In my vision, I saw those horses and their riders: they wear breastplates the color of fire, hyacinth and sulfur. The heads of the horses look like lions' heads; and fire, smoke and sulfur come out of their mouths.

Then, a third of humankind was killed by these three plagues: fire, smoke and sulfur, which the horses released, through their mouths, for the power of the horses was both in their mouths and in their tails. Their tails, in fact, look like serpents, and their heads are able to inflict injury as well.

However, the rest of humankind who were not killed by these plagues, did not renounce their way of life: they went on worshiping the demons, keeping those idols of gold, silver, bronze, stone and wood that cannot see, hear or walk. No, they did not repent of their crimes, or their sorcery, or their sexual immorality or their theft.

Then, I saw another mighty angel, coming down from heaven, wrapped in a cloud. A rainbow was around his head, his face was like the sun, and his legs, like pillars of fire. I could see a small book open in his hand. He stood, his right foot planted on the sea and his left on the land, and called, in a loud voice, like the roaring of a lion. Then, the seven thunders sounded their own message.

I was about to write what the seven thunders had sounded, when a voice from heaven said to me, "Keep the words of the seven thunders secret, and do not write them down."

And the angel I saw standing on the sea and land, raised his right hand to heaven, swearing by him, who lives for ever and ever, and who created the heavens, the earth, the sea and everything in them.

He said, "There is no more delay; as soon as the trumpet call of the seventh angel is heard, the mysterious plan of God will be fulfilled, according to the good news he proclaimed through his servants, the prophets."

And the voice I had heard from heaven, spoke again, saying to me, "Go near the angel who stands on the sea and on the land, and take the small book open in his hand." So, I approached the angel and asked him for the small book; he said to me, "Take it and eat; although it be sweet as honey in your mouth, it will be bitter to your stomach."

I took the small book from the hand of the angel, and ate it. It was sweet as honey in my mouth, but when I had eaten it, it turned bitter in my stomach. Then, I was told, "You must, again, proclaim God's words, about many peoples, nations, tongues and kings."

Then I was given a staff, like a measuring stick, and I was told, "Go and measure the temple of God and the altar, and count those who worship there. Do not bother to measure the outer courtyard, for this has been given to the pagans, who will trample over the holy city for forty-two months. Meanwhile, I will entrust my word to my two witnesses, who will proclaim it for one thousand two hundred and sixty days, dressed in sackcloth."

These are the two olive trees, and the two lamps, which are before the Lord of the earth. If anyone intends to harm them, fire will come out of their mouths, to devour their enemies: this is how whoever intends to harm them will perish. They have the power to close the sky, and hold back the rain, during the time of their prophetic mission; they also have the power to change water into blood, and punish the earth, with a thousand plagues, any time they wish.

But when my witnesses have fulfilled their mission, the beast that comes up from the abyss, will make war upon them, and will conquer and kill them. Their dead bodies will lie in the square of the great city, which the believers figuratively call Sodom, or Egypt, where their Lord was crucified. And their dead bodies will be exposed, for three days and a half, to people of all tribes, races, languages and nations, who will be ordered not to have them buried.

Then, the inhabitants of the earth will rejoice, congratulate one another, and exchange gifts among themselves, because these two prophets were a torment to them.

But after those three and a half days, a spirit of life, coming from God, entered them. They, then, stood up, and those who looked at them were seized with great fear. A loud voice from heaven called them, "Come up here." So they went up to heaven, in the midst of the clouds, in the sight of their enemies.

At that moment, there was a violent earthquake, which destroyed a tenth of the city, and claimed seven thousand victims. The rest were overcome with fear, and acknowledged the God of heaven.

The second woe has passed. The third is coming soon.

The seventh angel blew his trumpet; then, loud voices resounded in heaven:

> "The world has now become
> the kingdom of our God and of his Christ.
> He will reign for ever and ever."

The twenty-four elders, who sit on their thrones before God, bowed down to worship God, saying,

> We thank you, Lord God,
> Master of the universe,
> who are and who were,
>
> for you have begun your reign,
> making use of your invincible power.
>
> The nations raged
> but your wrath has come,
>
> the time to judge the dead
> and reward your servants the prophets,
>
> the saints and those who honor your Name—
> whether great or small—
>
> and destroy those who destroy the earth.

Then, the Sanctuary of God, in the heavens, was opened, and the Ark of the Covenant of God could be seen inside the Sanctuary. There were flashes of lightning, peals of thunder, an earthquake, and a violent hailstorm.

A great sign appeared in heaven: a woman, clothed with the sun, with the moon under her feet, and a crown of twelve stars on her head. She was pregnant, and cried out in pain, looking to her time of delivery.

Then, another sign appeared: a huge, red dragon, with seven heads and ten horns, and wearing seven crowns on its heads. It had just swept along a third of the stars of heaven with its tail, throwing them down to the earth.

The dragon stood in front of the woman, who was about to give birth, so that, it might devour the child as soon as it was born. She gave birth to a male child, the one who is to rule all the nations with an iron scepter; then, her child was seized, and taken up to God, and to his throne, while the woman fled to the desert, where God had prepared a place for her; there, she would be looked after, for one thousand two hundred and sixty days.

War broke out in heaven, with Michael and his angels battling with the dragon. The dragon fought back with his angels, but they were defeated, and lost their place in heaven. The great dragon, the ancient serpent, known as the devil, or Satan, seducer of the whole world, was thrown out. He was hurled down to earth, together with his angels.

Then, I heard a loud voice from heaven:

> Now has salvation come,
> with the power and the kingdom of our God,
> and the rule of his anointed.

> For our brothers' accuser has been cast out,
> who accused them night and day, before God.

> They conquered him, by the blood of the Lamb,
> and by the word of their testimony,

> for they gave up their lives,
> going to death.

> Rejoice, therefore, O you heavens,
> and you who dwell in them;

> but woe to you, earth and sea,
> for the devil has come to you, in anger,
> knowing that he has but a little time.

When the dragon saw that he had been thrown down to earth, he pursued the woman, who had given birth to the male child. Then, the woman was given the two wings of the great eagle, so that, she might fly into the desert, where she would be looked after for three and a half years. The serpent poured water out of his mouth after the woman, to carry her away in the flood, but the earth came to her rescue: it opened its mouth and swallowed the flood, which the dragon had poured from its mouth. Then, the dragon was furious with the woman, and went off to wage war on the rest of her children, those who keep God's commandments and bear witness to Jesus. And he stood on the seashore.

Then, I saw a beast, rising out of the sea, with ten horns and seven heads, with ten crowns on its horns. On each head was a title challenging God. The beast I saw looked like a leopard, with paws like a bear and a mouth like a lion. The dragon passed on his power, his throne and his great authority to the beast.

One of its heads seemed to be fatally wounded but this wound healed. The whole earth wondered and they followed the beast. People prostrated themselves before the dragon, who had given such authority to the beast, and they prostrated themselves before the beast, saying, "Who is like the beast? Who can oppose it?"

The beast was given speech; and it spoke boastful and blasphemous words against God; it was allowed to wield its power for forty-two months. It spoke blasphemies against God, his name and his Sanctuary, that is, those who already dwell in heaven.

It was allowed to make war on the saints and to conquer them. It was given authority over people, of every tribe, language and nation; this is why all the inhabitants of the earth will worship before it, those, whose names have not been written in the book of life of the slain Lamb, since the foundation of the world.

Let anyone who has ears to hear, listen:

> If your lot is the prison,
> to prison you will go;
> if your lot is to be killed by the sword,
> by the sword will you be slain.

This is, for the holy ones, the time of endurance and faith.

Then, I saw another beast rise out of the earth, with two horns like the Lamb but speaking like the dragon. This second beast is totally at the service of the first one, and enjoys its authority. So, it makes the world, and its inhabitants, worship the first beast, whose mortal wound has been healed. It works great wonders, even making fire descend from heaven to earth, in the sight of all.

Through these great wonders, which it is able to do on behalf of the beast, it deceives the inhabitants of the earth, persuading them to make a statue of the beast which, although wounded by the sword, is still alive. It has been allowed, to give a spirit to this statue; the statue of the beast speaks, and those who refuse to worship it are killed. So, this second beast makes everyone—great and small, rich and poor, free and enslaved—be branded on the right hand, or on the forehead, and no one can buy or sell, unless he has been branded with the name of the beast, or with the number of its name.

Let us see who is wise! If you are clever, you can interpret the number of the Beast; it is 666 and it is the name of a certain person.

I was given another vision: The Lamb was standing on Mount Zion, surrounded by one hundred and forty-four thousand people, who had his name, and his Father's name, written on their foreheads. A sound reverberated in heaven, like the sound of the roaring of waves, or deafening thunder; it was like a chorus of singers, accompanied by their harps.

They sing a new song before the throne, in the presence of the four living creatures and the elders, a song, which no one can learn, except the hundred and forty-four thousand, who have been taken from the earth. They are those who were not defiled with women, but were chaste; these are given, to follow the Lamb wherever he goes. They are the first taken from humankind, who are already of God and the Lamb. No deceit has been found in them; they are faultless.

Then, I saw another angel, flying high in the sky, sent to proclaim the definitive good news to the inhabitants of the earth, to every nation, race, language and people. He cried out with a loud voice, "Give God glory and honor, for the hour of his judgment has come. Worship him, who made the heavens, the earth, the sea and all the waters."

Another angel followed him, crying out, "Fallen is Babylon the great, fallen, the prostitute, who has made all the nations drunk with her unleashed prostitution!"

A third angel, then, followed, shouting aloud, "If anyone worships the beast, or its image, or has his forehead or hand branded, he will also drink the wine of God's anger, which has been prepared, undiluted, in the cup of his fury: he will be tortured by fire and brimstone, in the presence of the holy angels and the Lamb."

The smoke of their torment goes up for ever and ever; for there is no rest, day or night, for those who worshiped the beast and its image, and for those who were branded with the mark of its name.

This is the time for patient endurance among the holy ones, for those who keep the commandments of God and faith in Jesus. I heard someone from heaven say, "Write this: Happy, from now on are the dead who have died in the Lord. The Spirit says: Let them rest from their labors; their good deeds go with them."

Then, I had this vision. I saw a white cloud, and the one sitting on it, like a son of man, wearing a golden crown on his head and a sharp sickle in his hand. An angel came out of the Sanctuary, calling loudly, to the one sitting on the cloud, "Put in your sickle and reap, for harvest time has come, and the harvest of the earth is ripe." He, who was sitting on the cloud, swung his sickle at the earth and reaped the harvest.

Then, another angel, who also had a sharp sickle, came out of the heavenly Sanctuary. Still, another angel, the one who has charge of the altar fire, emerged, and shouted to the first, who held the sharp sickle, "Swing your sharp sickle, and reap the bunches of the vine of the earth, for they are fully ripe." So, the angel swung his sickle and gathered in the vintage, throwing all the grapes into the great wine press of the anger of God. The grapes were trodden outside the city, and blood flowed from the wine press, to the height of the horses' bridles, and over an area of sixteen hundred furlongs.

Then, I saw another great and marvelous sign in the heavens: seven angels brought seven plagues, which are the last, for with these, the wrath of God will end. There was a sea of crystal, mingled with fire, and the conquerors of the beast, of its name and the mark of its name stood by it.

They had been given the celestial harps, and they sang the song of Moses, the servant of God, and the song of the Lamb:

> Great and marvelous are your works, O Lord,
> God and Master of the universe.
>
> Justice and truth guide your steps,
> O King of the nations.
>
> Lord, who will not give honor and glory to your name?
> For you alone are holy.
>
> All the nations will come and bow before you,
> for they have now seen your judgments.

Then, the Sanctuary of the Tent of Divine Declarations was opened, and the seven angels, bringing the seven plagues, came out of the Sanctuary, clothed in pure and bright linen, with their waists girded with golden belts. One of the four living creatures gave the seven angels seven golden cups, full of the wrath of God, who lives for ever and ever. Then, the Sanctuary was filled with smoke that wraps God's glory and power, so that no one could enter, until the seven plagues of the seven angels were completed.

I heard a loud voice calling from the Sanctuary to the seven angels, "Go, and empty on the earth, the seven cups of the wrath of God."

The first angel went to empty his cup on the earth, and malignant and painful sores appeared on the people who bore the mark of the beast, and had bowed before its image. The second angel emptied his cup into the sea, which turned into blood, like that of the dead, and every living thing in the sea died.

The third angel emptied his cup into the rivers and springs, that turned into blood. And I heard the angel of the waters say,

> "You, who are and who were, O Holy One,
> you are just in punishing them in this way;
>
> since they have shed the blood
> of your holy ones and the prophets,
>
> you have made them drink blood;
> they rightly deserved it."

I heard another cry from the altar,

> "Yes, Lord and God, Master of the universe,
> your judgments are true and just."

The fourth angel poured out his cup on the sun, and its heat began to scorch people. They were severely burned, and began to insult God, who has power over those plagues, instead of acknowledging him.

The fifth angel emptied his cup on the throne of the beast, and suddenly his kingdom was in darkness, and the people bit their tongues in agony. They insulted the Most High God for their pain and wounds, but they did not repent.

The sixth angel poured out his cup on the great river Euphrates; then, its water was dried up, leaving a free passageway for the kings of the east. I saw coming from the mouths of the monster, the beast and the false prophet, three unclean spirits, which looked like frogs. They are, in fact, spirits of demons, that perform marvelous things, and go to the kings of the whole world, to gather them for battle on the great day of God, the master of the universe.

> "Beware! I come like a thief; happy is the one who stays awake, and does not take off his clothes; so he will not have to go naked, and his whole body be exposed for all to see."

Then, they assembled them, at the place called Armageddon in Hebrew (or the Hills of Megiddo).

The seventh angel emptied his cup into the air. Then, a voice came forth, from the throne, and was heard outside the Sanctuary, saying, "It is done." And there were flashes of lightning, peals of thunder and a violent earthquake. No, never has there been an earthquake so violent, since people existed on earth. The great city was split into three, while the cities of the nations collapsed. For the time had come for Babylon the Great to be remembered before God, and to be given the cup of the foaming wine of his anger.

Then, the continents withdrew and the mountain ranges hid. Great hailstones from heaven, as heavy as stones, dropped on the people, and the people insulted God, because of this disastrous hailstorm, for it was truly a terrible plague.

Then, one of the seven angels of the seven cups came to me, and said, "Now, I will show you the judgment of the sovereign prostitute, who dwells on the great waters. She, it is, who let the kings of the earth sin with her; and with the wine of her lewdness, the inhabitants of the earth have become drunk."

The angel brought me to the desert: it was a new vision. There, a woman was seated on a red beast. The beast, which had seven heads and ten horns, covered itself with titles, and statements that offend God. The woman was clothed in purple and scarlet, with ornaments of gold, precious stones and pearls. She held in her hands a golden cup, full of loathsome idolatry and impure prostitution. Her name could be read on her forehead, written in a mysterious way:

BABYLON THE GREAT,
MOTHER OF PROSTITUTES
AND OF THE LOATHSOME IDOLS OF THE WHOLE WORLD.

And I saw, that the woman was drunk with the blood of the holy ones and the martyrs of Jesus.

What I saw greatly surprised me, but the angel said to me, "Why are you surprised? I will reveal to you the secret of this woman, and of the beast with seven heads and ten horns that she mounts. The beast you saw has been, though, it, is not. It will come up from the abyss, and then go to perdition. What a surprise for the inhabitants of the earth, whose names are not written in the book of life, from the creation of the world! They will marvel, on discovering, that, the beast who has been, is not, and passes away.

Let us see if you guess: the seven heads are seven hills on which the woman sits. And they are also seven kings, five of which have already fallen, one is in power, and the seventh has not yet come, but will remain only a short while. The beast that has been but, is not, can be considered as the eighth, though it takes place among the seven; and it goes to perdition.

The ten horns are ten kings, who have not, yet, received power, but will have authority, for an hour, with the beast. They all have, only one aim, and they place their authority and power, at the service of the beast. They will fight against the Lamb, but the Lamb will conquer them, for he is Lord of lords and King of kings; and with him, will be his followers, who have been called, and chosen, and are faithful.

The angel went on, "Those waters you saw, on which the prostitute is seated, are peoples, multitudes, and nations of every language. The ten horns, and the beast itself, will plan evil against the prostitute. They will destroy her, and leave her naked; they will eat her flesh, and set her on fire. God makes use of them, to carry out his plan, so he has inspired, them with their common purpose, and they will place their power at the service of the beast, until the words of God are fulfilled. A last word: the woman you saw, is the great city which reigns over the kings of the whole world."

After this, I saw another angel, coming down from heaven. So great was his authority, that the whole earth was lit up with his glory. In a strong voice he cried out:

"Fallen is Babylon the great! Fallen!
She has become a haunt of demons,

a lodge for every unclean spirit,
a nest for any filthy and disgusting bird.

She has made all nations drunk
with the wine of her lewdness,

fornicated with kings of the earth,
and glutted the world's merchants
with her wantonness and wealth."

Then, I heard another voice from heaven:

"Depart from her, my people,
lest you share in her evil,
and so share in her punishments;

for her sins are piled up to heaven,
and God keeps count of her crimes.
Give back to her as she has given,
pay her twice, for what she has done.
Let her drink a double portion
of what she made others do.

> Give her as much torment and grief
> as the wantonness she enjoyed herself.

> For she said to herself,
> 'I sit as queen, I am not a widow,
> never, will I go into mourning!'

> And so, suddenly, her plagues will come—
> death, mourning and famine.

> She will be consumed by fire,
> for mighty is the Lord, the judge,
> who has passed sentence on her."

The kings, who shared her luxury, and committed adultery with her, will see the smoke as she burns, and they will weep and lament. They will, nevertheless, keep their distance, terrified at her punishment, and exclaim:

> "Alas, alas! Great city that you are,
> O Babylon, seat of power!

> Your doom has come in a single hour!"

The merchants of the world will mourn over her, for they will lose a market for their goods—their cargoes of gold and silver, precious stones and pearls, fine linen and purple garments, silk and scarlet cloth, fragrant wood, ivory pieces and expensive furniture, bronze, iron and marble, cinnamon and spices, perfume, myrrh and frankincense, wine and olive oil, fine flour and grain, cattle and sheep, horses and carriages, slaves and human lives. They will say:

> "Gone is the fruit you longed for.
> Gone are your luxury and splendor.
> Never will you recover them, never!"

The merchants who dealt in these goods, who grew rich from business with the city, will stand at a safe distance, for fear of her punishment. Weeping and mourning, they will cry out:

> "Woe, woe to the great city,
> to the linen and purple and scarlet you wore,
> to your gold and pearls, your finery,

> your great wealth, destroyed in an hour!"

Every captain and navigator, every sailor and seafarer, will stand afar, crying out, on seeing the smoke going up, as the city burns to the ground. "What city could have compared with this one?" They will pour dust on their heads and cry out in mourning:

"Alas, alas, great city,
where all, who had ships at sea,
grew rich, through her trade!

In an hour, she has been devastated."

Rejoice over her, O heavens!
Rejoice, prophets, saints and apostles!

God has rendered justice to you.

A powerful angel picked up a boulder, the size of a large millstone, and threw it into the sea, saying:

"With such violence will Babylon, the great city, be thrown down, never again to be seen.

Never again, will tunes of harpists, minstrels, trumpeters and flutists be heard in you. Never again, will an artisan of any trade, be found in you. Never again, will the noise of the mill be heard.

Never again, will the light of a lamp shine in you. The voice of bridegroom and bride will never, again, be heard in you.

Because your traders were the world's great, and you led the nations astray by your magic spell. In this city was found blood, of prophets and saints—yes, the blood of all who have been slain on the earth."

After this, I heard what sounded like the loud singing of a great assembly in heaven:

Alleluia!
Salvation, glory and might belong to our God,
for his judgments are true and just.

He has condemned the great harlot
who corrupted the world with her adultery.

He has avenged his servants' blood,
shed by her hand, in harlotry.

Once more, they sang:

Alleluia!
The smoke from her goes up, for ever and ever!

The twenty-four elders, and the four living creatures, fell down and worshiped God, seated on the throne. And they cried:

Amen! Alleluia!

A voice came from the throne:

> "Praise our God,
> all you, his servants,
>
> all you, who revere him,
> both small and great!"

Then, I heard what sounded like a great crowd, like the roaring of the waves, like peals of thunder, answering:

> Alleluia!
> The Lord now reigns,
> our Lord, the Master of the universe!
>
> Let us rejoice and be glad
> and give him glory!
>
> This is the time to celebrate the wedding of the Lamb,
> his bride has made herself ready.
>
> Fine linen, bright and clean,
> is given her to wear.

This linen stands for the good works of the holy ones.

Then, the angel told me, "Write: Happy are those invited to the wedding of the Lamb." And he went on, "These are true words of God."

As I fell down at his feet, to worship him, he said to me, "Beware, I am but a servant, like you and your brothers, who utter the testimonies of Jesus (these testimonies of Jesus are proclaimed through the spirit of the prophets). Worship God alone."

Then, I saw heaven opened, and a white horse appeared. Its rider is the Faithful and True; he judges, and wages just wars. His eyes are flames of fire; he wears many crowns, and written on him is his own name, which no one can understand, except himself. He is clothed in a cloak, drenched in blood. His name is the Word of God.

The armies of heaven, clothed in pure white linen, follow him on white horses. A sharp sword comes out of his mouth. With it, he will strike the nations, for he must rule them with an iron rod. He treads the wine press of the burning wrath of God, the Master of the universe. This is why, this title is written on his cloak and on his thigh:

KING OF KINGS AND LORD OF LORDS.

I also saw an angel, standing in the sun. He cried out with a loud voice, to all the birds of the air, "Come here, to the great feast of God. Come, and eat the flesh of kings, of generals and of the mighty; come, and devour the soldier and his horse, flesh of all, both free and slaves, both small and great."

Then, I saw the beast, with the kings of the earth, and their armies, gathered together, to fight against him, who rides on the horse, and his army. But the beast was captured, with the false prophet who served it, and performed signs, by which he deceived those, who had received the mark of the beast and worshiped its statue. The two were thrown, alive, into the fiery lake of burning sulfur, and all the rest were killed by the sword, which comes from the mouth of the rider who mounts the horse. And all the birds were fed with their flesh.

Then, an angel came down from heaven, holding in his hand the key to the Abyss, and a huge chain. He seized the monster, the ancient serpent, namely Satan or the devil, and chained him for a thousand years. He threw him into the abyss, and closed its gate with the key, then secured it with locks, that he might not deceive the nations in the future, until the thousand years have passed. Then, he will be released for a little while.

There were thrones, and seated on them were those with the power to judge. I, then, saw the spirits of those who had been beheaded, for having held the teachings of Jesus, and on account of the word of God. I saw all those, who had refused to worship the beast, or its image, or receive its mark on the forehead, or on the hand. They returned to life, and reigned with the Messiah for a thousand years. This is the first resurrection. The rest of the dead will not return to life before the end of the thousand years.

Happy and holy is the one, who shares in the first resurrection, for the second death has no power over them; they will be priests of God, and of his Messiah, and reign with him a thousand years.

At the end of these thousand years, Satan will be released from his prison; then, he will set out to deceive the nations of the four corners of the world, namely Gog and Magog, and gather them for war. What an army, so numerous, like the sand of the seashore! They invaded the land, and surrounded the camp of the holy ones, the most beloved city, but fire came down from heaven and devoured them.

Then, the devil, the seducer, was thrown into the lake of fire and sulfur, where the beast and the false prophet already were. Their torment will last day and night, for ever and ever.

After that, I saw a great and splendid throne, and the one seated upon it. At once, heaven and earth disappeared, leaving no trace. I saw the dead, both great and small, standing before the throne, while books were opened. Another book, the book of life, was also opened. Then, the dead were judged, according to the records of these books, that is, each one according to his works.

The sea gave up the dead it had kept, as did death and the netherworld, so that all might be judged, according to their works. Then, death and the netherworld, were thrown into the lake of fire. This lake of fire is the second death. All who were not recorded in the book of life were thrown into the lake of fire.

Then, I saw a new heaven and a new earth. The first heaven and the first earth had passed away, and no longer was there any sea. I saw the new Jerusalem, the holy city, coming down from God, out of heaven, adorned as a bride prepared for her husband. A loud voice came from the throne, "Here is the dwelling of God among mortals: He will pitch his tent among them, and they will be his people; he will be God-with-them.

He will wipe every tear from their eyes. There shall be no more death or mourning, crying out or pain, for the world that was, has passed away." The One seated on the throne said, "See, I make all things new."

And, then, he said to me, "Write these words, because they are sure and true."

And he said to me: "It is already done! I am the Alpha and the Omega, the Beginning and the End. I, myself, will give the thirsty, to drink without cost, from the fountain of living water. Thus, the winner will be rewarded: For him, I shall be God and he will be my son.

As for cowards, traitors, depraved, murderers, adulterers, sorcerers, and idolaters—all those who live in falsehood, their place is the lake of burning sulfur. This is the second death."

Then, one of the seven angels came to me, one of those with the seven bowls full of the seven last plagues. And he said, "Come, I am going to show you the bride, the wife of the Lamb." He took me up, in a spiritual vision, to a very high mountain, and he showed me the holy city Jerusalem, coming down out of heaven, from God. It shines with the glory of God, like a precious jewel, with the color of crystal-clear jasper.

Its wall, large and high, has twelve gates; stationed at them are twelve angels. Over the gates are written the names of the twelve tribes of the sons of Israel. Three gates face the east; three gates face the north; three gates face the south and three face the west. The city wall stands on twelve foundation stones, on which are written the names of the twelve apostles of the Lamb.

The angel who was speaking to me had a golden measuring rod, to measure the city, its gates and its wall. The city is laid out like a square: its length is the same as its breadth. He measured it with his rod and it was twelve thousand furlongs; its length, breadth and height are equal. Then, he measured the wall: it was a hundred and forty-four cubits high. The angel used an ordinary measure.

The wall is made of jasper, and the city of pure gold, crystal-clear. The foundations of the wall are adorned with every kind of precious jewel: the first is jasper, the second sapphire, the third turquoise, the fourth emerald, the fifth agate, the sixth ruby, the seventh chrysolite, the eighth beryl, the ninth topaz, the tenth chrysopraze, the eleventh hyacinth and the twelfth amethyst. The twelve gates are twelve pearls, each gate made of a single pearl, and the square of the city is paved with gold, as pure as transparent crystal.

I saw no temple in the city, for the Lord God, Master of the universe, and the Lamb, are themselves its temple. The city has no need of the light of the sun or the moon, since God's glory is its light and the Lamb is its lamp.

The nations will walk in its light, and the kings of the earth will bring their treasures to it. Its gates will not be closed at sunset, for there will be no night there. It is there, that the wealth, and the most precious things of the nations, will be brought. Nothing unclean will enter it, or anyone who does what is evil and false, but only those, whose names are written in the Lamb's book of life.

Then, he showed me the river of life, clear as crystal, gushing from the throne of God, and of the Lamb. In the middle of the city, on both sides of the river, are the trees of life, producing fruit twelve times, once each month, the leaves of which are for healing the nations.

No longer will there be a curse; the throne of God and of the Lamb will be in the city, and God's servants will live in his presence. They will see his face, and his name will be on their foreheads. There will be no more night. They will not need the light of lamp, or sun, for God, himself, will be their light, and they will reign forever.

Then, the angel said to me, "These words are sure and true; the Lord God, who inspires the prophets, has sent his angel, to show his servants what must happen soon."

"I am coming soon! Happy are those who keep the prophetic words of this book."

I, John, saw and heard all this. When I had seen and heard them, I fell at the feet of the angel who had shown me everything, to worship him. But he said, "No, I am a fellow servant, like you and your brothers, the prophets, and those who heed the words of this book. It is God you must worship."

He, then, said to me, "Do not keep secret the prophetic words of this book, because the time is near. Let the sinner continue to sin, and the defiled, remain in his defilement; let the righteous continue to do what is right, and he who is holy, grow holier."

"I am coming soon, bringing with me the recompense I will pay to each one, according to his deeds. I am the Alpha and the Omega, the First and the Last, the Beginning and the End."

Happy are those who wash their robes, for they will have free access to the tree of life, and enter the city through the gates. Outside are the dogs, sorcerers, the immoral, murderers, idolaters, and all who take pleasure in falsehood!

"I, Jesus, sent my angel, to make known to you these revelations concerning the churches. I am the shoot, and offspring of David, the radiant morning star."

The Spirit and the Bride say, "Come!" Whoever hears, let him say, "Come!" Whoever thirsts, let him approach, and whoever desires, let him freely take the water of life.

As for me, I warn everyone who hears the prophetic words of this book: If anyone adds anything to them, God will pile on him, the plagues described in this book. And if anyone takes away words from this book of prophecy, God will take from him, his share in the tree of life, and the holy city described in this book.

He who has declared all this says, "Yes, I am coming soon."

Amen! Come, Lord Jesus.

May the grace of the Lord Jesus be with you all!

ABOUT THE
CHRISTIAN COMMUNITY BIBLE

The Christian Community Bible (Catholic Pastoral Edition) is the first English translation of the Bible done and published from the Third World, specifically the Philippines. It is also unique for its pastoral commentaries on the biblical texts. After 19 years in Chile where he translated the Bible into Spanish—the "Biblia Latinoamérica"—Fr. Bernardo Hurault came to the Philippines in 1986 and with the Claretian Missionaries began the Christian Community Bible. Sr. Patricia Grogan FCJ, an Australian sister, came from England as the main editor and stylist, even as other religious and laypersons in the Philippines, shared in the work of translating the biblical texts and writing the pastoral notes. With Fr. Bernardo's extensive knowledge of New Testament Greek and profound reflection on the Word of God, he himself translated the New Testament of the Christian Community Bible.

His translation into contemporary English is at the same time fresh and with a somehow different "texture" from other translations as he tries to express the biblical texts in the language of people who use English as a second language, but at the same time remaining faithful to the original texts.

A revised edition of this Bible was published in 2013. Biblical scholars, linguists and copy editors from different countries worked together for several years for a completely new edition of the Christian Community Bible (CCB). It brought the text closer to the original languages in a number of passages, especially with a very careful revision of the text of the four Gospels.

The present edition (from the 62nd edition of the Christian Community Bible) does not contain the corresponding pastoral notes to the New Testament, but those interested can always refer to the Christian Community Bible (Catholic Pastoral Edition) for these. The complete CCB is available for free at www.bibleclaret.org. In addition, the new text of the New Testament in digital audio format is available, also for free from the above web page for listening or download.

The work of Fr. Bernardo continues with the Pastoral Bible Foundation. In the last 25 years this "Pastoral Bible" was translated into 12 languages and more than 120 million copies were distributed and sold around the world.

For Fr. Bernardo, the Risen Christ is at the very heart of the Bible and the Word becomes truly alive when we search for it with our sisters and brothers as we participate in a Christian community.

LECTIO DIVINA 1
THE VALUE AND VIRTUE OF LOVE

INVOCATION TO THE HOLY SPIRIT:

Come, Holy Spirit.

Come to our family as we call on you today.

We ask you to instruct our lives, our hearts, and our consciences.

Open our minds and our wills to understand what the Father wants to say to us through his Son, Jesus Christ.

We pray that your Word will permeate our lives and become life within us.

Make our family a living model, as we imitate Christ.

Amen.

BIBLE TEXT: 1 CORINTHIANS 13
Without love I am nothing.

Read the Bible text on page 128.

READING:
What does the text say?

When St. Paul visits Corinth, he discovers a variety of cultures in this very important port city. It is an essential point of transition, commerce and transport. But these cultures do not share the values of the early Christians. There are many dangerous pagan beliefs and practices to be found in Corinth. Therefore, Paul, after leaving the city, meditates and prays about what he has seen and then writes a letter to his friends in Corinth.

This well-known portion of Scripture is actually a continuation of an earlier text. Remember that originally the Bible was not divided into chapters or verses. Paul has been writing about the gifts of the Spirit and he reaches the climax of his argument when he states that love is the most important gift that God offers us.

This section begins by saying: *If I could speak all the human and angelic tongues, but had no love, I would only be sounding brass or a clanging cymbal.* In the ceremonies of the idolatrous cults in Corinth, gongs and bells were used. Paul compares the empty sounds that these pagan bells made with people who say they are speaking in tongues but do not show love. The same applies to those who present themselves as seers or proclaimers of messages from heaven but show no love to those who hear them. It is also true of those who have wisdom and knowledge but no love. Without love, we will be ineffectual in reaching out to people. Whether we have small gifts or great ones, without love, none of our gifts are of any consequence.

Paul begins by extolling the virtues of love, then later proposes a specific way that someone who loves should behave, and concludes the text by affirming that of everything we have, the most important and enduring is love.

Only by loving can we be truly Christian. And as we shall see, love is illustrated by concrete actions. It is not only an abstract theory; love is a way of life.

Now we have faith, hope and love. Faith is the certainty and the guarantee that leads us to believe in what we cannot see. Hope stimulates us and activates faith, especially regarding the coming of Christ. But when we see God face-to-face we will no longer need these two virtues. For we will no longer need to hope for something that has already happened. Yet love will remain beyond the limits of time. It is the only thing we will take with us.

Examine the text:

1. How does the story begin?
2. What comparisons does St. Paul use concerning gifts and love?
3. How does he describe a person who loves, step by step?
4. What does a person who loves do, and what should they not do?
5. What does Paul mean when he talks about looking into a mirror? To what does he refer?
6. What are the three most important virtues?
7. Of the three, which is the only one that endures? Why?

Review the text:

1. Underline the phrases that particularly caught your attention as you read them.
2. Highlight what you see as the most important part of the text.
3. Now look at all the verbs Paul uses; then choose the three you think are the most important.

MEDITATION:
What does the text say to me?

As a family, let us reflect on this Word of God to us. We will discuss our thoughts about what we have read using the following suggestions and questions. Anyone is welcome to read the suggestions and questions aloud, then we will all discuss them:

1. Let's share the phrases that caught our attention, what we see as the most important part of the text and the verbs each of us chose. This will help us discover what the text has to say to us individually and as a family.

2. We will all take turns to list aloud the good things we believe each of us does within as well as outside our family.

3. Then we will ask ourselves: Was each good deed done out of love? Or was it done for the sake of appearances, or to meet an obligation? St. Paul begins his message by making the point that good things that are not done out of love have no value.

4. We read again: *Love is patient, kind, without envy...* As we go through the list, let's share whether we are patient and kind, envious or boastful, proud or rude, self-seeking or easily angered. Do we delight in evil or rejoice in the truth? Do we forgive others, trust, hope, and persevere? By reviewing our actions in light of the text, we as a family can see whether we meet the standards Paul set out and where we need to improve.

5. Each member of the family has the opportunity to ask for help, and the rest of us express our willingness to assist one another to improve.

6. . There isn't a more loving atmosphere to be in than that of a family helping each other toward perfection. We can all grow if we truly help each other.

7. How can we grow in faith, hope and love? Let us pray together about how we can express this desire.

PRAYER:
What do I say to the Lord?

Let's think about what we have read in the Word of God and what we considered in our meditation; then we will pray to the Lord.

As we sit quietly, let's think about what we have covered so far.

We will begin by giving thanks to the Lord for all the gifts he has given to us—we each mention what we are thankful for.

Together we ask: **Lord, bless our family as we express our gratitude to you**.

We continue praying out loud together, asking God's forgiveness for the things we have not done well, or for the good things we could have done but did not do.

Then together we ask: **Lord, forgive us**.

We speak aloud to the Lord, asking him to help us so that we might improve in love and learn to love one another more every day.

Then together we ask: **Lord, help us to be more loving**.

CONTEMPLATION:
How do I implement the text in my life?

To contemplate means to consider, to think about in our minds and hearts, the ideas arising from the Word of God, so that they have a greater effect on our lives.

Let's repeat a phrase from the text together:

Without love I am nothing.

We will repeat this phrase several times now, and then again once we are at home, until it is engraved in our minds and hearts as the way we want our family to live.

ACTION:
How do I commit myself to act on what I have learned?

As we carry out the exercises of *Lectio Divina*, we make clear and concrete commitments to change certain things in our lives. If we do not follow through with actions, we are simply repeating ideas, nothing more.

The children can make a sign to hang somewhere in the house that reads,

Without love I am nothing.

As a family, choose to do something together that actively demonstrates love at home and in the wider world. At home, perhaps everyone can find a way to help one another, such as assisting with the cooking, doing housework, helping with school tasks, etc.

An activity of love outside the home could include visiting an ill person or helping a family in need. Whatever activities are chosen, they must be significant things that reveal how the family is changing and being truly Christian.

LECTIO DIVINA 2
THE VALUE AND VIRTUE OF RESPECT FOR LIFE

INVOCATION TO THE HOLY SPIRIT:

Come, Holy Spirit,
Come to our family as we call upon you today.
Clearly present to us the message of Jesus Christ for our family.
We want to be open to anything fresh that you have to say to us.
Your message is clear, and as a Christian family we want to do what
you ask of us.
Open our minds, strengthen our wills and give us the desire to always
be ready to understand and to adjust our attitudes.
We pray that your Word will permeate our lives and become life within
us.
Make our family be a model of life, as we imitate Christ.
Amen.

BIBLE TEXT: JOHN 10:1–18
I have come that they may have life, life in all its fullness.

Read the Bible text on page 382.

READING:
What does the text say?

St. John wrote his Good News, or Gospel, some sixty years after the death and resurrection of Jesus Christ. His text is his way of communicating to us his personal experience of his encounter with the resurrected Jesus.

There are several central themes in the Gospel of John and one of them concerns life. The next chapter of John — remembering that originally there would have been no chapter divisions—also focuses on the theme of life, as Jesus raises Lazarus from the dead.

If we were to read the Book of John from beginning to end, while keeping the rest of the Bible in mind, we would see that God, above all else, wants human beings to experience life. He is the Lord of Life. He offers it to us as a gift that we should take care of and respect. God wants us to have life in all its fullness.

Let us consider this text. Read the text with fresh eyes, taking it step by step. Remember that it is a speech made by Jesus. Note the phrase "I Am" bringing to mind God himself, the great *I Am*.

For those listening, Jesus presents the image of a pastor, a shepherd. This theme of a shepherd is often used in the Bible. God is the one who cares for his flock, in the same way that a shepherd takes care of his sheep. But Jesus begins by saying that before him there were false shepherds who took advantage of the sheep. However, Jesus is the shepherd, and also the gate through whom the sheep must pass to find pasture and life in all its fullness.

The text describes all that a shepherd does to look after the lives of his sheep. He cares for them and protects them from wolves who want to eat them. But there is something more basic and important; Jesus knows his sheep and they know him. Jesus gives his life for his sheep. He reminds us that he will surrender his own life to save the lives of his sheep. Life is a gift from God who offers himself as a sacrifice to give life to all of us who believe in him, and this is what we commemorate at Easter.

Jesus lays out the basic doctrine clearly and simply. The lives of his sheep are what is most important to him. Those who do not follow Jesus are like the false shepherds who steal and kill the sheep. It is important that as a family we remember this.

Examine the text:

1. How does the story begin?
2. What does Jesus say about himself? Why does he use these words?
3. What other image did Jesus use in reference to himself?
4. How should we understand the phrase that tells us Jesus came that we might have life?
5. Who are those who came but did not care for the lives of the sheep?
6. How does he deal with these evil people who did not care for the sheep?
7. How does Jesus describe the good shepherd?
8. Why does Jesus say that he lays down his life?
9. Jesus also says that he has authority to give life. What does that mean?

Review the text:

1. Underline the phrases that particularly caught your attention as you read them.
2. Highlight what you see as the most important part of the text.
3. Look at all the verbs used in the text, and choose the three you think are the most important.

MEDITATION:
What does the text say to me?

As a family let us reflect on this Word of God to us. We will discuss our thoughts about what we have read using the following suggestions and questions. Anyone is welcome to read the suggestions and questions aloud, then we will all discuss them:

1. Let's share the phrases that caught our attention, what we see as the most important part of the text, and the verbs each of us chose. This will help us discover what the text has to say to us separately and as a family.

2. The family is the main sanctuary of human life. Are we all aware of this?

3. Human life is a gift from God. It begins when a cell from the father is joined to one from the mother. This is the main reason why the family is open to God's most important gift: life. Do we respect life from the moment it begins? What help do we offer, as a family, to those who do not respect the life that has been conceived? Suggest a specific action.

4. Following birth, life is cared for by the family. Do we receive life with joy and help one another enjoy life in all its fullness?

5. How can our family, reflecting the image of the good shepherd, help other families accept their responsibility to care for everything in life?

6. We should also be interested in the growth of each person. We should show concern for the health, education, and spiritual growth of each of our family members. How do we do this?

7. There are also older people in our family who need more time and special attention. Are we aware that caring for everything in life also includes older adults? Do we care for them, pay attention to them, spend time with them and meet their needs? Can we be like Jesus, who gave his life for us? Will we give of our time, sacrificing our preferences and the things we want to do to care for the older generation?

8. From the beginning of life until its natural end, we share a responsibility with God to provide special care for each person he has entrusted to us. Do I have this awareness in my particular role as father, mother, child, grandchild, or grandparent?

9. What could I sacrifice to help others have life in all its fullness?

PRAYER:
What do I say to the Lord?

Let's think about what we have read in the Word of God and what we considered in our meditation; then we will pray to the Lord.

As we sit quietly, let's think about what we have covered so far.

Let's begin by thanking God for the life he has given us and each take a turn to share this in our own way.

Then together we will say: **Lord, bless our family as we express our gratitude to you**.

We continue praying together, asking forgiveness for the times we have failed to be responsible and have not helped other people with their needs.

Then together we ask: **Lord, forgive us**.

We ask the Lord aloud to grant us all that we need from him to help us be better people and to be more responsible about helping one another as well as defending life from its conception until he calls us home.

Then we all ask: **Lord, help us to care of life**.

CONTEMPLATION:
How do I implement the text in my life?

To contemplate means to consider, to think about in our minds and hearts, the ideas arising from the Word of God, so they may have a greater effect on our lives.

We repeat a phrase from the text together:

I have come that they may have life, life in all its fullness.

We will repeat this phrase several times now, and then again once we are at home, until it is engraved in our minds and hearts as the way we want our family to live.

ACTION:
How do I commit myself to act on what I have learned?

As we carry out the exercises of *Lectio Divina*, we make clear and concrete commitments to change certain things in our lives. If we do not follow through with actions, we are simply repeating ideas, nothing more.

Together, find photographs of everyone in the family. Then paste them onto a poster so that each family member is represented. The children can add this phrase in pretty letters:

Thank you, Lord, for life and our family.

Choose a family activity that shows respect and care for life. At home, help one another grow and be good companions. Do something special with the older adults, something that will show them how much they are loved. Maybe take them out somewhere special, or make something to show them how much they are appreciated.

Then organize an activity that expresses love outside the home. Perhaps visit an orphanage or a nursing home. Consider asking another family to join you as you do this. Whatever activities you choose, they must be meaningful things that reveal how your family members are changing and being true Christians who are responsible for life in all its stages.

LECTIO DIVINA 3
THE VALUE OF FORGIVENESS

INVOCATION TO THE HOLY SPIRIT:

Come, Holy Spirit,

As a family we ask you to teach us and guide us.

Come to our family as we call on you today.

We want the message of Jesus to be heard by and lived out in our family.

Open our minds and our hearts so we will be obedient to your will.

We do not want our plans to stand in the way as you show us how you want us to live as Christians.

Together we open our hearts so you can guide us.

We pray that your Word, Lord, will motivate us to be witnesses for the Christian faith.

Make our family a living model, as we imitate Christ.

Amen.

BIBLE TEXT: MATTHEW 18:15–35

Lord, how many times must I forgive the offenses of my brother or sister?

Read the Bible text on page 264.

READING:
What does the text say?

St. Matthew wrote his Gospel, or Good News, mainly for Jews who had converted to Christianity. This is why we see so many explanations of passages from the Old Testament. In this instance, Jesus is referring to Old Testament teachings on the Law and the Prophets, so we can have a new understanding of what God wants.

Throughout history as his plan of love has unfolded, God has been very patient with us. This text reflects God's patience. First, Jesus describes the proper way we should behave toward each other. Note he does not use the word "criticize," but rather, *"go and point out the fault to him."* When we see another Christian making mistakes, Jesus invites us first of all to help that person to stop, emphasizing that whatever we do, we should do it with a loving Christian attitude. He then proposes a clear plan for dealing fairly with a fellow Christians who refuses to listen. They will be corrected and forgiven for the faults they have committed.

Once Jesus has explained the need for patience when correcting faults,

Peter asks, *"How many times should we forgive someone?"* He suggests seven times, because the number seven has a special significance, symbolizing perfection. This seems like a more-than-acceptable number of times to forgive someone. But Jesus gives a much higher number, perhaps alluding to another text from the Old Testament (Genesis 4:24) where a similar multiplication is used. Jesus does not mean that we should count the number of times we forgive someone, until we reach 490—his point is we need to forgive freely.

Immediately afterward, Jesus tells the parable of two debtors. One owed a certain amount to the king, who forgave him his debt and wrote it off. However, when the debtor in turn was owed money, he refused to show mercy in the same way. Hearing of this, the king was angry and punished him because he did not demonstrate an attitude of forgiveness, despite having benefited from forgiveness himself. *Jesus added, "So will my heavenly Father do with you, unless you sincerely forgive your brothers and sisters."*

Examine the text:

1. How does the account begin?
2. What does Jesus say you should do when a fellow Christian offends you?
3. What is the process to follow when correcting a fellow Christian?
4. Jesus says something important about our prayers. What does he say?
5. Peter asks Jesus how many times he should forgive someone who offends him. How many times did Peter suggest?
6. How did Jesus respond to Peter's suggestion?
7. Jesus tells a parable about two debtors. What does the parable teach?
8. What happened to the debtor who was forgiven? How did he treat the person who was indebted to him?
9. How did the king react when he discovered that the man had not shown mercy in return?
10. How does Jesus refer to God's attitude toward those who do not forgive?

Review the text:

1. Underline the phrases that particularly caught your attention as you read them.
2. Highlight what you think is the most important part of the text.
3. Find all the verbs used, and select the three you think are the most important.

MEDITATION:
What does the text say to me?

As a family let us reflect on this Word of God to us. We will discuss our thoughts about what we have read using the following suggestions and questions. Anyone is welcome to read the suggestions and questions aloud, then we will all discuss them:

1. Let's share the phrases that caught our attention, what we see as the most important part of the text, and the verbs we chose. This will help us discover what the text is saying to each of us individually and as a family.

2. Jesus encourages us to help fellow Christians who have done something wrong. He proposes a friendly correction. Is that how we act? Do we severely criticize instead of lovingly correcting?

3. Can we as a family agree and establish a procedure to correct one another's mistakes? How should we do this?

4. How do we act in our home when a family member does something wrong? Do we forgive them? Do we ask for forgiveness when we have done wrong?

5. What do we gain individually, whether we are parents or children, when we ask forgiveness? Does it increase our respect for one another?

6. As human beings we all make mistakes. This is natural, and as Christians we should therefore develop a strategy that helps us be humble and ask forgiveness when we have done wrong. How can we do that? We should also foster a culture of forgiveness in our home. Can we clearly express this? How can we express this as a family?

7. We also understand that there are people outside the family whose actions can hurt us and others. How should we act from now on as a family when we notice other people's mistakes? What does the Lord ask us to do?

8. As a family we should be an example of forgiveness and love. How can we demonstrate forgiveness and love?

PRAYER:
What do I say to the Lord?

Let's think about what we have read in the Word of God and what we considered in our meditation; then we will pray to the Lord.

As we sit quietly, let's think about what we have learned so far.

Let's begin by thanking the Lord for the forgiveness he has offered to human beings and the salvation he offers us. Each person can share this in their own way.

Then together we ask: **Lord, bless our family as we give you thanks.**

We all continue praying aloud, asking forgiveness for the times we have not done what we should have, or when we have not done as well as we could have done.

Then together we ask: **Lord, forgive us.**

We each ask the Lord aloud for all that we need from him to help us be better Christians, who are committed to love and forgiveness.

Then we all ask: **Lord, help us to forgive others who do wrong.**

CONTEMPLATION:
How do I implement the text in my life?

To contemplate means to consider, to think about in our minds and hearts, the ideas arising from the Word of God, so they may have a greater effect on our lives.

Together let's repeat a phrase from the Lord's Prayer in Matthew 6:12: *Forgive us our debts, as we forgive those who are in debt to us.*

We will repeat this phrase several times now and then again once we are at home, until it is engraved in our minds and hearts as the way we want our family to live.

ACTION:
How do I commit myself to act on what I have learned?

As we carry out the exercises of *Lectio Divina*, we make clear and concrete commitments to change certain things in our lives. If we do not follow through with actions, we are simply repeating ideas, nothing more.

We all give one another a loving hug, we ask forgiveness from one another, and we forgive one another for any offense caused.

Organize an activity outside the home to demonstrate forgiveness. Find someone who has previously wronged your family, and tell the person that even though much time has passed, you all forgive them. In recognition of this, give them a small token, such as a homemade card with a meaningful message.

LECTIO DIVINA 4
THE VALUE OF FREEDOM

INVOCATION TO THE HOLY SPIRIT:

Come, Holy Spirit.

As our family gathers in prayer, we ask you to be present in our lives.

Father, we come before you, and we thank you for your inspired Word to us.

We want to follow Jesus, living out his and his disciples' teachings.

Come to our family as we call on you today for guidance.

As we open the Holy Scriptures, we ask you to help us understand your message

written by men inspired by you.

Help us to be obedient to your will.

Together as a family we open our hearts so that you can guide us.

We pray that your Word, Lord, will motivate us to be witnesses of the freedom we have found in Christ, so the world will believe in you.

Amen.

BIBLE TEXT: GALATIANS 5

Christ freed us, to make us really free.

Read the Bible text on page 158.

READING:
What does the text say?

St. Paul sends a very special letter to the Christians of Galatia. The Galatians' culture was Greek rather than Jewish. Paul's influence led them to an encounter with Jesus and then to form the community of the church in Galatia. It is a very important letter; Paul supports the new believers by laying out Christian doctrine very clearly. He places special emphasis on dealing with pagan cultures that surrounded them, as well as the values and virtues that should be evident in the life of a Christian.

Paul's letter to the Galatians teaches us important lessons that should influence the decisions we make as a family as well as the way we live the Christian life. This chapter begins with the phrase that is central to the theme: *Christ freed us, to make us really free.* What follows is a continuation of an ongoing debate: whether to be Christians it was necessary to adopt Jewish customs and live under the Law of Moses. Paul sets out his view very clearly, showing that Christ has set us free. Christ and his doctrine supersede Judaism, and acceptance of Jesus is sufficient to be able to live a new life. This is the central theme of Galatians and is often referred to as "new life according to the Holy Spirit."

For Paul, freedom also means not allowing ourselves to be dragged into practices and human passions that work against the Spirit. Liberty is not licentiousness—the freedom to do as you please. Rather, it is about living with joy under the guidance of the Holy Spirit. Paul lists many of the attitudes that are contrary to the Holy Spirit (verses 19–21).

The central idea is that true freedom comes through the fruit of the Spirit: love, joy, peace, tolerance, kindness, goodness, loyalty, humility, and self-control (verses 22–23).

Living according to the Spirit of liberty that Christ has granted us also leads us to accept his gifts, freely accept his doctrine, and live in his church.

Examine the text:

1. How does the account begin?
2. For St. Paul, what is more important: to live according to the law or according to the Spirit?
3. St. Paul says that we should appreciate our freedom. Why should we be careful not to misuse our liberty?
4. What does it mean to live according to the Holy Spirit's requirements?
5. What does Paul say is contrary to the Spirit?
6. What are the actions Paul lists as characteristic of those who give in and indulge the desires of the flesh?
7. What is the fruit of the Spirit?

Review the text:

1. Underline the phrases that particularly caught your attention.
2. Highlight what you see as the most important part of the text.
3. Find all the verbs used, and select the three you think are most important.

MEDITATION:
What does the text say to me?

As a family let us reflect on this Word of God to us. We will discuss our thoughts about what we have read using the following suggestions and questions. Anyone is welcome to read the suggestions and questions aloud, then we will all discuss them:

1. Let's share the phrases that caught our attention, what we saw as the most important part of the text, and the verbs we chose. This

will help us discover what the text is saying to each of us individually and as a family.

2. What do we each understand by the term freedom? Does our understanding coincide with what St. Paul tells us?

3. What are the things we can do to enjoy our freedom?

4. Today's world often presents us with things advertised as freedom. How does this "freedom" differ from freedom in Christ?

5. How can we, as a family, defend ourselves from these false offers of freedom that will harm us and lead us away from the Spirit of God?

6. How can we create a plan for our family that incorporates the nine fruit of the Spirit Paul presents?

7. What does Paul mean when he writes, *If we live by the Spirit, let us live in a spiritual way*?

PRAYER:
What do I say to the Lord?

Let's think about what we have read in the Word of God and what we considered in our meditation; then we will pray to the Lord.

As we sit quietly, let's think about what we have learned so far.

We begin by thanking the Lord for the salvation he offers us. We are grateful for the liberty we experience when we trust in him and live according to his freedom. We each can verbalize our gratitude.

Then together we all ask: **Lord, bless our family as we praise you for freedom.**

We continue praying aloud, asking God's forgiveness for the occasions when we did not live in freedom but as slaves to our passions.

Then we all ask: **Lord, forgive us.**

Let us ask the Lord aloud to help us be truly free and help others also to find freedom.

Together we ask: **Lord, help us to be free.**

CONTEMPLATION:
How do I implement the text in my life?

To contemplate means to consider, to think about in our minds and hearts, the ideas arising from the Word of God, so they may have a greater effect on our lives.

We repeat together a phrase from the text:

Christ freed us, to make us really free.

We will repeat this phrase several times now and then again once we are at home, until it is engraved in our minds and hearts as the way we want our family to live.

ACTION:
How do I commit myself to act on what I have learned?

As we carry out the exercises of *Lectio Divina*, we make clear and concrete commitments to change certain things in our lives. If we do not follow through with actions, we are simply repeating ideas, nothing more.

Each family member chooses one fruit of the Spirit: Love, joy, peace, tolerance, kindness, goodness, loyalty, humility, or self-control. Each person makes a poster or drawing depicting the theme of living freely according to the fruit they chose: Then they explain the drawing to the rest of the family.

As a family we also commit to do something outside the home that demonstrates to people what it means to be free and faithful in Christ.

LECTIO DIVINA 5
THE VALUE OF FAITHFULNESS

INVOCATION TO THE HOLY SPIRIT:

Come, Holy Spirit,
As a family we ask you for the gift of prayer.
We ask that you will enable us to understand your message,
as we read the Sacred Scriptures inspired by you.
Open our minds that have been closed by worldly influences;
open our hearts, hardened by the many mistakes we have made.
Come to our family as we call on you today.
We want to accept the life you offer us.
Holy Spirit, guide our family, leading us to the Father, through the Word.
We ask that your Word, Lord, guide us to live in faithfulness to Christ, our family,
And everyone in the world.
Amen.

BIBLE TEXT: MATTHEW 19
Let no one separate what God has joined.

Read the Bible text on page 265.

READING:
What does the text say?

St. Matthew writes his Good News, or Gospel, for Jews who have acknowledged Jesus as the Messiah. His community lived through the displacement and dispersal of people following the fall of Jerusalem. But most of them knew the laws of Moses. Matthew the evangelist presents Jesus as the great and unique legislator of the true Law. If Moses left them the first covenant, then Jesus Christ, the Lord and Messiah, brought them the true and definitive new covenant.

This chapter has a lot to teach us; the first and most important lesson is about marriage and family life. Jesus says Moses ended up accepting the separation of spouses. He agreed the husband could give his wife a document of "liberation." The only reason Moses agreed to this was because of the hard hearts of the men of that time. Jesus insists, *"Let no one separate what God has joined."*

It is obvious the central theme is based on the faithfulness of spouses.

Jesus is looking well beyond the established rules in which the wife was the "property" of a man. The coming together of two people creates a union: *"So they are no longer two, but one body,"* Jesus says. He is clearly opposed to divisions, once a formal decision to form a family has been taken. Therefore, the Christian family insists on the faithfulness of both spouses and their commitment to each other for all time.

The text immediately moves on to the fruit of the family: the children. Jesus loved children and always wanted them near him, to bless them and hold them up as an example of the kind of person who would enter the kingdom of heaven.

Matthew's text then gives us an important account about a rich young man. He wanted to have eternal life, but he was not willing to leave his possessions behind to follow the Lord. This is the bad example we should not follow.

Faithfulness is demonstrated in the Bible from the beginning. God reveals himself as the "faithful God." He is faithful to his promises and faithful to his people. He does not lie, he does not go back on his promises, and the Word—Jesus—does not return to the Father without fulfilling his mission. But God also requires the same faithfulness from those who love and follow him.

Jesus Christ is the model of faithfulness, since he committed himself "faithfully" to the will of his Father, surrendering himself and becoming a model for all the believers who call themselves "faithful." Faithfulness is the sign that marks all Christians from the time of their baptism. To become heirs of the kingdom, we must be faithful. As Paul says, *"Being stewards, faithfulness shall be demanded of us"* (1 Corinthians 4:2).

Examine the text:
1. How does the account begin?
2. Why do the Pharisees question Jesus about spouses being given permission to separate?
3. How does Jesus answer?
4. What did the true disciples of Jesus say when they heard him?
5. What does Jesus say about the ability to dedicate oneself faithfully to marriage, or to be consecrated?
6. Why did Jesus say the children should be allowed to come to him?
7. What was the intention of the rich young man?
8. Was his behavior acceptable?
9. What was the rich young man unwilling to do? What did he do after talking with Jesus?
10. What should we do to continue being "faithful"?

Review the text:

1. Underline the phrases that particularly caught your attention.
2. Highlight what you see as the most important part of the text.
3. Find all the verbs used, and select the three you think are most important.

MEDITATION:
What does the text say to me?

As a family, let us reflect on this Word of God to us. We will discuss our thoughts about what we have read using the following suggestions and questions. Anyone is welcome to read the suggestions and questions aloud, then we will all discuss them:

1. Let's share the phrases that caught our attention, what we saw as the most important part of the text, and the verbs we chose. This will help us discover what the text is saying to each of us individually and as a family.
2. For Jesus, faithfulness is about much more than what the world sees. How should we understand Jesus' command to be faithful?
3. Is faithfulness relevant only to marriage? Or does it go beyond the relationship between spouses?
4. God reveals himself to be faithful. Do we see God's faithfulness in our lives?
5. How should we prepare ourselves as a family to face a world that presents unfaithfulness as a value?
6. Do we recognize that books, advertisements, and propaganda often lead us toward unfaithfulness as a way of life? What can we do to remain alert and not be carried away by a non-Christian lifestyle?
7. Can our family, in conjunction with our community of faith, provide a program for living in faithfulness aimed at people who are in relationships and preparing for marriage?
8. What other aspects of faithfulness can we emphasize?

PRAYER:
What do I say to the Lord?

Let's think about what we have read in the Word of God and what we considered in our meditation; then we will pray to the Lord.

As we sit quietly, let's think about what we have learned so far.

We begin by thanking the Lord for his faithfulness toward us. We will take turns to verbalize our gratitude to God.

Then together we all say: **Lord, we thank you for our family and for your faithful love for us.**

We continue praying aloud, asking the Lord's forgiveness for not always being as faithful as he is and for all the times when we betrayed our faith and were unfaithful to those we love.

Then we ask: **Lord, forgive our unfaithfulness.**

Let us ask the Lord aloud to help us be his "faithful" disciples.

Together we ask: **Lord, help us to be faithful and genuine Christians.**

CONTEMPLATION:
How do I implement the text in my life?

To contemplate means to consider, to think about in our minds and hearts, the ideas arising from the Word of God, so they have a greater effect on our lives.

We repeat together a phrase from this text:

"Let no one separate what God has joined."

We will repeat this phrase several times now and then again once we are at home, until it is engraved in our minds and hearts as the way we want our family to live.

ACTION:
How do I commit myself to act on what I have learned?

As we carry out the exercises of *Lectio Divina*, we make clear and concrete commitments to change certain things in our lives. If we do not follow through with actions, we are simply repeating ideas, nothing more.

We will each write a personal prayer to the Lord, expressing that we want to be faithful to ourselves, our principles, our loved ones, and, above all, always faithful to Christ.

Together as a family we will become involved in a community project that helps people who are in relationships to understand the advantages of living a faithful life. We will emphasize the joy of faithfulness. This may be a creative activity, including posters and videos that focus on faithfulness as a lifestyle.

LECTIO DIVINA 6
THE VALUE OF RESPECT

INVOCATION TO THE HOLY SPIRIT:

Come, Holy Spirit,
As a family we come before you today, ready to pray.
We want to hear God speak to us through his inspired Word.
We don't want your Word to be one among many words. Help us to be attentive to it.
Holy Scripture offers us clear guidelines for our lives, and we do not want to ignore your instructions. They help us live better lives.
Today, we ask for your guidance and assistance, because we want to be better Christians.
May your Word show us the way and give us the will to truly live.
Help us accept your guidance.
We ask that your Word, Lord, motivate us to be witnesses worthy of respect, so the world might believe.
Amen.

BIBLE TEXT: EPHESIANS 4

Be humble, kind, patient, and bear with one another in love.

Read the Bible text on page 198.

READING:
What does the text say?

St. Paul writes a very special letter to the Christians at Ephesus. The entire letter is a great summary of the history of salvation. It relates God's actions from the beginning until the coming of Jesus Christ, as well as the truth that Christ brings to the world. It is important to read the entire letter, although we will concentrate on chapter 4.

To be humble, kind and well intentioned, to be patient and willing to put up with one another—this is the central theme of this recipe for living the Christian life. But the reason for living this way is very clear: there is only one God and Father, only one baptism that unites us, and together we form one body. What happens to one part of the body also affects the other parts of the body.

For this reason, we must respect each member of the church. Each has received different gifts according to their disposition. We must respect our differences because together we are all part of the same body. We are to maintain these bonds of unity and respect for the gifts and responsibilities

God has entrusted to us. If we do this, nothing will be able to separate us from one another or from this way of life.

St. Paul reminds the Ephesians to be aware of those who do not respect the law or the teachers, losing their sense of propriety that resulted in them giving themselves over to vices, impurity, and greed. Paul says it is better to renounce our former way of life and clothe ourselves in a new self, created to be like Christ.

We are required to embrace a new lifestyle. We must eliminate lying, always speak the truth, avoid anger, be understanding, and respect others. Christians are to behave in a way that distinguishes them from others. We are to renounce worldliness and clothe ourselves in the grace of Christ. St. Paul makes it clear that if Christ and Christ-like living are not a reality in our lives, then our faith is only theoretical. As Christians we are called to put our faith into practice and to share our joy with others through the Good News, as we live as witnesses for Jesus.

Examine the text:

1. How does the account begin?
2. What are the first recommendations Paul makes to us?
3. What is the unity we should respect? How can we justify unity with everyone?
4. What does it mean that each person has received a specific gift from God? What should we do with that gift in the community?
5. What is the body we share with others?
6. To be genuine Christians, what do we need to give up and what should we follow?
7. What does it mean to be a new person in Christ?
8. What are the requirements of a new life in Christ?

Review the text:

1. Underline the phrases that particularly caught your attention.
2. Highlight what you consider to be the most important part of the text.
3. Find all the verbs used and choose the three you feel are most important.

MEDITATION:
What does the text say to me?

As a family, let us reflect on this Word of God to us. We will discuss our thoughts about what we have read using the following suggestions and questions. Anyone is welcome to read the suggestions and questions aloud, then we will all discuss them:

1. Let's share the phrases that caught our attention, what we saw as the most important part of the text, and the verbs we chose. This will help us discover what the text has to say to each of us individually and to us as a family.

2. At the outset Paul exhorts us to be humble, kind, understanding, well intentioned, and respectful. How do I ensure my life meets all these requirements?

3. St. Paul reminds us there is only one God, one Spirit, one baptism, and one body—the church. What happens when one of the members does not act in unity with the rest of the body? Does the whole body experience pain?

4. What gifts has the Lord provided? Let's each describe the most important qualities that the gifts reveal. Then we all affirm and determine to support those gifts and qualities in one another.

5. St. Paul reminds us to stop acting like children who are tossed around by the waves, enticed away from our Christian lives by seductive alternative doctrines. How do we go about facing this challenge as a family? What are some of the ideas that are contrary to the Gospel that may seduce us as a family? What plans can we put in place to be aware of these challenges?

6. How can we be new people in Christ?

7. Which aspects of the new life are more difficult for us to live out in our daily lives? What can we do to help one another grow faithfully and be respectful of what the Lord offers us?

8. As we finish this reading, and before our time of prayer, let us ask ourselves this question: What do we understand about respect? Let's discuss the meaning of respect together as a family.

PRAYER:
What do I say to the Lord?

Let's think about what we have read in God's Word and what we considered in our meditation; then we will pray to God.

As we sit quietly, let's think about what we have learned so far.

We begin by giving thanks to the Lord for the teaching we have received in this text. It has taught us about the way we should treat one another. Let's each in our own way verbalize what we have learned

Then we all ask: **Lord, bless our family as we respect others.**

We continue, asking the Lord's forgiveness aloud, for the times when we have not been respectful toward others.

Then we all ask: **Lord, forgive our lack of respect for our brothers and sisters.**

We ask the Lord aloud to help us to be truly respectful and to help others be the same.

And we all ask: **Lord, help us to be respectful as good Christians**.

CONTEMPLATION:
How do I implement the text in my life?

To contemplate means to consider, to think about in our minds and hearts, the ideas arising from the Word of God, so they have an increasing effect on our lives.

Together we say a phrase from this text:

Be humble, kind, patient, and bear with one another in love.

We will repeat this phrase several times now and then again at home, until it is engraved in our minds and hearts as the way we want our family to live.

ACTION:
How do I commit myself to act on what I have learned?

As we carry out the exercises of *Lectio Divina*, we make clear and concrete commitments to change certain things in our lives. If we do not follow through with actions, we are simply repeating ideas, nothing more.

We will each promise out loud to be respectful, first towards ourselves and then towards others. Then we will ask each other to help us fulfil the promise we made.

As a family, we will be part of an activity together with our community. We will find a group of people who do not respect others. Then, kindly and joyfully, we will invite them to join us in doing something that demonstrates the virtue of respect.

LECTIO DIVINA 7
THE VALUE OF JOY

INVOCATION TO THE HOLY SPIRIT:

O Holy Spirit,
Beloved of the Father and the Son,
always inspire us in what we should think, in what we should say,
and in the way we should say it.
Teach us when we should stay silent and what we should do for God's glory.
Keep our understanding sharp and help us retain what we learn.
Set our minds in order and give us perceptiveness and subtlety to interpret what we see.
Grant us grace and effectiveness to proclaim your Word.
But, above all, grant us open hearts, in which your Word can live.
Amen.

BIBLE TEXT: PHILIPPIANS 4
Rejoice in the Lord, always!

Read the Bible text on page 212.

READING:
What does the text say?

St. Paul writes to the Christians in the region of Philippi, and he instructs them to keep the unity within the community. It is not possible to be a Christian in isolation; we cannot remain distant from others. We must joyfully share our Christian faith, our lives, and all we have in common.

St. Paul is insistent that we should *rejoice in the Lord, always!* Christians should be known for their joy and their goodwill. St. Paul adds a very important idea: *do not be anxious about anything.* This means that whatever happens in the lives of individuals or the community, we should be assured of the Lord's presence with us. In such times we are to pray and make supplication to the Lord with thankful hearts.

At the beginning of his letter, St. Paul reminds the Christians that he rejoices because of their lives. The Christian value of joy is very important, and in this letter Paul effectively emphasizes this.

A person who is joyful in Christ, and who expresses this joy, appreciates life from a different perspective and values what is true, noble, right, clean, and kind. In other words, we could say rejoicing acts like a lens through which we perceive all things and by which we appreciate their beauty.

Paul concludes this important letter by mentioning the great joy it brought him because the Christians of Philippi were concerned for him. Joyful people are concerned for other Christians, and by expressing their concern, they generate great joy.

Apply these insights as you read the brief letter to the Philippians; remember, rejoicing is a very worthwhile value all Christians should practice.

Examine the text:

1. How does the account begin?
2. What is St. Paul saying? Why did the Philippians cause him to be joyful?
3. Why is it important to live joyfully?
4. What should we do when we feel anxious about something?
5. When a person is joyful, how do they perceive life?
6. What does joy have to do with the other gifts God grants us?
7. Why is St. Paul so joyful?
8. What kind of life has St. Paul had? Does he simply want an abundance of material things?
9. St. Paul learned to live with poverty and hunger, as well as with riches and abundance. Did any of this separate him from Christ?

Review the text:

1. Underline the phrases that particularly caught your attention.
2. Highlight what you see as the most important part of the text.
3. Find all the verbs and choose the three you feel are the most important.

MEDITATION:
What does the text say to me?

As a family let us reflect on this Word of God to us. We will discuss our thoughts about what we have read using the following suggestions and questions. Anyone is welcome to read the suggestions and questions aloud, then we will all discuss them:

1. Let's share the phrases that caught our attention, what we saw as the most important part of the text, and the verbs we chose. This will help us discover what the text has to say to us individually and to us as a family.
2. Can we identify the things that make us lose our joy? How can we

prepare ourselves beforehand so that nothing takes away our joy?

3. What is St. Paul's recommendation to help us maintain our joy?

4. Together, let's make a list of situations or occasions when each of us might become discouraged. As we listen to one another sharing the list, let's think of ways to help one another prevent despair from gaining the upper hand, so that in the future we can all maintain our joy.

5. What are some other fruit of the Spirit that come from rejoicing?

6. Do we recognize that when we are joyful we have a better Christian testimony, and that as a result, we can evangelize more effectively?

7. How can we put together a plan to live joyfully?

8. Is our family joyful? What can we all do to contribute to a joyful relationship between us in Christ?

PRAYER:
What do I say to the Lord?

Let's think about what we have read in God's Word and what we considered in our meditation; then we will pray to God.

As we sit quietly, let's think about what we have learned so far.

We begin by giving thanks to the Lord for his command to be joyful. Let's each verbalize this in our own way.

Then we all ask: **Lord, bless our family with joy.**

We continue, each praying out loud, asking the Lord's forgiveness for the times when we have allowed despair to overcome us.

Then we all ask: **Lord, forgive us for not always being joyful as you have commanded us**.

Let's ask the Lord to give us everything we need to always rejoice, so we can demonstrate the joy that comes from knowing Christ.

Then we all ask: **Lord, help us to rejoice always as good Christians**.

CONTEMPLATION:
How do I implement the text in my life?

To contemplate means to consider, to think about in our minds and hearts, the ideas arising from the Word of God, so they have an increasing effect on our lives.

Together we say a phrase from this text:

Rejoice in the Lord, always!

We will repeat this phrase several times now and then again once we are at home, until it is engraved in our minds and hearts as the way we want our family to live.

ACTION:
How do I commit myself to act on what I have learned?

As we carry out the exercises of *Lectio Divina*, we make clear and concrete commitments to change certain things in our lives. If we do not follow through with actions, we are simply repeating ideas, nothing more.

As a family we each make it our purpose to live joyfully and to express our joy at home. We will all help one another to do this. We can write down the phrase: ***REJOICE IN THE LORD ALWAYS!*** Then put it somewhere we will all see it often. We can also paste another note on the bedroom or bathroom mirrors with something like this: "Try out a smile to reveal your joy in Christ." These reminders will help us develop joy.

Together as a family we will organize a gathering where our shared rejoicing in Christ is obvious. We will invite members of our community, as well as people from other communities, to rejoice with us. We will evangelize in a way that will show our joy.

LECTIO DIVINA 7
THE VALUE OF JOY

INVOCATION TO THE HOLY SPIRIT:

O Holy Spirit,
Beloved of the Father and the Son,
always inspire us in what we should think, in what we should say,
and in the way we should say it.
Teach us when we should stay silent and what we should do for God's glory.
Keep our understanding sharp and help us retain what we learn.
Set our minds in order and give us perceptiveness and subtlety to interpret what we see.
Grant us grace and effectiveness to proclaim your Word.
But, above all, grant us open hearts, in which your Word can live.
Amen.

BIBLE TEXT: PHILIPPIANS 4
Rejoice in the Lord, always!

Read the Bible text on page 212.

READING:
What does the text say?

St. Paul writes to the Christians in the region of Philippi, and he instructs them to keep the unity within the community. It is not possible to be a Christian in isolation; we cannot remain distant from others. We must joyfully share our Christian faith, our lives, and all we have in common.

St. Paul is insistent that we should *rejoice in the Lord, always!* Christians should be known for their joy and their goodwill. St. Paul adds a very important idea: *do not be anxious about anything.* This means that whatever happens in the lives of individuals or the community, we should be assured of the Lord's presence with us. In such times we are to pray and make supplication to the Lord with thankful hearts.

At the beginning of his letter, St. Paul reminds the Christians that he rejoices because of their lives. The Christian value of joy is very important, and in this letter Paul effectively emphasizes this.

A person who is joyful in Christ, and who expresses this joy, appreciates life from a different perspective and values what is true, noble, right, clean, and kind. In other words, we could say rejoicing acts like a lens through which we perceive all things and by which we appreciate their beauty.

Paul concludes this important letter by mentioning the great joy it brought him because the Christians of Philippi were concerned for him. Joyful people are concerned for other Christians, and by expressing their concern, they generate great joy.

Apply these insights as you read the brief letter to the Philippians; remember, rejoicing is a very worthwhile value all Christians should practice.

Examine the text:
1. How does the account begin?
2. What is St. Paul saying? Why did the Philippians cause him to be joyful?
3. Why is it important to live joyfully?
4. What should we do when we feel anxious about something?
5. When a person is joyful, how do they perceive life?
6. What does joy have to do with the other gifts God grants us?
7. Why is St. Paul so joyful?
8. What kind of life has St. Paul had? Does he simply want an abundance of material things?
9. St. Paul learned to live with poverty and hunger, as well as with riches and abundance. Did any of this separate him from Christ?

Review the text:
1. Underline the phrases that particularly caught your attention.
2. Highlight what you see as the most important part of the text.
3. Find all the verbs and choose the three you feel are the most important.

MEDITATION:
What does the text say to me?

As a family let us reflect on this Word of God to us. We will discuss our thoughts about what we have read using the following suggestions and questions. Anyone is welcome to read the suggestions and questions aloud, then we will all discuss them:
1. Let's share the phrases that caught our attention, what we saw as the most important part of the text, and the verbs we chose. This will help us discover what the text has to say to us individually and to us as a family.
2. Can we identify the things that make us lose our joy? How can we